INDUSTRIAL RELATIONS RESEARCH
ASSOCIATION SERIES

Contemporary Collective Bargaining in the Private Sector

EDITED BY

Paula B. Voos

First edition

Library of Congress Catalog Card Number: 50-13564

ISBN 0-913447-60-9

INDUSTRIAL RELATIONS RESEARCH ASSOCIATION SERIES
    Proceedings of the Annual Meeting
    Proceedings of the Spring Meeting
    Annual Research Volume
    Membership Directory (every fourth year)
IRRA Newsletter (published quarterly)
IRRA Dialogues (published semiannually)

Inquiries and other communications regarding membership, meetings, publications,
and general affairs of the Association, copyright requests, as well as notice of address
changes should be addressed to the IRRA national office.

INDUSTRIAL RELATIONS RESEARCH ASSOCIATION
4233 Social Science Building, University of Wisconsin–Madison
1180 Observatory Drive, Madison, WI 53706-1320 U.S.A.
Telephone: 608/262-2762   Fax: 608/265-4591

CONTENTS

PREFACE

This volume reflects the contributions of many individuals. In particular, the twenty-two chapter authors and commentators must be commended for their thorough and insightful work. They represent the leading authorities on the respective industries which they analyze.

Acknowledgment must also be given to the members of the IRRA Editorial Committee and past Editor-in-Chief, John F. Burton, Jr., for their encouragement and assistance in the publication of this volume. They recognized a need for this book and helped get it off to a sound beginning.

The Michigan State Project on Innovative Employment Relations Systems (PIERS), the Federal Mediation and Conciliation Service (FMCS), and the IRRA must be thanked for cosponsoring a three-day conference entitled, "The Changing Nature of Collective Bargaining in the Private Sector," held in February, 1993, in Detroit. The conference enabled chapter authors to present their preliminary findings and to receive feedback from labor and management practitioners and academics in attendance.

Kay Hutchison, IRRA Administrator and Managing Editor, who provided substantive suggestions, copy-edited the volume, and oversaw its production, deserves perhaps the greatest thanks of all for keeping the project on track. Finally, Mary Ann Twist, who did an excellent job of producing the first IRRA research volume on desktop publishing, should also be acknowledged.

The dedication and effort of all those mentioned above contributed to the final product. It seems to me that the study of industrial relations in particular industrial situations contributes greatly to our overall knowledge of labor-management relations. Hopefully, this volume will enhance our understanding of the recent past and future prospects of industrial relations.

Paula B. Voos, Editor

An Economic Perspective on Contemporary Trends in Collective Bargaining

PAULA B. VOOS
University of Wisconsin

The most recent IRRA volume to assess the condition of collective bargaining in North America was published in 1980 (Somers). That collection, which summarized collective bargaining developments through the latter 1970s, essentially covered the labor relations that emerged from the long period of post-World War II prosperity. In contrast, this volume, containing twelve chapters analyzing labor relations in particular industries from 1979 to 1993, shows the operation of a collective bargaining system in a very different economic environment—much less prosperous, much more competitive. Overall, these case studies detail both the resulting strains on our system of industrial relations and its amazing resiliency and adaptability given a difficult economic and legal situation.

The main purpose of this book is to analyze on a disaggregated basis what happened to private-sector labor relations during the tumultuous period since 1979. I would like to thank the authors of the various case studies in this volume for an outstanding research effort toward that end. I will not attempt to summarize their findings in this introduction because that is done in abstracts throughout the book. However, a careful reading of their work has helped me develop a new perspective on the key developments in collective bargaining of the last fifteen years, their interconnections, and their relationship to contemporary economic developments. In this introduction I will share my perspective and what I see as the implications for public policy.

A consensus has developed regarding some of the main developments of the 1980s in private-sector American industrial relations:

declining unionization, employers setting the agenda in bargaining, the spread of employee involvement programs and workplace innovations of various types, increased decentralization in bargaining structures, declining real wages, and heightened concern for job security. Various theoretical perspectives have been offered to understand the causal connections between these trends. Some argue that a fundamental transformation is underway in American industrial relations, while others suggest that recent developments reflect the expected response of established actors within a continuous IR system to dramatic changes in the economic and political environment.

While both views are represented in this volume, it seems to me that if there ever was an ongoing transformation of U.S. industrial relations, it is still incomplete. It is true that there have been many significant shifts in labor relations, including widespread experimentation with employee involvement programs and other workplace innovations aimed at increasing productivity, including decentralization of bargaining structures, and including employer-initiated confrontational bargaining. However, as I explain below, I view employee involvement programs as a new variant of an old phenomenon for American labor—productivity bargaining—not as evidence of a fundamental transformation. Neither decentralization nor confrontational hard bargaining is a new phenomenon either, although both have been accentuated in the last 15 years. The system is not transformed, but power has shifted from unions to employers as unionization rates have declined and as bargaining has faced a difficult economic and public policy context.

The case studies provide a deeper understanding of the causes, consequences, and importance of these developments. In particular, the economic context, associated public policy, and labor law of the period emerge as bedrock. Public policy has been the source of many economic shifts and it is always subject to future change and redirection, however. The question of what we might learn from these studies relevant to a redirection of public policy towards promoting a high wage yet an internationally competitive economy is considered at the end of these observations.

Main Trends

Confrontational Hard Bargaining

The 1980s witnessed a dramatic shift in bargaining power in management's favor, with employers setting the bargaining agenda in many industries (trucking, see Belzer; auto supply, see Cutcher-Gershenfeld; paper, see Eaton and Kriesky). As tactics to gain leverage, some employers used threats of work relocation, hired permanent replacements in strike situations, and/or unilaterally implemented terms and conditions of employment where workers decided a strike was ill-advised. The goal was typically cost control through reduction (or containment) of wage and benefit costs. The underlying context of high unemployment, increased competition, and the increasingly evident problems faced by unions in organizing workers and keeping them organized, all facilitated and encouraged confrontational bargaining.

In popular parlance, confrontational hard bargaining, starting with a management agenda of cost relief, is termed "concession bargaining." Most authors in this volume use that terminology. The careful reader will note, however, that the term "concessions" has come to be used in a diversity of situations ranging from drastic total compensation cuts (meatpacking), to reductions in selected elements of the total package of compensation (e.g. wage cuts taken to preserve health care benefits whose cost have escalated), and even to compensation increases which were in the form of lump sums rather than base pay adjustments (aerospace). Some have come to define situations in which unions agreed to modify work rules or pattern bargaining relationships as concessions. I prefer the concept of confrontational hard bargaining to that of concession bargaining both because this term focuses on the process rather than the outcome of bargaining and because the term "concessions" has come to be used so loosely.

Moreover, concessions—defined as actual reductions in total compensation—were not nearly so evident in the latter part of the 1980s as they were earlier. However, reduced union bargaining power has encouraged a confrontational hard-bargaining stance on the part of management in many companies continuing into the late 1980s and early 1990s. Hence confrontational hard bargaining is a more appropriate characterization of the dominant bargaining trend of recent times.

Even so, the direct reduction of wages and benefits was by no means the only management strategy for cost containment in the 1980s. Some companies concluded they could win the confrontational "battle" with labor but still lose the total cost containment "war" if poor relations with the work force led to adverse effects on labor productivity. Hence they adopted a less confrontational, "joint" approach to labor relations, emphasizing gains to productivity through shopfloor programs which involve employees, reorganize production, and reduce total costs—not just labor costs. Although management interest in employee involvement programs was widespread, appearing even in firms that made labor cost containment a bargaining priority, a joint approach was particularly likely to occur in industries that were still highly organized. Ford Motor, GM in the Saturn and Nummi projects, AT&T, National Steel, and Scott Paper would all be examples (see Katz and MacDuffie, Keefe and Boroff, Arthur and Konzelmann-Smith, Eaton and Kriesky).

Enhanced Productivity Through Employee Involvement

In this volume we see employee involvement, work reorganization, and innovative compensation programs aimed at increasing productivity in many firms. Employee participation's spread has been driven by reported savings in unit labor costs and in supervisory, material usage, and inventory costs. However, the involvement/participation programs described here are diverse. They encompass a wide range of practices which may or may not include any of the following: changing job classifications and the organization of work (e.g., team production), new compensation systems (e.g., pay for knowledge, gainsharing, profit-sharing), and efforts to improve union-management cooperation.

More critically, some involvement/participation programs have been initiated through a joint process of labor-management cooperation in which the union agrees to support the effort, whereas others have been implemented unilaterally by management. Union support typically involves agreement to major changes in work rules, payment systems and work organization in order to increase the likelihood of achieving continuous improvements in productivity; unilateral management implementation in an organized firm may ignore these supportive items or may involve attempting to force change through hard-bargaining tactics.[1]

While employee participation in its various forms has become widespread, the diversity of accompanying labor-management situations and the diversity of practices encompassed by the terms "involvement" and "participation" is a major factor in explaining the uneven track record of these programs.

The jury is still out on whether or not confrontational bargaining is compatible with employee involvement efforts in the long run, given the residue of bitterness visible in situations where employers essentially compel workers to participate. Companies that work with unions to establish a "joint" implementation of employee involvement are betting that union-management and worker-management relations are not separable and that a joint endeavor will ultimately prove more successful, especially if an improved economic climate in the future provides unions with more bargaining power. My judgment from the sketchy evidence available to date is that they will be proven correct, at least in situations where deunionization is not a viable option open to management.

The New Productivity Bargaining

In an era of reduced union bargaining power, confronted by demands for concessions and new shopfloor labor relations, unions have struggled to find a successful strategy. It is evident in this volume that at least some unions have arrived at what is essentially a modernized productivity bargaining strategy. That is, they have been willing to renegotiate work rules and to cooperate with management to improve productivity through employee involvement—in exchange for enhanced job security and a better economic package than could otherwise be negotiated (automobiles, telecommunications, steel, paper).[2] Where union leadership has taken this position, it has often occasioned a big debate within the union work force as to the appropriateness of union involvement in these schemes (auto assembly, telecommunications). It is not always clear that the perceived benefits to workers from participation programs (or from higher productivity itself) are greater than the perceived costs. In an economic climate in which it is difficult for companies to expand sales and in which it is hard for displaced workers to obtain equivalent jobs, employees may be reluctant to embrace productivity improvement plans which are likely to lead to work force reductions—unless the stark alternative is even greater job loss.[3]

On the other hand, many employees like the chance to exercise a degree of self-supervision, to change work tasks, to offer suggestions for quality or productivity improvement, and to be recognized as a part of the production "team." There is mounting evidence that these programs can increase labor's influence over some non-mandatory subjects of bargaining of importance to workers and that unions can gain increased member satisfaction by being involved in their operation. And in an era of economic limits and increased competitiveness, enhanced productivity is one way to maintain job security and compensation—to pay for things like ever more costly health insurance.

The debate within unions regarding employee participation, team production, or other workplace innovations is largely healthy and contributes to an improved chance of success in those situations where democratic debate results in union support for a participation effort and union involvement in the program's operation.[4] Participation programs in the union sector tend to be more serious and extensive than nonunion efforts, to result in more productivity improvement and to last longer (Rosow 1993). This occurs in part because unions act as representative institutions aggregating and communicating the views of individual workers regarding program operation; the nonunion environment lacks any comparable representative institution. As a result, programs in the union sector are more likely to balance management goals of increased productivity with worker goals of enhanced quality of worklife and better job security (Eaton and Voos 1992). Furthermore, in unionized settings these programs operate as new forms of a familiar phenomenon: productivity bargains in which unions and their members trade more productive work for economic goals. In the recent past this has often involved losing fewer jobs or seeing a smaller decline in hourly earnings than would otherwise be the case.

Finally, the democratic bargaining process may be more important than the outcome. There is a tendency for academics to define the latest managerial program as innovative and hence progressive, but that is an illusion. Actually, what is abidingly progressive is the opportunity for employees to determine what they want from their working lives— whether or not that includes agreeing to programs designed to improve productivity by involving workers in decision making.

Decentralization of Bargaining

Many chapter authors note a decreased use of multi-employer bargaining in recent years, a loosening of bargaining patterns, an increased tendency of collective agreements to be "tailored" to a particular company or particular operation's economic situation and a greater importance of locally bargained work rules in situations where companies are pursuing shopfloor participation or team production strategies. Bargaining has become more decentralized and patterns have loosened in aerospace (Erickson), meatpacking (Craypo), automobiles (Katz and MacDuffie) and other sectors. Steel, for instance, witnessed the demise of centralized multi-employer bargaining after the 1983 bargaining round. In the late 1980s, agreements at steel companies pursuing a cooperative joint path to increased productivity became somewhat different from those at companies which continued to take a confrontational approach to reducing direct labor costs, although in the early nineties the core group of basic steel producers appear to have settled into a new, looser form of pattern bargaining (Arthur and Konzelmann-Smith).[5] In trucking, the National Master Freight Agreement covered fewer companies and its role as a pattern setter lessened (Belzer).

It seems to me that such shifts demonstrate the adaptability and resiliency of collective bargaining in the face of changed conditions. This is not to say that pressures for decentralization do not create problems for unions or that tight pattern bargaining on economic issues may not be an appropriate economic solution in some circumstances—that somehow, it is always good for collective agreements to be crafted to reflect the economic position of individual employers or individual plants. We should be careful about adopting this position and about oversimplifying our understanding of "decentralization," which actually means quite divergent things in different contexts.[6]

Since employers have been the driving force behind the move to decentralize, it is important to try to understand what they are trying to achieve. Decentralization has accompanied increased attention to work rules and the implementation of employee involvement programs in several industries, sometimes supplemented by pattern bargaining to standardize economic compensation (e.g., auto assembly). Katz (1993) emphasizes this factor, along with a general trend toward management decentralization and increased diversity within both management and labor. However, it is evident from the case studies in this volume, that employers have pushed decentralization in order to gain increased leverage in union-management relations in several industries in which new forms of work organization are not widespread (e.g., meatpacking, trucking). In part, employers have been pushing decentralization in order to enhance bargaining power in an economic context of high unemployment in which they need not fear "wage drift" or union "whipsawing."[7] Another driving goal is that of gaining a cost advantage over competitors either by negotiating more advantageous terms with regard to direct labor costs, or through the ability to implement productivity-enhancing bargaining unit programs when competitors cannot. Of course, it is self-evident that all employers in an industry cannot gain a cost advantage through decentralized bargaining, so that employers who work hard to eliminate bargaining patterns may later discover that competitors are getting a better deal and that it is actually in their interest to return to patterns to stabilize competition.[8]

The Context of Collective Bargaining

An understanding of major collective bargaining developments requires careful consideration of the underlying economic, social, and political contexts. Author after author in this volume refers to the increased competitiveness of the economy as a whole and to the influence which greater competition within a particular industry has had on labor relations, typically by putting downward pressure on labor costs. Beyond the influence of increased competition, macroeconomic developments also played an important role in defining the economic context of collective bargaining. The 1980s witnessed three recessions, two deep ones at the beginning of the decade and one more typical downturn at the end. Throughout the period, economic policy was driven by a desire to stamp out inflation and reduce the size of government. Direct and indirect government policies resulted in a rate of unemployment high by historical standards. Unemployment and pressures for low product prices had a strong influence on collective bargaining, particularly before 1987. Even with economic recovery in the late 1980s, employment never returned to earlier levels in many industries but remained permanently depressed (e.g., steel) and was driven down still further by the recession which hit early in the 1990s. As this is being written in late 1993, the economy is characterized by excess labor supply for many types of labor and declining real wages overall.

Furthermore, these events transpired within the confines of a labor law that made it difficult for unions to maintain existing collective bargaining relationships much less to create new ones. The chapters in this volume reveal a number of ways in which labor law permitted management to escape or avoid collective bargaining. As a result, we see declining unionization in most private-sector industries (or the maintenance of low levels of union organization). Declining unionization and inadequate labor law protection for workers trying to exercise their legal right to form or join a union was a vitally important context for collective bargaining in this period.

This is not to claim that social and political factors were insignificant—indeed, they were related to the problematical public policy context. Unions did become politically less popular in the 1980s, and President Reagan did signal the increasing social acceptability of replacing striking workers in the PATCO situation—albeit in a very different legal context from that of the private sector. These factors reinforced the central economic and legal context of collective bargaining.

Finally, it is important to appreciate the extent to which these significant environmental determinants of collective bargaining are themselves the result of political choices, public opinion, and government policy. These are factors which can change or be changed in the long run, altering even the critical economic context of collective bargaining.

"It's the Economy, Stupid"

It has become commonplace to assert that the American economy has become markedly more competitive in the past decade. This theme runs throughout the volume, although the fundamental determinants of increased competition vary between different industries. One could easily conclude from the discussion that increased competition is a given—an inevitable and irreversible trend.

I must disagree. Competition increased in the '70s and '80s because of a series of policy choices made under the presumption that the benefits of increased competition (primarily lower prices) outweighed the costs. Product and labor markets are always an outcome of the institutions that create and maintain them. An example of a key institution would be the *rules of our financial markets* which facilitate takeovers, leveraged buy-outs, and other speculative financial restructuring designed to maximize returns to shareholders—but which put tremendous pressure on American managers to maximize short-run profitability, sometimes at the expense of long-run competitiveness or commitment to a line of business. The negative consequences of these fundamental institutional rules of financial markets are illustrated in several of the chapters in this volume (paper, textiles, trucking, steel). Beyond that, increasing product market competition during this period was the result of policy choices with regard to other institutions of the market. It is useful to consider some details of this process.

Deregulation was a policy initiative in response to economic theory proclaiming the virtues of competitive markets and to political mobilization on the part of large businesses consuming the products of regulated industries. For instance, in the telecommunications industry, business consumers of large amounts of long-distance services (the financial services industry, in particular) mobilized politically to achieve deregulation (Keefe and Boroff). They were successful in ending the earlier regulatory pricing policies that subsidized local telephone rates with above-cost long-distance rates.[9] In the trucking industry, business consumers of large-volume truckload services likewise mobilized to end the regulatory policies that had used above-cost pricing of truckload shipments to subsidize the shippers of smaller less-than-truckload freight. Again, they were successful in changing the regulatory environment of the industry (Belzer). In consequence, some large unionized trucking firms like UPS prospered.[10] Many other organized firms failed, and their employees were thrown out of work. In still others, workers' living standards were eroded by pressure to remain "competitive."

Deregulation was and is a concept supported by many economists because it is theorized that increased competition leads to lower overall prices. Within this intellectual context, it was a policy that was pursued by both Democratic and Republican administrations. The same is true for *increased international competition*. Democrat or Republican— presidents of the 1960s, '70s, and '80s have all negotiated lower tariff barriers and facilitated the integration of our economy with that of the rest of the world. Again, increased international trade was supported by conventional economic theory which stressed the benefits in terms of lower prices. It is important to remember that this didn't just happen— we made it happen.

Similarly, it seems today that *increased immigration*, legal and illegal, is inevitable. Greater legal immigration, however, was clearly a government policy, instituted by a series of legal changes in the '60s and '70s, capped by the Immigration Reform and Control Act of 1986. That law contained the Seasonal Agricultural Worker amendments under which 1.3 million persons have applied for residency in the United States, including an estimated one-sixth of the adult men in rural Mexico (Martin). High levels of illegal immigration are an example of policy by inaction. Several case studies investigate how immigration is affecting collective bargaining in agriculture, hotels and restaurants, and meatpacking (Martin, Cobble and Merrill, Craypo).

Finally, while government policy may not have created the *recessions* of the early 1980s (since the business cycle is a feature of all market economies), they were certainly deepened by policies adopted at that time to fight inflation and reduce the size of government expenditures. Federal Reserve Bank policies allowed the U.S. dollar to stay at a level that was seriously overvalued by historical standards, reducing the demand for American goods abroad and increasing the demand for artificially low-priced imports at home. This policy, coming at a time of severe recessionary conditions in the U.S., was devastating for many manufacturers, especially those in the durable goods sector. The maintenance of high interest rates by the Federal Reserve as another inflation-fighting strategy depressed the construction industry as well as those producing investment goods. To stimulate aggregate demand, federal income-tax cuts focused on high-income individuals were pushed by an administration bent on reducing the size of the public sector. As a result, inequality increased in the distribution of after-tax income at the same time real hourly earnings were falling rapidly for the less-educated groups who were suffering the most unemployment. Excess labor supply, unemployment, plant closings, an ample supply of replacement workers in the event of a strike—all these have haunted collective bargaining throughout the 1980s. The situation was, at least in part, the result of public policy choices (cf. Kochan and Piore 1984).

The combination of increased competition, surplus production capacity, and readily available labor led companies to look for ways to cut costs—the cost of supplies, the cost of inventories, but especially the cost of labor. Three strategies were widely used, sometimes in concert by the same employers. Some firms used capital mobility to avoid or escape collective bargaining. Others used confrontational tactics to get concessions from organized labor.[11] And finally others emphasized the reduction in unit costs (labor, supervisory, inventory, and material) through the enhancement of productivity through employee involvement or total quality management—the productivity bargaining response. Labor-management cooperation to raise productivity was particularly likely to arise in heavily organized industries where firms could not avoid or escape organization and where unions had sufficient bargaining power to encourage management to adopt the productivity bargaining path.

In short, the economic context is central to explaining collective bargaining trends in recent years. At the same time, it is vital to recognize the extent to which economic developments are themselves influenced by public policy initiatives. While it seems unlikely that some of the key policy initiatives identified above will be reversed in the near future (deregulation), others are presently politically very divisive (increased international competition as exemplified by NAFTA), and still others are perennial subjects of debate (macroeconomic policy, financial market regulation). Hence it seems entirely possible that some of these policies might be reversed or altered in the future.

Labor Law

Another crucial context for explaining outcomes in collective bargaining in the 1980s was the state of U.S. labor law. Many American employers have a deep and abiding distaste for labor unions. Contemporary labor law gives them ample latitude to move production to nonunion facilities, to legally or illegally avoid organization of new facilities,[12] and generally to fight unions in collective bargaining. This is not to suggest that all nonunion employees want to organize, or that unions themselves have played no role in union membership trends in recent years—just to state that our labor law makes new organization exceedingly difficult.

Under the NLRA, employees have the right to form or join unions and engage in collective bargaining if they so desire. That right is supposedly protected by government through the representation election process and through the outlawing of employer unfair labor practices which vitiate employee free choice (for instance, surface bargaining, threats to close organized plants, or the discharge of union supporters).

Yet, it is widely recognized that employers often manipulate the representation election process with the express purpose of delaying elections, delaying the disposition of unfair labor practice charges, and avoiding real bargaining to such an extent that employees are denied the effective right to organize and bargain collectively. In this regard, the textile industry case vividly documents the well-known weaknesses of the NLRA as amended and enforced (Chaykowski, Thomason, and Zwerling). Similar problems surface in other case studies, particularly in sectors in which collective bargaining is not well established (see the meatpacking and hospitality industry chapters, in particular).

Moreover, many employers have successfully recast employment to include a tiny supervisory element in many jobs, resulting in fewer and fewer employees being afforded protection under the NLRA.[13] Hence a smaller proportion of all employees have any protection whatsoever under the law should they desire to organize. There is evidence of this both in moderately organized sectors and even in highly organized sectors like telecommunications (Keefe and Boroff).

Other aspects of American labor law also create problems for collective bargaining. Although the discharge of employees who engage in concerted activity is illegal, the permanent replacement of strikers is not and is increasingly being used by employers. The studies of the paper, meatpacking, and hospitality industries all document the undesirable effects of the use of permanent strike replacements. Even when the collective bargaining relationship is not destroyed by the use of permanent replacements, there are long-run negative consequences for labor-management relations, employee morale, and productivity. For instance, after using permanent replacements at several plants, International Paper is now finding it difficult to gain employee trust and cooperation at other locations for an employee involvement effort to raise productivity (see Eaton and Kriesky). At the same time, other studies in this volume demonstrate that permanent strike replacements are rarely used in many sectors. Clearly, collective bargaining can work well without this source of employer leverage, as we also know from experience in Ontario, Canada where permanent replacements are legally prohibited.

These problems with organizing and bargaining under the current law are widely recognized. Other problems are more fundamental. Employers are currently provided enormous scope under U.S. labor law to evade organization or escape from existing union representation through the redirection of capital investment: relocation of production, outsourcing, discontinuation of product lines, mergers, acquisitions and sales of subsidiaries. These are all examples of legally acceptable strategies to avoid unionization and vitiate employee free choice. We witness this in a number of industries in this volume (restaurants, construction, auto supply, trucking, meatpacking). Furthermore, our current legal framework does not mesh well with union organizing along occupational or craft lines, as is demonstrated in the studies of construction and the restaurant portion of the hospitality industry. The spreading practice of double-breasting and the current difficulty under the law of effectively organizing jobs in the nonunion subsidiaries of union companies are of critical importance in construction and increasingly in other industries (for instance, trucking). It is important that we amend our labor law to deal with these increasingly evident problems of capital mobility as well as the longstanding ones attending representation elections and first contract negotiations.

Declining Unionization

Declining unionization is a major determinant of collective bargaining outcomes, but is itself an outcome of other more fundamental factors. As such, it occupies a peculiar place in this volume. It must be considered a very significant contemporary trend in collective bargaining and so is an important topic of discussion in nearly all the chapters.

In virtually every industry surveyed in this volume, we see some decline in the percentage of workers organized in the early 1990s compared to the late 1970s. The case studies give us considerable evidence regarding the effect of this trend on employees. The largest declines in real earnings occur precisely in those industries in which unionization plummets and collective bargaining becomes decentralized and destabilized as a result. Of industries which have exhibited at least moderate levels of unionization in the past, those which experienced a meltdown in the 1980s (auto supply, construction, meatpacking, trucking) also saw real hourly earnings decline precipitously.[14] On the other hand, where there were only moderate or slight decreases in unionization rates (auto assembly, telecommunications, steel, paper, aerospace) unions were more able to protect their members against adverse economic trends. A few chapters focus on industries where unions have not gotten off the ground, despite earlier hopes for unionization (hotels, agriculture, textiles). Here we can see the current economic and legal barriers to organizing.

Others have attempted to catalogue the reasons for deunionization into neat, if lengthy, lists. It is unnecessary to review here the literature regarding the multiple reasons for the gradual, long-run decline in the percent organized between 1954 and 1979—the changing locus of jobs, shifts in the composition of the labor force, management resistance to unionization through union substitution efforts, union organizing efforts, and other factors (see, for instance, Strauss, Gallagher and Fiorito 1991). Rather, we should ask what new insights emerge from the case studies in this volume regarding the sharp drop in union membership within particular industries since 1979. Two factors struck me as I read these cases: first, an economic environment which encourages competition based on low labor costs; and second, a legal framework which gives employers wide latitude to escape existing collective bargaining relationships and to avoid unionization.[15] Since I have just discussed the legal dimension, let me focus on the economic half of the story.

The importance of the economic context is demonstrated by the fact that while unionization levels are lower in 1992 than 1979 across the board, much of the decline took place early in the 1980s, with rates in the latter 1980s stabilizing or actually increasing in many industries. In construction, the low point came in 1985. For paper mills (though not container plants) it was 1987. In meatpacking, unions began to win major organizing campaigns after 1987. In trucking, most of the decline occurred early in the decade. In manufacturing generally, where declining unionization was typically the result of old-line producers reducing capacity while new domestic or foreign competitors added nonunion capacity, both trends slowed and rates of unionization tended to stabilize by the end of the 1980s. While this was true of auto assembly and steel, there were exceptions, including auto parts.

The economic context of excess production capacity stemming from a severe recession and an over-valued dollar is of great importance in explaining these trends—and this situation lasted until the middle of 1986, when the trade deficit (which had worsened in the early 1980s) began to diminish and unemployment finally fell below 7%. Excess capacity in the early 1980s put heavy pressure on unionized, high-wage companies with their typically older facilities. Companies which were not able to lower costs quickly lost market share. The result as it has played out in several industries (meatpacking, auto supply) was a cycle in which high-wage companies adopt strategies to lower costs and manage shrinking market share (including plant closings, relocating production, and diversification out of the industry) while nonunion employers continue to add new, low-cost capacity. The result is not only deunionization but also severe economic dislocation.

The observations contained in the case studies suggest that in explaining trends in labor organization we need to emphasize not only management resistance to unionization and the scope to which that is permissible under labor law, but also an economic environment which encourages competition based on low labor costs and the public policies which shape that economic environment.

Implications for Public Policy

At present, we are witnessing a major public policy debate over how to reverse several interrelated trends of the 1980s: declining real hourly earnings (especially for less-educated workers); increased inequality in the distribution of income; and less secure, more contingent employment. At the same time, there is an abiding concern to maintain and enhance the international competitiveness of the United States. The difficult and important question is how to achieve this competitiveness with a high and rising standard of living, not with low and declining labor standards.

High productivity, stemming from improved training, utilization, and motivation of our labor force, can play an important role in achieving both high earnings and international competitiveness (*America's Choice* 1990). High levels of product or service quality, rapid development of new products, and superior product design are also important. There is a growing consensus that workplace-level employee involvement programs can play a role in fostering quality, productivity, and more cooperative labor-management relations (termed the "mutual-gains workplace" by Kochan and Osterman 1993), although there is also recognition that employee involvement alone is not sufficient to create the high-performance workplace. Given this perspective, an important public policy issue becomes how we might foster labor-management cooperation and real employee involvement.

Let me stress that real employee involvement is what is needed, not some company-dominated, go-through-the-motions exercise in which workers appease management by pretending to participate! That alternative is not likely to have much success in raising productivity. Real employee involvement programs must serve worker goals (improved quality of worklife, dignity and democracy, enhanced job security and compensation) as well as company goals. The evidence suggests that this is most likely to occur in a situation of independent employee voice (Eaton and Voos 1992). However, even in the union sector, participation programs often fall short of their promise.

What do we learn from these studies of private-sector collective bargaining in the 1980s that is relevant to this policy debate over how to foster real employee involvement, high-productivity growth, and labor-management cooperation? Even though the union sector is only part of the economy, it includes crucially important industries, particularly in terms of our ability to be internationally competitive.[16] The studies in this volume, taken as a whole, support a number of conclusions that should be central to public policy in the labor area.

First, when managements choose to reduce cost per unit by raising productivity through true shopfloor participation programs, unions are typically receptive to these initiatives. There has been widespread joint union-management operation of employee involvement programs in parts of the auto assembly, steel, paper, and telecommunications industries. This has not occurred without internal union debate, without growing pains, or without management hesitation (some companies have opted for a unilateral management or compulsory approach to "participation"). It is also true that in some sectors, the parties have been satisfied with a more traditional, arms-length labor-management relationship (e.g., in much of aerospace).[17] Nonetheless, on the whole, American unions are not married to a system of narrow job classifications or adversarial shopfloor labor relations; they are willing to cooperate and participate.

In return for cooperation and participation, labor unions typically demand that management forswears hard bargaining and direct reductions in wages, unless the economic situation is truly dire. Moreover, unions commonly expect employers to desist from deunionization strategies. Unions negotiate accretion agreements or neutrality pledges pertaining to nonunion facilities where they are strong enough[18] and settle for vague understandings where they are not. Of course, unions also see the maintenance or enhancement of employment security and compensation as important goals in the productivity bargaining from which these programs derive. These goals have been pursued in different ways in different situations.

In very dire economic circumstances, management may be able to successfully combine hard-bargaining strategies of direct labor cost reduction or containment with shopfloor productivity programs. Certainly, many companies closed or threatened to close particular U.S. operations in the early to mid-1980s to obtain cost relief and even used such tactics to get employees to accept new workrules and shopfloor labor relations. However, there is mounting evidence that forcing employees to accept new work organization and "participation" leaves a residue of bitterness that limits the effectiveness of these programs. In the end, I doubt that management can successfully coerce meaningful participation, especially in organized situations.

In sum, organized labor has proven itself more than willing to cooperate in fostering employee involvement and other workplace initiatives designed to increase productivity and product quality, in exchange for attention to its own goals (recognition as an equal partner, limits on deunionization, enhanced job security and compensation, workplace democracy). At the same time, it is important that policymakers recognize that productivity-focused employee involvement initiatives are not labor's programs to the same extent they are management programs. Reducing costs by increasing productivity and improving competitiveness by enhancing quality are management goals—legitimate management goals—but management goals nonetheless. Organized labor can be encouraged to buy into these efforts if increased productivity is used to fund enhanced job security and improved compensation in an era of economic limits.[19] But it is unrealistic to ask organized labor to lead in promoting productivity improvement-oriented employee involvement programs.

Instead, public policy should facilitate what is occurring in some parts of the private sector: the new productivity bargaining involving joint labor-management initiatives to promote high-performance workplaces through employee involvement and work reorganization. The most important thing government can do to promote joint involvement initiatives is to foreclose or discourage other currently available alternatives— low-wage strategies involving deunionization and/or confrontational bargaining to reduce direct labor costs. In order to promote high-wage, high-productivity outcomes as a matter of public policy, government must do more than publicize best-case companies and urge management to take the high road. Instead, public policy needs to change the economics of the fundamental management choice—either to outlaw things like coercive antiunion behavior or to make the low road more difficult, more expensive, and therefore less attractive to management. It is important to reform labor law so that employers will not be able to escape collective bargaining or thwart their employees' legitimate desires to organize. The law should encourage labor and management to effectively resolve problems through negotiation.[20] It is also necessary to change an economic and political terrain that has often encouraged confrontational bargaining, rather than joint union-management initiatives and productivity bargaining.

Government has considerable power to shape both the macroeconomic environment and the microeconomic situation of many sectors through taxation, interest, trade, and regulation policies. For instance, we might recast the institutional rules of the financial marketplace to reduce pressures for short-run profit maximization as opposed to investments to increase long-run competitiveness. Or we might reconsider ways to "manage" trade—to carefully craft the institutional context of trade— much as the Europeans are doing as they construct the social regulations of the Common Market—and to select appropriate trading partners. The issue is not whether we are for or against trade or for or against markets, but rather how government can shape a fundamentally open, free market economy to serve the society's goals of high living standards, employment security, and democracy both on and off the job.[21] A full-employment economy would ease many of the strains witnessed in this volume, for instance reducing worker opposition to labor-displacing productivity improvements or trade agreements. It would facilitate productivity-enhancing employee training, because both employers and workers would perceive real benefits to such training. It would help reverse the recent decline in the standard of living. And of course, full employment remains an important goal in its own right.[22]

Public policy will be more realistic and will enjoy a better chance of success if we ground it in the unpopular but fundamental truth that labor and management have some natural, inescapable differences of interest as well as some common goals. In recent years, as fundamental economic trends have shifted the balance of power, management has been more aggressive in exercising its economic interest. Where that shift has been most pronounced, hard bargaining, deunionization, and declining living standards have dominated the landscape. Where unions have been relatively stronger, productivity bargaining and joint union-management initiatives on the shopfloor to promote productivity have emerged. If we want to foster cooperative joint efforts—and our public policy interest in promoting high-wage, high-productivity outcomes suggests that we should—it will be necessary to change both the economic terrain and the laws that govern organizing and collective bargaining. That is a hard truth but it is a more realistic prescription than one which emphasizes moral suasion, government showcasing of successful labor-management situations, or any other form of organized cheerleading. In order to encourage managers to take the high road, government must foreclose other options and do a better job of managing the economy. These are the key lessons for public policy which I would draw from the studies in this volume.

Acknowledgments

Special thanks are due to my graduate student, Jody Knauss, and as well as to various colleagues, including Dale Belman, Charles Craypo, Adrienne Eaton, Tom Kochan, Ray Marshall, Don Nichols, and Craig Olson.

Endnotes

[1] Union members have not always been willing to give up protective work rules, however, without a "significant emotional event"—a plant closing or other threat making employee participation under changed workrules more palatable. This is one reason why hard bargaining, direct labor cost concessions, and employee participation or profit-sharing have sometimes gone hand in hand in the 1980s.

[2] The new productivity bargaining differs from the older productivity bargaining primarily in that it involves union agreement to programs that continually increase productivity, as opposed to one-time deals associated with the installation of new technology, etc. The new productivity bargaining requires the positive commitment of bargaining unit members to a much greater extent than did the old productivity bargaining and, hence, requires a continuing positive labor-management relationship.

[3] Furthermore, only a handful of involvement efforts are meaningful attempts at economic democracy, truly integrating the work force into the decision-making process. Most are designed specifically to get workers to endorse corporate goals, notably higher productivity. Despite a rhetoric of trust and empowerment, plans are often unilaterally imposed.

[4] Jill Kriesky has pointed out to me that sometimes within the paper industry, internal local union battles over the correct position on employee involvement consumed considerable energy and caused divisions that continued even after a local decided to support the participation process, reducing worker solidarity.

[5] Arthur and Konzelmann-Smith emphasize the retreat from multi-employer bargaining in steel and from the CWS attempt to standardize labor grades and wages. They emphasize the extent to which "remanning" and other work reorganization is being negotiated locally. Nonetheless, it seems to me that a more sophisticated and subtle type of pattern bargaining has emerged in steel from union attempts to equalize the employee cost burden across companies. That is, because benefit costs have become a major percentage of total compensation, and companies differ strikingly in the age composition of their work forces (and, hence, in the cost of providing pensions and health insurance), the union discovered that equalizing wage rates and benefit provisions no longer allowed it to equalize labor costs and thereby remove labor from competition. The Steelworkers have not dropped the elimination of competition based on labor costs as a goal. Instead, they are now using pattern bargaining of a more subtle form to achieve this end. This year, the "Cooperative Partnership" accords at Inland, Bethlehem and National Steel set the pattern for the industry, including U.S. Steel (a classic hard bargainer which once dominated the multi-employer bargaining process). The deal apparently trades union representation on corporate boards and enhanced job security for productivity improvements (*Wall Street Journal*, August 2, 1993:2).

[6] In auto assembly, the focus on shopfloor changes in the auto industry (just-in-time production, work teams, employee involvement) has led to increased emphasis in collective bargaining on local issues at the same time pattern bargaining on economic issues still predominates for everything except profit-sharing (the vast bulk of compensation), despite some variation in the pattern for Saturn and the organized transplants. In trucking, in contrast, economic patterns have become much more decentralized.

[7] Unlike Katz, I also see decreased unionization as a cause of decentralization in bargaining, not as an example of decentralization. The fact that the trend to decentralization has occurred worldwide does not demonstrate the paramount importance of workrule flexibility in the context of work reorganization and employee involvement,

precisely because most advanced market economies have similar high levels of unemployment, making the leverage explanation just as plausible.

[8] This discussion suggests that decentralization is as much of a problem as a solution. For those who sympathize with employer desire for individually tailored solutions, this might suggest the need to consider what is needed to encourage competition on the basis of increased productivity or quality, rather than lower hourly compensation.

[9] This subsidization benefited smaller business and creating virtually universal telephone service for even lower-income consumers. Technological innovation in the delivery of telecommunication services, along with political factors, also influenced the deregulation decision.

[10] UPS may have prospered for other reasons as well. It has been suggested to me that this firm benefited from the deregulation of the airline industry which allowed it to break into the airfreight-overnight package market. The essential point, however, is that the less-than-truckload segment of the industry has grown more concentrated because of deregulation (see Belzer).

[11] Unions, pressured by members to save jobs, often gave relief to hard-pressed firms. The experience of several industries, however, was that concessions tended to spread from one firm or plant to another, from those who were truly on the edge of survival to competitors who merely demanded equal concessions and had the leverage to insist (e.g., steel, meatpacking, auto supply, trucking). In this manner, concession bargaining may have preserved some jobs and some companies but the reemergence of labor cost-based competition did tremendous harm to other enterprises and their employees.

[12] It is undoubtedly important to distinguish between legal and illegal tactics used to influence workers engaged in deciding whether or not to organize. The current minimal cost of illegal behavior results in a considerable number of violations of the law. It is important to reduce these either by increasing the penalties for violation or by redesigning the choice process to forestall opportunities for illegal behavior.

[13] This is occurring despite contractions with contemporary trends in work organization which are returning elements of supervisory responsibility to the bargaining unit work group.

[14] Belzer points out that declines in trucking are uneven and that union membership has held up in the less-than-truckload sector to a greater extent than has been realized; he considers the term "meltdown" inappropriate for the trucking industry. It seems to me that union membership declined sharply enough in trucking, that along with deregulation, decentralization of bargaining and sharp shifts in employment between companies, trucking collective bargaining destabilized radically in the early 1980s. This is what I mean by a meltdown.

[15] Here we are discussing within industry rates of labor organization; in the economy as a whole, inter-industry shifts in employment are also significant. Interestingly, there is little evidence in this volume that changing employee characteristics play a significant role in explaining declining levels of labor organization. Recent immigrants, women, and other growing groups in the labor force, have been heavily

involved in organizing attempts in several industries in this volume (hotels and meat-packing).

[16] Aerospace manufacturing, steel, automobile assembly, and paper all are very important, highly unionized industries with a significant volume of international trade. Obviously there are other industries in this category not examined in this volume (e.g., agricultural equipment, construction equipment, coal, electrical products, and rubber are some examples).

[17] See Erickson for a discussion of the aerospace case and the role of aerospace technology, along with international union positions, in limiting profit-sharing. My own interpretation is that the aerospace economic situation in which employment/job security is not related closely to labor costs or productivity is fundamental along with the factors discussed by Erickson.

[18] This has been the quid pro quo in auto assembly, paper, and telecommunications.

[19] This is partly because increased productivity growth in a particular company or industry does not necessarily or automatically translate into improved compensation, labor standards, or job security (e.g., meatpacking). Increased productivity may be the key to higher American living standards and international competitiveness in the long-run without necessarily helping workers in any particular company or industry in the short-run. In the short run in a particular firm or industry, higher productivity may generate job losses and weaken labor's bargaining power.

[20] For instance, problem solving requires sufficient information, so we might re-examine legal information requirements. It is also important to reconsider mandatory/permissive/illegal categories to facilitate the use of collective bargaining to resolve issues that either party deems important. The definition of bargaining units and the exclusion of lower-level supervisors from the protection of the law is another issue that relates to the effectiveness of collective bargaining. So too are issues related to particular industries, like construction, where occupational rather than industrial organization is the norm. Another issue would be the coverage of the NLRA across industries and sectors.

[21] The earlier discussion also suggests that we might consider ways to manage competition in industries in which deregulation has proven destabilizing. At the present time, however, reregulation of these industries does not seem to be on the political horizon.

[22] I am reminded of Clark Kerr's suggestion that to reduce labor-management conflict, we need to avoid depressions and wars (Kerr 1954). Of course it is important to avoid major depressions and wars for other reasons! Similarly, while full employment would have a salutary effect on collective bargaining, it is an important public policy goal in and of itself.

References

America's Choice: High Skills or Low Wages. 1990. The Report of the Commission on the Skills of the American Workforce. Rochester, NY: National Center on Education and the Economy.

Eaton, Adrienne E., and Paula B. Voos. 1992. "Unions and Contemporary Innovations in Work Organization, Compensation, and Employee Participation." In L. Mishel and P. Voos, eds., *Unions and Economic Competitiveness*. Armonk, NY: M.E. Sharpe.

Katz, Harry C. 1993. "The Decentralization of Collective Bargaining: A Literature Review and Comparative Analysis." *Industrial and Labor Relations Review*, Vol. 47, no. 1 (October), pp. 3-22.

Kerr, Clark. 1959. "Industrial Conflict and Its Mediation." *American Journal of Sociology*, Vol. LX (November), pp. 230-245.

Kochan, Thomas A., and Paul Osterman. 1993. *The Mutual Gains Enterprise: Human Resource Strategies and National Policy*. Manuscript, Massachusetts Institute of Technology.

Kochan, Thomas A., and Michael Piore. 1984. "Will the New Industrial Relations Last? Implications for the American Labor Movement." *The Annals of the American Academy of Political and Social Science*, Vol. 473 (May), pp. 177-189.

Rosow, Jerome. 1993. Work in America Institute. Testimony to the Commission on the Future of Worker Management Relations, U.S. Departments of Labor and Commerce. Washington, DC.

Somers, Gerald G., ed. 1980. *Collective Bargaining: Contemporary American Experience*. Madison, WI: Industrial Relations Research Association.

Strauss, George, Daniel G. Gallagher, and Jack Fiorito. 1991. *The State of the Unions*. Madison, WI: Industrial Relations Research Association.

Wall Street Journal. 1993. "Steelworkers Get Accords With 2 Concerns." August 2, p. 2.

CHAPTER 1

Collective Bargaining in the Paper Industry: Developments Since 1979

ADRIENNE EATON
Rutgers University

JILL KRIESKY
University of Oregon

Editor's Abstract

The paper industry is highly unionized nationwide (especially in basic paper production, less so in plants converting paper to products), although unionization has declined somewhat in recent years. Bargaining is quite decentralized, reflecting both the different paper submarkets (newsprint, tissue paper, writing paper, diapers, etc.) and basic paper's location in geographically dispersed small towns adjacent raw materials and water. Labor costs are a small portion of total costs, wages are high, and the range of jobs include some that are quite skilled. Technology has been undergoing a revolution in recent years, with a shift to computer-automated production. This has required a transformation of traditional blue-collar paper-making skills. Long-term economic factors have been favorable, despite recession-related problems in the early 1980s and again in the early 1990s. There has been strong long-term growth in paper demand. The U.S. industry enjoys a raw material advantage in the world market.

In recent years, team production, employee involvement, and labor-management cooperation have become increasingly common in basic paper mills. Work reorganization, more "flexibility" in job descriptions and staffing arrangements, and increased training have often accompanied technological modernization efforts. Several large paper companies have signed national agreements with the United Paperworkers International Union (UPIU) indicating their willingness to cooperate with the union in jointly making the transition. Moreover, industry compensation has held up reasonably well. While real hourly earnings declined after 1986, it was a much less severe decline than for most manufacturing workers.

The current cooperative turn, however, follows a period of labor strife. Paperworkers themselves perceive the 1980s as a period in which they were often forced to make concessions on weekend premium pay, holiday closings, job descriptions and work rules, subcontracting, even health care. For a period, lump sum payments largely replaced base pay increases. These concessions were more severe at some companies than others and at some locations than others. They were often forced by hard-bargaining strategies in which companies used or threatened permanent striker replacements, plant closures, or lack of new technological investment. International Paper is the premier example. Eaton and Kriesky review the efforts of the UPIU to fight these trends and chronicle the problems for the union caused by (1) a decentralized bargaining structure, (2) NLRB interpretation of labor law, (3) technological changes which facilitated the replacement of strikers, and (4) union weakness and lack of preparation.

The reader will be struck by the thoughtful discussion of the mixed legacy of this period of labor strife for today's cooperative efforts. Employee involvement and team production in some locations may be hampered by the labor strife of the 1980s which leads part of the work force to view "flexibility" as a concession to management. On the other hand, some hard bargainers, like Champion, appear to have been successful in managing a turn to a more cooperative relationship with the union and have jointly implemented team programs in some locations. Other companies, like Scott or James River, who never demanded sensitive concessions (e.g., elimination of holiday closing), have a good relationship with the union and appear to be poised to take maximum advantage of employee involvement and teams. It remains to be seen whether or not the hard bargainers really achieved a cost advantage over their competitors. However, while organized labor suffered some setbacks in the 1980s, it continues to be a presence in the industry today. Modernization and productivity improvement initiatives are unlikely to be successful without taking this into account.

o   o   o

Listen my friends to the message I gots,
This is another message from Big Ed Potts.
Listen I say and read, and listen real keen
About the way they want to screw us,
     Mr. Champeen.

To them it seems okay, but to me it's unfair,
If he's up to cut our premium pay, it'll
     be his woist nightmare.
He might think we're just blowing smoke,
But try to cut our pay, and he'll surely choke.
We're in this together, ONE AND ALL,
When negotiations come, CHAMPEEN will fall.

We'll stand together, it's not just talk,
Give it your best shot . . ., we won't balk.
Between the fence post is what I usually write,
And premium pay is worth a fight.
We don't want much, not the silver spoon.
This is Big Ed Potts, you'll hear from me soon.

These lines from a pseudonymous paperworker-poet sum up the tenor of labor relations in the paper industry in the 1980s and highlight a contentious issue. They also point to continuing problems in the industry today resulting from the conflicts of the 1980s. The author, a worker at a Champion mill in Florida in the late 1980s, informs the reader that management's demand for the elimination of the decades-old overtime premium for weekend work will result in intense conflict with the workers and their union, a prediction that came true repeatedly in the industry through the 1980s. His call for paperworker solidarity, however, was less often heeded and, even when heeded, often failed to deter management's demand for concessions.

Many, though not all, paper companies eliminated weekend premium pay, reorganized work through the use of production teams, and established participative programs during the 1980s. Increased decentralization in an already decentralized system, widespread and successful attempts to operate during strikes for the first time in the industry, and the growth of a modest yet significant nonunion sector, all strengthened management's bargaining power. In the early 1990s, however, the concession movement waned, and several large companies established labor-management cooperation programs at the corporate or strategic level.

The reasons for these changes are complex. The beginnings of significant international competition, tremendous technological change, a spurt of merger and acquisition activity leading to increased debt, and changing management philosophies, all contributed to management's drive for concessions. Yet despite short-term cyclical problems, the industry remained relatively prosperous throughout the decade, leading some to conclude that companies pursued concessions simply because they could, not because they needed to. This lingering suspicion on the part of many workers and union leaders makes the path to greater cooperation a difficult one, at least in those companies who bargained hard and successfully for concessions.

This chapter explores these themes. It is organized as follows. It begins with a discussion of the industry—its primary product groups, its long-term prospects, and its employers. We then turn to the level of unionization and a discussion of the important unions in the industry. Next, we review the major challenges shaping the industry's economics, including globalization, environmental issues, and technological change. We conclude with a detailed examination of bargaining relationships and outcomes, with a particular focus on the high levels of conflict and cooperation that have characterized the recent past.

The Industry and Its Institutions

The Employers

In 1991 the Commerce Department ranked the paper and allied products industry as the ninth largest in manufacturing in the U.S. (U.S. Department of Commerce 1992:10-11). Its ranking in the world economy is similar, employing approximately 3.5 million persons (ILO 1992:4).[1] Further, it is a growth industry. Contrary to some predictions, the paper industry has clearly benefited from the information revolution. Use of computers, facsimile machines and other electronic reporting devices has increased worldwide demand for paper. In addition, the rise of consumers' environmental concerns has strengthened demand for biodegradable corrugated containers and other box products. The prognosis for the long term is for continued growth for paper in general, though the demand for certain specific products will likely decline.

Indeed, the industry is a diverse one in terms of products. The fundamental split within the industry is between the production of its basic products—pulp (some of which is sold on the open market) and seven basic paper grades[2]—and "converting," the side of the industry that produces the final products with which consumers are familiar such as disposable diapers, paper bags, and cardboard boxes. This division is meaningful in labor relations terms, in particular because the "converting" end is less unionized. Within these broad categories there are numerous specific products. For the most part, they are not especially important in terms of differences in labor relations. Differences in the future prospects for particular products have implications for particular mills but mean less for overall trends.

While long-term trends in demand appear strong, the industry, along with the rest of the U.S. economy, has experienced two serious downturns since 1979.[3] On the other hand, the years from 1987 to 1989 set records in terms of profits and production levels (Vogel and Weber 1989:47; *The Paperworker* March 1991; see Table 1).

TABLE 1

Profits Rates and Productivity: U.S. Paper Industry 1975, 1979-1993

Year	Return on Net Worth[a]	Return on Sales[b]	Index of Output per Production Employee Hour[c]
1975	12.1%	5.7%	63.2
1979	16.0	9.8	75.5
1980	11.6	7.2	75.5
1981	11.7	7.5	74.8
1982	5.5	3.5	80.7
1983	8.5	5.3	86.3
1984	10.7	6.7	87.4
1985	9.7	6.2	89.8
1986	10.5	7.1	96.7
1987	14.1	9.3	100.0
1988	18.8	11.4	101.2
1989	15.4	9.6	101.8
1990	10.6	6.3	103.8
1991	4.4	2.9	105.5
1992	4.4	1.5	113.2
1993	-0.6	1.0	118.2

[a]Net profit after taxes to net worth. Source: American Forest and Paper Association from Quarterly Financial Report for Manufacturing, Mining and Trade Corporations.

[b]Net profit before taxes to net sales. Source: American Forest and Paper Association from Quarterly Financial Report for Manufacturing, Mining and Trade Corporations.

[c]1987=100. Source: U.S. Department of Labor, Bureau of Labor Statistics via American Paper Institute.

It is difficult to specify who the largest employers are given that the ranking has changed enormously in the last two decades and that there is a degree of overlap with the wood products industry (which uses the same raw material). Table 2 presents sales and earnings figures in 1992 for 26 paper and allied products companies. Based on 1992 sales through the third quarter, the ten largest companies in the U.S. rank as follows: International Paper, Kimberly-Clark, Stone Container, Champion International, Scott, James River, Mead, Boise Cascade, Union Camp, and Temple-Inland. However, in a separate listing of paper *and* forest products company sales for 1991, Georgia-Pacific and Weyerhaeuser are included and rank second and third behind IP (*Pulp and Paper* March 1992:25).

TABLE 2

Sales and Income for 26 U.S. Paper Companies, 1992
(thousand dollars)

Company	Sales	Income
Badger Paper Mills Inc.	54,952	(1,674)
Boise Cascade	2,831,150	(123,060)
Bowater-US	1,095,019	(60,047)
Chesapeake	876,611	13,151
Consolidated Papers	872,076	2,575
Champion International	3,889,032	52,019
Federal Paperboard	1,008,254	66,470
Glatfelter	411,003	42,311
International Paper	10,200,000	312,000
James River	3,586,501	47,806
Kimberly-Clark	5,281,800	413,500
Longview Fibre	503,442	22,272
The Mead Corp.	3,586,100	54,500
Mosinee Paper Co.	169,747	631
Nashua Paper Co.	407,317	3,836
Pentair	917,764	28,465
Potlatch Corp.	1,003,048	68,374
Scott Paper	3,660,800	122,400
Pope & Talbot	400,477	(5,084)
Sonoco Products Co.	1,353,969	80,112
Stone Container Corp.	4,189,900	(94,700)
Temple-Inland	2,014,600	121,700
Union Camp	2,320,014	68,977
Westvaco	1,722,664	103,060
Wausau	370,935	40,009
Willamette	1,775,702	68,303

Source: American Paper Institute. (Figures are through the third quarter only.)

Since paper mills are typically located near their most important input, trees, they are concentrated in the Northeast, Midwest, Northwest and South. While many of the newer plants, built in the 1960s and later, were located in the South, it is less likely that this was due to the region's nonunion reputation than to the relatively plentiful and fast-growing forests.[4]

Unions and Unionization

Paper is one of the most organized industries in the U.S., although accurate measures are hard to identify. Industry observers indicate that there are substantial differences between industry segments. Further, while levels of organization are high, they are declining. In 1982 a Bureau of Labor Statistics economist stated that approximately 96% of production workers in pulp, paper and paperboard mills were organized (Larson 1984). One industry observer estimates that in 1979 approximately 91% of the primary side was organized, a figure which has dropped to roughly 85% in 1992.[5] The figures for converting are much lower; a union representative estimated that approximately 25% are organized.[6]

Various scholars have used data collected through the Current Population Survey to estimate unionization rates. Unfortunately, since they rely on individual reports regarding industry as well as union membership and contract coverage, these estimates lack complete accuracy. Table 3 presents these estimates for the years 1975 and 1979 through

TABLE 3

Unionization Rates for the Paper Industry, Selected Years
(Contract Coverage in Parentheses)

Year	Pulp, Paper, and Paperboard Mills	Miscellaneous Paper Products	Paperboard Containers and Boxes
1975	67.6%	43.9%	49.2%
1979	69.1	42.7	53.3
1980	67.1	42.1	52.9
1983	59.2	33.9	45.2
	(62.7)	(35.2)	(48.0)
1984	58.9	39.9	42.8
	(60.6)	(43.1)	(43.7)
1985	60.0	28.9	38.7
	(61.2)	(31.8)	(40.4)
1986	59.8	27.3	34.1
	(62.5)	(29.3)	(35.8)
1987	57.7	26.1	33.7
	(58.0)	(26.4)	(35.9)
1988	53.9	23.7	34.6
	(55.3)	(24.4)	(37.5)
1989	50.0	22.9	28.6
	(51.9)	(25.2)	(30.4)
1990	53.2	21.0	28.3
	(54.3)	(22.9)	(29.0)
1991	53.9	23.7	34.6
	(49.6)	(25.4)	(34.4)

Sources: 1975, 1979, 1980: From the Current Population Survey as estimated by Kokkelenberg and Sockell (1985). 1983-1991: From the Current Population Survey as estimated and supplied by Hirsch and Macpherson (1993).

1991. The CPS divides the industry into three segments: pulp, paper and paperboard mills; miscellaneous paper and pulp products; and paperboard containers and boxes. While the absolute numbers do not match the estimates of industry observers, they do support the three observations described above. The levels on the primary side, consisting of pulp, paper and paperboard mills, are significantly higher than other segments of the industry. Further, although the numbers fluctuate, there is an overall downward trend in all three categories. Finally, these rates are among the highest reported in manufacturing. For the earlier years, only subsets of primary metals and transportation equipment and glass and glass products surpassed unionization in paper mills.

One factor—the difficulty of building new mills on new sites—is largely responsible for these trends and differences (Birecree 1991:5). This is due to both the enormous capital investment required to build new mills and environmental regulations and permitting procedures. Yet, it is the building of new facilities that has reduced unionization levels in the paper industry. One paper industry labor relations expert indicates that of 27 new mills built in the past twenty years, 18 are nonunion.[7] Further, the much smaller investment involved in building new converting operations has allowed for more greenfield and, therefore, nonunion sites. For example, Union Camp has one new, nonunion paper mill but approximately 20 new, nonunion converting facilities.[8]

Unions have found establishing local unions in new facilities difficult. Not surprisingly, labor and management differ on the reasons. The unions blame defects in labor law and its administration. Management points to the terms and conditions of employment in the nonunion facilities, which tend to equal or surpass those in unionized facilities. Moreover, once organized, only about half of the new locals actually secure first contracts,[9] an experience which also parallels that in other industries. At the same time, only one multi-mill company, Fort Howard Paper, has successfully resisted unionization in all of its mills. Decertifications of existing facilities have not been significant in number, although those resulting from the replacement of strikers at some IP mills are notable in the message they send and the attention they have received. In fact, IP recently announced that it would prefer to operate nonunion, an important departure from past practice in the industry (BNA *Daily Labor Report* [henceforth *DLR*] May 13, 1992).

While unionization rates in the industry remain relatively high, membership in the primary unions has shrunk. Membership in the United

Paperworker International Union (UPIU), the single largest union in the industry, declined in the 1980s due to improvements in paper making technology, the opening of nonunion mills (especially in converting) and to a lesser extent, subcontracting of some union work (see Table 4). To counter these factors and the obstacles to organizing mentioned above, the union instituted a new organizing department in 1987. (Previously, international representatives conducted most organizing on their own, and historically, much organizing was "top-down" with companies automatically recognizing the union.)

TABLE 4
Membership Figures for UPIU, 1981-1994

Year	Membership
1981	271,915
1982	263,653
1983	254,127
1984	250,799
1985	242,074
1986	239,321
1987	236,026
1988	229,267
1989	226,464
1990	222,681
1991	222,024
1992	218,086
1993	212,669
1994	264,236

Source: UPIU Research Department, April 1994.

UPIU represents approximately 218,000 production, technical, and maintenance workers. (The clericals in mills are not typically organized.) They are organized into 1075 locals, including 30 amalgamated locals. Membership is most heavily concentrated in New England, the Southeast, and North Central states. Approximately 2000 members belong to locals in Manitoba and Ontario, Canada. The union is the product of several mergers, the most important of which culminated in the current organization in 1972.[10] Largely due to the creation of UPIU through mergers, it is common in some parts of the country to find three or four different UPIU locals within a single plant.[11] Typically the unions negotiate major issues collectively in a plant-wide agreement.

There is one other significant paper workers' union in the U.S., the Association of Western Pulp and Paper Workers (AWPPW), an independent that operates on the West Coast from Alaska to California. Its membership has also shrunk. In 1979 there were just over 20,000 members; as of January 1993, only 14,000 remained. The loss is due both to technological change and the closure of mills.[12] The membership is similar to that of the UPIU, although multiple locals are a rarity. AWPPW is engaged in virtually no organizing at this time; there are few new plants opening in their region, and they have made a determination not to go outside the industry for members.[13]

A few additional unions represent some paper mill workers. In particular, the International Brotherhood of Electrical Workers, the Pipefitters, and the Boilermakers represent a few skilled maintenance units in plants across the U.S. Occasionally these smaller locals coordinate bargaining with the paper worker locals in the plants. The Graphic Communications International Union has significant membership in converting plants, while the Steelworkers, the Allied Industrial Workers, and the Operating Engineers each represent production workers at a single paper mill.[14]

Several mergers involving industry unions have occurred recently. Possible merger partners for UPIU within the paper industry have included both the AWPPW[15] and the Canadian forest products unions (*The Paperworker* Nov. 1992:6). However, in the summer of 1993, the AWPPW membership turned down a merger proposal which both its executive board and convention delegates had endorsed.[16] UPIU has also pursued talks with potential partners outside the industry. The newest partner is the 50,000 member Allied Industrial Workers of America (AIW) which merged with UPIU in fall 1993. Mergers and increased organizing efforts have recently helped UPIU turn around the ten-year downward trend in membership. (See Table 4).

Challenges Facing the Industry

Aside from the two cyclical downturns the industry faced since 1979, there have been a number of other forces for change. The following section reviews the challenges facing the industry including international competition, environmental and other public policies, mergers and acquisition, and technological change.

Foreign competition. While it is clear that the markets for paper products have and will continue to become increasingly international, it is less clear how much of a threat foreign competition presents to U.S.

companies. The U.S. is the largest producer of pulp and paper products in the world, with Japan and Canada following a substantial distance behind (*ICEF Info* 1992). However, the U.S. is also the largest importer of paper goods, in part because of the large percentage of newsprint and other products purchased from Canada. Imports from other countries are a small but growing threat.[17] While historically the Scandinavian countries were the other major producers, today countries throughout the world make paper. The countries of Southeast Asia and South America have rapidly expanded production using their vast and fast-growing forest resources (*PIMA Magazine* [henceforth *PIMA*] Dec. 1987, March 1990; *ICEF Info* 1992).

Beyond the export activity it generates, the emergence of these competitors has additional implications for U.S. paper production. Foreign producers, primarily the Japanese, purchase inputs (wood) from the U.S. for their own domestic production. In doing so, they compete for those resources with domestic producers particularly in the Northwest.[18] Though controversy rages over whether to blame environmentalists (and protection of the spotted owl) or the Japanese, it is clear that the resource base and, therefore, paper production is on the decline in the Northwest.

Globalization has also meant growing export activity by U.S. companies. Until recently, U.S. producers used other countries as "markets of convenience" in which they sold surplus output when demand was slack at home. The ability of U.S. companies to export has depended, in large part, on the relative value of the dollar. Hence exports declined sharply in the early 1980s with the rise in the dollar. Unfortunately, this worsened the industry recession since the strengthening of the dollar occurred at the exact moment when weakness in domestic markets created the need to export. Exports recovered later in the decade as the dollar fell (Birecree 1991).

Increasingly, U.S. producers are exporting even when demand is strong at home. Between 1979 and 1989, U.S. exports of paper rose 140%; market pulp rose 100%; and paperboard rose 54% (*Pulp and Paper* March 1991:59). Continued or improved access to foreign markets will be important to the future of the U.S. industry. Japan's annual per capita consumption of paper products is second only to that of the U.S. (Tetrick 1992:77), but it imports only 4.2% of its products (*Pulp and Paper* July 1989). An agreement was signed between the U.S. and Japan in April 1992 that has the potential to further open the Japanese market to U.S. paper products.

The unifying European market provides another important challenge for U.S. producers. In this case, some U.S. producers have responded by establishing production facilities in those countries. Several of the large U.S. corporations, including International Paper, James River, and Scott, invested there in anticipation of the 1992 European Community agreements (*PIMA* June 1991:36). However, other than in Europe, Scott Paper alone appears to have invested substantially in "bricks and mortar" in growing foreign markets (*PIMA* June 1991). Facilities operated by U.S. companies in other countries are, by and large, for consumption in those countries. Thus imports from foreign operations of U.S.-based companies have not provided a significant challenge to U.S. production facilities as happened, for instance, in the auto industry. These operations may instead reduce the export of U.S.-produced goods.

Finally, significant changes in North American trade policy occurred in the 1980s and may continue to be influential with the passage of the North American Free Trade Agreement (NAFTA). The U.S.'s historic trade deficit with Canada in paper declined significantly in 1991 after the adoption of the new trade agreement with Canada. Many, including the U.S. Commerce Department (1992:10-13), credit the free trade agreement with the change. Others point to Canada's slow adjustment to the demand for newsprint manufactured from recycled inputs.[19]

Exports to Mexico have been increasing over the last five years and are expected to accelerate with the passage of NAFTA. Because paper is a heavily capital-intensive industry, it is not likely that much paper production will move to Mexico due to NAFTA. However, industry representatives indicated in 1992 that the Mexican paper industry expected to expand in the wake of NAFTA. Indeed, Kimberly-Clark's 43% owned subsidiary, already the largest producer in Mexico, is expanding (*Pulp and Paper* April 1992:33). But both the lack of a good natural resource base (trees) and the difficulty of raising sufficient capital for a new facility, when ample capacity exists in the U.S., limit the growth possibilities in Mexico. UPIU representatives admit that converting operations could move there as easily as many other manufacturing operations.[20] But the difficulties of shipping cartons, tissues, etc., make proximity to the market important; converting operations are typically located near their major metropolitan markets.

The extent to which globalization of the industry has driven change in labor relations is unclear. On the one hand, the industry is and has been well positioned for the international market. Many industry executives emphasize that the U.S. (and Canadian) forest resources provide a distinct advantage over many competitor nations (see, for example, an interview with Champion's Sigler [*PIMA*, Sept. 1989:27]).[21] Further, there is widespread agreement that its capital, natural resources, and even labor inputs, make U.S. production extremely competitive, if not dominant in the world (Rooks 1991:33). The editor of one trade magazine observed in 1989 that "paper company managers have a double advantage. They have resisted union demands because of the weakened state of organized labor and *avoided the intense international competition . . .* that caused labor unions to lose their power" (emphasis added, Rooks 1989).

Certainly union representatives discount the importance of international competition and have viewed it as essentially an attempt to legitimize "unreasonable" concessionary demands.[22] Still, some industry executives point to growing competition as a central impetus for bringing down bargained wage increases in the early 1980s.[23] A third view which accommodates both positions holds that while international competition was not severe enough to create the need for concessions in the short run, the industry has positioned itself to successfully compete in world markets for the long term, in part by reducing labor costs and improving productivity.

Public policy. Three areas of public policy other than labor law itself have affected recent paper industry labor relations: enforcement of antitrust regulation, environmental protection, and occupational safety and health laws. The first is a phenomenon of the 1970s that has had a lasting impact on the industry. Paper industry representatives consistently report that competition in the industry grew in the 1980s, though as described above, this was only partly a result of increased foreign competition. It may also have resulted from "a series of notorious price-fixing cases involving folding cartons, paper boxes, and other products [that] swept paper companies into criminal prosecutions" (Stewart 1993:59). These criminal and civil cases involved a wide range of products and most of the major companies in the industry. They resulted in a variety of outcomes including guilty verdicts with fines and jail terms, innocent verdicts, and out-of-court settlements (*Wall Street Journal,* June 12, 1980, Sept. 29, 1980, Dec. 3, 1980; *New York Times,* Feb. 29, 1980, April 28, 1980, Sept. 19, 1980, Nov. 10, 1980). Thus policy decisions to enforce antitrust laws may have increased price competition in a traditionally "monopolistically competitive" industry (Birecree 1991:3).[24]

A second area of regulation increasingly important to the industry is environmental protection. The emission of by-products into water and, to a lesser extent, air represent the primary concerns. Further, increased emphasis on recycling of paper has changed the raw material inputs into the manufacture of some paper products. Thus environmental regulations have led to significant capital expenditures and have affected siting decisions. Closely related to these issues, of course, is the worldwide movement to protect existing forests. To the extent that this movement focuses successfully on the vast forests in the developing world, the U.S. paper industry may actually benefit as foreign-based production facilities lose easy and/or cheap access to those forests. On the other hand, as mentioned above, decreased logging in the Northwest, due in part to concerns over environmental impact, has reduced the raw material inputs for pulp and paper mills (wood chips). Some observers blame environmental regulations for mill closures in that part of the country.[25]

Occupational safety and health regulation, linked by many to environmental issues, has also affected the paper industry. Since the mid-1980s, OSHA has proposed significant fines on several large paper companies for various violations inside paper plants.[26] UPIU locals have frequently requested OSHA inspections at their worksites both because of increased awareness of the dangers to workers' health posed by the chemicals with which they work (*The Paperworker* Sept. 1991, Nov. 1991) and as a bargaining tactic (BNA *Union Labor Report* May 16, 1991:145-46). Indeed, some industry representatives have suggested that the union has made similar use of the environmental regulation apparatus.[27]

Mergers and acquisitions. As was the case in most industries in the 1980s, mergers and acquisitions altered company size, product mix, and industrial relations in the paper industry. Since 1974 one-third of the top 100 companies in the industry (worldwide) disappeared as independent entities, primarily through merger and acquisition (Kalish 1990). Many of the remaining largest paper companies increased in size dramatically through these transactions.[28]

This corporate restructuring and the "alarmingly high" debt-to-equity ratios (Matussek and Pearson 1991) acquired by many companies undoubtedly affected industrial relations. Georgia-Pacific, recognized by unions as one of the industry's hard bargainers, reportedly abolished existing contracts in plants it acquired in favor of its own "model" contract.[29] Champion's "white knight" takeover of St. Regis created debt that led to a reduction by half of the combined companies' work force through layoffs and division sales (American Paper Institute [henceforth API] 1986:32; J. Brooks 1987:188-89). Heavy debt also put pressure on Champion management to search for new ways to increase productivity and reduce costs. Coincidentally, the acquisition of additional facilities resulted in the near simultaneous expiration of contracts at several locations. This presented UPIU with the opportunity to "pool" its contract ratification voting, a tactic discussed in more detail below.

Technological change and the labor force. Paper, though historically a product of a continuous-flow process, has experienced additional automation over the last dozen years. F. Keith Hall, president of the Technical Association for the Pulp and Paper Industry (TAPPI), recently reported that "the pulping process has been exploding with the improvements in computerization" (Rice 1992). Indeed, capital spending largely on new automation (and to a lesser degree on environmental controls) increased rapidly in the industry in the early 1980s after decades of little change. For instance, IP began a seven-year, $6 billion automation program in 1979 (Birecree 1991). Spending declined somewhat in the mid-1980s but rebounded again in recent years (*Pulp and Paper* Jan. 1991:102).

Not surprisingly, the actual pace and degree of change varies enormously from company to company and from mill to mill. While IP was an early automater, a Champion executive admits his company was relatively slow to upgrade; Champion is currently in the midst of a substantial, five-year spending program.[30] One industry representative indicates that virtually all paper manufacturing facilities have some computerization, but the extent and level of sophistication in using the technology vary widely.[31]

In its most "advanced" forms, computerization has distanced the papermaker from the manufacturing process. Where once a papermaker relied on his (rarely her) senses to monitor production, now the monitoring is done largely through the intermediary of the machine. The traditional papermaker listened to the sounds made by the machine, touched and smelled the pulp. In the most advanced plants today, operators are now largely confined to control rooms where they monitor the production process on computer screens (Zuboff 1988). Computerization has also allowed for significant improvements in quality through the generation of a tremendous amount of data about the production process. Finally, the new machines are larger and produce high volumes of very wide paper more efficiently. These changes have had a number of consequences for jobs and job content. First, the greatest impact has been on employment levels which have remained flat while production has increased. As Table 5 shows, the industry as a whole (SIC code 26) employed 522,700 production employees in 1980; in 1991, 520,100 production employees were working. The number of workers in the industry fell significantly in the 1981-82 recession; in some cases employment rolls fell by as much as 30% (*Pulp and Paper* July 1985). But by 1984 when the industry began to rebound and companies stopped laying off workers, few returned to prerecession employment levels. In mid-1985, *Pulp and Paper* reported that of the 21 major companies it surveyed, none were increasing their work force levels.

TABLE 5
Earnings, Hours, and Employment
Paper and Allied Products, 1980-1993

Year	Avg. Hourly Earnings Paper	Real Hourly Earnings Paper	Avg. Hourly Earnings All Mfg.	Total Emp'ees Paper (1000s)	Prod. Emp'ees Paper (1000s)	Avg. 1st Year Wage Increases Paper(%)
1973	4.20	9.46	4.09	704.6	543.1	NA
1979	7.13	9.75	6.70	706.8	535.6	9.6
1980	7.84	9.46	7.27	692.8	522.7	9.2
1981	8.60	9.41	7.99	688.5	518.4	8.7
1982	9.32	9.62	8.49	662.0	493.4	6.9
1983	9.93	9.95	8.83	661.2	494.5	5.6
1984	10.41	10.08	9.18	680.9	511.6	3.3
1985	10.83	10.13	9.53	677.7	512.1	2.1
1986	11.18	10.29	9.73	673.7	511.0	0.3
1987	11.43	10.16	9.91	679.0	515.7	0.4
1988	11.65	9.96	10.19	689.9	517.3	0.9
1989	11.96	9.76	10.48	697.4	521.8	1.1
1990	12.31	9.54	10.83	699.3	524.3	2.5
1991	12.72	9.47	11.18	687.9	517.4	2.2
1992	13.07	9.46	11.46	687.3	517.7	2.5
1993	13.42	9.44	11.76	680.1	515.4	NA

Sources: Data for 1980-1982 from *Employment & Earnings*, January 1984. Data for 1983-1987 from Supplement to *E&E*, August 1988. Data for 1988-1991 from *Employment & Earnings*, January 1992. Average first-year-increase series from American Paper Institute. Real earnings computed using the CPI-W, 1982-1984=100.

Secondly, the skills required by workers have changed substantially and are expected to evolve further in the future. Both technical and interpersonal skills are assuming much greater importance. Further, pulp and paper production takes place primarily in rural areas. For several decades plants have drawn on the local, high school-educated population for workers who were trained at work for the semi-skilled and skilled jobs (*New York Times* December 28, 1986; Birecree 1993). Over the last decade, the source for paper mill employees remained the same, but their numbers and skills are changing dramatically. As one industry representative put it, paper companies have relied on high wage levels to attract the "cream" of the local work force, but "the cream is becoming seriously diluted."[32] Training efforts in the industry thus far appear to lag behind skill requirements.

The increasing use of computers require technology-based skills which Zuboff (1988) has labeled intellective. Workers need to make sense of data using inferential reasoning, procedural and systemic thinking rather than responding to the physical cues (the sight, feel, smell, even taste of pulp) which, in the past, made a worker a good papermaker. Zuboff's accounts of two paper mills using state-of-the-art technology suggest that the existing work force is being trained in the new methods. She notes, however, that in the newer of the two plants, the workers were younger and many had some college education (which may be associated with intellective skills).

Birecree (1993) notes that workers need more sophisticated math and reading skills than was previously the case, and she reports that workers receive formal classroom training. Indeed, many experts argue that traditional on-the-job training will no longer suffice (*Pulp and Paper* Dec. 1989). Industry journals are filled with recommendations that management enlist automation vendors, human resource departments, training consultants, educational technology (videos and interactive computer training), and community colleges in aggressive efforts to teach workers both the intellective skills and the relationship between their job and the rest of the papermaking process (*PIMA* May 1989:7, Feb. 1989:28, July 1989:42, Oct. 1989, April 1991:30-31).

The need for interpersonal skills is closely tied to the move toward team-based production. Paper journal articles increasingly advocate training on a variety of problem solving, consensus building, communication, even self-management techniques which will allow teams or crews of workers in one phase of papermaking to coordinate and integrate their activities with teams involved in production "upstream" or "down-stream." Managers in the paper industry, as in others, attest to the improved productivity which results when people learn to work together.

Collective Bargaining

Dunlop and Healy have described collective bargaining as resembling a poker game, a debating society, a rational process and an exercise in power politics. It is the latter which most correctly characterizes bargaining in the paper industry in the 1980s. In 1979 relations among the major unions and the major employers in the industry were relatively cordial, and contracts featured double-digit wage increases in response to a high rate of increase in consumer prices. Marked changes occurred in the following decade. Wage increases moderated considerably, and decades-old work rules and wage supplements disappeared from many contracts. Some bargaining relationships, notably that between International Paper and UPIU, had deteriorated into open warfare, while others sought to avoid such conflict through the development of corporate and/or plant level cooperation programs.

A wide variety of issues became contentious for the parties during the 1980s, some common to other industries, others not. Bargaining structure itself was a source of conflict, as the parties struggled to create or keep the structures that would yield the best results for themselves. Overall, while UPIU sought to increase centralized or coordinated bargaining, the industry trend moved toward even greater decentralization. Labor and management also clashed over the size and structure of wage payments. Lump-sum bonuses reduced or eliminated percentage increases and many wage supplements. In addition, management sought and often won both changes in work rules that increased their flexibility and measures that shifted health care costs onto workers.

Because of the decentralized structure in the industry in the early 1980s, some contracts, typically three years in length, were bargained every year. However, in two years out of every three, considerably more contracts were bargained. Regional emphasis shifted from one year to another as well. (*Pulp and Paper* Jan. 1987:39; API 1992).

New negotiating tactics. In the late 1970s the collective bargaining process in the paper industry mirrored that of other manufacturing industries. As mentioned above, labor relations were fairly cordial. When bargaining broke down, locals went on strike. Management rarely attempted to operate during stoppages. The UPIU successfully used mill-by-mill bargaining to whipsaw local management into substantial wage increases as well as numerous wage supplements.[33] Annual wage increases hovered around 10%. Indeed, percentage wage increases in the first year of paperworkers' contracts were well above the manufacturing average (API chart ER90096). Change was on the horizon, however, as the character and concerns of management and the tactics they were willing and able to use began to change. In particular, sometime in the late 1970s an event took place that was to have a rippling effect throughout the industry over the course of the next decade: a mill on the West Coast operated during a strike.[34] What was never viewed as a realistic possibility suddenly became a choice.

Thus when UPIU President Wayne Glenn announced in 1981 that cost-of-living clauses, improved occupational safety and health provisions, and advance notice of an employer's plans to lay off workers or close a plant were top bargaining priorities, industry executives had other ideas (BNA *DLR*, Feb. 19, 1981:A-6). Company managers, increasingly recruited from the ranks of financial managers and attorneys rather than operations management, gradually turned their attention toward labor costs. Their efforts to hold down wages and benefits developed somewhat differently in the South, Northeast, and Midwest (where UPIU represents most organized paperworkers) and the West Coast (where AWPPW predominates).

One industry executive indicates that CEOs from the major companies met in 1980 and agreed to limit wage increases; specifically, the goal was to cap them at 8%. Champion and Scott mill management in Alabama led the charge. UPIU unions struck at both locations, but salaried personnel successfully operated the mills. Managements' success with bouts of hard bargaining emboldened them to pursue it more broadly and to widen their bargaining agenda to include wage supplements and work rules.[35] In the following year the single most important centralized structure in the industry, International Paper's Southern Kraft Multiple (SKM) began experiencing difficulties which eventually led to its breakup. The SKM dated back to 1938 and, at one time, had included as many as 10 mills. It set the pattern for bargaining in the South and strongly influenced settlements throughout the country (excluding the West Coast).[36] In 1981 IP argued that the Georgetown, South Carolina, mill required contract language concessions allowing for greater flexibility in production work before the company would consider capital investment at those locations. The UPIU agreed that Georgetown should withdraw from the multiple to make an agreement that would secure the mill's future but which would have been unfavorable to the other locals in that group.

Events took a slightly different turn on the West Coast. A bitter and disruptive strike involving the major companies in 1978 led both the union and larger employers to search for a means to stabilize relations three years later.[37] In 1981 seven companies formed the Pulp and Paper Employer Bargaining Council (PPEBC) and reached an agreement peacefully with the AWPPW.

The economic downturn in the following years provided further impetus for lowering labor costs nationwide. Profits in the industry plummeted in 1982 (Table 1). Prices fell to 1979 levels and capacity utilization dipped to 86% (Birecree 1991). Still, widespread demands for concessions were slow to emerge, although wage increases had begun their downward creep (Table 5, last column). By 1984 the worst in terms of industry performance was over; the worst for the industry's unions and workers was just beginning.

In the South the SKM collapsed. In the multiple's 1983 negotiations only six mills bargained together. In 1984, IP argued that "diversity in size, vintage of capital stock, products produced and performance of these mills made it impossible to deal with the needs of each with respect to growing product market problems when all were covered by a common agreement" (Birecree 1991:12). As in other cases, power bargaining tactics accompanied rational arguments. UPIU agreed to dissolve the multiple because it believed IP would close mills down rather than modernize them (*Pulp and Paper* May 1985:140; Beck 1988). The union also agreed to stagger contract expiration dates of the participating mills (Birecree 1991:9-11).

On the West Coast, opposition to the PPEBC was running high on both sides despite its earlier success. Only three companies returned to the council in 1984. (One company was absorbed by another of the six, and two dropped out.) In that year the council unilaterally implemented their final offer which included small (uncontested) pay increases, revisions in health and welfare, and elimination of mandatory shutdowns on Christmas and July 4th. The latter was strongly opposed by the union. Nearly 43 AWPPW contracts covering 14,000 workers expired in both 1981 and 1984 when the PPEBC and AWPPW bargained. Their agreement set a pattern for the industry on the coast in both years (BNA *DLR* March 6, 1984:A-1,2; June 15, 1984:A-6,7).[38]

Bargaining in the industry was at a low ebb in 1985, but the settlements made that year foreshadowed substantial changes to come in the rest of the decade. API predicted at the start of the year that health care cost containment, increasing flexibility, elimination of production restrictions, and team concept would all be considered at the bargaining table (*Pulp and Paper* Jan. 1985:77). Proposals to increase flexibility included loosening of traditional job classifications and broadened subcontracting. Overall wage settlements continued their downward path from 3.3% in 1984 to 2.6% in 1985.[39]

Conflict escalates. UPIU began to fight back. In 1986 strike activity increased for the first time in three years (*Pulp and Paper* Jan. 1987:39). Management, however, countered with equally aggressive tactics, including the hiring of permanent replacements. Permanent replacements had been used to win strikes in the summer of 1985 by Georgia Pacific (Crossett, Arkansas) and Pentair's Miami Paper (West Carrollton, Ohio).[40] Workers at Boise Cascade's Rumford, Maine, mill struck on July 1, 1986, when asked to agree to flexibility language, a limited two-tier wage system, revocation of work rules, and increased insurance costs (BNA *DLR*, Sept. 18, 1986:A1-3). A month and a half later, management began hiring some 342 replacements. In September the company threatened to subcontract the work of another 350 workers. The move forced workers to accept contracts similar to the final offer (BNA *DLR* 181:A-1).

At the same time, the union developed a strategy that sought to establish some de facto centralization to bargaining and thus end the whipsaw. It consisted of holding off on signing a contract at a given location until all locals willing to coordinate had reached agreements. An early use of the strategy came in the 1986 negotiations with Champion International where the union coordinated bargaining among locals at several mills making white paper. Though some concessions were made on flexibility and health care, the union did not give up the overtime premium for Sunday work. While Champion asserts that the corporation was not interested in eliminating the Sunday premium in this year,[41] UPIU hailed the pool as a successful strategy and attempted to widen its use.

In general, however, the unions failed to beat back the concessionary trend. Management held first-year average wage increases to 0.3% in 1986, and 60% of the agreements used lump-sum cash payments in the first year to hold down labor costs.[42]

Locals in 61 mills lost restrictions on holiday operations (API: ER89047). Saturday/Sunday premium pay was eliminated in 33 contracts in 1986, over half of which were in the South (API:ER89047). Many of these were IP locals, since in 1985 and 1986 combined, 37 IP locals gave up Sunday premium pay (Birecree 1991).

In 1987 the locals representing IP workers in four locations began to fight back in what became the most bitter and well-publicized conflict in the industry. When IP demanded from the five locals at its Mobile, Alabama, mill the by-now routine concessions of increased use of team concept, flexibility between production and maintenance, loss of Saturday and Sunday premium pay, and greater subcontracting rights (Birecree 1991:14), the locals refused to accept them. On March 21, 1987, IP initiated a lockout. Later the Mobile locals joined locals from three other IP locations in an attempt to ward off the same demands. In a May 1987 meeting, they agreed to create a voting pool. As individual contracts expired, locals would join the pool. The union planned to pool ratification votes from all participating locals. None would sign an agreement until all received acceptable contracts. (BNA *DLR*, June 17, 1987:A-8).

After IP locked out the Mobile workers, it began operating with salaried personnel and temporary replacements. In the following months, locals struck at three plants in Maine, Pennsylvania, and Wisconsin. IP immediately hired permanent replacements at the three plants. UPIU responded with a number of bargaining strategies including a corporate campaign; involvement in town politics (Jay, Maine) to pass legislation prohibiting use of strikebreakers and temporary housing and appropriating town money for enforcement of state environmental laws; "caravans" of strikers speaking throughout New England and the South to enlist community support for their cause and stepped up reporting of alleged health and safety violations to OSHA. (BNA *DLR*, June 17, 1987:A-8,9; Aug. 6, 1987:A-12,13; Aug. 20, 1987:A-9-11; Oct. 28, 1987:A-12,13; Nov. 2, 1987:A-15,16; Dec. 2, 1987:A-10,13; Jan. 25, 1988:A-5-7; April 25, 1988:A-16,17; Feb. 12, 1992:A-8,9).

None of these tactics moved IP. Moreover, the failure of other IP locals to join their pool further hurt the striking/locked-out locals. According to Getman and Marshall (1993:1831), "the key defection came . . . in the fall of 1987 when the local union at the mill in Pine Bluff, Arkansas, decided by a large vote not to join the pool."[43] This failure points up the inability of the international union to control local union decisions and, therefore, to centralize the struggle against IP and other companies. After 16 months on strike (and 19 months locked out in Mobile), the union abandoned the strike (BNA *DLR*, Oct. 12, 1988). It was later decertified at the three struck mills.[44]

Thus despite the fact that company profit levels were now rebounding (see Table 1), the unions continued to take a beating. Average first-year wage increases only reached 0.4% in 1987. Locals continued to lose weekend premium pay and accept flexibility. On the West Coast centralized bargaining was abandoned, while contracts expired for nearly three-fourths of AWPPW members. Many of the new contracts followed the trend of wage freezes and lump-sum bonuses evident throughout the industry (BNA *DLR*, Jan. 19, 1990:A-1,2).

UPIU continued its attempts to centralize bargaining, pursuing a formal voting pool at other IP mills and again at Champion in 1989. Thirty-six locals at 24 mills joined a pool agreed upon by the IP council in June 1989. IP filed unfair labor practice charges against the union, and the NLRB issued a complaint. The Champion locals at white paper mills that coordinated bargaining in 1986 formed a voting pool in 1989.[45] This time the company was determined to eliminate the Saturday/Sunday premium pay. Locals balking at the demand reached impasse, and Champion implemented management's terms. Eventually, however, all locals ratified the contracts. Champion also filed charges against the union; these were later dropped as part of the effort to build a more cooperative relationship.[46]

Champion's implementation of terms became part of a new trend. As the use of replacements made strikes increasingly futile, UPIU shifted its approach to bargaining impasses. Locals increasingly chose to work under terms unilaterally implemented by management. In some of the cases, the union attempted to use in-plant tactics (Beck 1990). API figures show an average of roughly seven implemented "contracts" each year from 1988 to 1991.

Aftermath of Hard Bargaining

By 1992 much of the concessionary activity was over, and labor-management relations were moving in a number of different directions. It is clear, however, that hard bargaining in the 1980s significantly altered wages and work rules.

Despite the low levels of wage increases in the mid-1980s, wage levels for the industry still stood well above the manufacturing average by the end of the period (Table 5). In fact, comparisons of wage levels throughout this period show that the percentage increases in paper wages still outstripped those in manufacturing generally until 1988. However, after that year nominal paper industry wage percentage increases did not exceed the manufacturing average again until 1991.[47] Still, paperworkers generally fared better than other manufacturing workers in real terms. Between 1979 and 1992, all manufacturing workers lost real income, but paperworkers' real wages fell 3% compared to a 9.5% decline for manufacturing as a whole (see Table 5).

By the early 1990s most companies wanting the elimination of Saturday/Sunday premium pay had probably won it. According to API figures, by 1992, 133 contracts featured no premium pay for Saturday/ Sunday work (API:ER89047). Other companies, notably Scott and James River, never pressed strongly for such concessions. Likewise, management eliminated restrictions on holiday operations in 122 mills between 1986 and late 1992 (API:ER88025). Despite the relatively high wage rates in the industry, workers remain bitter about these concessions, especially given the perceived financial strength of the industry in recent years. Further, union leaders indicate that the loss of the overtime premium translated into a significant (7% to 12%) loss in income.[48]

Substantial movement has also been made toward increased flexibility, though many plants are still operating traditionally. Unionized mills frequently operate with team production systems similar to those found in newer nonunion operations. Production teams in the paper industry typically reduce the number of job classifications within a line of progression. In maintenance, teaming (or multicrafting) has reduced the number of (usually craft) classifications from as many as twelve to as few as two. Flexibility has also increased management's ability to assign production workers to other job classifications (outside of their teams or lines of progression). In some cases it has also meant that nonbargaining unit employees could do bargaining unit work, even when there was not an emergency. Some agreements provide for production workers to do routine maintenance and minor repairs usually assigned to maintenance employees (BNA *DLR*, Sept. 18, 1986:A1-3). From 1988 through 1990, management secured some kind of flexibility in 77 agreements (API:ER88023). There were fewer changes of this type in 1991 and 1992, but by this time management may have already secured them in chosen locations.

These same issues have been important in the West, although that region had tended to lag behind. In the past, West Coast producers argued that they needed wage freezes to compete with Southern and Northeastern mills. Since 1990 they have demanded more flexibility to compete with Southern producers who have already secured relaxed work rules in bargaining. The demand has met with resistance on the part of AWPPW, which is determined to fight the reduction in employment that flexibility may bring. (*Pulp and Paper* July 1985:58-59).

Throughout the country the increasing use of flexible work arrangements and teams may be tied to other emerging bargaining phenomena. Since 1987 (at least), contract length has increased beyond those previously negotiated and beyond the average for manufacturing. One observer indicated that in 1989 more than 90% of contracts were for at least three years and *more than 50%* of those were for at least four years (*Pulp and Paper* Sept. 1989). API figures confirm a growing percentage of contracts in paper that are three years or longer: 1987, 63%; 1988, 79%; 1989, 79%; 1990, 85%; 1991, 70%; 1992, 69%. There has also been a rash of early settlements/extensions of contracts beginning in 1988 (API:ER89065). In all but one year (1990), the majority of these occurred in the South. Further, since 1988 there have also been 146 settlements that have added or adjusted some form of nonconventional compensation (API:ER89059).

There are a number of possible explanations for these changes. Most importantly, companies may want an extended period of labor peace in which to establish flexible and, perhaps, cooperative work arrangements. Unions are also anxious to lock in acceptable contract terms, given the exhausting concessionary battles of the last decade. Management is increasingly relying on contingent compensation schemes to adjust wages during these lengthy contracts and to aid the development of participative and cooperative activities.

Attempts by UPIU to bring greater centralization in bargaining have largely failed. Companies clearly understand that a decentralized structure helps them achieve their bargaining demands in the current climate. Industry representatives argue strongly that centralized bargaining is simply not feasible in an industry with such diversity in products, technology, and region of operation. Yet it is also clear that ultimately power is at stake. One executive went so far as to suggest that "one of the biggest assets we've got in this industry [is] local bargaining, as opposed to industry-wide bargaining" (API 1986:54).[49]

Experiments with Labor-Management Cooperation and
Employee Involvement

The paper industry, like many others in recent years, has experimented with various forms of union-management cooperation and employee involvement (EI).[50] Interestingly, these innovative activities are intimately tied to the conflict discussed above. In some cases the implementation of certain types of EI programs exacerbated tensions between labor and management, while in others, cooperative programs were adopted to repair the damage done by conflict.

Surveys of paper industry representatives suggest widespread experimentation with cooperative and participative programs. A 1985 industry survey of 271 mill managers found that 80% had some form of labor-management committee (*PIMA* April 1985:20-23). Five years later a survey of UPIU locals found that almost two-thirds of respondents had experience with some form of employee involvement. Nearly 75% of the programs reported were established since 1986, with one-quarter put in place in 1989 alone (Kriesky and Brown 1992).

Kriesky and Brown's survey indicates that programs carry a wide variety of titles, many including the words "quality" or "team" or both: quality circles, quality improvement process, total quality, team concept, team management, team development or production quality teams are some of the common titles. Such labels reflect the fact that many programs encompass the reorganization of work into more "flexible" arrangements. The most common issues reportedly discussed in these programs include plant effectiveness (88%), safety and health (65%), statistical process control (54%) work flow and job duties (52%), and work environment (51%) (Kriesky and Brown 1992).

The survey results also make clear that few of these programs are jointly developed. Management initiated and solicited union involvement in 53% of the programs. In 22%, management established programs with no role for the union. Not surprisingly, the unilateral nature of much of this activity has created a great deal of suspicion about these programs on the part of union leaders.[51] Indeed, the open-ended comments in Kriesky and Brown's survey repeatedly express the sentiment that management has not demonstrated genuine interest in greater employee involvement in decisionmaking. Typical is a respondent from a local in Tennessee who reported that the program "was discontinued because [the] company wasn't willing to put sufficient effort into [the] program to make it work." A recent study of 12 Southern mills similarly indicates that work reorganization was not implemented in a participatory or joint manner (Simpson 1992).

A particularly interesting case is the IP mill at Jay which had a history of unilateral EI programs in the years before the 1987 strike. The first of these efforts, "Operation Breakthrough," encouraged workers to make suggestions directly to upper level management without union involvement. Management replaced it with "QIP" (quality improvement process) which involved workers and managers in discussions about production and working conditions. The union participated in QIP for a time but eventually withdrew. Shortly before the strike, management asked workers to help write training manuals for their jobs. This was sharply resisted, as the union viewed this as a training aid for potential striker replacements. Finally, as part of the proposal that produced the strike, management introduced "Project Productivity." This program sought to reorganize work by reducing job classifications, setting up work teams, and allowing supervisors more leeway in assigning work. Significantly, management did not build a role for the union into "Project Productivity" (Getman and Marshall 1993:19-23, 92).

This is not to say that all EI programs in the paper industry are management dominated. In fact, there are a growing number of cases where *unions* have participated in reorganizing work. In fact, unions' resistance to the adoption of team systems has often pushed management toward a more inclusive method of implementing work reorganization. For instance, Boise Cascade managers in Jackson, Alabama, won team language in 1989 contract negotiations over strong objections of UPIU local members. However, after signing the contract, both sides agreed to establish a joint mill improvement team to interpret the new, general contract language and to set up the system through which all workers receive training. This, in turn, improves their wages. In addition, the team has evolved into a "super grievance committee" solving problems before they become grievances. Boise Cascade hopes to replicate this system in its other mills (see Kriesky and Brown 1993). Similarly, when Union Camp purchased a new paper machine for its Savannah, Georgia, mill a new work system was designed jointly with the union and the workers with excellent results reported.[52] (For other examples, see *PIMA* April 1992:34-37, June 1985:41-44.)

Most recently there have been joint efforts to tackle another contentious issue. James River and UPIU agreed to work jointly for health insurance reform calling for the formation of a national health care policy (*Pulp and Paper* June 17, 1991:3-4). Champion has encouraged locally based joint efforts to control health costs.[53]

Finally, Scott (1989), James River (1989), and Champion (1991) have all entered into national agreements with UPIU expressing their willingness to cooperate with the union. The agreements call for continuous improvement in product quality and output, worker training, job improvement and security, and a fair and competitive return to stockholders. The national agreements provide for periodic meetings at which high-level managers and union officials can exchange ideas and information. In addition, the national agreements and related structures provide support for local initiatives. Some of these cooperative efforts are reaching into the bargaining process itself as some bargaining pairs are attempting mutual gains or "win-win" bargaining.[54] Moreover, both Scott and James River have also guaranteed that they will not interfere with organizing efforts in their unorganized plants (James River Corp. 1989a, 1989b).

Executives of several paper companies cite the decline in labor relations brought by strikes in the 1980s as a primary reason for undertaking some form of cooperation (Hoerr 1989:61; *Pulp and Paper* July 1, 1991:7).[55] Scott and James River chose an alternative path early on, a component of which is that they did not ask for the most offensive of the concessions demanded by other companies, particularly the end to Sunday premium pay. Champion, on the other hand, pursued hard bargaining first; although they had won the resultant contract "battles," they found themselves losing the productivity "war." Both union and management officials recognize that the company that took the most aggressive stand against the union—IP—and historic adversary Georgia Pacific have little chance of establishing such programs in many of their plants. Indeed, there is some evidence that IP, at least where replacements were used, paid a big price in reduced profits and productivity due to its adversarial behavior. IP's recent attempt to patch up relations with the UPIU with a nonbinding "peace accord" to work toward a "cooperative atmosphere" failed to attract rank-and-file support (see Getman and Marshall 1993:82; *The Paperworker* April 1993:4).[56]

The fact that the 1990s began with these different patterns of labor relations has led some to argue that companies' labor relations can be categorized as either cooperative or adversarial (see, for instance, Cutcher-Gershenfeld, McKersie and Walton 1989; Birecree 1993). This analysis falls short for at least two reasons. First, because bargaining is decentralized, particularly on the union side, labor relations actually occur at the mill level. Even within one company, mill relations may cover the spectrum of cooperative to adversarial.[57] Secondly, labor relations "strategies" in paper are constantly changing. Thus at one point in time, Champion and its locals could have been described as adversaries, while now they pursue a more cooperative approach in many locations.[58]

One must also consider that the activity at Champion (and other companies that have tried aggressive bargaining and cooperation) may be qualitatively different from that at Scott or James River. Champion only considered cooperation once it had won the concessions it sought. Moreover, it has not signed a neutrality agreement. It is not yet clear if national-level agreement can overcome the stale taste left in the mouths of workers after forced concessions or a failed strike. Indeed, recent research indicates that poor labor relations and concession bargaining contribute to the failure of employee involvement programs (Eaton 1994). Thus Champion and other companies that now think cooperation sounds appealing may find it more elusive than employers who never pursued a hard-bargaining strategy.

Conclusion

There is no doubt that the decade of the 1980s was a significant one for labor-management relations in the paper industry. As ingredients strengthening management's position at the bargaining table coalesced, the union suffered setbacks. The final outcome, however, is not necessarily a clear management victory.

Both technology and economic factors contributed to the industry's willingness and ability to gain the upper hand in negotiations. Improved technology had reduced the number of workers required to run a paper mill, which in turn contributed to management's ability to continue operations during a strike. Further, management used investment in new technology to gain bargaining leverage as mills could be threatened with closure if concessions were not forthcoming. Though the most recent improvements were embodied in greenfield mills infrequently, their owners' success in keeping a significant number of them nonunion provided management with another chip at the bargaining table.

Economic conditions seemed to favor management's position too. Despite the industry's recovery during the mid-1980s and strong performance by the decade's close, it held out plausible economic arguments for concessions from the unions. In some cases the merger and acquisition activities of the 1980s forced employers to find ways to reduce costs to pay off debts incurred in the transactions. More importantly, however, the announced increase in international competition meant that flexibility on the job and moderation in wages and benefits must replace the "restrictive" work rules and large income gains once enjoyed by the unionized work force. Whether the competitive threat is real or perceived, few trade unionists dismiss it completely given the experiences of other manufacturing industries in recent years.

Finally, management's strength and resolve in contract negotiations grew as it experimented with new aggressive methods of responding to strikes. New management in the late 1970s and early 1980s began to produce paper during strikes—first with supervisory personnel and later with permanent strike replacements. Bolstered by the antiunion mood prevailing in business and government throughout the decade, they tried methods that were previously unthinkable. And they succeeded. While management's muscles grew, the unions' atrophied at the hands of technological change and the NLRB. UPIU, unaccustomed to hard bargaining on the part of employers, only gradually began to fight back. However, the mill-by-mill bargaining structure that had served them well in earlier decades now hindered the union's efforts to broaden bargaining conflicts and impose higher costs on management. The NLRB and reluctance on the part of some workers and local union leaders to join the fight hindered efforts to centralize that structure.

Despite their losses in bargaining battles in the 1980s, we cannot conclude that the paper industry unions are without potential for improving wages and working conditions for their members. Real wages in the paper industry declined much less than elsewhere in the 1980s, in part due to continued union organization. The emergence of EI plans on the local level and wider cooperative efforts on the corporate level are clear indications that management recognizes that contract language and wage concessions alone will not improve productivity and quality. In exchange for their willingness to involve their members in cooperative efforts, unions have already gained from various companies' pledges not to seek reductions in Saturday/Sunday premium pay, not to interfere in organizing campaigns, and not to lay off members of the existing work force. In some mills, unions have made significant gains in worker participation in decision making. If unions are able to use these commitments by management to secure job protection for their members, a voice in decisions about production in the workplace, and new bargaining units in the industry, the 1990s may again see a readjustment of bargaining relations in the paper industry.

Endnotes

[1] Canada also has a large and internationally significant paper industry which will not be discussed in this chapter. Its main products, newsprint and pulp, have suffered a decline in demand in recent years. Lowered U.S.-Canada trade barriers,

increased recycling of newspapers, and improved newsprint production technology in the U.S., historically Canada's biggest customer, have created a crisis in the industry and in relations between the Canadian paper unions and producers.

[2] For instance, one industry publication, *Pulp and Paper*, profiles a different product each month. These are: Kraft linerboard, tissue, coated free-sheet paper, uncoated free-sheet, coated groundwood, market pulp, Kraft paper, and newsprint.

[3] The first recession lasted from 1982 to 1983. The second began in late 1990, early 1991.

[4] Indeed, Region V of the United Paperworker International Union (UPIU) includes Florida, Georgia, South Carolina, and Alabama and has the second largest membership of the union's eleven regions.

[5] Personal communication with Richard Klinzing, Jan. 1993.

[6] Interview with Gordon Brehm, Special Assistant to the President, United Paperworkers International Union, Nov. 9, 1992 and Feb. 19, 1993.

[7] Interview with Richard Klinzing, Vice President for Employee Relations, American Forest and Paper Association, Dec. 8, 1992 and Jan. 5, 1993.

[8] Interview with Russell Boekenheide, Vice President for Human Resources, Union Camp, Jan. 18, 1993.

[9] Interview with Gordon Brehm (op cit).

[10] In 1972 the International Brotherhood of Pulp, Sulphite, and Paper Mill Workers (IBPSPMW), an AFL union established in 1906 to represent unskilled and semi-skilled paperworkers, joined the United Papermakers and Paperworkers (UPP) to form the United Paperworkers International Union. The second most significant merger took place in 1957 after the AFL and CIO merged. The formerly AFL union representing machine tenders, the International Brotherhood of Paper Makers, and the formerly CIO union, the United Paperworkers of America, joined to form the UUP (UPIU 1986:25-30).

[11] The existence of different locals also stems in part from the history of racially segregated job classifications and union locals (Northrup 1969).

[12] Interview with James A. Thompson, Vice President and Research Director, Association of Western Pulp and Paper Workers, Jan. 13, 1993.

[13] The two major paperworker unions in Canada, the Canadian Paperworkers Union (CPU) and the Communications and Electrical Workers of Canada, and the Energy and Chemical Workers Union merged in 1993 creating the Communications, Energy, and Paperworkers Union of Canada. The Pulp, Paper, and Woodworkers of Canada, a second important union, is considering a merger with the Canadian Association of Smelter and Allied Workers. The smaller Federation of Paper and Forestry Workers (FTPF) represents some workers in the industry in Quebec.

[14] Personal communication with Beck, 1993.

[15] Interview with Gordon Brehm (op cit).

[16] AWPPW is apparently exploring other possible partners as well (interview with Thompson).

[17] Foreign ownership of U.S. capacity has also increased dramatically—500% in the last half of the 1980s (*PIMA* Aug. 1991:45).

[18] Seventy percent of U.S. wood exports to Japan are raw materials which, in 1990, contributed to the production of an additional one million tons of paper in Japanese factories (*The Paperworker* June 1992). Since 1988 Japanese efforts to import hardwood chips from the U.S. for paper production have raised concerns. (See *The Paperworker* June 1992 for a discussion of this issue.)

[19] Indeed, prior to the agreement, "More than 70% of U.S. paper industry exports to Canada were dutiable, while less than 10% of Canadian products entering the U.S. were dutiable" (Handelsman 1993).

[20] Interview with Gordon Brehm (op cit).

[21] Nor should U.S. producers be troubled by a shift toward recycled raw material inputs. The U.S. is one of the largest consumers of paper products and, therefore, producers of paper waste. Indeed, some claim that New York City's largest export is wastepaper.

[22] Interview with Gordon Brehm (op cit).

[23] Interview with Byron Trefts, Vice President for Corporate Labor Relations, Champion International Corporation, Jan. 19, 1993. See also Birecree (1990).

[24] Birecree (1991:4-5), on the other hand, argues that IP lost the ability to control prices when it became more reliant on more price-competitive foreign markets to absorb overproduction in the late 1970s. Further, both current and former UPIU staff argue that tacit, if not explicit, price collusion still exists in the industry (interviews with Brehm and Beck).

[25] Interview with James A. Thompson (op cit).

[26] Violations have included failure to report work-related injuries, failure to provide respiratory protection for workers in hazardous jobs, failure to safely operate industrial trucks, etc. (BNA *DLR*, Sept. 27, 1987:A-2; Dec. 9, 1987:A-7; Dec. 28, 1987:A-4, A-5; Sept. 20, 1989:A-2-4; March 27, 1991:A-1; Oct. 30, 1991:A-4,5).

[27] Interview with Russell Boekenheide (op cit).

[28] For example, between 1980 and 1983 James River purchased the Brown Company, acquiring an in-house source of pulp; American Can's Dixie/Northern operations, securing two more pulp mills; and Diamond International, increasing its pulp and paper capacity. As a result, the company more than doubled in size (*PIMA* Jan. 1991:84-85).

[29] Interview with Mark Brooks, Special Projects, United Paperworkers International Union, Nov. 9, 1992.

[30] Interview with Byron Trefts, Vice President for Corporate Labor Relations, Champion International Corporation, Jan. 19, 1993. Unfortunately for both companies, the new production came on line when the economic environment did not permit rapid recovery of the investment. Indeed, the unfortunate timing of IP's investment and consequent stress on the costs of production has been cited as a major factor in IP's forceful pursuit of concessions (Birecree 1991).

[31] Interview with Richard P. Klinzing (op cit).

[32] Ibid.

[33] Indeed, since 1960 wage rates in the industry have exceeded the manufacturing average, at least in part because labor costs are not a high percentage of total costs. Birecree (1991), for instance, puts labor costs as a percentage of total costs at about 24% for IP. Payroll as percentage of the value of shipments (as calculated from *Census of Manufacturers* data) ranges from approximately 10% to 20%, depending on the industry segment. This figure has declined somewhat during the 1980s, reflecting increased capital substitution for labor.

[34] Some paper managers recall this as happening in 1979 (interview with Trefts). One IP executive suggests that IP operated during a strike for the first time in 1976-77 at its pulp mill in Gardiner, Oregon.

[35] Interview with Byron Trefts (op cit).

[36] Interview on Dec. 2, 1992 with Joe Bradshaw, a UPIU Regional Vice President and leader of the union bargaining team for the SKM, in which he claims that the agreement set a pattern for the entire paper industry throughout the country including converting plants.

[37] Though the strike was mainly over wages and pensions, the AWPPW also sought two-year contracts so as to align itself with contracts in the wood products industry. Strife over the bargaining structure itself worsened the conflict. An earlier centralized structure (the Uniform Labor Agreement) had broken up in the late 1960s. While it was replaced by company-wide bargaining in some cases (e.g., Boise Cascade, Weyerhaeuser) and mill-by-mill bargaining in others, disagreements developed in 1978 over the informal structure, specifically who would set and who would follow any pattern that might emerge (interview with Thompson).

[38] Interview with James A. Thompson (op cit).

[39] Companies first demanded these concessions from UPIU locals primarily in the South. They were not frequently contentious issues on the West Coast until later in the decade.

[40] They were also used by Alaska Land and Pulp (Sitka, Alaska 1986), Boise Cascade (Deridder, Louisiana), and Potsdam Paper (interviews with Beck and Brehm; BNA *DLR*, Sept. 26, 1990:A-6,7).

[41] Interview with Byron Trefts (op cit).

[42] This is close to double the 35% average for all of manufacturing. The number of paper industry agreements including these payments tripled between 1984 and 1986 (API:ER88020).

[43] According to Frank Bragg, Outreach Coordinator, Special Projects Dept., United Paperworkers International, and the former president of Local 265 (IP, Mobile), members at his location viewed as the key defection the refusal of the Moss Point, Mississippi, locals to join their efforts. The contract at Moss Point expired after the lockout and strikes began but before UPIU officially established the pool. (Interview with Bragg on June 22, 1993.)

[44] When the strike ended, the union leadership claimed that it would continue to use its corporate campaign and a boycott against IP products (see BNA *DLR*, Oct. 12, 1988:A-15).

[45] Each local's votes were sent to UPIU headquarters for counting. The international allowed individual locals that voted against the agreement accepted by the pool to either strike or work under implemented terms.

[46] In November 1992 the NLRB ruled the IP pool a violation of the duty to bargain in good faith, noting that the structure and operation "impermissibly injects extraneous and irrelevant nonunit considerations into the bargaining process." (BNA *DLR*, Feb. 10, 1992:A8; see Getman and Marshall 1993 for a detailed discussion of the related legal issues). The UPIU notes that the Board had upheld pools in an earlier USWA case (Brooks).

[47] First-year lump-sum bonuses are not included in either manufacturing or paper industry figures. Their widespread use in paper in the late 1980s may have contributed to higher wage rates in the first year of the contract than the data indicate. However, management frequently used bonuses to buy out the Saturday/Sunday premium pay. Since the lost premium pay typically exceeded the size of the bonus, paperworkers saw their annual nominal wages fall.

[48] UPIU leaders and members also find the loss of the overtime premium particularly galling given its importance in the original agreements to work seven days a week decades ago (interviews with Brooks and Brehm). Management, on the other hand, points out that paper was the last continuous process industry to carry these provisions.

[49] Despite the decentralized bargaining, both parties attempt to set strategy and goals centrally within their organizations. For instance, UPIU has member councils for each of the large employers. However, without the ability to coordinate bargaining through the pooled voting procedure, they can only work together informally. Corporate labor relations offices similarly set strategy and some bargaining goals for mill management, although specific bargaining objectives may be left to local managers. Some paper firms, for instance, have made clear that health care cost containment is a necessity, but find that containment solutions are best framed locally (interviews with Boekenheide and Trefts). At the industry level, the American Paper Institute (now the American Forest and Paper Association) has provided a forum for the exchange of information and strategic discussion of labor relations issues.

[50] As defined here, EI programs include any program that involves workers in decisionmaking about work-related issues. Importantly, such programs may or may not involve the union as an institution. Union-management cooperation, on the other hand, by definition involves the union as an institution in joint decisionmaking outside of the traditional issues and processes of collective bargaining. In paper, these joint activities are common at the mill level and have recently emerged at the strategic or corporate level.

[51] Both UPIU and AWPPW agree to employee involvement efforts only after evaluation on a case-by-case basis. They support those in which the union plays a strong role (interviews with Brehm and Thompson).

[52] Interview with Byron Trefts (op cit).

[53] Interview with Richard P. Klinzing (op cit).

[54] Interview with Byron Trefts (op cit).

[55] Interview with William Peterson, former Corporate Manager for Employee Relations, Boise Cascade Corporation, Aug. 23, 1992.

[56] IP offered the "peace accord" to the Primary Mill Joint Pension Council in conjunction with a pension plan that included many improvements over those negotiated in recent years. Despite the positive recommendation of the union negotiators, membership at the thirteen participating mills rejected the proposal largely because of their anger over IP's past hard bargaining tactics. When put to a vote a second time, the membership accepted the proposal in part to ensure that IP would not insist upon bargaining pension plans on a mill-by-mill basis. Union leadership recognizes that it may take years for many members to show a true willingness to work with IP management (interview with Brehm).

[57] IP's relations are generally regarded as adversarial, but in the Pine Bluff (Arkansas) mill, a local cooperates with management's safety program (interview with Brehm).

[58] Cutcher-Gershenfeld et al. (1989) acknowledge that the adversarial posture may be reversible, pointing to a changed negotiations process at Boise Cascade's Rumford mill (p. 477).

References

American Paper Institute. 1993. "Industry Collective Bargaining Review." Employee Relations Committee and Labor Relations Subcommittee Meeting, Phoenix, Arizona, November.

_____. 1986. Transcript of Employee Relations Conference, January.

Antos, Jeff. 1991. "Step-by-Step System Helps Involve Line Employees in Quality Program," *Pulp and Paper*, pp. 152-53.

Beck, John P. 1988. "The Pattern Bites Back: The Dominance of the South in Paper Industry Bargaining and Worklife." Society for the Study of Social Problems Meeting, Atlanta, Georgia, August 21-23.

_____. 1990. "The Possibilities and Limitations of In-Plant Strategies." University and College Labor Education Association Southern/Midwestern Regional Conference, Iowa City, Iowa, November.

Birecree, Adrienne. 1990. Unpublished notes of interviews with J. Gilliland, Director of Employer Relations, International Paper.

_____. 1991. "Capital Restructuring and Labour Relations: The International Paper Company Strike." *International Contributions to Labour Studies*, Vol. 1, pp. 1-28.

_____. 1993. "Corporate Development, Structural Change and Strategic Choice: Bargaining at International Paper Company in the 1980s." *Industrial Relations* (Fall), Vol. 32, No. 3, pp. 343-66.

Blackman, Ted. 1991. "'Team Concept' Involves Crews in All Aspects of Mills." *Forest Industries*, Vol. 118, No. 9 (November), pp. 14-15.

Briggs, Jean A., and Adam Snitzer. 1986. "Here We Go Again?" *Forbes*, September 22, pp. 68, 72.

Brooks, John. 1987. *The Takeover Game*. New York: Truman Talley Books.

Bureau of National Affairs. *Collective Bargaining, Negotiations, and Contracts*. Washington, DC: BNA.

_____. *Daily Labor Report*. Washington, DC: BNA.

_____. *Union Labor Report*. Washington, DC: BNA.

Champion International Corporation and the United Paperworkers International Union. Undated. "Champion-UPIU Forum Proposed Joint Mission and Philosophy Statement."

Cohen, Avi J. 1984. "Technological Change as Historical Process: The Case of the U.S. Pulp and Paper Industry, 1915-1940." *Journal of Economic History*, Vol. 44, No. 3 (September), pp. 775-799.

Cutcher-Gershenfeld, Joel, Robert McKersie, and Richard Walton. 1989. "Dispute Resolution and the Transformation of U.S. Industrial Relations: A Negotiations Perspective." *Labor Law Journal* (August), pp. 475-83.

Eaton, Adrienne. 1994. "Factors Contributing to the Survival of Employee Participation Programs in Unionized Settings." *Industrial and Labor Relations Review*, Vol. 47, No. 3 (April), pp. 371-89.

Getman, Jack and Ray Marshall. 1993. "Industrial Relations in Transition: The Paper Industry Example," *Yale Law Review*, Vol. 102, No. 8 (June), pp. 1804-95.

Graham, Harry Edward. 1970. *The Paper Rebellion: Development and Upheaval in Pulp and Paper Unionism*. Iowa City: University of Iowa Press.

Handelsman, Jacob. 1993. "International Competitive Environment for the Paper Industry." Internal memo, American Forest and Paper Association, January 13.

Hirsch, Barry T., and David A. Macpherson. 1993. "Union Membership and Coverage Files from the Current Population Surveys: Note." *Industrial and Labor Relations Review*, Vol. 46, No. 3 (April), pp. 574-78.

Hoerr, John. 1989. "The Payoff from Teamwork," *Business Week*, July 10, pp. 56-62.

ICEF Info. 1992. No. 2. International Federation of Chemical, Energy and General Workers' Unions. 1992.

International Labour Organisation (ILO). 1992. *Social and Labour Issues in the Pulp and Paper Industry*. Geneva.

James River Corporation, and the United Paperworkers International Union. 1989a. "Memorandum of Agreement." October 23.

_____. 1989b. "Joint/Cooperative Understanding on Union Organizing Neutrality." November 30.

Kalish, John. 1990. "Restructuring in an Age of Globalization." *Pulp and Paper International*, October, pp. 44-50.

Kien, Julian M. 1989. "Labor Year in Review," *Pulp and Paper*, January, p. 200.

Kokkelenberg, Edward C., and Donna R. Sockell. 1985. "Union Membership in the United States, 1973-1981." *Industrial and Labor Relations Review*, Vol. 38, No. 4, pp. 497-543.

Kriesky, Jill, and Edwin Brown. 1991. "Employee Involvement Programs: A Survey of Pulp and Paper Industry Unions." Unpublished paper, University of Alabama at Birmingham.

_____. 1992. "Implementing Employee Involvement: How Paper Companies Gain Local Union Support." *Employee Rights and Responsibilities Journal*, Vol. 5, No. 2 (June), pp. 117-129.

_____. 1993. "The Union Role in Employee Involvement Programs: A Case Study at the Boise Cascade Company's Jackson Mill." *Labor Studies Journal*, Vol. 18, No. 3 (Fall), pp. 17-32.

Larson, David. 1984. "Wages in the Paper Industries among Highest in Manufacturing." *Monthly Labor Review*, Vol. 107, No. 3 (March), pp. 52-54.

Levine, Jonathan B. 1989. "Papermakers Will Be as Busy as Beavers." *Business Week*, January 9, p. 101.

Lush, Patricia. 1992. "B.C. Pulp Strike Over as Firms Give in on Holiday." *Toronto Globe and Mail*, July 18, pp. B1-B2.

Matussek, Heide, and John Pearson. 1991. "The Predators Turn into Poodles." *Pulp and Paper International*, September, pp. 41-56.

Monthly Labor Review. 1979. "Occupational Pay and Benefits in the Papermaking Industries." Vol. 102, No. 5 (May), pp. 46-47.

New York Times. 1986. "Maine Town Divided by Bitter Strike." December 28, Section 1, p. 36.

Northrup, Herbert R. 1969. *The Negro in the Paper Industry*. Philadelphia: Industrial Relations Unit, Wharton School, University of Pennsylvania.

The Paperworker. Nashville, TN: United Paperworkers International Union.

PIMA Magazine. Arlington Heights, IL: Paper Industry Management Association.

Pulp and Paper. New York: Miller Freeman Periodicals.

Rice, Marc. 1992. "Paper Industry Seeks Balance between Business, Environment." *Birmingham (AL) Post-Herald*, March 3, p. B5.

Rooks, Alan. 1989. "Labor and Management: Forging a New Relationship." *PIMA Magazine*, Vol. 57, No. 2 (February), p. 5.

Sherbanowski, Janet. 1991. "Recycling an Industry." *Canadian Banker*, Vol. 98, No. 4 (July-August), pp. 48-52.

Simpson, Jimmy C. 1992. "Job Classification Consolidation and Workrules Flexibility in Southern Paperplants." Diss., University of Alabama, Tuscaloosa.

Stewart, James B. 1993. "Annals of Law: Michael Milken's Biggest Deal." *New Yorker*, March 8, pp. 58-71.

Tetrick, Nicholas. 1992. "Paper." *Standard and Poor's Industry Surveys*, May 14, pp. 75-79.

United Brotherhood of Carpenters and United Paperworkers International Union. Undated. *BE&K Campaign Alert*, Issue No. 3.

United Paperworkers International Union. 1986. *Stewards Training Manual*. Nashville, TN: UPIU.

U.S. Bureau of Labor Statistics. *Employment and Earnings*, January 1984, January 1992, August 1988 Supplement. Washington, DC: GPO.

U.S. Department of Commerce. 1985. *1982 Census of Manufacturers*, Industry Series: Pulp, Paper and Board Mills, March. Washington, DC: GPO.

_____. 1990. *1987 Census of Manufacturers*, Industry Series: Pulp, Paper and Board Mills. Washington, DC: GPO.

_____. 1992. *1992 U.S. Industrial Outlook—Paper and Allied Products*, Washington, DC: GPO.

Vogel, Todd, and Joseph Weber. 1989. "Turn Out the Lights, Paper's Long Party Is Over." *Business Week*, November 6, pp. 47-8.

Wilkinson, Norman B. 1975. *Papermaking in America*. Greenville, Delaware: The Hagley Museum.

Zuboff, Shoshana. 1988. *In The Age of the Smart Machine: The Future of Work and Power*. New York: Basic Books.

CHAPTER 2

Meatpacking: Industry Restructuring and Union Decline

CHARLES CRAYPO
University of Notre Dame

Editor's Abstract

Craypo contends that developments in meatpacking illustrate the tendency for product market competition to drive down wage rates in an unregulated or inadequately organized industry. The chapter focuses on beef packing, the largest portion of the industry and a bellwether for developments in pork packing and, to a lesser extent, processed meats and chicken.

By the 1960s the Meatcutters and the Packinghouse Workers had largely organized beef packing and had established strong wage patterns. Wages were 26% above the average for nondurable manufacturing in 1968, when the two unions merged. However, this was soon to change, with the entry of Iowa Beef Packers (IBP). IBP was followed by other "new breed" imitators: Cargill and Excel. IBP introduced "boxed beef" to the industry, reducing transportation costs while improving convenience and quality. Iowa Beef located large, new plants on the High Plains, closer to livestock to minimize weight loss. It simultaneously followed a low-wage strategy of resisting unionization and/or refusing to accept industry wage patterns if organized. Iowa Beef repeatedly used permanent strike replacements to defeat attempts to extend the industry wage pattern to its organized operations.

Craypo details the resulting problems. As new capacity was continually added in the High Plains states, old plants became uncompetitive. Plant closures idled large numbers of workers. This produced pressures for concessions, which were exacerbated by the recessions of the early 1980s. Concession bargaining turned into a free-fall between 1979-83, when the United Food and Commercial Workers (established by a merger of the Meatcutters and the Retail Clerks in 1979) became unable to establish or maintain a new industry pattern. By 1986 wages in meatpacking were 9% below the average for all nondurable manufacturing. Conditions began to mirror those found at the turn of the century: low wages, immigrant labor, high turnover, and unsafe working conditions.

Labor relations in pork packing, and to a lesser extent poultry, have largely followed beef. Pressures for lower labor costs were central to the bitter Hormel strike of 1984. Again, permanent strike replacements were an important source of employer advantage. As in beef, there has been a substantial decline in real earnings in pork packing. Poultry processing is largely a Southern industry and is less organized than the other parts of the meat packing industry. Health and safety are a primary worker concern and problems in the area, along with low wages and expanding employment, may create a better climate for organizing in the future.

Since 1987 the UFCW has begun to regroup in beef packing, following success in a strike/lockout at Dakota City's IBP plant in which the UFCW publicized company falsification of plant safety records. The union subsequently organized another IBP plant, a plant at National Beef, and another Monfort facility in 1993. By 1992 the UFCW had succeeded in gaining representation for workers in plants producing 70% of the total volume of beef. Nonetheless, union/nonunion wage differentials in the industry still reflect union weakness. The future is uncertain, but the UFCW has shown determination to invest the resources necessary to reorganize all parts of the meatpacking industry.

o   o   o

At the turn of the century, meatpacking was characterized by relatively low wages, immigrant labor, and dangerous working conditions (Commons 1904). That changed as a result of collective bargaining and government regulation. By the 1960s meatpacking wages were high, production jobs stable, and conditions much safer. But the subsequent entry of new packers weakened the union and put labor back in competition. Bad labor standards drove out good. Earnings and employment reverted to the earlier period—low wages, immigrant labor, unsafe conditions.

This chapter describes recent trends in meatpacking with the emphasis on beef, although the story is much the same in pork and poultry. Events can be divided into three time periods: 1946 to 1968, when industrial unionism swept the industry; 1969 to 1986, when industry changes eroded union power and lowered labor standards; 1987 to 1993, when the union began to reverse things. Before turning to these evolutionary stages, it is useful to describe beefpacking and its work force and to identify the sources of union bargaining power.

Industry and Labor Force Changes

Meat products (SIC 201) is divided into three parts: meat packing (2011), meat processing (2013), and poultry slaughter and processing

(2015). Beef historically dominated the industry but poultry now is the fastest-growing segment, followed by branded pork products.[1] Beef plants typically convert cattle to boxed beef cuts within a single complex. Production consists of slaughtering the animal and then disassembling the carcass into thick cuts of chucks, rounds and loins; thin cuts of briskets, steaks and short ribs; and ground beef. These final cuts are shrink-packed in vacuum-protected bags, placed in sealed containers and shipped in refrigerated trucks to retail stores and restaurants. The process minimizes dehydration and shrinkage, improves shelf life and eliminates the need for skilled meat cutters. Although employment in meat products grew by one-third between 1960 and 1990, as Table 1 shows, growth was unevenly distributed. Jobs increased significantly in poultry and meat processing but by 1984 had declined nearly one-third in packing.

TABLE 1

Changes in Employment of Production Workers
in Selected Industries and Time Periods

	Years				
	1960-1990			1985-1990	
Industry (SIC)	Workers (thousands)	%		Workers (thousands)	%
Food products (20)	-13	-1		81	7
Meat products (201)	103	40		57	19
Meat packing (2011)	-48	-29		1	1
Meat processing (2013)	30	86		10	18
Poultry (2015)	121	205		46	34

Source: Bureau of Labor Statistics, *Employment Hours and Earnings, United States, 1909-1990, Volume I,* Bulletin 2370, March 1991; and *Supplement,* June 1991.

Hundreds of firms slaughter and process beef and pork, but only a handful dominate. Oligopolistic control has been the historical experience. Predecessors of Swift, Armour, Wilson and Cudahy pioneered in refrigerated rail-car shipment of dressed beef from Great Lakes' packing plants to Eastern markets. This advance enabled them to locate plants nearer to cattle and hog supplies and to take advantage of economies of large-scale production. Immigrant labor provided cheap, tractable labor. Despite anti-trust restrictions on vertical integration and technological changes favoring small packers, the Big Four retained dominant market shares into the 1960s. Then they began getting out of beef slaughtering in response to narrow profit margins and increased competition from independent packers and, instead, concentrated more on branded pork products (Carpenter and Handler 1961:26-31; Arnould 1971).

The power of the old-line companies ended with entry of the "new breed" packers. Armed with a government loan and an alternative production strategy, Iowa Beef Packers (later IBP) was the first such newcomer. The company was founded by experienced packing men who understood the industry and the weaknesses of the Big Four. Success in meatpacking historically went to those most able to (1) locate plants close to livestock in order to minimize weight loss and damage during transportation; (2) buy enough animals to operate plants at efficient levels of capacity; (3) hire and extract labor at the lowest cost; (4) remove bone and fat, maximize extraction of by-products, and thus ship only the edible cuts to market; and (5) offer consumers both convenience and quality. Therefore, instead of shipping carcasses, IBP shipped boxed beef. Instead of building plants near urban rail centers, it built and renovated them in rural areas, often in right-to-work states. Instead of accepting unions and pattern bargaining, it resisted both and developed its own (enterprise) wage standard. None of these practices was unknown to the rest of the industry, but IBP was the first to combine them in an aggressive operating strategy aimed at existing packers and practices.

By 1976 IBP was the nation's leading beefpacker. It also was the most profitable producer with an average 24.7% rate of profit on equity over the preceding five years, compared to the industry average of less than 10% (*IBP Annual Report* 1976:5). In 1976 it expanded into pork and, within a decade, was the country's largest porkpacker. Its success attracted integrated companies ideally positioned to diversify into packing (*Financial World* 1989). ConAgra, a major food producer, acquired Armour in 1983, half the assets of Swift Independent (SIPCO) in 1987, and Monfort of Colorado the same year. Swift and Armour had been owned by conglomerates and Monfort was a large, family-owned packer. Cargill, a global grain merchant, acquired MBPXL (previously Missouri Beef Packers) in 1978 and later renamed it Excel, which then made additional acquisitions. By the late 1980s, IBP, ConAgra, Excel, and National Beef, the fourth member of the new Big Four, together controlled about 80% of domestic beefpacking (Nelson 1985:5-10; Robbins 1988).

The new firms moved the locus of meatpacking from the Corn Belt to the High Plains, an area with plentiful grain supplies, cattle-fattening feedlots and a nonunion labor force. Table 2 shows the shift in shares of feedlot cattle from states such as Iowa and Illinois to a geographic arc extending from the Texas Panhandle through western Kansas and Colorado into Nebraska. Although total packing jobs declined 41% during 1963-1990, employment shares increased in each of these states (BLS 1991).

TABLE 2
Regional Shares of Cattle in Feedlots: 1960 and 1990

Region	Percentage Share 1960	1990
Northern Plains: KA, NE, ND, SD	18.4	34.0
Southern Plains: TX, OK	4.3	20.9
Western Corn Belt: IA, MO, MN	30.1	11.8
Eastern Corn Belt: IL, IN, MI, WI, OH	18.8	9.4
All Other	28.4	23.5

Source: Michael J. Broadway, "Recent Changes in the Structure and Location of the Meat- and Fish-Processing Industry." State University of New York, Geneseo, unpublished paper (no date).

Kansas, which increased its share of slaughtered cattle from 7.3% to 17.6% during 1975-85 and is now the nation's leading producer, more than doubled its employment share in 1980 when IBP built the world's largest beef plant in Garden City. Altogether, by 1987 the new beefpackers had five huge plants in southwest Kansas employing 9500 workers and slaughtering nearly 21,000 head of cattle daily. ConAgra meanwhile opened another big plant in Grand Island, Nebraska. In view of declining red meat consumption during the 1980s, this expansion had to occur at the expense of older, higher-paying urban plants. For example, 14 of the 16 plants located in Wichita and Kansas City, Kansas, were closed between 1959 and 1987 (Broadway 1990; Stull and Broadway 1990).

Movement to the High Plains gave the new packers an operating edge over old-line companies but also made it difficult for them to find enough industrial workers in this sparsely populated area. They solved the problem by going outside the area to hire immigrant and refugee labor, mainly Hispanic but also Asian.[2] In 1987 IBP's Garden City plant employed an estimated 900 Asians, 750 Hispanics and 750 Anglos in hourly jobs; the same year the Monfort plant there employed 671 Hispanics, 335 Anglos, 60 Asians and 27 African Americans (Stull, Broadway and Erickson 1992:50). The U.S. Equal Employment Opportunity Commission does not report data at the 4-digit SIC level. Therefore, figures on workers by race and ethnic origin are available for the meat products industry (SIC 201) but not for the sub-categories meatpacking and poultry.[3] Even so, total numbers are less important in determining the impact of immigrant and refugee workers in beefpacking than is their concentration in the large, relatively new plants of the High Plains states. Industry labor standards are being set in these plants because their highly competitive products are marketed nationally, just as the immigrants who fabricate those products are recruited nationally from among disadvantaged labor groups.

The advantages employers gain from segmented labor markets change constantly, however, and the use of Asian workers in these plants apparently is on the decline and that of Hispanic and Anglo women on the rise. Service providers and plant workers estimated that in 1990 half to three-fourths of the work force at IBP's Lexington, Nebraska, plant was Hispanic, but they reported few Asians and African Americans. They also estimated that one-third of the hourly workers were women. IBP reportedly was targeting area women, especially farm wives, to work in the plant because they are less mobile than foreign workers and probably either unemployed or underemployed. It even began to provide day care service at the plant (Stull, Broadway, and Erickson 1992:51; Gouveia and Stull 1992:15-6).

Three Stages of Labor and Industrial Relations in Beefpacking

To understand why the union lost power in meatpacking it is necessary to identify the theoretical sources of union bargaining power (Craypo 1986:Chap. 2). For a union to have economic bargaining power, the firms (industry) must have the ability to pay higher labor costs, either by raising product prices or by making labor more productive. Assuming this to be the case, the union must establish and maintain three conditions: organize the relevant labor force, eliminate competitive unionism, and establish appropriate bargaining structures.

The relevant work force includes all groups of workers employed in the production of goods or services that compete in the same sales markets. Inability to organize the relevant work force makes unionized workers vulnerable to competition from comparable products made with cheap labor. The union also must eliminate the possibility of being undermined at the bargaining table by the inferior contracts or destructive behavior of a competitor union. Competitors are distinguished from rivals in that the latter seek to outperform one another by improving labor standards, while the former settle for inferior terms and conditions and, in the event of labor disputes, may continue working or go back to work before another union settles. A competitor union also may try to obtain "sweetheart" recognition. Finally, the bargaining structure must permit the union to strike effectively. In practice, this requires sufficient centralization to give the union direct access to company decision makers and enable it to strike the industry or, more likely, to target one firm for a pattern settlement.

Stage I: The Triumph of Industrial Unionism, 1946-1968

During the first stage of labor relations in beefpacking, firms had the ability to pay, and unions established each of the conditions necessary for bargaining power. Two unions were involved: the Amalgamated Meat Cutters and the United Packinghouse Workers of America (UPWA). The Amalgamated was organized in 1887 as an AFL affiliate and given jurisdiction over meatpacking. A craft union with industrial union sympathies, it struck the major packers unsuccessfully in 1904 and again in 1921. Passage of the Wagner Act opened the way for unionization by it and the CIO organizing committee that became the UPWA.

Both unions made significant organizing gains and together had most of the relevant work force under contract by the end of World War II. UPWA had the bulk of the Big Four's multiplant operations and the Amalgamated the remainder, as well as most of the independent packers. The Amalgamated also represented skilled meat cutters in grocery stores and wholesale distribution centers, giving it a much larger membership than UPWA. Leaders in both organizations understood the importance of avoiding competitive unionism and, by the late 1940s after some feuding and failure to harmonize strike activities, established coordinated bargaining and master contracts. In 1953 they signed a no-raiding pact and in 1968 merged the two organizations.[4]

Meatpacking was among the basic industries in which unions achieved the necessary conditions for bargaining power. By the early 1960s, UPWA and the Amalgamated together represented more than 95% of hourly workers in multiplant packers outside the South (BLS 1964:4), negotiated nearly uniform changes in master agreements throughout the industry, and were not competitors. Stoppages involved individual companies that refused to negotiate or follow the industry settlement pattern. Armour was the preferred pattern setter, and Swift the most resistant. Wages and conditions were not identical among firms and plants but varied depending on the industry's historical and regional structures and the product niches and production volumes of individual firms. Pattern bargaining also brought most independent packers into wage conformity (Carpenter and Handler 1961:4). And, finally, it enabled unions to narrow many historic wage differentials among plants (especially those at Swift) and to extend master agreements to previously uncovered plants and the various processing and distribution centers[5] (Brody 1964:Chap. 11; Purcell 1960:Chap. 14; Perry and Kegley 1989:Chap. 8).

Table 3 shows the results of union bargaining success during Stage I. In 1947 average hourly earnings of production workers were 12% higher than those in the nondurable manufacturing sector and slightly lower than in all manufacturing. By 1968, after two decades of union bargaining power with large firms having the ability to pay, packinghouse wages were considerably higher than in nondurables and manufacturing generally, and also above those in meat processing, which employed skilled meat cutters. The institutional power of meatpacking unions is indicated by the fact that they made these gains at a time when production employment was steadily declining due to plant closings. Between 1958 (the earliest year for which separate employment figures for meatpacking are available) and 1969, the number of production workers fell by 27,000 (16%). Most losses occurred as packers closed slaughter operations in the Great Lakes.

The final bargaining round in which the unions were able to take the pattern settlement to the rest of the industry was in 1967. That year, with Armour as the target, most packers settled before the contracts expired, even Rath Packing, which was experiencing financial difficulty and eventually would be bought out by the employees. Swift was last and most reluctant to settle. It resisted further narrowing of wage differentials among plants and a package of job protections that had been agreed upon by the other Big Four packers.

Stage II: The Decline of Union Power, 1969-1986

Union decline in beef packing begins with the 1969 round of bargaining at IBP's plant in Dakota City. IBP opened the unit in 1966 and

TABLE 3

Average Hourly Earnings and Earnings Differentials,
Selected Industries and Years: 1947-1990

| Year | Average Hourly Earnings* | | | | | | Hourly Earnings Differentials: Meatpacking vs. | | | | |
	Meat Packing	Meat Processing	Poultry	Food	Non-durable Mfg.	All Mfg.	Meat Processing	Poultry	Food	Non-durable Mfg.	All Mfg.
1947	$1.19	—	—	$1.06	$1.14	$ 1.22	—	—	12%	4%	-2.5%
1968	3.45	$3.24	—	2.80	2.74	3.01	6%	—	23	26	15
1986	8.24	8.76	$5.92	8.75	8.95	9.73	-6	39%	-6	-9	-18
1990	8.73	9.03	6.83	9.63	—	10.84	-3	28	-10	—	-24

*Current Dollars

began producing boxed beef the following year. The Amalgamated organized it in 1968, but IBP told the union it would not accept the industry wage pattern. Indeed, workers struck for several months to get a first contract and then had to settle for base wages below industry averages and accept an unprecedented $0.61 per hour differential between slaughter and fabricating wages in the same plant. This contract began to put meatpacking labor back in competition.

Five more rounds of bargaining at Dakota City between 1969 and 1986 completed the process. Each ended in a lengthy dispute, ranging in duration from four to fourteen months. Each arose from IBP's refusal to follow industry pattern settlements and often from its insistence on wage freezes or cuts. Each also ended with the company remaining below the base wages paid by traditional union packers. The union lacked the power to force IBP into pattern bargaining because it could not strike the Dakota City plant effectively against the use of replacement workers and the company's alternative sources of beef production. This was the only major IBP plant the union had under contract at a time when IBP was building and acquiring a number of rural plants in right-to-work states.

With these advantages in hand, IBP pursued its aggressive bargaining policy. In three of the five contract rounds it locked out union workers and in all five it brought in replacement workers following the strike or lockout. This made it one of the earliest large employers to use replacements consistently in labor disputes beginning in 1969. The international union supported the Dakota City local financially during these confrontations because it understood the threat posed by substandard conditions at IBP to all of its unionized packing. The fact that the union nevertheless was unable to maintain industry standards suggests that labor law reform to restrict the use of replacement workers must be part of any policy to restore a balance of power in labor relations and, by implication, to revive the high-wage economy.

In defense of its actions IBP argued that as a beef producer it was more in competition with the independent packers than with the Big Four. Therefore, because the independents, both union and nonunion, had lower wage structures than the majors, IBP would be at a competitive disadvantage if it had to pay Big Four wages. It also claimed that hourly jobs in boxed beef plants require less skill and experience than those in fabricating plants and, therefore, should pay less. The union countered that IBP was using the comparability standard in a self-serving way. Because most beef products compete in the same national markets, regardless of where they are produced, it argued, workers fabricating these products should be paid comparable wages. To do otherwise is to make groups of workers compete with one another to determine which will work for the lowest pay. In addition, the union pointed to IBP's superior profit and productivity as evidence of its ability to match industry patterns.

These opposing arguments were brought to bear during a six-month dispute at Dakota City in 1973. IBP locked out union workers there after they voted to strike against company contract demands. Two weeks later federal mediators persuaded the parties to submit the issues to a panel chaired by a neutral fact-finder. The panel's final report concluded that an appropriate wage level for Dakota City would be one which neither inhibited the old-line packers from expanding beef operations nor encouraged them to try to avoid negotiated labor standards by contracting work to IBP or low-wage independents. At the same time, rates should not be so high as to threaten IBP's competitiveness.

At that point the parties agreed to settle the dispute in binding arbitration. The subsequent award narrowed wage differentials between IBP and the Big Four by 42% in slaughtering and 46% in processing (BNA 1974; Perry and Kegley 1989:138-43). But the decision was a pyrrhic victory for the union because it ratified and preserved the interplant wage differentials that were putting packinghouse workers back in competition. From the policy perspective of the Wagner Act, collective bargaining is preferred in market economies precisely because it takes labor out of competition and prevents wages from being driven to the lowest denominator and eroding consumer purchasing power.

Subsequent outcomes confirmed union concerns. IBP's bargaining policy, based on the new power relationship, prevented the union from eliminating competitive differentials between it, the largest employer, and other packers. The arbitration award institutionalized wage differences and set in motion a downward wage spiral. It narrowed the gap between IBP and other large packers but only temporarily. Union power continued to decline, allowing IBP to further widen the differential in subsequent bargaining rounds. Nor did the compromise achieve the panel's objectives of preserving the Big Four packers as viable competitors, or of preventing the unionized independents from continuing to chop wages and benefits or simply ridding themselves altogether of unions and collective bargaining. Eventually, the old-line packers would essentially be gone from beef slaughter and processing, and the smaller independents often closed or reorganized as nonunion, low-wage operations.

In 1979 the Amalgamated merged with the Retail Clerks International Union to form the United Food and Commercial Workers (UFCW), at that time the largest AFL-CIO affiliate. This also would be the last year the unions negotiated uniform settlements with old-line packers. Wage and benefit erosion occurred after that in both beef and pork. Wilson and Armour negotiated 44-month mid-term wage freezes at $10.69 an hour in late 1981 under the threat of pork plant closures. Other packers soon got similar concessions in return for promises not to close plants for 18 months. The union intended the $10.69 hourly rate to be a uniform wage floor in pork but in 1983 Wilson filed for bankruptcy, voided its master contract, and unilaterally slashed wages and benefits. Eventually it negotiated a court-approved concessionary agreement with the union. Following a management buyout, Dubuque Packing closed three plants and reopened them two weeks later at $6.50 an hour rather than $10.69. Unable to hold the line on plant-by-plant givebacks, the UFCW eventually agreed to lower base wages in pork to $8 to $9 an hour, but with scheduled increases to $10 an hour across the industry in 1985.

The union's target base wage in beef was $10.20 an hour in 1981, reflecting traditionally lower wages in that part of the industry, but all of the large beefpackers and most of the others actually paid less than that (Cappelli 1985:94). Even so, this did little to improve the competitive position of the old-line firms, which were disadvantaged by both smaller plants and higher wages (Duewer and Nelson 1991). An industry analyst estimated that, even with the concessions, slaughter costs at Wilson and Armour were $30 to $35 per head of cattle compared with $18 for IBP (Cox and Guyon 1981). IBP meanwhile used replacement workers to break a 1982 strike at Dakota City and, a year later, forced the union to accept a 12% wage cut for 42 months. It then reduced wages proportionately at its nonunion plants. Other beef packers followed the lead. Monfort, still an independent producer, closed its Greeley, Colorado, plant during a labor dispute in 1980 and reopened it nonunion two years later. ConAgra acquired thirteen Armour beef plants from Greyhound and closed and reopened nonunion at twelve of them. Excel meanwhile acquired Spencer Packing and resumed operations after gaining union concessions.

These trends effectively destroyed national bargaining and uniform wage increases in meatpacking. More than 400 beef and pork slaughter plants were closed and some 40,000 jobs lost between 1972 and 1987 (LaGanga 1990:D7). The number of hourly workers covered by master agreements declined from 70,000 in 1976 to 30,000 in 1983 (Lublin 1983). Four years later, according to a report by the union's packing-house director, wages in beef still had not recovered from the earlier rollbacks. UFCW plants generally paid $7 to $8 an hour in base wages, many others less than that. Moreover, actual earnings were lower than the base rates because starting wages, usually in effect for up to two years, were as much as $2 an hour below base wages, and labor turnover rates in these plants sometimes exceeded 100% annually. As a result, the union claimed 40% to 50% of the workers actually earned less than the base. The report conceded that IBP, Excel, ConAgra, and National had effectively replaced negotiated wage standards in the industry with a non-negotiated standard that emanated from IBP (Anderson 1987).

The impact on industry wages was devastating. Between 1968 and 1986 average hourly earnings in meatpacking dropped from 6% above to 6% below those in processing and from 23% above to 6% below those in all of food manufacturing (see Table 3). In the 1950s it was estimated that labor costs represented roughly 10% of sales in meatpacking (Carpenter and Handler 1961:28); by the 1980s the figure was a little more than 5%; and by the early 1990s, 3.4% (Bjerkie August 1992:35).

During Stage II beefpacking became one of the few basic industries in which wage changes occurring outside the negotiated pattern became the basis for changes inside union contracts. In the same 1973 bargaining round that legitimized wage differentials at Dakota City, IBP negotiators presented an alternative wage-setting formula to the union. They called it the Beef Industry Wage Index, or BIWI. It is an index of current base wages in all union and nonunion plants that slaughter a thousand or more cattle per day, weighted according to the volume in each plant. Thus, the base wage in a plant that accounted for one-tenth the total slaughter would determine one-tenth the value of the index. IBP prevailed upon the union to incorporate the BIWI into its Dakota City contract in 1973 and still adjusts wages there in accordance with changes in the index.[6]

Competitive unionism also emerged during Stage II. The only previous threat to UFCW's predecessor unions, and a relatively mild one at that, was the National Brotherhood of Packinghouse Workers, a consolidation of independent locals at several Swift plants. The Brotherhood competed directly with the Packinghouse Workers, especially during and after World War II, when it negotiated contracts similar to the master agreements but never joined union strikes (Purcell 1960:Chap. 2, 228, 242-4). Later, its fortunes suffered along with those of the company, and it merged with UFCW in 1989 (Gollas 1992:1660).

The Teamsters (IBT) represent a more recent competitive challenge. In 1992 the IBT had beefpacking contracts with IBP at Pasco, Washington (a relatively small plant) and Amarillo, Texas; with ConAgra at Garden City, Kansas; and with Excel at Ft. Morgan, Colorado. It also had contracts in porkpacking. Whether these contracts undermine the UFCW is difficult to determine in an industry characterized by large wage differentials among unionized plants.[7]

In some instances, however, the IBT has directly jeopardized UFCW bargaining rights. One case involved the Monfort-ConAgra plant in Marshalltown, Iowa. In July, 1989, local management informed the UFCW local there that the plant would close in three months, the day the labor contract expired. Monfort intended to lease the plant to a company that bargained with a Teamster local in Kansas. Workers were told they should apply to the other company for jobs that reportedly paid up to 85 cents an hour more than under the existing UFCW agreement. Federal, state, and local politicians immediately called for investigations into what they saw as a sham operation. UFCW also revealed that counsel for the leasing company had been involved in similar transfers involving IBP (*Mason City Dressed Beef, Inc.*, 231 NLRB No. 102 [1977]) and an independent beefpacker in Wisconsin (*Whitehall Packing Company, Inc.*, 257 NLRB No. 43 [1981]). The negative uproar continued until Monfort reversed its decision to close Marshalltown and entered into contract negotiations with UFCW (Erb 1989a, 1989b).

A reform group also emerged inside the UFCW during this time. REAP (Research, Education, Advocacy, People) was organized in 1990 under the leadership of Lewie Anderson, the union's former packinghouse director who by then had become a UFCW local business agent. REAP claimed some 2000 members in 20 mainly meatpacking locals. The group went on record against contract concessions, especially two-tiered wage systems, and urged changes in the union's constitution, including referendum election of international officers.

Anderson, who had been instrumental in developing the international's policy in meatpacking before being fired as director in 1989, claimed that the union was agreeing to low-wage contracts in return for voluntary recognition by major packers and was discouraging locals from coordinated bargaining efforts in single companies. He argued that when he was director in the early 1980s contract concessions were unavoidable because of industry overcapacity and the availability of replacement workers, but they no longer were because the economy had improved and there was a labor shortage (BNA 1990b). Phillip Immesote, who succeeded Anderson as director, responded that the problem is not with union policy but with the power of the new breed packers. While he regretted that industry patterns were gone, the job of the union now, he said, was to rebuild plant by plant (BNA 1990d).

Union decline thus weakened one form of labor market regulation in meatpacking. The other, government rule-making and enforcement, also deteriorated during this time, particularly in the area of occupational health and safety. High levels of job injuries are historical in meatpacking. In the mid-1980s, however, they reached epidemic proportions and received considerable media attention. In 1987 Congressman Tom Lantos (D-CA), Chairman of the House Employment and Housing Subcommittee of the Committee on Government Operations, initiated an investigation focusing on safety and health violations in IBP's Dakota City plant and in meatpacking generally (U.S. House of Representatives 1987).

Among other things, the Subcommittee learned that for workers meatpacking is the most dangerous industry in America. As Table 4 shows, the rate of job injuries and illnesses historically exceeds that in processing, especially during the 1980s, when the differential widened. By 1990-91, the risk in packing matched that in poultry during the 1960s, when poultry workers had neither unions nor protective job safety laws. Moreover, meatpacking wages were decreasing during this time, not increasing to compensate workers for the greater risks they were taking.

The two most frequent injuries in packing are knife wounds and punctures (about one-fourth) and nerve and tendon damage (one-third); the latter is caused by rapid, repetitive motions that can leave arms, hands and wrists permanently damaged (carpel tunnel syndrome). Other injuries also can be brutal (e.g., getting kicked or pinned by dying cattle; being hit by large chunks of meat; slipping on greasy floors; catching fingers and hands in slicing and chopping machines).[8]

The higher injury rates in meatpacking also coincided with faster production lines and increased use of immigrant labor. No formal data

TABLE 4

Worker Injury and Illness Rates: 1972-1990

Sector and Industry	Average Annual Injury and Illness Rates Per 100 Full-Time Workers			
	1958-70	1972-81	1982-91	1990-91
Total private sector	—	9.6%	8.2%	8.6%
All Manufacturing	12.9%	13.6	11.4	12.9
Meatpacking	32.4	32.9	34.9	43.9
Meat processing	27.4	22.9	21.7	21.7
Poultry°	43.1	24.1	26.1	25.0

° Poultry Dressing Plants and Packing (SIC 2016) until 1988, when SIC 2016 was combined with Poultry and Egg Processing (SIC 2017) as Poultry Slaughtering and Processing (SIC 2015)

Source: U.S. Department of Labor, Bureau of Labor Statistics, *Occupational Injuries and Illnesses in the United States*, various years.

are available on line speeds but those who study the industry agree that dramatic increases occurred with the introduction of boxed beef and the opening of the high-volume plants in the High Plains. An animal sciences specialist at Texas A&M, for example, reported in 1986 that some lines in IBP plants "have gone from a kill speed of 125 carcasses an hour to 400 an hour" (Greenhouse 1986:26). University of Kansas anthropologist Donald Stull and others interviewed workers and floor supervisors from IBP's Garden City plant which has been called the "Cadillac" of U.S. beef plants. He described the labor process:

Between 350 and 400 head are killed, bled, skinned, gutted, sawed, boned, cut, trimmed, shrink-wrapped, boxed and loaded every hour. If the workers are really "humping" and nothing breaks down, they may even get 425-450 head an hour. Chain speed is regulated by those in management—they can speed it up or slow it down. This frustrates workers, who often sacrifice safety and quality to keep up. But they must keep pace and do the job right, or face reprimand or terminations (Stull 1992:47).

During the 1986-87 strike-lockout at Dakota City, the union claimed that since 1981 the slaughter line speed had increased 22% and some processing lines up to 55%, without any increase in the number of workers. IBP officials refused to confirm or deny these estimates but emphasized that the company conducts industrial engineering studies before increasing the speeds in order to guard against worker injuries or damage to the equipment (Risen 1987).

These changes occurred in the absence of significant technological advances in the labor process. Meatpacking does not lend itself to extensive automation because it occurs in an environment that is hostile to sensitive machines—cold, damp atmospheres, slick surfaces, and raw material that varies in size and shape. The last round of major technical changes in meatpacking occurred in the 1950s and consisted mainly of electrification of hand tools and manual processes used before the turn of the century. About 80% of packinghouse work involves meat cutting. "However," a 1982 BLS report concluded, "most cutting tasks must still be performed manually, and the industry remains relatively labor intensive." (BLS 1982:1) Computers, lasers, and micro chips are found in modern packing plants, and machines have automated much of the material handling and product packaging, but most workers still use the tools and equipment introduced in the 1950s. Thus the combined effect of new meat products, different work forces, and faster line speeds probably explains the industry's sizable productivity gains in the 1960s and 1970s. Culmination of these trends in the 1980s may explain the more recent slowdown in productivity in the industry.[9]

Thus in Stage II of labor relations in meatpacking, the union lost each of the three conditions necessary for bargaining power. In beefpacking at least a third of the relevant work force no longer worked under union contracts; more importantly, the nonunion labor force was concentrated in efficient plants that make highly competitive products and was located far from the historical locus of the unionized industry. Second, companywide, pattern bargaining had broken down. And, finally, competitive unionism had become an obstacle to attempts by any single union to organize the relevant work force and establish effective bargaining structures.

Stage III: Reversing the Trend, 1987-1993

By 1987 it was apparent that to be effective UFCW had to organize the new packers and standardize base wages. By 1993 it had made progress in the former but was only beginning to build the structural foundations for the latter.

Tables 5 and 6 show how far the union had come by mid-1992 in rebuilding its organization and bargaining structures and how far it had yet to go. UFCW contracts covered slightly more than two-thirds of beefpacking. Of thirty-one plants handling a thousand or more cattle per day twenty were unionized: seventeen by UFCW and three by IBT.

TABLE 5

Beefpacking Plants by Organizational Status: June 1992

Organizational Status	Number of plants	Slaughter + Processing Production Volume°	% Total Volume	Weighted Average Base Wage
Union	21	117,417	70	$8.03
Nonunion	10	50,311	30	7.84
Total	31	167,728	100	$7.97

° Cattle per day.

Source: IBP, "Beef Industry Wage Index," June 22, 1992.

Union plants accounted for 70% of the total volume of production and paid a weighted average base wage of $8.03, or 19 cents per hour more than the $7.84 rate paid by nonunion plants, a union wage differential of just 2.4% among the major producers. A narrow union/nonunion wage differential can indicate that nonunion employers voluntarily pay high wages in order to avoid unionization. In beefpacking, however, it indicates union weakness, an inability to negotiate wage increases in union plants that are much above those paid in nonunion plants.

Table 6 disaggregates the organizational and wage data in Table 5 by individual company. It shows that union representation was complete but divided in Excel's multiplant system. UFCW contracts with five of the six plants called for above average wages despite the relatively low rates under the lone Teamster contract. The union also had all of the Beef America plants but wages there were below average, perhaps because the company is a consolidation of small, former independents in Nebraska and does not have strong ability to pay because it has not performed well financially.

UFCW had contracts with all of the single-plant independents except Hyplains, a more important packer strategically than its size would suggest because it sits as a small but low-wage competitor in the heart of the beef slaughter region. The union's highest wages were at a relatively small beef plant operated by Morrell, a leading pork packer, but in 1992 the company announced it was closing that unit. National Beef was a recent organizational victory for the UFCW and also in the process of raising wages nearer the average level as a result of its initial contract.

The union's major problems were extensive nonunion operations at IBP (six of nine plants) and ConAgra (three of six plants). ConAgra's

TABLE 6
Union and Nonunion Beefpacking Plants by Company: June 1992

Company (number of plants)	Volume° Slaughter	Processing	% of Volume Slaughter	Processing	Average Base Wage Slaughter	Processing
Beef America						
UFCW (5)	5,600	6,000	6.5	7.3	$7.94	$7.43
Champion (Litvak)						
UFCW (1)	—	1,300	—	1.6	—	8.35
ConAgra						
Union (3)	10,900	9,400	12.7	11.5	8.22	7.89
UFCW (2)	7,700	6,700	9.0	8.2	8.43	8.13
IBT (1)	3,200	2,700	3.7	3.3	7.70	7.30
Nonunion (3)	10,300	10,800	12.0	13.2	7.75	7.75
Monfort (2)	10,300	9,400	12.0	11.5	7.75	7.75
Excel						
Union (6)	20,100	18,450	23.4	22.6	8.30	8.14
UFCW (5)	16,400	15,250	19.1	18.7	8.40	8.20
IBT (1)	3,700	3,200	4.3	3.9	7.75	7.75
Hyplains						
Nonunion (1)	2,000	—	2.3	—	6.40	—
IBP						
Unions (3)	12,566	16,376	14.6	20.0	8.17	7.97
UFCW (2)	7,316	11,199	8.5	13.7	8.24	7.88
IBT (1)	5,250	5,177	6.1	6.3	8.39	8.14
Nonunion (6)	15,580	11,624	18.1	14.2	8.03	7.88
Kansas plants (2)	8,605	10,424	10.0	12.8	8.11	7.98
Morrell						
UFCW (1)	1,525	1,100	1.8	1.3	8.45	8.45
National						
UFCW (1)	5,000	4,700	5.8	5.7	7.60	7.40
Packerland						
UFCW (1)	2,400	2,000	2.8	2.5	7.45	7.45
Total	85,971	81,750	100.0	99.9	$8.03	$7.84

° Cattle per day

Source: Calculated from data in IBP, "Beef Industry Wage Index," June 22, 1992.

SIPCO plants were unionized, having been part of the old Swift system, but its two large Monfort plants were not. Located in Colorado and Nebraska, they accounted for 12% and 11.5% of the total volume of slaughter and processing production. In addition, IBP's two large Kansas plants represented more than 10% of both slaughter and processing capacity. Thus, the nonunion operations of these two packers combined accounted for more than one-fifth of the slaughter and processing done in large beef plants. Base wages at these plants were below the BIWI average. Nor could UFCW make independent packers adhere to negotiated industry standards. Events involving three Denver-area independents show the importance of wage differentials among plants producing for the same markets. Litvak, Pepper, and United negotiated as a group and, along with Monfort's plant in Greeley, followed the Big Four pattern precisely; until 1976, when they broke ranks in response to competition from IBP, National, and other low-wage producers. UFCW made concessions to the Denver packers and Monfort that year, but not in the 1979 round; whereupon Monfort closed Greeley, and the Denver companies demanded further relief from $10 an hour wages. Again the union made concessions. But Pepper closed anyway in 1985, and Litvak shut its slaughter operations and began fabricating beef as Litvak-Champion, although only after the union agreed to $5.90 an hour starting wages (Gollas 1992:1623-28, 1633-54).

UFCW began to regroup in beefpacking in a dispute at Dakota City that eventually involved contract concessions, but which otherwise might have ended in union decertification. Following a lockout in December, 1986, and use of replacement workers three months later, IBP appeared to have successfully replaced much of its union work force and could have been ready to try for a decertification election, one in which replacements but not strikers would have been eligible to vote. Suddenly, however, IBP offered contract terms better than those contained in its last offer. It did so following investigation of job safety charges the union filed against the company after management brought in the replacements. The complaint alleged IBP had falsified required plant safety records.

Top executives denied the charges in testimony before the Lantos Subcommittee but later had to admit improper recordkeeping and false testimony, which they claimed were unintentional. Nevertheless, amidst talk of perjury and possible jail sentences IBP softened its contract demands and a settlement was reached, albeit a concessionary one for the union, including a two-tiered wage system. Lantos strongly rebuked the company but dropped the perjury matter (Craypo 1993).[10]

In 1991 the parties negotiated their first contract at Dakota City without a dispute. It called for minimum wage increases of 70 cents an hour for workers hired before the 1987 settlement and shortened wage progression periods for those hired after that. "Labor-management relations were better during this cycle of negotiations because of an attitude of mutual respect," observed a company representative (BNA 1991a). Excel had acquired a plant in Colorado and reopened it union but with a $0.60 an hour wage cut, saying it could not pay more than IBP, ConAgra, and National. The company took the same position regarding its two Texas plants. In subsequent contract talks, however, it agreed to raise base wages in Texas to $8.70 an hour over three years and to shorten the progression time needed to earn the base rate. "You just can't attract people, particularly the higher skilled, at the previous starting rate of $6 an hour," the manager at one plant explained. UFCW's packinghouse division director said the contract represented "very substantial movement (in beefpacking) for the first time in about ten years." He interpreted Excel's move as evidence that packers knew they could not keep a satisfactory work force with lengthy progression rates and at base wages slightly above those in service jobs that are much less strenuous and dangerous than meatpacking (BNA 1990c:437).

The union intended to use the Texas contracts as the model in an effort to rebuild industry wage standards (BNA 1990d:495). It succeeded in negotiating similar rates at Excel's Colorado slaughter plant, which at the time paid lower wages than the company's Texas plants had paid before the negotiated increases. According to a UFCW representative, Excel management agreed to the increase because the union had effectively coordinated bargaining activities among its Excel locals, had survived the Dakota City dispute, had a certification election pending at National Beef, and appeared to be making progress in organizing Monfort (Gollas 1992:1663-77).

UFCW had assured Excel it would organize National and remove that plant as a low-wage competitor. It did so a few months later in 1991 when production workers there gave the union its biggest meatpacking victory in a decade. The vote showed that the union, which had assigned Asian organizers from the start, could organize the industry's new work force. A plant accident that took the lives of three workers early in the six-month campaign also solidified union sentiment. Within three months the union had a four-year contract with National that boosted entry wages $2.05 an hour in processing and $1.30 in slaughter, increases comparable to those at Excel's Kansas and Colorado plants, although, as Table 6 shows, wage levels at National still were lower than those elsewhere (BNA 1991b; *AFL-CIO News* 1992). This was an important gain for the union because National accounted for 6% of beef slaughter and is located in the middle of the Plains region. Monfort was a problem for the union before ConAgra acquired it in 1987. In the early 1970s, chairman and CEO Ken Monfort complained publicly and to the union about the impact of IBP on other producers. In 1979 contract negotiations he demanded large concessions. The union struck for ten weeks before making an unconditional offer to go back to work after Monfort began hiring replacements. Production resumed without a contract, but the plant closed a few months later. Meanwhile, the company prepared to begin slaughtering at the former Swift plant it had acquired in Grand Island, Nebraska. Before reopening, however, Monfort illegally recognized the National Maritime Union as bargaining agent in order to avoid the UFCW (*Monfort of Colorado*, 256 NLRB 612 [1981] p. 613). A UFCW official claimed the NMU contract had called for wages and benefits $3 to $4 an hour less than those at Monfort's non-union plant in Greeley (Gollas 1992:1631). UFCW lost the certification election that followed but charged unfair labor practices. The Board found that Monfort had committed a host of violations and ordered a re-run election (*Monfort of Colorado*, 284 NLRB 1429 [1987]). The union again lost and again appealed to the National Labor Relations Board.

Monfort then reopened its Greeley plant nonunion. UFCW tried to regain representation rights there but lost a 1983 election. After seven years of legal proceedings, the NLRB ruled that Monfort had discriminated against former employees for union activities and then conducted an improper election campaign (*Monfort of Colorado*, 298 NLRB No. 16 [1990]). It instructed Monfort to rehire the union workers and ordered another election. The union finally won in April, 1993, when the predominantly Hispanic work force at Greeley voted for UFCW representation (BNA 1993a).

Thus by 1993 the UFCW had made visible progress in rebuilding its organizational base in beefpacking. Whether it will be able to continue doing so against the formidable opposition confronting it remains to be seen. But it is a large organization with considerable resources and has demonstrated determination and willingness to use those resources to achieve the objective.

Labor Relations in Pork and Poultry

Most of the important trends found in beefpacking also are present in pork and poultry. Both industries are dominated by huge, vertically integrated firms. Work is hard and dangerous and wages low by manufacturing standards, although often high compared with alternative employment in the rural communities in which plants are concentrated. Key segments of each industry remain unorganized, although unions have made inroads.

Pork

Pork is largely a Corn Belt industry but production has increased significantly in Virginia, North Carolina, and Mississippi. In 1992 the largest four producers—IBP, ConAgra, Morrell, and Excel—accounted for nearly half the total output in Table 7. UFCW had large Excel and ConAgra plants under contract but only two of IBP's four large plants. The remaining nonunion plants included in the table belonged to independent packers and represented only 15% of total production. Moreover, in 1993 UFCW won a certification election at Lundy Packing, the largest independent. The higher degree of unionization perhaps explains the higher union wage differential in pork: 8.8% in 1992 compared to 2.4% in beef.

TABLE 7
Porkpacking Plants by Organizational Status: June 1992

Organizational Status	Number of Plants	Production Volume°	% Total Volume	Weighted Average Base Wage
Union	27	244,500	73	$8.50
Nonunion	12	91,700	27	7.81
Total	39	336,200	100	$8.32

°Hogs per Day
Source: IBP, "Pork Industry Wage Index," June 22, 1992.

Porkpackers nevertheless are in the same kind of competition to lower labor costs. IBP again is the major force. The company calculates a monthly Pork Industry Wage Index (PIWI) the same way it does the BIWI and also applies it to union and nonunion pork plants just as it applies the BIWI to beef plants. Thus the average weighted base wage in 1992 was $8.15 an hour in IBP's union plants and $8.18 in its nonunion plants. Base wages varied widely among all the plants included in Table 7, from $6.75 to $9.80 in union plants and from $6.60 to

$9.25 in nonunion pork plants. As in beef, individual porkpackers there-fore are motivated to resist unionization and uniform wage bargaining, either because the low-wage plants of other producers pressure them to do so, or because large wage differentials create the opportunity for them to widen profit margins by doing so. Such conditions foster hostile labor relations and acrimonious strikes.

In the most widely publicized dispute, Hormel unilaterally cut base wages in 1984 at its Austin, Minnesota, plant from $10.69 to $8.25 an hour. In contract negotiations the following year, management agreed to $10 an hour base wages for regular workers but wanted to start new hires at $9. UFCW had negotiated a $10 base wage elsewhere after hav-ing to abandon its previous standard of $10.69 an hour in view of rates as low as $6 an hour in nonunion, reopened and threatened pork plants. UFCW Local P-9 nevertheless demanded retention of the $10.69 rate on the grounds that Austin was the logical place to draw the line on con-tract concessions: Hormel was profitable, the Austin plant was among the industry's newest and most efficient, and the local had made Hormel more vulnerable to a job action as a result of a "corporate campaign" it was conducting against the company.

When the local struck, however, Hormel dug in its heels and eventu-ally hired replacement workers in a bitter, violent confrontation. Neither the corporate campaign nor the walkout caused Hormel to meet the local's demands, nor did local union efforts to widen the dispute to the company's other plants. Finally, in June, 1986, the international imposed a harsh trusteeship on P-9 and, a few months later, negotiated a compa-nywide agreement with Hormel that raised base wages to $10.70 an hour but retained the company's two-tiered wage system (Green 1990; Moody 1988:314-27). Hormel later threatened to terminate its Austin slaughter operation, although not the processing plant, unless the local took a wage cut in slaughter, which the new P-9 officers refused to do. Instead Hormel leased the slaughter operation to Quality Pork Pro-cessors. In 1989 the union accepted a $7 an hour start-up wage at the leased plant, progressing to $9; in 1993 it negotiated a $9.50 base rate over four years.[11]

By the 1990s the industry shake-out in pork appeared to have run its course and union strike effectiveness improved as a result. UFCW signed a three-year master agreement with Wilson in 1992, following a three-week strike affecting some 2,000 workers in four plants. The con-tract contained no union concessions and instead boosted base wages to

$9.70 an hour and improved health care (BNA 1992b). Considering the reverses of the 1980s, the Wilson contract was a victory for the union. As in beef, however, UFCW has a long way to go to restore its previous bargaining power. The immediate obstacle continues to be IBP's large, nonunion plants. But a long-term threat involves the ability of low-wage independents and major nonunion producers to enter into "co-packer" agreements with high-wage union processors. Such transactions among firms effectively transfer processing and packaging operations from high-wage to low-wage plants. They are more likely to occur in pork than in beef because processed products and brand labels are more important in pork than in beef. Widespread use of this practice, however, could create a new and formidable type of wage competition throughout the industry.

Poultry

Poultry is now a Southern industry. Most of the recent growth has been in Arkansas, North Carolina, Georgia, and Alabama, and along the Chesapeake Bay Peninsula. Wages are lower than in beef and pork but, as Table 3 shows, have been rising faster, doubtless due to the industry's rapid expansion. Poultry also has been a dangerous industry for workers (see Table 4), even more so than meat processing, which it closely resembles. Injury and illness rates in poultry did decline appreciably following enactment of federal safety laws, but workers in large plants work at dangerous speeds, sometimes processing as many as 90 chickens a minute. Such speed requires individual workers to make thousands of swift, repetitive hand and wrist motions per shift, which results in high rates of cumulative trauma disorder. Lack of effective workplace regulation and arbitrary labor relations create even more hazardous conditions, as demonstrated in 1992 by a fire inside the locked doors of a North Carolina poultry plant that took the lives of 25 workers. Thus, even though they often pay the highest wages in town, labor turnover in poultry is high, as it is in meatpacking (Applebome 1989).

Precise figures on unionization rates in poultry are unavailable but general estimates are 15% to 20%. UFCW and the Retail, Wholesale and Department Store Union (RWDSU) are the most active unions in the industry. Each has organized large plants after multiple, legally contested elections and each has negotiated first contracts after protracted talks and strikes. They are not competitor unions and, indeed, have merged. However, the lack of clear negotiated industry standards makes it difficult for them to take union workers out of competition and prompts individual employers and plants to resist vigorously. RWDSU, for example, won representation elections covering more than a thousand workers at two Choctaw Maid poultry plants in Mississippi in October, 1990. Due to legal appeals, however, the union was not certified until mid-1992 and then could not get contracts until January, 1993 (Colatosti 1992; Rosier 1993). Even so, the industry's size, growth rate, and labor-intensive processes invite sustained union organizing efforts.

Industrial Organization and Labor Relations in Beefpacking

Case studies, past and present, show that labor markets are highly structured systems in which interested parties have uneven shares of economic and institutional power. Competition is the driving force in market systems and individual and organizational responses to it are the dynamics that determine productive outcomes. This was the insight of John R. Commons. It is the "menace of competition," he maintained, that explains labor-management conflict in market economies (Commons 1909:68-9, 78-9). For this reason, as Robert Hoxie observed, union structures evolve in response to changes in the organization of production: "The union organic structure shows a tendency to parallel the capitalistic, a union unit to meet each capitalistic unit" (Hoxie 1917:99).

Industrial organization thus is central to understanding the rise and decline of industrial unionism in the U.S., because labor relations in this country are decentralized at the company and firm levels. In meatpacking it took organized labor more than a half-century to organize the multiplant structures of the old oligopoly and another decade to bring them under companywide pattern bargaining. Industrial unionism succeeded because it matched the organizational structure of the leading firms; it survived the decentralization of meatpacking that occurred during the immediate postwar decades, but not the restructuring that new breed packers engineered in the 1970s and 1980s. The new oligopoly advanced the industry but left the union behind.

Old and new packers alike had to imitate IBP's anti-union model once its competitive effectiveness was evident. Each of the large, new packers chose to operate union-free if possible and, at a minimum, to avoid multiplant, uniform contract settlements. Once committed to this approach, however, the industry had nothing to offer the union in place of the postwar bargaining system, nothing that would give organized labor a legitimate role in the changed industry. The new firms destroyed the balance of power inherent in postwar labor relations, but the strategy they used to do so made the parties even greater adversaries and essentially precluded labor-management cooperation involving either them or the old-line packers.[12]

So the union, in a response that was defensive and adaptive, set out to organize the new relevant work force, establish new bargaining structures and replace indexed wage adjustments (i.e., the BIWI and PIWI formulas) with negotiated wage increases. Union policy had to be defensive rather than offensive because the labor relations environment had changed in ways that undermined established union power. It had to be adaptive rather than reactionary because the old system of three-year, pattern settlements and master contracts had become irretrievable. Nevertheless, the business of U.S. unions is to organize workers and negotiate and administer contracts, thus, the UFCW strategy is to find innovative ways of restoring the bargaining power that had given it effective countervailing power against the old oligopoly.[13]

The relevant question in a case like this is not whether union wages priced workers out of competition. Market competition destroys existing practices and institutions, those of unions and companies alike. In this instance a new firm introduced practices that simultaneously increased labor's productive value and devalued its price, the former through new products and processes, the latter through division of labor, plant relocation, and recruitment of workers from low-wage labor pools. The more relevant question therefore is whether it is good economic practice and wise public policy to reduce production costs by reducing living standards. Or should we try instead to regulate the way in which labor and management create and distribute wealth?

The issue is not whether supply and demand determine wages, for they do, but what determines supply and demand? In this case the answer reinforces the view that under certain conditions unregulated labor markets can become low-wage markets. As a result of the changes described, labor was put back into competition and wages fell, conditions worsened, and a vulnerable labor force emerged. Meatpacking thus represents a uniquely American version of the new global economy. It incorporates the "Toyotist" version of Japanese lean production—work speed-ups, job stress, health and safety problems—without subscribing to the positive labor aspects—employment security, employee participation, union-management acceptance and cooperation. It also differs from the practices of European industries that have not tried to avoid unions or drive down labor costs, although they might be prompted to do so in the future in response to similar kinds of competitive forces (Sengenberger 1993).

The new meatpackers produce quality products in efficient workplaces, but they do not offer good wages, safe working conditions, and stable communities.[14] The second relevant question, therefore, is can they continue to be successful performers without also having to exhaust human resources, depend on disadvantaged labor, and make war against organized labor? And can they contribute to a strong domestic economy at the same time they alleviate Mexico's unemployment problem by hiring Hispanic immigrants?

These questions arise from analysis of the interaction between labor standards and productive systems (Wilkinson 1983). Institutional processes are filled with unintended consequences, and the new oligopoly has not had its way with labor without a cost. As each large packer drives down labor standards in order to maintain or improve its competitive position, the combined effect is to eliminate a large segment of the traditional labor force and to replace it with a transient population that has no stake in or commitment to the industry and in whom the industry has no abiding interest.

A certain number of high-performance packers can compete and thrive in the industry for a time using low-wage strategies, but it is a fallacy of composition to think that a major economic sector can function this way indefinitely. By the late 1980s meatpacking as a productive system was producing unacceptable results when measured in terms of social stability, job safety, and worker living standards. The virtuous circles that characterized it and other basic industries in the postwar years—self-sufficient earnings, steady jobs, experienced and reliable work forces—had given way to vicious circles of an opposite nature. So much so that the editor of the industry's leading trade journal was moved to warn the packers that human resources, like natural ones, are not limitless. "They cannot be exploited forever," he observed, "without risk to the very survival of the exploiters" (Bjerklie October 1992:40).

Endnotes

[1] Beef consumption peaked in 1976 at 94 lbs. per person before falling to around 80 lbs. in the mid-1980s; pork peaked in 1980 at 70 lbs. and declined slowly to 62 lbs.; chicken rose steadily from 40 lbs. in the mid-1970s to nearly 60 lbs. by 1986 (Greenhouse 1986:1).

[2] Asians losing jobs in aircraft and packing plants in eastern Kansas were recruited to work in Garden City. IBP has had considerable success recruiting Hispanics from California and Texas (Farney 1990:A1). According to California officials, the company utilized their labor recruitment services nearly one hundred times between July 1990 and August 1991 (Rhoads 1992:9).

Dependence on immigrant labor can be risky. The Immigration and Naturalization Service fined Morrell a total of $450,000 for violations of the Immigration Reform and Control Act of 1986 involving 748 workers at two plants. Violations mainly concerned work authorization forms rather than illegal employment (BNA 1990e).

[3] In the meat products industry (SIC 201), 53,072 Hispanic and 9,734 Asian blue-collar workers were employed in 1991, or 21% and 4%, respectively, compared to 23,264 (9%) and 1,827 (0.7%) in 1978. African-Americans' share increased from 22% to 24%, although their numbers rose by 40%, from 44,562 to 62,295. (U.S. Equal Employment Opportunity Commission, *Survey of Private Employers 1991*, Washington, DC.) Most of the increases in Hispanic and Asian workers appear to be in meatpacking and that of African Americans in poultry and fish processing plants in the Southeast (Broadway, no date).

[4] Although it occurred as IBP was becoming an important force in the industry, the merger was motivated by other, often conflicting trends in meat packing. "Sharp changes in the composition of the industry and its operations were influencing the decision to join forces. An increasing share of the market had been captured by relatively new, small nonunion producers; major meatpacking companies decided to decrease the size of their production units and to decentralize operations into rural areas; several had become merger targets of conglomerates" (Dewey 1971:65-6).

Some but not all of the conglomerates weakened their meatpacking subsidiaries by treating them as cash cows. For example, "LTV bled Wilson thoroughly. LTV closed down plants and took tax credits, sold off the meatpacking business and took the cash, and didn't put much back in" (Williams 1983).

[5] In the 1964 round of bargaining, for example, the Amalgamated brought more than 5,000 workers in 34 plants under master contracts for the first time. A spokesman said the union felt "morally bound" to establish the union pattern in the rest of the industry in order to protect the covered companies from low-wage competition (Perry and Kegley 1989:134).

[6] The union subsequently agreed to incorporate the BIWI into its first contract at the IBP beef plant in Joslin, Illinois.

[7] As Table 6 shows, the IBT contract at Amarillo paid higher wages than the UFCW contract at Dakota City, but IBT wages were lower than UFCW's at Excel and ConAgra. In 1992 IBT negotiated a four-year contract at Pasco which included interim wage increases to $7.33 in processing and $7.83 in slaughter, compared to UFCW average wages at IBP that year of $7.97 and $8.17 (BNA 1992a). Like UFCW, the Teamsters sometimes accepted wages below those paid in certain nonunion plants. Its contract at ConAgra's Garden City plant, for example, paid 40 cents an hour less than IBP's nearby nonunion plant (Stull and Broadway 1990:13).

[8] For testimony and affidavits on these and other packing plant injuries, see U. S. House of Representatives 1987: Part I, pp. 38-61; Stull 1992:25-33. The Subcommittee

investigation revealed improper recordkeeping by IBP at Dakota City, and by Morrell and Company at its Sioux City, Iowa pork plant. In July 1987, IBP was fined $2.6 million—the largest such levy to date—for more than a thousand recordkeeping violations. A few months earlier Morrell had been fined $690,000 for similar infractions, and the next year a record $4.3 million for safety violations at Sioux City, where seven out of eight production workers had experienced recordable injuries or illnesses the preceding year (BNA 1988b).

[9] Output per worker hour in packing rose annually by 2.8% during 1967-79 and by 1.3% during 1979-90; by contrast, in processing it rose annually by 5.5% in 1973-79 and remained flat during 1979-90 (Carnes 1987; Kronemer 1993).

[10] A year later IBP, UFCW, and the Labor Department signed an agreement in which the company conceded dangerous working conditions in its plants, especially the high incidence of cumulative trauma disorders, and promised to implement a comprehensive preventive ergonomic program in cooperation with the union.

In 1990 Excel and UFCW agreed on a similar health and safety program affecting 8,600 workers in seven beef and three pork plants. Union officials called the company action "enlightened" because it occurred in the absence of OSHA fines and citations, although Cargill, Excel's parent company, had been cited for violations in its poultry plants. Excel had previously recognized the union on the basis of authorization cards at the Ottumwa, Iowa plant it leased from Hormel (BNA 1988a, 1990a).

Resolution of the Dakota City conflict also facilitated IBP's voluntary recognition of UFCW at its Joslin, Illinois beef plant (Bernstein 1988).

[11] A lesser known but more important dispute involved two large Morrell pork plants. An anti-concession strike at Sioux City, Iowa, triggered a sympathy walk-out at Sioux Falls, South Dakota. Morrell broke both using replacements and imposed its own terms and conditions. Fewer than half the Sioux Falls strikers were recalled. But six years later a federal appeals court ruled that Morrell had to arbitrate their recall rights, another instance in which exceedingly lengthy proceedings seemed to abrogate the practical intent of protective labor legislation (BNA 1987, 1989, 1993b).

[12] Prior to its 1983 bankruptcy filing and 40% wage cut, Wilson, for example, "enjoyed one of the most cordial and progressive labor-management relationships in the meatpacking industry." It had not been struck since 1959 and experienced few contract grievances. Employee involvement was high and most Wilson plants had quality circles (*Business Week* 1983:71).

[13] During the 1970s and 1980s wage bargaining in U.S. manufacturing shifted from deferred and automatic increases based on comparability, inflation, and productivity, to contingent adjustments based on diverse performance variables. In the past, unions usually rejected substantial and permanent concessions to firms that did not have the ability to pay, correctly anticipating that the profitable ones would then demand equal treatment on competitive grounds. Declining union densities and increasingly persuasive threats of plant closings eroded union power in the 1980s and changed the standards of bargaining (Craypo 1986:Chap. 9).

[14] For more detailed discussions of community disruption by the industry, see "Special Issue, When the Packers Came to Town: Changing Ethnic Relations in

Garden City, Kansas," *Urban Anthropology* 19, no. 4 (Winter 1990); Hackenberg et al. 1993; Craypo 1993:200-4.

References

AFL-CIO News. 1992. "UFCW Negotiates First Contract at National Beef." January 8, p. 9.

Anderson, Lewie G. 1987. *Report on Wages in the Beef Sector of Meat Packing: IBP Set Wage Pace for Beef Industry.* United Food and Commercial Workers International Union, March 6.

Applebome, Peter. 1989. "For Poultry Industry, Worker Injuries Rise as Business Booms." *New York Times,* November 6, pp. A1, A20.

Arnould, Richard J. 1971. "Changing Patterns of Concentration in American Meat Packing, 1880-1963." *Business History Review* XLV, no. 1 (Spring), pp. 18-34.

Bernstein, Aaron. 1988. "How OSHA Helped Organize the Meatpackers." *Business Week,* August 29, p. 82.

Bjerklie, Steve. 1992. "No Way Up?" *Meat & Poultry.* A Three-Part Series: August, pp. 35-41; September, pp. 39-46; October, pp. 33-40.

Broadway, Michael J. 1990. "Recent Changes in the Structure and Location of the U.S. Meatpacking Industry." *Geography* 75, no. 1, pp. 76-79.

_____. (no date). "Recent Changes in the Structure and Location of the Meat- and Fish Processing Industry." State University of New York, Geneseo, Unpublished paper.

Brody, David. 1964. *The Butcher Workmen: A Study of Unionization.* Cambridge: Harvard University Press.

Bureau of Labor Statistics. 1964. *Industry Wage Survey: Meat Products.* Bulletin No. 1415, June. Washington, DC: GPO.

_____. 1982. *Technology and Labor in Four Industries.* Bulletin No. 2104, January. Washington, DC: GPO.

_____. 1991. *Industrial Wage Survey: Meat Products,* Bulletin 1415 (April).

Bureau of National Affairs. 1974. "Arbitrator Rules in Iowa Beef Dispute." *Daily Labor Report* May 9, p. A-16.

_____. 1987. "UFCW Ends Six-Month Sympathy Strike by 2,500 at South Dakota Morrell Plant." *Labor Relations Week* 1 November 11, pp. 1046-7.

_____. 1988a. "Workers at Excel Slaughtering Plant Choose UFCW as Bargaining Agent." *Labor Relations Week* 2 July 27, pp. 728-9.

_____. 1988b. "OSHA Proposes Record Fines for Alleged Morrell Safety Violations." *Labor Relations Week* 2 November 2, p. 1045.

_____. 1989. "John Morrell Implements Terms, Cuts Wages 18% at Sioux Falls Plant." *Labor Relations Week* 3 February 22, p. 174.

_____. 1990a. "UFCW, Excel Reach Ergonomic Pact; Voluntary Agreement Affects 10 Plants." *Labor Relations Week* 4 January 3, p. 17.

_____. 1990b. "UFCW Members Hold Founding Meeting for Rank-and-File Reform Organization." *Labor Relations Week* 4 April 11, pp. 351-2.

_____. 1990c. "Excel, UFCW Negotiate Contract for 1,500 at Friona, Texas Plant." *Labor Relations Week* 4 May 9, pp. 437-8.

_____. 1990d. "UFCW Packinghouse Director Looks to 1990s as Time to Rebuild Contracts." *Labor Relations Week* 4 May 23, pp. 495-6.

_____. 1990e. "INS Hits Morrell & Co. with $345,000 in Proposed Fines." *Labor Relations Week* 4 September 5, pp. 819-20.

_____. 1991a. "UFCW Local 222 Ratifies Contract Covering IBP Inc.'s Flagship Plant." *Labor Relations Week* 5 July 31, p. 707.

_____. 1991b. "Employees of National Beef Vote for UFCW Representation." *Labor Relations Week* 5 September 18, p. 853.

_____. 1992a. "IBP and Teamsters Negotiate Pact for 1,200 Workers at Washington Plant." *Labor Relations Week* 6 April 1, p. 317.

_____. 1992b. "UFCW Approves Master Wilson Foods Pact Ending Three-Week Strike at Four Plants." *Labor Relations Week* 6 May 27, p. 516.

_____. 1993a. "NLRB Seeks Contempt Citation against Meatpacker for Continuing Violations." *Labor Relations Week* 7 April 21, p. 374.

_____. 1993b. "Morrell Must Arbitrate Issues over Recall of 1987 Strikers." *Labor Relations Week* 7 May 12, p. 457.

Business Week. 1983. "The Slaughter of Meatpacking Wages." June 27, pp. 70-1.

Cappelli, Peter. 1985. "Plant-Level Concession Bargaining." *Industrial and Labor Relations Review* 39, no. 1 (October), pp. 90-104.

Carnes, Richard B. 1987. "Meatpacking and Prepared Meats Industry: Above-Average Productivity Gains." *Monthly Labor Review* 111, no. 1 (January), pp. 37-42.

Carpenter, Walter H., Jr., and Edward Handler. 1961. *Small Business and Pattern Bargaining.* Boston: Babson Institute Press.

Colatosti, Camille. 1992. "Poultry Industry Organizers Making Slow Progress under Difficult Conditions." *Labor Notes* #165 December, pp. 1,14-5.

Commons, John R. 1904. "Labor Conditions in Meat Packing and the Recent Strike." *Quarterly Journal of Economics* 19 (November), pp. 1-32.

_____. 1909. "The American Shoemakers, 1648-1885." *Quarterly Journal of Economics* 24 (November), pp. 39-84.

Cox, Meg, and Janet Guyon. 1981. "Food Union Extends Its Wage Concessions to 2 Meatpackers, Seeks National Pattern." *Wall Street Journal*, December 24, p. 22.

Craypo, Charles. 1986. *The Economics of Collective Bargaining.* Washington, DC: Bureau of National Affairs.

_____. 1993. "Strike and Relocation in Meatpacking." In *Grand Designs: The Impact of Corporate Strategies on Workers, Unions and Communities.* C. Craypo and B. Nissen, eds., Ithaca, New York: ILR Press, pp. 185-208.

Dewey, Lucretia M. 1971. "Union Merger Pace Quickens." *Monthly Labor Review* (June), pp. 63-67.

Duewer, Lawrence A., and Kenneth E. Nelson. 1991. *Beefpacking and Processing Plants: Computer-Assisted Cost Analysis.* Commodity Economics Division, Economic Research Service, U.S. Department of Agriculture. Staff Report No. AGES 9115. Spring.

Erb, Gene. 1989a. "Monfort Plans at Marshalltown Called Despicable." *Des Moines Register,* August 20, pp. 1G, 2G.

_____. 1989b. "Monfort Backs Down, Says Marshalltown Plant Won't Be Leased." *Des Moines Register,* September 2, pp. 1A, 6A.

Farney, Dennis. 1990. "A Town in Iowa Finds Big New Packing Plant Destroys Its Old Calm." *Wall Street Journal*, April 3, pp. A1, A8.

Financial World. 1989. "Boxed In." 158, no. 6, March 21, pp. 50-1.

Gollas, Al. 1992. Transcript of Testimony in *United Food and Commercial Workers Locals 951, 588, 7, 1036 and 576*, NLRB Case No. 16-CB-3850, July 23, pp. 1603-1735.

Gouveia, Lourdes, and Donald D. Stull. 1992. "Dances With Cows: Beefpacking's Impact on Garden City, Kansas and Lexington, Nebraska." Unpublished paper, National Conference on New Factory Workers in Old Farming Communities, Queenstown, Maryland, April 12-14.

Green, Hardy. 1990. *On Strike at Hormel: The Struggle for a Democratic Labor Movement*. Philadelphia: Temple University Press.

Greenhouse, Steven. 1986. "Can the Cow Make a Comeback?" *New York Times*, September 28, pp. 1, 26; sec. 3.

Hackenberg, Robert A., David Griffith, Donald D. Stull and Lourdes Gouveia. 1993. "Creating a Disposable Labor Force." *AQ* 5, no. 2 (Spring), pp. 78-101.

Hoxie, Robert F. 1917. *Trade Unionism in the United States*. Chicago: University of Chicago Press.

Kasler, Dale. 1988. "Union Wins Battle at Illinois Plant." *Des Moines Register*, September 21, p. 3A.

Kronemer, Alexander. 1993. "Productivity in Industry and Government: 1973-91." *Monthly Labor Review* 116, no. 7 (July), pp. 44-51.

LaGanga, Maria L. 1990. "Meat Market Slaughter." *Los Angeles Times*, April 22, pp. Dl, D7.

Lublin, Joanns. 1983. "Effort to Save Pay Scales in Meatpacking Brings Lewie Anderson Many Spats, Not All with Firms." *Wall Street Journal*, August 4, p. 46.

Moody, Kim. 1988. *An Injury to All: The Decline of American Unionism*. New York: Verso.

Nelson, Kenneth E. 1985. *Issues and Developments in the U.S. Meatpacking Industry*. Washington, DC: U.S. Department of Agriculture.

Perry, Charles R., and Delwin H. Kegley. 1989. *Disintegration and Change: Labor Relations in the Meat Packing Industry*. Philadelphia: Industrial Relations Unit, University of Pennsylvania.

Purcell, Theodore V. 1960. *Blue Collar Man: Patterns of Dual Allegiance in Industry*. Cambridge, MA: Harvard University Press.

Rhoads, Alexander. 1992. "Shattered Promises: Immigrants and Refugees in the Meatpacking Industry." *Poverty and Race* 1, no. 5 (November), pp. 5, 9.

Risen, James. 1987. "Injury Rate Soaring, Workers at Meatpacking Plant Say." *Los Angeles Times*, March 2.

Robbins, William. 1988. "A Meatpacker Cartel Up Ahead?" *New York Times*, May 29, p. 4.

Rosier, Sharolyn A. 1993. "Perseverence Is Rewarded at Choctaw." *AFL-CIO News*, February 15, pp. 1, 12.

Sengenberger, Werner. 1993. "Lean Production: The Way of Working and Producing in the Future?" In *Lean Production: Labour Aspects of a New Production Concept*. Geneva: International Institute for Labour Studies, International Labour Organization, pp. 1-22.

Stull, Donald D. 1992. "Knock 'Em Dead: Work on the Killfloor of a Modern Beefpacking Plant." Louise Lamphere, Guillermo Grenier and Alex Stepick, editors, *Newcomers in the Workplace: New Immigrants and the Restructuring of the U.S. Economy.* Philadelphia: Temple University Press.

Stull, Donald, Michael J. Broadway, and Ken C. Erickson. 1992. "The Price of a Good Steak: Beef Packing and Its Consequences for Garden City, Kansas." In *Structuring Diversity: Ethnographic Perspectives on the New Immigration,* L. Lamphere, ed. Chicago: University of Chicago Press, pp. 35-64.

U. S. House of Representatives. 1987. *Underreporting of Occupational Injuries and Its Impact on Workers' Safety.* Subcommittee of the Committee on Government Operations, 100th Congress, 1st Session, Part I, March 19; Part II, May 6; Part III, September 21.

Wilkinson, Frank. 1983. "Productive Systems." *Cambridge Journal of Economics* 7, pp. 413-29.

Williams, Monci J. 1983. "The Return of the Meatpackers." *Fortune* May 2, p. 257.

CHAPTER 3

Collective Bargaining in the Aerospace Industry in the 1980s

CHRISTOPHER L. ERICKSON
UCLA

Editor's Abstract

Aerospace is a highly organized industry in which American companies have maintained a technological edge and remain export competitive, despite the recent growth of the European consortium Airbus Industrie. The industry has a pyramid structure, with a few prime contractors at the top and many subcontractors and parts manufacturers further down. Boeing, the only prime contractor that mainly manufactures commercial aircraft, is the United States' single largest exporter. Major companies on the military/space side include Hughes, Lockheed, Northrop, and Rockwell. McDonnell Douglas is active on both sides of the industry. Both military and commercial production is quite cyclical. This is due to the nature of the production process, as well as to the speculative vagaries of the commercial airline industry and to political/military policy shifts. Both sides of the industry are now in a downturn after the boom years of the 1980s, with the slump particularly severe on the military side.

Worker representation in aerospace is split between two major unions with different origins and philosophies: the International Association of Machinists and Aerospace Workers (IAM) and the United Automobile, Aerospace and Agricultural Implement Workers (UAW). Large engineering and technical unions, most notably the Seattle Professional Engineering Employees Association (SPEEA), also are active.

Erickson organizes his survey of aerospace collective bargaining around two fundamental insights:

1. In many respects, industrial relations in aerospace retains many vestiges of the postwar system. It has developed neither a widespread lean production system, nor profit sharing, nor other significant forms of worker participation. Attempts to utilize total quality management have had uneven success, and one of the two main unions, the IAM, has declared its opposition to team concept programs.

2. Nonetheless, the 1980s and 1990s have been decades of major change in wage bargaining. Increased competition is largely responsible. Product markets have been shaken by the deregulation of the airlines, the emergence of Airbus, the "end of the cold war," and the tightening of government budgets and procurement contracting procedures. With these developments, the differing market positions of the aerospace manufacturers have taken on greater importance in determining bargaining outcomes, and both intra- and interindustry patterns have weakened.

In 1983, aerospace broke from the "auto-aero-implement" pattern of earlier years, when lump sum payments were negotiated in aerospace in lieu of the profit-sharing provisions in the auto industry. While the aerospace lump sum payments were less advantageous to employees than the base pay adjustments of the prior era, they were more valuable than profit sharing proved to be for auto workers. Strong intra-industry patterns significantly weakened in 1989, when Boeing employees received substantial pay increases after a strike (in the context of a strong market for commercial aircraft), while the employees at the military contractors received less (in the context of slumping military/space demand). Recent bargaining outcomes suggest further weakening of the intra-industry pattern, although the rest of the industry still looks to the Boeing settlement as a trendsetter.

o   o   o

This chapter examines recent collective bargaining developments in one of the few highly unionized U.S. industries that maintains a technological edge and remains export competitive into the 1990s, the aerospace industry. Table 1 presents the union coverage for the companies in this industry with the most production workers represented in major bargaining units;[1] these are the bargaining relationships on which this study will focus.

The industry has a pyramid structure, with a few prime contractors at the top and many subcontractors and parts manufacturers further down the pyramid. The companies represented in Table 1 are mainly prime contractors, except for two engine manufacturers (United Technologies and General Electric) and one subcontractor (Rohr). While there are many military contractors and parts suppliers, and most of these companies produce products for both the military and commercial sectors, three final assemblers of large commercial transports essentially control the world market, suggesting that the final market for commercial turbojet aircraft is highly oligopolistic.

The industry is also distinguished by the fact that worker representation is essentially split between two major unions, the International

TABLE 1

Largest Union Representation of Production Workers
in Aerospace Divisions of Companies in the 1980s

Company	Locations	Primary Union	Range of Workers Covered by Major Settlements During 1980s[a]
Boeing	Washington Oregon Kansas	IAM	26,000-58,000
	Pennsylvania	UAW	1,200-3,300
McDonnell Douglas	Missouri Southern California	IAM	13,000-18,300
	Southern California Oklahoma	UAW	6,600-15,000
Lockheed	Southern California Northern California Georgia	IAM	18,000-30,000[b]
United Technologies (Pratt & Whitney)	Connecticut Connecticut	IAM IBT	13,800-22,000 6,200-6,600
General Dynamics	Southern California Texas	IAM	10,000-16,600[c]
(Cessna)	Kansas	IAM	2,000-6,000
Rockwell	Southern California Ohio Oklahoma	UAW	7,500-17,000
Hughes	Southern California Arizona	CJA IAM	11,500-13,500 1,500-2,200
General Electric	Ohio Massachusetts	UAW IUE	5,000[d] 5,000[d]
Raytheon (Beech)	Kansas Colorado	IAM	3,900-7,800
Rohr	Southern California	IAM	4,200-5,050
Martin Marietta	Maryland Florida Colorado	UAW	2,300-6,000

Source: U.S.B.L.S., Current Wage Developments
[a] Employment ranges based on contract reports in Current Wage Developments in the 1980s.
[b] Includes clerical workers.
[c] Aerospace divisions sold to Hughes and Lockheed in 1992.
[d] Part of master agreement covering most unionized GE employees.

Association of Machinists and Aerospace Workers (IAM) and the United Automobile, Aerospace and Agricultural Implement Workers (UAW). These unions, which have different origins and philosophies, can have considerable bargaining power due to the nature of the production process and the output markets.

There has been a shift in the environment of collective bargaining in this industry from rent sharing to a more competitive system during the 1980s. The driving forces behind this shift have been fundamental changes in the nature of the product markets: deregulation of the airlines and the appearance of viable foreign competition on the commercial side and the end of the cold war, the government budgetary crisis, and tightening of procurement contracting procedures on the military/ space side.

With the tightening of these constraints, pattern bargaining has significantly weakened over the course of the 1980s. The military and commercial sides of the industry have never had coincident business cycles, but this fact was less important when rents were ample; in the 1980s, the widening differences in the fortunes of the companies in a situation of reduced rents contributed to a weakening of the strong intraindustry wage growth pattern that held throughout the postwar period. In addition, the parties have moved away from the interindustry pattern established in the automobile industry and, with it, the stable postwar wage rule of "3% AIF plus COLA."[2]

Nevertheless, a major premise here is that in order to understand the general trajectory of the aerospace industry as well as the major changes in its collective bargaining practices, one must focus on a single company, Boeing, both because it is the largest and most profitable (also clearly the most viable now in an environment of shrinking military expenditures) and because it has maintained its status as the pattern setter for the industry in its collective bargaining relationship with the IAM (in terms of contract innovations, if not actual growth rates of wages). Of particular import was the 1983 settlement between Boeing and the IAM, which was the first major aerospace contract in the 1980s to contain lump sum provisions, a weak form of two-tier wage scales, and significant language on technological change.

Beyond the weakening of previous wage rules and patterns and the introduction of lump sums, there has been little innovation in industrial relations in this industry as a whole compared to other leading unionized industries. It has not developed a widespread lean production system, employment stabilization provisions, profit sharing, or significant forms of worker participation on a large scale. Attempts to utilize total quality management have had uneven success, and one of the two main unions has openly declared its opposition to team-concept programs in principle. In many ways, industrial relations in this industry retains many vestiges of the postwar arms-length system, due to a variety of technological, market, and political factors.

The next section describes the industry and its main segments, as well as the nature of product market competition in these segments. The following section describes the nature of the labor markets, the unions, and the bargaining structures they have developed with the unionized employers. Next, having laid out this context, the bargaining outcomes of the decade are detailed. A conclusion follows a review of the nature of the domestic nonunion sector and workplace level developments.

The Industry, Major Employers, Product Markets, and Key External Influences

This study defines the aerospace industry as those companies classified in SIC (Standard Industrial Classification) 372, Aircraft and Parts, and SIC 376, Guided Missiles and Space Vehicles.[3] The aerospace industry is thus defined here as those companies engaged in the production of aircraft, guided missiles, space vehicles and parts, but not defense electronics, avionics, instruments, or related products and services. These neglected industries accounted for 31% of total aerospace employment and 7% of aerospace production workers in 1991 (Aerospace Industries Association 1992:142).

There are two principal ways to break down the industry into subsectors. The first is by the nature of the product, regardless of whether the final customer is military or commercial. Under this rubric the three main sectors are Airframes, Aircraft Engines and Parts, and Guided Missiles and Space Vehicles. These are the categories for which employment figures are available. Table 2 gives the total employment and the share of all manufacturing employment in these three sectors from 1968 (the peak of the Vietnam War employment boom) through 1991. The table shows that employment grew both in absolute terms and as a share of all manufacturing employment in all three sectors during the 1980s. By 1991 the industry, as defined here, accounted for 4.5% of all workers in manufacturing, or 838,000 workers. Note as well that employment grew most steeply in Guided Missiles and Space Vehicles, though it

TABLE 2

Aerospace Industry Employment: 1968-1991

Year	Airframes (SIC 3721)		Aircraft Parts and Engines (SIC 3724, 3728)		Missiles & Space (SIC 376)	
	Number (1000s)	% of Mfg.	Number (1000s)	% of Mfg.	Number (1000s)	% of Mfg.
1968	468	2.4	364	1.8	150	0.8
1969	457	2.3	348	1.7	124	0.6
1970	370	1.9	299	1.5	98	0.5
1971	288	1.5	243	1.3	88	0.5
1972	287	1.5	208	1.1	93	0.5
1973	301	1.5	224	1.1	93	0.5
1974	308	1.5	232	1.2	94	0.5
1975	293	1.6	221	1.2	93	0.5
1976	281	1.5	206	1.1	86	0.5
1977	270	1.4	211	1.1	83	0.4
1978	288	1.4	239	1.2	93	0.5
1979	333	1.6	259	1.2	102	0.5
1980	349	1.7	284	1.4	111	0.5
1981	344	1.7	282	1.4	123	0.6
1982	320	1.7	264	1.4	131	0.7
1983	305	1.7	257	1.4	141	0.8
1984	306	1.6	269	1.4	154	0.8
1985	326	1.7	291	1.5	177	0.9
1986	339	1.8	317	1.7	200	1.1
1987	356	1.9	322	1.7	206	1.1
1988	369	1.9	315	1.6	208	1.1
1989	382	2.0	329	1.7	194	1.0
1990	381	2.0	331	1.7	185	1.0
1991	357	1.9	314	1.7	167	0.9

Source: U.S.B.L.S., "Employment and Earnings" and Aerospace Industries Association estimates.

dropped in this sector after 1988 and that employment in the aircraft sectors was particularly volatile. Figure 1 shows employment indexes (1980 = 100) for Aircraft and Parts and all manufacturing for the period 1968-1991. This cyclicality will be discussed in more detail below.

Although this division is the one for which reliable employment figures are available, it is not the most meaningful for examining the nature of product markets, as the classification Aircraft and Parts includes both commercial and military aircraft. For examining product market developments, the more useful distinction is between civil aircraft, on the one

FIGURE 1
Employment Indexes, 1980 = 100

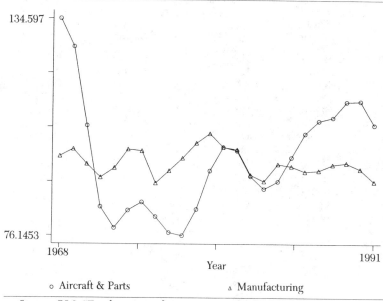

o Aircraft & Parts   ∆ Manufacturing

Source: BLS, "Employment and Earnings."

hand, and aerospace products sold to the U.S. (and, increasingly, foreign) governments on the other hand (military aircraft, guided missiles, and space vehicles).[4] Table 3 displays total sales for these sectors from 1974 through 1991 at 1982-84 prices. Commercial sales fluctuated through the 1980s (though they were higher in 1991 than in 1979), while military plus space sales nearly doubled (though taken together they fell after 1987).

Table 4 displays industry trade figures from 1970 through 1991 at 1982-84 prices. Note that both imports and exports rose in both the commercial and military sectors over the course of the 1980s. Perhaps most remarkably, aerospace exports accounted for 10.4% of all exports of U.S. merchandise in 1991. The nature of the commercial and military/space segments of the industry and their product markets will now be examined in more detail.

Commercial

The civil aircraft side of the industry is very concentrated. Though there are a number of general aviation (or small aircraft) companies,

TABLE 3

Aerospace Industry Sales: 1974-1991
($ millions 1982-84)

Year	Civil Aircraft	Military Aircraft	Missiles	Space	Related Products and Services[a]
1974	12,819	17,337	8,333	8,949	8,249
1975	12,013	18,532	7,017	8,710	8,907
1976	10,557	17,661	6,452	8,413	9,334
1977	10,203	17,830	6,776	8,252	10,073
1978	12,610	19,712	6,285	8,768	10,449
1979	18,219	18,120	6,581	9,015	10,627
1980	19,763	18,421	7,851	9,642	10,703
1981	18,072	21,601	8,405	10,328	11,974
1982	11,380	25,391	10,744	10,895	11,803
1983	12,423	30,179	10,310	14,002	13,383
1984	10,289	30,043	10,910	15,719	13,392
1985	12,760	34,156	10,630	17,245	14,958
1986	14,341	37,123	10,916	18,335	16,147
1987	13,614	38,489	8,996	19,600	16,140
1988	16,077	35,391	8,681	20,551	16,140
1989	17,664	31,973	10,985	20,382	16,201
1990	23,995	30,674	10,849	20,234	17,135
1991	27,645	28,248	8,025	21,058	16,995

[a] Related Products and Services = Sales of electronics, software, and ground equipment in support of aerospace products, plus sales by aerospace manufacturing establishments of systems and equipment which are generally derived from the industry's aerospace technological expertise in design, materials, and processes, but which are intended for applications other than flight.

Source: Aerospace Industries Association.

among them Cessna (General Dynamics), Beech (Raytheon) and Piper, just three final assemblers of large commercial jet aircraft control 95% of the world market; two of them are located in the United States. The Boeing Company is unambiguously at the top of the commercial pyramid and is the only company in history to make an overall profit on the production of large commercial transports such as the 747 (MIT Commission on Industrial Productivity 1989); it is the only prime contractor whose sales are primarily commercial. McDonnell Douglas is the other U.S. integrator of commercial airframes such as the MD-11, but still has most of its sales on the military side.[5] Below the final assemblers in this commercial pyramid are subcontractors (such as the nonunion, and often prime contractor, Northrop Corporation for the Boeing 747) and parts suppliers dependent on the fortunes of Boeing and McDonnell Douglas.

TABLE 4

Aerospace Industry International Trade: 1970-1991
($ millions 1982-84)

Year	Civil Transports		Other Civil[a]		Military		Total		Aerospace Share of All Exports of U.S. Merchandise
	Imports	Exports	Imports	Exports	Imports	Exports	Imports	Exports	
1970		3,307		3,178		2,291	794	8,776	7.9%
1971		3,869		3,736		2,773	921	10,378	9.5%
1972		2,677		4,390		2,012	1,352	9,079	7.6%
1973		3,748		4,784		3,050	1,761	11,581	7.2%
1974		5,385		5,310		3,696	1,511	14,391	7.1%
1975		4,455		5,441		4,587	1,388	14,483	7.2%
1976		4,337		5,640		3,807	1,012	13,784	6.7%
1977		3,195		5,137		4,178	1,206	12,510	6.2%
1978		3,923		5,307		6,109	1,446	15,339	6.9%
1979		6,884		6,576		2,720	2,327	16,180	6.3%
1980		8,164		7,914		2,740	4,313	18,818	6.9%
1981	216	7,899	4,085	6,746	651	4,755	4,950	19,409	7.4%
1982	239	3,973	3,776	5,983	717	6,212	4,734	16,169	7.2%
1983	189	4,702	2,750	5,936	521	5,492	3,460	16,130	7.8%
1984	260	3,075	3,385	6,221	1,096	5,149	4,741	14,445	6.7%
1985	557	5,128	4,075	6,900	1,067	5,375	5,699	17,402	8.6%
1986	677	5,726	5,161	7,824	1,372	4,448	7,210	18,000	8.7%
1987	485	5,614	5,157	8,267	1,317	5,910	6,959	19,789	8.8%
1988	951	7,410	5,477	9,748	1,254	5,622	7,681	22,779	8.4%
1989	1,034	9,930	4,773	10,731	2,281	5,235	8,087	25,896	8.8%
1990	564	12,770	5,749	11,344	2,716	5,789	9,029	29,903	9.9%
1991	943	15,331	5,861	10,769	2,742	6,049	9,547	32,150	10.4%

Note: Detailed imports only available for these categories after 1980.

[a] Other Civil = General aviation, helicopters, engines, spacecraft, used aircraft, gliders, airships, and parts.

Sources: Aerospace Industries Association; U.S. Bureau of the Census, "U.S. Imports for Consumption and General Imports, TSUSA Commodity and Country of Origin"; International Trade Administration.

The jet aircraft engine portion of the commercial market also has three main competitors, two of them located in the U.S.: United Technologies (Pratt and Whitney), General Electric, and Rolls Royce of Great Britain; together they controlled 67.5% of the civil turbojet engine market in 1991.[6] They compete to be chosen by the airframe

assembler (Boeing, McDonnell Douglas, and Airbus) or the final customer (airlines) for inclusion in the final product.

The nature of product market competition on the commercial side of
the industry has changed radically over the course of the last decade.
Through the 1970s, the U.S. companies that controlled the vast majority
of the noncommunist world's market for large commercial transports
were all unionized, were within the stable auto-aero-implement collective
bargaining pattern (and thus had similar rates of change in their labor
cost structures), and sold to the same (mainly domestic, regulated) customers. Analysts tended to conclude that "price turns out to play a relatively minor role (in selling in the aircraft industry) . . ., whereas performance, maintainability, and most importantly, on-time delivery will most
often decide who reigns as the current king of the mountain or who drops
out of the market completely" (Bluestone, Jordan, and Sullivan 1981:9).[7]

Yet by the end of the decade, a new study of the commercial aviation
industry by the MIT Commission on Industrial Productivity (1989) concluded that the "particular constellation of factors" allowing for performance-based rather than price-based competition "has gone forever"
and that new developments in the product markets have fundamentally
"shifted customer relationships away from engineering and toward
finance."[8]

There were two key developments in the external environment facing the domestic industry that drove this change. The first was the entry
of Airbus Industrie of Europe, now the world's second-ranked integrator
of large commercial jets.[9] Airbus has followed an aggressive strategy of
price-based competition and low-interest leasing arrangements made
possible, the U.S. companies argue, by subsidies and inducements from
the European governments.[10] Figure 2, which displays the world market
share of large commercial transports from 1970 to 1991, indicates that
Airbus' share of the world market for large commercial transports rose
from zero in the early 1970s to more than 20% in 1991. Airbus also
clearly has different unit labor cost structures than the U.S. companies.
While unit labor costs are not necessarily lower in Europe, the entry of
Airbus puts wages back into competition compared to the previous situation when the world's main commercial producers were within the
same collective bargaining pattern.

A further complicating factor is that there is also significant cross-
continental subcontracting and strategic partnering. In addition to the
recent discussions of a joint venture among Boeing and the Airbus partners to build a super-jumbo jet, there are more than 400 U.S. suppliers

FIGURE 2

World Market Share of Large Commercial
Transport Airplanes: 1970-91

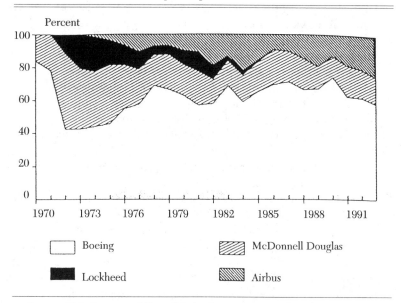

Source: U.S. Congress, Office of Technology Assessment [1991], p. 352.

in more than 30 states for Airbus aircraft, and current U.S. content of Airbus aircraft including U.S. engines ranges from 22% for the A340 to 39% for the A330.[11]

The second key development was the deregulation of the domestic airlines by the U.S. Civil Aeronautics Board (CAB). While regulated the airlines could not compete on the basis of price and so competed on the basis of product differentiation, including the quality of the aircraft (Carroll 1975). Once deregulated in 1978 the airlines began to compete among each other more on the basis of price and saw their product market rents evaporate, which plausibly (but arguably) led them to be more concerned with the costs of their airplanes, thereby spurring more competition on the basis of price among the aircraft manufacturers. While it is conceivable that heightened price competition among the airlines might have increased air traffic and thus demand for aircraft, it is also likely that deregulation exacerbated the cyclicality of air traffic and thus the cyclicality of aircraft production and employment, to be discussed below.

Nevertheless, it is worth stressing again the continued dominance of Boeing, though its share has slipped over the course of the decade. Boeing continues to control more than half of the world's market for turbojet aircraft (Figure 2), has produced the majority of these aircraft in service in the world airline fleet (excluding those produced in the former Communist countries), and is the United States' single largest exporter, accounting for $17 billion in exports in 1991 (*Los Angeles Times* March 1, 1992; Aerospace Industries Association).[12] One key result of Boeing's long-term dominance of the commercial industry is that it is closer to the standardized mass production paradigm, with fewer basic configurations for its jets. McDonnell Douglas, on the other hand, is more of a niche player, offering more configurations to meet the specialized needs of its customers.

The commercial side of the industry is subject to the speculative vagaries of the world commercial airline industry and, increasingly, leasing companies that buy in bulk and make long-term hunches about air traffic demand. Orders and backlogs for aircraft jumped in the mid-1980s, peaking in 1989, but have dropped since as the volume of new orders has fallen precipitously—some of the financially strapped airlines have even canceled previous orders, and as of this writing surplus jets sit in storage in the Mojave Desert in southeastern California (*Los Angeles Times* November 22, 1992). The boom and subsequent drop in orders can be largely attributed to changes in long-run forecasts of world airline traffic; the effect of the business cycle on this part of the industry thus operates through these forecasts as well as through cancellations of existing orders by airlines in distress.

Military and Space

The noncommercial side of the market is much less concentrated and also accounts for a larger portion of total aerospace sales, though less foreign trade (Tables 3 and 4). Among the main producers on this side of the market during the 1980s were McDonnell Douglas, General Dynamics, Hughes, Martin Marietta, Lockheed, Rockwell, and Boeing as well as Northrop and Grumman, the principal nonunion companies.

Two main changes have affected the nature of market and budgetary pressures on this part of the industry. First, U.S. government procurement contracting has slowly moved from cost-plus to fixed-price policies. Cost-plus contracting, which automatically reimburses all project costs including those for labor, has some technological justification (basically, the inability to precisely calculate costs in advance due to technical uncertainties associated with the start of a new project); it also allowed the companies to directly pass on their costs to the taxpayers, however. Explicit cost-plus contracting was largely gone by the early 1970s, and starting in 1983 the Department of Defense (and more specifically the Defense Contracts Auditing Agency [DCAA]) directly put pressure on the aerospace companies during their negotiations with the unions, threatening to not award contracts to companies granting "excessive" wage increases. Although there is evidence that the DCAA is now taking a less activist role in challenging union-negotiated wage rates (and it is an open question as to whether the earlier pressure had a significant effect on bargaining outcomes), it is nevertheless clear that with fixed-price, competitively bid contracts, labor costs become more of a direct concern for the contractors.

Second, with the end of the cold war and the emerging government budgetary crisis, military and space spending, both procurement and research and development, have been shrinking in absolute terms. This in turn has led to a crisis atmosphere among the military contractors. As Table 4 indicates, one response has been an increased emphasis on sales to foreign governments (along with intensified lobbying of the U.S. government to obtain access to these markets). Another response has been an active environment of mergers and acquisitions,[13] suggesting a trend toward increased concentration on the military/space side of the market.

Common Pressures

The commercial and military/space sides of the market have been subject to some common pressures during the course of the 1980s. The most important have been the growth of strategic joint ventures as well as co-production and offset arrangements with domestic competitors and international interests.[14] The companies enter into joint arrangements with foreign companies and governments as inducements for sales and sources of working capital, and also join forces with competitors to share risks. Obviously these sorts of arrangements lead to many complicated issues of information sharing and technology transfer.

Joint ventures and subcontracting also allow the unionized companies the opportunity to operate de facto on a nonunion basis by moving production to sites without unions. These arrangements are therefore a subject of concern for the unions, although they have been unsuccessful in their attempts to bargain limits on them thus far.

A second important common pressure on the commercial and military sectors involves the influence of state and local laws and, more specifically, the environmental and workers' compensation laws of California, which are viewed as being particularly onerous by the many aerospace companies located in that state.[15] A result has been the beginnings of an exodus of aerospace companies from California. In some instances, actual and proposed transfers are from unionized to nonunionized settings and have resulted, in any case, in massive displacement of former aerospace workers in California.[16]

Workers, Unions, and Bargaining Structures

Workers and Labor Markets

Product and re-equipment cycles for commercial aircraft are very long, lasting decades (MIT Commission on Industrial Productivity 1989); the product cycle for the military side is clearly more inherently politically determined. Production is also very cyclical, with engineers and various combinations of production workers needed at different stages of the long process between product conception and final production. There is much movement among companies by workers, particularly on the West Coast, and a general perception that "when one aerospace company is hiring, another is laying people off," although the employment figures presented in Table 2 and Figure 1 indicate cyclicality in the entire industry as well. While the unions are concerned about employment security, their demands (largely unsuccessful to date) tend to take the form of limits on subcontracting rather than explicit employment guarantees. Given the inherent cyclicality of production and the increasing volatility of the commercial market, many in the industry view such guarantees as infeasible.[17]

This cyclicality also poses a dilemma for companies regarding their provision of on-the-job-training. The movement of workers among companies limits the returns to the company that actually provides the training. The industry has a higher proportion of skilled craft workers and professional and technical workers and a lower proportion of less-skilled operatives than manufacturing as a whole: in 1990, 45% of all aerospace workers were production workers, while 27% were engineers, scientists and technicians (Aerospace Industries Association, taken from company annual reports and *Employment and Earnings*). Much of the actual general training takes place in the military and at vocational-technical schools. According to the Current Population Survey (CPS) Outgoing

Rotation Group, in 1990 1% of aerospace production workers were in the military in World War II, 4% in the Korean War, 12% in the Vietnam War, and 12% during other periods; 71% had not been in the military. Before the recent downturn, employers claimed that the industry was facing a severe shortage of experienced, blue-collar skilled labor (Schwartz et al. 1987:266), and even now there is evidence of employer difficulty in finding qualified engineers (*Los Angeles Times* August 22, 1992). Some in the industry claim, however, that the introduction of numerically controlled machine tools and automation are diminishing the severity of the skills shortage. Finally, the fact that workers on certain classified government programs require security clearance restricts the labor pool available for those programs.[18]

Unions

The aerospace industry remains highly unionized, though the share has dropped over the course of the decade. The CPS Outgoing Rotation Group indicates that union membership among production workers fell from 53.8% in 1985 to 44.5% in 1991, and among all workers from 28.9% in 1985 to 24.8% in 1991.[19]

The two unions representing the most production workers in the industry are the IAM and the UAW. As indicated in Table 1, the main plants at Boeing, Lockheed, General Dynamics, United Technologies (Pratt and Whitney Engines), Raytheon (Beech Aircraft), and Rohr are primarily organized by the IAM, while the main plants at Rockwell, Martin Marietta, and General Electric (Engines) are primarily organized by the UAW. Two of the companies in this table deviate from this rule of essentially exclusive representation by one or the other of these unions.[20] McDonnell Douglas has major plants represented by both unions, with the workers in its main military plant organized by the IAM and those in its main commercial plant organized by the UAW. Hughes is primarily organized by the Carpenters and Joiners' Association (CJA), an artifact of the company's production of the wooden Spruce Goose in the 1940s. This study concentrates on the relationships with the IAM and the UAW.

The two unions have different origins, craft for the IAM and industrial for the UAW, and they engaged in intense jurisdictional disputes in the industry during the 1930s and 1940s. They eventually signed a "no-raid" pact in 1949 prohibiting organizing activities by either union in plants where the other union had agreements or NLRB certification.[21] The two have coordinated bargaining to varying degrees through the years, as will be discussed below.

Recently, however, there have been basic philosophical differences between the unions: the IAM is generally considered to be a traditional, arms-length union while the UAW is more interested in union-management cooperation, as will be discussed in more depth below. Furthermore, the UAW has always been part of a larger "orbit of coercive comparison."[22] UAW-represented bargaining units and the units they strongly influence tended to follow the actual terms of automobile industry settlements more closely than did IAM-represented and influenced units before the break of the interindustry pattern in 1983.

In addition, the aerospace branch of the union is seemingly more influential within the IAM, where former local union officials in the aerospace industry have risen as high as the vice presidency of the international union. Within the UAW the aerospace department has been considered as secondary to automobiles and agricultural implements.

Finally, while the UAW and the IAM are perhaps working less closely together now, the IAM has been consciously trying to increase coordination within its organization. While representatives of the internationals at both unions have traditionally engaged actively in the bargaining process, providing information to local negotiators and participating in the negotiations, the IAM locals now share even more information about their experiences and strategies with each other, and the presidents of the locals at the major companies represented by the IAM meet together at the beginning of bargaining with each company. This new higher level of coordination was initiated prior to the 1986 bargaining round.

Another distinctive feature of unionization in this industry is the existence of large engineering and technical unions, most notably at Boeing, where the Seattle Professional Engineering Employees Association (SPEEA) represents close to 30,000 workers. Such unions also represent engineers and technicians at McDonnell Douglas and Lockheed (Southern California Professional Engineering Employees Association, Engineers and Scientists Guild). The negotiations carried out by these unions and the companies differ from those with the production worker unions in that they primarily negotiate wage floors and wage pools, which are then distributed on the basis of merit. In the 1992 bargaining round, SPEEA became involved in a dispute with Boeing over the union's desire to limit the discretion of supervisors in

awarding the merit portion of the pay increases. The following sections
will primarily concentrate on the production worker unions.

Bargaining Structures

The bargaining structures developed by the companies and the
unions vary significantly across the companies that make up the industry. A brief description of some of the most prominent gives a sense of
the wide range of different structures. Boeing and the IAM negotiate a
corporate-wide master agreement which is then voted on by each of its
three main locals in the Puget Sound region, Wichita, and Portland.
Lockheed, which has its main facilities in Georgia and both northern
and southern California, negotiates the "major economics" with the
IAM across the three main plants, but bargains noneconomic issues on a
decentralized basis.[23] McDonnell Douglas, on the other hand, has a
much more decentralized bargaining structure across its IAM-represented plants in St. Louis and southern California and its UAW-represented plant in southern California, with wages and benefits more likely
to be negotiated locally than at the other two companies. The other
companies tend to fall within this spectrum: Rockwell, for example,
signs a master agreement with its Aerospace Group, while General
Dynamics (before selling its aerospace divisions to Lockheed and
Hughes in 1992) was more decentralized.

As for informal bargaining structure, the industry has traditionally
followed a tight intra-industry pattern, as will be discussed below. It
should be noted, however, that not all of the companies with major
union representation listed in Table 1 have been strongly associated
with this pattern. Negotiators at Hughes claim to be little influenced by
the other aerospace settlements in their negotiations with the CJA. In
general, the relationship between Hughes and the CJA local tends to be
more "locally oriented" than the relationships between the other companies and the international union-influenced IAM and UAW locals.
The Hughes-CJA contract cycle has been moved so far out of sync that
they now settle two years after Boeing; unlike the rest of the West Coast
aerospace companies, they eliminated COLAs in their 1982 contract.

The two major domestic engine manufacturers are also not very
closely associated with this pattern. They are located in the Midwestern
and Northeastern parts of the country and, thus, lack physical proximity
(and commonality of labor markets) with the vast majority of the aircraft
and missile/space producers located in the West and the South. The

contracts at United Technologies' Pratt and Whitney division have tended to significantly deviate from the other aerospace companies, particularly in the phasing down of cost-of-living clauses during the early 1980s and the return to general wage increases before the rest of the industry. General Electric negotiates a master agreement with most of its main unions across its different industry segments; the company's aerospace workers are covered by the same contract as the other (mainly IUE) unionized workers in that wide-ranging corporation. Having noted these deviations, the next section will examine the development of inter- and intra-industry wage patterns during the 1980s among companies that were strongly associated with the pattern.

Bargaining and Bargaining Outcomes

Earnings

Aerospace workers have traditionally been highly paid. Table 5 presents average hourly earnings (including overtime and lump sum payments) in the industry and in all manufacturing for production workers from 1970 to 1991 at 1982-84 prices. The table indicates that the hourly earnings premium for workers in Aircraft and Parts over all manufacturing rose from 22% to 24% in the 1970s to 34% in 1983, then remained stable within the range of 34% to 39% until 1991, when it rose to 42%. Figure 3 presents production worker hourly earnings (including overtime) in Aircraft and Parts (both with and without lump sums), Automobiles (excluding lump sums and profit-sharing payouts due to lack of availability of the data in hourly form), and all manufacturing over the period 1960 to 1991 at 1982-84 prices. This figure indicates that aerospace workers have recently done relatively better than their traditional comparison group, automobile workers, as will be discussed below.

History of Pattern Bargaining Prior to 1980s[24]

The aerospace industry has traditionally followed a tight intra-industry pattern, with later contracts generally following the first contract to be negotiated in a given round. In addition, aerospace settlements have traditionally followed closely the terms negotiated in the automobile industry, jointly forming (with the agricultural implements industry) the "auto-aero-implement" pattern. One stylization of the wage portion of this pattern is that the bargaining units within it closely adhered to the wage rule of "3% AIF plus COLA" during much of the postwar period.

After resolving their jurisdictional disputes in the 1930s and 1940s, the two unions held joint aerospace industry bargaining conferences

TABLE 5

Average Hourly Earnings,
Aerospace Production Workers: 1970-1991
($ 1982-84)

Year	Aircraft (SIC 372)	Missiles and Space (SIC 376)	Manufacturing
1970	10.59		8.63
1971	10.74		8.81
1972	11.24	11.36	9.14
1973	11.28	11.31	9.21
1974	10.99	11.12	8.97
1975	11.15	11.19	8.98
1976	11.32	11.39	9.17
1977	11.42	11.62	9.37
1978	11.56	11.60	9.46
1979	11.38	11.36	9.23
1980	11.26	11.19	8.82
1981	11.34	11.07	8.79
1982	11.64	11.35	8.80
1983	11.87	11.64	8.87
1984	11.99	11.47	8.85
1985	11.87	11.42	8.87
1986	11.92	11.25	8.88
1987	11.87	11.27	8.72
1988	11.66	11.29	8.61
1989	11.65	11.27	8.45
1990	11.55	11.23	8.29
1991	11.62	11.08	8.21

Note: Includes overtime premiums; SIC 372 and SIC 376 earnings also include lump sum payments.

Sources: U.S.B.L.S., "Employment and Earnings" and Aerospace Industries Association Estimates.

before the start of several of the bargaining rounds in the 1950s and 1960s. The two unions jointly targeted Boeing, Lockheed, McDonnell Douglas, Rockwell or United Aircraft—presumably the one that was most prosperous—to create the "key settlement" to form the pattern, with both unions waiting to negotiate with the other companies until this first settlement had been reached; and the later settlements generally fell into line with the pattern setter.

Particularly notable were the bargaining rounds in the early 1950s, when the UAW consciously attempted to match the GM settlement provisions at the aerospace companies it represented. According to Levinson

FIGURE 3
Real Average Hourly Earnings

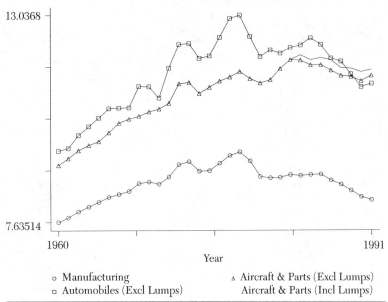

13.0368	
7.63514	
1960	1991

Year

o Manufacturing   ᴀ Aircraft & Parts (Excl Lumps)
▫ Automobiles (Excl Lumps)   Aircraft & Parts (Incl Lumps)

Source: BLS "Employment and Earnings."

(1966:53), in 1953 an arbitration panel found that "automobile wage rates and wage movements (were) relevant to a determination of wages in the airframe industry" and viewed its award "as a step toward narrowing the differential." The UAW in particular pushed for parity with the automobile industry down through the years. While the differential was never fully eliminated until the 1980s (as indicated in Figure 3), the prominence of the UAW in the aerospace industry, particularly in those years when one of its bargaining units formed the "key settlement," ensured that the aerospace industry closely followed the "3% plus COLA" wage rule established in the automobile industry through the end of the 1970s.

Katz (1985:27-28) notes the functions served by wage rules in the automobile industry: orderly adjustment of wages during multiyear agreements, reduction of the potential scope of disagreement over compensation, provision of structure for negotiations, provision of political stability for labor and management leaders, and reduction of the likelihood that overt conflict might break out in the face of a negotiations impasse. The same functions likely applied to the aerospace industry as well, along with the extra political stability provided by overtly following the settlements in the automobile industry. In the 1980s, however, both the wage rule and the interindustry pattern came to an end, while the intra-industry pattern weakened considerably.

Major Developments in Bargaining in 1980s[25]

Table 6 presents the general wage increases (GWI), lump sum bonuses (LSB), and profit-sharing provisions negotiated by four of the prime contractors and the unions representing their production workers (Boeing-IAM, Lockheed-IAM, McDonnell Douglas-IAM, and Rockwell-UAW) and one highly unionized subcontractor (Rohr-IAM), as well as the most recent previous General Motors-UAW agreement during the 1980s and 1990s. It is important to note that this table does not include benefits, which tend to show more variance across these companies. The role of benefits, particularly health care coverage, in contract negotiations in the 1980s will be discussed below. In addition, cost-of-living provisions are not included in this table. COLAs tend to be provided on a cents-per-hour per point change in the CPI basis in this industry, though Boeing moved to a proportional system in 1989; otherwise, there were not major changes in COLA provisions in the 1980s (except for the diminution of coverage at Pratt and Whitney and Hughes, discussed above). Finally, wage changes due to classification and auto-progression systems are not included in the table. What the table does tell us is how the wage growth pattern changed over the course of the decade.

The 1980 bargaining round was the last that followed the "3% plus COLA" wage rule. Even under this regime, the first year was seemingly more negotiable, with the second and third years more likely to stand at exactly 3%.[26] Note the similarity of the settlements across the five aerospace companies presented here, as well as the similarity with the General Motors settlement—clear evidence of a tight pattern.

In 1983, however, Boeing broke with past practice and did not offer any across-the-board GWI, instead offering LSB of 3% of the employee's previous year's earnings in each of the three years of the contract and selective wage increases to the top labor grades. In the crisis atmosphere of the early 1980s, the union accepted the offer without much objection, though they later became more critical of lump sum payment systems. This settlement was also significant because it deviated from

TABLE 6

Wage and Bonus Settlements at Selected Aerospace Companies and General Motors in the 1980s & 1990s[1]

Bargaining Round		Boeing	Lockheed	McDonnell Douglas	Rockwell	Rohr	General Motors
		IAM	IAM	IAM	UAW	IAM	UAW (most recent)
1980-1981	first year increase	7% gwi	7% gwi	7% gwi	7% gwi	7% gwi	3% + 24¢ gwi
	second year increase	3% gwi	3% gwi	3% gwi	3% gwi	4% gwi	3% gwi
	third year increase	3% gwi	3% gwi	3% gwi	3% gwi	3% gwi	3% gwi
1983-1984	first year increase	3% lsb[2]	3% lsb	3% lsb	3% lsb	3% lsb	profit sharing: 10% of pre-tax profits in excess of sum of 10% of net worth & 5% of other assets
	second year increase	3% lsb	3% lsb	3% lsb	3% lsb	3% lsb	
	third year increase	3% lsb	3% gwi	3% lsb	3% gwi	3% lsb	
1986-1987	first year increase	12% lsb	12% lsb	3% gwi + 3% lsb	3% gwi + 2% lsb	10% lsb	9¢-50¢ gwi + $180
	second year increase	5% lsb	5% lsb	2% gwi + 2% lsb	6% lsb	6% lsb	2.25% lsb
	third year increase	5% lsb	5% lsb	4% lsb	5% lsb	6% lsb	2.25% lsb
							profit sharing cont.
1989-1990	first year increase	4% gwi + 10% lsb	4% gwi[3]	5.5% gwi + 4% lsb	4% gwi	3% gwi	3% gwi
	second year increase	3% gwi + 5% lsb	3% gwi + 4% lsb	3% gwi + 4% lsb	3% gwi + 2% lsb	4% gwi + $1200	3% lsb
	third year increase	3% gwi + 4% lsb	3% gwi + 4% lsb	3% gwi + 4% lsb	6% lsb	4% gwi + $1700	3% lsb
							profit sharing cont.
1992-1993	first year increase	12% lsb	$1500 lsb	4% lsb	4% lsb	$1600 lsb	3% gwi
	second year increase	3.5% gwi	3% lsb	4% lsb	4% lsb	2.5% gwi	3% lsb
	third year increase	3.5% gwi	3% lsb	4% lsb	3% lsb	3% gwi	3% lsb
							profit sharing cont.

Source: U.S. Department of Labor, Current Wage Developments, various issues.

lsb = lump sum bonus payment as percentage of previous year's earnings

gwi = increase in hourly base wage (general wage increase)

[1] Boeing negotiates a corporate-wide agreement with the IAM. Lockheed signs separate agreements with the IAM at its three main plants, but negotiates with them on wages and benefits as a group. McDonnell Douglas negotiates with its plants separately; the settlement with the IAM-represented Torrance-Huntington Beach plant is reported, although until 1986 the settlements at the other McDonnell Douglas plants were usually similar (the 1992-93 settlement is for St. Louis). The Rockwell Aerospace Group agreement with the UAW is reported, as is the agreement between Rohr and the IAM for the company's two plants in Southern California.

[2] Workers in the top labor grades did receive some wage increases.

[3] Workers in the bottom third labor grades received no wage increases and lump sums of 4%, 7% and 7% in the first, second, and third years, respectively.

the form of concessions negotiated in the most recent automobile contracts, opting for LSB rather than profit sharing. Thus, in this year, when the industry was in a deep trough (see the employment figures in Table 2), both the interindustry pattern based on the settlement negotiated in the auto industry and the stable postwar wage rule of "3% plus COLA" apparently came to an end.

As regards the form of the concessions, the auto industry (along with much of the rest of unionized manufacturing) started using lump sum bonuses later in the 1980s, following Boeing's innovation.[27] On the other hand, explicit profit sharing has not been attempted to any significant extent in the aerospace industry.[28] There are several possible explanations for this lack of profit sharing in aerospace, which is particularly striking given the previous importance of the automobile industry in setting the interindustry pattern. The actors tend to emphasize the technical infeasibility of profit sharing in this industry due to the cyclicality of employment and the long lag between product conception and break even (rendering employment guarantees problematic and project-based profits long in coming), as well as the low level of trust between the unions, particularly the IAM, and the companies. In addition, government contracting poses particular problems for bonus schemes: considering that there is already much disagreement over who will ultimately pay for bonuses that are based on annual earnings ("How much of the year did a particular worker work on a particular project?"),[29] one can see how much more complicated it would be to define "profits" on this side of the industry.[30]

It is also possible that the bonus schemes allowed the companies to provide the workers with more money than their counterparts in the auto industry, which was in comparatively much worse financial shape during much of the 1980s, without making this difference explicit (and thus directly upsetting orbits of coercive comparison) and without putting the money permanently into the base wage. According to Katz and Meltz (1991), profit-sharing payouts at GM, Ford, and Chrysler between 1982 and 1989 totaled $1,754, $13,365, and $4,306 per employee, respectively. Except for the Ford payouts, this is clearly less than the bonus payouts in the major aerospace companies.[31] Note, however, that the union movement generally views lump sum payments much less favorably than profit sharing.[32] In any case, Figure 3 does indicate that, even disregarding lump sums, aerospace workers' average earnings caught and passed auto workers' average earnings during the 1980s.

Although the table suggests that the intra-industry pattern still held in 1983, the nature of the bargaining after the key settlement had been reached also constituted a break from the past. The unions consciously tried to break the pattern established at Boeing, in contrast to past practice when the unions generally tried to enforce (or build upon) the pattern. The Lockheed and Rockwell contracts did deviate somewhat, providing for 3% GWI rather than LSB in the third year. Although the UAW held a long and bitter strike at McDonnell Douglas to fight the imposition of the terms of the Boeing settlement and to attempt to follow the terms of the Lockheed settlement, the rank and file ended up accepting essentially the same contract as Boeing's, as had the IAM-represented workers at McDonnell Douglas over the objections of the union leadership. It is notable that the UAW tried to follow the pattern established at Lockheed rather than the one established in the automobile industry or the "key settlement" within the industry, in contrast to past practice. This suggests both that profit sharing may not have been viewed as feasible and that the Boeing settlement was viewed as concessionary.

Finally, the 1983 round was important because it saw the introduction of a weak form of two-tier wage systems (in the form of expanded rate ranges) at several of the companies (most notably Boeing and Lockheed), though most were later phased out. The Boeing contract alone also contained the industry's first significant language on technological change, which will be described in greater detail below.

The 1986 round saw Boeing and the IAM again negotiate no GWI, but LSB of 12%/5%/5%. Lockheed and the IAM soon signed a similar agreement. McDonnell Douglas and the two unions became engaged in a bitter dispute over the company's attempt to initiate a medical insurance co-payment provision. After months of "working to rule," the unions signed settlements that did contain the co-payment provisions; whether health care should be substantially contributory (on the part of workers) remains a contentious issue in the industry. The agreement also contained a combination of GWI and LSB, in contrast to those at Boeing and Lockheed. In addition, the "intra-company" pattern at McDonnell Douglas was broken as the UAW signed a five-year agreement with the company while the IAM signed an agreement with the traditional three-year duration. This break appears to have been driven by the company's desire to separate the two contracts and thus diminish their influence on each other as well as the influence of the Boeing settlement on the UAW negotiations; in general, the breakup of the intra-industry patterns have been company driven. Rockwell and the UAW negotiated a combination of GWI and LSB as at McDonnell Douglas and General Motors, while Rohr and the IAM signed an agreement with only LSB, as at Boeing and Lockheed.

At first glance the table would seem to indicate that the intra-industry pattern broke down in 1986-87 with the variety of combinations of GWI and LSB in the different contracts. Consider, however, the following rule of thumb related by negotiators. If you consider the cost of the two types of provisions within the life of a single contract and disregard compounding and the time value of payments as well as issues such as anchoring points for future contracts (the hourly base wage often serves as an anchor), a GWI of 1% in the first year of a three-year contract is approximately equivalent to an LSB of 3% in the first year, considering that the GWI will also be received in the second and third years. Similarly, a second-year GWI of 1% is equivalent to a second-year LSB of 2% and third-year GWI and LSB are directly comparable.[33] If you convert all of the GWI to LSB in this manner for the aerospace companies in Table 6 in the 1986-87 bargaining round and then add up the total value of the settlements, they all add up to 22%. While seemingly nonrational on its surface, a reasonable stylization of the wage rule in 1986-87 in the aerospace industry was thus 22%.

The 1989 bargaining round, however, saw further significant weakening of the intra-industry pattern. The negotiation of the "key settlement" was exceptional because Boeing was in extraordinarily good shape, with backlogs and orders unprecedented for the 1980s (the commercial aircraft order boom of the late 1980s peaked in that year), and resultant high expectations among the union and the rank and file. After a 48-day strike, the first at Boeing in 12 years, the settlement finally reached provided GWI of 4%/3%/3% and LSB of 10%/5%/4%.[34]

The settlements at the other companies, which were not in as good financial shape as Boeing (nor had that company's long-term prospects) due to the decline in military expenditures, deviated from both the exact terms and the overall value of the Boeing settlement (no equivalent of the 22% rule holds). The Lockheed settlement was notable because it paid workers in the lowest labor grades lump sums alone with no increase in the hourly wage and also moved to a preferred provider medical arrangement with large deductibles (by industry standards). At the end of the Lockheed negotiations, the chief negotiator for the IAM local stated, and the chief negotiator for the company agreed, that this was the first time in 50 years that the first contract settled in the aerospace industry had not set a pattern.

The 1992 round saw further variance in settlement outcomes. The Boeing contract contained an LSB of 12% in only the first year of the contract, along with GWIs of 3.5% in the second and third years. It is notable that neither the main stated concern of the union (limiting subcontracting) nor the main stated concern of the company (inducing workers to bear more of the burden of health care costs) were addressed in the final contract. The settlements reached at Lockheed, McDonnell Douglas, and Rockwell provided only lump sums in each year, with the amounts varying across these companies. The Rohr contract provided a first-year LSB and second- and third-year GWIs. As in 1989, it appears as though the diverging fortunes of the companies, due to their concentrations in one or the other segments of the industry, has led to further collapse of the intra-industry pattern.

Yet it is worth emphasizing that the bargainers in the rest of the industry still look to the Boeing settlement as the trendsetter. It is also worth noting that in 1983 at Boeing and 1990 at Lockheed, the contracts provided for selective increases in the base wage for workers in the higher labor grades, allowing the companies to widen the skills differential that tends to be narrowed by cents-per-hour COLA clauses. This suggests that, at least in these two instances, the companies obtained latitude to differentially reward higher skill levels, and that lump sum payments helped to ease this differential treatment.

Overall, regarding wage rules and patterns, "3% plus COLA" and the strong interindustry pattern (whereby aerospace contracts followed closely the terms of automobile industry contracts) came to an end in the 1983 round, while the strong intra-industry pattern started to weaken in the 1986-87 round and significantly weakened further in the 1989-90 and 1992-93 rounds.

In fact, except for the introduction of LSB and the breakdown of the old rules and patterns of wage bargaining, the contracts in this industry have been remarkable for their *lack* of innovation, especially when compared to the employment or income security, profit sharing, and other cooperative arrangements developed elsewhere (such as the auto industry).

The Domestic Nonunion Sector

There are at least three primary reciprocal influences between aerospace industry collective bargaining and labor relations in the nonunion

U.S. companies. First, even two of the main nonunion companies, Northrop and TRW, do have smaller IAM-represented bargaining units. Second, and more importantly, the union and nonunion aerospace companies draw from the same labor markets. This induces the nonunion companies to engage in "union substitution" strategies. Northrop even distributes the document "Working with Northrop," which resembles a union contract in some respects. It includes rules on seniority, layoffs, and recalls; promotions and transfers; grievance procedures; and pay determination. People in the industry claim that wages are generally comparable or even higher at the large nonunion companies.

Most of the companies, union and nonunion, also participate in the same specialized compensation surveys which obviously exert influence on, as well as being influenced by, collective bargaining outcomes. This influence also works through the DCAA, which uses 14% above the average pay for a classification in its definition of the "labor market"[35] as the criterion for an audit for *over*payment at the companies. One major difference is that the nonunionized companies have much more latitude to pay workers on government contract projects differently from those working on commercial projects.

Finally, the widespread joint venturing between the unionized and nonunionized companies also suggests a strong mutual influence of the two sectors. As discussed above, a major concern of unions in the 1980s has been the unionized companies' ability to operate de facto on a nonunion basis through these joint ventures and subcontracting arrangements.

The nonunion sector has been growing, as evidenced by the decline in the unionization rate cited above. Two plausible explanations for this relative growth in the nonunion sector are the movement of unionized companies to right-to-work states and the recent increase in subcontracting by the (relatively highly unionized) prime contractors.

Workplace-Level Developments

Production System, Technology, and Employee Involvement

The aerospace industry has been moving toward a leaner production system in fits and starts, with mixed union acceptance and involvement. One key element of the industry's bargaining history, perhaps related to the technology, is that the parties claim that they do not negotiate production standards such as productivity, speed of the line, or other aspects of the "effort bargain." Some of the companies do, however, discuss technological change with their unions (and, in general, the parties claim that the companies have been more forthcoming with information recently), and some have attempted to implement total quality management systems (TQMS), with mixed success.

In a recent study of the impact of technological change on labor relations in the commercial aircraft industry, Schwartz et al. (1987:266) identify five major technological changes in commercial aircraft production, which also apply to military aircraft production and, to some extent, guided missiles and space vehicle production: (1) the increasing use of light-weight materials of comparable strength, (2) changes in the assembly process which have eliminated welding after forming and have improved the efficiency of die-making, (3) the production of large jets from refractory alloys (with electrochemical machining), (4) the increasing use of computer-aided design, and (5) the introduction of numerically controlled machine tools. Nevertheless, these authors still classify aircraft production technology as primarily batch production.

The IAM was a pioneer in demanding union voice on technological change and negotiated language on technological change in the 1983 agreement with Boeing. The contract outlined the company's obligation to brief the union on new technology, created a joint training advisory committee with equal participation by the union and management to make advisory decisions on training for those affected by technological changes, and set up pilot projects aimed at improving the quality of work life and productivity (Verma and McKersie 1985; Schwartz et al. 1987). These programs were continued in the 1986, 1989, and 1992 agreements and the Quality Through Training Program was eventually funded at 10 cents per bargaining unit hour for training, tuition, facilities, staff, administration, publicity, equipment, and materials. These particular forms of explicitly bargained technological consultation and adjustment arrangements did not spread to the other bargaining relationships in the industry, however.

Boeing also formed quality circles on an experimental basis without the involvement of the union starting in 1980 (Verma and McKersie 1985). Yet the IAM remains suspicious of the team concept. In fact, the national union has issued a white paper on team concept programs that says, in part, the following:

> By their very nature, these (team concept/TQM/QWL/EI) programs interfere with the union's obligations (1) to represent each and every member of the bargaining unit, (2) to enter into collective bargaining over wages, hours and working

conditions, (3) to abide by and enforce the terms and conditions of any collective bargaining agreement already in effect, and (4) to preserve the integrity of the union as an autonomous, democratic organization according to the laws of the land and the IAM's constitution and By-Laws. . . . Therefore, it is the policy of the IAM to resist any team concept program. (IAM 1990).[36]

On the other hand, TQMS has been attempted more extensively at the UAW-represented plants at McDonnell Douglas and Rockwell, as the dominant faction of that union is generally more receptive to participating in EI (for internal union debate about UAW involvement in EI at NUMMI, which was used as a model for the system at McDonnell Douglas (see *New York Times* articles by Parker and Slaughter December 4, 1988 and Lee December 25, 1988). The McDonnell Douglas plan is generally viewed as a failure, perceived as chaotic by the production workers and falling victim to the existing highly adversarial environment at that plant; the gallows humor among the highly mobile skilled production workers was that TQMS meant "Time to Quit and Move to Seattle." The Rockwell program, though more limited in scope, has been viewed as more successful, and reference to the parties' joint commitment to EI was included in the 1990 contract. The U.S. government has been encouraging TQMS as a condition for receiving military/space contracts; the experience in this industry suggests that such mandates can lead to wildly different outcomes when implemented depending on the existing culture and the commitment of the parties to genuine change.

Thomas (1991) studied union-management cooperation during the course of three technological changes at a major aerospace manufacturing firm that had forged with its union a set of agreements in the early 1980s committing both sides to pilot projects in work redesign, retraining for employees displaced by new technology, and advance consultation on the company's plan for technological change. Among his findings were that the union was ambivalent about the true costs and benefits of cooperation, had concerns about perceived co-optation by management, and had little advance involvement in the introduction of the new technology; the industrial relations staff played only a marginal role.

In their study of a quality circle program at a Fortune 100 aerospace company that introduced quality circles without the involvement of the union, Verma and McKersie (1987) found that participation in the program increased workers' identification with the company and its goals.

Strikes and Grievances

Table 7 reports the strikes in the industry involving major bargaining units from 1982 to 1991. The table indicates that no more than four strikes took place at major bargaining units in the industry during any given year during this period. Perhaps the two most notable strikes in the decade were the UAW strike at McDonnell Douglas in 1983-84 over the company's attempt to follow the Boeing contract and the IAM strike at Boeing in 1989 discussed above; in neither case did the strikes spread to the rest of the industry.

TABLE 7

Aerospace Industry Strikes Involving
1,000 or More Workers: 1982-1991

Year	# of Strikes	# of Workers Involved	Work-Days Idle	Bargaining Units
1982	4	11,900	45,200	Avco—UAW General Electric—UAW Goodyear Aerospace—UAW Textron—UAW
1983	2	8,700	369,200	McDonnell-Douglas—UAW
1984	4	14,600	188,200	Beech Aircraft—IAM General Dynamics—IAM McDonnell-Douglas—UAW
1985	4	19,700	289,800	General Dynamics—IAM General Electric—UAW, IAM Textron—UAW, IAM United Technologies—IAM
1986	—	—	—	
1987	—	—	—	
1988	3	10,600	415,800	General Electric—UAW, IAM Loral—UAW Textron—UAW
1989	2	58,500	1,848,000	Boeing—IAM Textron—IAM
1990	1	2,300	56,700	Lockheed Service—IAM
1991	1	1,500	—	Textron—UAW

Source: U.S.B.L.S., "Current Wage Developments" (Workers involved and work-days idle tabulated by Aerospace Industries Association).

Nevertheless, workers in this industry can have enormous strike leverage, depending on the state of the product-market cycle. Interruptions of production have always been costly for the commercial manufacturers (given the importance of on-time delivery), and are particularly costly during boom times in the newly competitive environment such as 1989 at Boeing. In addition, the government has a policy to refuse delivery from plants on strike.

Kleiner, Nickelsburg, and Pilarski (1988) found a surprising positive relationship between grievance activity and productivity in a large unionized commercial aircraft manufacturing firm that had attempted to follow "Japanese style" management techniques, with a significant employee involvement program, during the latter two years of their period of study, 1978-87. This finding led them to question whether "zero is optimal" when it comes to grievances.

Conclusion

The aerospace industry remains among the few highly unionized and export competitive parts of the U.S. economy, largely because of the market position of one company, Boeing—the country's largest single exporter and home of one of the country's largest union locals, an unusual combination, indeed, for the early 1990s. Distinctive features of the industry's collective bargaining system are that it is organized by two major unions and has seen relatively little innovation regarding employment guarantees, profit sharing, employee involvement and other cooperative arrangements. It was previously part of the strong auto-aero-implement interindustry pattern, but moved away from this pattern in the early 1980s and, with it, the stable postwar wage rule of "3% plus COLA." Intra-industry pattern bargaining also weakened later in the decade. During recent years, market and budgetary constraints have tightened considerably in both the commercial and military/space sectors of the industry; the question that remains is whether more profound changes in the collective bargaining system will be necessary to adequately adapt to the rapidly changing competitive environment.

Acknowledgments

I thank the people involved with labor relations in the aerospace industry who generously shared their time and insights with me. In addition, I benefited from comments by Reggie Newell (a discussant for this paper) and other participants at the joint PIERS, FMCS, and IRRA conference "The Changing Nature of Labor Relations in the Private Sector" (Detroit, February 1993), as well as seminar participants at U.C. Santa Barbara. I particularly thank Jonathan Leonard and Paula Voos for helpful discussions and feedback. Mark Jerger provided stellar research assistance. During this research period, I was partially supported by the UCLA Institute of Industrial Relations.

Endnotes

[1] Defined as more than 1,000 workers.

[2] AIF (Annual Improvement Factor) and GWI (General Wage Increase) are used interchangeably in this paper.

[3] Companies not primarily classified in these SIC codes are given less emphasis in this study; SIC codes that might be included in a broader definition of the "aerospace industry" are SIC 3663 (Radio and Television Communication Equipment), SIC 3812 (Search, Detection, Navigation, Guidance, Aeronautical and Nautical Systems, Instruments, and Equipment), and SIC 3829 (Measuring and Controlling Devices, NEC). This broader definition is used by the Aerospace Industries Association.

[4] Reliable employment figures are not available according to this output-market distinction; at some companies the same workers work on commercial and military aircraft, and the exact size of employment in some secret programs is not released. More obviously, parts makers can supply the same parts to final assemblers of either commercial or military aircraft.

[5] Lockheed produced a jumbo jet in previous decades (the L-1011, many of which are still in service), but ceased doing so during the 1970s.

[6] Source: Aerospace Industries Association. Pratt and Whitney and General Electric are also the primary suppliers of jet engines for military aircraft produced in the U.S.

[7] While some analysts (notably Carroll [1975]) put more emphasis on the importance of price competition, it was nevertheless true that wages were "out of competition."

[8] MIT Commission on Industrial Productivity (1989:1). This view is also expressed in Schwartz et al. (1987).

[9] The four partners in Airbus are Deutsche Aerospace, a subsidiary of Daimler-Benz A.G., with a 37.9% stake; the French state-owned Aerospatiale, which also has a 37.9% stake; British Aerospace, with a 20% stake; and the Spanish state-owned Construcciones Aeronauticas S.A., with a 4.2% stake (New York Times, Jan. 7, 1993). Majumdar (1987) provides an analysis of the new competitive environment facing the airframe manufacturers with the entry of Airbus.

[10] See Tyson (1993) for an analysis of industrial policies toward the aerospace industries in the U.S. and Europe; she notes that a key difference is that European government support has generally been more commercially motivated.

[11] Source: IAM.

[12] It is also the most significant private employer in the Pacific Northwest area: Pascall Pederen and Conway (1987:7) estimated that in 1989 one out of every six, or 389,000 jobs in Washington state were linked to Boeing, and that the company's operations directly and indirectly supported between 15% and 20% of the state's total economic activity.

[13] Two recent examples have been General Dynamics selling its missile operations to Hughes and its military aircraft operations to Lockheed, and General Electric selling its military electronics operation to Martin Marietta (*New York Times* Nov. 24, 1992, Dec. 10, 1992).

[14] Some notable recent examples are the Strategic Defense Initiative contract awarded by the Air Force to a team of Rockwell and TRW, over Lockheed and Martin Marietta, and the new military plane F-22 being jointly developed by Lockheed and Boeing (*Los Angeles Times* Dec. 9, 1992, Dec. 12, 1992). Pratt and Whitney and Rolls Royce are both members of the International Aero Engines consortium and McDonnell Douglas has had on-again off-again talks with Taiwan about a partnership to build a new jumbo jet (*Air Transport World* Nov. 1992, *New York Times* Aug. 11, 1992). Perhaps most significantly, Boeing has reportedly entered into an agreement with the Airbus partners to develop a next-generation super-jumbo jet (*New York Times* Jan. 6, 1993), as mentioned above.

[15] In 1988, 36% of all establishments in SIC 376 were located in California, employing 53% of all workers and accounting for 55% of total payroll in SIC 376. In total, 258,000 aerospace workers were employed in California, or 31% of the national total (U.S. Department of Commerce, *County Business Patterns*).

[16] Recent examples include Hughes' announced transfer of its missile-building operations to Arizona, Lockheed's transfer of its nonclassified work to its facilities in Georgia, and McDonnell Douglas' decision to build its new commercial airliner MD-12 in one of eight other states rather than at its existing commercial plant in southern California (*New York Times* Dec. 18, 1991, *Los Angeles Times* Sept. 10, 1992). Ong and Lawrence (1993), who define the aerospace industry to include aircraft and parts, guided missiles and space vehicles, and search and navigation systems and equipment (SIC 381) find that California lost more than 130,000 aerospace jobs between 1988 and 1993, and that "few laid off aerospace workers have been able to gain meaningful work, with a majority remaining out of work and an increasing number running out of employment benefits" (p. 3).

[17] Schwartz et al. (1987) discuss in more detail this cyclicality and its relationship to the issue of job security.

[18] The security requirements also tend to wreak havoc on seniority progression systems when both classified and nonclassified programs are part of the same ladder.

[19] This particular measure (based on the CPS Outgoing Rotation Group) is not available prior to the mid-1980s. Freeman and Medoff (1979) estimated that over the period 1973-75, 60% of aerospace production workers belonged to a union. Kokkelenberg and Sockell (1985) estimated that the unionization rate among all workers in aircraft and parts was 41.6% over the period 1973-75, 41.0% over the period 1974-76, 38.7% over the period 1975-77, 37.0% over the period 1976-78,

39.8% over the period 1977-79, 42.6% over the period 1978-80, and 43.5% over the period 1979-81. Curme, Hirsch, and Macpherson (1990) estimated that the unionization rate among all workers in aircraft and parts was 38.1% over the period 1983-85, 37.3% in 1986, 34.3% in 1987 and 32.2% in 1988; among all workers in guided missiles and space vehicles, 16.8% over the period 1983-85, 16.9% in 1986, 17.4% in 1987, and 18.7% in 1988.

[20] The Boeing Vertol Helicopter Unit in Pennsylvania is represented by the UAW but did not have more than 4,000 members during the 1980s, compared to the West Coast IAM unit, which approached 60,000 members.

[21] For a comprehensive early history of industrial relations in this industry, see Levinson (1966).

[22] Ross (1956) first defined this concept of the psychological and organizational forces of equitable comparison driving wage equalization.

[23] Lockheed is distinctive because the IAM also represents its clerical workers (about one-quarter of the membership).

[24] This section draws from Levinson (1966), McCann (1989), and U.S. Department of Labor (1974, 1976a, 1976b).

[25] This section draws from Bureau of National Affairs (1992), Erickson (1992), and various issues of *Current Wage Developments.*

[26] See Erickson (1992) for further evidence that "3% plus COLA" showed variability, particularly in the first year of the contracts during the 1970s.

[27] From the end of 1987 through the third quarter of 1991, the percentage of all private-sector workers under major collective bargaining settlements covered by lump sum provisions was between 40% and 43%; recent evidence suggests that these provisions are becoming less common, however. By the third quarter of 1992 the share had fallen to 33% (U.S. DOL 1992). See Erickson and Ichino (1994) for further analysis of lump sum bonuses in union contracts.

[28] Gainsharing was attempted with reportedly limited success at the UAW-represented McDonnell Douglas plant; Lockheed imposed an ESOP program that was viewed with hostility by the IAM because the company was perceived to be designing the program so as to thwart a hostile takeover rather than addressing the workers' and the company's legitimate joint interests.

[29] In fact, there has been much disagreement over whether the U.S. Department of Labor should include lump sums in its calculations of industry earnings, which are used in the negotiations between the government and the companies over reimbursements.

[30] There have been nascent attempts to define gains on the basis of reducing hours to finish a particular project, but people in the companies tend to complain that the government thinks in terms of reimbursing *costs* while refusing to share *gains.*

[31] Consider from Table 6 that the total bonus payouts at Boeing during the 1980s for a worker earning $40,000 per year (including overtime) would have amounted to $14,000.

[32] For example, the UAW (1989) cites "lump sum wage settlements instead of percentage improvement factors" as a major cause of the situation that "the aerospace industry continues to enjoy a period of rising profits while the workers' spendable income has remained relatively stable," while also arguing that "workers should be able to share in the fruits of their labor by the establishment of a true profit-sharing program."

[33] One management negotiator referred to this metric as "percentile units," indicating that it is often used in discussions among company negotiators and with the unions.

[34] In addition to wages and bonuses, other main points of contention were the pension formula and the extent of mandatory overtime.

[35] This is a slippery and contentious definitional issue; both union and nonunion companies inside and outside of the industry have been included in the various surveys that have been used.

[36] However, a more recent (undated) paper on "High Performance Work Organization Partnership" by the IAM acknowledges that "It is clear that both defense and commercial workplaces in the private and public sectors have to convert from traditional North American work systems to high performance if they are going to compete globally." The paper also provides advice on how to negotiate "full-partnership" high performance work system, which it sharply distinguishes from both the Taylor model and TQM model.

References

Aerospace Industries Association of America. 1980-1993. *Aerospace Facts and Figures*. Washington, DC: Aerospace Industries Association of America.

Air Transport World. 1992. "A Broad Battle on Many Fronts: Aircraft Engines."

Bluestone, Barry, Peter Jordan, and Mark Sullivan. 1981. *Aircraft Industry Dynamics: An Analysis of Competition, Capital and Labor*. Boston, MA: Auburn House.

Bureau of National Affairs. 1992. "Wage Patterns in Aerospace." In *Collective Bargaining Negotiations and Contracts*. Washington, DC: BNA, pp. 18:1-18:19.

Carroll, Sidney. 1975. "The Market for Commercial Airliners." In *Regulating the Product: Quality and Variety*, R. Caves and M. Roberts, eds. Cambridge: Ballinger.

Curme, Michael, Barry Hirsch, and David Macpherson. 1990. "Union Membership and Contract Coverage in the United States, 1983-1988." *Industrial and Labor Relations Review*, Vol. 44 (October), pp. 5-33.

Erickson, Christopher. 1990. "Union Wage Determination in Manufacturing in the 1980s: Three Empirical Investigations." Unpublished dissertation, MIT.

_____. 1992. "Wage Rule Formation in the Aerospace Industry." *Industrial and Labor Relations Review*, Vol. 45 (April), pp. 507-22.

Erickson, Christopher, and Andrea Ichino. 1994. "Lump-Sum Bonuses in Union Contracts." In *Advances in Industrial and Labor Relations*, Vol. 6, pp. 183-218.

Freeman, Richard, and James Medoff. 1979. "New Estimates of Private Sector Unionism in the United States." *Industrial and Labor Relations Review*, Vol. 32 (January), pp. 143-74.

International Association of Machinists and Aerospace Workers. 1990. "IAM White Paper on Team Concept Programs." Unpublished memo.

Katz, Harry. 1985. *Shifting Gears.* Cambridge: MIT Press.

Kleiner, Morris M., Gerald Nickelsburg, and Adam M. Pilarski. 1988. "Grievances and Plant Performance: Is Zero Optimal?" *Proceedings of the 41st Annual Meeting.* Madison, WI: Industrial Relations Research Association.

Kokkelenberg, Edward, and Donna Sockell. 1985. "Union Membership in the United States, 1973-81." *Industrial and Labor Relations Review,* Vol. 38 (July), pp. 497-543.

Levinson, Harold M. 1966. *Determining Forces in Collective Wage Bargaining.* New York: John Wiley and Sons.

Los Angeles Times. 1992a. "Boeing Runs into Some Turbulence." March 1, p. D1.

_____. 1992b. "Hughes Cuts 4,500 Jobs in Southland." Sept. 10, p. A1.

_____. 1992c. "Mayday for Aerospace: Worldwide Slump Grounds Commercial Jet Makers." Nov. 22, p. D1.

_____. 1992d. "Rockwell, TRW Win Major 'Star Wars' Contracts," Dec. 12, p. D1.

_____. 1992e. "Southland Aerospace Firms Suddenly Lack Engineers," Aug. 22, p. A1.

Majumdar, Badiul. 1987. "Upstart or Flying Start? The Rise of Airbus Industrie." *The World Economy,* Vol. 10 (December), pp. 497-518.

McCann, John. 1989. *Blood in the Water: A History of District Lodge 751 of the International Association of Machinists and Aerospace Workers.* Seattle, WA: District Lodge 751, IAM.

MIT Commission on Industrial Productivity. 1989. *Made in America: Regaining the Productive Edge.* Cambridge: MIT Press.

New York Times. 1988a. "Behind the Scenes at NUMMI Motors." Dec. 4, p. F2.

_____. 1988b. "Worker Harmony Makes NUMMI Work." Dec. 25, p. F2.

_____. 1991a. "Breathing Easier at McDonnell Douglas." Sept. 29, p. F1.

_____. 1991b. "Nine Towns Spare No Effort to Snare New Plant." Dec. 18, p. A1.

_____. 1992a. "G.E. Will Sell Aerospace Unit for $3 Billion." Nov. 24, p. A1.

_____. 1992b. "General Dynamics Will Sell Lockheed its Fighter Division." Dec. 10, p. A1.

_____. 1992c. "McDonnell Realigning Operations." Aug. 11, p. C1.

_____. 1993a. "Confusion on Plans for a Giant Plane." Jan. 7, p. C4.

_____. 1993b. "Germans Join Boeing in Jet Study." Jan. 6, p. C5.

Ong, Paul, and Janette Lawrence. 1993. "The Employment Crisis in Aerospace." Report Series, UCLA Graduate School of Architecture and Urban Planning.

Pascal, Glen, Douglas H. Pedersen, and Richard S. Conway, Jr. 1989. "Boeing Company Economic Impact Study." Unpublished report.

Ross, Arthur. 1956. *Trade Union Wage Policy.* Berkeley: University of California Press.

Schwartz, Arthur R., et al. 1987. "The Impact of Technological Change on Labor Relations in the Commercial Aircraft Industry." In *Workers, Managers, and Technological Change: Emerging Patterns of Labor Relations,* D.B. Cornfield, ed. New York: Plenum Press.

Thomas, Robert. 1991. "Technological Choice and Union-Management Cooperation." *Industrial Relations,* Vol. 30 (Spring), pp. 167-192.

Tyson, Laura D'Andrea. 1993. "Industrial Policy and Trade Management in the Commercial Aircraft Industry." Chapter 5 of *Who's Bashing Whom?* Washington, DC: Institute for International Economics.

United Automobile, Aerospace, and Agricultural Implement Workers. 1989. "Collective Bargaining Recommendations to the Twenty-Seventh UAW Aerospace Collective Bargaining Conference." Unpublished memo.

U.S. Congress, Office of Technology Assessment. 1991. "Government Support of the Large Commercial Aircraft Industries of Japan, Europe and the United States." In *Competing Economies: America, Europe and the Pacific Rim.* Washington, DC: Office of Technology Assessment.

U.S. Department of Commerce. *County Business Patterns.* Various issues.

U.S. Department of Labor. *Current Wage Developments.* Various issues.

_____. 1974. *Collective Bargaining Summary: Aerospace Industry.* Washington, DC. DOL.

_____. 1976a. *Wage Chronology: The Boeing Company and Machinists' Union, June 1936-October 1977.* Washington, DC: DOL.

_____. 1976b. *Wage Chronology: Lockheed California Company and Machinists' Union, March 1937-October 1977.* Washington, DC: DOL.

_____. 1992. "Major Collective Bargaining Settlements in Private Industry, Third Quarter 1992." Press release, USDL:92-687.

Verma, Anil, and Robert B. McKersie. 1985. "Industrial Relations at the Boeing Company: A Case-Study." Unpublished paper.

_____. 1987. "Employee Involvement: The Implications of Noninvolvement by Unions." *Industrial and Labor Relations Review,* Vol. 40 (July), pp. 556-68.

CHAPTER 4

The Transformation of Industrial Relations in the American Steel Industry

JEFFREY B. ARTHUR
Purdue University

SUZANNE KONZELMANN SMITH
Indiana University at South Bend

Editor's Abstract

Arthur and Smith argue that economic, technological, and institutional changes in the 1980s have fundamentally transformed the industrial relations system in the American steel industry. Prior to the 1980s, the bargaining structure in steel matched the concentrated and centralized nature of the industry as a whole. Not only did a multi-employer bargain set the pattern for the wider industry, but also there was coordination of pay for particular jobs through the Cooperative Wage Survey. Strikes, and the resulting substitution of imports for U.S. steel, were avoided through top-level labor-management committees and the Experimental Negotiating Agreement.

In the early 1980s, all this fell apart. Increased foreign imports, stagnating steel consumption (both secular and cyclical), lagging U.S. technology, and a rapidly growing nonunion mini-mill sector, all occasioned massive employment losses in the integrated steel companies. The steel industry eliminated over 40 million tons (25%) of capacity in the 1980s and reduced employment by more than half (250,000 jobs). Developments included plant closures, bankruptcies, U.S. Steel's diversification out of the industry, and investment in new continuous casting technology (funded in some companies through ties to foreign steelmakers). There were substantial reductions in real wages. Multi-employer bargaining disappeared. Since 1989, there has been establishment of pattern bargaining in the industry, but this coexists with considerable diversity in plant-level industrial relations practices.

This diversity reflects company and plant-level differences in business strategy, technology, and products, as well as labor-management relations. The authors contrast plant-level labor relations at National Steel and USX's steel producing operations at Gary. National Steel responded to changes in the competitive environment by asking for the union's cooperation and participation. In contrast, USX generally attempts to change work practices with a minimum of union involvement. The authors examine the resulting difficulties encountered so far in USX's Gary steel producing operation and relate those problems to the company's history of adversarial labor relations.

The crucial question for the future is whether the "Cooperative Partnership" negotiated at Inland, Bethlehem, and National Steel will successfully spread to other firms. The Steelworkers are pushing this model. It involves giving workers enhanced job security, employee involvement, considerable information sharing, and unprecedented union participation at all levels of decision making, in exchange for significant quality and flexibility-enhancing work restructuring, and a linking of compensation to firm performance.

American steel has apparently regained its long-run competitiveness but a number of problems remain. The integrated firms still face strong competition from domestic mini-mills (half of which are non-union) and foreign steelmakers. Arthur and Smith are concerned that the focus on staying competitive by reducing direct labor costs may create barriers to more cooperative, productivity-enhancing labor relations.

o   o   o

In 1950 more than 45% of the world's steel was produced in the U.S. The conditions under which the U.S. steel industry thrived during this period consisted of steadily increasing demand for steel and the superiority of U.S. production technology and productivity in the world market. Under these conditions, industrial relations mechanisms were set up whereby the U.S. steel oligopoly could ensure labor force stability with the union through the establishment of coordinated bargaining and standardized work organization.

The U.S. steel industry was hit particularly hard by the changes in the economic environment occurring over the last 10 to 15 years. Historical data from the last 50 years indicate that the period from 1975 to 1991 represented a dramatic shift from earlier periods. The large integrated sector of the steel industry experienced wrenching changes in terms of declining demand for its products as well as an increase in foreign and domestic minimill competition. The impact of these changes included low operating rates, large financial losses for steelmakers, bankruptcies, and massive plant closures and employment reductions through the mid-1980s. Steel firms reacted in different ways to the crisis. Some, like U.S. Steel, diversified corporate assets outside of the steel industry; others, like National Steel and Inland Steel, joined with foreign producers to increase steel investments. As a whole, the industry eliminated more than 40 million tons (25%) of capacity in the 1980s and reduced employment by more than 250,000 employees (60%) during this period (American Iron and Steel Institute, various years).

This combination of environmental and strategic-level changes in the industry put severe pressures on the traditional system of industrial relations that had developed in the steel industry in the post-World War II period. These changes contributed to the breakdown of a number of institutional mechanisms that had helped to maintain centralization of power and standardization of industrial relations practices and collective bargaining outcomes. As a result, we have seen an increasing amount of decentralization and diversity in steel industry industrial relations. We find evidence that multiple patterns of industrial relations practices are emerging which reflect company and plant-level differences in technology, products, business strategy, as well as the labor-management histories and institutions.

One of the industrial relations patterns that has emerged, and the one the international leadership of the United Steelworkers of America appears to be advocating, is a new cooperative partnership, modeled after the 1986 National Steel Agreement. This new industrial relations model includes significant quality and flexibility-enhancing work restructuring coupled with an increased share of compensation linked to firm performance and productivity in exchange for job security guarantees and unprecedented employee and union participation and information sharing at all levels of the company. Whether, in fact, this model spreads to other unionized steel firms in the industry will depend on the choices and actions made by unions, management, and government actors as they struggle with the transition from a traditional to a new work system.

Distinct Steel Industry Segments

While changes in economic conditions affected all firms in the steel industry, all firms were not affected in the same way. The steel crisis in the 1980s highlighted the heterogeneity in the industry. What is normally thought of as "the steel industry" is, in fact, composed of three distinct industry segments: the integrated sector, the specialty steel sector, and the minimill sector (U.S. Bureau of Labor Statistics [henceforth BLS] 1985). The integrated sector is the best known and by far the largest of the three, accounting for approximately 65% of domestic steel production. The term "integrated" refers to the fact that firms in this sector are involved in every aspect of steel making—from preparing the iron ore, limestone, and coal to be melted down in a blast furnace, to reheating and rolling the semifinished steel billets, slabs, and blooms into a wide range of carbon and alloy steel products.

What are known as "specialty steel mills" currently account for about 7% of domestic production. Some of the larger firms in this segment are Al Tech Specialty Steel Co., Allegheny Ludlum Steel Corp., Crucible Steel, and Carpenter Technology. Because of the highly specialized nature of their products and the type of high-quality steel alloys that they use, there are basic differences between this sector and the traditional, primarily carbon steel, integrated and minimill sector producers. For example, Hirshhorn (1986) estimates that the employment cost per ton of steel shipped in the specialty steel sector was approximately 1.6 times that in the integrated sector and 2.6 times that in the minimill sector. These differences reflect both the higher skill level required in these mills and a more labor intensive, low-volume production process than that in either the integrated or minimill sectors.

Steel Minimills

The final sector of the steel industry, known as steel "minimills," has traditionally differed from the two other sectors in terms of their technology, products, size, and market orientation. Minimills are "nonintegrated" in the sense that they use steel scrap as their main input or "charge" which is melted down in electric furnaces. The molten steel is then continuously cast into semifinished shapes which are rolled into a number of steel products such as wire rods, concrete reinforcing bars, and structural shapes (e.g., angles, channels, I-beams). Because of their technological configuration, minimills are able to achieve economies of scale at a much lower volume of output than integrated mills. The average annual capacity of these mills is about 400,000 tons of raw steel, compared to about 3 million tons in a typical integrated facility (Hogan 1987). Most of the minimill plants are operated as independent firms. There are approximately 58 minimill plants in the U.S. owned by 37 separate firms (Association of Iron and Steel Engineers 1989).

In contrast to the integrated sector, minimills have, on average, done quite well over the last 20 years.[1] Their market share has increased from less than 10% in 1970 to almost 30% today, and they have almost completely taken over the market for bar shape products from both integrated firms and imports. Until recently, minimill-sector growth has been limited by their inability to compete in the market for flat-rolled steel which accounts for about 60% of the carbon steel market. The development by Nucor Steel of a new technology called "thin-slab casting" at its Crawfordsville, Indiana, plant offers the potential for minimills to significantly increase their market share by competing directly with integrated producers in the market for flat-rolled products. Nucor's success with this technology has already led other producers to follow. In addition to a second flat-rolled Nucor mill in Arkansas, two minimill companies, Birmingham Steel and Oregon Steel, have also announced plans to build similar mills.

Currently, however, there is some question as to how far this sector can continue to expand. One inhibiting factor is the cost of steel scrap which is used as the input to minimill steelmaking process. The use of steel scrap increased by 67% between 1982 and 1988, and prices increased by 40% (*Business Week* June 13, 1988:122). Scrap accounts for about half the cost of production so producers are obviously sensitive to any large price increases. Scrap supply does not appear to be a big problem in the U.S., where there is an estimated 800 million tons of scrap which could come to market if that became profitable (p. 122). Most of this supply, however, is not the high-grade scrap required for most flat-rolled products.

Alternatives to the use of high-grade scrap are quickly developing. One is the use of direct reduced iron (DRI), a type of purified iron which can be combined with scrap to produce higher steel grades. To date, this alternative has been too costly (relative to scrap) for most producers to use. As the demand and price for high-grade scrap continues to rise, however, one would expect increased use of DRI. Nucor has already announced plans to build a relatively small DRI producing plant in Trinidad (*Wall Street Journal* Jan. 7, 1993:A4). However, as the price of input (scrap or other) goes up for minimills, their cost advantage vs. modern integrated production begins to disappear.

Minimill Industrial Relations

The United Steelworkers of America (USWA) has had only limited success in organizing the new minimills. Approximately half of the minimill firms and about 40% of the minimill plants in the U.S. are unionized (Smith 1991) compared to the nearly 100% unionization rate in the integrated and specialty steel producing firms. In general, the USWA has been more successful in gaining representation rights in older mini-mill plants than in newer (and more technologically efficient) ones (Arthur 1990).

Contrary to the popular image that minimills represent a "new" cooperative industrial relations system (e.g., Piore and Sable 1984; Barnett and Crandall 1986), Arthur (1990, 1992) found that there is considerable variation in labor relations approaches used by both union and nonunion minimills. Among the 14 unionized minimill plants in his study, about half had industrial relations practices and wage levels that followed closely the basic steel "pattern" set in the integrated sector. Only about one-quarter of the unionized mills were found to have a highly cooperative set of industrial relations practices including extensive employee involvement, training, and information sharing.

This same broad spectrum of practices was also present in the nonunion minimills. About half of these mills followed a traditional "control" human resource strategy (Walton 1985) with jobs characterized by relatively low wages and benefits, low skill requirements, little or no use of employee involvement programs or due-process mechanisms, and high employee turnover. Other nonunion patterns included a modified piece-rate type system as well as a "sophisticated nonunion" or "human resource management" system (Katz and Kochan 1992).

Somewhat surprisingly, Arthur (1990) did not find a large difference in employment costs per hour between the union and nonunion minimills. The union mills reported an employment cost (including wages, benefits, bonuses, etc.) of $20.15 per hour, while the average in the nonunion mills was $19.19. Given the large variance in wages in both sectors, this difference is not statistically significant. It is also fairly close to the $22.80 employment cost per hour reported for the integrated sector in 1988 (AISI 1989). Because of the large productivity differences between nonunion and union minimills (as well as unionized integrated plants producing similar products), however, the nonunion sector of the steel industry maintains a substantial unit labor cost advantage over unionized producers.

In general, the nonunion minimill companies have been quite strong in their opposition to unions and have used a combination of union suppression as well as union substitution tactics. For example, Florida Steel, a company with four minimill plants in the South, was found by the NLRB to have engaged in a "pattern of attempting to defeat the union at all cost by a sustained campaign of varied and repeated unfair labor practices . . ." throughout the 1970s (BNA August 10, 1982:D-1). Because of these violations, the company was ordered to pay $3.3 million in back pay in 1982, the third largest settlement issued by the NLRB at that time (*AFL-CIO News* May 10, 1982:6).

Other minimill companies, such as Nucor Steel and Chaparral Steel, have relied on other means to avoid unions. For example, Nucor Steel, which is the largest of the minimill companies with more than 3.5 million tons of annual capacity in its seven minimill plants, pays its employees a base salary that is below the industry average but provides the opportunity to earn much higher salaries based on a group productivity or gainssharing program (Savage 1981). Because Nucor has been one of the only steel companies to remain profitable through the 1980s, these bonus payments put Nucor's total compensation consistently at or above that paid to unionized steelworkers. In addition, because of their market success, Nucor can boast a record of never having laid off its production employees. These compensation and job security policies, combined with the fact that most of Nucor's plants have been built in relatively rural areas with low union density and few other comparable opportunities for employees, have made them particularly resistant to unionization.

A critique of the Nucor incentive compensation system is that it puts pressure on employees to cut corners and take safety risks. Eleven people died at Nucor plants between 1980 and 1991. That equals a fatality rate of 23.4% per 100,000 production workers compared to the industry average of just under 12% (*Wall Street Journal* May 10, 1991:1). Nucor denies the claim that they are less safe than other steel companies. They cite the fact that their record reflects the fact that they had more new start-ups than other mills (an especially dangerous time) and that they employ younger, less experienced workers (who are more at risk of injury) (p. 1).

We discuss the impact of the growing minimill sector on steel industry industrial relations in the concluding section. We now turn our attention to developments in the integrated sector of the industry since it is the largest of the steel industry segments and its industrial relations practices tend to spill over into the union and nonunion portions of the other segments as well. Firms in this segment of the industry also have a rich, well-documented industrial relations history. Since this segment was clearly hit the hardest by the environmental changes in industry, it provides an excellent opportunity to examine the impact of these changes on traditional industrial relations structures and practices in the industry.

Traditional Industrial Relations Structure in Steel

The three-tier structure of industrial relations (Kochan, McKersie, and Cappelli 1984; Kochan, Katz, and McKersie 1986) provides a useful model for analyzing steel industry industrial relations. This model differs from the traditional industrial relations systems framework (i.e., Dunlop 1958) in that it emphasizes the choices that are available to parties within a set of environmental and technological constraints. Instead of the traditional focus on the practice and outcomes of collective bargaining, personnel policies, and the development and administration of public policies governing labor-management relations, the three-tier framework posits that industrial relations activities and outcomes are best understood by additionally examining union and management activities both above and below this level. It is only by examining all three levels that we can understand the entire IR system in a given industry.

Using this framework, the traditional IR system in the steel industry, which developed in the post-World War II period and lasted through the late 1970s, is presented in Table 1. We argue in this chapter that economic, technological, and institutional changes in the 1980s fundamentally transformed this traditional system. In order to appreciate the significance of these changes, it is first necessary to understand the structure and characteristics of this traditional system.

Steel Industry Structure

Since the formation of the United States Steel Corporation under the leadership of Judge Elbert H. Gary in 1901, which consolidated 65% of the nation's steelmaking capacity under one management, the U.S. steel industry has been characterized by a highly concentrated, oligopolistic industry structure. As it emerged from World War II, the eight largest firms in the industry accounted for 80% of U.S. raw steel production with the U.S. Steel Corporation alone accounting for 34% of that production.

In addition, U.S. steel firms held a substantial percentage of world markets (Barnett and Schorsch 1984). U.S. steelmakers had sizable advantages over foreign competitors in nearly every aspect of production including technology, process, scale, and productivity. These characteristics gave U.S. steelmakers a competitive advantage in benefiting from the growth in steel demand following World War II. The start of the Korean War in 1950 served to accelerate this demand growth because of war-related production required by government and the resulting

TABLE 1

Three-Tier Structure of Traditional IR System in Steel

	Labor	Management	Government	Institutional Mechanism
Strategic	Centralization of bargaining and standardization of outcomes	Industry concentration and "friendly" domestic competition	Wage and price policies	Human Resource Committee
		"Conservative" technological investments	National security interests and aid to foreign producers	Joint Advisory Committee on Productivity
		Independence from both government and labor		
Functional	Improve wages, benefits and income security across the industry	Emphasis on continued production [avoid strikes]	Intervene or threaten to intervene to avoid strikes or "unfavorable" outcomes	Experimental Negotiating Agreement
		Maintain full "management's rights" over business issues		Coordinated bargaining
Workplace	Detailed, standardized wages and work rules;	"Rationalize" and standardize wages and work organization	Enforce EEO order on seniority	Cooperative Wage Survey
	Local issues	Maintain distinction between employee and supervisor		
	Incentives			

stockpiling by customers against the possibility of steel rationing. Internationally, the steel industry was being called on during this period to help rebuild a war-devastated Europe and Japan, including the need for a substantial amount of steel-intensive infrastructure in the cities. Much of the growth during this period was coordinated by the industry's stabilizing leader, the U.S. Steel Company, which accounted for nearly 30% of the industry's total shipments in 1950. Market shares for the Big Six integrated steel makers remained relatively stable through the mid-1970s. This balance was maintained in part because the rest of the industry was fearful of U.S. Steel's market power in the event of unrestrained competition. U.S. Steel, meanwhile, could not afford to push its market advantage too far for fear of government antitrust action (Tiffany 1988).

Union Structure

The structure of USWA, the industry's union, mirrored, in large part, the concentrated and centralized structure of the industry. The Steelworkers' first president, Philip Murray (1942-52), and other early leaders came directly from the United Mine Workers where the power of the national organization was firmly established (see Clark, Gottlieb, and Kennedy 1987). Ulman (1961) points to a number of historical factors that pushed the burgeoning union toward centralization, including the need to deal in a unified way with government agencies and actions. Perhaps most importantly, effective bargaining power in the steel industry required matching the structure of the industry itself. As Stieber (1980:158) observes:

> Since it dealt with an industry dominated by one giant, U.S. Steel, and many mini-giants whose policies were well coordinated, it was important for the union to speak with one voice. Success depended on a strong central organization and solidarity towards the industry.

Thus at the level of collective bargaining, centralized negotiations and the emphasis of national over local interests were in the interest of both union and management leaders. This common interest was formalized through a series of institutional mechanisms.

Institutional Mechanisms

Centralized bargaining. De facto centralized negotiations across steel industry firms were formalized first in 1955 when the top six companies agreed to a USWA proposal to meet in separate committees in Pittsburgh so that Steelworkers' then president McDonald could personally lead each negotiation. By 1959 the major companies had authorized a four-member committee (two from U.S. Steel and one each from Bethlehem and Republic) to negotiate all issues on their behalf (Stieber 1980; Hoerr 1988). One outgrowth of centralization was a high degree of standardization of collective bargaining outcomes across firms within the steel industry and across plants within firms, including smaller firms not directly involved in coordinated bargaining—which all followed the basic steel pattern. From the union's standpoint, this also had the beneficial effect of removing wages as a primary source of competition between U.S. steel producers. As long as the government was willing, the steel producers could pass on additional labor costs in the price of its products.

Top-level labor-management committees. While the two sides maintained a traditional arms-length negotiation posture with regard to collective bargaining issues, there have been several attempts at top-level cooperation between industry and union leaders. Top-level cooperation began to develop after the bitter 116-day steel industry strike in 1959. The period from 1960 to 1980 has been labeled the "harmonious years" in steel industry industrial relations (Stieber 1980:182). In contrast to the 1946-59 period when the industry experienced five major strikes, there were no major strikes in the 20 years that followed. Significantly, 1960 was also the first year in which steel imports exceeded exports. The steel import "problem" was seen as resulting from customers seeking protection from uncertain steel supply associated with each labor negotiating round. The need to restrict the influx of foreign steel was an issue behind which both labor and management could rally and present a united front to government.

The first of the top-level cooperative efforts in steel, the Human Relations Research Committee, later named the Human Relations Committee (HRC), was formed in 1960. It consisted of top-level company and union officials and was designed to handle ongoing bargaining issues in order to avoid long, debilitating strikes in the future. The HRC ended with the election of I.W. Able as USWA president in 1965. It was followed by the Joint Advisory Committee on Productivity in 1971. While helpful in terms of promoting common interests at the top level of the IR structure, both of these efforts failed to garner strong employee involvement or support at the middle and workplace levels (Camens 1982:310; *Business Week* August 18, 1980:103).

Experimental Negotiating Agreement. In contrast, the Experimental Negotiating Agreement (ENA), signed in 1973, had a direct impact on the collective bargaining relationship in the steel industry. In this groundbreaking agreement, the union and the steel companies agreed not to strike or lockout during the term of the agreement and to submit all unresolved issues to binding interest arbitration. In return, the companies agreed to a $150 "share-the-wealth" bonus for each employee, a guaranteed yearly minimum wage increase of 3% and a 1-cent COLA for every 0.3% increase in the CPI (BNA 1987:233).

The primary purpose of the ENA was to halt the surge of imports and stockpiling that occurred during contract years by eliminating the threat of a major work stoppage. Past experience had shown that strikes, or the threat of a strike, had hurt both labor and management by allowing foreign competitors to increase their U.S. market shares. The ENA "worked" to the extent that there was no work stoppage in 1974, 1977, or 1980, the three contract years in which the ENA was in effect.

Cooperative Wage Survey. In the steel industry, standardization applied not only to general issues of wage and benefit increases through centralized collective bargaining, but also to specific job definitions, structures, and responsibilities at the plant or workplace level. Standardization was achieved at this lower level through a unique institutional mechanism known as the Cooperative Wage Survey (CWS).

The CWS arose out of a 1944 War Labor Board directive instructing the U.S. Steel Corporation and the Steelworkers Union to set out to eliminate wage inequities, both within and across plants (Stieber 1959). Steel industry union and management worked jointly on this program which affected some 500,000 steelworkers or about 4% of all U.S. manufacturing production workers in 1960 (p. xix). The CWS consisted of a job evaluation system in which jobs were described in terms of their primary function, materials used, source of supervision, direction exercised, and working procedure (United Steelworkers 1971:7). Jobs were then rated across 12 areas that covered the training, skill, effort, responsibility, and working conditions required on the job. A complex formula was developed to determine job rates based on the weighted categories and to maintain a 3.5-cent distance between each of the 30 wage categories that were developed.

The CWS codified and made explicit a system in which the rights of the worker were tied directly to the job.[2] This was particularly true with regard to pay. In a 1950 U.S. Steel arbitration case involving a pay dispute, the arbitrator states: "It is clear that it is jobs and not men that are classified in the agreement" (United Steelworkers 1981:472). The CWS was, in effect, a formal agreement between the parties that the performance of certain job duties would be paid a specific amount, regardless of who performed them.

Summary. The institutional mechanisms developed during this period (the CWS, coordinated bargaining, and the ENA) strengthened and rigidified the existing trends toward centralization and standardization in this industry. These characteristics appeared to fit with the environmental and economic conditions of the postwar period. Living standards and conditions of steelworkers clearly improved dramatically during this period, and steel companies continued to thrive. It was only in the face of dramatic changes in the economic environment in the late 1970s and 1980s that some of the weaknesses of these institutional mechanisms began to become apparent. We turn next to these environmental changes and describe the impact they have had on industrial relations structures and activities in the 1980s and 1990s.

Environmental Changes

During the early 1980s, integrated steel producers faced competitive pressure from foreign steel producers and domestic steel minimills in an economic context characterized by stagnant demand for steel products. As a result, a large proportion of their steel-producing capacity exceeded total domestic demand for the product. In addition, much of the existing U.S. capacity was in serious need of technological upgrading to compete with the relatively more efficient steel minimills (for bar and rod products) and modernized facilities of many foreign producers.

The effects of the decline in the product market for integrated firms and the changing economic and technological environment in the late 1970s and early 1980s had a profound effect on steel companies' profits and competitive status. Integrated steel firms reacted to these challenges by dramatically reducing capacity and employment and by seeking foreign investors to finance massive modernization programs. The effects of these actions began to become apparent in the period since 1985 in which steel industry profitability, capital utilization, and productivity all improved significantly over the previous 5- to 10-year period.

As we argue below, however, the steel industry that emerged from the recession in the late 1980s was fundamentally different from the one that existed prior to that time in terms of its size, competitive structure, technology, and most important for us, its industrial relations institutions.

Stagnating growth in steel consumption. Table 2 shows the changes in apparent consumption (defined as shipments plus imports minus exports). This table indicates that consumption grew fairly steadily from 1940 through the early 1970s, with peaks during the Korean War years and again in the early 1970s. Since that time, however, consumption has fallen steadily from a high of more than 122.6 million tons in 1973 to 88.3 million tons in 1991. As can be seen from Table 2, the sharpest declines in apparent consumption and production occurred in the late 1970s and again in 1982 and 1983 following the oil shocks and associated general economic downturns of those two periods.

For the integrated sector of the U.S. steel industry, the overall decline in apparent consumption understates the total amount of decline in their customer base. In addition to a declining total domestic market, the integrated firms' share of that market was also declining due to the rise in imports and domestic steel minimills. Table 2 shows that from 1975 to 1984, the percent of domestic steel consumption accounted for by steel imports nearly doubled from 13.5% to 25.2%. U.S. steel exports, on the other hand, declined from approximately 3 million tons in 1975 to less than a million tons in 1985. Further, much of this import growth came from "nontraditional" steel exporters outside of Japan and Europe (AISI, various years).

The percent of imports has declined steadily since the mid-1980s. Part of the change in imports was related to exchange rates. The value of the dollar soared against most foreign currencies in the early to mid-1980s but has declined dramatically since 1985. In addition to the change in exchange rates, the Voluntary Restraint Agreements (VRAs), signed in 1984 and extended in 1989, restricted imports to 20% of the U.S. market. These agreements expired in March 1992 and, with the breakdown of the Multilateral Steel Agreement, have left the industry without government protection from imports for the first time since 1982 (McManus 1992). The reaction by some industry firms has been to invoke antidumping and illegal subsidy laws and to file suit against individual nations (which they were unable to do under the VRA). In a somewhat surprising recent ruling, the U.S. International Trade Commission cleared foreign steelmakers of the bulk of these suits, causing steel stock prices to fall and all but eliminating the hope of U.S. steel firms to enforce higher steel prices on most products (*Wall Street Journal* July 28, 1993:A3; July 29, 1993:A2). Unless something else is done, it appears the result of the new ruling will reverse the recent decline in the percent of steel imports (see Table 2) and put pressure on the Clinton administration to establish a new trade policy for steel.

In addition to imports, domestic minimills were also increasing their share of the domestic market. The percent of domestic steel shipments accounted for by steel minimills increased from approximately 10% in 1975 to 20% in 1985 (Locker Associates 1989; Barnett and Crandall 1986) and close to 30% today. Until recently, minimills were limited to producing "long" steel products such as steel bars, rods, and light structural shapes—which account for approximately 25% of the total market

TABLE 2

Annual U.S. Steel Industry Imports, Exports, Production, and Apparent Domestic Consumption

Year	Imports (000,000 tons)	Exports (000,000 tons)	Apparent Domestic Consumption[a] (000,000 tons)	Production (000,000 tons)	Percent Imports
1945	.054	4.354	52.942	79.702	0.1
1950	1.014	2.639	90.607	96.836	1.1
1955	.973	4.061	81.629	117.063	1.2
1960	3.359	2.977	71.531	99.282	4.7
1965	10.383	2.496	100.553	131.462	10.3
1970	13.364	7.053	97.109	131.514	13.8
1975	12.012	2.953	89.016	116.642	13.5
1980	15.495	4.101	95.247	111.835	16.3
1981	19.898	2.094	105.444	120.828	18.9
1982	16.663	1.842	76.388	74.577	21.8
1983	17.070	1.199	83.454	84.615	20.5
1984	26.163	0.980	98.922	92.528	26.4
1985	24.256	0.932	96.367	88.259	25.2
1986	20.692	0.929	90.026	81.606	23.0
1987	20.414	1.129	95.939	89.151	21.3
1988	20.891	2.069	102.622	99.924	20.3
1989	17.321	4.578	96.943	97.943	17.9
1990	17.169	4.303	97.847	98.906	17.5
1991	15.845	6.346	88.345	87.896	17.9

Source: AISI; *Annual Statistical Reports*, various years.

[a] Equal total U.S. shipments plus imports minus exports.

for steel products. Because of their relative technological efficiency in producing these types of products (as compared to integrated producers), they have virtually taken over these product markets from the integrated producers in the 1980s.

As argued previously, a foundation of the traditional IR system in steel was the ability of the union to set wage standards and to take wages out of competition. Rising market share for imports and domestic minimills (many of which are nonunion) means that this ability has severely eroded.

Capacity and employment reductions. The immediate effects of the changes in economic and competitive conditions were increasing problems with excess capacity and low operating rates for most integrated steel companies in the early 1980s. The average capacity utilization rate (production/capacity) in the steel industry between 1980 and 1985 was only 65%, compared to an average of 82% in the preceding five-year period (AISI, various years). Further, as was described above, it became painfully clear by the early 1980s that the excess capacity problem was not simply a result of a cyclical downturn in demand for steel products. Rather, it reflected a worldwide structural decline in steel consumption in industrialized countries (Bain 1992).

The reaction to these changes by the U.S. steel companies has been a relatively swift and dramatic reduction in U.S. integrated steel capacity and employment. As a whole, the U.S. steel industry reduced capacity by 40 million tons (or 25% of total industry capacity) between 1975 and 1991 (AISI).[3] Between 1977 and 1988, 21 of the 48 integrated steel plants in the U.S. had closed (Deily 1991:257), while numerous others had experienced partial shutdowns of their facilities (Barnett and Crandall 1986:Tables 3-5).

As expected, capacity reductions and plant closures were associated with a large decline in steel industry employment in the 1980s. Table 4 shows that since 1980 employment in the steel industry has declined by more than 60% as more than 250,000 jobs have been lost. The effects of these massive employment losses on communities and families is difficult to overestimate. Pennsylvania was clearly hit hardest by the capacity reductions. Production declined by more than 11 million tons in the state between 1980 and 1990 (AISI, various years). In contrast, the Midwest fared relatively well, with Indiana, Ohio, and Michigan actually showing slight increases in production over the period (AISI, various years).

TABLE 3

U.S. Steel Industry Capacity, Capacity Utilization, Continuous Casting,
and Net Income

Year	Capacity (000,000 tons)	Capacity Utilization Rate[a] (percent)	Continuous Casting (percent)	Net Income ($000,000)
1945	NA	NA		184
1950	NA	NA		767
1956	129.9	88.7		1,113
1960	142.8	69.5		811
1965	148.2	88.7		1,069
1970	153.8	85.5		532
1975	157.4	74.1		1,595
1980	153.7	72.8		681
1981	154.3	78.3		1,653
1982	154.0	48.4	29.0	(3,384)
1983	150.6	56.2	32.1	(2,231)
1984	135.3	68.4	39.6	(31)
1985	133.6	66.1	44.4	(1,834)
1986	127.9	63.8	55.2	(4,150)
1987	112.2	79.5	59.8	1,077
1988	113.0	88.4	61.3	(567)
1989	115.9	84.5	64.8	1,597
1990	116.7	84.8	67.4	54
1991	117.6	74.7	75.8	(2,072)

Source: AISI; *Annual Statistical Reports*, various years.

[a] Equals annual production divided by capacity.

Table 4 shows that while the bulk of employment reductions focused on the blue-collar wage earners, salaried employees were also profoundly affected. The number of salaried employees was reduced in this period from 107,000 in 1980 to 41,000 in 1991.

It should be noted that steel industry job losses were not confined to the U.S. Other industrialized countries experienced similar downturns as well. From 1980 to 1990, for example, total steel industry employment declined 53% in Great Britain, 38% in Canada, 36% in Germany, and 28% in Japan (Bain 1992:6).

Financial strains and lagging technology investments. Because of the capital-intense nature of steelmaking, low capacity utilization rates increase the costs per ton significantly. Given the new competitive environment, however, steel producers were not able to pass these added costs on to customers in the form of price increases. Domestic steel prices remained essentially constant in absolute dollars from 1981 to

TABLE 4

Employment and Productivity in the U.S. Steel Industry

Year	Total Employment	Number of Wage Earners	Number of Salary Workers	Productivity[a]
1945	515,003	438,825	76,178	.182
1950	592,261	503,309	88,952	.192
1955	624,764	519,145	105,619	.225
1960	574,552	449,888	121,664	.221
1965	583,851	458,539	125,312	.287
1970	531,196	403,115	128,081	.324
1975	457,162	339,945	117,217	.343
1980	398,829	291,483	107,346	.384
1981	390,914	286,219	104,695	.422
1982	289,437	198,477	90,960	.376
1983	242,745	168,852	73,893	.501
1984	236,002	170,694	65,308	.542
1985	208,168	150,906	57,262	.584
1986	174,783	128,418	46,365	.635
1987	163,338	120,865	42,473	.738
1988	168,897	125,289	43,608	.798
1989	168,853	124,218	44,635	.788
1990	163,963	119,683	44,280	.826
1991	146,140	105,045	41,095	.836

Source: AISI; Annual Statistical Reports, various years.

[a] Equals total yearly production divided by the total number of wage earners.

1991 (McManus 1992) reflecting oversupply in the world market. Without the ability to compensate higher costs with higher prices, integrated steelmakers' income declined significantly in the early 1980s as shown in Table 3. From 1976 through 1985, the average integrated producer's common stock price fell by nearly 50% while the average New York Stock Exchange share rose by about 30% (Barnett and Crandall 1986: 14). Since 1977, 25 steel companies have filed for Chapter 11 banruptcy protection including such established companies as Wheeling Pittsburgh (1985) and LTV Steel (1986), the nation's second largest steel company. This financial trouble was not limited to firms in the integrated sector. In 1985-86 alone, five minimill plants went bankrupt and closed down. Between 1982 and 1986, 19 of the 59 minimill plants had changed ownership (Arthur 1990:150). Some minimill companies, however, such as Nucor Steel, were able to operate at a profit even during this period.

Under the financial conditions described above, it was obviously difficult for large steel firms to generate funds for much needed capital improvements which they had failed to make prior to the 1980s. In 1983, for example, only 32% of the total raw steel production in the U.S. was produced using continuous casting (a process which significantly reduces production costs), compared with 86% in Japan and an average of 61% in Europe.

Changes in ownership patterns. Lacking the internal funds to support their much needed technological investments, U.S. steel firms have increasingly moved toward joint ventures with foreign (especially Japanese) steel companies and investors in the 1980s. At present, every major U.S. integrated steel company, except Bethlehem Steel, is involved in at least one joint activity with a Japanese partner.[4] Examples include USX and Pohand Iron and Steel Company, Ltd. (S. Korea, 1986); National Intergroup and Nippon Kokan Steel (Japan, 1986); Inland Steel and Nippon Steel (Japan, 1987 and 1990); LTV and Sumitomo Metal (Japan, 1986) (Smith 1991:53). These ventures provide U.S. steelmakers with much needed new capital and technology, while foreign steelmakers gain access to both protected U.S. markets and domestic and foreign steel customers.

Unlike in the auto industry, the presence of Japanese ownership in the steel industry has not been associated with a move toward increasing the nonunion sector of the industry. In part, this may be because, unlike the auto industry, all of the Japanese investment to date in the integrated sector has taken the form of joint ventures with unionized U.S. steelmakers where the USWA still has a substantial amount of bargaining power. There have been no "greenfield" integrated steelmaking facilities built in the U.S. by either U.S. or Japanese steel companies since Bethlehem Steel's Burns Harbor plant in 1962.[5]

Response by Steelworkers Union

As an institution, the United Steelworkers of America also underwent a number of changes in the 1980s. The USWA lost 494,000 members between 1979 and 1983 alone and moved from the fourth largest union in the U.S. in 1979 to the ninth largest in 1988 with about 730,000 members (Gilford 1990). The AFL-CIO reports dues-paying steelworker membership at 459,000 in 1991, down from 1,062,000 in 1975 (AFL-CIO 1991). As the number of dues paying members declined, so did the union's ability to support its staff of 1,460 (Hoerr 1988:369). Many of the older union employees took advantage of an early retirement program which reportedly reduced the union employment 25%

overall and 50% in the Pittsburgh headquarters (*Industry Week* June 1, 1987:28).

In response to declining membership in steel and other related industries, the USWA has stepped up its organizing and other activities to attract new members. They added 75 full-time district organizers to the 25 on the payroll in 1984 and further diversified their membership to include hospital and food workers, cab drivers, security guards and paramedics (*Wall Street Journal* May 23, 1991:1). They also attempted to attract associate members and began offering a steelworkers' credit card to USWA members. These new organizing efforts appear to be showing some results. USWA membership increased by 40,000 members between 1983 and 1988 (Katz and Kochan 1992). The future of the union, however, still depends on the fate of blue-collar workers in steel and other industries. Office and technical jobs constitute only about 6% of union membership (*Wall Street Journal* May 23, 1991:1).

In the midst of this industry downturn, the Steelworkers elected their fifth president, Lynn Williams, in 1984. Williams had taken over for the previous USWA president, Lloyd McBride, who died during his term of office in 1983. In the election the following year, he defeated Frank McKee in a fairly close election. Williams, a Canadian, actually got fewer votes than McKee in the U.S. but won overwhelmingly in Canada, which represents about 20% of the USWA's total membership.

Coming into office in the midst of the downsizing in the steel industry, Williams' approach to the union presidency differed somewhat from his predecessors. In part because of his background in the Canadian labor movement, he has tended to take a more "internationalist" and long-term perspective—emphasizing political action and long-term industry policy in addition to more short-term bargaining issues (Hoerr 1988:411). This perspective is illustrated in the international's position toward plant closings and dislocated workers. The USWA position is that since the company is responsible for managing the business and government is responsible for managing the overall economy in which the plant closing occurred, they (not the union) should bear the major social responsibility for assisting displaced workers (U.S. Department of Labor 1989:48).

The Steelworkers' experience with plant closing illustrates some of the problems with government policies in this area. Since 1983 the USWA has had a contract provision calling for a 90-day notice of a plant or department closing including a 30-day period for the USWA "to review and propose an alternative to closure." In practice, however, steel companies, particularly U.S. Steel, have been reluctant to formally announce the closing of a plant until long after the plant had been operationally shut down. Formally declaring a plant closed triggers expensive pension, severance, and other benefits and has implications for the company in terms of taxes (i.e. depreciation) and stock prices. In the meantime, however, steelworkers who have been unemployed for years are considered on "temporary" layoff, have exhausted their unemployment benefits, and are not eligible for job search or retraining assistance from the JTPA or Trade Adjustment Assistance programs (U.S. Dept. of Labor 1989). USWA-initiated programs have attempted to deal with these problems by gaining the support of company and government agencies when they occur (before official notice).

In terms of bargaining, Williams has shown two faces to company negotiators seeking contract changes (Hoerr 1988:408-14; *Business Week* October 5, 1984:154-56). For those perceived to be taking advantage of the current situation to exploit or eliminate the union, Williams has shown himself to be a tough, pragmatic negotiator—leading a corporate campaign against the Phelps-Dodge cooper company and sanctioning strikes against Wheeling-Pittsburgh and USX. In other situations (where union security doesn't appear at risk), Williams has demonstrated a considerable amount of flexibility and innovation in working out new compromises with steel companies. An open supporter of effective labor-management cooperation, he has provided leadership for the Steelworkers' advances in this area at companies such as LTV and National Steel. The union's role in these new cooperative initiatives is discussed below.

An additional response by unionized workers to the financial difficulties of their plants and companies in the 1980s has been to increase their ownership share in these firms. By early 1988, USWA members owned substantial stock (though less than 15%) in Wheeling-Pittsburgh, Bethlehem, LTV Steel, and Kaiser Aluminum. Companies like Weirton, Northwestern Steel and Wire, McCluth Steel, and others became employee owned through employee stock ownership plans (ESOPs) (Hoerr 1988:453). In most companies where the USW negotiated an ESOP, it also demanded a voice in the company's policy making at all levels of decision making, including a seat on the board of directors.

Effects of Industry Reactions to Crisis—Post-1985 "Recovery"?

By the mid- to late 1980s, the actions taken by industry firms and their unions, combined with a modest economic recovery, began to show some positive economic results. For example, the dramatic cuts in steel capacity and a modest upturn in the demand for domestic steel products boosted capacity utilization rates to an average of close to 80% since 1985 (compared to the 62% average utilization rate from 1980 to 1985). The financial picture for the industry also improved significantly in the second half of the 1980s. Table 3 shows that steel companies in the aggregate had positive net income figures in 1987 (for the first time in five years) and again in 1989 and 1990.

Perhaps more importantly from the point of view of a long-term recovery, steel industry modernization and productivity figures had increased substantially by the late 1980s. For example, Table 3 shows that the percent of U.S. steel production cast using continuous casting had increased from 29% in 1982 to nearly 76% in 1991. Some of this change reflects additional investment in technology by firms—particularly in the minimill sector whose added capacity during this period uses all continuous casting. Some of this increase in the use of continuous casting also reflects the closing of plants with older technology. The pattern of plant closings is described in more detail below.

The increased use of continuous casting and other technological and industrial relations changes has been associated with a rapid increase in labor productivity in the 1980s. As shown in Table 4, yearly production per wage earner in the steel industry more than doubled between 1980 and 1991—from 383 tons per year in 1980 to 836 in 1991.[6] These increases mean that U.S. productivity in terms of labor hours per ton is now equal to, if not exceeding, that of major competitors in Japan and Europe.

Summary of Effects of Environmental Changes

At the beginning of the 1990s, the U.S. steel industry appears to be in a reasonably stable position compared to its position a decade earlier. The industry continues to face, however, a number of challenges (discussed in the concluding section of the chapter), and it is still too soon to conclude that a full "recovery" has been achieved.

What is clear is that the structure of the industry has been transformed by the economic and other environmental changes in the 1980s. As noted above, the industry lost over half of its total employment and one-quarter of its capacity during the period. The steel industry's centralized, oligopolistic structure also appears to have eroded significantly. Minimills now control a large portion of the steel market with a potential to grow even larger. U.S. Steel, once the stabilizing leader of the industry, now depends on the oil and gas industry for the majority of its income and sales. Instead of a highly centralized industry with standardized outcomes and practices which characterized the industry throughout much of the postwar period, the current period is increasingly being characterized by diversity and experimentation.

These company and plant-level differences became apparent in the patterns of plant closings in the industry as firms were forced to choose which facilities to shut down. In her study of steel industry plant closures between 1977 and 1987, Deilly (1991) found that steel firms were most likely to close small plants, plants whose products competed directly with minimills or sold products to contracting industries, plants without electric-arc furnaces, as well as those plants whose coastal location made them particularly vulnerable to steel imports. Deilly (1991) also found firm differences in their propensity to close plants, controlling for other factors.

These intercompany and interplant differences had a profound effect on the centralized industrywide industrial relations structures and uniform policies of the previous period. We turn next to the specific industrial relations implications of the economic changes and steel industry restructuring in the 1980s.

Effect of Environmental Changes on Industrial Relations Structures and Collective Bargaining Outcomes

Table 5 shows the aggregate wage and benefit outcomes in the U.S. steel industry since 1945. As can be seen from this table, wage increases accelerated rapidly in the industry in the 1970s under the ENA but slowed considerably in the 1980s with the first-ever wage decreases in the industry occurring in 1983 and 1984 and then recovering somewhat in the late 1980s. The 47% increase in absolute hourly earnings in the steel industry between 1979 and 1991 lagged behind the all manufacturing increase of 54% and the 63.6% increase in the CPI. It was also considerably less than the increases in comparable industries such as autos and mining which had hourly wage increases of 69% and 67%, respectively, during this period. (BLS, *Employment and Earnings*, various years). Even with this real wage decrease during the 1980s, however, steel industry hourly earnings remained the highest among the durable goods producers in 1991 (ibid.).[7]

As shown in Table 5, employment costs (both hourly and salaried) have historically accounted for 35% to 40% of total costs.[8] Because of productivity increases and other cutbacks, the percent of employment costs to total costs has decreased to about 28% (or about 20% for hourly workers). This trend would suggest that the focus on further labor cost reduction as a primary source of cost cutting may be decreasing. In addition, Table 5 indicates that the percentage of the employment cost for hourly workers accounted for by employee benefits increased sharply in 1982 and has remained at approximately 40% since that time, reflecting both increased health insurance costs, as well as employee retirement and pension obligations.

TABLE 5
U.S. Steel Industry Wages and Benefits, 1945-1991

Year	Total Hourly Employment Cost[a,b]	Base Wage[a,c]	Percent Benefits[d]	Employment Cost[e] as a Percent of Total Cost
1945	9.91	9.08	8.2	NA
1950	10.79	9.49	11.9	NA
1955	13.82	12.10	12.7	36.4
1960	17.58	14.22	19.0	NA
1965	19.37	14.49	25.0	38.6
1970	19.90	14.88	25.4	41.0
1973	23.56	17.45	25.9	37.0
1975	26.80	18.30	31.8	37.0
1979	29.87	20.67	30.8	35.3
1980	30.50	20.02	34.3	37.3
1981	30.20	20.12	33.4	36.0
1982	33.55	19.84	40.9	38.0
1983	30.36	18.63	38.7	31.6
1984	27.92	18.00	35.5	30.6
1985	28.88	18.07	37.4	29.1
1986	28.89	18.18	37.1	25.9
1987	28.42	17.42	38.7	29.9
1988	28.37	16.91	40.4	28.0
1989	27.03	16.47	39.1	27.4
1990	26.70	16.39	38.6	27.6
1991	27.64	16.56	40.1	28.6

Source: AISI, Annual Statistical Reports, various years.

[a] CPI adjusted, 1991 dollars.

[b] Total hourly employment cost equals base wage plus other payroll costs (i.e., vacation pay, pay for holidays not worked, profit sharing, gain sharing, stock plans, etc.), plus employee benefits cost per hour (active and retired employees).

[c] Base wage defined as pay for hours worked including standard hourly wage rate, incentive pay, shift differentials, Sunday, holiday, and overtime premiums.

[d] Benefit costs include those for active as well as retired employees.

[e] Employment cost equals total employment cost for both hourly and salaried employees.

These wage and benefit outcomes, however, provide only a partial indication of the extent of industrial relations changes that have occurred in the industry in the 1980s. Underlying these outcomes have been a series of institutional and structural changes in the industry which represent a radical departure from the traditional industrial system described earlier. We argue that it is these structural changes, rather than any particular collective bargaining outcome, that signal a fundamental transformation in industrial relations in the industry.

Institutional IR Changes

Breakdown of wage standards. The 1980 bargaining round was the last time that all nine major U.S. producers bargained together for a uniform, nonconcessionary agreement with the USWA. These negotiations produced two notable changes: First, the parties decided not to renew the ENA for future negotiating rounds. Second, the parties agreed to establish an experimental program of "labor-management participation teams" (LMPTs) designed to deal with job-related issues at the plant level that were not covered by the contract and to encourage increased productivity.

Under increasing environmental pressures described above, wage standards began to erode quickly following the 1980 bargaining round. The first "off-pattern" agreements were negotiated with the USWA in firms that had filed for bankruptcy under Chapter 11—McLouth Steel and Penn-Dixie Steel (later renamed Continental Steel). The McLouth agreement, signed in 1982, reduced hourly labor costs to $17, or about $6 less than that called for in the prevailing master contract in the industry. The Penn-Dixie agreement undercut the master contract by about $2 per hour. Other firms followed quickly. Wheeling-Pittsburgh received wage cuts of $1 per hour. Smaller steelmakers, many of whom competed with minimills, also asked for (and eventually received) wage cuts.

By agreeing to these "off-pattern" wage settlements, the USWA obviously put itself into a very difficult position. It was clear that these agreements would eventually undercut the competitive position of other steel companies which would soon be demanding similar reductions. The union's research department recognized that there was overcapacity in the industry and that some of that capacity would have to be eliminated if the industry was going to remain healthy. However, as Hoerr (1988:63-70) describes, the USWA, under the leadership of Lloyd McBride, faced a number of dilemmas in dealing with financially weak steel companies. McBride feared that in the absence of concessions these firms would not be shut down but would instead be sold to new buyers who would attempt to reopen the plant with low-cost, nonunion labor. There had been a number of examples of this already in the industry. Secondly, the employees at the local plants themselves voted for the wage concessions to keep their mill and jobs alive. The international, rightly or wrongly, was understandably reluctant to tell these workers that they would have to sacrifice their jobs for future good of the industry and the union.

Soon the wage concessions spread to the basic steel contract. The 1983 national agreement included a pay cut of $1.25 an hour which was to be restored in three annual installments over the life of the contract. The COLA provision, while retained in the contract, was sharply reduced. In addition, the contract included reductions in holidays, vacations, and Sunday premiums. In return for these concessions by the union, the steel companies agreed to reinvest labor-cost savings in steel facilities, make "good faith" efforts to curb subcontracting, and increase their payments in the supplemental unemployment benefit (SUB) fund by 50 cents per hour (BNA 1987:18, 239).

End of coordinated bargaining. In 1985, partly in recognition of different wage settlements in the industry, the last vestiges of institutional coordinated bargaining broke down. On May 2 the industry leaders decided unanimously not to continue bargaining as a group. Instead, each company would bargain separately with the USWA (*Business Week* May 20, 1985). This decision by the steel companies represented both the divergence of interest that had developed between steel companies as well as the growing disillusionment among many of the companies with the bargaining leadership of U.S. Steel, which had begun to develop highly visible antagonistic relations with the USWA. National Steel, the first company to break from coordinated bargaining, was trying to forge a more cooperative relationship with the USWA and did not want to have their fate determined by USX negotiators (Hoerr 1988). In addition, USX, now a diversified oil company, was in a better position to take a strike than others such as Inland or Bethlehem Steel, who remained dependent on the steel industry (Hoerr 1988:474-76).

The USWA, while not anxious to see the end of coordinated bargaining, had already acknowledged company differences through their earlier policy on concessions for "distressed" firms. In recognition of these differences, it changed the way in which its contracts were ratified. In the past, the master contract had been voted on by the Basic Steel Industry Conference (BSIC) which is made up of local presidents. In the January 1986 meeting of the BSIC, it was decided that beginning that year, contracts would be ratified by a direct vote of the members of the firm covered by the contract.

The impact of these changes soon became clear. First, in July 1985, there was a strike/lockout at Wheeling-Pittsburgh, which was in bankruptcy at the time. It was the first authorized work stoppage in the industry since 1959. The strike lasted until October 1985, when the sides settled on an employment rate of $18 per hour, about $5 below the industry average. In return, the union gained a substantial say in the company through stock ownership and direct participation at every level of company decision making (see Hoerr 1988:461-63).

Next, LTV, National, Inland, Armco, and Bethlehem Steel all agreed to early negotiations before the 1986 deadline. Only USX refused early negotiations. Negotiations began with LTV Steel, the second largest U.S. steel company, which included plants formerly owned by Jones and Laughlin Steel and Republic Steel. This agreement set an unofficial "standard" for the other firms. The agreement consisted of cuts in wages and benefits of $3.60 per hour and a guarantee by the union to help to improve productivity. Instead of repaying concessions in guaranteed scheduled wage increases, the new agreement called for increases to take the form of profit sharing or preferred stock. This type of payment formula further opened the door for increased variation in wages across steel industry firms.

At Armco the union went even further in rejecting the uniform wage pattern by negotiating separate contracts with each of the five plants owned by the company. The result was that wage settlements varied from no wage increases at the Middletown and Ashland facilities to a $3.25 decrease at the Baltimore plant. According to one USWA official, the different outcomes at these plants "takes into account different competitive realities at each of the company's locations" (BNA 1992:18, 242).

National Steel and USX

Nowhere were the differences between steel companies as apparent as between National Steel and USX. The 1986 negotiations with National Steel resulted in a 39-month contract (labeled a "cooperative partnership") that reduced wages and benefits by $1.50 an hour and opened the door to radical changes in job definitions and work rules while at the same time providing employees with an employment security guarantee for the life of the contract and an unprecedented degree of information and problem-solving involvement at all levels of the company.

In contrast, negotiations with USX resulted in a six-month lockout/ strike. At issue was the company's demand to get wage and work rule concessions similar to the other financially troubled steel firms, while not giving in to the union's demand for a National Steel-type agreement on employment security and information sharing. In particular, the sides disagreed strongly on contracting-out rules at the plants. The final agreement, ratified in January 1987, was a compromise settlement similar to that negotiated earlier with other steel companies. The company received some of the wage relief it was demanding and an agreement to eliminate more than 1,300 union jobs. The union got some of the contracting-out restrictions it was looking for as well as improved early retirement benefits. The four-year agreement was not set to expire until 1991, compared to a 1989 expiration date for contracts signed with most of the other steel firms.

What explains these different outcomes? U.S. Steel and National Steel represent opposite ends of the spectrum of labor relations approaches in the steel industry, yet many of their actions in response to the steel crisis in the early 1980s were similar. Both companies cut back their existing work force significantly in the early 1980s. Both companies also went through corporate reorganizations in which the company's steel division became independent from the other holdings of the corporation.

In spite of these similarities, the companies differed in terms of the way that they managed their corporate downsizing and reorganization. Hoerr (1988:426-29), for example, describes the often brutal way in which salaried employees at U.S. Steel were dismissed with no consultation or advance notice. There were reports of some universities "blackballing" USX recruiters because of the company's reputation in dealing with their managers. In laying off unionized employees, there were also a number of management decisions that soured relations between the union and management, including USX's decision to try to import steel slabs from British Steel, their strong insistence on contracting out bargaining unit work, and their apparent backtracking on agreements with the union to keep plants open if certain conditions were met (see Chap. 16).

More than anything, these management decisions and the differences between National and USX had to do with different management philosophies reflected by the leadership of the firms. The leadership of USX, including CEO David Roderick, U.S. Steel President Thomas

Graham, and Industrial Relations Vice President and chief negotiator Bruce Johnson, was from the "old school" of labor relations which treated unions as adversaries and viewed even limited cooperation with skepticism at best. As Hoerr (1988:440) states: "The idea of power-sharing with the union ran counter to U.S. Steel's ideology and concept of good management practice."

In contrast, National Steel CEO Pete Love decided in 1981 that a fundamental change in corporate culture would be needed. In 1984, in part to begin to try to establish a different type of relationship with the union, National was the first of the integrated companies to pull out of coordinated bargaining. The top company negotiator, Stanley Ellspermann, began informal problem-solving meetings with the union in December 1984, in which the company and the union began to discuss difficult issues of work restructuring and employment security. Although the parties faced a number of large hurdles to overcome along the way, the relationships and processes that developed in these ongoing meetings set the stage for the eventual cooperative partnership agreement in 1986 (Ball et al. 1989).

1989 Contract: Return to "Pattern"?

As noted earlier, the steel industry experienced a modest recovery in 1987-89, with the steel companies reporting a positive net income in 1987 for the first time in seven years. The year 1989 was also relatively profitable for U.S. steelmakers with an aggregate net income in excess of $1.5 billion for the industry (see Table 3). Within this context, the Steelworkers were intent on restoring the wage and benefit cuts that had been made in the 1986 round and requested early negotiations with the steel companies. In May, the Steelworkers reached an agreement with Bethlehem Steel Corp. on a 50-month contract which restored wages to their pre-1986 levels as well as the restoration of holidays and Sunday premium pay. Profit sharing was continued as well as new provisions on family care leave and "excessive" overtime. In addition, the plan calls for the return of a cost-of-living clause, called an "inflation recognition payment plan," a quarterly adjustment of 1% for each 1% rise above 3% in the Consumer Price Index. In the event that the company is not profitable, adjustment will be paid with stocks (BNA 1990a:18, 244).

The Bethlehem contract also included an innovative career development program which was to be financed by company contributions of

$300,000 per month. This program was joined later by National, Inland, Armco, and USX who agreed to share in the funding (at somewhat lesser monthly amounts) and to jointly administer the program with the union. As stated in an appendix to the 1989 Bethlehem-USWA agreement, the purpose of the program is to provide "support services for the education, training, and personal development" of employees, including basic skills training, in order to enhance workers' "ability to absorb craft and noncraft training, their ability to progress in the workplace, and their ability to perform their assigned work tasks to the full extent of their potential, and their knowledge and understanding of the workplace, and of new and innovative work systems." (BNA, 1990b:16, 64.)

The agreements with the rest of the companies, including those with LTV in 1990 and USX in 1991, followed the "pattern" set by the Bethlehem agreement. This return to an industry-level contract pattern gives rise to the question of whether the changes and decentralization that we observed in the industry were really just temporary adjustments rather than a fundamental "transformation" in the industry (Kochan, Katz, and McKersie 1986; Ready 1990; Cappelli 1990). Certainly, some of the features of the changes in the early 1980s, such as different wage and benefit outcomes across integrated mills and the elimination of the COLA, appear to have been reversed in the latest contracts. The forces of centralization and standardization, discussed at the beginning of the chapter, continue to be strong in the U.S. steel industry for both union and management.

We believe, however, that these similarities in collective bargaining outcomes at the firm level belie a large amount of industrial relations diversity at the plant level. Instead of one dominant industrial relations pattern for the industry, there appears to be a series of patterns emerging for plants whose products compete in different segments of the industry's market with different levels of product market competition and technology changes.

The Battle Over Plant-Level Work Restructuring at USX's Gary Works[9]

Given this new, more decentralized approach to management and industrial relations, it is becoming increasingly apparent that some of the most fundamental and radical changes from the traditional industrial relations system in the steel industry are occurring at the individual plant level. Across the industry, job and work restructuring has been accomplished on a plant-by-plant basis. Thus the plant-level work organization has become in many ways the new "battleground" for industrial relations restructuring in the steel industry. The following changes occurring at the Gary Works of the U.S. Steel Division of USX illustrate both the extent of work restructuring in steel as well as the problems and challenges faced by the parties in implementing these changes.

History of changes. The Gary Works, built in 1906, is the principal integrated steelmaking facility of the U.S. Steel Division of USX. Since 1980 the company spent approximately $1 billion to upgrade technology, including a changeover to 100% continuous casting on the steel producing side of the mill and upgrades and computer controls in many other areas of the mill. As a result, despite the plant's age, its process technology is among the most advanced in the industry. Work restructuring can be seen as part of this overall effort to effectively utilize the latest manufacturing process technology in order to compete effectively in the new steel industry product market environment.

Labor and management approached the work reorganization issue at both the functional (collective bargaining) and workplace levels. The 1987 collective bargaining agreement between U.S. Steel and the USWA mandated the "remanning" of all plants within the U.S. Steel Division. In essence, remanning represented an agreement to renegotiate the 30-year-old work structuring agreement (the CWS) by reexamining the content of every job and realigning job structures to achieve greater efficiency. The contract specified that remanning was to be accomplished between February 1 and June 30, 1987, eliminating 268 jobs on the steel processing side of Gary Works and another 123 jobs in the finishing mills. An implementation committee was established, consisting of three local management and three local union appointees, to implement the realignments specified in the contract.

Like many local unions (and management groups), the leaders of USWA Local 1014, which represents 4200 production and maintenance workers on the "steel-producing side" of the Gary Works, approached the remanning task with a great deal of distrust and skepticism. Nevertheless, despite resistance from both local labor and management, there were important motivations for reaching an agreement on work restructuring at this plant—most notably, the threat of job loss in the absence of change. Employees at Gary Works had recently witnessed massive layoffs at both Gary Works and South Works, a connected U.S. Steel facility. At its peak, Gary Works employed 25,000 people; by 1988 it employed only 7,800, including management and union personnel. South Works is now completely closed. An additional motivation was the threat of a potentially unfavorable arbitration decision (for both sides) concerning the job restructuring issue should the parties not agree on their own.

Nature of changes. Work restructuring at the Gary Works has resulted in realigned production and maintenance job structures, the creation of the team leader position, and changes in the supervisory structures. Production job restructuring has largely involved the combination of existing jobs into one through job elimination and the reallocation of tasks. One exception is the equipment tender position which combines maintenance and operator responsibilities. This position thus blurs the clear distinction between production and maintenance work, a hallmark of the traditional IR system institutionalized by the CWS. Union opposition to this type of restructuring has been strong. Currently there are still no equipment tender positions on the steel-producing side of the Gary Works (although some equipment tenders exist on the finishing side of the mill).

In addition to production jobs, maintenance job structures have also undergone substantial changes which are designed to increase the ability and authority of maintenance workers to perform a wider variety of tasks. In doing so, these changes have blurred the distinct craft demarcations embedded in the traditional workplace system. At U.S. Steel's Gary Works, expanded craft positions include the millwright (expanded), motor inspector (expanded), ironworker, systems repairman, and mechanical and hydraulic repairman job titles. According to a Gary Works management representative, the objective in creating these new positions is to broaden the job content, responsibility, and skills of maintenance workers and to reduce the reliance on their specific crafts in which labor shortages may exist. In exchange, new positions are compensated at higher rates of pay, based on the assigned job classifications of new versus original positions. These changes are described in Table 6.

Movement to one of these expanded craft positions requires greater skill and responsibility as well as expansion in the task content of jobs. As shown in Table 6, the "employment training and experience" element of the job increased in 89% of the restructured jobs. Mental skills requirements as well as other job responsibilities also increased in most cases. These changes have important implications for the type of new employee skills and training that will be required in the industry in the wake of technological change and work restructuring.

The team leader. One of the most dramatic changes in traditional steel industry job structures found at Gary is the creation of the position

TABLE 6

Requirements for Advancement
to Expanded Craft Positions from Existing Positions

Original Position JC[°]		Expanded Position JC[°]		Factor Class's[°°] Which are Increased	Factor Class's[°°] Which are Decreased
Welder	14	Ironworker	19	2,3,5,6,8,12	
Rigger	14			2,3,4,5,6,9,11	
Boilermaker	15			2,3,5,6,8,11	
Instrument Repairman	16	Systems Repairman	20	2,3,5,7,8,12	
Electronics Repairman	18			5,7	
Machinist	16	Mechanical and Hydraulic	19	2,7,8,10,11,12	5
Millwright- Expanded	16	Repairman		2,3,6,8	
Motor Inspector	14	Motor Inspector- Expanded	16	2,3,4,6	
Millwright	14	Millwright- Expanded	16	2,4,5,6,9	

[°] Job classification number based on classification in the 1963 USWA Job Classification Manual for original positions; and negotiated job descriptions/classifications supplied by USWA Local Union 1014 in 1989 for expanded positions.

[°°] Factor classifications are identified below.

Factor	Percent of Expanded Positions with Increase	Percent of Expanded Positions with Decrease
2. Employment training and experience	89	
3. Mental skill	67	
4. Manual skill	33	
5. Responsibility for materials	67	11
6. Responsibility for tools and equipment	67	
7. Responsibility for operations	22	
8. Responsibility for the safety of others	56	
9. Mental effort	22	
10. Physical effort	11	
11. Surroundings	33	
12. Hazards	33	

Source: Union Interviews, USX Gary Works, 1989; Published Job Descriptions supplied by USWA Local Union 1014 in 1989; Job Classification Manual, USWA, 1963.

of team leader. This is an entirely new bargaining unit position which effectively assigns supervisory responsibility and authority in all areas except discipline to a production or maintenance worker. According to the 1987 collective bargaining agreement, "A Team Leader shall be responsible to lead the overall task execution by the work team, perform administrative functions and participate in hands-on performance of his team's work." Compensation is set at three job classifications above the highest classified job in the seniority unit over which the team leader exercises leadership. Team leaders have the advantages and contractual protection associated with union membership while at the same time assuming the authority and responsibility associated with shopfloor management.

Again, this change represents a radical departure from traditional job structures in steel which emphasized a sharp distinction between supervisory and bargaining unit work and authority. It effectively transfers traditional supervisory functions to a new union position.

Supervisory and managerial restructuring. Along with the creation of the team leader position, Gary Works has also been adjusting managerial structures. During the 1980s, supervisory structures, which had not been significantly changed since the early twentieth century, have been or are in the process of being substantially altered. According to a union representative, prior to 1980 the ratio of supervisory to production and maintenance personnel was approximately 1:7; it is now approximately 1:25.

As shown in Table 7, the plant remains organized into levels of supervision that include plant, division, department, and seniority unit levels. The number of management positions, however, in each of these levels has been reduced in an effort to reduce costs and improve the responsiveness of various channels of decision-making authority within and between each level of supervision in the plant. Because the heaviest supervision has traditionally existed at the level of the shopfloor (the seniority unit), it is this level which has been most radically affected by recent efforts at restructuring supervision. As shown in Table 7, the changes dissolve approximately four levels of shopfloor supervision into one position, the front line manager.

Resistance to change. Despite joint labor and management involvement in this massive work restructuring effort, implementation has been met with a great deal of resistance. In part, this is a result of a history of conflict and mistrust at the plant. According to a management representative, "The

TABLE 7
Managerial Hierarchy Before and After Restructuring

Pre-1980	1989
(PLANT) Plant Superintendent Assistant Plant Superintendent	(PLANT) Plant Manager
(DIVISION) Superintendent (for each division) Assistant Superintendent	(DIVISION) Division Manager (for each division)
(DEPARTMENT) Superintendent (for each department) Assistant Superintendent	(DEPARTMENT) Department Manager (for each department)
(SENIORITY UNIT) General Foreman Relief Foreman Vicing Foreman Shopfloor Foreman	(SENIORITY UNIT) Front Line Manager (for each seniority unit)

Source: Management Interviews at US Steel's Gary Works, 1989.

Gary Works has always been looked at as the toughest place in U.S. Steel to work in labor relations because the unions are so aggressive." Other union officials talked about a strong distrust of management, especially at the corporate level. According to one, "U.S. Steel is not an honorable company. Its industrial relations policy is the same as it was 30 to 40 years ago. I don't think that they care about their employees or that they can be trusted."

Amid an atmosphere of distrust, broadening the tasks performed by production and maintenance workers is seen by some as another form of "speed-up" which poses significant safety risks to workers as well as changing the wage-effort bargain (see e.g., Parker and Slaughter 1988). Similarly, there is evidence that the team leader position has created new friction on the shopfloor. USWA agreements forbid one worker from testifying against another. Thus the team leader is put in an uncomfortable spot when asked to testify against a worker involved in a shopfloor grievance. Finally, and perhaps most importantly, there has been strong resistance from supervisory personnel who are especially vulnerable to job loss due to the restructuring and yet have been called upon to oversee many of these changes.

Clearly, some resistance would be expected in any change effort of this magnitude. The especially strong resistance at this plant, however, provides a good illustration of the link between the strategic and workplace levels of industrial relations in this industry. Much of this mistrust toward these changes by the union appears to be directed at the corporate or strategic level of the company. Union officials cited strategic decisions by USX to close down plants even after the employees have engaged in pay concessions and work restructuring as evidence of the company's lack of commitment to steelworkers.

Which Industrial Relations Model?

The Gary Works case described above is significant because it represents a model of industrial relations changes and work restructuring in the steel industry that attempts to limit the involvement of the Steelworkers Union. The question in the 1990s is no longer whether or not some form of workplace restructuring will take place. The environmental, technological, and product market changes described earlier have necessitated changes in the traditional industrial relations system in steel. The breakdown of traditional institutional structures signifies that these changes will likely be both profound and long lasting. The important remaining question in steel is what will be the role of the union in both shaping these changes and in operating within this transformed industrial relations system.

In answering this question, the comparison between the approaches of National Steel and U.S. Steel is again instructive because they represent very different paths to achieving industrial relations restructuring. The approach used at USX in the 1980s was to drive productivity improvement and work force reductions by invoking its managerial right to close unprofitable plants and operations and using its relatively strong bargaining power to implement work restructuring in the form of job combinations, "remanning," and contracting out. The local union has been placed in a traditional reactive position of resisting these changes through the strike, grievance and arbitration mechanisms (in the case of contracting out and remanning), and resistance at the workplace level.

It now appears within the industry, however, that further gains in productivity and especially quality cannot be easily achieved simply by cutting additional employees. Instead, there is some indication that even USX now sees cooperation as the way to achieve additional quality and productivity gains (Miles 1989). Their approach to employee cooperation, however, appears to be consistent with their earlier position on restructuring. As stated in a recent *Business Week* article (Miles 1989:151):

> Instead of working with the union, USX is mounting a management-driven strategy to build worker involvement outside of the union contract. The point: to go around top USWA leaders and form alliances directly with workers . . . Says one top USX insider, "We've screened the International out. We want worker cooperation, but we don't want to broker it through the union."

Under this scenario, the Steelworkers Union would have little involvement and control over the process of industrial relations changes at the plant level. An appeal of this path is that it requires the least amount of change for both union and management. While the outcomes of collective bargaining and the structures under which the parties interact may differ significantly from previous periods, the nature of the relationship is essentially unchanged.

Against this backdrop, the National Steel Cooperative Partnership model stands out in dramatic relief. Here the union plays a vital and active role in shaping future restructuring in the steel industry. The Cooperative Partnership (CP) model consists of a set of changes in the union-management relationship which spans all three tiers of the industrial relations system discussed earlier. Like the management-initiated change model at USX, the CP model includes extensive work restructuring and job combinations, as well as the increased use of profit sharing and gains-sharing compensation. The difference between the CP model and the model used at USX is that in exchange for these "concessions" in the CP model, the union gets employment security over the life of the contract and an unprecedented level of information sharing and influence over managerial decisions (Ball et al. 1989).

Employee and union involvement is achieved in the collective bargaining contract through the establishment of joint labor-management cooperation committees with equal numbers of management and union members at corporate, division, and departmental levels. As stated in a 1986 Memorandum of Understanding on the Cooperative Partnership:

> [T]he parties have committed themselves to a set of relationships in which the company will share information with the union about the business, including, among other things, investment plans, marketing plans, cost performance, and financial

results. In addition, the union will be allowed input to major decisions before those decisions are made.

Thus these new labor-management committees structures are designed to be both information-sharing and decision-sharing vehicles—enabling the union to be an informed participant in policy decision making as opposed to reacting to the implementation of unilaterally imposed policies. USWA international leadership as well as the 120-member Wage Policy Committee (consisting of local union leaders) have taken a strong and fairly specific position on work restructuring and cooperation: They are willing to support work restructuring, profit sharing, and cooperation as long as it is negotiated as a package with the other changes that are part of the CP model. This position was articulated in a recent Wage Policy Committee statement concerning goals for the upcoming 1993 negotiations:

> In many enterprises, experience has shown that the task of management is far too important to be entrusted to the managers. Given a proper voice in management decisions, our members are much more likely to insure that the plant is run in such a way as to provide long-term employment security and a decent income for themselves and a fair profit for their employer. Workers have more at stake in that kind of outcome because their alternatives are so much more limited (BNA 1993:8, 656).

The position regarding union involvement in management in this document is not entirely new. It has its roots in some of the early SWOC writing on this topic in the 1930s and 1940s (e.g., Golden and Ruttenberg 1942).

Outcomes from the 1993 bargaining round with Inland Steel, Bethlehem Steel, and National Steel indicate that the union has been successful in negotiating CP-type agreements with all three companies. The new contracts are six-year agreements which include increased union participation at all levels of the company, including a new provision for a union-designated seat on the board of directors, in addition to a no-layoff provision and substantial increases in pension payments for senior workers (*New York Times* August 2, 1993:D1). In turn, the company secured the ability to continue to reduce its work force through attrition and to improve productivity by eliminating "restrictive" work rules and jurisdictional boundaries as well as some control over rising health care costs. As in the previous agreement with National Steel, the level of information sharing with the union concerning strategic business decisions is extensive. At Bethlehem, for example, a memorandum of agreement is reported to provide for union access to detailed business plans involving "products, pricing, markets, capital spending, short- and long-term cash flow forecasts, and the method and manner of funding or financing the business plan" (p. D1).

It is precisely this high level of union involvement that appears to be the sticking point in negotiations with USX, whose contract does not expire until January 1994, as well as with the smaller Armco Steel Co., where the parties agreed to continue working under the previous contract. Both Armco CEO, Thomas Graham (former head of USX's Steel division), and U.S. Steel's head, Thomas Usher, have been outspoken critics of the type of union involvement called for in the previous settlements. With the rest of the industry having settled, the pressure will be on USX to accept a similar type of agreement. Upcoming negotiations with USX will undoubtedly provide a test of the resolve of both sides on this issue.

While the institutional characteristics of the CP model appear to have spread across most of the industry, the success of this model and the nature and extent of union influence is still very much in doubt. As illustrated by the case of U.S. Steel's Gary Works, the contractual creation of plant-level union-management committees or even a seat on the board of directors does not in itself signify a transformed relationship in which the union becomes a true partner in shared decision making (e.g., Camlin, Scharf, and Walton 1993). Rather, the joint committee structure provides an opportunity or vehicle for a transformed labor-management relationship. We propose that the realization of this opportunity will depend on other factors such as those discussed below.

Challenges and Choices Facing Steel Industry Unions and Management in Achieving a New Labor-Management Partnership

Clearly, the transformation from an adversarial to a partnership relationship requires a fundamental change in the attitude and behaviors of both labor and management actors involved in the relationship (e.g., Cutcher-Gershenfeld 1991; Camlin et al. 1993). Equally important from our perspective, however, is the broader context or environment in which these changes are taking place and the strategic choices made by the parties in dealing with the changing competitive pressures in the industry. Stated differently, the successful adoption of the CP model depends on the ability of the plants and firms using this model to effectively compete within their chosen product markets.

Continued overcapacity and downsizing. While the industry emerged from the dramatic restructuring of the early 1980s with much more competitive and efficient operations, the industry is still highly vulnerable to a continued domestic economic recession. U.S. steel capacity still exceeds domestic consumption by some 20 million tons which indicates that unless something changes rather dramatically, further plant closings and capacity reductions will be necessary.

This continued threat of downsizing presents a number of threats to the emerging cooperative partnership programs. The crisis situation which surrounds downsizing generally increases management's bargaining leverage to force union acceptance of workplace reforms (such as the remanning at Gary) under the threat of a plant closure and job loss. Changes made under these conditions are unlikely to lead to real partnership arrangements and may engender a vicious cycle in which the lack of union involvement and commitment to these reforms decreases their effectiveness in improving plant performance (Cooke 1992). The lack of effectiveness puts the plant more at risk for closure. If the facility does eventually close or the work force is severely reduced, then it appears that union acceptance of the new partnership arrangement was misplaced, making further attempts at reform even more difficult.

We propose then that successful defusion of the CP model depends on the ability of union, management, and government decision makers to effectively manage further downsizing (or employment security) in the industry (see e.g., Smith 1991). This is a complex issue. As we have seen, the likelihood of any given plant or facility shutting down will depend on a number of factors including its age, size, location, plant layout and technology, competitive position vis-à-vis minimills, imports, and other integrated producers, as well as labor-management relations. In addition, national policy area choices with regard to foreign trade, technology development and investment, exchange rates, and employee training and placement are also critical. Thus an effective response to further employment adjustments will require a coordination of activities and policy choices by labor, management, and government decision makers across the three levels of the IR system described in Table 1 (see e.g., Katz and Kochan 1992:Chap. 15).

Centralization vs. decentralization. The breakdown of coordinated bargaining and the new company-level contract ratification procedure has opened the door to a much greater degree of decentralization in steel industry industrial relations than was possible in the past. While this decentralization can be seen as a positive development from the point of view of local autonomy and flexibility, there are dangers as well. Renewed intercompany competition over labor costs could lead to a downward spiraling bidding war over wages and benefits, which would be harmful from the point of view of steelworkers' living standards. In addition, we propose that the focus on reducing direct labor costs as a means to staying competitive in the industry creates significant barriers to achieving the kind of cooperative partnership described earlier. Wages and benefits are classic "distributive" labor-management bargaining issues (Walton and McKersie 1965). If these issues become the primary focus, then it seems inevitable that the traditional adversarial relationship will dominate—impeding other more cooperative adjustments (Kochan, Katz, and McKersie 1986). Thus some level of centralized coordination of collective bargaining outcomes in this area appears to be necessary for the cooperative model to flourish.

Pension costs. A related issue at the collective bargaining level is the need for steel firms and the USWA to deal with large pension liabilities and the growing costs of employee benefits such as health care and retirement. The steel industry tops the list of industries with underfunded pensions covered by the Pension Benefit Guarantee Corporation, with the formerly bankrupt LTV Steel Corporation topping the list with almost $3 billion in pension liabilities. Needless to say, these pension liabilities and retirement payments played a big part in the recent contract negotiations with LTV and other steel companies as well (*Wall Street Journal* July 7, 1992:A4; *Business Week* March 16, 1992:40). The lack of these liabilities for the new steel minimills gives them a built-in labor cost advantage.

Technological change and minimill competition. As noted earlier, new casting technology has enabled low-cost, nonunion minimills to begin to compete directly with integrated mills in the large market for flat-rolled products. In dealing with this competitive challenge from minimills, integrated firms face several strategic choices. One option is to attempt to compete directly with minimills based on cost for similar products by building flat-rolled minimill plants of their own. Armco Steel has announced plans to build its own flat-rolled minimill in Ohio. Dofasco Steel, a Canadian integrated producer, will also build a U.S. plant with Co-Steel. U.S. Steel has plans to build a new minimill facility as well (*Wall Street Journal* April 8, 1993:A4). We propose that steel firms following this option will have a difficult time developing and maintaining a cooperative partnership model. This option puts strong pressure on unionized producers in this area to match the nonunion compensation practices and work rules and would tend to pit one integrated firm's plant against another. The incentive to try to avoid the union altogether at a "greenfield" minimill site will also be quite strong, which would seriously undermine the "partnership" concept.

A second alternative is to move increasingly into the high-value, high-quality steel product market, particularly for autos which minimills have not as yet been able to penetrate. This has been the historical reaction by integrated firms to minimill competition. While this business strategy choice would appear to be more consistent with the development of a cooperative partnership, there are risks as well. It is not clear, for example, how much demand there is for truly "high-end" steel products (i.e., those commanding a price premium). Current estimates of the size of this market vary from 9 to 20 million tons (Hess 1992), which means that minimills would gain control over a vast majority of the carbon steel market.

A third option would be to continue to develop and invest in new technologies which would make existing integrated production more cost competitive with minimills. There are a number of technologies which are currently being developed that would dramatically change the way that steel is produced in integrated facilities. These include the use of coal injection and direct steelmaking, which eliminates the need for traditional coke ovens and blast furnaces, and direct casting, which would bypass the casting step. All of these technologies are attempts to both eliminate stages in the steelmaking process and move increasingly toward a continuous process method, as opposed to batch production method. There is certainly no guarantee, however, that new technology will be developed fast enough to allow integrated firms to "leapfrog" the minimills before they have been able to take control of significantly larger amounts of market share (Hess 1992:19).

As can be seen from the above discussion, there is currently a great deal of uncertainty about the future direction of industrial relations in the U.S. steel industry. We have seen in the past decade traditional IR structures break down under the weight of economic changes providing an historic opportunity for the creation of a new industrial relations system in steel embodied in the cooperative partnership model. The building of the new structural basis for this transformed relationship, however, is taking place within a context of high economic, regulatory, and technological uncertainty. It is the interaction between these challenges created by changing conditions and the choices made by the parties reacting to these challenges that will determine which industrial relations model emerges in the 1990s.

Acknowledgments

We would like to thank Paula Voos and the participants at the conference on "The Changing Nature of Private-Sector Bargaining," Detroit, Michigan, February 8-10, 1993, for helpful comments on a previous draft of this paper and union and management representatives at U.S. Steel's Gary Works for their participation and comments.

Endnotes

[1] For a good discussion of minimills, see Barnett and Crandall (1986).

[2] Katz (1985) labeled this type of system in the U.S. auto industry, "job control unionism."

[3] Again, this figure understates the reduction in the integrated sector of the industry since minimills continued to add capacity during this period.

[4] Bethlehem is involved in a joint venture with National Steel which is 70% owned by Japan's NKK Steel Company.

[5] The new IN/TEC IN/KOTE facility described in the chapter is a steel-finishing facility. There is one steel minimill, Auburn Steel, built in the mid-1970s, which is fully owned by a Japanese company and is nonunion.

[6] The productivity data available do not allow us to determine the degree to which subcontracting in the industry (which increased during this period) contributed to the productivity gains.

[7] In 1979 the ratio of steel industry earnings to all manufacturing was 1.55. This ratio declined to 1.37 by 1991.

[8] AISI published data do not allow for a separate calculation of the percentage of employment costs for hourly employees to total costs (without salaried employment costs). Historically, however, salaried employment costs have been approximately 30% of the total employment costs.

[9] This case description is based primarily on interviews with labor and management representatives conducted by the second author during plant visits in 1989 and 1993 and supplemented by other archival records.

References

AFL-CIO. 1991. *Report to the Executive Council of the AFL-CIO to the 19th Constitutional Convention* (Detroit, MI), November.
AFL-CIO News. 1982. May 10, p. 6.

American Iron and Steel Institute (AISI). Various years. *Annual Statistical Reports*. Association of Iron and Steel Engineers. 1989. *Directory of Iron and Steel Plants*.

Arthur, Jeffrey B. 1990. *Industrial Relations and Business Strategies in American Steel Minimills*. Ph.D. Dissertation, Cornell University.

_____. 1992. "The Link Between Industrial Relations Strategies and Business Strategies in American Steel Minimills." *Industrial and Labor Relations Review*, Vol. 45, No. 3 (April), pp. 488-506.

Bain, Trevor. 1992. *Banking the Furnace: Restructuring of the Steel Industry in Eight Countries*. Kalamazoo, MI: W.E. Upjohn Institute.

Ball, Judith S., Pamela A. Kennedy, Lee M. Ozley, and E. Douglas White. 1989. *Cooperative Partnership: A New Beginning for National Steel Corporation and the United Steelworkers of America*. U.S. Dept. of Labor, BLMRCP.

Barnett, Donald F., and Robert W. Crandall. 1986. *Up From the Ashes: The Rise of the Steel Minimill in the United States*. Washington, DC: The Brookings Institution.

Barnett, Donald F., and Louis Schorsch. 1984. *Steel: Upheaval in a Basic Industry*. Cambridge, MA: Ballinger Publishing Co.

Bureau of National Affairs (BNA). Various dates. *Daily Labor Report*. Washington, DC: BNA.

_____. 1987. "Wage Patterns and Data: Steel." *Collective Bargaining Negotiations and Contracts*, Vol. 1, Bulletin Nos. 1093 and 1105, pp. 18:231-18:242.

_____. 1990a. "Wage Patterns and Data: Steel." *Collective Bargaining Negotiations and Contracts*, Vol. 1, Bulletin No. 1168, pp. 18:242-18:245.

_____. 1990b. "Current Bargaining Issues: Worker Training Programs." *Collective Bargaining Negotiations and Contracts*, Vol. 1, Bulletin No. 1167, pp. 16:51-16:64.

_____. 1991. "Wage Patterns and Data: Steel." *Collective Bargaining Negotiations and Contracts*, Vol. 1, Bulletin No. 1198, pp. 18:245-18:256.

_____. 1993. "Bargaining Preview: Steelworkers Bargaining Goals." *Collective Bargaining Negotiations and Contracts*, Vol. 1, Bulletin No. 1234, pp. 8:651-8:662.

Camens, Sam. 1982. "Capital Formation and Industrial Policy: Crises in the Steel Industry." *Hearings before the Subcommittee on Oversight and Investigations of the Committee of Energy and Commerce*, House of Representatives, Ninety-seventh Congress. Washington: U.S. GPO, pp. 305-324.

Camlin, Scott P., Kathleen R. Scharf, and Richard E. Walton. 1993. "Union-Management Partnerships: A Context for Joint Decision-Making." Paper presented at the Conference on Innovations in Negotiation and Grievance Handling in the New Industrial Relations Order. Harvard University, May 20-21.

Cappelli, Peter. 1990. "Is Pattern Bargaining Dead? A Discussion." *Industrial and Labor Relations Review*, Vol. 44, No. 1 (October), pp. 152-59.

Clark, Paul F., Peter Gottlieb, and Donald Kennedy, eds. 1987. *Forging a Union of Steel*. Ithaca, NY: ILR Press.

Clark, Gordon L. 1988. "Corporate Restructuring in the Steel Industry: Adjustment Strategies and Local Labor Relations." In J. Hughes and G. Sternlieb, eds., *America's New Economic Geography*. New Brunswick, NJ: Center for Urban Policy Research, Rutgers University.

Congressional Budget Office. 1984. *The Effects of Import Quotas on the Steel Industry.*

Cooke, William N. 1992. "Product Quality Improvement Through Employee Participation: The Effects of Unionization and Joint Union-Management Administration." *Industrial and Labor Relations Review*, Vol. 46, No. 1 (October), pp.
119-134.

Cutcher-Gershenfeld, Joel. 1991. "The Impact of Economic Performance of a Transformation of Workplace Relations." *Industrial and Labor Relations Review*, Vol.
44, No. 2 (January), pp. 241-260.

Deilly, Mary A. 1991. "Investment Activity and the Exit Decision." *Review of Economics and Statistics*, Vol. 70, pp. 595-602.

_____. 1991. "Exit Strategies and Plant-Closing Decisions: The Case of Steel."
Rand Journal of Economics, Vol. 22, No. 2 (Summer), pp. 250-263.

Dunlop, John T. 1958. *Industrial Relations Systems.* New York: Henry Holt.

Gilford, Courtney D. 1990. *Directory of U.S. Labor Organizations*, 1990-91 Edition.
Washington, DC: Bureau of National Affairs.

Golden, Clinton S., and Harold J. Ruttenberg. 1942. *The Dynamics of Industrial
Democracy.* New York: Harper.

Hess, George W. 1992. "Minis Move Closer to Maxi Status." *Iron Age* (October), pp.
18-22.

Hirshhorn, Joel S. 1986. "Restructuring of the United States Steel Industry Requires
New Policies." In W. Goldberg, ed., *Ailing Steel.* (New York: St. Martin's Press),
pp. 205-246.

Hoerr, John P. 1988. *And the Wolf Finally Came: The Decline of the American Steel
Industry.* Pittsburgh, PA: University of Pittsburgh Press.

Hogan, William T. 1984. *Minimills and Integrated Mills: A Comparison of Steelmaking in the United States.* Lexington, MA: D.C. Heath.

Industry Week. 1987. June 1, p. 28.

Katz, Harry C. 1985. *Shifting Gears.* Cambridge, MA: MIT Press.

Katz, Harry C., and Thomas A. Kochan. 1992. *An Introduction to Collective Bargaining and Industrial Relations.* New York: McGraw-Hill.

Kochan, Thomas A., Robert B. McKersie, and Peter Cappelli. 1984. "Strategic Choice
and Industrial Relations Theory." *Industrial Relations*, Vol. 23, pp. 16-39.

Kochan, Thomas A., Harry C. Katz, and Robert B. McKersie. 1986. *The Transformation of American Industrial Relations.* New York: Basic Books.

Locker Associates, Inc. 1989. "Minimills: Challenges and Opportunities." Report
presented to United Steelworkers of America, AFL-CIO-CLC, February 9.

McManus, George J. 1992. "MSA Failure Leaves Steel in a Confused State." *Iron
Age*, May, pp. 24-26.

Miles, Gregory L. 1989. "Suddenly, USX Is Playing Mr. Nice Guy." *Business Week*,
June 26, p. 151.

Pare, Terence P. 1991. "The Big Threat to Big Steel's Future." *Fortune*, July 15, pp.
106-8.

Parker, Mike, and Jane Slaughter. 1988. *Choosing Sides: Unions and the Team Concept.* Boston, MA: South End Press.

Piore, Michael J., and Charles F. Sable. 1984. *The Second Industrial Divide: Possibilities for Prosperity.* New York: Basic Books.

Ready, Kathryn J. 1990. "Is Pattern Bargaining Dead?" *Industrial and Labor Relations Review*, Vol. 43, No. 2 (January), pp. 272-79.

Savage, John. 1981. "Incentive Programs at Nucor Corporation Boost Productivity." *Personnel Administrator*, Vol. 26 (August), pp. 33-36.

Smith, Suzanne K. 1991. "Technological Integration and Fragmented Labor Market Structures: The Decline and Restructuring of the U.S. Steel Industry." *International Contributions to Labor Studies*, Vol. 1, pp. 27-57.

Stieber, Jack. 1959. *The Steel Industry Wage Structure*. Cambridge, MA: Harvard University Press.

————. 1980. "Steel." In G. Somers, ed., *Collective Bargaining: Contemporary American Experience*. Madison, WI: Industrial Relations Research Association, pp. 151-208.

Tiffany, Paul A. 1988. *The Decline of American Steel*. New York: Oxford University Press.

Ulman, Lloyd. 1961. *The Government of the Steel Workers' Union*. New York: John Wiley.

United Steelworkers of America. 1971. *Job Description and Classification Manual.*

————. 1981. *Handbook of Arbitration Decisions.*

U.S. Bureau of Labor Statistics. Various Years. *Employment and Earnings*. Washington, DC: GPO.

————. 1985. *The Impact of Technology in Four Industries*. Bulletin 2228 (May), pp. 20-34.

U.S. Department of Labor, Bureau of Labor-Management Relations and Cooperative Programs. 1989. "Cooperative Labor-Management Worker Adjustment Programs." Washington, DC: GPO.

Walton, Richard A. 1985. "From Control to Commitment in the Workplace." *Harvard Business Review* 63 (2), pp. 77-84.

Walton, Richard E., and Robert B. McKersie. 1965. *A Behavioral Theory of Labor Negotiations*. New York: McGraw-Hill.

CHAPTER 5

Collective Bargaining in the U.S. Auto Assembly Sector

HARRY C. KATZ
Cornell University

JOHN PAUL MACDUFFIE
University of Pennsylvania

Editor's Abstract

In the recent past, the assembly sector of the automobile industry has witnessed widespread experimentation with new work designs and human resource practices. Collective bargaining outcomes across companies and plants have become more varied. Katz and MacDuffie link these developments to increased competitive pressures and to the challenge posed by lean production.

The Big Three (GM, Ford, and Chrysler) increased their market share in the early 1990s. This, however, followed a period of intense competitive pressure in which the Big Three lost ground. Japanese market share rose from 22% in 1979 to 33% in 1991. These figures include both direct imports and the output of "transplants," the largely nonunion assembly plants established by Japanese producers in the 1980s in the U.S. and Canada. Despite the upturn in sales in the early 1990s, the Big Three hourly work force continued to fall, from 740,000 in 1978, to 455,000 in 1990, to approximately 400,000 in 1993.

One source of Japanese advantage appears to be the lean production system. This involves both a set of production practices (designed for manufacturing, just-in-time inventory, closer links to supplier firms, more product variety, and more rapid model development) and a set of human resource practices (work teams, fewer job classifications/multi-skilling, increased worker training, employee involvement, and pressures for "continuous improvement"). Aspects of this new HRM and production system have been adopted by the Big Three in various auto plants, but these practices are by no means universal. This is one source of increased diversity.

In the early 1980s, there was a sharp shift in automotive collective bargaining with the demise of the traditional bargaining formula of a 3% annual improvement factor plus COLA. Profit sharing was instituted. Although profit sharing has never been substantial relative to base pay, it has produced different results for GM, Ford, and Chrysler employees. Concession bargaining emerged repeatedly in plant-level negotiations in the 1980s—largely in the form of company demands for changed work rules. Management has utilized investment decisions to gain leverage in these negotiations. However, Katz and MacDuffie point out that new HRM systems like teams typically have been more successful when they are not forced upon the hourly work force.

In an era of reduced employment and continued plant closing, management has held a strong position. However, the UAW has been able to maintain itself as a formidable force in the industry. The real base wage rate for auto assemblers actually rose slightly between 1980 and 1993, despite the economywide decline in real hourly earnings. The UAW has also focused on increased job security through SUB plans, job banks, and through cooperation aimed at enhancing productivity. A primary remaining challenge is organization of the largely nonunion transplants.

Katz and MacDuffie point out that there is a range of opinions within both management and labor about these collective bargaining and human resource developments. Controversy remains regarding the success of the Saturn agreement, the experience at NUMMI, and, indeed, the whole gamut of work design and human resource experiments at other facilities. The future is uncertain, but those who support a cautious, incremental approach to change, employee involvement, and lean production are likely to be reinforced by the recent success of the Big Three.

o   o   o

The auto industry has historically played a prominent role in American collective bargaining, introducing many now common features—multiyear contracts with cost-of-living-adjustment escalators and built-in annual real wage increases, supplementary unemployment benefits, "30-and-out" pensions, and quality of working life (QWL) programs—and upholding a strong structure of pattern bargaining for many years.[1] In the 1980s automotive labor relations was again in the forefront in taking actions to modify this long-established model, under pressure from both foreign and domestic competitors and from new production models linked to new human resource practices.

The cumulative outcome of these pressures has been increased diversity and decentralization of collective bargaining outcomes, at both company and plant levels; widespread experimentation with new work designs and human resource practices at individual plants, both new and old; and continued debate within both union and management ranks about the best way to deal with these changes. Modifications of the industry's collective bargaining model have included so-called "concessionary" contracts that replace traditional bargaining formulas with company-specific profit-sharing plans and work rule changes; extensive new income and job security programs to cope with industry restructuring; joint labor-management efforts around training and quality; and the use of new work structures at the shop floor level, such as teams combined with very few job classifications, that challenge the principles of "job control" unionism.

The auto industry also remained newsworthy during the 1980s and 1990s as a result of the expansion of Japanese ownership and influence and the prominence of new models of worker and union participation. As Japanese companies became owners or co-owners (along with American company partners) of new assembly plants, the fact that virtually all of the solely owned Japanese plants operated without a union introduced the threat of nonunion operations to what had been one of the few remaining fully unionized sectors in the American economy. The presence of Japanese plants in the U.S. also gave impetus to the diffusion of "lean production," a Toyota-derived model combining new manufacturing methods such as just-in-time inventory systems and statistical process control with new human resource practices focused on worker motivation and multiskilling.

The perception of lean production as economically superior to traditional mass production increased the pressure on the U.S. industry to move toward more flexible ways of automating plants and organizing work, and launched a debate within the unions about the advantages and disadvantages of lean production from the workers' viewpoint. Meanwhile, the extensive form of worker and union involvement (even in business decisions) that emerged in the expanding Saturn facility, a subsidiary of General Motors, was viewed by many as an American alternative to (or extension of) lean production and quickly attracted both proponents and opponents among management and union ranks.

Before we describe these recent developments in automotive industrial relations more fully, we will first review the industry and its innovative history of labor-management relations. We focus in this chapter on the automotive assembly sector—those auto companies that assemble cars and trucks (and also produce many vehicle parts that are supplied to these assembly operations). In the next section, we describe the primary parties involved in U.S. automotive labor relations: the unions and the companies. Subsequent sections focus on the competitive and technological environment affecting the bargaining context for the U.S. automotive industry, the structure of collective bargaining in this industry historically, new developments in collective bargaining from 1979 to the present, and a look to the future that sketches out three possible scenarios for automotive industrial relations.

The Parties

The Unions

The United Automotive Workers (UAW) is the primary union representing workers in the auto industry.[2] The International Union of Electricians (IUE) also represents some hourly workers in the assembly firms (primarily in the electrical products plants of these firms). By the late 1940s the UAW had organized all hourly workers in the companies that assembled cars and trucks.[3] Until 1985, the UAW was an international union as it included Canadian auto workers. In 1985 the Canadian auto workers voted to secede and a separation agreement was negotiated between the U.S. and Canadian parts of the UAW to form the Canadian Auto Workers (CAW).

The UAW is a large and fairly centralized union. The internal structure of the union includes departments organized along company lines in the auto industry and an agricultural implements department. National union staff coordinate bargaining within each department and also assist in the implementation of benefits, employee assistance, health and safety, and quality of working life programs.

The central figure in the union over the postwar period was Walter Reuther who, along with his brothers, was active in the union's sit down strikes and organizing efforts in the 1930s. Reuther served as president of the UAW from 1947 until his death in 1970. During his tenure, Reuther led a coalition (the "administrative caucus") that dominated the national affairs of the union, and while he was alive, Reuther's influence and imagination encouraged an innovative spirit within auto bargaining (Steiber 1962). Under Reuther's guidance the UAW also was very active in national and local politics and a strong supporter of the Democratic Party. Yet, even with the dominance of the Reuther coalition, the UAW historically has had strong democratic traditions which appeared recently in the debates occurring within the UAW between the "New Directions Movement" and the "Administrative Caucus." These debates are reviewed later in this chapter.

The Companies

The American assembly companies are commonly referred to as the "Big Three"—General Motors (GM), Ford, and Chrysler. They produce a number of car and truck parts and they assemble these parts into final vehicles, although the extent to which these assemblers are "vertically integrated" (use parts produced in their own plants) varies. Estimates of the degree of integration as of 1990 are GM—70%, Ford—40%, and Chrysler—30%.[4] The Big Three's production and skilled trades workers are completely unionized, and their national (companywide) collective bargaining agreements cover the companies' final assembly and parts plants. In addition, the Saturn Corporation, a subsidiary of GM, operates a sizeable unionized auto assembly complex in Tennessee, covered under a separate contract that differs substantially from the national GM agreement. Table 1 contains basic information about these companies.

There are also a number of assembly plants with Japanese ownership involvement, referred to in the industry and in this chapter as the "transplants." Table 2 contains summary information on these plants. The three unionized transplants acquired this status by virtue of their joint venture arrangements with U.S. companies. These arrangements have been somewhat fluid; they have been altered at two of these plants since they opened.[5] The contracts at these plants, like at Saturn, represent a substantial departure from the national UAW-Big Three agreements. Five of the transplants are nonunion plants, and they appear to represent the dominant trend for new investment, with both BMW and Mercedes-Benz now building new nonunion plants.[6]

Japanese companies have historically been much less vertically integrated than the Big Three, and this pattern is also true for the transplants. Estimates indicate that Toyota, Nissan, and Mazda are the most vertically integrated of the Japanese companies at 30%, and that Suzuki is the least vertically integrated at 16%; the industry average is just under 25%.[7] The transplants initially sourced many of their parts from Japan but have made a strong effort in recent years, accelerated by political pressures related to the U.S.-Japan trade deficit and the rise in the value of the yen, to increase the "local content" of their U.S.-built vehicles.[8]

The Bargaining Context

The Competitive Environment

From 1946 until 1979, the auto industry in the U.S. was on a prosperous growth path, even in the face of the industry's periodic sharp

TABLE 1
U.S. Automotive Companies:
North American Assembly Operations, 1990-1993

Company	Number of Assembly Plants			1990 NA Production	1991 NA Producttion	1990 U.S. Employment	1993 est. Employment
	US	Canada	Mexico				
GM	26	4	2	2,654,302	2,401,077	287,000	233,000
Ford	15	2	2	1,378,146	1,172,384	100,000	87,000
Chrysler	7	4	2	726,753	510,147	68,000	55,000

Source: Automotive News; Annual Reports; unpublished reports, UAW.

TABLE 2

Japanese Automobile Assembly Plants Based in the United States, 1982-90

Company	Location	Production Began	1989 Production	1990 Production	Current Capacity	Unionized
Total			1,262,876	1,493,884	1,815,000	
Honda	Marysville, OH	1982	1,363,274[1]	1,435,437[1]	360,000[1]	No
Nissan	Smyrna, TN	1983	238,641	235,248	265,000	No
New United Motor Manufacturing (Toyota and General Motors)	Fremont, CA	1984	192,471	205,287	240,000	Yes
Mazda (with Ford)	Flat Rock, MI	1987	216,501	184,428	240,000	Yes
Diamond-Star (Mitsubishi and Chrysler)	Normal, IL	1988	90,741	148,379	240,000	Yes
Toyota	Georgetown, KY	1988	151,099	218,155	200,000	No
Subaru-Isuzu	Lafayette, IN	1989	11,160	66,950	120,000	No
Honda	East Liberty, OH	1989	0[1]	0[1]	150,000	No

[1]Honda Marysville production level includes Honda East Liberty production as well.

Sources: Motor Vehicle Manufacturers Association and *Automotive News*, Detroit, MI: Crain Communications, Inc., various issues.

Christopher J. Singleton. 1992. "Auto Industry Jobs in the 1980s: A Decade of Transition," *Monthly Labor Review*, Vol. 115, no. 2, pp. 18-27.

cyclical swings. Over these years domestic production of cars and trucks increased from 5 million to 13 million vehicles. From 1946 to 1979 the number of production workers grew 20% and periodically fluctuated substantially along with vehicle production. The combination of large vehicle output growth and modest employment growth was due to the significant productivity gains accomplished by the industry. This productivity and output growth helped produce strong profit figures for the industry and provided support for substantial growth in auto workers' real earnings.

From the end of World War II until the late 1970s, the economic environment of the auto industry was conducive to steady improvements and general stability in labor relations. Three environmental factors were critical—growth in domestic auto sales, a low level of imported vehicle sales, and a high degree of unionization. Yet, in the early 1980s, a labor and management that had grown accustomed to long-run growth in total vehicle sales and profits were confronted by a number of fundamental changes in the auto market.

One important aspect of the change was an increase in international competition in the form of increased vehicle imports. While the level of imports increased steadily during the 1960s and 1970s from a postwar low of 5% in 1955, it surged during the 1980s. As reported in Table 3, the total import share of American new car sales rose from 22.2% in 1979 to a peak of 30.8% in 1987, although a variety of developments in the early 1990s, as noted below, caused an equally sharp decline in import share to 21.7% in 1993.

In the early 1980s American auto makers also confronted sizeable declines in sales induced by a sluggish American economy. As shown in Table 4, from 1979 to 1982 employment in the auto industry (SIC 371) declined by 29.4% (from 990,400 to 699,300). Ford and Chrysler were hardest hit during this downturn. Then, in mid-1983, auto sales began to rebound strongly and employment in the industry and the financial status of the auto assemblers markedly improved. By 1985 employment had recovered to 883,500; these numbers reflect not only the recovery of the Big Three but also the strong growth in transplant employment during the early 1980s. Profits also rebounded; the combined profits of the Big Three (GM, Ford and Chrysler) were $6.3 million in 1983 and $9.8 million in 1984, and the Big Three continued to be profitable into the late 1980s.

Despite the return to profitability in the mid-1980s, the Big Three faced increasing competition not only from imports but also from the

TABLE 3

U.S. New Car Sales of American Automakers, Japanese Transplants and Imports,
and Total Imports, 1979-90

(Numbers in thousands of Units)

Year	American Automakers		Japanese Transplants		Japanese Imports		Total Imports		American Automakers—All Motor Vehicles
	Sales	Percent of Total	Sales	Percent of Total	Sales	Percent of Total	Imports	Percent of Total	Production
1979	8,163	76.7	0	0	1,848	17.4	2,328	21.9	11,098
1980	6,401	71.3	0	0	1,977	22.0	2,397	26.7	7,667
1981	6,044	70.8	0	0	1,892	22.2	2,326	27.3	7,614
1982	5,665	71.0	0	0	1,801	22.6	2,222	27.9	6,785
1983	6,660	72.5	50	0.5	1,916	20.9	2,386	26.0	8,900
1984	7,744	74.5	134	1.3	1,906	18.3	2,442	23.5	10,462
1985	7,906	71.6	221	2.0	2,218	20.1	2,841	25.7	11,095
1986	7,675	67.0	446	4.1	2,386	20.8	3,249	28.3	10,688
1987	6,402	62.6	618	6.0	2,173	21.3	3,144	30.7	10,097
1988	6,735	63.6	766	7.2	2,103	19.8	3,067	28.9	10,122
1989	6,064	62.4	1,009	10.4	1,911	19.7	2,698	27.8	9,615
1990	5,500	59.2	1,343	14.4	1,721	18.5	2,453	26.4	8,152

Note: For the purposes of this table, the term, "American Automakers," denotes General Motors, Ford, Chrysler, and American Motors.

Source: Motor Vehicle Manufacturers Association and *Automotive News* (Detroit, MI., Crain Communications, Inc.), various issues.
Christopher J. Singleton. 1992. "Auto Industry Jobs in the 1980s: A Decade of Transition," *Monthly Labor Review*, February 1992, Vol. 115, No. 2, pp. 18-27.

TABLE 4

U.S. Automobile Industry Employment in Motor Vehicles and Equipment (SIC 371)

Year	Employment (thousands)
1979	990.4
1980	788.8
1981	788.7
1982	699.3
1983	753.7
1984	861.7
1985	883.5
1986	872.4
1987	866.6
1988	857.4
1989	857.0
1990	800.9
1991	789.0
1992	812.2
1993	820.4
February 1994	851.4

Sources: Figures (except for February 1994) are annual averages from various issues of Employment and Earnings, Bureau of Labor Statistics, Washington, DC: GPO.

sizeable growth in Japanese transplant auto production. Table 3 shows that Japanese transplant car sales grew from zero in 1982 to 14.8% of the U.S. market by 1993, with transplant sales projected to approach a 20% share of the American market by the turn of the century. With a relatively constant level of Japanese imports through most of the 1980s, this represented a growth in the market share of nearly 15 percentage points for Japanese companies, from 17.6% in 1979 to 32.1% in 1991—representing most of the lost market share for the Big Three, since European and Korean imports gained less than 4% of the U.S. market during this period.[9]

When a sluggish economy returned in the early 1990s, it had dramatic effects on both employment and profits among the Big Three. By 1991, auto industry employment was down to 789,000; most of this drop reflected job losses for the Big Three, since the transplants continued to bring new capacity on-line during this period. In 1991 financial losses in the core automotive businesses at GM, Ford and Chrysler were $5.2 billion, $1.9 billion, and $0.8 billion, respectively.[10] GM's losses led to the company's decision to close 22 plants by 1995 and cut white- and blue-collar employment by 80,000.

Some good news for American companies came in the early 1990s with a small but significant increase in Big Three market share, up from 60.5% in 1991 to 63.6% in 1993, brought on by sluggish sales of vehicles imported from Japan, partly due to an unfavorable exchange rate and the Big Three's successful unveiling of some popular new products and willingness to show price restraint to gain sales. Profits also rebounded at the Big Three in 1993, with GM, Ford, and Chrysler all reporting profits of around $2.5 billion.[11] Along with this sales and profit rebound, employment also rebounded but not as strongly as the auto companies made extensive use of overtime (particularly at Ford and Chrysler) and benefited from productivity improvements.

Even in the face of periodic profit rebounds, the increase in international and domestic competition led to sizeable declines in employment at the Big Three and UAW membership. From 1978 to 1990, the number of hourly jobs at Big Three assembly operations declined by 39% (from 740,000 to 455,000). This trend continued despite the most recent upturn, with 1993 estimates of 400,000 hourly jobs. Meanwhile, overall UAW membership declined 37% from 1979 to 1990 (from 1,510,000 to 950,000).[12]

In addition to intensified competitive pressures, the economic environment of the U.S. auto assemblers was altered from the 1980s on through the Big Three's decision to forge coproduction agreements with their Japanese counterparts, as noted above.[13] The primary motivation for the U.S. companies was to fill gaps in their product lines, particularly for small cars. Yet, the Big Three have also been influenced, to varying degrees, by the desire to use these co-owned but Japanese-managed plants to experiment with new production systems and to develop demonstration models for their wholly owned plants.[14]

The importance of the transplants for industrial relations arises from the fact that they utilize innovative practices in both work organization, employee involvement, and manufacturing practice (discussed below) and that the plants solely built by the Japanese are unorganized. The emergence of sizeable domestic nonunion competition in the auto assembly sector represents a significant new pressure on the UAW. Although the UAW had seen its representation decline in the independent auto parts sector (plants that make auto parts but are owned by companies other than the Big Three) over the post-World War II period, the assembly sector had remained completely unionized. Indeed, the Big Three essentially abandoned its efforts to create a nonunion sector when the UAW successfully resisted GM's "Southern Strategy" of opening nonunion assembly plants in the 1970s. Through the new nonunion transplants the UAW came to face the same threat that plagued so many other American unions over the last 30 years. Although the UAW has launched various organizing drives in unorganized transplants in recent years, none of these drives have come close to being successful.

Also significant for collective bargaining has been the formation of more extensive linkages between the assembler companies and their parts suppliers. Most assemblers dramatically reduced the number of their parts suppliers and initiated longer term contracts with the select group of suppliers that remained. At the same time, they increased the percentage of the parts purchased from non-captive suppliers through increased outsourcing from their wholly owned "inside" suppliers. The immediate effect of this trend was to increase the pressure for cost reduction on the parts plants owned by the assemblers and to reduce union density in the auto parts sector, since the vertically integrated suppliers are 100% unionized, while the U.S.-owned independent sector is about 50% unionized, and the Japanese supplier transplants are nearly 100% nonunion. The formation of stronger links across the assembly companies and between assemblers and parts suppliers eventually also may produce complicated problems regarding bargaining structure and union jurisdiction.[15]

The increased use of just-in-time (JIT) inventory systems, in which assemblers receive multiple parts deliveries from suppliers close to the time of production and substantially shrink their buffers of incoming parts and work-in-process inventories, placed new demands for quality and on-time delivery on suppliers. Those suppliers able to meet these demands, often larger U.S. independent parts companies or Japanese supplier transplants already familiar with just-in-time, benefited greatly, thus accelerating the trend away from vertical integration.

As the level of inventory held by the Big Three dropped during the 1980s (Haimsen 1992), the interdependence of assembler and supplier plants increased dramatically, affecting labor relations in unpredictable ways. For instance, while the lean buffers of JIT provide an incentive for suppliers to avoid labor conflict that might interrupt parts deliveries (and for assemblers to do business with suppliers who can manage labor relations effectively), the greater interdependence between assembly and parts plants also gives a new potential source of strike leverage.[16]

Plant-Level Performance Differentials

In the face of heightened competition, the Big Three and the UAW made substantial changes in their industrial relations practices over the 1980s and early 1990s, as discussed below. An important force for change was the perception that Japanese-owned plants, both in Japan and in the U.S., had substantial productivity and quality advantages over the typical Big Three plant because of their use of lean production, a system developed by Toyota and used to varying degrees by all Japanese companies.

Lean production is described (Womack, Jones, and Roos 1990) as combining a different way of thinking about production goals (quality and productivity as mutually attainable, not a tradeoff) with new production methods aimed at boosting efficiency through the elimination of waste (reducing buffers through just-in-time inventory systems; "building in" rather than "inspecting in" quality) and human resource practices aimed at motivating workers and developing their skills (work teams, job rotation, problem-solving groups, increased worker training, performance-based bonus pay, reduction of status barriers). Underpinning the entire system is the idea of *kaizen* or continuous improvement in production processes and in productivity and quality outcomes. According to this model, buffer reduction reveals production problems and creates the pressure to solve them. Then, if workers are sufficiently skilled and motivated, they will respond by extensive participation in the improvement process.

The perception of lean production as the source of Japanese competitive advantage represented an important shift away from Japan-specific factors such as lower wage rates, longer working hours, cooperative enterprise unions, lifetime employment, and cultural traits (e.g., a strong work ethic and a group orientation conducive to teamwork). These culturally based explanations were undermined by the performance of the Japanese transplants in the 1980s. Data from MIT's International Assembly Plant Study indicated that the transplants, using American workers, engineers, managers and (at some plants) union officials, achieved performance results, in terms of both productivity and quality, that matched or surpassed most American plants (Krafcik 1986; Krafcik and MacDuffie 1989).[17]

Furthermore, the source of the transplants' performance advantage appeared to be their implementation of lean production methods very similar to those used in plants in Japan (Shimada and MacDuffie 1987;

Gelsanliter 1989; Florida and Kenney 1993). The transplant wages and benefits are similar to U.S. plants (although, with a new young work force and less generous programs, their pension and health care costs are much lower). Their level of technology ranged from moderate to high, but was often less in amount and sophistication than the most advanced U.S. plants.

The NUMMI case was particularly influential, because unlike the "greenfield" nonunion plants of Honda and Nissan, it occupied a former GM plant in California and hired its employees from the ranks of the former GM work force. Union officials from what had been one of the most militant local unions at GM were brought back as well. Yet within a year of opening, NUMMI had the best quality and productivity of any GM-affiliated plant and the lowest absenteeism and grievance rates as well (Krafcik 1986; Brown and Reich 1989; Adler 1992).

Observations about the transplants were supported by broader statistical analyses from the MIT Assembly Plant Study (MacDuffie 1991, 1994a; MacDuffie and Krafcik 1992). In an international sample of 62 assembly plants, there was a strong relationship between the use of buffers and the use of human resource practices (i.e., the "leaner" the buffers, the more extensive the reliance on work teams, job rotation, high levels of worker training, contingent pay, and so forth). The study also found that the use of buffers and human resource practices were strong predictors of productivity and quality, both as separate indices and when combined into a single "production organization" measure.

This view of lean production has been challenged on two points. Some researchers question whether lean production is indeed a distinctive paradigm with performance advantages, pointing to industry and company-level statistics on inventory levels and financial performance that show only modest variation across U.S. and Japanese companies (Williams and Haslam 1992). Whatever cost advantages Japanese companies may have are attributed to lower wages in the various tiers of the supply system.[18]

More widespread are critiques that acknowledge the performance advantages of lean production, but argue that these are attained not through greater dependence on worker skill and motivation but through exploitation of workers. For example, the Mazda plant in Flat Rock, Michigan has achieved some notoriety for the harsh treatment of workers during its launch period, as reported in Fucini and Fucini (1990). It is interesting to note that this account suggests that many of the problems at the Flat Rock plant were due to management's inability to implement lean production effectively under the financial and time pressures of the product launch.

Other accounts of the transplants develop a broader critique of "lean production" as relying on "sweating" workers through a faster work pace, rigid job standardization, intensive peer pressure for higher work effort within teams, and continual stress from the lack of buffers and from *kaizen* efforts to remove work content from jobs (Parker and Slaughter 1988; Babson 1993; Graham 1993). From this perspective, the challenge to unions is to develop a strategy for eliminating or at least containing the exploitative aspects of lean production.[19] For researchers, these critiques highlight the importance of gathering more information on the consequences of lean production for workers and workers' perceptions of lean work practices.

These critiques have influenced debates within auto workers' unions in North America, as discussed below. The Canadian Auto Workers (CAW) have prepared the most fully developed position on lean production, based on their research at the GM-Suzuki joint venture transplant in Canada known as CAMI (CAW 1993; Robertson et al. 1993).

Meanwhile, the idea of lean production as a new production paradigm capable of superior performance has taken hold strongly among corporate management at the U.S. companies. However, the implementation of lean production at U.S. plants has been relatively slow, and varies for different aspects of this system. Most quickly adopted have been lean production policies on the reduction of buffers. The pace of implementation of new human resource practices has been slower, particularly in the cases where new work structures such as teams are being implemented at existing plants. The area in which U.S. companies have followed the lean production model least is product variety and manufacturing flexibility, as noted below.

Forces for Flexibility

In the post-World War II period, the auto industry was noteworthy as a model of the success of mass production techniques with steady, but incremental, technological change. In the early 1970s it appeared that these mass production techniques would be extended through the development of "world cars" assembled with interchangeable parts manufactured all over the world. A number of aspects of the new competition in the world auto market, however, raised doubts about the world car strategy and the future efficacy of mass production techniques. The new economic environment placed a premium on flexibility in the production process, and placed demands on labor and management to reorient labor relations accordingly (Katz and Sabel 1985). However, the response of the Big Three companies to these demands has varied considerably.

Factors contributing to the need for greater flexibility in the production process include: developments in the product market, new technologies, and macro-economic events. On the product market side, U.S. consumers have responded enthusiastically to the growing variety of vehicle types offered for sale by both domestic and foreign auto producers, a reflection of the world-wide erosion of distinct national auto markets (Altshuler et al. 1984). Much of this variety has resulted from an increase in "niche" products produced in relatively low volumes. Japanese companies have been able to exploit their more rapid product development cycle to meet these new market niches more quickly than the Big Three.

There has been a proliferation of models offered in the U.S. market, as shown in Table 5. From the 1940s through the 1960s, the American auto companies designed family size cars, produced each model in large volumes and made much of their profits from these cars. In 1955, for example, three models (two Chevrolets and one Ford) made up 50% of all cars sold in the U.S. By 1991, it took 24 models to cover half of U.S. sales, and these models were produced by seven companies (three American, three Japanese, and one joint venture).

This shift in product market strategy has important implications for the production process because production schedules for niche vehicles are more subject to changes in consumer preferences or competitive offerings. Consequently, on the shop floor there is greater need for the capacity to rapidly adjust production volumes and type, particularly the mix of different products within a certain level of production. One way to acquire this sort of flexibility is to replace the traditional assembly-line production techniques and highly formalized industrial relations practices with team forms of work organization and more informal work rules.

A second factor is the move toward new microprocessor-based technologies that has made it easier to build multiple models in the same assembly plant. The increased use of robotics and other "flexible" automation provides additional pressure for more flexible work rules

TABLE 5

Fragmentation of the American Auto, Van, and Light Truck Market 1955-1989

	1955	1973	1986	1989
Total				
Products on Sale	30	84	117	142
Annual Sales per product ('000s)	259	169	136	112
American Products				
Products on Sale	25	38	47	50
Annual Sales per product ('000s)	309	322	238	219
European Products				
Products on Sale	5	27	27	30
Annual Sales per product ('000s)	11	35	26	18
Japanese Products				
Products on Sale	0	19	41	58
Annual Sales per product ('000s)	0	55	94	73

Source: James P. Womack et al. 1990. The Machine that Changed the World. New York: Rawson Associates.

since the ability to rapidly switch product types appears to be the critical advantage robots have over earlier forms of automation.[20]

A third factor is the volatility in product demand generated by macro-economic flux and structural economic developments: oil price shocks, government policy responses to the inflation-unemployment tradeoff, and the increased exposure of the U.S. economy to world economic events.[21] This trend, which seems likely to continue, exacerbates the fluctuations in consumer demand that result from increased product variety, and further increases the need for companies to be able to rapidly adjust production volumes and model mix in any given plant.

Given these trends, the American auto companies faced a double problem in the early 1980s. While they were racing to adjust to the new volatility and variety in product demand and technology, they were simultaneously struggling to reduce the cost and quality advantages of Japanese producers. A complicating factor during this period was that it was not clear exactly what was the source of the Japanese performance advantage. Initially, U.S. companies suspected that the Japanese auto companies had lower costs and higher quality because they had a better way of performing mass production.[22] In addition, since Japanese products sold in the U.S. at that time were small cars with few option combinations, some U.S. observers concluded that Japanese factories faced substantially less manufacturing complexity than American factories, another cost advantage.[23]

At the same time, Japanese production systems seemed to be better suited than American practices to providing the flexibility demanded in a world of volatile markets and technologies.[24] Thus, the American companies were confused as to whether to focus their strategy around performing mass production in a less costly manner, or whether the world industry required a radically redesigned production system oriented toward flexibility and adaptability.[25] This confusion had important consequences for the conduct of industrial relations, as discussed below.

By the early 1990s, all of the Big Three spoke quite openly about their intention to speed the transition to lean production approaches in their assembly operations. For the most part, however, this has not included the lean production emphasis on high levels of product variety. Indeed, most Big Three plants are probably more narrowly focused on a single platform than they were in the early 1980s, and the number of options offered has been reduced dramatically as well, both in the interest of cost reduction.[26] Current strategic choices of the Big Three suggest that this "variety gap" with Japan will continue.[27] The fact that the Big Three will not be asking their plants to handle high levels of product variety implies that there will be less pressure to introduce flexible forms of production at these plants.

Locational Effects

The locational consequence of the changes underway in the world auto market has been a movement toward the recentralization of production. Although the concurrent trend toward the outsourcing of certain parts to low-wage locations such as Mexico receives much attention, the more significant trend has been toward a greater geographical concentration of auto-related manufacturing. The rationale is in part to capture the benefits of just-in-time inventory procedures and in part to allow more intensive communication between product design and manufacturing functions. This has occurred through the tendency for plant closings to occur in plants located far from Detroit; the creation of clusters of plants, such as Buick City and Saturn at GM, that bring together engine plants, transmission plants, assembly plants, and other parts plants to one central location; and the consolidation of stamping operations and other operations into assembly plants.

It is also noteworthy that a number of the new "greenfield" assembly plants are clustering in an area close to Interstate I-75, in a north-south corridor of Midwestern states that extends well south of the traditional Detroit-area home of the industry. These include Honda's two Ohio plants, the Saturn complex, and the Nissan plant in Tennessee, the Toyota assembly plant in Georgetown, Kentucky, the Mitsubishi plant in Illinois, and the Subaru-Isuzu plant in Indiana. No doubt the construction of these plants in the South was partially induced by management's belief that workers there would be more willing to avoid unionization and/or accept nontraditional industrial relations practices.[28] This I-75 corridor has also become the home for new independent parts suppliers, many of them Japanese-owned or Japan-U.S. joint ventures, that supply the transplants. These new suppliers are also overwhelmingly nonunion.

The Structure of Collective Bargaining

Pattern Bargaining

Prior to 1979, the bargaining structure among the auto assembly firms involved very strong pattern following within and across the auto companies. The degree of pattern following has declined across the Big Three and cross-company variation has increased with the entry of Japanese transplants as described more fully below.

In the traditional bargaining structure that prevailed at the Big Three compensation is set by national company-specific, and multi-year (since 1955 they have been three-year) agreements. Some work rules such as overtime administration, employee transfer rights, and seniority guidelines are also set in the national contracts. Local unions, in turn, negotiate plant-level agreements which supplement the national agreements. These local agreements define work rules such as the form of the seniority ladder, job characteristics, job bidding and transfer rights, health and safety standards, production standards, and an array of other rules which guide shop floor production. The local agreements do not regulate either wages or fringe benefits which are set in the national contract. Some indirect influences on wage determination do occur at the plant level in the definition and modification of job classifications provided through the local agreements.

Local bargaining over work rules allows for the expression of local preferences and some adjustment to local conditions. This facilitates the sort of shop floor "fractional bargaining" described by Kuhn (1961). In this system the grievance procedure with binding third-party arbitration serves as the end point of contract administration although disputes concerning production standards, new job rates, and health and safety issues are not resolved through recourse to arbitration.

The influence of the agreements reached in the auto assembly firms has traditionally extended out to the auto supplier industry and beyond. The UAW, for example, has used the auto assembly agreements as a pattern setter in their negotiations in the agricultural implements industry.[29] Other unions, especially those linked to auto production such as the rubber industry, also looked to the contracts in the auto assembly firms as pattern setters. From the early 1950s until the late 1970s the extent of interindustry pattern following varied somewhat over time, but generally there was a high degree of pattern following. In the 1980s, the pattern leading role of the Big Three settlements declined (Budd 1992).

Wage Rules and Fringe Benefit Determination

From 1948 until 1980, formulaic mechanisms have been utilized to set wage levels in collective bargaining agreements in the Big Three.[30] The formulaic wage-setting mechanisms traditionally included in the contracts were an annual improvement factor (AIF) that after the mid-1960s amounted to 3% per year, and a cost-of-living adjustment (COLA) escalator that often provided full or close to full cost-of-living protection.

The importance of these formulaic mechanisms is that they provided continuity in wage determination across time and across the assembly companies at any given point in time. The continuity across time was provided by the fact that, except for minor adjustments, the formula mechanisms rigidly set wages from 1948 until 1979 among the Big Three companies.[31] Continuity across the industry was provided by intercompany pattern following and by the fact that in the plants covered by the company agreements, the national contract wage was not modified in local bargaining.

Along with increases in real hourly earnings, auto workers received steady improvements in their fringe benefit package. A number of these fringe benefit advances such as supplementary unemployment benefits, "30-and-out" pensions, and paid personnel holidays were innovations that eventually spread to the auto supplier firms and to a number of other industries. Over the postwar period fringe benefits became a larger share of total worker compensation.

Job Control Unionism

At both national and shop floor levels, the labor relations system in the Big Three traditionally relied on contractually defined procedures to regulate disagreements between labor and management. The contractual regulation of these procedures was heavily focused on "job control."[32] Wages were explicitly tied to jobs and not to worker characteristics. In addition, much of the detail within the contract concerns the specification of an elaborate job classification system with much attention paid to the exact requirements of each job and to seniority rights that were tied to a job ladder guiding promotions, transfers and layoffs (Piore 1982). The dominance of a job control focus did not lead to a complete stabilization of shop floor labor-management relations. Labor and management often engaged in struggles over the exact terms of working conditions and the bounds of union or worker involvement in decision making. Frequently these issues were addressed through informal day-to-day relations between workers and their supervisors, but occasionally disputes produced either authorized or unauthorized local strike actions.

Furthermore, there was not perfect standardization in the tenor or outputs of shop floor labor relations because the focus of collective bargaining was on standardizing *contractual terms*. Significant variation emerged in the tenor and practical conduct of shop floor labor-management relations across plants and across work groups within given plants. In some plants there was a constant acrimonious relationship, while in others the parties developed a more cooperative interaction.[33]

From the late 1940s until the late 1970s, the application of wage rules and job control unionism produced steadily rising real compensation to auto workers and long-term growth in auto employment and production. With limited import penetration in auto sales, this was a bargaining process where the geographic bounds of union organization closely matched the relevant product market. The consistency the bargaining process had with the economic environment was one of the primary factors contributing to the system's attractiveness to both labor and management. Important political functions for labor and management also were served by the stability and continuity in the auto negotiation processes.

New Developments in Collective Bargaining, 1979-94

Concession Bargaining

By the late 1970s the economic environment in the world auto industry had changed substantially from its former pattern, and labor and management struggled to respond to many economic pressures. The wage rules traditionally used to set wage levels were modified significantly, first as part of efforts to avoid bankruptcy at Chrysler in 1979 and 1980. In agreements reached at the Big Three after 1979, the traditional formulaic wage rules were replaced by lump sum increases, periodic base pay increases, and profit sharing.[34] The 1993-96 contracts provide a 3% base pay increase in the first year and 3% lump sum pay increases in the second and third year of the contracts and continue the company-based profit-sharing programs.

Table 6 reports the hourly wages (including COLA payments) received by auto assemblers at GM from 1980 to 1993.[35] The figures in Table 6 show the limited growth in real earnings received by auto assemblers over the 1980s and early 1990s as a result of the abandonment of the regular 3% per year AIF wage increases. Yet, given the declines in real earnings suffered by many other American workers, auto workers' hourly wages rose sizably relative to other production workers over this period as shown in column C of Table 6.

Table 6
Auto Assembler Hourly Wages, 1980-1993

	(A) Auto Hourly Wage	(B) Auto Real Hourly Wage	(C) Ratio of Auto to Average Production Worker Hourly Wage
1980	9.77	11.86	1.47
1985	13.15	12.22	1.53
1990	15.69	12.00	1.57
1993	17.42	12.06	1.61

(A) This figure is the hourly base wage (including COLA payments) received by assemblers at General Motors. It is from an unpublished series of the UAW.

(B) This figure is the hourly wage reported in Column A divided by the consumer price index, as reported by the Bureau of Labor Statistics, *Monthly Labor Review*, various issues (1982-84 = 100).

(C) This figure is the hourly auto assembler wage reported in Column A divided by the average hourly earnings of production or non-supervisory workers on private non-form payrolls, as reported by the Bureau of Labor Statistics, *Monthly Labor Review*, various issues.

The introduction of profit sharing received much attention in the press, particularly in light of the traditional pattern setting role the auto assemblers have played in American collective bargaining. The payouts of the profit-sharing plans adopted in the Big Three from 1982 on have varied substantially, in large part due to differences in the financial performance of the companies. The profit-sharing payouts between 1982 and 1989 at GM, Ford, and Chrysler totaled $1,754, $13,365, and $3,752, respectively.[36] In 1993 Chrysler workers on average received a profit-sharing payout of $4,300, while Ford workers received $1,350, and GM's profit sharing plan provided no payout to hourly workers.[37] The variation in profit-sharing payouts received by workers across companies was the source of some controversy within the work force and the UAW.

The contracts at the Big Three after 1979 also included a number of new income and job security programs; programs that were induced by the layoffs and plant closings that were occurring at the Big Three. These programs include "guaranteed income stream benefits," joint national employee development and training programs at each company funded by company contributions, and "jobs bank" programs protecting workers displaced by non-market (i.e., non-sales) related causes.[38] A worker's seniority heavily influenced the level and duration of benefits they received in these programs, although the specific benefit criteria varied across the programs.

The 1990-93 and 1993-96 Big Three contracts provided extensive additions to the income security package. A significant new element in these contracts was the provision that workers could not be laid off for more than 36 weeks *whatever the cause*. These income and employment security programs became a costly and controversial issue at GM as a result of the extensive layoffs and plant closings that were occurring there. GM exhausted the $4.2 billion that had been allocated for income and employment security protections in the 1990-93 contract and in the winter of 1993 had to provide supplemental funding into the SUB funds (and divert $400 million from the joint GM-UAW training fund) to continue benefits until the contract was renewed. The 1993-96 contract at GM replenished the SUB funds and provided a total of $4 billion to cover the income and employment package. The income and employment security protections at GM included an early retirement program in an effort to more quickly reduce the work force.

These job security measures served a number of purposes. The job security measures appear to serve a symbolic function by providing some direct assurance to the workers that pay and work rule concessions would in fact lead to an improvement in their job security. It appears that this sort of explicit linking of concessions and employment enhancement is often necessary to convince workers of the value of such concessions.

The UAW also favored income security programs as a device to raise the cost of layoffs to the companies. The union hoped that as the relative cost of employment declined (given the rise in benefits paid to laid off workers) the companies would have a greater incentive to maintain employment. Unfortunately, increased income security programs also exerted a downward "income effect" on employment (by reducing the companies' total assets). It is unclear whether the relative cost or income effects dominated. In any case, large scale layoffs and plant closings continued at GM in the 1990s even in the face of the high income security penalties paid by the company.

Another explanation for the UAW's support of the income and job security programs was that these programs represent, in part, the union's effort to negotiate acceptable severance payments for workers. Under a severance approach, the UAW is essentially accepting the inevitability of plant closings and layoffs and uses the income security programs to ease workers' acceptance of this outcome.

The severance payment programs may even encourage further employment declines by stimulating complacency within workers and the UAW by reducing the costs to workers of further employment declines. On the other hand, the employment security programs, particularly those oriented toward training, may be facilitating changes in work practices that contribute to cost and quality improvements and thereby help encourage employment expansion. A potential positive benefit of the programs is to allay workers' fears that the participation in productivity improvement will jeopardize their own or other workers' employment prospects. Our field work suggests that the effects of income and job security programs vary substantially across plants and are closely linked to the dynamics of labor-management relations at the plant level.

It is interesting to note that the existence of very costly income and employment security programs at GM did not completely settle employment security issues. In the winter and spring of 1994, as sales began to recover at GM, in the local bargaining over the local contracts that supplemented the company contract the UAW pressured the company to extend even further employment protections. In many cases the union was successful at using whipsaw tactics and the threat of strikes at critical part plants whose shutdown would harm production throughout the GM system. For example, at a major parts making complex in Flint the company agreed to add a third shift and drop plans to cut employment while at its Shreveport plant the company agreed to specific employment increases to relieve work pace pressures (Templin and White 1994; *Daily Labor Reports* 1994b).

With respect to fringe benefits, the agreements reached at the Big Three after 1979 included a number of concessions. For example, all paid personal holidays (nine per year in the 1979-1982 agreement) and one regular holiday were eliminated. Although the companies have sought medical care copayments, to date the Big Three agreements have not included copays, but rather have been modified after 1979 to require steps such as second opinions and encouraged the use of preferred providers. In addition, the 1993-96 Big Three contracts diverted 22 cents in COLA adjustments to pay for fully paid medical benefit coverage.

The Increase in Diversity and Decentralization

The pay concessions and the move to contingent compensation schemes that tied wages to company performance increased the variation in employment conditions across the auto assembly companies. In addition, sizeable variation was created through the addition of the unionized Japanese transplants and the Saturn subsidiary, each of which had a separate agreement with the UAW, and through wage and benefit policies at the nonunion transplants.[39]

Further variation resulted from the fact that work rules and work organization were being modified in different ways and at a varied pace across auto assembly plants. The threat of increased employment loss due to either the further outsourcing of parts production, plant closings due to excess capacity, or production volume reductions due to demand fluctuations all created pressures to lower costs and improve product quality. Ultimately, the pressure for increased interplant work rule divergence came from the same source as the pressure for intercompany pay variation: the fear that even greater losses in employment would result if previous policies were maintained. Companies often used investment decisions as explicit leverage for these changes, in a strategy unions saw as "whipsawing," that is, forcing plants to compete against each other through concessions.

Some of these work rule changes involved increases in the "effort bargain" through a tightening of production standards. Other work rule changes include efforts to lower production costs by increasing the flexibility with which labor is deployed. Common examples of the latter include classification consolidation, limits imposed on job bidding rights, the use of work teams to promote multiskilling through job rotation, and a pushing down of certain responsibilities, such as quality inspection, from specialized staff to the shop floor. Finally, in many plants the modification of work rules interacted closely with ongoing worker involvement programs. In this way, the emergence of more decentralized collective bargaining was linked to a shift away from the job control focus that characterized postwar auto bargaining.

The extent of changes in work organization and employee involvement at different plants can be arrayed along a continuum, with the most change occurring at "greenfield" sites such as the Japanese transplants and Saturn. Anchoring the other end of the continuum are "brownfield" plants with ongoing operations that have changed very little, typically because of opposition to change in management and/or union ranks and because the demand for the plant's product has remained strong.[40]

There are two intermediate points along this continuum. Most similar to the new "greenfield" sites are those plants that are closed for several months for a major retrofit. The lengthy shutdown creates the opportunity for substantial change, both by signalling a new approach to labor-management relations or manufacturing methods and by allowing the time for extensive training. Changes in these cases are typically less extensive than in the pure "greenfield" cases and vary depending on the company's overall strategy and on the credibility of company threats to withhold investment unless changes are made.[41]

Another intermediate category would be "brownfield" plants in continuous operation that attempt a major "on-line" retrofit. These plants typically agree to make changes in their traditional procedures out of concern for their long-term competitiveness, prompted either by their management or union leadership, or by some kind of investment "carrot" or "stick."

There can be high variation within this group, in terms of motivation to change and the mechanisms of change. For example, the Oklahoma City and Shreveport plants of GM are both relatively new, built in the late 1970s and early 1980s, and both began as nonunion plants with a "team concept" during GM's "Southern Strategy" years. Although both were quickly unionized, the team concept was retained at Shreveport and was reaffirmed in three referenda at the plant during the 1980s. Shreveport became an important model for plants considering teams within and outside of GM. At Oklahoma City, however, the team concept was thrown out as soon as the plant was unionized. Only in the late

1980s was a revised and renamed version of teams implemented at the plant, along with a variety of initiatives that helped the plant make the J.D. Power "Top 10" list for quality in 1991.

Chrysler's Newark and Sterling Heights plants also reflect two different approaches to bringing about new work practices. The Newark plant is one of six Chrysler plants (two are assembly plants) covered under an innovative collective bargaining contract known as the Modern Operating Agreement (MOA). Modeled on the team system at GM's Shreveport plant, the MOA consists of a consolidation of job classes, a pay-for-knowledge system, work teams, extensive training, and the removal of status barriers between managers and workers. It is overseen by elaborate joint governance arrangements, involving union and management representatives at both plant and corporate levels, and a crew of union and management MOA facilitators to support the program. For the Newark plant, voting in favor of the MOA was the quid pro quo required by Chrysler before it would commit to investing in retrofitting the plant for a new product line.[42]

The Sterling Heights plant, on the other hand, is not an MOA plant and is covered by a mostly traditional collective bargaining contract. However, management initiated what is known as a Progressive Operating Agreement (POA), involving greater flexibility in labor deployment (i.e., fewer classifications) but not team structures or new compensation schemes. Chrysler installed the POA after ascertaining that there was little chance of convincing the local union to adopt the MOA and no opportunity to apply the leverage of an investment decision.

Often the more a plant is forced to make changes toward a flexible, team-based model by the threat of plant closure or disinvestment, the greater the difficulty with implementation, because workers perceive the changes as concessions. Chrysler's Newark plant first voted down the MOA and only voted in favor when it became clear that the alternative was a plant shutdown. After the second favorable vote, implementation was very slow. GM's Van Nuys plant in California was intended to become the next "NUMMI" and GM arranged for many members of NUMMI to go there as advisors and trainers. But the vote on moving to the team concept was bitterly divided, and at the same time that employees approved it, they also elected a new president opposed to the team concept. The changes never took hold, and the Van Nuys plant was closed in the fall of 1992.

The diversity and decentralization of collective bargaining arrangements has posed challenges for both management and the union (Katz

1993). While management has spurred much of the diversity by taking advantage of opportunities to apply the leverage of investment decisions to different plants, the resulting mix of contract arrangements creates considerable administrative complexity. This is particularly true when national-level wage, benefit, seniority, and job security policies must be synchronized with local-level variation in such areas as pay-for-knowledge and classification consolidation.

For the UAW, the decentralization of collective bargaining makes it difficult to develop a unified national strategy with respect to management-initiated reforms. The potential for "whipsawing" is particularly distressing for the union during a period of plant closings. For example, when GM's December, 1992 announcement of several plant closings left unclear which of two plants making large rear-wheel-drive vehicles would be closed, each plant undertook a campaign to convince the company to keep them open. This implicit pressure for local concessions infuriated the UAW and seriously strained relations with GM, while also creating conflict between plants. Finally, the close interaction between decentralization in bargaining and movements away from traditional "job control" unionism creates special problems for union strategy.

From Job Control to Increased Worker Involvement in Business Decision-Making

The expansion of worker and union involvement and the introduction of team forms of work organization in some plants has led to significant movements away from the traditional job control orientation of shop floor labor relations. The earliest worker participation programs were the QWL programs at GM. QWL programs were initially conceived of as experimental efforts designed to address worker concerns with the work environment and the climate of the relationship between workers and supervisors. Yet, in response to the industry's decline, at corporate and local levels, the distinction between QWL activities and "normal collective bargaining" often disappeared. Rather, worker involvement became inextricably linked with other aspects of labor relations. In the process, labor and management took significant steps away from the traditional job control orientation, and thereby contributed further to the erosion of the old labor relations system.

Early corporate-level steps toward greater union involvement in decisions included the placement of Douglas Fraser, then President of the UAW, on the Chrysler Board of Directors; "mutual growth forums" initiated at the Big Three where business decisions such as investment and outsourcing are discussed; and an informal exchange of information between national company and union officials. Joint (and often informal) activities underway at the local level include worker involvement in shop floor quality circles; local mutual growth forums analogous to national forums; and wide-ranging discussions between plant management and union officials concerning outsourcing, new technologies, quality, and production problems.

The range of worker participation now varies widely across plants.[43] In some plants a sizeable number of hourly workers participate regularly in quality circles or problem solving groups. A more extensive form of worker involvement occurs in the plants utilizing "team," "natural work group," or "modern operating" concepts. In these plants there are few and in some cases only a single, classification for production workers and often a "pay-for-knowledge" system which rewards workers for learning a wider variety of jobs. The teams or work groups receive advance warning regarding new technology and production plans, can voluntarily create job rotation schemes, and have input into the work area layout and production decisions. Informal dispute resolution mechanisms drive down the level of formal grievances. Often the introduction of teams has led to substantial reductions in the number of supervisors and a shift in the remaining supervisors' role toward that of a facilitator and coordinator.[44] At the same time, in some other plants labor-management relations are much as they were years ago.

The most extensive participatory labor-management relationship in the auto industry (and perhaps the most extensive anywhere) occurs at the Saturn Corporation. In July 1985, GM and the UAW reached agreement on the design of labor relations at Saturn. Saturn, a subsidiary of GM, is a complex of plants in Spring Hill, Tennessee, can now produce approximately 325,000 small cars a year. As this volume went to press, GM announced plans to place the Saturn unit in an expanded small-car group.[45]

The organizational structure of Saturn includes a number of committees, each of which includes worker or union representation (Rubenstein, Bennett, and Kochan 1993; Saturn Corporation 1985). At the shop floor level there are work units made up of 6 to 15 workers and a single production worker classification. Work units participate as a problem-solving group and make decisions concerning job assignments, job rotation, overtime, and recruitment.

Workers perform a variety of job tasks in their work area and also perform some of the planning and control tasks traditionally carried out by supervisors. At the top level of Saturn is a "strategic advisory committee" which engages in long-run business planning and includes the president of the UAW local union.

All employees of Saturn are paid on a salary basis. Currently production workers receive base wages that are 95% of the wage received by other GM auto workers and are eligible for a bonus based on how well training targets are met. This bonus has lifted Saturn worker earnings modestly above the earnings received by auto workers in other parts of GM. The intent is to expand the bonus to roughly 20% of the workers' earnings and shift the performance target to cost and quality objectives when Saturn is producing at full capacity.

Saturn sets out to provide a more permanent form of employment security for its work force than the traditional layoff system. Over the long run, 80% of the Saturn work force will be protected by a pledge that layoffs will not occur "except in situations arising from unforeseen or catastrophic events or severe economic conditions." The remaining 20% of the work force will be "associate members" and will not receive this protection. Issues such as the practical meaning of the employment security pledge and the mechanisms to be used to decide when a catastrophic event or severe economic conditions have occurred, have not yet been resolved.

There are two extremely novel aspects of shop floor industrial relations at Saturn. For one thing, the Saturn complex has no local seniority agreement. Thus, there is no formal role for seniority in matters such as job assignments, job bidding, overtime, and shift assignments. Most of these decisions are made informally by the work units (i.e., by workers themselves). Perhaps most revolutionary is the presence of union and management "partners" who co-manage decisions within the Saturn complex. Although the union does not have a formal place on the GM Board of Directors which makes the ultimate decisions concerning Saturn's investments, products, and pricing, the strong role played by union partners at Saturn gives the union a level of involvement in decision making that is unparalleled in contemporary American industrial relations.

Internal Union Debates

There have been heated debates inside the UAW and the auto work force concerning the virtues and effectiveness of worker and union involvement processes. Often these debates occur informally, in some cases they are triggered by specific events occurring at a plant such as a local contractual dispute or contract renegotiation. In the 1980s, the New Directions Movement emerged as an important organization that opposed the joint programs underway in the Big Three. Some candidates in the various elections occurring at the plant level identify themselves as part of this "movement." In addition, the leader of the movement, Jerry Tucker, has run for executive offices in the UAW under the heated opposition of the administrative caucus (the "party" that has dominated the internal affairs of the UAW since the rise of Walter Reuther). Tucker was soundly defeated in his 1992 bid to unseat Owen Bieber as President of the UAW, yet New Directions candidates have been more successful in a number of local UAW elections.[46]

Although the New Directions Movement represents the most formal and effective opposition to the administrative caucus that has surfaced in the UAW over the last twenty years, it is important to keep in mind that the UAW has a long tradition of democratic politics in its many local unions. The intensity of debates at the plant level may well have increased in recent years in the face of economic pressures and alternative restructuring methods, but this debate builds on longstanding traditions.

Debates inside the UAW about new work practices are exacerbated by the wide variation occurring in the form and consequences of new practices. The content and meaning of teams, for example, varies significantly across plants and at some plants, even across work groups. Teams at NUMMI, for instance, exhibit a "Japanese" orientation with their emphasis on standardized job assignments, continuous improvement, and a relatively strong role for supervisors. At some other plants, including Saturn, work teams are linked to the broadening of worker roles and worker autonomy. As a result, the UAW is under pressure to formulate positions toward teams and joint processes in the midst of wide experimentation and ambiguities in the new work practices.

While developments in Canada are largely beyond the scope of this chapter (see Kumar and Meltz [1992] for an overview), it is worth noting that the Canadian Auto Workers (CAW) has taken positions similar to New Directions on work restructuring and developed them into an "active opposition" strategy for dealing with the Big Three and the one Canadian unionized transplant (CAMI) (Kumar and Holmes 1994).

In the case of CAMI, the CAW carried out a longitudinal research study of worker attitudes after the plant opened and detected a steady decline in worker support for key provisions of lean production (Robertson, Rinehart, and Huxley 1992). This culminated in a strike of CAMI by the CAW in the fall of 1992, partly over an economic issue involving wage parity with other Canadian plants, but also over various concerns about lean production as implemented at the plant, most prominently a demand that team leaders be elected rather than appointed. The contract settling the strike includes provisions establishing crews of relief workers, constraints on the use of *kaizen* to change production processes without a review of staffing requirements with the union, election and recall procedures for team leaders, and other language restricting management flexibility in allocating labor. It is not yet clear how the CAW position on lean production—limiting certain practices while attempting to seize control of new work structures such as teams that can increase worker power in the production process—will influence the UAW position at the unionized transplants and at Saturn.

A Look to the Future

Currently labor and management in the auto assembly sector (and more generally in U.S. industrial relations) confront a choice regarding how to adjust industrial relations in the face of many environmental pressures. The interconnected nature of the auto (and any) labor relations system constrains the range of alternatives facing the parties. The auto assembly sector remains so interesting because it so starkly illustrates those choices.

On the one side stands the participatory approach represented by Saturn and the many other auto plants that have expanded worker and union involvement. A key step in this participatory direction are the elaborate joint programs coordinated at the corporate and national union levels in the Big Three, with the joint programs between Ford and the UAW standing out as an exemplar case (Ferman et al 1991). In the participatory approach, training programs are used to redeploy the work force which along with the reorganization of work and participatory processes help bring work back into Big Three plants.

The decentralization underway within the structure of collective bargaining and the expansion of Japanese transplants give local labor and management more flexibility than ever to promote a participatory approach if they so choose. In this sense, Saturn and the transplants have had a powerful "demonstration effect" in raising awareness of the viability of this participatory route.

At the same time, there are some within the ranks of both labor and management who would prefer to continue traditional approaches. These individuals either prefer the old system or doubt the efficacy of participation. The option here is to make small incremental changes in collective bargaining practices rather than bold reforms. Recent events involving GM and the UAW illustrate this approach. In the face of the cutbacks in GM plant capacity and employment, GM management and the GM department of the UAW agreed to provide more extensive early retirement benefits hoping that this would ease the tensions associated with the downsizing of the corporation. Fitting with an incremental approach, contracts in 1987, 1990, and 1993 substituted lump sum payments for previous annual improvement pay increases, but kept the profit-sharing segment only as a small component of the total pay package. Contracts negotiated at the Big Three in 1993 extended this approach by providing further income and job security programs functioning as severance payments to permanently laid off workers.

Another manifestation of this conservative path is found in resistance to the diffusion of "special case" collective bargaining agreements to a broader number of plants. The UAW leadership, while still accepting the Saturn and NUMMI pacts, has made it clear that they do not regard these pacts as a precedent to be followed by other plants and at times, has even expressed doubts regarding the value of those agreements. Many managers at Big Three plants also have been cautious and/or skeptical about the value of changing toward these new models, given the threat they pose to traditional roles.

Militants within either the work force or the UAW prefer to aggressively resist the downsizing of the Big Three by trying to limit the companies' ability to close plants and lay off workers. The New Directions movement supports this approach. Although it is not exactly clear how the militants could gain the job security they seek, at least a militant program in the years ahead could extend New Directions' opposition to joint programs.

The management counterpart to this militant strategy would promote the further outsourcing of production and seek further contractual pay and work rule concessions. In this strategy, at some point, management at the Big Three might seek to emulate their Japanese counterparts and operate on a nonunion basis by trying to win a strike with the UAW through the hiring of permanent striker replacements.

As one speculates about the form and likelihood of success for any of these strategies, it is clear that the choices made by labor and management influence one another. In the Big Three, a participatory approach by the union, for example, is unlikely to succeed in the face of managerial efforts to go nonunion. Likewise, managerial efforts to promote participatory restructuring are unlikely to progress where the union (or the work force) pursue a militant agenda.

The parties face choices in how they respond to the options before them and consequentially our predictive powers are limited. At the same time, it does appear that militancy (and possibly complacent acceptance of the status quo) by either side could override any interest in the other side to participatory restructuring. It seems clear that if participation is to become the centerpiece of auto assembly industrial relations in any of the Big Three, then both labor and management will have to promote this strategy more forcefully than they have in the recent past. At the time of the writing of this chapter, the rebound of sales and profits at the Big Three makes a conservative approach—including incremental changes in collective bargaining practices—a more likely outcome in the near term.

The Japanese transplants, while primarily utilizing practices common to Japanese auto plants (i.e., work teams with job rotation and standardized job assignments), have evolved toward a hybrid mixture including some practices typical of American auto plants (i.e., wage rates tied to jobs, no rotating shift schedule, election rather than appointment of team leaders), and some new practices (i.e., the peer review discharge procedure used at Honda). It remains to be seen if major modifications occur within the transplants' practices as the work forces in these plants age and the plants confront the periodic severe downturns common in the American auto market. The variation among the transplants may also increase over time. The unionized transplants may move toward a different hybrid model than the nonunion ones, and the transplants of the smaller Japanese companies may face more difficulties coping with the turbulence in the competitive environment as compared to the plants of Toyota, Honda, and Nissan who can rely on more substantial corporate resources.

The UAW is certain to focus sizeable future resources and energy around the unionization of the transplants, even in the face of the limited returns they have to date received from those efforts. The nonunion BMW and Mercedes-Benz plants that will open in South Carolina and Alabama, respectively, in 1996-97 will presumably also be targets for organizing. The success of these organizing efforts in turn is likely to be influenced by the image projected by the UAW and the union's decisions concerning the strategic choices discussed above. In this way, the fate of industrial relations at the Big Three and the Japanese (and now German) transplants may become closely intertwined. The results of the UAW's organizing efforts also will have significant ramifications for the auto parts sector and for the American labor movement overall, given the traditional interindustry pattern-setting role of the UAW.

Whatever strategies labor and management choose at the Big Three and the Japanese transplants, the central role played by industrial relations in the future of the auto assembly sector is likely to persist. Indeed, the dynamics of industrial relations in the next five years may be the most important influence on the three central issues confronting the industry—the competitive success of the Big Three in relation to Japanese rivals, the extent to which the Japanese transplants evolve away from the "lean production" model as practiced in Japan, and the degree to which the UAW articulates a clear strategy toward industry restructuring and new production methods.[47]

Endnotes

[1] Thirty-and-out pensions provide that a worker can retire and receive pension benefits after 30 years of service regardless of age.

[2] For an analysis of the internal political operation of the UAW, see Steiber (1962).

[3] For lively accounts of the early history of the UAW, see Reuther (1976) and Howe and Widick (1949). An interesting account of the UAW during World War II is provided in Lichtenstein (1982).

[4] Womack, Jones, and Roos (1990). Ford was by far the most vertically integrated of the Big Three early in the century, approaching 100% in the heyday of the Rouge complex. However, it reduced this level to about 50% after World War II and then to 40% during the 1980s.

[5] The Flat Rock plant, which opened in 1987, was initially owned 100% by Mazda. However, Ford has had an important relationship with the plant from the start: Ford owns 25% of Mazda, provided the land from a former foundry for the new plant, was instrumental in arranging Mazda's pre-launch recognition of the UAW, and purchases up to half of the plant's output, badged as Ford products. In 1992, when Mazda was faced with an extreme financial crunch, it sold half of the plant to Ford, and AutoAlliance Inc. was formed. In a reversal of the Ford-Mazda arrangement, Chrysler and Mitsubishi owned the Diamond-Star plant jointly from the time it opened in 1989, but in 1992 Chrysler sold its share back to Mitsubishi to raise cash. Thus the Diamond-Star plant is the only wholly owned Japanese plant to be unionized.

[6] Although we cover only U.S. plants here, there are four transplants (three Japanese and one Korean) in Canada as well: a GM-Suzuki joint venture known as CAMI, which has union representation through the CAW; a Honda plant in Alliston, Ontario; a Toyota plant in Cambridge, Ontario; and a Hyundai plant in Bromont, Quebec. The latter three plants are all nonunion.

[7] These are 1986 estimates, but the degree of vertical integration has changed little at Japanese companies in recent years. See Nishiguchi (1994).

[8] There is no universally accepted definition of local content, but the most common formulation was developed by the Environmental Protection Agency in the late 1970s. It calculates "domestic content" as the declared value of imported components divided by the average dealer wholesale price of the vehicle, subtracted from 100; by this measure, labor costs, advertising costs, and other "local" expenditures are included. Both American and Canadian parts are considered "domestic," under terms of the U.S.-Canada Auto Pact of 1965. On this basis, the average domestic content for the Big Three is 89% and for the transplants is 57%, with Honda of America Manufacturing, the first transplant operation, at a level of 68%; both Honda and Toyota have set targets of 75% domestic content within the next few years. Critics of the transplants use measures that attempt to evaluate the value of domestic parts directly and exclude other costs, and derive a lower "domestic content" estimate for the transplants of 48% (Economic Strategy Institute 1992).

[9] At this time, the U.S. and Japanese governments established the Voluntary Reduction Act (VRA) agreement to keep Japanese automotive imports at this level.

[10] The year 1992 was somewhat better for the Big Three, with automotive business losses of $1.5 billion at GM, $0.4 billion at Ford, and a profit at Chrysler of $0.7 billion. These gains from the low point of 1991 were overshadowed, however, by GM and Ford's decision to adopt new accounting standards requiring that pension liabilities be fully reflected on the company's books. As a result, they reported historic losses: $7.4 billion at Ford and $23 billion at GM. Chrysler adopted this accounting standard in 1993.

[11] Chrysler's 1993 operating profit of $2.4 billion was offset by adoption of the new accounting standards on pensions that were adopted by GM and Ford in 1992. With this charge, Chrysler reported a loss of $2.55 billion in 1993.

[12] We were not able to identify official Big Three employment or UAW membership statistics. The figures cited in the chapter are from unpublished UAW series, various years.

[13] The coproduction arrangements created in the assembly sector also have a broader impact on the competitive environment, as companies join in the exchange of parts, joint product development, or collaborative R&D projects.

[14] These factors are also apparent in some new coproduction arrangements, not involving joint ownership, in which U.S.-owned and managed plants build niche vehicles for Japanese companies. For example, in the early 1990s, Ford-owned and managed plants in Avon Lake, Ohio and Louisville, Kentucky began to manufacture vehicles for sale under Nissan and Mazda badges, respectively. While there is no direct management role for Nissan or Mazda, these plants (and the Ford plants in

Wayne, Michigan and Hermosillo, Mexico that make Mazda-designed Escorts) are more likely to implement Japanese-style work organization policies (e.g., teams, reduced job classifications) than other Ford plants.

[15] See Joel Cutcher-Gershenfeld and Patrick McHugh's chapter on the auto parts sector in this volume.

[16] An illustration of this leverage came in the summer of 1992 when a strike at GM-owned parts plants in Lordstown, Ohio forced the Saturn plant in Tennessee to stop production of its hot-selling new product. While this accelerated the settlement of the strike on terms favorable to the local union, it also prompted public criticism of the strike by the president of the Saturn local union. It is not yet clear what lessons are being drawn from this experience by both parties. GM may decide to boost its inventory buffers to avoid a recurrence or may work harder to avoid future strike activity. The UAW may use this leverage in more local disputes or may pressure locals to avoid such action for the sake of GM's overall financial health.

[17] This research used a methodology for productivity that adjusts for differences in vertical integration, product size, option content, and absenteeism in order to ensure comparability across plants. Quality data are derived from J.D. Power's Initial Quality Survey, adjusted to include only those defects that the assembly plant has some control over. The average labor productivity for the Japanese transplants was 20.9 hours per vehicle, compared with 16.8 hours per vehicle for Japanese plants in Japan and 24.9 hours per vehicle for Big Three plants in the U.S. For quality, the transplant performance, at 54.7 defects per 100 vehicles, was virtually equivalent to plants in Japan, at 42.1 plants per 100 vehicles, and substantially better than the Big Three plants at 78.4 defects per 100 vehicles.

[18] Williams and Haslam claim that performance differentials observed in the MIT Assembly Plant Study are not valid because such plant-level comparisons cannot be made accurately. However, their own case rests on shaky empirical evidence, including national industry data that includes both car and truck producers as well as suppliers, and company data that is unadjusted for vertical integration, among other problems.

[19] These issues were the focus of a conference in May 1993 at Wayne State University, entitled "Lean Production and Labor: Critical and Comparative Perspectives," proceedings forthcoming.

[20] The impact of programmable technologies on plant performance with respect to cost, quality, and variety appears to vary substantially based on the prevailing approach to organizing the production systems. Jaikumar (1986) notes the tendency for U.S. metalworking plants to use Flexible Manufacturing System (FMS) technology primarily for a small number of high-volume parts, both because of a legacy of large-batch mass production and in order to meet return-on-investment criteria. Japanese and German plants used the same technology to make many more parts in low-volume runs. The MIT Assembly Plant Study also revealed a difference in the relationship between the level of automation and labor productivity at plants with different production systems. A large subset of "high-tech" plants with relatively traditional mass production systems (including several Big Three plants) have much lower levels of performance on average—36% more hours per vehicle and 61% more

defects per 100 vehicles—than the plants that combine lean production methods with high levels of automation.

[21] See Piore and Sabel (1984) for a more elaborate discussion of how macroeconomic and structural changes in the world economy have increased the need for flexibility on the shop floor.

[22] The Japanese use of just-in-time inventories appeared to lower inventory costs and the Japanese *nenko* pay system with fewer job classifications and fewer links between specific job duties and pay seemed to contribute to lower production costs. For further description of labor relations and work organization practices in the Japanese auto industry see Cole (1971, 1979).

[23] In fact, even in the late 1970s and early 1980s, Japanese companies produced quite high levels of product variety for their *domestic market*, and that capability has facilitated their move into new market segments for larger, more option-laden (and higher margin) vehicles.

[24] Data from the MIT Assembly Plant Study suggests that Japanese "lean production" plants are able to absorb relatively high levels of product variety without any adverse impact on cost and quality, in contrast with U.S. and European mass production plants (MacDuffie, Sethuraman, and Fisher 1993).

[25] The few efforts of the American companies to produce niche vehicles at low volumes were relatively unsuccessful (e.g., the Fiero and the Reatta at GM). These failures may have had more to do with product design than with manufacturing cost and quality, but they did have the effect of curtailing support among the Big Three for moving very far toward a more flexible form of production system.

[26] Product variety trends at other plants are mixed. Most Japanese companies, in their plants in Japan, are also now reducing product variety, particularly in terms of the number of model variants and major options (e.g., engine/transmission combinations) offered for a given platform. The Japanese transplants, on the other hand, have tended to start their operations with very low complexity and then to add more models, more body styles, and more options over time.

[27] For example, central to General Motors' current drive to regain profitability is a steady cutback in platforms and product variants. The number of car platforms will be reduced to five and the number of product development teams to just three. Models are being trimmed from 144 in 1991 to 126 in 1992 and 117 in 1993 (*Automotive News*, May 17, 1993). Ford has also revived the "world car" strategy with a new product jointly developed between the U.S. and Europe known as the Mondeo, launched in Europe in March 1993 and replacing the Tempo/Topaz line in the U.S. for the 1994 model year. Unlike the Escort of the early 1980s, where the European and American versions shared almost no parts due to rivalries between design groups and different market requirements, the two versions of the Mondeo are said to share 70% to 80% of their parts. It remains to be seen whether this design achievement makes the "world car" strategy more feasible this time around.

[28] Another reason for this locational clustering is population movements which make this location a convenient distribution point.

[29] See Chris Erickson's chapter in this volume for a discussion of the relationship between auto and agricultural implement collective bargaining settlements.

[30] The history of wage setting in the U.S. auto industry is discussed in more detail in Harbison (1950), Reder (1949), Ross (1949), and Katz (1985).

[31] A chronology of postwar bargaining in the U.S. auto industry is in Bureau of National Affairs (various years) and U.S. Department of Labor (1969).

[32] Job control unionism is not synonymous with business unionism. The latter refers to the political philosophy of the labor movement. There are labor movements such as the Japanese that could be characterized as business unionist but not job control oriented.

[33] The wide diversity in shop floor relations is revealed by the variation in plant-level industrial relations performance indicators from two GM divisions. See Katz (1985: Chapter 5).

[34] See Katz (1985, 1988) for descriptions of early and mid-1980s bargaining.

[35] Assembler hourly wages at Ford were nearly identical to those at GM, while earnings at Chrysler were lower in the early and mid-1980s due to the special concessions described above. Skilled trades workers (such as tool and die makers and electricians) earned base hourly wages that were approximately 18% higher than the earnings of auto assemblers over the 1980s.

[36] See Katz and Meltz (1991).

[37] Note, the 1993 profit-sharing payout at Chrysler was the highest ever received by hourly workers at the Big Three. Profit-sharing bonuses were also very large for executives at Ford and Chrysler in 1993. In 1993, 200 Chrysler executives received bonuses that amounted to 100% of their annual salaries (Lavin 1994).

[38] These and other job and income security programs are described more fully in Katz (1985, 1988).

[39] The transplants, both union and nonunion, typically pay wages that are close to Big Three levels. However, the transplants have pension, medical care, and other fringe benefits that differ substantially from the benefits provided at the Big Three (the transplants often provide lower benefits) and from one another, often based on local labor market conditions.

[40] These are often relatively new plants where no major technological upgrading is needed to remain relatively viable economically, but can include old plants where a popular product allows a continuation of the status quo. Included in this category would be plants such as Chrysler's St. Louis #2 minivan plant, GM's Lake Orion plant making the Cadillac DeVille, and Ford's Chicago plant making the Taurus/Sable. According to Kumar and Meltz (1992), many Canadian plants of the Big Three also fit into this category.

[41] Included in this category would be plants such as NUMMI, where the same work force and union officials returned to an old GM facility under Toyota management (albeit after a two-year shutdown and a rehiring process that screened out some of the old employees); the Ford plant in Wayne, Michigan which, while closed

to prepare for producing the new Escort, introduced a new contract to implement a team system in part of the plant, while retaining a traditional contract for the rest of the plant; the Ford plant in Avon Lake, Ohio, which introduced a new contract with flexible work practices during the shutdown period before production of the new Ford-Nissan jointly designed minivan; and the Jefferson North plant of Chrysler, a new plant built to produce a new Jeep model but retaining the work force from the old Jefferson East plant which had been torn down.

[42] An account of the evolution of Chrysler's MOA plants by a research team from MIT and George Washington University, prepared initially for Chrysler and the UAW, will soon be released in abridged form by the Department of Labor.

[43] Evaluation of the impact of work restructuring on plant-level industrial relations and economic performance is provided in Katz, Kochan and Keefe (1987) and Katz, Kochan and Gobeille (1983).

[44] The role of supervisors does vary substantially even across sites that have introduced some sort of team system. As described below, at Saturn UAW members take on most of the responsibilities performed traditionally by supervisors while at NUMMI and some other sites relatively strong supervisory roles persist.

[45] The innovative contract at Saturn and where any additional Saturn assembly plant should be located has been the source of much controversy within the UAW at times exacerbating the tension that exists between the president of the UAW local union at Saturn (Michael Bennett) and Stephen Yokich, the head of the GM department of the UAW (see *Daily Labor Reports* 1994a).

[46] A chronology of the conflict between the New Directions Movement and the Administrative Caucus is provided in Katz and Kochan (1992:159).

[47] Further thoughts on the implications of lean production for workers and unions can be found in MacDuffie (1994b).

References

Adler, Paul. Forthcoming. "The 'Learning Bureaucracy': New United Motor Manufacturing, Inc." In B.M. Staw and L.L. Cummings, eds. *Research in Organizational Behavior*, Greenwich, CT: JAI Press.

Altshuler, Alan et al. 1984. *The Future of the Automobile*. Cambridge: MIT Press.

Babson, Steve. 1993. "Lean or Mean: Lean Production at Mazda," *Labor Studies Journal*, Vol. 18, no. 2 (Summer).

BNA (Bureau of National Affairs). 1980. "Ford Motor, EEOC Settle Nationwide Job Bias Action." *Daily Labor Report*, November 25, A-3, A-4.

_____. 1982a. "Auto Workers Held Entitled to Enforcement of Neutrality Pact with Dana Corporation." *Daily Labor Report*, June 8, A-3, A-4.

_____. 1982b. "General Motors Accepts Union Proposal to Pass Labor Costs Savings to Consumers." *Daily Labor Report*, January 12, A-11.

_____. 1983a. "Autoworkers Accept New Contract at Dana as Parties Sever Link with Auto Pattern." *Daily Labor Report*, December 12, A-1.

_____. 1983b. "EEOC, General Motors Sign $42 Million Agreement to Settle 10-Year-Old Charge." *Daily Labor Report*, October 10, A-3-A-5.

_____. Various years. *Collective Bargaining Negotiations and Contracts: Wage Patterns.* Washington, DC.

Brown, Clair, and Michael Reich. 1989. "When Does Union-Management Cooperation Work? A Look at NUMMI and GM-Van Nuys," *California Management Review*, Vol. 31, No. 4.

Budd, John W. 1992. "The Determinants and Extent of UAW Pattern Bargaining." *Industrial and Labor Relations Review*, Vol. 45, no. 3 (April), pp. 523-39.

CAW. 1993. *Work Reorganization: Responding to Lean Production.* North York, Ontario: The Canadian Auto Workers Union.

Cole, Robert E. 1979. *Work, Mobility and Participation*, Berkeley and Los Angeles: University of California Press.

_____. 1971. *Japanese Blue Collar*, Berkeley and Los Angeles: University of California Press.

Daily Labor Report. 1994a. "UAW Leaders Agree Saturn Must Expand Despite Problems With Current Contract," January 13, pp. A-7 and 8.

_____. 1994b. "UAW Accepts Local Agreement At Truck Plant," January 19, pp. A-17 and 18.

Economic Strategy Institute. 1992. "The Future of the Auto Industry: It Can Compete, Can It Survive?," Washington, DC.

Ferman, Louis A., et al. 1991. *Joint Training Programs: A Union-Management Approach to Preparing Workers for the Future.* Ithaca, New York: ILR Press.

Florida, Richard, and Martin Kenney. 1993. *Beyond Mass Production: The Japanese System and Its Transfer to the U.S.* New York: Oxford University Press.

Fucini, Joseph, and Suzy Fucini. 1990. *Working for the Japanese: Inside Mazda's American Auto Plant.* New York: Free Press.

Gelsanliter, David. 1990. *Jump Start: Japan Comes to the Heartland.* New York: Farrar, Straus, Giroux.

Haimsen, Joshua. 1992. "Just-In-Time, Supplier Proximity, and Productivity in the U.S. Auto Industry." Working paper, IMVP, MIT, Cambridge, MA.

Harbison, Fredrick H. 1950. "The General Motors-United Auto Workers Agreement of 1950." *Journal of Political Economy* Vol. 58 (October), pp. 397-411.

Howe, Irving, and B.J. Widick. 1949. *The UAW and Walter Reuther.* New York: Random House.

Jaikumar, Ramchandran. 1986. "Post-Industrial Manufacturing," *Harvard Business Review* (Nov.-Dec.), pp. 69-76.

Katz, Harry C. 1985. *Shifting Gears: Changing Labor Relations in the U.S. Automobile Industry.* Cambridge, MA: MIT Press.

_____. 1988. "Automobiles." In D. Lipsky and C. Donn, eds., *Collective Bargaining in American Industry.* Lexington, MA: D.C. Heath, pp. 13-54.

_____. 1993. "The Decentralization of Collective Bargaining: A Literature Review and Comparative Analysis." *Industrial and Labor Relations Review*, Vol. 47, no. 1 (October), pp. 3-22.

Katz, Harry C., and Thomas A. Kochan. 1992. *An Introduction to Collective Bargaining and Industrial Relations.* New York: McGraw-Hill.

Katz, Harry C., Thomas A. Kochan, and Kenneth R. Gobeille. 1983. "Industrial Relations Performance, Economic Performance, and QWL Programs: An Interplant Analysis." *Industrial and Labor Relations Review*, Vol. 37, no. 1 (October), pp. 3-17.

Katz, Harry C., Thomas A. Kochan, and Jeffrey H. Keefe. 1987. "Industrial Relations Performance and Productivity in the U.S. Automobile Industry." *Brookings Papers on Economic Activity*, Vol. 3, pp. 685-715.

Katz, Harry C., and Noah Meltz. 1991. "Profit Sharing and Auto Workers' Earnings: The United States vs. Canada," *Relations Industrielles*, Vol. 42, No. 3, pp. 513-530.

Katz, Harry C. and Charles F. Sabel. 1985. "Industrial Relations and Industrial Adjustment in the Car Industry," *Industrial Relations*, Vol. 24 (Fall), pp. 295-315.

Krafcik, John F. 1986. "Learning from NUMMI." Working paper, IMVP, MIT.

Krafcik, John F., and J.P. MacDuffie. 1989. "Explaining High Performance Manufacturing: The International Assembly Plant Study." Working paper, IMVP, MIT.

Kumar, Pradeep, and Noah Meltz. 1992. "Industrial Relations in the Canadian Automobile Industry." In R. Chaykowski and A. Verma, eds., *Industrial Relations in Canadian Industry*. Toronto: Dryden.

Kumar, Pradeep, and John Holmes. Forthcoming. "Change, But in What Direction? Divergent Union Responses to Work Restructuring in the Integrated North American Auto Industry." In F. Deyo, ed., *Global Capital, Local Labour*. London: Macmillan.

Lavin, Douglas. 1994. "Chrysler Aides To Get Bonuses Equal to Salaries," *Wall Street Journal*, p. A-3.

Lichtenstein, Nelson. 1982. *Labor's War at Home*. London: Cambridge University Press.

MacDuffie, John Paul. Forthcoming. "Human Resource Bundles and Manufacturing Performance: Flexible Production Systems in the World Auto Industry." *Industrial and Labor Relations Review*.

_____. 1994b. "Workers' Roles in Lean Production: The Implications for Worker Representation," forthcoming in volume of papers from "Lean Production and Labor: Critical Perspectives" conference at Wayne State University, May 1993.

_____. 1991. "Beyond Mass Production: Flexible Production Systems and Manufacturing Performance in the World Auto Industry." Ph.D. dissertation, Sloan School of Management, MIT.

MacDuffie, John Paul, and John F. Krafcik. 1992. "Integrating Technology and Human Resources for High Performance Manufacturing: Evidence from the World Auto Industry." In T.A. Kochan and M. Useem, eds., *Transforming Organizations*. New York: Oxford University Press.

MacDuffie, John Paul, K. Sethuraman, and M.L. Fisher. 1994. "Product Variety and Manufacturing Performance: Evidence from the International Automotive Assembly Plant Study," under revision at *Management Science*.

Nishiguchi, Toshihiro. 1994. *Strategic Industrial Sourcing: The Japanese Advantage*. New York: Oxford University Press.

Parker, Mike, and Jane Slaughter. 1988. *Choosing Sides: Unions and the Team Concept*. Boston: South End Press.

Piore, Michael J. 1982. "American Labor and the Industrial Crisis." *Challenge 25* (March-April), pp. 5-11.

Piore, Michael J., and Charles F. Sabel. 1984. *The Second Industrial Divide*. New York: Basic Books.

Reder, Melvin W. 1949. "The Structure of the 1948 General Motors Agreement." *Review of Economics and Statistics* Vol. 31 (February), pp. 7-14.

Reuther, Victor G. 1976. *The Brothers Reuther and the Story of the UAW: A Memoir.* Boston: Houghton Mifflin.

Robertson, David, et al. 1993. *The CAMI Report: Lean Production in a Unionized Auto Plant.* North York, Ontario: CAW-Canada Research Department.

Robertson, David, James Rinehart, and Christopher Huxley. 1992. "Team Concept and Kaizen: Japanese Production Management in a Unionized Canadian Auto Plant." *Studies in Political Economy* Vol. 39 (Autumn), pp. 77-107.

Ross, Arthur M. 1949. The General Motors Wage Agreement of 1948. *Review of Economic and Statistics* Vol. 31 (February), pp. 1-7.

Rubenstein, Saul, Michael Bennett, and Thomas A. Kochan. 1993. "The Saturn Partnership: Co-Management and the Reinvention of the Local Union." In B. Kaufman and M. Kleiner, eds., *Employee Representation: Alternatives and Future Directions.* Madison, WI: Industrial Relations Research Association.

Shimada, Haruo, and John Paul MacDuffie. 1987. "Industrial Relations and 'Humanware': Japanese Investments in Automobile Manufacturing in the United States," Working paper, Sloan School of Management, MIT.

Stieber, Jack. 1962. *Governing the UAW.* New York: Wiley.

Templin, Neil, and Joseph B. White. 1994. "GM to Add Truck Capacity; Union Says Firm Dropped Plans to Slash 1,200 Jobs," *Wall Street Journal*, February 16, p. A-4.

U.S. Department of Labor, Bureau of Labor Statistics. 1969. "Wage Chronology—General Motors Corporation, 1939-68." Bulletin 1532. Washington, DC: GPO.

Womack, James P., Dan Jones, and Dan Roos. 1990. *The Machine that Changed the World*, Rawson Associates, New York.

Chapter 6

Competition and Divergence: Collective Bargaining in the North American Auto Supply Industry

Joel Cutcher-Gershenfeld and Patrick P. McHugh
Michigan State University

Editor's Abstract

The auto supply industry contains both producers of original equipment components for auto manufacturers (the OEMs) and companies which produce replacement parts used in motor vehicle repair. GM, Ford, and Chrysler each have their own parts supply division and also buy components from independent companies. Historically, this has been a source of linkage between auto supply and auto assembly collective bargaining. Moreover, the same union, the UAW, represents employees in both auto assembly and auto supply, although other labor organizations also have contracts at some parts plants. The Japanese auto manufacturers do not have separate parts divisions, but are tightly linked to particular suppliers through "kiretsu" structures of shared stock ownership, financing arrangements, and management exchange programs.

Auto component manufacturers have been under constant cost pressures from the OEMs for more than a decade. Increased competition in the auto parts industry is driven partially by increased competition in the automobile market itself. It has also been increased by mobile capital and a surge in both domestic nonunion and foreign production. At the same time, the automakers (the OEMs) have shifted to just-in-time production and, hence, are demanding improved quality and tightly scheduled, guaranteed delivery from parts makers. Tighter integration of operations between a select group of suppliers and OEMs coexists with a sharply competitive overall market environment.

As a result, collective bargaining in the auto supply sector is diverging toward extremes. In one group of independent supply firms and in the components facilities of the OEMs themselves, employee involvement has emerged as a key component of labor-management cooperation. Good labor relations and employee involvement facilitate timely delivery, high-quality output, and labor flexibility. This is one extreme. On the other hand, other employers have chosen to compete primarily on the basis of price, have demanded deep concessions, and have taken initiatives to undermine the institutional integrity of organized labor. Union representation in the auto parts industry has declined sharply over the 1980s and early 1990s. After 1985, average hourly earnings in auto parts fell relative to those in auto assembly, and relative to manufacturing more generally (which themselves were declining in real terms).

Cutcher-Gershenfeld and McHugh contend that nonunion firms are increasingly setting the agenda for industrial relations in the auto supply industry. The nonunion firms have set the agenda on concession bargaining—for instance, around employee health care copayments—and in flexible work practices centered on continuous improvement (*kaizan*). Large unionized independents like Budd and the Big Three parts divisions have demonstrated leadership in bargaining employee involvement, training, investment in new technology, and other items previously excluded from negotiations by management rights clauses. Still, with the growth of the largely nonunion Japanese supply networks, and as TRW and other independent suppliers have shifted employment to new nonunion facilities, nonunion labor relations practices and employment conditions have become increasingly important in this industry.

o   o   o

Collective bargaining in the North American auto supply industry is diverging toward both contentious and cooperative extremes. International and domestic nonunion competition provide a turbulent context in which auto suppliers and unions are making key strategic choices about the very nature of their relationships. At the contentious extreme there are employer initiatives in this industry aimed at undermining the core institutional legitimacy and status of unions. At the cooperative extreme there are joint partnerships in this industry that represent a fundamental transformation in industrial relations.

The central role played by automobiles in our society ensures that the overall North American auto industry is closely followed by the business press, with collective bargaining developments regularly reported to the general public. In contrast, the auto supply sector of our economy is poorly understood—even by experts—and is largely hidden from the general public. As a result, we will begin this chapter with a definition of the industry and a detailed look at the structure of the auto supply sector. This background information is essential to an understanding of recent collective bargaining developments, which are at both the cooperative and contentious extremes.

Industry Definition

There is no typical auto supply firm, just as there is no typical part or component in an automobile. Consequently, the automotive supply industry extends across several standard industrial classifications. Motor-vehicle parts and accessories (SIC 3714) accounted for 68% of the total value of shipments in the industry in 1984; automotive stampings (SIC 3465) accounted for 18%; engine electrical equipment (SIC 3694) composed 6%; carburetors, pistons, and rings (SIC 3592) and storage batteries (SIC 3691) consisted of 3% each; and vehicle lighting equipment (SIC 3647) accounted for 1% (U.S. Senate Investigation 1987). Other industries also produce motor vehicle parts, including fabricated rubber products (SIC 3069), steel springs (SIC 3493), and internal combustion engines (SIC 3519).

Because of the complex makeup of the auto supply sector, the exact number of firms involved is unknown. Estimates of the number of firms in the industry range from 4,000 to 15,000 (U.S. Senate Investigation 1987; U.S. Department of Commerce 1986b). Two factors account for discrepancies in estimates of the number of firms in the industry. First, an automobile is a complex network of parts originating from an assortment of firms ranging from producers of carpet and upholstery to paints and chemicals to refrigeration and heating equipment. The Motor-Vehicle Manufacturers Association (MVMA 1985) lists 36 different industrial types which provide parts and components to the original equipment manufacturers (OEMs). Most of these firms are not exclusive producers for the automotive sector (for example, steel companies or chemical companies) and do not get classified in those SIC codes which are normally regarded as members of the automotive supply industry. Therefore it is difficult to discern exactly how encompassing the automotive supply industry is in terms of the number of firms and the number of employees involved. Second, it is unclear how smaller job shops, which act as suppliers-to-the-suppliers, are treated in automotive supply industry statistics.

In 1990, total employment in the automotive supply industry (defined in this case as SIC 3465, 3592, 3647, 3691, 3694, and 3714) was estimated at 604,000, while production worker employment was at about 482,000 (U.S. Department of Commerce 1992a). Table 1 presents the changes in employment for the industry over the 12 years prior to 1990. Peak employment in the industry occurred in 1978 with total employment at 759,000 and production worker employment at 627,000. During the next 12 years, total employment dropped by 20% and production worker employment dropped by 23%. Despite increases in industry shipments, some projections indicate that total employment is likely to continue to fall in the years to come partially due to improved productivity and the introduction of new technologies and partly due to continued cost pressures on auto suppliers (U.S. General Accounting Office 1988).

TABLE 1
U. S. Auto Supply Employment, 1976-90[a]

	1976	1978	1980	1982	1984	1986	1988	1990
Total employment (in thousands)	659	759	595	522	619	614	647	604
Production workers (in thousands)	546	627	468	409	500	490	521	482
% Production workers	82.8	82.6	78.6	78.3	80.7	79.8	80.5	79.8

Source: U.S. Department of Commerce 1987, 1988, 1989, 1992a.
[a]Automotive Parts and Accessories (SIC 3465, 3592, 3647, 3691, 3694, 3714).

Industry and Market Structure

To understand collective bargaining in the auto supply industry, it is important to first understand the structure of the marketplace and of the companies in the industry. Key issues of bargaining leverage derive from the industry and market structures.

Two Market Segments

The automotive supply industry is split between two distinct market segments. The largest segment contains producers of original equipment parts and components for motor vehicle manufacturers (referred to as original equipment manufacturers or OEMs). The second segment involves the production of replacement parts for the motor vehicle aftermarket. Although some firms are producers in only one portion, many firms are involved in production for both market segments.

OEM Suppliers. Historically, in the first part of this century, innovative auto supply firms were carefully nurtured by auto manufacturers

(Helper 1991b). These close relations were increasingly undermined in the post-war years as the OEMs shifted to competitive bid processes where cost became the primary criteria driving supplier contracts. Under the competitive system, there was little information sharing between suppliers and OEMs, with multiple suppliers often receiving contracts for a given component—both of which increased OEM leverage vis-à-vis suppliers. As a result, cost pressures from OEMs have long been a factor in auto supply industry collective bargaining.

More recently, pressure to meet OEM customer requirements is having an even further impact on the content and process of bargaining. First, the cost pressures have become even more intense in the past decade—reflecting the competitive pressure associated with a doubling of the number of companies building cars in North America and very little growth in demand. The OEMs have successfully demanded constant prices or even annual reductions in product costs of 1% to 3% throughout the 1980s and have continued into the 1990s. For example, GM has implemented a 3-2-2 plan in which it hoped to secure 3% cuts in 1991, 2% in 1992 and in 1993.[1] Similarly, Ford is asking its parts producers to cut costs by 1% annually until 1997. Ford's own Automotive Components Group (ACG) is afforded no advantages in this process, the bidding system requires internal suppliers to compete against outside suppliers (U.S. Department of Commerce 1992a).

Concurrent with the cost pressures is a return to the historic pattern of closer relations between OEMs and suppliers. Based on Japanese manufacturing methods, there is increased willingness on the part of OEMs to award long-term contracts to a core group of key suppliers in order to also promote joint product design, just-in-time delivery and sharing of cost savings (U.S. General Accounting Office 1988; Womack, Jones, and Roos 1991). A recent survey by Helper (1991a) indicates that customer-supplier contracts have been getting longer and that relations between suppliers and OEMs are broadening—with some variance across OEMs. For example, in 1984, 30% of GM's contracts with outside suppliers were multi-year, while 70% of Ford's were multi-year in 1985. There has also been an increase to 2.3 average contracts per year with a given supplier compared to 1.2 contracts per year in 1984 (Helper 1991a, 1991b).

As part of these more tightly integrated relationships, OEMs are pressuring suppliers to meet highly restrictive quality and delivery standards. Each OEM has its own program along these lines, such as "Targets of Excellence" (GM), "Q1" (Ford), and "Pentastar" (Chrysler).

As an example of the scope of these programs, consider a report on an audit at Simpson Industries, an engine parts maker. The General Motors audit team inspected the company's research and design efforts, financial situation (including the cost of its medical plans), and interviewed line workers without management present to assess the labor relations climate (Treece 1987). The most restrictive programs are found at the Japanese manufacturing operations in North America, which include Toyota, Honda, NUMMI (Toyota/GM), Diamond Star, AAI (Mazda/Ford) and others. Matching these higher Japanese standards are a new generation of programs from the U.S. companies, such as Ford's more comprehensive "Total Quality Excellence" standard. As one auto supply manager commented, "The goalposts are moving all the time." The supplier inspection programs ensure that issues of quality, safety, and the continuous improvement of operations (which typically involves team-based work systems) appear on the collective bargaining table—alongside management demands that emanate from the cost pressures.

Suppliers who meet OEM standards are accorded first-tier status which provides an opportunity for attaining a long-term contract. This allows for longer-term collective bargaining agreements as well. It also enables a select group of auto suppliers to take seriously union pressures for increased employment security (as a quid pro quo for participation in continuous process improvement efforts).

As a core group of supplier firms receive an increasing number of long-term contracts from the OEMs, however, the status of other supplier firms shifts. They may move into second-tier status (suppliers to the first-tier suppliers), they may seek business outside the industry, or they may go out of business. The potential impact is vast. For example, Ford reduced the number of its suppliers for North American operations from about 3,200 in 1980 to 2,100 in 1987, with further cuts since then (Moskal 1987). Similarly, during the late 1980s, there were 600 to 800 suppliers per model at Chrysler. By contrast, the new 1993 LH and 1994 PL car lines have 170-140 suppliers. Through its SCORE (supplier cost-reduction effort), Chrysler claims to have saved $150 million (U.S. Department of Commerce 1992a). Overall, the number of firms in the U.S. auto supply industry may be cut by more than half by the turn of the century, which has led some observers to characterize this marketplace as a "blood bath."

Suppliers to the Aftermarket. The decision to sell in the aftermarket liberates the supplier's labor-management relations activities from direct

OEM pressure. Moreover, general manufacturing wages and working conditions become an alternative point of comparison for collective bargaining for aftermarket suppliers. As a consequence, employers have sought to reduce compensation levels and alter working arrangements within the firm to better coincide with various local manufacturing referents (most likely not OEMs).

Historically this portion of the industry has been counter-cyclical, since people fix cars rather than replace them during economic downturns. By contrast, OEM sales are a primary element of the business cycle. Thus, the aftermarket is further separated from the economic dynamics in the OEM market. Also, any consideration of employment security is likely to be constrained in the aftermarket since long-term business contracts are not common. There are some possibilities for long-term contracts here—for example contracts with large retail organizations that do auto repair such as Sears and Montgomery Wards. Still, there is not the same sharply defined multi-tier structure, so there is not the same sharply differentiated array of collective bargaining practices.

Size and Ownership Structure

Overlaid on the two markets (and the multiple tiers within the OEM market) are a mix of small, medium-sized and large firms. Most of these firms are independent companies, but each of the OEMs has its own parts supply divisions. The Japanese firms do not have separate parts divisions, but are tightly linked through what is termed a "kiretsu" structure of shared stock ownership, common bank financing arrangements, and management/worker exchange programs.

First-Tier Divisions Within OEMs. The parts subsidiaries of General Motors, Ford, and Chrysler are the largest producers in the auto supply industry. Most of these producers are separate operating units or divisions within the automotive manufacturing firms (for example, AC/Rochester in General Motors). These internal supply operations account for approximately 60% of the shipments in the motor-vehicle parts and accessories component of the automotive supply industry (U.S. Senate Investigation 1987).

In terms of labor-management relations, the subsidiaries have traditionally inherited many of the provisions originating from negotiations between their respective parent organizations and the UAW. As pressures for improved performance mounted throughout the auto supply industry in the 1970s and 1980s, subsidiaries have been constrained in departing from the automobile assembly pattern. Specifically, union leadership at UAW organized facilities have been reluctant to disengage from pattern bargaining. As a result, there has been mounting pressure from the OEMs to outsource parts.

An interesting contrast is afforded by the IUE, which represents employees at GM's Packard Electric Division, which produces electrical components. This union has adopted a somewhat different strategy from the UAW. The IUE has been more willing to restructure compensation, for example, in the form of a multi-tier wage plan (*Business Week* 1983). There is some evidence to suggest that the increased flexibility on wages has been associated with a reduced rate of plant closings and layoffs. For example, by the late 1980s, not a single IUE GM employee was on layoff. Note, however, that an equally important explanatory factor in this case is the increased use of electronics in automobiles—which has been a source of increased demand for Packard Electric products.

On the one hand, these supply operations at the OEMs benefit from capital investment and dedicated supply arrangements. As well, they benefit from supportive institutions created under national UAW agreements which provide for a range of joint committees dedicated to issues such as training, quality, job security, employee involvement, and safety. On the other hand, these plants and divisions are burdened by both corporate systems and national contracts (for example, management can be constrained by corporate accounting systems, while the local union can be constrained by the national contract regarding wages and benefits).

There is a constant pressure on these plants to justify keeping their work in-house (resulting in what some UAW activists term pitting plants against plants and workers against workers). For example, during the mid to late 1980s, product lines in the GM system were designated with green, yellow, or red lights (Krebs 1987). A green light meant that the plant was a world-class competitor in cost and quality. A yellow light indicated that the plant still had a possibility of being saved. These were most prevalent—a plant with an 8% cost disadvantage would be an example here. The operation may be able to develop a plan to eliminate the disadvantage through evaluating product design, manufacturing processes, geographic location, and the labor-management relations in the plant and area. The labor-management situation ranks near the top in importance. A red light meant the operation could not compete in terms of cost and quality at GM and was at imminent risk of closing.

This includes plants with a 15% or more disadvantage on a cost basis. Thus, despite the many advantages of being an internal OEM components operation, there are still pressing competitive issues and some unique constraints all of which impact on collective bargaining.

Large First-Tier Independents. There are several large independent diversified suppliers that account for substantial shares of automotive supply industry sales. The top four independent suppliers, Borg Warner (producer of engine transmissions and suspension components, turbo chargers, plastic parts, and other miscellaneous parts), Budd (producer of body stampings and frames, wheels, brakes, and plastic related parts), Rockwell International (producer of axles, brakes, electronic vehicle management systems, plastic body panels, seat recliners, and other various parts), and TRW (producer of electronic parts, electromechanical devices, piston rings, power steering systems, seat belts, and other parts) accounted for almost 10% of the sales in motor-vehicle parts and accessories (U.S. Senate Investigation 1987). Of these top four independent suppliers, only Budd is concentrated in the automotive supply industry. The other three companies are diversified, receiving the majority of their net sales outside the automotive sector (U.S. Senate Investigation 1987). Other notable large independents include: Kelsey-Hayes, Eaton, Dana, Sheller-Globe, Magna International, Nippondenso, Tenneco Automotive, Lear-Siegler, Allied Corporation, DuPont, ITT, and Litton.

Large independent suppliers have had a longstanding relationship with unionization, particularly with the UAW. The Kelsey-Hayes Wheel Company in Detroit was the scene of the first successful sit-down strike and effective organizing effort by the UAW (Babson 1986). Afterward, the focus of UAW efforts quickly shifted to the OEMs, where success at the automotive manufacturing level set the configuration for auto supply reliance on pattern bargaining and the predominance of the UAW. Thus, until the 1970s, large independent suppliers tended to follow patterns set at national negotiations with the Big Three or Big Four automobile producers and the UAW. Though there was usually a lag, workers at supplier firms came to expect wage and benefits commensurate with those at Ford, GM, and Chrysler.

Since the rise of concessions in the early 1980s, the link to OEM wage, benefits, and other gains has eroded. The first-tier suppliers were quick to follow Chrysler's pattern of concession bargaining and layoffs, but have had many more rounds of concessionary demands and layoffs. According to figures reported by Herzenberg and Shaiken, while Big

Three components employment has declined by over 30% from 1978 to 1988, employment in U.S. unionized independent auto parts suppliers has fallen by almost 50%. Interestingly, employment in U.S. nonunion independent part supplier has risen 33%, while Canadian and Mexican parts employment from 1978 to 1988 has risen by 9% and 178%, respectively (Herzenberg and Shaiken 1990). Clearly the patterns among the independent suppliers are more divergent than within the OEMs.

The growth of employment in the nonunion operations and in Mexico and Canada reveals a critical point of leverage among the large independent manufacturers. These firms are best able to utilize capital investment as a strategic tool for transforming the nature of employment relations. One study of a large independent supplier, for example, documented its transformation from being almost entirely unionized to being almost entirely nonunion—all through the selective use of investment in new technology and the sale or purchase of plants (Verma 1985; Verma and Kochan 1985).

Nonetheless, the large independent suppliers continue to be deeply influenced by OEM labor relations. For example, nearly all of the large independent suppliers have experimented with various cooperative labor-management innovations based on OEM models. These include employee involvement initiatives, health and safety committees, joint training committees, employee assistance programs, and team-based work systems.

Smaller Second-Tier and Third-Tier Independents. Despite the large market share held by the top handful of companies, there are thousands of smaller firms that also serve OEM supply operations, first-tier independent suppliers, or the aftermarket. According to the Department of Commerce, approximately 34% of the firms in SIC 3714 have less than 10 employees, while only 7% have greater than 500. The other SIC components of the automotive supply industry have similar structural patterns (U.S. Department of Commerce 1986b). Table 2 displays industry concentration for the motor vehicle parts and accessories portion of the auto supply industry. This table illustrates both the large market share held by several large firms and the much smaller percentage of shipments accounted for by the multitude of smaller producers. Therefore, the industrial structure of the automotive supply industry, for the most part, consists of a small number of very large diversified firms and vast numbers of small focused firms.

Historically, smaller firms in the auto supply industry have tended not to be organized. Intensive performance pressures—especially over

TABLE 2

U.S. Auto Supply Industry Concentration, 1977-87[a]

	1977	1982	1987
Number of companies	2,194	2,000	2,306
Percent of the value shipments accounted for by:			
4 largest companies	62%	61%	60%
8 largest companies	70%	69%	66%
20 largest companies	79%	77%	76%
50 largest companies	86%	84%	83%

Source: U.S. Department of Commerce 1987.
[a]Motor Vehicle Parts and Accessories (SIC 3714).

the past decade—have driven many of these less resource-rich suppliers to make immediate and drastic changes in employment relations. They have always been the first to absorb fluctuations in production volume, reflected in constant rounds of layoffs and rehiring. Frequently, employers did not feel that they had sufficient resources (or time) to create new labor-management relationships, so they opted either to downsize, escape to a new nonunion facility or close operations altogether. There are some interesting instances, however, where concerns for organizational survival and/or the assistance of outside third parties have led to far-ranging forms of cooperation within smaller auto supply firms (Block et al. 1990).

For small independent suppliers, the relevant point of comparison for labor negotiations is most likely to be the standard of living in the community in which the plant resides. Thus it is important to consider the firm and community, as well as the industry structure, as central to the context for negotiations. Still, there is a key area of OEM influence in that many of the large independent manufacturers are adopting quality target programs along the same lines as the OEM programs. As a result, new pressures are created in the smaller suppliers to present evidence of worker-led quality inspection, continuous improvement efforts, joint labor-management committees, and other forms of innovation.

In sum, car lines are becoming more varied, creating needs for flexible machining processes that will allow production changes to be made at minimal cost. First-tier suppliers are shifting to be high-tech providers that join automakers in designing parts and in tightly integrated just-in-time delivery arrangements. Diverse innovations are emerging in first-tier collective bargaining, reflecting competitive pressures to break from pattern bargaining combined with resources that allow for innovation. Beneath this first-tier are multiple tiers of subsuppliers who are more constrained for resources, more vulnerable to cyclical demand and increasingly likely to either leave the auto supply sector or go out of business. Collective bargaining in the second and third tiers reflects the resource constraints in rounds of concession bargaining, punctuated by plant closings.

Competitive Challenges

Throughout its history, the automotive supply industry's economic fortunes have been a function of the ebb and flow of the American motor-vehicle manufacturing industry, while economic success for motor-vehicle producers has been tied to the business cycle. During recessions, used-car sales are robust and home maintenance of automobiles increases, which creates prosperity in the smaller aftermarket segment of the industry. On the other hand, prosperity in the original equipment market varies directly with changes in national income. This pattern was broken during the oil price hikes of the 1970s and subsequent recessions when both the aftermarket and original equipment market experienced declines due to reductions in the amount of driving (Dorfman 1984). Overlaid on the economic pressures resulting from the business cycle and shifts in driving patterns are two key additional sources of competitive pressure—the impact of nonunion and international competition on collective bargaining in unionized operations.

Nonunion and New Foreign-Owned Domestic Competitors

The auto supply sector has always had a lower union density in comparison with auto assembly, but recent developments have dramatically increased the importance of the nonunion sector. This industry typifies the thesis in the Kochan, Katz, and McKersie (1986) study of *The Transformation of American Industrial Relations*, which held that the non-union sector was replacing the unionized sector in setting the agenda for employment relations. In auto supply we find nonunion locations setting the agenda on concessions, around employee health care co-payments, for example, and around employee participation innovations, such as the use of team-based work systems. In fact, many of the larger independent suppliers have union and nonunion plants under their umbrella, and they use the nonunion plants as a model for and a source of leverage regarding changes in the employment relationship at unionized facilities. At the same time, unionized parts and components operations of OEMs have been particularly innovative with regard to joint consultation over investment, training, employee involvement, and product development.

As direct competitors, the nonunion facilities tend to be newer. As a result, they have competitive advantages in terms of newer equipment, less entrenched work practices, and reduced pension costs. In the case of brand new "greenfield" facilities, there is a perceived additional competitive advantage associated with beginning production with a new work force carefully selected to match the work system.

A newly emerging group of largely nonunion suppliers is comprised of the Japanese suppliers following Japanese OEMs who have been increasing production capacity in North America. In the 1980s Japanese firms invested more than $5 billion dollars in U.S.-based assembly facilities including seven Japanese-affiliated auto manufacturers and more than 100 Japanese-affiliated auto parts suppliers (U.S. General Accounting Office 1988). Recent estimates suggest that there are now between 120 to 300 Japanese-affiliated suppliers in the U.S., with about 42% being joint ventures (Herzenberg and Shaiken 1990; U.S. Department of Commerce 1992a). These new auto supply firms represent a further competitive challenge since many of them bring a new array of work practices centered on teamwork and continuous improvement, both of which are linked to just-in-time delivery, integrated product design, preventative maintenance, reduced in-process inventory, and other manufacturing innovations. Table 3 illustrates the seriousness of the competitive challenge associated with the new manufacturing methods. The new manufacturing methods are evolving and taking on a unique character in North America, demonstrating that the competitive threat is not just from abroad and that it is not dependent on a Japanese work force (Cutcher-Gershenfeld et al. 1993).

Altogether, Japanese, European, and Canadian firms had invested in about 475 auto parts plants in the U.S. (351 or 74% are foreign owned, while 124 or 26% are joint ventures) as of 1992. There are also 10 foreign-owned auto parts R&D centers in the U.S., 9 Japanese and 1 German (U.S. Department of Commerce 1992a). Most of these facilities are nonunion (though exact estimates are difficult to locate), which means that the nonunion domestic operations with Japanese links need to be further understood as part of a larger pattern of international investment in the U.S. auto supply sector.

TABLE 3

Average Supplier Performance
Comparison of Average Japanese and American Suppliers[a]

	Japan	U.S.
Supplier performance[b]		
Die change times (minutes)	7.9	114.3
Job classifications	2.9	9.5
Machines per worker	7.4	2.5
Inventory levels (days)	1.5	8.1
Number of daily JIT deliveries	7.9	1.6
Supplier/Assembler Relations[c]		
Number of suppliers per assembly plant	170	509
Proportion of parts delivered JIT (%)	45.0	14.8
Proportion of parts single sources (%)	12.1	69.3

[a]Adapted from Womack, Jones, and Roos 1990, p. 157.

[b]From a 1989 study of 18 supplier plants in Japan and 10 supplier plants in the U.S.

[c]From a 1990 assembly plant survey.

International Competition

In 1972 the U.S. automotive supply industry had a $821 million trade surplus which steadily increased until 1981 when it peaked at close to $3 billion (U.S. Department of Commerce 1988). As Table 4 indicates, the industry encountered its first trade deficit in 1984, which was $976 million. Since then, the deficit has been steadily increasing. In 1989 the deficit was over $5 billion.

TABLE 4

U.S. Auto Supply Industry Trade Data, 1980-89[a]

	1980	1982	1984	1986	1989
Value of imports (millions of $)	5,559	5,118	6,513	12,125	15,370	18,729
Value of exports (millions of $)	6,918	7,253	8,555	11,149	10,658	13,302

Source: U.S. Department of Commerce 1988, 1989, 1992a.

[a]Motor Vehicle Parts and Stampings (SIC 3465, 3592, 3647, 3691, 3694, 3714).

The growth in the trade imbalance is partly attributed to rising imports associated with expanded production by Japanese transplants which still maintain important ties to overseas suppliers. Concurrently, the number of Japanese-affiliated automotive suppliers operating facilities in the United States has doubled from 1984 to 1988 to over 100. The rise in Japanese-affiliated suppliers coincides with Japanese manufacturers' investment in transplant firms in the U.S., which has been driven by current voluntary import restraints, currency fluctuations, and other factors. Table 5 indicates that U.S. locations are importing substantial quantities of parts from Japanese suppliers while Japanese plants are importing relatively little from the U.S.

TABLE 5
Regional Trade Data, 1990-92 (in billions of dollars)
U.S. Automotive Parts Trade[a]

	1990			1991			1992[b]		
	Exp	Imp	Bal	Exp	Imp	Bal	Exp	Imp	Bal
Canada	13.7	9.2	4.5	13.6	7.9	5.7	13.1	9.1	4.0
EC	1.7	4.3	-2.6	1.8	4.2	-2.4	1.5	3.8	-2.3
Japan	0.8	10.6	-9.8	0.8	10.0	-9.2	0.8	10.5	-9.8
Mexico	4.5	4.5	0.0	5.4	4.9	0.5	5.3	6.2	-0.9

Source: U.S. Department of Commerce 1992a; Exp=exports, Imp=imports, Bal=balance of payments

[a]Motor Vehicle Parts and Stampings (SIC 3465, 3592, 3647, 3691, 3694, 3714)
[b]Estimate

Domestic motor-vehicle producers are also outsourcing greater amounts of automotive supplies overseas, especially to lower wage countries, such as Brazil, South Korea, and Mexico. The data on Mexico in Table 5 reflects this trend. In Mexico employment in the auto supply industry has risen from less than 10,000 in 1978 to close to 100,000 in 1989 (Herzenberg and Shaiken 1990). According to Herzenberg and Shaiken, Mexico's export-oriented plants are now achieving high levels of quality and productivity, which suggests that they will continue to grow in the future. Many automakers are implementing significant expansion efforts in Mexico. The North American Free Trade Agreement has important implications for the future of this portion of the industry.

The intense competition from abroad is partly responsible for auto supply industry pricing remaining relatively stable through the 1980s (U.S. Department of Commerce 1989). Stable prices along with customer pressure to keep prices low, have been critical factors driving management bargaining initiatives in the automotive supply industry—in particular, management attempts to constrain payroll costs, increase flexibility, and enhance effort.

Several suppliers have reacted to the international challenge by trying to penetrate the transplant market, seeking out joint ventures, and establishing facilities in other countries. For example, Champion has opened new production facilities in India and South Korea (Phillips 1988). Sheller-Globe is not only trying to expand foreign operations but is also infiltrating the transplant market by building relationships with decision makers in Japan who are building assembly plants in the U.S. (Kertesz 1987; Sheridan 1988) and is one of 23 U.S. parts companies with offices in Japan (Treece 1987).

Changes in Technology, Products and Materials

Adding to the contextual turmoil in the auto supply sector are rapid changes in technology, products, and materials. Shifts in all three areas often translates into threatened plant closings and work displacement. The changes also create new opportunities for jobs and training.

In terms of materials, customers are demanding an increased use of plastics in car bodies (because of weight and corrosion protection advantages) which will imperil some steel and stamping facilities but create opportunities for the plastics industry. In addition, new engines will include more aluminum and less cast iron which will imperil some foundries while opening opportunities in the aluminum casting industry. CAFE (corporate average fuel economy) standards, emissions standards, and safety regulations reinforce interest in using alternative materials (typically replacing steel and cast iron with aluminum, plastics, and ceramics).

Product and technology changes can have equally dramatic implications for supply operations. The former Rochester Products Division of General Motors, for example, built its reputation around making a state-of-the-art line of carburetors. In a very short period of time, the rise of fuel injection technologies undercut the company's competitive advantage and forced a complete strategic reorientation around building capabilities for producing fuel injection modules. Similar shifts have been required for supply firms producing products associated with rear wheel drive cars or vinyl interiors, for example, while vast new opportunities are being created around the increased use of electronic components in cars.

Intense competition in the industry and technological changes have blurred the presumed connection between business conditions and supplier success. For example, Champion has faced a shrinking market for spark plugs at a time when automotive shipments in general have been rising. The major reason for Champion's problems result from technological changes (smaller modern engines need fewer spark plugs and require less frequent tune-ups) and competitive pressures from overseas producers (Phillips 1988).

In production operations, new technologies also impact on employment relations via the increased use of robots and programmable machines. Issues of deskilling, retraining, and downsizing often emerged as a consequence. Also, many unionized suppliers have contracts with work rules that protect employment or limit machine utilization. For example, many pattern-making shops have contracts with clauses that specify one operator for each milling machine, even though multiple programmable machines can operate virtually unattended.

The combination of changes in products, materials, and technology raise core strategic issues that have been incompletely addressed (at best) in the auto supply sector. Some large independent suppliers, such as Budd, have formed labor-management committees in which some of these issues are being given consideration. For the most part, however, the responses of unions to issues of new technology, materials and products has been ad hoc—with no clear strategy emerging in this sector.

Shifts in Plant Location

The industry is geographically concentrated in the Midwest—especially in Michigan (which leads in terms of employment and production for the auto supply industry and motor vehicle manufacturing), Ohio, Indiana, and New York. Other states such as Illinois, Wisconsin, Pennsylvania, New Jersey, Massachusetts, and California also have significant number of suppliers (1982 Census of Manufacturers; Motor Vehicle Manufacturers Association 1985). Geographic concentration of the industry is consistent with the history of the automotive parts sector which has maintained a close proximity between itself and vehicle manufacturers. Propinquity is more important for the original equipment segment of the industry versus the aftermarket.

Over the past decade, there has been substantial movement by supply firms to rural Midwest locations (seeking reduced union influence, relatively lower wages, and tax advantages). We noted the power implications of these new locations in our discussion of the nonunion portion of the industry. The mobility of capital in the auto supply sector can be understood as a reflection of two factors. First, as Table 6 indicates, a

higher than average proportion of capital is tied up in equipment, which
is generally more mobile than buildings.

TABLE 6
Assets per Employee
U.S. Auto Supply and All Manufacturing, 1985

	Total Assets Per Employee[a]	Buildings Per Employee	Machinery Per Employee
Auto Supply (SIC 3714)	$60,918	$9,713 (16% of total)	$50,350 (84% of total)
Total Manufacturing (SIC 20-39)	$46,918	$10,829 (23% of total)	$36,089 (77% of total)

[a]Total assets includes "building and other structures" and "machinery and equipment."

Source: U.S. Department of Commerce 1985, 1986a.

Second, as Table 7 indicates, wages represent a higher than average
proportion of operating costs. While the data in Tables 6 and 7 both
help to explain capital mobility, it is important to recognize that the
numbers in both tables are still relatively close to industry averages—
with much higher mobility, for example, in an industry such as textiles.

TABLE 7
Labor Cost as a Percentage of Total Costs
U.S. Auto Supply and All Manufacturing, 1985

	Cost of Material[a]	Labor Cost Total[b]	Labor Cost % of Total Cost[c]
Auto Supply (SIC 3714)	$31,551,500	$15,079,100	32%
Total Manufacturing (SIC 20-39)	$1,276,013,400	$488,603,800	28%

[a]Cost of materials includes energy, raw materials, semi-finished goods, parts, contract work, and other factor inputs not including direct labor or services such as advertising, insurance, and telephone or depreciation charges.

[b]Labor cost includes payroll, social security, and other legally required payments, employer benefits payments, and other programs.

[c]Total cost equals cost of materials plus labor cost.

Source: U.S. Department of Commerce 1985, 1986a.

Recently, however, there has been a reverse shift in the power issues associated with geography. With the growing emphasis on cost saving and quality improvement through just-in-time inventory techniques, there are new, more compelling strategic pressures associated with the geographic location of automotive parts suppliers. This development accords some bargaining leverage to unions in what would otherwise be older, less competitive facilities since they are often close to OEM manufacturing operations.

Unions in the Auto Supply Industry

Prior to the mid-1970s, the automotive supply industry was heavily unionized. The United Automobile, Aerospace and Agricultural Implement Workers (UAW) predominated, but other unions such as the Allied Industrial Workers (AIW), the International Brotherhood of Teamsters (IBT), the International Brotherhood of Electrical Workers (IBEW), and the International Association of Machinists (IAM) had significant memberships in the industry. For all of these unions, the turbulence in the auto supply sector has eroded union density and created substantial internal organizational pressures—both of which are only beginning to be recognized and addressed.

History, Key Unions, and Union Density

Historically, the relatively high degree of union density and the predominance of a single union (the UAW) have resulted in an emphasis on pattern bargaining in the industry. The pattern has traditionally begun among the OEMs, where the UAW would pick one employer to be the "target" and other OEMs would be expected to adopt similar contracts. As we noted earlier, the provisions would then flow from the OEMs to the large independent suppliers. Examples of issues that have diffused through this sector after being included in OEM/UAW agreements include: annual improvement factors (AIF) and cost-of-living adjustments (COLA) starting in the late 1940s; supplementary unemployment benefits (SUB) in the mid-1950s; and prepaid prescription drug plans, dental plans, and vision care plans in the 1960s and '70s. All of these settlements have been diffused both in the union and nonunion sectors of the auto supply industry, as well as into many other sectors of the U.S. economy (McCaffery 1988; Katz 1985).

In addition to pattern bargaining where substantive issues have come from the OEMs to the auto supply firms, there is also a high degree of similarity in the way bargaining has historically been structured.

Auto suppliers with multiplant operations have tended to follow the OEM structure of conducting national bargaining for the firm, followed by supplementary local negotiations. The combination of substantive and procedural patterns have been characterized as a "connective" bargaining structure (Katz 1985).

All of the developments already noted in this chapter—including OEM pressures on cost, quality, and employment relations practices; growing nonunion and international competition; new materials, products and technologies; and the strategic nature of geographic location—have been serving to undermine the connective structure of collective bargaining in the auto supply industry. A key consequence for unions has been a dramatic decline in union density.

As Table 8 indicates, there has been a general decline in union density for the overall auto industry. Table 9 indicates that there are many ways to estimate the specific decline in union density for the auto supply sector and all methods of calculation point to the same result—an even sharper decline in union density.

TABLE 8

Total U.S. Automobile Industry (Manufacturing and Supply[a])
Percent Unionized

	1976	1978	1980
Percent organized	72.0	69.3	66.0

Source: Kollelenberg and Sockell 1985. "Union Membership in the United States: 1973-1981," Industrial and Labor Relations Review (July) (three-year moving average).

[a]Motor Vehicles and Motor Vehicle Equipment (Census Industry Classification 219).

The declining percentage of auto supply industry workers represented by unions reflects the closing of unionized facilities, the outsourcing of work in unionized facilities, the continued nonunion status of new facilities, the increased market share held by imports, and some decertification elections. As a result, the UAW and other unions in the industry face a difficult set of institutional challenges. Each of the factors associated with the decline in union density in this industry is complex and not easily reversed. Some of the answer will lie, of course, in new organizing strategies, but these depend on the unions in this industry fashioning new approaches to employee representation that are

TABLE 9
Percent Unionized
U.S. Auto Parts Industry

(1) Estimates for independent parts firms in the BLS industry data[a]

	1969	1974	1983
Percent organized	80.0	80.0	58.0

(2) Estimates using UAW membership data and SIC employment figures[a]

	1976-78	1982-84	1987-88
Percent organized			
Including Big Three parts plants	82.0	68.0	58.0
Excluding Big Three parts plants	59.0	37.0	24.0

(3) Independent auto suppliers whose workers belong to unions[b]

	1976	1980	1984	1988
Percent organized	62.0	50.0	30.0	22.0

[a]*Source:* Herzenberg and Shaiken 1990.
[b]*Source:* Gardner and Lupo 1989.

responsive to the emerging issues around employment security, new approaches to manufacturing, closer links between suppliers and customers, increased capital mobility, and sophisticated programs aimed at building employee commitment.

Intraorganizational Issues

Though less visible, a key issue that parallels the decline in union density is increased turbulence within the organizational structure of auto supply unions. One particularly salient internal dynamic emerged during the 1980s around concessionary pressures from employers. When these issues first surfaced, it was often the international union staff and some local union leaders who first recognized the legitimacy of the competitive pressures facing auto supply firms. Other local leaders and the majority of members often did not receive the same economic briefings and, as a result, treated the dire warnings as standard bargaining rhetoric. When the warnings of job loss came true, there was often surprise and disillusionment. Consider the comments of one international union official regarding a meeting to present a concessionary contract to local members in a Budd facility during the early 1980s:

At the plant level workers were told [by some local union activists] that things were fine. There were two messages being sent. We had a ferocious membership meeting. Talk about being scared, we had to be escorted out of the meeting. They never believed it until they disassembled the machines.[2]

After a few rounds of massive layoffs in the early and mid-1980s the dynamic shifted. Local union leaders and their memberships were anxious to stem any further job loss, and they agreed to a wide range of local experimental agreements. Suddenly, the same international union staff who had been struggling to educate local unions about the seriousness of the competitive pressures were scrambling to achieve some order and consistency among the various local contracts. Local union members went from resisting change to embracing it in ways that created equity problems, and that sometimes directly undermined union solidarity. The net effect of these dynamics has been pressure for decentralization of internal power in auto supply unions.

Combined with the pressure for decentralization has been growing internal debate over the merits of union-management cooperation and the implications of new work systems. One aspect of this debate is reflected in the emergence of the "New Directions" faction in the UAW, though the issues are part of internal local politics even where there is not a strong New Directions presence. One very new development along these lines involves informal links occurring among union leaders representing workers in Japanese-affiliated operations, which may prove an important source of innovation regarding union strategies around new work systems (Cutcher-Gershenfeld et al. 1993).

Bargaining Processes and Outcomes

Given the many complex developments in the auto supply industry, it should come as no surprise to learn that collective bargaining processes and outcomes are changing in fundamental ways.

Bargaining Processes

Prior to the 1970s, industrial relations strategies in the automotive supply industry typified the "New Deal system of industrial relations." Analogous to the New Deal system, automotive supplier labor-management interactions were dominated by the negotiation and implementation of collective bargaining agreements. In addition, strategic decisions concerning investment and human resource policies were left to management, while the shop floor was governed by job control unionism in which worker rights and obligations were formally spelled out and adjudicated through formal grievance procedures. The rise of the nonunion sector in the 1970s, documented by Kochan, Katz, and McKersie (1986), was also reflected in a prototypical way in the automotive supply industry. In the 1980s, the pattern bargaining and the bargaining structure among the OEMs both began to break down. As we have noted, Chrysler broke from the pattern on substantive issues as part of its bailout package in the early 1980s. This set the stage for concession bargaining in a number of industries, including auto supply. Thus even though pattern bargaining itself was breaking down, it was still the OEMs that were setting the agenda for negotiations within the supplier firms. As well, by the mid-1980s, local negotiations within the OEMs were taking on greater significance and the national bargaining structure was becoming more fragmented. Again, this breakdown flowed through to bargaining among the supplier firms. Today, both the concession bargaining and the fragmentation of the structure has gone further in the auto supply firms than it has in bargaining between the UAW and the OEMs. Thus an important question for the future involves the degree to which relations between the UAW and the OEMs will continue to serve as the frame of reference for negotiations in the auto supply industry.

Perhaps the most important aspect of the shift in the bargaining process has involved management taking the lead in making demands during bargaining. One international UAW representative explained a recent bargaining experience this way:

> This was not traditional negotiations. The whole process was different. I was shocked by their demands. . . . They came out demanding, and I don't like bargaining this way. It was 'this or else,' with the demise of a couple of plants as a possibility held over our heads.

When Mitchell (1985) first examined what he termed shifts in the norms of collective bargaining, there was an open question as to whether the shifts were likely to be enduring. Certainly in the auto supply sector we continue to see managements bringing the bulk of the issues to the bargaining table.

Not all of the managerial demands involve economic concessions. Many employers have been aggressive, for example, in seeking early settlements with their unions and in negotiating long-term agreements.

Both of these employer demands are aimed, of course, at assuring customers of uninterrupted production. For example, one UAW local president stated that:

> The company notified us of a desire to negotiate early in order to be able to bid better on new work with better cost predictions. . . . We were told that this would help get the company into a more competitive position. The window would be open now on bids. We were persuaded that this was a legitimate situation.

The employer in this case, which was involved in a bitter strike in the prior negotiations, made these comments on the negotiations:

> The customers became antsy and wanted a buildup of inventory. The agreement included a sharing of the cost saved from not having to build up inventory. Having a four-year contract in this industry is quite unique, especially for us.

A UAW official further elaborated on the decision to agree on a long-term contract:

> We went with a four-year agreement rather than three years because the company has the ability to say we have a long-term contract. Their ability to go in the market and bid for work is improved. Ford and GM look at the company and union to have a good relationship. Ford did an audit of the plant about three weeks ago and they wanted to talk to the union. In the future, unions will have to help companies compete for work. These companies want to know that we can work out our problems.

Union leaders in these situations have also demonstrated an increased willingness to operate via letters of agreement and more continuous or administrative forms of bargaining. These arrangements, which are sometimes characterized as "living agreements" often center on regular joint meetings that address issues such as product quality and health insurance cost containment. These innovative arrangements often have an emergent character. For example, in the late 1980s, the Budd Company established a national joint labor-management committee with an initial charge to focus on health care cost containment. Since the bargaining committees were meeting in this committee on a quarterly basis, other issues began to also appear on the agenda. Within a year of its establishment, the committee had become a critical forum for dialogue on a wide range of collective bargaining issues.

Interestingly, many of the joint efforts involved union-management dialogue and even decision making on issues that have previously been excluded from negotiations under management rights clauses of contracts. These include issues such as product development, manufacturing methods, investment in new technology, product quality, training, and employee involvement. The furthest reaching initiatives along these lines are found in the parts and components divisions of the OEMs. In a typical Ford facility, for example, there will be a joint plant-wide steering committee (matched by joint area committees in larger plants), a network of employee involvement problem-solving groups, a joint training committee, a mutual growth forum, a joint health and safety committee, a joint apprenticeship committee, and various task forces on topics of mutual concern. Even though all of these joint activities are constrained from engaging in collective bargaining, numerous issues come up in these committees that are channelled to the bargaining table. Similarly, issues arise at the bargaining table and are sent to these various joint committees. Thus an elaborate two-way exchange emerges between collective bargaining and the joint activities.

A further change in the dynamics of auto supply sector negotiations involves the presence of new faces at the bargaining table—particularly from management. Both line managers and financial officers are taking more active roles in collective bargaining and general union-management relations. One UAW international representative explained a 1987 round of negotiations with a large first-tier supplier as a dramatic change from the past:

> There was a change in the way they did business. On a daily basis the traditional role of IR was not there. They lacked authority at the table.

The production manager in one of these plants confirmed the shift in his comments:

> I communicate with the union all of the time. I go with the local president to seminars on quality and high-level meetings. I don't ignore IR, but I look to do the job myself. When you bring in IR or if a committeeman gets involved, that's just more problems.

An employment relations executive for a large independent supplier also commented on the increased presence of financial managers:

> For the first time in 1985, the assistant controller was actually present during the negotiations. This is a financially sensitive time and we need to focus on cost analysis. Their presence and input forced analysis of expense and cost, an issue which is foreign to negotiators. Before it was always after the fact, and we ate the expense.

Most of the shifts in the bargaining process that we have documented are emerging from the management side of the table, whether they involve increased demands, longer-term and earlier agreements, or a higher profile for line and financial managers. For the most part, the unions in this industry have been adjusting to the changes in the bargaining process, but they have not matched management with a clearly articulated alternative set of approaches to bargaining. As one UAW international representative stated:

> You better start looking at the year 2000 if you want work in old facilities. We started way back in 1985 with long-range planning. But it's hard to get the membership thinking long term, especially when the people are working all the overtime they want, actually more than they want to. It is hard to convince them that their job is in jeopardy.

Thus management is left to setting the agenda and shaping the process by which these issues are being addressed. The result has been the emergence of a managerially oriented mix of bargaining outcomes in the auto supply sector.

Bargaining Outcomes

Nearly every major development in the 1980s concerning wages and benefits has been reflected in the auto supply industry. In the early 1980s, concession bargaining quickly spread throughout this industry. The UAW developed expertise in analyzing a firm's financial statements, since "opening up the books" was often a precursor to such bargaining. As well, the restructuring of compensation around a two-tier system was attempted in many auto supply firms. More recently, efforts to reduce health care costs and to introduce various forms of contingent compensation have been common in the auto supply industry. Forms of contingent compensation include gainsharing, profit sharing, and bonus payments.

Lump sum payments are a common (and cost saving) substitute for percentage increases in base wages.

Of course, it is the competitive pressures that account for the auto supply industry being at the leading edge of managerial initiatives aimed at moderating wage and benefit costs. The simple fact that prices have remained relatively constant during the 1980s in many firms helps to explain the downward pressure on labor costs. Table 10 presents data on average hourly earnings in auto parts, compared with motor vehicle equipment generally and all manufacturing. The story is quite compelling. During the 1970s and early 1980s, average hourly earnings in auto parts closely matched earnings in motor vehicle equipment generally and were well above the average for all manufacturing. Further, the rate of change followed the same pattern. Even with a decline in the rate of change during the early 1980s (reflecting wage concessions), auto supply followed the OEM pattern and both were wage leaders. For the subsequent period from 1985 to 1990, however, average hourly earnings for all manufacturing increased at a faster rate (13%) than motor vehicle equipment (9%), which in turn outpaced auto supply (4%).

TABLE 10

Average Hourly Earnings, 1970-90
U.S. Auto Parts, Motor Vehicle Equipment, and All Manufacturing

	1970	% Change 1970-80	1980	% Change 1980-85	1985	% Change 1985-90	1990
Motor vehicle parts and accessories (SIC 3714)	$4.17	127%	$9.42	35%	$12.69	4%	$13.22
Motor vehicle equipment (SIC 3714)	$4.22	133%	$9.85	36%	$13.39	9%	$14.56
All manufacturing	$3.35	117%	$7.27	31%	$9.54	13%	$10.83

Source: U.S. Employment, Hours, and Earnings 1909-1990. Bureau of Labor Statistics Bulletin #2370, U.S. Department of Labor 1991.

But the focus goes beyond labor costs. A survey of 328 parts suppliers listed the following UAW contractual issues from most to least important: (1) work rules, (2) labor costs, (3) benefits, (4) employee involvement, and (5) employee security (Arthur Anderson and Company 1985). The first issue—work rules—reflects growing managerial demands for what are termed "modern-operating agreements." These agreements generally feature a limited number of job classifications, few restrictions on job assignments, provisions for cross-training (which may be tied to pay-for-skill incentive systems), and team-based work structures. These work redesign issues have come relatively late to the auto supply industry.

While some work redesign in the auto supply sector arose out of QWL initiatives begun in the early 1980s, there has been relatively little of the complete reorganization according to sociotechnical principles that characterized some continuous production industries or even some new facilities built by the OEMs. Issues of work redesign have really surfaced with increased attention to Japanese production systems, with practices such as just-in-time delivery, statistical process control, total quality management, and the Toyota "pull" system.

Employment security has been fairly elusive in this industry. As we saw earlier, Table 1 illustrates total employment has declined by about 10% over the past two decades, with a slightly higher decline for production workers. In fact, these numbers understate the full extent of job loss among auto suppliers during this period since there was an influx of new auto supply jobs created over the past decade due to outsourcing on the part of OEMs and the arrival of Japanese supplier operations. Also, the numbers mask the shift from union to nonunion employment noted earlier (see Tables 8 and 9).

The difficulties of making employment security guarantees are best illustrated by the experiences at Packard Electric, a parts supply division of General Motors that is organized by the IUE. In the late 1970s, the parties were pioneers in the establishment of quality of worklife processes to foster employee involvement. At the time, management indicated that no employees would lose their jobs as a result of their participation in the QWL process. By the early 1980s, no new jobs had been created in Packard Electric's home manufacturing facility in Warren, Ohio, while new plants were being built in southern U.S. states and in Mexico. When some Ohio work was slated to move to Mexico, a sharp confrontation erupted over whether the intent of the initial assurances about job security and QWL had been violated. After a complex negotiations, the parties reached a unique labor agreement. The unions agreed to a multitier wage system, the movement of labor-intensive work to Mexico, and increased use of temporary workers in exchange for an explicit lifetime job security for the current union membership in Warren, Ohio. Far more common than formal "no layoff" pledges, however, have been informal accommodations where the scope of layoffs has been greatly reduced from what might have happened otherwise. From a negotiations perspective, however, such informal arrangements are harder to specify, which means they are more likely to be addressed through more continuous informal negotiations than periodic formal collective bargaining.

Conclusion

Collective bargaining in the auto supply industry embodies cooperative and contentious extremes in labor-management relations. A close look at this sector of the economy reveals powerful economic, structural, and institutional forces that are driving relations at both extremes. The conflicts often revolve around fundamental issues of survival—for the business and for unions. Underlying the conflicts are more than a decade of constant cost pressure, overlaid with mobile capital and competitive pressures from domestic nonunion locations and from abroad. The cooperation encompasses issues traditionally reserved as management rights. Underlying the cooperation we find tighter integration of operations between suppliers and customers, manifest in the form of just-in-time delivery arrangements, total quality audits, and supplier involvement in product design.

Given these turbulent developments of the past decade, what does the future hold for collective bargaining in the auto supply industry? By way of conclusion, we would like to highlight six key unresolved questions. The answers to these questions will be important for this sector of the economy and will likely have broader implications in our society.

First, is the North American auto supply industry moving to a more sharply separated core and periphery structure? Though there have long been primary and secondary labor markets in this country, the current trends will sharpen rather than temper the distinction between high-paying, stable auto supply jobs and volatile, low-paying jobs. This has implications for collective bargaining, which might then be similarly bifurcated into stable partnership arrangements, on the one hand, and constant erosion, on the other.

Second, who will be the future customers in this industry? Historically, the Big Three or Big Four original equipment manufacturers have—as primary customers—set the tone in this sector. With increased foreign production capacity in North America and increased efforts to sell on a global basis, the future customers for the North American auto suppliers are going to be more heterogeneous and more demanding (as competition among them continues). It will be important to assess the degree to which collective bargaining agreements reflect the shifting customer base.

Third, will the cooperative and the contentious paths both lead to the same mix of labor relations practices? Along both paths it is employers who are setting the agenda, with a focus on issues of cost, quality, schedule, work practices, and safety. However, the focus is primarily on cost, schedule, and work rules when employers are demanding concessions. In contrast, employers are pushing cooperative initiatives to focus especially on issues of quality, teamwork, and safety. Most labor-management relationships feature simultaneous employer initiatives that are cooperative and contentious in nature, but one orientation usually dominates. It will be important to assess the long-term competitive and labor-management relations implications of these alternative paths.

Fourth, will unions fashion effective strategies in response to the turmoil in this sector of the economy? The ascendancy of employers is reflected in declining union density and the erosion of traditional pattern bargaining. The whip-saw tactic—which was once a powerful union weapon—has become a primary tool for auto supply employers. In order to effectively respond, unions will be challenged to better coordinate across locations (and even companies). They will also have to adjust internally to better handle the current mix of decisive debates around how best to respond to the changed context.

Fifth, what new organizational forms will emerge among auto supply firms? Decentralized cooperative networks of supply firms have been emerging in Europe for over a decade (Piore and Sabel 1984). Will similar multifirm arrangements emerge here? There are already some initiatives around issues of training and apprenticeships, school-to-work transitions, and global marketing. The potential in this domain is vast—matched only in degree by the intensity of the competition among these firms. Thus key issues remain regarding the ultimate nature of future relations among auto supply firms (which may be unionized or non-union).

Finally, how will developments in the auto supply sector figure in larger debates over the future of industrial relations policy in the United States and Canada? Industrial relations issues are in the public agenda in many forms, including: training and adjustment issues associated with the North American Free Trade Agreement, laws concerning union organizing and the hiring of permanent replacement workers, laws and policies concerning various forms of worker participation, and policies regarding workplace training and school-to-work transitions. Developments in the auto supply sector encompass all of these policy issues and, in some cases, are key driving forces in the policy debates (for example, NAFTA). As new policies emerge in these various domains, it is likely that the auto supply sector will be a rich testing ground where early indications of policy impacts will be most visible.

The story of the 1980s in the North American auto supply industry has been one of competition and divergence. So far, the 1990s have featured more of the same. Yet, the six unresolved questions that we have highlighted all suggest potential limits on the competition and divergence or the institutionalization of these patterns. Thus the balance of the decade is not likely to be any more congenial for collective bargaining in this sector of the economy. But developments here bear watching since this is a sector where we are likely to find early clues about the future nature of the institutions of collective bargaining.

Acknowledgments

This chapter builds on research conducted for two companion books on negotiations: *Strategic Negotiations: A Theory of Negotiated Change in Labor-Management Relations* by Richard Walton, Joel Cutcher-Gershenfeld, and Robert McKersie, and *Pathways to Change: Strategic Choices in Labor Relations* by Joel Cutcher-Gershenfeld, Robert McKersie, and Richard Walton. We are grateful for the many contributions that Richard Walton and Robert McKersie have made to our understanding of the material presented in this chapter. Additionally, most of the quotes from union and management officials and other factual material that is included in this chapter is drawn from material in these two books.

Endnotes

[1] GM's aggressive demands for cuts in supplier prices achieved high visibility under Ignacio Lopez who broke from the trend toward single supplier contracts and initiated new rounds of competitive bidding among suppliers, accompanied by detailed on-site audits. Lopez also drew attention for his unique personal style, such as what he termed his "warrior diet" and his practice of wearing his watch on the opposite wrist as a constant reminder of GM's need to regain profitability. With his departure for Volkswagen, the cost cutting goals remain, but early indications suggest that GM's tactics will not be as aggressive (Fleming 1992a, b, and c).

[2] Note that this quote and most of the quotes that follow are drawn from Walton, Cutcher-Gershenfeld, and McKersie (forthcoming) or Cutcher-Gershenfeld, McKersie, and Walton (forthcoming).

References

Arthur Anderson and Company. 1985. *Cars and Competition: Manufacturing Strategies*. Royal Oak, MI: Arthur Anderson and Company.

Babson, Steve. 1986. *Working Detroit: The Making of a Union Town*. Detroit, MI: Wayne State University Press.

Block, Richard, Joel Cutcher-Gershenfeld, Ellen Kossek, Michael Moore, Debra Gash, Patrick McHugh, and Almira Gilles. 1991. *Research Report on: Innovative Labor-Management Practices in Small Firms*. Washington, DC: U.S. Department of Labor.

Business Week. 1983. "The Revolutionary Wage Deal at GM's Packard Electric." August 29, pp. 54-56.

Cutcher-Gershenfeld, Joel, Robert McKersie, and Richard Walton. Forthcoming. *Pathways to Change: Strategic Choices in Labor Negotiations*.

Cutcher-Gershenfeld, Joel, Michio Nitta, Betty Barrett, Nejib Belhedi, Cherly Coutchie, Takashi Inaba, Iwao Ishino, Seepa Lee, Wen-Jeng Lin, William Mothersell, Jennifer Mulder, Stacia Rabine, Shobha Ramanand, Mark Strolle, and Arthur Wheaton. 1993. "Japanese Team-Based Work Systems in the United States: Explaining the Diversity." Working paper, Michigan State University.

Dorfman, John R. 1984. "Auto suppliers." *Forbes*, January 2, pp. 101-104.

Fleming, Al. 1992a. "Suppliers Buzz over 100 Days of Lopez." *Automotive News*, August 3, pp. 1, 35.

_____. 1992b. "Call to Arms: Lopez Shows Charisma in Role as General of GM's Cost War." *Automotive News*, August 31, pp. 1, 33.

_____. 1992c. "GM Insider's Notes Outline Lopez Cost-cutting Meeting." *Automotive News*, September 28, p. 34.

Gardner, Greg, and Nunzio Lupo. 1989. "UAW Reeling from Big Defeat at Smyrna." *Detroit Free Press*. July 28, pp. 1a, 14A.

Helper, Susan. 1991a. "How Much Has Really Changed between U.S. Automakers and Their Suppliers?" *Sloan Management Review*, Summer, pp. 15-28.

_____. 1991b. "Strategy and Irreversibility in Supplier Relations: The Case of the U.S. Automobile Industry." *Business History Review*, Vol. 65, pp. 781-824.

Herzenberg, S., and H. Shaiken. 1990. "Labor Market Segmentation in the North American Auto Industry." Paper presented at the Annual Meeting of the Canadian Industrial Relations Research Association, Victoria, British Columbia.

Katz, Harry C. 1985. *Shifting Gears: Changing Labor Relations in the U.S. Automobile Industry*. Cambridge, MA: MIT Press.

Kertesz, Louise. 1987. "Sheller-Globe Strategies." *Automotive News*, July 27, E32-E33.

Kochan, Thomas A., Harry C. Katz, and Robert B. McKersie. 1986. *The Transformation of American Industrial Relations*. New York: Basic Books.

Kokkelenberg, Edward C., and Donna R. Sockell. 1985. "Union Membership in the United States." *Industrial and Labor Relations Review*, Vol. 38, no. 4, pp. 497-540.

Krebs, Michelle. 1987. "GM Products to Die If They Can't Compete." *Automotive News*. March 30, p. 56.

McCaffery, Robert. 1988. *Employee Benefit Programs: A Total Compensation Perspective*. Boston, MA: PWS-Kent Publishing Company.

Mitchell, D. 1985. "Shifting Norms in Wage Setting." *Brookings Papers on Economic Activity*.

Moskal, Brian S. 1987. "Fearing Darwin Was Right." *Industry Week*, June 29, pp. 28-30.

MVMA. 1985. *Motor Vehicle Facts and Figures*. Detroit, MI: Motor Vehicle Manufacturers Association of the United States, Inc.

Phillips, Stephen. 1988. "Champion Is Starting to Show a Little Spark." *Business Week*, March 21, p. 87.

Piore, Michael J., and Charles F. Sabel. 1984. *The Second Industrial Divide*. New York: Basic Books.

Sheridan, John H. 1988. "Cracking the Transplant Market." *Industry Week*, March 7, pp. 41-42.

Treece, James B. 1987. "U.S. Parts Makers Just Won't Say Uncle." *Business Week*, August 10, pp. 76-77.

U.S. Department of Commerce. 1985. *Annual Survey of Manufacturers*. Washington, DC: Bureau of the Census.

_____. 1986a. *Annual Survey of Manufacturers*. Washington, DC: Bureau of the Census.

_____. 1986b. *County Business Patterns*. Washington, DC: Bureau of the Census.

_____. 1987. *U.S. Census of Manufacturers*. Washington, DC: Bureau of the Census.

_____. 1988. *U.S. Industrial Outlook*. Washington, DC: International Trade Administration.

_____. 1989. *U.S. Industrial Outlook*. Washington, DC: International Trade Administration.

_____. 1992a. *U.S. Industrial Outlook*. Washington, DC: International Trade Administration.

_____. 1992b. *1987 Census of Manufacturers*. Washington, DC: Bureau of the Census.

U.S. Department of Labor. 1991. *U.S. Employment, Hours and Earnings, 1909-1990*. Bulletin #2370. Washington, DC: Bureau of Labor Statistics.

U.S. General Accounting Office. 1988. *Foreign Investment: Growing Japanese Presence in the U.S. Automotive Industry*. GAO/NSIAD-88-111. Washington, DC: U.S. GAO.

U.S. Senate Investigation. 1987. "U.S. Global Competitiveness in the U.S. Automotive Parts Industry." *Report to the Committee on Finance*. U.S. Senate Investigation No. 332-232 USITC Publication 2037, December.

Verma, Anil. 1985. Relative Flow of Capital to Union and Nonunion Plants Within a Firm. *Industrial Relations*, Vol. 24, no. 3, pp. 395-405.

Verma, Anil, and Thomas A. Kochan. 1985. "The Growth of the Nonunion Sector Within a Firm." In T. Kochan, ed., *Challenges and Choices Facing American Labor*. Cambridge, MA: MIT Press, pp. 89-117.

Walton, Richard, Joel Cutcher-Gershenfeld, and Robert McKersie. Forthcoming. *Strategic Negotiations: A Theory of Change in Labor-Management Relations.* Boston: Harvard University Press.

Womack, James P., Daniel T. Jones, and Daniel Roos. 1990. *The Machine That Changed the World.* New York: Rawson Associates.

CHAPTER 7

The Motor Carrier Industry: Truckers and Teamsters Under Siege

MICHAEL H. BELZER
Cornell University

Editor's Abstract

Here the focus is on the general freight portion of the trucking industry and the pattern-setting National Master Freight Agreement. In the 1980s and '90s, collective bargaining in trucking has seen enormous changes, resulting from deregulation and the recession of the early 1980s. These include:

1. A decline in real hourly earnings to 1962 levels by 1990; the decline was much larger in the trucking industry than in manufacturing.

2. A marked decline in the number of employers, particularly union employers. This occurred largely in the period 1980-86. At the same time, the growth of big firms (for instance, UPS) has resulted in a more concentrated general freight industry.

3. A sharp loss of union jobs, particularly in the early 1980s. These have not been regained in the later 1980s, when employment grew heavily in nonunion companies. Membership in the Teamsters (about 400,000 of whom were truck drivers in 1985) peaked in 1974 at a high of 2 million; in the late '80s membership stabilized at about 1.6 million.

4. Decreased coverage of the National Master Freight Agreement—movement toward more decentralized bargaining and widespread concession bargaining. This was accompanied by internal union debate regarding the appropriateness of concessions and their form. This debate continues today particularly with regard to regional freight carriers.

5. Changed Teamster leadership since 1991, when Ron Carey was elected by a direct membership vote. This occurred in a three-way race, under a consent order with the U.S. Justice Dept. settling its RICO suit. Carey has abolished the Teamster conference structure (the regional level of the union). Groups opposed to Carey, however, retain political control of many locals. Moreover, the union faces financial

problems resulting from the unwillingness of the membership to raise dues to offset increased strike pay.

Belzer focuses on the impact of trucking deregulation in explaining major trends. He explains how deregulation led to a fundamental reorganization of the industry, from one in which most firms carried both truckload (TL) and less-than-truckload (LTL) shipments, into two economically distinct segements. LTL firms must charge rates sufficient to cover the cost of their "hub-and-spoke" systems with terminals in which small shipments can be routed nationwide. Upon deregulation, some firms specialized in TL freight, which requires no hub-and-spoke system. Many were new entrants with a lower cost structure than their pre-existing competition both for this reason and also because they were often nonunion. They captured the TL market. This, along with the 1980-82 recession, caused massive employment loss and economic dislocation in the early 1980s.

Unionization has survived in the LTL sector (69% organized), where economies of scale present barriers to entry, but the TL segment is becoming rapidly nonunion (with less than 25% now organized). Wages are much lower in TL ($9.62 an hour in 1991) than in LTL ($13.18). While the severe post-deregulation shakeout is probably over, the Teamsters and the industry face a number of continuing dilemmas, including how union firms can remain economically viable, while delivering good earnings to union members.

o   o   o

Regulatory restructuring and tough economic times during the 1980s brought dramatic change to the trucking industry and its labor-management relations. High inflation, interest rates, and fuel prices exacerbated the cyclical decline in tonnage caused by the recession of the early 1980s. Many firms went bankrupt or were acquired by other carriers, while others expanded rapidly. The basis of competition shifted from service to price. For nonsupervisory workers, high unemployment put downward pressure on real wages.

Recession and deregulation also combined to force radical changes in the collective bargaining environment. In less than a decade, trucking changed from an almost completely unionized industry, following a centrally-bargained pattern, to a partially unionized industry with a fragmented bargaining structure. Deep wage declines among nonunion drivers and concession bargaining at unionized carriers created a volatile political atmosphere within the Teamsters, the leading truck drivers' union.

Economic pressure on wages and working conditions provided a fertile environment for the growth of internal opposition to the established leadership. Rank-and-file forces within the union rode a growing groundswell of member dissatisfaction throughout the decade, rebuffing Teamster leaders in a series of legal rulings and member votes.

In 1988 the Justice Department took civil action against the union under the Racketeer Influenced and Corrupt Organizations (RICO) provisions of the 1970 Organized Crime Control Act. Faced with a trial, the union's executive board agreed to an out-of-court settlement that gave court-appointed officers a strong hand in running many of the union's internal affairs. The consent decree gave court officers extraordinary authority to bring charges against union leaders and forced the union to elect its national officers under court supervision. In 1991, after the first direct membership election of top officers in the union's history, a leader from outside the executive board was elected to head the Teamsters: Ron Carey. Economic, institutional, legal, and political turmoil thus produced dramatic changes in the nation's largest union and in its collective bargaining relationships.

The Industry[1]

Characteristics

The for-hire trucking industry provides transportation of goods for manufacturers and distributors of commodities.[2] In 1990 the trucking industry employed over 1.6 million persons, plus a significant number of owner-operators.[3] Although most trucking companies are small and most trucks are used locally, large interstate common carriers operate most miles.[4]

Although sensitive to the business cycle in the short run, trucking has been a long-run growth industry and is likely to remain so. Employment in the trucking industry increased at an average annual rate of 2.63% since 1947. This increase reflects the steady shift of freight from railroads to trucks, as well as the general increase in goods production following World War II. The Federal Highway Administration (FHWA) expects ton-miles to increase 3.4% per year through the end of the century (Taff 1986:61). Further, the Bureau of Labor Statistics (BLS) expects truck driver employment to increase by 23.8% between 1986 and 2000 (U.S. Dept. of Labor, Bureau of Labor Statistics [henceforth BLS] 1988:Table A-1).

This chapter, like most studies of the trucking industry, will focus on general freight. While truckers haul a wide variety of specialized products, commodity handling in the general freight segment is relatively uniform. Researchers can simplify complex industry segmentation to

FIGURE 1
Employment

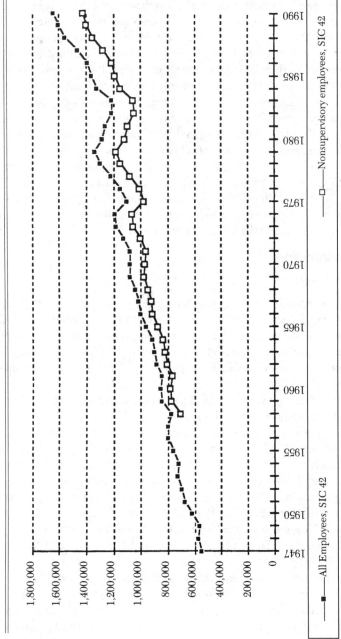

Source: BLS 1991a, 1991b. SIC 42 is Trucking and Warehousing.

shipment size and weight. Moreover, collective bargaining for intercity general freight carriers traditionally sets the pattern for the industry, influencing special commodity and local cartage pay rates. The National Master Freight Agreement (NMFA) is the key settlement.

The structure of the trucking industry plays a crucial role in defining industrial relations. The market segment within which each motor carrier operates directly affects the wages and working conditions of the labor force, including local drivers, long distance drivers, dock workers, and others. The carrier's market also affects the union's ability to organize and represent its workers. The union can easily locate, organize, and communicate with local and long-distance drivers and dock workers. However, long-distance drivers working for carriers without terminals and dock facilities can be difficult to identify, locate, and organize.

The Interstate Commerce Commission (ICC) defines a truckload (TL) shipment as one weighing more than 10,000 pounds. A less-than-truckload (LTL) shipment weighs less than 10,000 pounds. While LTL shipments are small, averaging 1260 pounds, the average TL shipment weighs 26,600 pounds (Belzer 1990:61). Although general freight truckers hauled a mix of LTL and TL freight before 1980, deregulation forced the general freight industry to break into segmented markets. This market segmentation weakened the union's hold on the industry and contributed to the fragmentation of the bargaining structure.

Companies specializing in LTL freight employ a sophisticated network of pickup-and-delivery trucks that "peddle freight" on a local basis. Dispatched from a terminal with a load of small shipments to deliver, they deliver and pick up freight throughout the day, returning with a load of small shipments destined for locations throughout the carrier's network. Dock workers unload these city trailers and distribute the freight to linehaul trailers heading to other terminals for subsequent delivery by pickup-and-delivery drivers in another city. Most large LTL carriers also have "break bulk" terminals in strategic locations throughout their systems, which replicate this process for whole regions of the country.

This elaborate system, akin to multiple hubs and spokes with multiple layers of centralization, is unnecessary for TL freight. The trucker typically loads freight at the shipper's dock and delivers it directly to one or more consignees. The infrastructural requirements are different: terminals and freight docks, required to handle LTL freight, are unnecessary. Consequently, LTL carriers are capital intensive while TL carriers are not. Organizationally, the employees of TL carriers relate to each other on a sporadic basis, while LTL employees see each other regularly. Hence unions face a great organizational problem trying to organize and represent TL drivers.

Economic Regulation and Deregulation

The ICC regulated interstate motor freight following the Motor Carrier Act of 1935. Over the next four decades, trucking became the dominant mode of transportation for the nation's shipment of goods. During the Carter administration, the ICC used its discretionary authority to reduce its economic control. The Motor Carrier Act of 1980 codified this reduced level of economic regulation, significantly loosening entry, rate setting, and other rules.

Regulation. The Motor Carrier Act of 1935 closed the for-hire trucking industry to most new common carrier entrants. Existing carriers had to apply to the ICC for certification, and new common carriers had to establish, to the ICC's satisfaction, that there was a need for service that existing carriers could not meet. Carriers had to meet fitness standards proving they were capable of meeting the demand for service specified by their authority and certifying insurance coverage. Following the railroad model, the ICC required rates to reflect the value of service.[5] Although the ICC allowed carriers to set their own rates, common carriers were encouraged to set rates collectively using rate bureaus. Regulation created a legal and structural taxonomy that remains substantially unchanged (for a detailed analysis, see Sweeney, McCarthy, Kalish, and Cutler 1986; Anderson and Huttsell 1989).

Congress enacted motor carrier regulation to establish a sound foundation for the development of the industry. The Depression experience of high business failure rates among trucking companies, combined with freight rates that severely undercut the railroads, convinced legislators to intervene in the market for motor carriage (Felton 1989a:3-13). State regulators, unable to enforce rules to protect the safety of the motoring public, demanded federal intervention for a decade. The used-truck market, awash in surplus equipment from bankrupt carriers, offered unemployed workers with little or no knowledge of the industry an opportunity to buy themselves a job. Unfortunately, these would-be entrepreneurs found themselves in the same destructively competitive environment. Their tendency to price at marginal cost drove their wages to very low levels and stretched their hours beyond those humanly possible, exacerbating the states' safety problems (Childs 1985).

Economists thought the fundamental problem was that competition in transportation tends to be "destructive." According to this argument, marginal cost pricing in competitive transportation markets tends to produce rates too low to provide funds for sufficient maintenance and reinvestment. Once a trucker has carried freight to its original destination (front haul), it will take on a return shipment (back haul) at a price that may just cover marginal costs rather than running the truck back empty.[6] In particular, markets may produce prices below fully distributed costs because front-haul prices compete with prices of other truckers for whom this freight movement is a back haul.

Thus, with unregulated pricing and continual entry of new carriers, everyone's front haul is someone else's back haul. As these low back-haul prices tend to become market prices, they lead to unpredictable entry and exit, overcapacity, inadequate service, high bankruptcy levels, low wages, and long hours (Locklin 1972).

Shippers also worried about the effects of rate discrimination, first prohibited by the Interstate Commerce Act of 1887, which banned railroad rebates solicited by the trusts. In competitive markets, trucking companies tended to set lower rates for large shippers than for small shippers to deliver identical freight. These lower rates reflected the greater market power of big firms engaged in rate negotiations. In the political context of the 1930s, smaller shippers successfully argued that such price discrimination was inherently unfair. Hence regulation that prohibited discrimination ensured that truckers charged all shippers the same rates for the same service.

Deregulation. Between 1977 and 1980, with the encouragement of the Carter administration, the ICC increased the competitiveness of the market for trucking services. It allowed a dramatic increase in entry and reduced the power of the rate bureaus, forcing a transformation of the market (Anderson and Huttsell 1989:20, 22, 37-41). The Motor Carrier Act (MCA) of 1980 codified the various changes made by the ICC and formally restructured the economic regulations within which the industry operates.

Economic deregulation occurred in part because of a change in economic philosophy to foster low prices for the benefit of consumers by encouraging more competition among carriers. However, since the demand for trucking service is derived from the demand for goods, the transfer of benefits to the consumer are indirect and difficult to measure with precision. In addition, since truckers have always been competitive, deregulation's biggest effect was to change the framework of that competition.

Political support for deregulation was bipartisan. Manufacturers and other shippers of goods agitated for changes, giving economic clout to the political battle. Large shippers clearly benefited along with some large trucking companies that were able to take advantage of the new environment, but many small shippers and most existing trucking companies were harmed. Freight rates fell, especially for large shippers and for truckload shipments. Operating rights owned by existing trucking companies became nearly worthless. Carriers had to write off as losses the intangible value of these operating rights, accumulated over decades, for which they paid real money during the regulatory era (Felton 1989b:158-61).[7] Employees in the industry also bore the brunt of change.[8]

Other regulatory changes. Other public policy changes besides deregulation affected the industry in the 1970s and 1980s. Productivity declined in 1973-74 due to the 55 mph speed limit. Recognizing this cost, in 1975 the federal government permitted states to increase maximum weights from 73,280 to 80,000 pounds. Uneven implementation by states resistant to the higher weights led to the Surface Transportation Act of 1982, which mandated higher weight limits as well as states' acceptance of both 48-foot single trailers and 28-foot doubles. The 1983 appropriations act for the Department of Transportation (DOT) further permitted 102-inch trailer widths, replacing the old 96-inch standard (Taff 1986:43-46). These regulatory changes enhanced labor productivity, allowing carriers to haul larger, heavier loads.

The Commercial Vehicle Safety Act of 1986 mandated the Commercial Driver's License (CDL). Implemented in the spring of 1992, it requires standardized testing, certification, and recordkeeping for licensed commercial truck drivers. Enacted to control the quality of driver licensing and to prevent the issuance of multiple state licenses, the CDL also restricted the supply of labor. It is no longer possible for anyone with an ordinary state driver's or chauffeur's license to drive a truck in interstate commerce.

Finally, DOT regulations issued in the fall of 1988 mandated extensive drug testing, and drug tests are required in all preemployment physicals. The DOT also requires companies to test randomly and without warning, if they have "reasonable suspicion" of drug use, within 32 hours of a DOT reportable accident, and with periodic physical exams.

The Economic Context of Deregulation

The trucking industry is very sensitive to business cycles, which strongly influence the volume of commercial shipments. Regulatory restructuring occurred at the beginning of the 1980-82 recession. Trucking companies thus confronted significant institutional change just when freight tonnage and revenue declined.

The intensification and globalization of manufacturing competition also has affected trucking companies. Although truckers have limited competition from outside the U.S., they experience the impact of global competition on their customers. Manufacturing companies aggressively cut costs throughout the 1980s, and the distribution of goods is a significant cost item. As lean production systems and just-in-time inventory control have grown, truckers have come under pressure to do more for less. At the same time, the minimal buffer created by just-in-time production may make industry more vulnerable to transportation strikes.

The Economic Effects of Institutional Change

The MCA of 1980 restructured competition in the trucking industry, with enormous consequences for industrial organization and labor relations. Before 1980 the industry was built around a balance of LTL and TL freight movements. Since LTL and TL freight were symbiotic parts of the freight movement process, common carriers structured operations to handle both kinds of shipments. Since the industry was heavily unionized, industrial relations practices and work rules developed to reflect this mixed-freight environment as well as the job control unionism prevalent within the U.S. industrial relations system. City drivers picked up and delivered both LTL and TL shipments out of city terminals, while over-the-road drivers performed intercity transport.

Economic deregulation abruptly discarded rigid entry, price, and service requirements, forcing the structure of the industry to change. The formerly efficient strategy of hauling both LTL and TL freight became inefficient. Carriers' carefully cultivated business bases, built over decades, abruptly vanished. The business strategy of carriers had to change accordingly. For instance, carriers began to discriminate in favor of large shippers by granting deep volume discounts.

Regulatory change caused a rapid transformation of the industry. Large, general freight carriers restructured quickly as either LTL or TL specialists. Interlining became difficult without collective rate making,[9] and carriers without a national infrastructure lost their interregional and national shipper clientele. The small special commodities section of the industry suddenly became nearly indistinguishable from TL general freight, and the line between general and specialized commodities blurred. New TL general freight carriers, now carrying both common and contract freight, quickly emerged without a developed pickup and delivery framework. Because these new entrants formed and folded quickly and had no fixed base of operations, they remained nonunion. Their low wages, low capitalization, and correspondingly low rates took a large share of existing common carriers' business.

Many existing general freight carriers were disadvantaged in the new environment. Their experienced, unionized work force would not readily accept dramatic cuts in wages and conditions forced by the influx of low-wage TL carriers. Also, many carriers lacked the management expertise or financial reserves to react quickly enough to the new rules. These difficulties were compounded by their shaky balance sheets caused by the loss of the financial value of their operating rights. Existing terminal structures became a burdensome overhead for carriers attempting to compete for TL business, turning former assets into liabilities. High overhead and low revenues forced many firms into bankruptcy. Others survived at the margin, offering a mix of LTL and TL service on a regional or local basis.

Carriers already specializing in LTL freight had an advantage, taking advantage of network efficiencies. A few large carriers became transcontinental by making aggressive acquisitions. They capitalized on network economies available to carriers that could pick up small shipments and deliver them anywhere.

Since most of the general freight industry was unionized, the dislocation cost thousands of Teamster jobs. In 1983 the Teamsters estimated 32.5% of the employees covered by the National Master Freight Agreement (NMFA) were on layoff (BNA 1983b:A-9; 1983c:D-1).

While the initial effects of deregulation are difficult to separate from the recession of 1980-82, the change was both cyclical and secular. Many unionized trucking firms disappeared permanently in the early 1980s. By May 30, 1993, the Teamsters identified 140 class I and II interstate general freight carriers covered by the NMFA in 1980 (of a total of 728) that ceased operations following deregulation. When the MCA of 1980 passed, these firms employed 175,022 people and had operating revenues of over $8 billion in 1979 dollars. They employed

48% of the class I and II general freight work force and earned 48% of the revenues (Conyngham 1993).

The union was at a disadvantage because the sudden devaluation of operating authority gave surviving carriers limited incentive to purchase the business of failed carriers. Since union members' transfer rights were based on the orderly transfer of authority from one carrier to another, existing contractual job-protection mechanisms became ineffectual. This institutional discontinuity exacerbated the effects of industrial restructuring and recession.

Although some dislocated employees found work within surviving LTL firms, others went to work in the TL sector for up to 40% less (Belzer 1993, forthcoming). While new TL carriers have entered and surviving LTL carriers have picked up much of the remaining work, the magnitude of the dislocation is indisputable. Deregulation completely restructured the business environment within which collective bargaining functions and hence had enormous ramifications for the work force.

Market Segmentation and Concentration

Motor carrier deregulation restructured the trucking industry and general freight transport. Before deregulation, most carriers hauled a mix of TL and LTL freight. After deregulation, the freight industry segmented into TL and LTL niches.

In addition, general freight split into national, regional, and local segments, as well as particular commodity markets. This niche specialization makes it somewhat difficult to measure competition by conventional market structure measures.

The number of certificated carriers more than doubled following deregulation. However, most new entrants are very small, so the number of large (class I and class II) general freight carriers actually declined. The general freight industry thus has become much more concentrated.

Within market segments the picture is more complex. While LTL carrier concentration has increased dramatically, TL concentration may have declined. However, the largest TL carriers continue to grow in size and sophistication. As shippers have become more concerned about reliability of service, they have reduced their lists of carriers to the ones they know are most efficient and dependable (Enis and Morash 1987; Corsi and Stowers 1991).

FIGURE 2
1977 General Freight Distribution

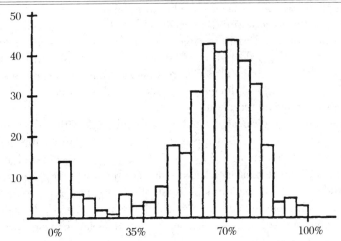

Note: The vertical axis is the number of carriers. The horizontal axis is the ratio of LTL revenue to total revenue for each carrier.
Source: Tape of *Motor Carrier Annual Reports*, American Trucking Associations.

FIGURE 3
1987 General Freight Distribution

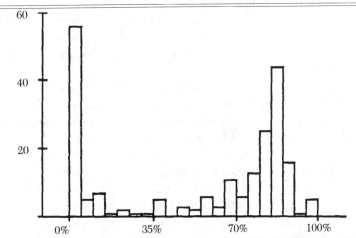

Note: The vertical axis is the number of carriers. The horizontal axis is the ratio of LTL revenue to total revenue for each carrier.
Source: Tape of *Motor Carrier Annual Reports*, American Trucking Associations.

TABLE 1
Market Concentration of Class I General Freight Carriers, Including UPS

Carrier	1977	1982	1987	1990
Roadway	4.9%	5.6%	6.5%	5.4%
Consolidated Freightways	4.0%	5.0%	6.4%	5.7%
Yellow	3.7%	4.4%	7.1%	6.2%
Total Big 3	12.6%	15.0%	20.0%	17.3%
United Parcel Service (UPS)	15.1%	23.7%	33.0%	31.9%
4-Firm Concentration Ratio	27.7%	38.8%	53.0%	49.2%
Herfindahl-Hirschman Index	231.6	471.3	823.3	1,147.5
Total number of carriers	396	291	266	501

Source: Computer data files of 1977, 1982, 1987, and 1990 *Motor Carrier Annual Reports*, American Trucking Associations.

Note: See Belzer 1994 for details.

TABLE 2
Concentration by Market Segment

Segment		Share of Revenues Held by		
		Top 4	Top 8	Top 20
LTL	1977	18.3	26.4	40.6
	1987	36.9	48.9	66.6
	% change	102.4	85.1	64.3
TL	1977	14.4	21.6	32.8
	1987	10.9	19.1	36.5
	% change	-23.9	-11.8	11.1

Source: Corsi and Stowers 1991; Table 2 (excludes UPS)

Industrial Relations Institutions

The Legal Environment

A unique blend of laws governs the trucking industry. The National Labor Management Relations Act covers trucking, unlike the railroads and airlines, which are governed by the Railway Labor Act.

Unlike workers in most other private industries, employees of motor carriers subject to the Motor Carrier Act are exempt from maximum hour (overtime) provisions of the Fair Labor Standards Act of 1938 (FLSA). This provision exempts approximately 1.25 million employees of ICC-DOT regulated carriers, whether they are city or road drivers or mechanics.

In 1981 the Minimum Wage Study Commission (MWSC) concluded this exemption was acceptable because union contracts covered 80% of all over-the-road drivers. Although these contracts usually provide overtime pay for city drivers, they rarely provide overtime pay for road drivers. However, the commission considered contractual provisions for daily guarantees, pay for nondriving work, and trip minima to be adequate protection (Fritsch 1981:151-86).

Unfortunately, the MWSC based its report on prederegulation data that were between 5 and 15 years old at the time. The substantial growth of nonunion TL carriers after deregulation created an environment in which wage and work rule exploitation could thrive. Furthermore, while the MWSC report specifically credits collective bargaining contracts which assure drivers pay for their nondriving labor, TL and nonunion drivers now are significantly less likely to be paid for nondriving labor time (Belzer 1993, forthcoming). Moreover, low-wage, nonunion competition has forced concessions resulting in longer hours of work without overtime pay on many local unions. For example, during the 1980s, Chicago's powerful Local 705 agreed to allow carriers covered by the tank contract to break down the distinction between city and road seniority boards. After a driver works 40 hours locally at an hourly rate, the company can force him onto the road for the remaining 30 hours at a straight road rate. In addition, city drivers' overtime standards were raised from 8 hours per day to 45 hours per week, allowing companies to force drivers to work 15-hour days without overtime compensation.

Nonunion competition has forced many union drivers to accept percentage pay. For example, intermodal (piggyback and container) drivers frequently are paid a percentage of the revenue. Since the rate does not increase along with a driver's weekly hours, all driver compensation is on a straight piecework basis. In addition, if the rate falls, the driver's wage falls also. Drivers absorb all delay time at rail and container terminals, and percentage rates reduce shipper incentives to improve timeliness and productivity. Most piggyback carriers also operate locally so they are not subject to DOT regulation, and drivers may work an unlimited number of hours each week. The expansion of the TL sector and the resulting significant deunionization of the industry leaves the conclusions of the commission quite out of date.

The Unions

The International Brotherhood of Teamsters (IBT) represents most unionized trucking industry employees along with workers in many other industries. Initially, the Teamsters sought only to represent "craft teamsters," those engaged in local delivery of specific commodities such as bread, coal, oil, milk, and beer. Local general freight drivers demanded representation during the 1930s and brought over-the-road freight drivers with them. By the end of the decade, the IBT started to organize support workers (warehouse, inside sales, and clerical employees) to protect its primary base.

In the Midwest in the 1930s, Farrell Dobbs and the Minneapolis Teamsters used an industrial model to spread unionization (James and James 1965:100; Dobbs 1972; Sloane 1991:18-22).[10] At the same time, Dave Beck on the West Coast supported a similar approach to Teamster organizing, expanding membership aggressively among support workers and within associated industries (Garnel 1972:87-88, 197). In the late 1950s, International President James R. Hoffa transformed widespread pattern bargaining into centralized bargaining, culminating in the National Master Freight Agreement (NMFA) in 1964. Unconstrained, following the Teamsters' expulsion from the AFL-CIO in 1957, Hoffa also sought to expand Teamster influence and membership throughout various industrial sectors (James and James 1965:136-140).[11]

In 1985 approximately 400,000 Teamsters out of approximately 1.6 million members were truck drivers, but less than half of those worked under the NMFA (Methvin 1985:2; BNA 1985a:A-8). Thousands more work as dock workers and other support personnel. Nonetheless, the trucking industry is extremely important to the Teamsters, because of its historic importance as its core jurisdiction and because of its close economic relationship to the jobs of other members. As most firms depend on trucking for the delivery of a wide range of goods from general freight to overnight letters, control of the trucking industry also gives the union great bargaining leverage in other disputes.

Teamster membership levels have declined by 17.8% since their 1974 high of 2,019,300. Most of the decline likely reflects the problems specific to trucking rather than a generalized loss of members. Almost all of the drop in membership occurred between 1980 and 1986 during the severe shakeout period following deregulation.

One may derive figures for the proportion of trucking industry workers represented by all unions from the Current Population Survey (CPS), although these data are known to be unreliable in some

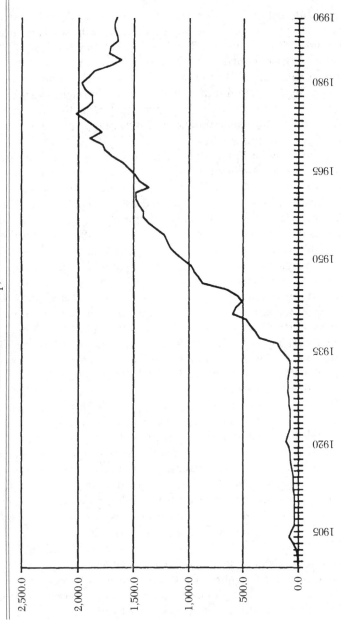

FIGURE 4
Teamster Membership, in Thousands

Sources: Troy and Sheflin 1985; LM-2 reports 1984-1990; Bureau of Labor Information 1984-1990.

respects.[12] Data from the CPS show union density declining. However, unionization data collected by the author in 1991 suggest union decline in general freight is modest—at least until 1990 when the quality of the data deteriorates sharply. In fact, the employment gains at large LTL carriers offset some but not all of the dislocation caused by extensive bankruptcies. Since most of these carriers are unionized, union density in general freight remains quite high.[13]

The Teamsters evolved as a relatively decentralized union. Local unions wield considerable power within the union, employ most of the individuals who engage in organizing, bargain many contracts, and handle grievances. Locals have some discretion over how the pattern-setting NMFA will be applied within their jurisdiction and how that pattern affects other contracts. The union has always been troubled by assertions that some locals cut under-the-table deals to gain employment or negotiate "sweetheart" contracts for certain employers.[14] Given the power of locals within the union, this problem has been difficult for the international or even the regional conferences to control.

Although certain pockets of union truck drivers have resisted affiliation or control, the Teamsters continue to dominate trucking industry collective bargaining.[15] Clearly the union had developed considerable bargaining power by the 1960s and 1970s, given its extensive organization of the relevant work force, its centralized and pattern bargaining, and its ability to make its strikes effective. Although union density within the industry has declined, the Teamsters continue to enjoy significant bargaining power in selected sectors of the trucking industry.

Bargaining Structure

The trucking industry's bargaining structure is complex. First, the National Master Freight Agreement is a multiemployer agreement which covers less than 10% of the union's membership; other trucking contracts use the NMFA as a pattern. Second, the NMFA determines pay increases, but not the base rate. Regional supplements, local riders, and individual company addenda determine actual wages; these are technically part of the NMFA. In addition, many carriers covered by the NMFA operate under profit-sharing schemes that reduce wages up to 15%.

Regional, local, industry, and company contracts cover the rest of the Teamsters' trucking members. For example, United Parcel Service (UPS) employs some 260,000 workers. Approximately 150,000 of these are Teamsters who work under a national contract.[16] About half the

TABLE 3
Union Density

Year	Hirsch A	N	Hirsch B	N	Belzer A	N	Belzer B	N
73-78	0.599	1,533						
1977					0.847	380	0.878	382
1978								
1979	0.566	175						
1980	0.564	94						
1981	0.607	84						
1982					0.804	278	0.861	280
1983	0.504	127	0.432	1,034				
1984	0.304	79	0.375	1,158				
1985	0.288	111	0.341	1,154				
1986			0.319	1,093				
1987			0.276	1,136	0.727	256	0.846	256
1988			0.300	1,161				
1989			0.269	1,166				
1990			0.241	1,264	0.476	189	0.651	190

Notes: Hirsch A uses only May public use CPS samples; N = number of drivers sampled in the for-hire sector. Hirsch B uses all 12 monthly CPS samples for each year; N is the same as Hirsch A. Hirsch analysis published in Hirsch 1993. Belzer A excludes United Parcel Service; N is the number of carriers analyzed. Belzer B includes United Parcel Service; N is the number of carriers analyzed.

unionized UPS work force works part time, mostly as freight handlers and loaders (Solomon 1992).[17] Separate national, regional, or local contracts cover carhauler carriers, tank and bulk carriers, food distributors, grocery firms, bakeries, and other private carriers.

Grievances

Master freight also defines noneconomic provisions, especially the grievance procedure. The NMFA, like many other trucking contracts, has an open-ended grievance procedure governed by evenly matched union and management committees. It is open-ended because either side can strike or lock out if a deadlock occurs. Grievance panels at the local, joint council, conference, and national levels resolve grievances deadlocked at lower levels.[18] Only the national panel can call a strike under the NMFA. Similar panels govern non-NMFA contracts, and only the highest panel governing any contract can reach a final deadlock (Levinson 1980).

This equal-panel approach is less expensive than arbitration, and some experts contend it is a powerful tool for the union (James and James 1965; Sloane 1991:216-37). However, critics charge the process encourages union and management representatives to cut deals. This system also allows union leaders to retaliate against dissidents or political challengers, thereby controlling local union officials. Local leaders need to win grievances if they hope to be reelected, and officials at higher levels of the organization control the panels (James and James 1965:178-81; Fox and Sikorski 1976:26-8, 42; Teamsters for a Democratic Union [TDU] 1990:14; Sloane 1991:228, 236).

Employer Organization for Collective Bargaining

General freight carriers created Trucking Employers Incorporated (TEI) in 1963 to present a united front to the Teamsters for negotiating the first National Master Freight Agreement. At its height, TEI represented between 800 and 1000 carriers; it was led by a 36-person board of directors and a 9-person negotiating committee. However, by 1976 TEI was an unwieldy organization, governed by a 102-member executive policy committee elected by about 30 regional carrier associations. At its peak, the NMFA negotiated by TEI directly covered between 300,000 and 500,000 workers. Many non-TEI carriers followed the TEI lead and signed the NMFA contract or followed the pattern (Levinson 1980:104-106).

The diversity of needs put a great strain on TEI unity. This internal tension caused TEI to break up in September 1977. Seceding employers created Carrier Management Incorporated (CMI), claiming its members represented 50,000 employees at ten regional carriers. Local cartage organizations, such as the powerful Chicago-based Motor Carrier Labor Advisory Council (MCLAC), remained outside TEI, further weakening employer unity. TEI and CMI reunified under Trucking Management Incorporated (TMI) in April 1978, healing the breach. However, this association retained the same representational structure as its predecessor (Levinson 1980:139-144). It thus inherited its predecessor's diverse constituency, needs, and internal tensions.

However, the new TMI that negotiated the 1979 contract only represented about 400 carriers, half the number of carriers represented by TEI in 1976. By 1982 TMI represented only 284 carriers (BNA 1985a: A-8). Given the dislocation in the industry caused by deregulation and the recession of the early 1980s, large and small carriers, often in regional and truckload markets, began negotiating their own independent contracts. By 1985 TMI only represented between 34 and 36 carriers.

Both TMI and the union claimed they represented an unchanged proportion of the industry's employees. However, while the 1985 master freight contract covered between 150,000 and 160,000 employees, the union estimated between 40,000 and 50,000 of these workers were on indefinite layoff (BNA 1985a:A-8). Thus the increasing relative importance of MCLAC and Regional Carriers Incorporated (RCI) and the persistent demand of small carriers to negotiate separate terms suggests weakened centralized bargaining and a declining pattern by 1985.

MCLAC, representing 115 carriers employing between 40,000 and 50,000 employees, ultimately was forced to accept the 1985 TMI agreement. RCI, a new association representing small and medium-sized regional carriers employing 20,000 unionized workers, did not sign and left its members to negotiate independent settlements (Perry 1986:105-10).

By 1988 bargaining representation clearly was even more decentralized. TMI retained its representation of the 34 largest carriers, but MCLAC represented only 50 carriers and RCI represented 18. Published reports claimed the NMFA included about 180,000 workers (BNA 1988a:A-5), although the number was probably closer to the roughly 150,000 covered in 1985, less layoffs. By 1991 TMI had dwindled to 24 carriers, although it is likely that they represented the same number of workers as in previous years (BNA 1990), given that consolidation in LTL continued to concentrate both freight and employees in the largest carriers.

In 1994 the Teamsters and TMI negotiated their first master contract since the election of Ron Carey as Teamster president. TMI, directly representing 23 carriers, led the bargaining for management, which again included MCLAC and RCI. The NMFA covered approximately 120,000 workers, with 75,000 of those working for TMI carriers and the remainder employed by carriers represented by MCLAC, RCI, and other management associations.

Industrial Relations in Transition: Hard Bargaining

Pressure to reopen the 1979-82 NMFA began soon after passage of the Motor Carrier Act of 1980. By 1981 many carriers, faced with either impending bankruptcy or expansion opportunities, asked for relief from many of the more expensive work rules. Concession demands included the elimination of fixed starting times, elimination of the Monday-through-Friday work week, reduced wages for new hires and casuals, wage cuts (some direct and some camouflaged in bogus employee stock ownership plans, or ESOPs), and a switch from hourly or mileage pay to a percentage of freight revenue.

Concession bargaining was intense. For example, Roadway used a provision in the 1976 NMFA that allowed locals to vote independently on scheduling, thereby whipsawing terminals and locals against one another to force acceptance of flex time. As the concession bandwagon gained steam, intensive local bargaining began. Large companies pitted locals and worksites against each other, and small companies demanded contract reopeners that reduced wages and conditions.

Persuading rank-and-file Teamsters to vote for concessions was difficult. Wage cuts disguised as loans began to appear, bargained at the local level. A large LTL carrier, Cooper-Jarrett, became the first to demand and later default on such a loan. Cooper-Jarrett's program, a loan of 15% of wages to the company paid back from profits in excess of $500,000, became a pattern that scores of carriers later followed, either to stay in business or to take advantage of a favorable bargaining environment. A Minnesota carrier, Glendenning Motor Ways, even asked its employees to donate the last two months of labor in 1981 to the company, to help it raise the $1.25 million it needed to stay in business. Glendenning successfully convinced most of its workers to donate

$4500 each to the company by converting its labor-time giveaway into an ESOP on which the company defaulted when it went bankrupt (La Botz 1990:197-208).

The 1982 master freight contract contained many concessions. Wages were frozen for three years, and COLA payments were diverted into health, welfare, and pension funds. New work rules, designed to make NMFA carriers more competitive with nonunion carriers, allowed road drivers to make one pickup and delivery of a full truckload shipment within the city drivers' territory, reversing the rule that reserved all customer deliveries to city drivers. It also allowed regional supplements and local addenda to resolve many of the previous years' bargaining issues, diminishing the importance of centralized bargaining (BNA 1982a:A-8; 1982b:D-1; Perry 1986:105-8).

Concessions were widespread. A survey of the general freight industry by the Industrial Research Unit of the University of Pennsylvania found that more than 50% of all responding unionized common carriers had received some kind of concessions, including wage reductions, free labor time, reduction or elimination of daily and weekly guarantees, and premium and overtime pay reductions. "The result was a further proliferation of the under-the-table arrangements of the 1970s, to the point where they were more a rule than an exception among small and/or truckload carriers" (Perry 1986:106-7).

While President Roy Williams' 1982 NMFA passed with a 61.5% majority, workers' dissatisfaction with concessions given to UPS surfaced. UPS, with a near monopoly in the small package business, netted $227.4 million after taxes in 1982 (for a 45.2% return on equity), yet demanded and received a pay freeze.[19] The UPS contract passed by a slim majority.

Concession bargaining occurred against a backdrop of legal problems for the union. General President Roy Williams was convicted of attempting to bribe Senator Cannon of Nevada to block deregulation, and the government forced him to resign. On April 21, 1983, the general executive board announced it had elected Jackie Presser to replace Williams. Presser quickly called a meeting of officers and proposed a national rider creating a two-tier wage system that would pay new hires and workers recalled from layoff at a 31% lower rate of pay. Terms of the proposed rider included a reduction of hourly pay from $13.23 to $11.00, a reduction of mileage pay from 32¢ to 22¢, a reduction of guarantee pay, a reduction to $5.50 for breakdown and delay time, and elimination of COLA adjustments and sick pay (BNA 1983a; Hirsch 1988:317, note 19). Members defeated Presser's proposed concessions by 94,086 to 13,082 (BNA 1983d:A-7).

However, the concessions drive continued amid bad economic conditions in the industry. The 1985 agreement included a two-tier wage system similar to the one rejected in 1983, although it was paired with an 11% wage hike for currently employed members. This time the second tier was temporary, which was more acceptable to union members. New hires started at 70% of scale, came up to 80% after one year, 90% after two years, and reached full scale after three years.

Although these reduced-wage, second-tier employees were new hires, they were not new to the industry or the union. Companies hiring reduced-wage drivers generally were hiring experienced union drivers laid off from carriers that had either cut back employment or closed down. The contract also cut the hourly wages of casuals from $13.26 to $11.00, putting them $2.76 below scale the first year. Since casuals' pay was frozen, it dropped $3.76 (25.5%) below NMFA scale by 1988 (BNA 1985b; Pustay 1989:252).

Contract opponents, both union and employer, charged the contract disproportionately benefited large, growing carriers. They claimed those carriers able to hire new regular or casual employees would put other unionized carriers at a competitive disadvantage. This contract change arguably gave large carriers the ability to gain at the expense of small carriers, further exacerbating the concentration of the LTL general freight industry.

The 1985 contract passed by a narrow 53.2% majority, but the Teamsters' ratification procedures prompted a lawsuit from Teamsters for a Democratic Union (TDU), the rank-and-file reform organization. Charging the vote excluded tens of thousands of casuals and citing the narrow vote margin, TDU demanded the union include its casual members in contract ratification votes. They argued that since casuals would lose more than 25% of their wages in this contract, they likely would have provided enough votes to reject the contract. The Teamsters claimed there were only 3,000 casuals, and the union only needed a one-third vote in favor of the contract to pass it regardless. In an out-of-court settlement, the Teamsters agreed that in future contract votes, they would allow casuals to vote if they worked at least 80 days the previous calendar year (BNA 1985c).

The 1988 NMFA negotiations produced an annual wage increase of 2.38%, applicable to all employees. It also improved the two-tier structure to 85-90-95 and cut the catch-up period to 18 months. However, members rejected the contract by an overwhelming 64%, whereupon the general executive board imposed it. Jack Yager, cochair of the negotiating committee, signed a statement to the members claiming the union constitution bound it to accept a final offer unless more than two-thirds of the members reject it (BNA 1988c:D-1; 1988d:A-5; 1988e:A-9). Presser, dying of cancer, resigned soon afterwards.

TDU members quickly sued the union, claiming it had gerrymandered the election to produce the most favorable vote. TDU cited extensive voting irregularities and claimed the "two-thirds rule" violated the "equal right to vote" provision of the Landrum-Griffin Act (BNA 1988f:A-11). This lawsuit did not prevent the implementation of the 1988 NMFA. Nonetheless, in an October 17, 1988, out-of-court settlement, new IBT General President William McCarthy agreed to amend the IBT Constitution to provide majority vote for contracts, except when a majority of all covered members do not vote.

ESOPs made their first formal appearance in the 1988 NMFA. Introduced at the local and company level in previous years as a mechanism to cut wages and save carriers from bankruptcy, the 1988 NMFA institutionalized them (Davis and Weintraub 1990). Under the new NMFA, if a carrier could get support from 75% of its Teamster employees, it could implement a wage deduction up to 15% (to a maximum of $2.25 per hour). Many members and local leaders saw it as a wedge that would effectively drive down the scale (BNA 1988d:A-5). Under the cover of profit sharing, these new ESOPs intensified the employers' whipsaw capability, as many companies (many of them admittedly in trouble) scrambled to set them up.

The 1991 contract provided a $1.40 raise for hourly workers (3% annually), bringing hourly wages to approximately $17.16 by 1994 and a 3.5¢ per mile wage increase for road drivers. It eliminated the COLA in all but name, fixing COLA payments contractually. Casuals received the same wage increase, bringing them to $14.45 by the end of the contract. The contract retained the two-tier schedule but removed the 95% step (BNA 1991:A-2).

The 1994 NMFA was important both for Carey and the trucking employers. LTL trucking companies wanted freer access to the intermodal market, as well as the right to assign work flexibly to match increasingly cyclical shipping schedules which demanded just-in-time delivery. The new Teamster leadership sought to bargain a contract that preserved union wages and conditions while allowing the carriers to meet intense competitive pressures. TMI bargained hard, and their final offer demanded the right to employ local workers on a part-time, temporary basis, paying $9 per hour (up to 24% of all local hours worked at approximately half the regular rate, with little or no benefits). They also demanded the right to rail up to 35% of freight, reduce starting pay to 70% of scale with a two-year catch-up, and replace the open-ended grievance procedure with binding arbitration.

The Teamsters struck for 24 days, the longest strike in the history of the Master Freight Agreement. The resulting contract, ratified by a four-to-one margin, did not provide for regular part-time employees, although it did allow carriers to rail up to 28% of freight mileage. Wage increases of $1.30 per hour (3.25¢ per mile) over the life of the four-year contract were modest (less than 2% per year), and the total economic package was only $3.20. Dock casuals' wages were frozen at $14.45 per hour for four years, and combination driving/dock casuals' wages will increase only $1.11 over four years. The two-tier wage system worsened, as new hires will start at 75% of scale and catch up in two years.

The contract made major changes to the grievance structure. Binding arbitration replaced the right to strike over deadlocked grievances. However, the contract created an innovative arbitration panel consisting of one company representative, one union representative, and one impartial arbitrator. The panel will issue decisions the same day as the hearing, and a new ten-point Grievant's Bill of Rights spells out grievants' rights to information, transcripts and written decisions. In addition, except for " 'cardinal' infractions," employees are presumed innocent and employers cannot fire them without a hearing. This last reform constitutes a major victory for which reformers fought for more than 15 years.

Finally, the contract provides that employees who go to work for the union, either by appointment or by election, will retain the right to return to their former position without loss of seniority. This provision reduces the pressure on union officials to win election by any means necessary, in order to avoid unemployment and destitution, and reduces the institutional imperative that helped develop a professional class of union officials, insulated from the members. In sum, the 1994 contract provided the carriers with important productivity tools while it allowed the union to advance the process of reform begun in 1992.

Wages in the Trucking Industry

Wage levels in the trucking industry reflect these economic and bargaining developments. Since 1978 real wages among all nonsupervisory employees have declined more than 24%. By 1990 real wages in the trucking industry had returned to 1962 levels. See Figure 5.

The periods of wage gain and loss correspond to significant changes in the economic and political climate. The first period of increase corresponds to Hoffa's struggle to gain centralized bargaining. During that period real wages increased approximately 3% per year. However, real wages stabilized during the Hoffa-negotiated NMFAs.

The power struggle that ensued after Hoffa was out of power brought extremely large annual increases. During the 1970 negotiations, the Chicago locals broke away from the national pattern and, following a 13-week strike, settled for a contract that increased wages by $1.65, favoring local over linehaul drivers. Not to be outdone, Fitzsimmons returned to the bargaining table and won an increase of $1.85 (Levinson 1980:119-120).

In general, labor and political strikes were common during the spring of 1970, contributing to pattern-breaking wage gains in many industries. Since the late 1970s, however, economic deregulation, high unemployment, and the concession bargaining it engendered have brought steady declines in employee earning power.

Figure 6 compares trucking to other industrial wages. In 1958 trucking wages were similar to those in durable goods manufacturing. Although never as high as construction, trucking wages rose and became comparable to primary metals and auto manufacturing. However, since regulatory restructuring, trucking wages have declined faster and farther than have those in other industries. While most blue-collar workers have suffered absolute wage declines since the late 1970s, truck drivers' wages have fallen so far they are again comparable to durable goods manufacturing wages. In sum, they lost ground along with other manufacturing workers while also losing the advantage they had gained over those workers.

Recent research indicates these low wages are not spread uniformly across the industry. In general freight, union carriers pay an average of 35.7¢ per mile, while nonunion carriers pay only 24.3¢. The average

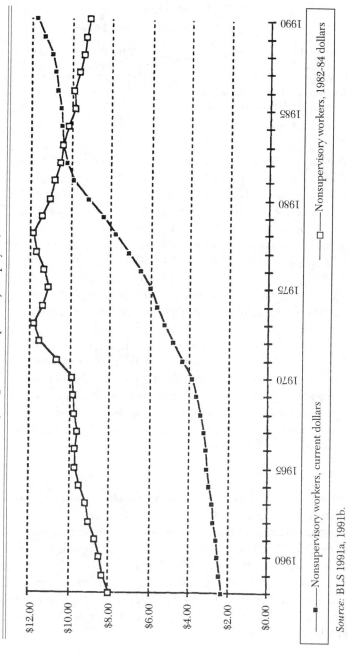

FIGURE 5
Hourly Wages of Nonsupervisory Employees, SIC 42

■——— Nonsupervisory workers, current dollars

□——— Nonsupervisory workers, 1982-84 dollars

Source: BLS 1991a, 1991b.

TABLE 4

Average Annual Change in Real Earnings

Hoffa consolidates bargaining	1959-1964	3.02%
NMFA #1 & #2	1965-1970	0.67%
Post-Hoffa power struggle	1971-1973	6.14%
Weak union leadership; stagflation	1974-1979	-0.51%
Weak union leadership; deregulation	1980-1990	-2.16%

Source: BLS 1991a, July 1991b.

union carrier pays $14.21 per hour for local hourly wages, while the average nonunion carrier pays $9.57. Also, while LTL carriers pay an average of 33.5¢ per mile, TL carriers pay only 23.8¢. The average LTL carrier pays $13.19 per hour, while the average TL carrier, if it pays by the hour, pays its local drivers $9.62. Perhaps most interesting, both TL and nonunion carriers are significantly less likely to pay road drivers any compensation for nondriving labor or delay time (Belzer 1993, forthcoming).

Finally, mileage and hourly rates, while suggestive of total compensation, underestimate the union-nonunion difference. Examining 1981 ICC data, Perry discovered benefits contributions of class II union carriers were nearly twice as high as corresponding nonunion carriers. According to Perry, by 1983, average annual wages of nonunion class I carriers were 32% lower than those of their union counterparts, and average total compensation was 37.8% lower. The benefits costs of the nonunion carriers were 78% lower. Hence, while nonunion wages are lower than union wages, "the greatest relative compensation advantage of nonunion over union carriers is in the area of benefits rather than wages" (Perry 1986:101, 104).

Political Turmoil

The Teamsters have a long history of dissent, much of it related to the strength of individual locals and conferences within a relatively decentralized organization. The Professional Drivers Council for Safety and Health (PROD), created in 1972 to promote health and safety and union reform, was the Teamsters' first national rank-and-file reform organization. It produced an important critique of corruption in the Teamsters. This report called on federal agencies to utilize existing law, especially Landrum-Griffin, to support members' reform efforts (Fox and Sikorski 1976).

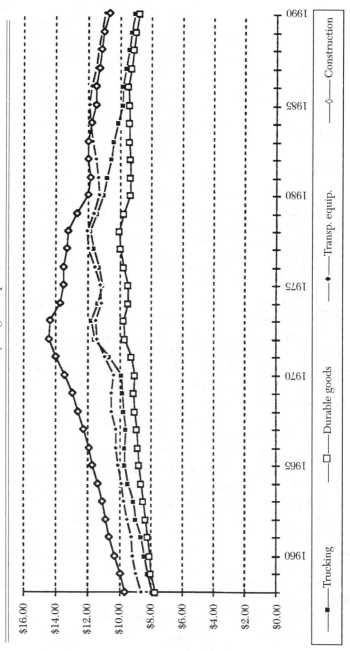

FIGURE 6

Interindustry Wage Comparison

Source: BLS 1991a, 1991b.

TABLE 5
Local Hourly Wage Distribution

	Average rate	Percent of grand mean
Grand Mean	$12.37	100.0%
Union	$13.88	112.1%
Non-union	$ 9.57	77.4%
LTL	$13.19	106.6%
TL	$ 9.62	77.8%
LTL/union	$14.21	114.9%
LTL/nonunion	$10.17	82.2%
TL/union	$11.50	93.0%
TL/nonunion	$ 8.82	71.3%

Source: Data collected by author, 1991; published in Belzer (1993).

Notes: All differences significant at better than the .05 level. For these calculations, a union carrier has at least a trace of representation (between 0% and 12.5%), and a nonunion carrier has no representation.

Teamsters for a Democratic Union (TDU), founded after a rank-and-file campaign to secure contract improvements in 1976, joined the effort with a particular emphasis on collective bargaining issues and structural reform. Both organizations focused on fighting corruption within the union and they merged as TDU in 1979 (La Botz 1990; Benson 1992). TDU garnered several victories in union locals during the 1980s. Although most of these victories were short-lived, they demonstrated, along with contract ratification problems, the breadth of member disaffection (Crowe 1993).

TDU opposed most of the contracts negotiated by the international during the 1980s. At first this opposition had little effect, but the Teamster leadership found it increasingly difficult to pass contracts. The UPS and Master Freight contracts in 1984 and 1985 passed by narrow margins.

Member dissatisfaction with contracts increased the credibility of TDU, which supplied members with contract bulletins and organization. Carhaul drivers rejected the 1985 contract by more than 80% (La Botz 1990:271). In 1987 and 1988 members rejected the UPS and NMFA contracts by 50.75% and 64% margins, respectively (BNA 1987:A-9; 1988e:A-9). Teamster Presidents Jackie Presser and Weldon Mathis further incurred the ire of the membership when they invoked the "two-thirds rule" to impose each of these contracts on the majority.[20]

When drivers rejected the 1988 carhaul contract by a 72.1% margin, McCarthy was forced to renegotiate for better terms. These contract defeats portended broad disapproval of the IBT leadership and were organizational triumphs for TDU.

Campaigning for delegate positions at the 1986 IBT convention, TDU members stepped up their demand for the right to vote for top union officers. While supporting Sam Theodus, president of Cleveland general freight Local 407, TDU collected 100,000 signatures on a national right-to-vote petition, demonstrating significant support for structural reform. Although only 24 delegates of more than 2000 voted for Theodus, 100 delegates signed an open letter supporting democratic elections (La Botz 1990:286-88). While symbolic, the extent of floor dissent in a Teamster convention again exposed the leadership's weakness.

Legal Turmoil and Reform

Corruption in the Teamsters has been a political issue since the mid-1950s. President Tobin, while unable to root out corruption at the local level, kept the international above reproach during his 45-year tenure. However, four out of the next six international presidents were either charged with or convicted of various crimes, including jury tampering, bribery, extortion, and misappropriation of union and benefit funds. Beck, Hoffa, and Williams went to prison. Frank Fitzsimmons escaped government prosecution, but his successor identified him as a tool of organized crime, following his own bribery conviction (Brill 1978; President's Commission on Organized Crime 1985:63-119; Methvin 1985:39). Presser defended his illegal actions by claiming they were sanctioned by the FBI, for which he was an informant. He died before he could be tried.

The AFL-CIO, the Justice Department, reformers within the union, and rank-and-file Teamster organizations have all tried for decades to rid the union of corrupt elements. In 1957, thirteen New York rank-and-file members sued the IBT to block Hoffa's election as IBT president, alleging he had sandbagged the convention with paper locals created to get their convention votes. To resolve the suit, Hoffa agreed to allow the court to supervise the international. A board of monitors served from 1958 to 1961, the first judicial attempt to clean up the international; it was ineffectual (Goldberg 1989; 1990:934, 984-94).

After decades of indifferent Labor Department enforcement of the Landrum Griffin Act, the Justice Department tried a new approach. On June 28, 1988, the Justice Department brought civil charges against the

Teamsters under the Racketeer Influenced and Corrupt Organizations (RICO) provisions of the 1970 Organized Crime Control Act. This was the first use of RICO against an entire national union. The power of RICO comes from three elements. First, since it empowers the Justice Department to take civil action, RICO replaces the criminal law standard of "beyond a reasonable doubt" with the much looser civil "preponderance of evidence" standard. Second, a judge can interpret a union official's refusal to testify on the grounds of self-incrimination as an admission of guilt sufficient to order him banned from the union (a civil rather than criminal penalty). Third, since labor unions have a legal obligation to act against racketeers, the failure to act against a union official who engages in criminal activity or associates with organized crime constitutes evidence of tolerance of labor racketeering. In a RICO trusteeship, the court can expel union officials who knowingly fail to take action (Methvin 1992).

Some scholars believe the use of RICO is risky, potentially infringing on union members' civil rights, including the fundamental right not to incriminate oneself (Geoghegan 1988; Goldberg 1990:927-945).[21] Opposition to the use of RICO against the Teamsters received support from other labor unions, the AFL-CIO, and 246 congressmen concerned about RICO's threat to the labor movement (Carlson 1991). In testimony before the Senate Governmental Affairs Committee's Permanent Subcommittee on Investigations on April 12, 1989, AFL-CIO President Lane Kirkland argued that government trusteeships are "wrong as a matter of principle. Government-dominated trade unions, no matter what the excuse, are contrary to freedom of association" (BNA 1989b:A-12).

TDU very carefully balanced its position on the 1987 RICO lawsuit. Although TDU opposed the court-appointed trusteeship because it opposed government control of unions, as an intervenor it supported the court-ordered direct election of officers in order to increase union democracy.[22]

Facing imminent trial under the RICO statute, the Teamsters general executive board signed a consent order on March 13, 1989. This order provided for the judicial appointment of three court officers (an administrator, an investigations officer, and an election officer) with powers comparable to those of the general president. Most important, the consent order required the direct democratic election of all international officers (Goldberg 1990:996-97).

The incumbent union leadership split in the ensuing election, running two candidates: Vice-Presidents R.V. Durham and Walter Shea.

UPS Local 804 President Ron Carey assembled a slate of vice presidential candidates from around the country and ran a grass-roots campaign. Although Carey was not a member of TDU, that group enthusiastically lent its national organization to Carey and this provided crucial support (Crowe 1993). In the 1991 election, Carey defeated Durham and Shea in the race for general president. Carey received 48.5% of the vote and swept his entire slate with him, providing support for the view that democracy could play an important role in union reform (Jennick 1992; Crowe 1993; for a profile of Carey, see Brill 1978:155-201).

Since the election, Carey has introduced ethics rules, reduced excessive compensation and luxuries, and reinvigorated the international's organizing, educational, and research efforts. He has put several corrupt locals into union trusteeship, including Chicago's important Local 705.

Court officers' efforts under the federal trusteeship resulted in charges against 214 officials and three locals. Actions by the investigations officer resulted in 51 expulsions, 64 resignations, 53 suspensions, and 30 other settlements (Carberry 1993).[23] A permanent independent review board will retain oversight over the Teamsters' internal efforts to root out organized crime.

Carey's leadership remains controversial, however, at least among local and regional officials. The 1991 convention vote to raise strike benefits to $200 per week, without a commensurate raise in the per capita tax, left the international in serious financial difficulty. In early 1994, the members rebuffed Carey's attempt to stanch the flow of funds, rejecting a dues increase by a three to one margin in a first-ever national referendum. During the Master Freight strike, the union paid out approximately $45 million in benefits, forcing it to borrow $30 million from the AFL-CIO. Strike costs drove the union treasury to $15 million, compelling the general executive board to suspend further strike payments and implement a constitutional provision mandating a $1 per member dues levy on local unions until International funds exceed $25 million.

These financial woes prompted Carey to ask the executive board to revoke the charters of the area conferences, thereby immediately saving the union $14 million per year (although Carey promised the international would replace any services lost in the transition). Conference officials opposed this move, charging political motivation, but Carey convinced the court that the move involved long-needed reforms rather than an infringement on the free speech rights of conference officials. After 60 hours of testimony, the Board voted 14-3-2 to revoke the charters, making a major change in the structure of the union.

The union leader, as the elected leader of a democratic institution, must gain and retain the respect of his members by negotiating good contracts. Carey passed his first test by successfully negotiating a carhaul contract that had been overwhelmingly rejected by the membership. His second great test came in the 1993 UPS negotiations, which produced one of the highest wage packages in the nation as well as significant process reforms. The National Master Freight Agreement represented the greatest challenge. The core of the union can be found in the beleaguered freight industry, which has economic problems that make bargaining particularly difficult. While the long strike produced mixed results, Carey appeared to produce a credible contract for his constituents under difficult circumstances.

Finally, the political conflict within the union is not over, and many of Carey's political opponents retain control of important locals and regional bodies. They will pounce on any missteps he makes and will blame him for any further concessions to the employers.

Conclusion

The spectacular shakeout in the trucking industry that resulted from deregulation has moved from crisis to chronic decay. Consolidation within the industry is likely to continue, and large carriers will improve their market positions by expanding in selected markets. Market segmentation likely will be a permanent feature of the trucking industry. Large LTL carriers and railroads will buy out smaller carriers that fit their strategic plans.

Public policies have replaced economic regulation with safety and environmental regulation. First, the trucking industry case causes us to ask whether public policy is best served by direct labor market regulation or by economic regulation. Since the nation has relied upon private collective bargaining to regulate the industry, declining collective bargaining coverage has further shredded the regulatory fabric and subjected an increasing number of industry employees to low labor standards (see Belzer 1994).

Second, can declining unionization be turned around? Existing labor laws that support capital mobility coincidentally encourage deunionization. Current laws encourage instability in labor relations by permitting companies to start nonunion (even in highly organized environments like trucking) and permitting unionized carriers to start nonunion subsidiaries capable of replacing them.

While union influence has declined in the truckload industry, it has not disappeared. Direct and indirect union effects are evident in TL general and specialized freight, and union influence in LTL remains strong. Although real wages have declined, the decline is less severe among unionized carriers. The Teamsters' weakness in TL and regional markets remains a problem for the organization. The IBT is down but not out; it retains considerable membership support, organizing appeal, and potential bargaining power based on its ability to mount effective strikes. It must use these assets to reestablish a presence in the truckload market. Regional LTL markets (where carriers can mix LTL and TL work and customers expect premium service) are the next battlegrounds in collective bargaining.

At present, nonunion TL firms complain of a labor shortage, especially in long-haul operations. This may be a market failure, as the labor shortage exists at the same time thousands of qualified drivers are out of work. Although potential employees exist, they are so far down the queue that they are unqualified according to federal law or are unacceptable to truckers insurance companies. In short, these carriers cannot attract sufficiently skilled and responsible employees at the low-wage rates the industry pays. If the trucking industry is to attract and retain stable, literate, careful employees, it must improve wages and living and working conditions. That is, higher wages and better working conditions would likely increase the supply of high-quality employees to the industry.

A further problem looms in the future. The North American Free Trade Agreement (NAFTA) currently provides no protection for truck drivers or trucking companies. Unless prohibited by a sidebar agreement, Mexican companies or Mexican subsidiaries of U.S. companies may be free under NAFTA to operate within the U.S., using Mexican driver's licenses and standards. If so, extremely low-wage Mexican labor could flood the U.S. trucking market with disruptive consequences for domestic firms and workers.

The deregulation experience demonstrates that increased product market competition reflects back into labor markets, as firms attempt to gain a competitive edge by cutting wages and allowing labor standards to deteriorate. To date, public policy efforts to protect workers by directly regulating labor markets have been ineffective and incomplete, although such regulation might be improved in the future. Only collective bargaining protects trucking companies and their employees from this downward spiral, and it has been seriously weakened in the past decade. Nonetheless, barring new shocks from NAFTA or other sources, the worst industry dislocation appears to be over. The Teamsters retain a presence in the industry and a power base for the future. The challenge to the "New Teamsters" under Ron Carey is to turn the tide by reestablishing their strength in the trucking industry.

Endnotes

[1] A definition of trucking industry terms can be found in the appendix to this chapter.

[2] Most trucks are used privately. Only 14.4% of 4,886,200 working trucks on the road are operated for hire, although for-hire trucks account for 40.4% of all truck miles (Taff 1986:3-17).

[3] Individuals who own and drive their own trucks operate approximately 210,000 (30%) of all for-hire trucks; 43% of these owner-operators lease their trucks to certificated carriers (U.S. Department of Commerce 1990-91:Table 2).

[4] Less than one-fourth of all trucks belong to fleets larger than 20, although fleets of 20 trucks or more run 42.8% of the miles. Local cartage occupies 62% of all trucks, and only 10% of all trucks operate more than 200 miles from their base of operations. However, this interstate hauling accounts for 69.2% of all for-hire mileage, and common carriers log 69.5% of these interstate for-hire miles.

[5] Transportation pricing theory has been debated for more than one hundred years. Value-of-service theory contends efficient transportation pricing requires rates to reflect the relative value to the shipper of moving the freight. Since the law of supply and demand forces those with inelastic demand to pay higher rates, the value of the commodity proxies the value of service, and optimum efficiency results (Locklin 1972:142-170). Many economists argue value-of-service pricing is a contrivance of regulators and claim cost-of-service tariffs are more efficient. However, recent research suggests value-of-service theory explains pricing in the unregulated environment (Beilock 1985).

[6] The precise components of marginal costs are difficult to determine. For instance, owner-operators may accept a rate that pays for fuel but not wages.

[7] Since the MCA of 1935 limited entry, the legal right to haul a particular commodity between specified points granted by the ICC became a scarce and valuable commodity. Carriers expanded by purchasing the rights of other carriers, and carriers purchased other carriers for their operating rights.

[8] For a detailed account of changes wrought by deregulation and the effect of deregulation on industrial relations, see Belzer (1994).

[9] Interlining requires competitors to cooperate in scheduling, rate setting, billing, and a division of the revenues.

[10] Dobbs and other Trotskyists played a pivotal role in the expansion of the Teamsters union. Major unionization battles and strikes led by Dobbs and his comrades

directly contributed to the unionization of drivers in the Midwest, leading to the first multistate general freight contract.

[11] The International Brotherhood of Teamsters received its charter from the American Federation of Labor on August 22, 1903. It has had ten presidents:

1903-1907	Cornelius P. Shea	1981-1983	Roy Williams
1907-1952	Daniel J. Tobin	1983-1988	Jackie Presser
1952-1957	David D. Beck	1988-1988	Weldon Mathis[°°]
1957-1971	James R. Hoffa[°]	1988-1992	William J. McCarthy
1971-1981	Frank E. Fitzsimmons	1992-	Ronald R. Carey

[°]Hoffa went to prison on March 7, 1967. General Vice President Frank Fitzsimmons assumed day-to-day authority in his absence.
[°°]Acting President while Presser was on extended sick leave.

[12] For instance, one individual answers questions for members of the entire household, and there may be considerable error in that individual's knowledge of whether or not other household members are represented by labor organizations. Truck drivers who are single heads of households also may be difficult to locate and sample, as many virtually live on the road. In addition, the CPS includes workers who drive any kind of truck in any operation, which indiscriminantly lumps general freight drivers with those who deliver pizza.

[13] My analysis uses a population consisting of class I general freight carriers, as reported to the ICC and obtained from the American Trucking Associations. I calculated that 50% of all carrier employees in 1990 were drivers of company equipment and generalized that proportion to previous years. These calculations were necessary because the number of drivers at each company was available on tape only after 1990. The generalization is conservative because the industry-wide proportion of production to supervisory employees rose between 1977 and 1990. I multiplied the number of drivers by the union density at each carrier; the latter data were obtained from my 1991 survey and related research. Finally, this analysis assumes failed union carriers were union shops, as most were.

Finally, in 1990 the ATA reclassified carriers on their own initiative to reflect their own interpretation of the restructuring of the industry. While the reclassification may have been necessary, it doubled the population of general freight carriers and abruptly changed the population's character. See Duke (1992) for a critique and Belzer (1994) for further clarification.

In sum, while CPS data include all truck drivers from DOT-regulated intercity truck drivers to unregulated couriers, ICC data are limited to the general freight market. This approach avoids confounding broad changes in service markets with changes in the general freight trucking industry.

[14] In a decentralized bargaining environment, however, it may be hard to tell a sweetheart from a legitimate concession without evidence of kickbacks.

[15] Chicago IBT Local 705 continues to bargain its own freight contract. Chicago Local 710 bargains an independent contract for dock and office workers and also for regional UPS employees. The Chicago Truck Drivers Union (CTDU), an independent teamsters union, historically represented about one-half of all local freight drivers in the Chicago area, although it now also represents over-the-road drivers. In

Texas the Union of Transportation Employees (UTE) represents drivers for many intrastate carriers. Unique circumstances have led to representation at specific carriers by the United Steelworkers Union and the International Association of Machinists. Finally, private-carrier drivers often belong to the same union as production workers.

[16] Chicago Locals 705 and 710 represent an additional 10,000 to 12,000 employees in separate contracts, and Local 2727 represents airline mechanics. In its entirety, UPS employs some 75,000 drivers.

[17] ICC Motor Carrier Annual Reports indicate part-timers average 15 hours per week.

[18] Joint councils are formed wherever there are three or more locals in one city. Locals from surrounding cities will usually affiliate in the large city's joint council, and state and multistate joint councils may also be created. Conferences and trade divisions may be established at the state, area, multi-area, trade, national company-wide, or industry-wide level (IBT Constitution Articles XV and XVI).

[19] Data from Motor Carrier Annual Report submitted to the ICC.

[20] While "[c]ontracts may be accepted by a majority vote . . .," and "a majority of such members may direct further negotiations before a final vote on the employer's offer is taken," if the local union's executive board determines the "employer has made a final offer of settlement, such offer must be submitted to the involved membership and can be rejected only by a two-thirds (2/3) majority." (Constitution of the IBT, June 1981:Article XII, Section 1). This section, pertaining to strikes by local unions, was applied by the international executive board in these extraordinary circumstances.

[21] Goldberg argues that for decades state and federal governments have had ample authority under existing common law to impose receiverships for corrupt, discriminatory, or undemocratic practices. The federal government's failure to use existing laws to reinforce members' own efforts to keep the union honest makes the use of RICO particularly disturbing. Goldberg shows how prosecutors turned membership rights into property rights covered by RICO, while they ignored RICO's threat to union members' free speech and freedom of association (Goldberg 1990:927-945). However, Goldberg supports the use of RICO in the Teamsters' case if the court limits its actions to removing criminals and establishing a basis for democratic control by the membership and does not interfere in collective bargaining.

[22] Since its inception, TDU's "Rank and File Bill of Rights" demanded direct election of international officers. TDU always supported the enforcement of Landrum-Griffin's Bill of Rights for Union Members and fair elections procedures (Paff 1987; TDU 1987; BNA 1989a:A-4).

TDU also tried for many years to convince the Labor Department to enforce Landrum-Griffin's requirement for democratic election of international officers. For two years before the Justice Department filed the RICO suit, TDU battled with them to force the Labor Department to interpret Landrum-Griffin as requiring the direct election of international officers. As Goldberg opined, it is "very ironic" that the Justice Department that opposed enforcement of Landrum-Griffin chose to use the much more radical RICO instead (Riley 1987).

[23] As of September 1993, 12 charged individuals await the Independent Administrator's Opinion and five others face repeat charges.

APPENDIX
Glossary of Trucking Terms

Term	Definition
Back haul	The secondary freight loading from a point near the consignee, a region often outside the trucker's primary customer base, returning to the trucker's home terminal.
Casuals	Workers hired on an irregular basis and without a position on a seniority board; they may be hired out of hiring halls.
Certificated carrier	A carrier authorized to offer common carrier service to the public on the basis of published tariffs.
Class I	Carriers grossing more than $5 million annually.
Class II	Carriers grossing between $1 million and $5 million annually.
Common carrier	A carrier that offers its services to the public according to published rates.
Contract carrier	A for-hire carrier whose services are available only through a private contract between trucker and shipper.
Dock workers	Persons who work on a loading dock, loading and unloading freight.
Exempt carrier	Carriers exempt from ICC regulation: haulers of certain commodities, haulers of shipments that are part of continuous airfreight movements, intrastate and local cartage, and private carriers.
For-hire carrier	A motor carrier that offers its services to the public.
Front haul	The primary freight loading from a trucker's home terminal to the consignee.
General freight	Non-specialized freight that generally requires no special handling or equipment.
Interline	A single freight movement shared by at least two carriers, neither of which can deliver the freight within its own system.
Less-than-truck-load (LTL)	A shipment weighing less than 10,000 pounds; also, a carrier primarily hauling these small shipments. A full load for an LTL carrier typically consists of more than thirty shipments. LTL operations require elaborate terminal and pick-up and delivery operations.
Linehaul	An "over-the-road" freight movement; also drivers who do inter-city and inter-state work, either from terminal to terminal or shipper to consignee.

Local cartage	Trucking operations limited to a single city or metropolitan area.
Operating authority	The ICC grants operating authority to for-hire carriers, specifying the commodities to be hauled and services to be offered.
Owner operator	Persons who own and drive their own trucks, either under their own authority or under contract to a carrier. Some owner operators own more than one truck and employ other drivers.
Piggyback	An intermodal configuration in which a railroad flatbed carries a complete semi-trailer. In a related usage, the rail car holds a container, which is a semi-trailer box or tank without wheels, undercarriage or king pin.
Private carrier	A company that uses its own trucks to deliver goods it produces or distributes. Deregulation allows private carriers to do limited for-hire hauling.
Special commodities	Specialized freight that requires special handling and special equipment; e.g., bulk solids or liquids, refrigerated commodities, automobiles.
Ton-mile	An output measure defined as the transportation of one ton of freight the distance of one mile.
Truckload (TL)	A shipment weighing more than 10,000 pounds; also, a carrier primarily hauling these large shipments. A full load for a TL carrier typically consists of between one and four shipments. TL operations do not require terminal infrastructure.

References

American Trucking Associations. 1977, 1982, 1983, 1990. *Motor Carrier Annual Report*. Data collected by the Interstate Commerce Commission on tape and disk. Alexandria, VA: Financial & Operating Statistics Service, Department of Statistical Anaylsis.

Anderson, Dale G., and Ray C. Huttsell. 1989. "Trucking Regulation, 1935-1980." In J. R. Felton and D. G. Anderson, eds., *Regulation and Deregulation of the Motor Carrier Industry*. Ames, IA: Iowa State University Press, pp. 14-41.

Beilock, Richard. 1985. "Is Regulation Necessary for Value-of-Service Pricing?" *Rand Journal of Economics* Vol. 16, No. 1 (March), pp. 93-102.

Belzer, Michael H. 1990. "The Transformation of Labor Relations in the Trucking Industry Since Deregulation." M.S. Thesis, Cornell University.

_____. 1993. "Collective Bargaining in the Trucking Industry: The Effects of Institutional and Economic Restructuring." Ph.D. diss., Cornell University.

_____. 1994. *Paying the Toll: Economic Deregulation of the Trucking Industry*. Washington, DC: Economic Policy Institute.

_____. Forthcoming. "After Deregulation: Do the Teamsters Still Matter?" *Industrial Relations Review*.

Benson, Herman. 1992. "Union Democracy Triumphs Over Organized Crime." *Dissent* (March), pp. 138-142.

Brill, Steven. 1978. *The Teamsters*. New York: Pocket Books.

Bureau of Labor Information. Various years. *Directory of Labor Organizations in Canada*. Ottawa: Bureau of Labor Information.

Bureau of National Affairs (BNA). 1982a. "Wage Freeze, Diversion of COLA Money Highlights of New National Truck Pact." *Daily Labor Report*, No. 23 (February 3), p. A-8.

_____. 1982b. "Preliminary Draft of Teamsters' National Master Freight Agreement and Central States Supplement and Rider." *Daily Labor Report*, No. 23 (February 3), p. D-1.

_____. 1983a. "Teamsters Schedule Mid-August Membership Vote on Revisions of Master Freight Pact." *Daily Labor Report*, No. 150 (August 3), p. A-6.

_____. 1983b. "Talks on Truck Rider Concluded, Teamsters Say; Union Survey Shows Layoff Rate of 32.5 Percent." *Daily Labor Report*, No. 160 (August 17), p. A-9.

_____. 1983c. "Report by Teamsters on Layoffs Under National Master Freight Agreement." *Daily Labor Report*, No. 160 (August 17), p. D-1.

_____. 1983d. "Contract Rider Endorsed by Presser Overwhelmingly Rejected by Teamsters." *Daily Labor Report*, No. 181 (September 16), p. A-7.

_____. 1985a. "Teamsters, Employer Groups Begin National Master Freight Bargaining." *Daily Labor Report*, No. 11 (January 16), p. A-8.

_____. 1985b. "Teamsters Negotiate Pay Hikes, Lower Entry Rates in New Freight Agreement." *Daily Labor Report*, No. 63 (April 2), p. A-10.

_____. 1985c. "Teamsters Modify Voting Eligibility Policy to Settle Challenge to Master Freight Vote." *Daily Labor Report*, No. 114 (June 13), p. A-2.

_____. 1987. "Teamsters Locals Ratify New Contract Raising Pay and Benefits for UPS Employees." *Daily Labor Report*, No. 162 (August 24), p. A-9.

_____. 1988a. "Trucking Industry Talks Get Underway." *Daily Labor Report*, No. 10 (January 15), p. A-5.

_____. 1988b. "Economic Terms of Tentative Master Freight Pact Released by Teamsters; Local Reps Meet in Chicago." *Daily Labor Report*, No. 68 (April 8), p. A-5.

_____. 1988c. "Teamsters Summary of Union's Proposed 1988 National Master Freight Agreement." *Daily Labor Report*, No. 68 (April 8), p. D-1.

_____. 1988d. "Teamsters to Vote on Freight Pact; Ratification is in Doubt, However." *Daily Labor Report*, No. 75 (April 19), p. A-5.

_____. 1988e. "Teamsters Announce Ratification of National Master Freight Agreement." *Daily Labor Report*, No. 98 (May 20), p. A-9.

_____. 1988f. "Dissident Teamsters Members Sue Union Over Ratification of National Freight Pact." *Daily Labor Report*, No. 104 (May 31), p. A-11.

_____. 1988g. "Complaint Filed by Individual Members of Teamsters on Ratification of National Master Freight Agreement." *Daily Labor Report*, No. 104 (May 31), p. D-1.

_____. 1989a. "Dissent Teamsters Group Seeks to Intervene in Government's RICO Case Against International." *Daily Labor Report*, No. 15 (January 25), p. A-4.

_____. 1989b. "Witnesses Disagree on Whether Trusteeships Deal With Organized Crime's Ties to Unions." *Daily Labor Report*, No. 70 (April 13), p. A-12.

_____. 1990. "Teamsters and Freight Carrier Group Begin Talks on Master Trucking Accord." *Daily Labor Report*, No. 228 (November 27), p. A-6.

_____. 1991. "Teamster Members by 2-1 Ratify Nationwide Master Freight Contract." *Daily Labor Report*, No. 85 (May 2), p. A-2.

Carberry, Charles M. 1993. "Investigations Officer's Report." (July 22).

Carlson, Peter. 1991. "Teamster Glasnost." *Washington Post Magazine* (December 8), p. W15.

Childs, William R. 1985. *Trucking and the Public Interest: The Emergence of Federal Regulation 1914-1940*. Knoxville, TN: University of Tennessee Press.

Conyngham, Michael. 1993. "I.C.C. Regulated Motor Carriers of General Freight Under the National Master Freight Agreement that Terminated General Freight Operations from July 1, 1980 to May 30, 1993." *Teamsters Research Department Report* (June 4). Washington, DC: International Brotherhood of Teamsters.

Corsi, Thomas M., and Joseph R. Stowers. 1991. "Effects of a Deregulated Environment on Motor Carriers: A Systematic, Multi-Segment Analysis." *Transportation Journal* 30, No. 3 (March), pp. 4-28.

Crowe, Kenneth C. 1993. *Collision: How the Rank and File Took Back the Teamsters*. New York: Charles Scribner's Sons.

Davis, Grant M., and Norman A. Weintraub. 1990. "Labor-Management Relations: ESOPs in the Trucking Industry." In M. Roomkin, ed., *Profit Sharing and Gain Sharing*. Institute of Management and Labor Relations Series, Vol. 2, edited by James Chelius. Metuchen, NJ and London: IMLR Press/Rutgers University and The Scarecrow Press.

Dobbs, Farrell. 1972. *Teamster Rebellion*. New York: Monad Press.

Enis, Charles R., and Edward A. Morash. 1987. "Some Aspects of Motor Carrier Size, Concentration Tendencies, and Performance After Deregulation." *Akron Business and Economic Review*, Vol. 18, No. 1 (March), pp. 82-94.

Felton, John Richard. 1989a. "Background of the Motor Carrier Act of 1935." In J. R. Felton and D. G. Anderson, eds., *Regulation and Deregulation of the Motor Carrier Industry*. Ames, IA: Iowa State University Press, pp. 3-13.

_____. 1989b. "Motor Carrier Act of 1980: An Assessment." In J. R. Felton and D. G. Anderson, eds., *Regulation and Deregulation of the Motor Carrier Industry*. Ames, IA: Iowa State University Press, pp. 143-162.

Fox, Arthur L., and John C. Sikorski. 1976. *Teamster Democracy and Financial Responsibility: A Factual and Structural Analysis*. Washington, DC: PROD, Inc.

Fritsch, Conrad F. 1981. "Exemptions to the Fair Labor Standards Act, Transportation Sector." *Report of the Minimum Wage Study Commission*, June. Washington: U.S. GPO.

Garnel, Donald. 1972. *The Rise of Teamster Power in the West*. Berkeley: University of California Press.

Geoghegan, Thomas. 1988. "Union Suit: A Wrong Cure for the Teamsters." *The New Republic* 199, No. 8 (August 22), p. 14.

Goldberg, Michael J. 1990. "Cleaning Labor's House: Institutional Reform Litigation in the Labor Movement." *Duke Law Journal*, No. 4, pp. 903-1011.

_____. 1989. "The Teamsters' Board of Monitors: An Experiment in Union Reform Litigation." *Labor History*, Vol. 30, No. 4 (September), pp. 563-584.

Hirsch, Barry T. 1988. "Trucking Regulation, Unionization and Labor Earnings: 1973-85." *Journal of Human Resources*, Vol. 23, No. 3 (June), pp. 296-319.

_____. 1993. "Trucking Deregulation and Labor Earnings: Is the Union Premium a Compensating Differential?" *Journal of Labor Economics*, Vol. 11, No. 2 (April).

International Brotherhood of Teamsters. 1981. *Constitution*. Washington, DC: IBT.

James, Ralph, and Estelle Dinerstein James. 1965. *Hoffa and the Teamsters: A Study of Union Power*. Princeton: D. Van Nostrand Company.

Jennick, Susan. 1992. "Union Democracy Defeats Organized Crime in the Teamsters Union." *Union Democracy Review*, No. 86 (February), p. 1.

La Botz, Dan. 1990. *Rank-and-File Rebellion*. New York: Verso.

Levinson, Harold M. 1980. "Trucking." In G. Somers, ed., *Collective Bargaining: Contemporary American Experience*. Madison, WI: Industrial Relations Research Association, pp. 99-150.

Locklin, D. Philip. 1972. *Economics of Transportation*, Seventh ed. Homewood, IL: R. D. Irwin.

Methvin, Eugene H. 1985. "Additional Views of Commissioner Eugene Hilburn Methvin." *The Edge: Organized Crime, Business, and Labor Unions Appendix*. October. Washington, DC: GPO.

_____. 1992. "The Liberation of the Teamsters; End of Organized Crime Influence on Labor Union." *National Review*, Vol. 44, No. 4 (March), p. 35.

Paff, Ken. 1987. "Let the Teamsters Vote; We Need Union Democracy, Not a Government Takeover." *Washington Post*, Outlook (June 21), p. B15.

Perry, Charles R. 1986. *Deregulation and the Decline of the Unionized Trucking Industry*. Philadelphia, PA: Wharton Industrial Research Unit.

President's Commission on Organized Crime. 1985. "In the Matter of Roy L. Williams, a Witness Subpoenaed by the President's Commission on Organized Crime." *The Edge: Organized Crime, Business, and Labor Unions Appendix*. October. Washington, DC: GPO.

Pustay, Michael W. 1989. "Deregulation and the U.S. Trucking Industry." In K. Button and D. Swann, eds., *The Age of Regulatory Reform*. Oxford: Clarendon Press, pp. 236-256.

Riley, John. 1987. "Debate Continues on Teamster Tactics." *The National Law Journal* (November 3), p. 3.

Sloane, Arthur A. 1991. *Hoffa*. Cambridge, MA: MIT Press.

Solomon, Mark B. 1992. "Teamsters Chief Slams UPS For Boosting Part-Timers." *Journal of Commerce* (September 24), p. A 1.

Sweeney, Daniel J., Charles J. McCarthy, Steven J. Kalish, and John M. Cutler, Jr. 1986. *Transportation Deregulation: What's Deregulated and What Isn't*. Washington, DC: National Small Shipments Traffic Conference.

Taff, Charles A. 1986. *Commercial Motor Transportation*. Centreville, MD: Cornell Maritime Press.

Teamsters for a Democratic Union. 1987. *Convoy Dispatch*, November/December.

_____. 1990. "Should We Dump the Grievance Panels?" *Convoy Dispatch* (April), p. 14.

Troy, Leo, and Neil Scheflin. 1985. *U.S. Union Sourcebook*. West Orange, NJ: Industrial Relations Data and Information Services.

U.S. Department of Commerce, Bureau of the Census. 1991. *Census of Transportation, 1987; Truck Inventory and Use Survey*. Washington, DC: GPO.

U.S. Department of Labor, Bureau of Labor Statistics. 1991a. *Employment, Hours, and Earnings, United States, 1909-90*. March. Washington, DC: GPO.

_____. 1991b. *Supplement to Employment and Earnings*. July. Washington, DC: GPO.

_____. 1988. *Occupational Projections and Training Data: A Statistical and Research Supplement to the 1988-1989 Occupational Outlook Handbook; Bulletin 2301*. April. Washington, DC: GPO.

CHAPTER 8

Telecommunications Labor-Management Relations: One Decade After the AT&T Divestiture

JEFFREY KEEFE
Rutgers University

KAREN BOROFF
Seton Hall University

Editor's Abstract

The telecommunications industry is in turmoil. Since September 1993, telecommunications employers have announced plans to eliminate 98,000 jobs. On average, AT&T has eliminated 1,000 jobs per month since divestiture. Not surprisingly, job security has emerged as a major subject of bargaining, both at AT&T and at the various Regional Bell Operating Companies (RBOCs), where considerable deregulation is still pending. Employment and union security are also threatened by technological developments that make telecommunications and cable television companies either collaborators or competitors.

Keefe and Boroff assess the impact of the breakup of AT&T in 1984 on employment, productivity, compensation, unionization, employee involvement, and other industrial relations outcomes. These issues were largely ignored by proponents of increased competition in telecommunications. Indeed, they are still being ignored in discussions of the "information super highway," as is witnessed by legislation recently introduced in Congress. Both state regulators of the RBOCs and federal policymakers need to be more conscious of the human consequences of further changes in the telecommunications business environment.

Keefe and Boroff demonstrate that post-divestiture productivity growth in telecommunications has fallen to half of its predivestiture trend. This is not due to a slackening of technological change, but rather to reduced economies of scale and scope, to unproductive excess capacity brought about by multiple long-distance carriers, to the replacement of R&D expenditures by marketing expenditures, and to a serious reduction in employee morale stemming from the new employment insecurity. The econometric studies that consistently demonstrated economies of scale and scope in the Bell System were apparently correct. Productivity issues as well as industrial relations consequences should inform future telecommunications policy. Unionization of the industry has fallen with the entry of new nonunion competitors. Moreover, organized companies have shifted toward more supervisory or managerial jobs. Foreign equipment manufacturers, along with MCI, were big winners from deregulation. Both groups have been vigorously antiunion. Keefe and Boroff document how these employers remain nonunion in the face of union organizing drives, both by exploiting current labor law and by selectively violating it. They also review the 1992 Workplace of the Future agreement at AT&T. Here the Communications Workers of America (CWA) gained enhanced ability to influence restructuring and downsizing and to shape the structure and format for employee participation. Organizing should be facilitated because the CWA got neutrality and card check provisions at AT&T—except for the subsidiary which was formerly National Cash Register. Nonetheless, Keefe and Boroff conclude that it is at best uncertain whether the cooperative Workplace of the Future vision can become a reality in a downsizing environment.

Keefe and Boroff detail union gains in recent contracts at several RBOCs with regard to employment security, union institutional security, and influence over the employee participation process. The central issue for the future at the Regional Bell Operating Companies is whether or not they can gain sufficient control over their economic environment to manage restructuring and phase in employment changes. The alternative is that restructuring will be abrupt and employee morale, union organization, and productivity will all suffer.

o   o   o

The purpose of the divestiture is to establish conditions which will prevent the type of anticompetitive activities which the government had charged in its complaints. . . . These activities, and hence the settlement of the lawsuits, do not involve AT&T labor relations and, more particularly, they have nothing to do with the Communications Workers of America or its relationship with the Bell System.

Judge Harold H. Greene, August 11, 1982
Consent Decree Opinion, p. 80

Throughout most of the 20th century, the Bell System was the telephone industry, a public utility organized as a unified natural monopoly. The network of Bell Telephone Companies and AT&T Long Lines provided both local and long-distance telephone services for most Americans, while Western Electric manufactured almost all the telephone equipment used by the Bell System. The unexpected AT&T divestiture fundamentally restructured the American telecommunications industry.

On January 1, 1984, AT&T divested its 22 Bell operating companies (BOCs), the providers of local telephone service, to settle an antitrust case initiated by the U.S. Justice Department in 1974. The Justice Department insisted that the company be restructured into competitive and regulated entities. Telecommunications equipment and long-distance service were designated as competitive, while the provision of basic dial tone would continue to take place through regulated monopolies. AT&T chose to retain Western Electric (equipment manufacturing), AT&T Long Lines (long-distance service), Bell Laboratories, and its newly formed competitive products subsidiary, American Bell (renamed AT&T Information Systems or ATTIS). The 22 BOCs were reorganized into seven regional holding companies that were prevented by the settlement from entering the competitive long distance, information services and equipment manufacturing markets.

On the eve of divestiture, AT&T was the world's largest private employer with over one million employees. With $138 billion in assets, it was the wealthiest private institution in the world; its profits totaled $7.3 billion, and it ranked first in corporate net income. It had three million shareholders, 95% of whom held less than 600 shares, and since 1885 AT&T had never missed or lowered its dividend. Its revenue amounted to almost 2% of U.S. GNP, and its investments accounted for over 9% of U.S. domestic investment. The local Bell companies provided over 80% of the U.S. local telephone service, while AT&T Long Lines handled over 95% of U.S. long-distance calls. Western Electric was the world's largest manufacturer of telecommunications equipment, and if it had been independent, it would have ranked as the twelfth largest industrial corporation on the *Fortune 500*. In addition, Bell Laboratories was America's premier research institution, employing over 10,000 PhDs, with a research budget that surpassed the total research budget for the rest of U.S. industry. Under Bell's leadership, the telephone industry was characterized by above-average productivity growth (6% annually), technological innovation, long-term capital planning, universal service, and employment stability.

One decade after the AT&T divestiture, Congress is considering several new major legislative initiatives to reform the Communications Act of 1934, to reduce the lines of business restrictions contained in the divestiture agreement, and to promote the development of the national information infrastructure through greater competition. Just as Judge Greene explicitly excluded all employment issues from the scope of his review of the consent decree, no current reform bill addresses the labor, employment, or productivity effects of the proposed telecommunications industry restructuring. This chapter will show that the divestiture settlement profoundly affected the industry's labor relations and, more particularly, greatly impacted the Communications Workers of America (CWA) and its relationships with all the former Bell System companies. Since divestiture, downsizing and chronic employment insecurity have become the major employee concerns. These considerations, however, remain excluded from the public discourse over the alternative configurations of America's new information super highway.

Labor-Management Relations in Telecommunications

At divestiture, approximately two-thirds of the industry's employees were union members. The CWA remains the dominant union, but the International Brotherhood of Electrical Workers (IBEW) has a sizable membership as well. AT&T also bargained with the Telephone Independent Union, which disbanded at divestiture; its locals affiliated with either CWA or the IBEW. In the decade prior to divestiture, labor-management relations in the Bell System matured with AT&T's acceptance of national bargaining in 1973. Collective bargaining was conducted in a two-tier framework in which economic issues were resolved at a national table. As a result of national bargaining, workers experienced a rising standard of living through deferred wage increases and a cost-of-living escalator, and their health and pension benefits were some of the best in American industry. The Bell System also provided employment security for its workers and managers through comprehensive human resource planning. Western Electric, however, was excluded from this employment security system, and during the 1970s it experienced declining employment. Displaced manufacturing workers received negotiated early retirement incentives and severance packages. At the local operating company level (the second tier), bargaining focused on work administration issues. National bargaining stabilized labor-management relations, and the industry experienced no major strikes during the decade prior to the announcement of the consent decree. Transcending the collective bargaining and workplace relationships, however, was the vigorous political campaign jointly undertaken by AT&T and its unions to prevent the breakup of the Bell System.

After the divestiture announcement on January 8, 1982, this labor-management relationship abruptly changed. In August 1983, CWA conducted a three-week national strike against AT&T involving some 600,000 hourly employees—the second largest strike in U.S. history. The eight new companies rejected a national bargaining structure in favor of corporate or subsidiary-level bargaining. In 1986 CWA conducted a 26-day strike against AT&T over wages and COLA elimination. The strike ended when the IBEW accepted the company's final offer. The CWA also mobilized its members to oppose layoffs and continuous downsizing, even picketing the home of Robert Allen, chairman of AT&T, attacking him for a "Frank Lorenzo" stance toward unions. Since divestiture AT&T has eliminated some 140,000 bargaining-unit jobs, while it has established and purchased major nonunion subsidiaries. It competes with aggressively antiunion MCI and Sprint in long distance. In the equipment markets the company faces challenges from major multinational competitors such as Northern Telecom, Siemens, Ericsson, and Alcatel which operate in the U.S. with varying degrees of "union-free" militancy. Since 1991 AT&T has stabilized its market share in long distance and increased its market share in the equipment business. During 1992 the company and the two unions sought to rebuild their relationship by negotiating new contract language on a "Workplace of the Future" that creates a framework for working collaboratively in transforming their organizations.

In contrast to the post-divestiture AT&T trauma, the regional Bell operating companies (RBOCs) retained the Bell System approach of managing change gradually. The first round of post-divestiture collective bargaining negotiations in 1986 was relatively uneventful, except for a ten-day strike at NYNEX over health care. In 1989 however, disputes over health insurance produced four major strikes involving over 200,000 workers. The companies insisted on managed care networks and some cost shifting. At NYNEX a four-month strike by the CWA and the IBEW defeated the company's health insurance demands, while managed care was accepted in all other agreements. In 1992 collective bargaining was once again peaceful. Although downsizing had begun, it was handled voluntarily with some financial inducements in most companies.

The relative stability of the regional Bells, however, is ending. Since divestiture many state and local services have been deregulated or placed under incentive regulation. The only remaining monopoly segment has been the local telephone loop, the line between the subscriber and the local central office switch. On September 17, 1992, the FCC ruled that competing local networks must be allowed to connect with the local Bell exchanges (co-location), thus opening local telephone service to competition. The legality of co-location has been successfully challenged by NYNEX in federal court.

New broad-band fiber-optic cable technologies create the potential for interactive multimedia services, which require the integration of cable TV and telephone to become economically feasible. A new generation of wireless communications is also about to begin. These new digital wireless networks will substantially reduce the costs of mobile communications, while greatly improving quality and accelerating the diffusion of wireless communications.

As a result of this new industry structure the RBOCs may undergo a restructuring in the next five years similar to AT&T's, as they transform themselves from public utilities into financial and market-driven organizations. The major issue facing the RBOCs and the unions is whether change can be managed without permanently scarring incumbent employees, or whether competitive conditions will demand radical and traumatic restructuring. Since October 1993 major corporate restructurings accelerated at the RBOCs, leading to job loss.[1] In contrast to AT&T, most of the RBOCs will be able to implement these reductions largely through attrition, early retirements, and voluntary severance.

From the standpoint of labor-management relations, this massive industrial restructuring is in jeopardy of severing the traditional link between high productivity growth through rapid technological change and rising employee incomes with employment security. When compared to the decade prior to divestiture, post-divestiture productivity growth has fallen by one-half as networks are duplicated and many of the one million employees in the industry now face chronic insecurity, displacement, and stagnating incomes. Breaking the industry's social contract through this uncoupling may have serious long-term consequences for productivity, service quality, and stable labor-management relations.

The new digital interactive technologies and the fiber optic and wireless networks will radically redefine temporal and spatial relations in a postindustrial society. For symbolic workers, the location of their work activity is already becoming less important. As skill sets shift from electromechanical to electronic, from analog to digital, and from hardware to software, the traditional work forces are often downsized. Simultaneously, new workers are hired as such companies are at the forefront of using these new technologies to reorganize their own work systems, thus creating new technical occupations. Today's environment stands in sharp contrast to the 75 years of organizational stability under the Bell System.

Evolution of Labor-Management Relations in the Bell System

AT&T's Bell System had a long history of paternalism, ironically captured by the phrase "Ma Bell." Throughout the first half of the 20th century AT&T also vigorously opposed independent unionism. During World War I, the IBEW had considerable success in organizing telephone operators and affiliating with their independent organizations. Yet early IBEW efforts to organize telephone workers were eventually defeated by a combination of union suppression and substitution policies.

AT&T set up company unions during the American Plan era of the 1920s to inoculate the Bell System against independent unions, and here lie the roots of the CWA, the major telephone union. The company developed a centrally directed personnel program aimed at preventing unionism, promoting administrative efficiency, and presenting a favorable public image. In 1913 AT&T established a benefit plan that included company-paid pensions, vacations, and sickness and disability benefits. In 1915, it added employee stock purchase options. By the 1920s, it had gained a reputation for providing secure and continuous employment (Schacht 1985). In 1932, however, that reputation would be tarnished as Bell companies opted to lay off workers rather than cut the AT&T dividend.

Starting in the late 1930s, AT&T's company unions were slowly transformed into an industrywide union with the assistance of the National Labor Relations Act's Section 8(2) prohibition against company-dominated unions. Between 1935 and 1937 more than 180 labor organizations were formed in the Bell System. Without exception they directly descended from the network of company unions that AT&T had put in place to thwart the growth of independent unions. In 1938 many of these former company unions met to found the highly decentralized National Federation of Telephone Workers (NFTW). Section 8(2) had required AT&T to separate itself from its company unions; however, company domination would remain informally intact in many locals until the founding of the CWA in 1947.

This transformation in labor relations received further assistance from the National War Labor Board (NWLB) during World War II. Militant telephone operators would once again be the driving force in this metamorphosis, as they had been during World War I. On November 17, 1944, a strike of telephone operators in Dayton, Ohio began when Ohio Bell refused to alter its unequal pay practices for temporary transfers who received a higher rate of pay than the regular work force. The strike was settled after the President threatened seizure. The NWLB then created a National Telephone Panel to address this dispute and other issues. The panel legitimated the independent NFTW by including two NFTW members as labor representatives on the tripartite panel. In the spring of 1945 a dispute arose involving AT&T Long Lines, the Traffic Employees Association of New York (independent), and Branch 101 Federation of Long Lines Telephone Workers (NFTW) when both unions attempted to enforce a weekly wage increase recommended by the panel. A settlement was eventually reached without a strike. Partly as a result of this dispute, however, the NWLB upgraded the panel to a commission with the authority to enforce its decisions.

In 1947 the CWA (the successor to the NFTW) was formed to attain national bargaining with AT&T. Although the company controlled employee benefits, set the community wage standards for employee pay, and established the administrative practices of the Bell System, it insisted on local collective bargaining. Local negotiations were used to demonstrate to state utility commissions that Bell companies had autonomy and that labor costs were determined by the local labor market. According to AT&T, state regulation, not federal regulation, was the most appropriate method for determining the costs, prices, and profits for each Bell telephone company. To defend the local negotiations framework, the company defeated a four-week national strike in 1947. Ironically, this defeat strengthened those union activists who advocated a more highly centralized and disciplined union as essential to countervail the company's centralized coordination of local bargaining.

The new union, the CWA, attempted to use its political leverage in Washington to get the company to agree to national bargaining. Starting in 1951 during the Korean War, then CWA President, Joseph Beirne, served on the Wage Stabilization Board which granted telephone workers a 10% wage increase. In that same year the union prompted a Senate Education and Labor Committee investigation into AT&T's control over the BOCs labor relations. The 62-page report concluded that the telephone industry's poor labor relations was primarily attributable to the company's control of collective bargaining, which prevented meaningful negotiations at the local level. The Senate report, however, did not alter the company's approach to collective bargaining.

During the 1950s the local bargaining framework proved to be unstable, producing violent strikes at Indiana Bell, Southern Bell, and Ohio GTE, as union leaders and the rank-and-file members grew increasingly frustrated. Peaceful strikes were not effective because they did not disrupt the increasingly automated telephone system. Many local leaders firmly believed that local bargaining was a farce.

Beginning in 1959, an informal pattern-bargaining relationship developed between CWA and the Bell operating companies. This pattern method worked well until 1968, when the union conducted a brief national strike (the first since 1947) to secure the pattern. The IBEW in Illinois, however, refused to follow the pattern and conducted a four-month strike, which Illinois Bell eventually defeated.

In 1971 CWA conducted a national strike against the Bell System, developing its first mobilization campaign. The unions gained COLA and agency shop with a grandfathering provision that permitted non-union employees already on the payroll an exemption from paying the agency fee. When the parties settled, AT&T Board Chairman, H. I. Romnes, called President Nixon to notify him of the settlement; Nixon, 33 hours later, announced wage price controls. CWA in the New York City Plant Department, however, stayed on strike against the advice of its national leaders. This strike lasted for seven months and cost the union $11 million in strike benefits. The New York agreement granted an agency shop clause without grandfathering and a small increase in the city allowance. The CWA was defeated on every major issue. Furthermore, during the strike New York Telephone, using hundreds of newly promoted supervisors from across the country, upgraded its plant and equipment and thus alleviated a major three-year service crisis in downtown Manhattan. AT&T won the strike, but pressures were building to change the bargaining procedure, and they gained further momentum with the settlement of a massive Equal Employment Opportunity complaint against the company.

In 1970 the Equal Employment Opportunity Commission (EEOC) and several civil rights organizations sought to intervene in an AT&T rate case before the Federal Communications Commission (FCC). After two years of administrative hearings and negotiations between the company and the federal government—represented by the EEOC—the Justice Department, and the Labor Department, a consent decree was approved in January 1973 by a U.S. District Court. The decree provided for a $38 million wage adjustment package and a six-year program to restructure AT&T's personnel system.

Women constituted the majority of the nonmanagement, union-eligible work force in the Bell System. Until 1970 occupations within the company were sex segregated. Table 1 reports the trends in company employment between 1950 and 1980. During this period, the expansion of telephone service resulted in a steady growth of the telephone crafts and management, a relative decline in the female nonmanagement work force, and a dramatic decrease in the number of operators.

The EEOC demonstrated that sex discrimination was the fundamental organizing principle for Bell's personnel system. It found that 92% of all Bell System employees worked in sex segregated jobs (using a standard of 90% of the occupation being of one sex to determine sex segregation). To break down gender segregation, the EEOC consent decree contained an affirmative action override. The override permitted the company to bypass seniority and the well-established trainability standards for identifying the best qualified candidate and to select a candidate from the pool of basically qualified applicants if this procedure was necessary to meet the decree's goals and timetables. The union was deluged with grievances filed by male plant-craft workers who were being bypassed for promotion. Given the broad base of dissatisfaction with the affirmative action override, local strikes appeared likely in 1974. Consequently, the consent decree pushed the company further toward national bargaining.

The company's main concern, however, was the growing number of challenges to its role as the public manager of the nation's telephone network. In 1968, the FCC issued its Carterfone decision, which started the process of the deregulation of customer premise equipment. The following year, the FCC handed down a decision allowing MCI to begin building a private-line network. MCI would use this decision as the opening round in a 15-year contest to deregulate long-distance telephone service. As the forces of deregulation gathered momentum at the national level, AT&T instituted a process of corporate strategic planning in 1969. It moved to solidify the support of state regulators and independent telephone companies by increasing the long-distance cross subsidies for local service through the Ozark Settlement Plan in 1971. Its

TABLE 1

AT&T's Employment Distribution by Occupation and Gender 1950-1980

	1950	1960	1970	1980
Total AT&T Employment	523,251	735,766	1,005,380	1,044,041
Bell System	523,251	580,405	772,980	847,768
Western Electric	73,458	143,352	215,380	174,372
Bell Labs	5,757	12,009	17,020	21,901
Bell System Employment				
Bell System Management	70,630	105,833	169,401	248,562
Management Percent of Total	13%	18%	22%	29%
Bell System Nonmanagement	446,129	466,795	574,534	589,939
Nonmanagement distribution				
Plant craft forces	24%	30%	35%	44%
Traffic-operators	47%	34%	29%	16%
Office-clerical	19%	23%	24%	10%
Other	10%	12%	12%	31%
AT&T Female Employment				
AT&T Women	363,363	378,070	503,728	517,439
Percent of AT&T total	65%	51%	50%	50%
Bell System Women	340,504	331,780	425,428	443,819
Women as percent of total	65%	57%	55%	52%
Women in management	23,266	34,084	56,749	95,739
Women in nonmanagement	310,998	290,914	341,989	339,369
Percent of management	33%	32%	33%	39%
Percent of nonmanagement	70%	62%	60%	58%
Women in Bell System nonmanagement				
Plant craft forces	69	353	1,939	60,281
Traffic operators	208,067	159,946	165,461	83,597
Office-clerical	79,795	101,575	129,310	53,740
Other	23,078	29,040	45,279	141,770
Women as percent of plant				
craft forces	0%	0%	1%	23%
Traffic operators	100%	100%	93%	90%
Office-clerical	92%	93%	93%	93%
Other	54%	52%	64%	79%
Women's average age (yrs)	30	34	33	37
Average service (yrs)	9	11	9	12
Annual turnover	19%	20%	27%	na

Source: Bell System Statistical Manual 1950-1980. June 1982, AT&T's Comptroller's Office, New York, pp. 701-8.

response to efforts to deregulate the telephone industry would emphasize that the unified Bell System was the solution to the nation's communications needs.

As this campaign took shape under AT&T's aggressive new chairman, John DeButts, corporate labor relations proposed a national two-tier framework for collective bargaining in 1973. This structure would promote stability and reduce the likelihood of service disruptions. Bargaining on economic issues was conducted at a national negotiations table. The outcome of these negotiations would produce a national "Go Down" agreement, which would then be added to each local agreement. AT&T held over 150 agreements with its unions that were subject to the national provisions. Once a national agreement was reached, local bargainers were usually given a week to reach a settlement. A local contract had to be ratified before the national "Go Down" agreement for wages and benefits could be implemented in that unit. Local negotiators could not discuss issues settled at the national level, which were subject to a separate national ratification. This procedure deterred the local bargainers from engaging in pattern-breaking strikes over economic issues. The bottom level of the two-tier structure, however, was relatively removed from the shop floor. To address workplace job pressures, AT&T and CWA negotiated a Quality of Work Life (QWL) Program in 1980, and by 1983 over 1200 QWL groups were in place that eventually involved over 100,000 employees in QWL committees.

The two-tier bargaining structure matched the Bell System structure. Negotiations henceforth took place at the organizational levels where the decisions about the respective bargaining issues were being made. Between 1973 and 1982, the national collective bargaining framework provided the stability the parties had sought, and it allowed them to turn their efforts and considerable resources toward their unsuccessful campaign to prevent the deregulation of telecommunications and the divestiture of AT&T. Divestiture and deregulation changed the structure of the industry and, consequently, of collective bargaining.

Stakeholders in Regulation and Deregulation

Local and long-distance telephone service was regulated as a natural monopoly in a two-tier federal and state system throughout most of this century. The first modern state regulatory commissions were established in Wisconsin and New York in 1907. By 1913 almost two-thirds of the states had established regulatory commissions. In 1910 Congress authorized the Interstate Commerce Commission (ICC) to oversee interstate common carrier communications. In 1934 it was superseded by the FCC.

Regulators sought to achieve three major goals: efficiency, reliability, and universal service. Efficiency was principally realized through network-scale economies, the nonduplication of telephone facilities, regulatory review of costs, and regulated pricing. Reliable high-quality service was provided through a highly integrated network and a service-oriented organization and work force. And universal service was accomplished by subsidizing the price of basic telephone service and rate averaging, which reduced the rates for rural customers by charging uniform rates for service.

Under FCC regulation, AT&T functioned as the public network manager. It provided all local companies access to the long-distance network. Local operating companies were required to serve everyone within their region and were guaranteed a rate of return without any competition. Regulators established a fair and reasonable rate of return and prevented entry into the market. Under this system, 92% of American homes had telephones, and most Americans were satisfied with their service. However, the rate structure made the Bell System vulnerable to potential competitive entry. Long-distance and business equipment rental rates were deliberately set above their costs. The revenue surpluses were used to reduce the price of basic telephone service below its cost. This cross-subsidized rate structure, designed to promote universal service, also created strong incentives for outside firms to devise ways to enter high-priced subsidized markets such as long-distance and business equipment. It also stimulated heavy users of the high-priced services to seek alternative sources of supply. Specifically, a concentrated group of large businesses in financial and computer services increasingly subsidized local rates for residential users. These large users became well organized into political action groups that supported MCI's challenge to the Bell System's long-distance monopoly and blocked AT&T's efforts at Congressional reform of the Federal Communications Act.

During the 1970s, the long-distance rates increasingly cross subsidized local service. The Ozark Plan for separations and settlements negotiated in 1971 by federal regulators, AT&T, other telephone companies, and state regulators increased the recovery costs of nontraffic-sensitive local facilities in the long-distance rate structure. A separations and settlements procedure had been originally mandated in *Smith vs. Illinois Bell* (1931) when the Supreme Court ruled that because long-distance calls require the use of local exchanges on both ends for connection, the long-distance carrier must reimburse the local exchange carrier for use of the local facilities. The new cost allocation methodology embedded in the Ozark Plan shifted more costs from local to long-distance rates. By the mid-1970s long-distance rates paid for one-third of the local plant costs while accounting for less than 8% of local plant usage. By 1980 long-distance rates contributed two dollars to the cross-subsidy for each dollar it cost to operate the long-distance network. State regulators found such a cost reallocation politically attractive partly because technology was driving down long-distance costs while local access costs were relatively stagnant.[2] Largely as a result of the Ozark Plan, the inflation-adjusted average monthly local telephone bill fell by 29% during the 1970s (Teske 1990:2-4). At the same time, the Ozark Plan stiffened the resolve of major corporate long-distance users to escape from the Bell System monopoly and the cross-subsidized rate structure.

Over the objections of the FCC and AT&T, MCI gained entry to the publicly switched long-distance market through a federal court ruling in 1978. Once MCI entered this market, the cross-subsidy scheme was doomed. During the last decade, as the cross-subsidies were eliminated, prices for long-distance telephone service have declined by 40% and long-distance calling volume has more than doubled, while basic local residential service rates have increased by more than 60% from $11.58 to $18.66.[3] Deregulation led to substantial economic gains for concentrated large corporate interests that are major users of the long-distance network and widespread losses for residential consumers and former Bell System employees (Teske 1990:126). Not surprisingly, public opinion polls at the time of divestiture indicated that over 70% of telephone customers opposed the Bell System breakup.

Residential consumers largely have not benefited from the changes in the industry. Deregulation, as expected, has led to rate increases for local telephone service. State regulators approved $10.5 billion in rate hikes between 1982 and 1986, out of $70 billion in annual BOC revenues (Teske 1990:40). Since 1987, however, local rates have been relatively flat. Consumers have also experienced significant transactions costs from the deregulation in selecting a long-distance carrier and confusion over service problems and billing, and there are at best only a few new services that are in demand by residential consumers. A significant segment of the consuming public is also unlikely to be interested in the new multimedia services. According to a 1991 AT&T study, almost 40% of American households still use a rotary-dial telephone. In addition, less than two-thirds of American households purchase cable TV service, although it is available to 90% of homes.

Many of the costs of deregulation and restructuring have been borne by employees. We estimate that more than 300,000 jobs have been eliminated within the former Bell System since divestiture. Telephone deregulation has led to the breaking of lifetime employment security pledges and the abrupt elimination of many managerial and union-represented jobs. Not surprisingly, since 1982 divestiture has also contributed to a steady increase in labor-management conflict in the industry.

At the same time and somewhat unexpectedly, shareholders have greatly benefited from deregulation and divestiture. Between 1984 and 1992, the seven RBOCs and AT&T have each increased their shareholders' wealth in excess of 300%; with AT&T, Ameritech, Pacific Bell, and Bell Atlantic exceeding 350% and Southwestern Bell yielding over 400% growth. In 1982, after the divestiture announcement, the market value of AT&T stock was $47.5 billion. By 1993 the combined equity value of the former AT&T companies was in excess of $180 billion, almost a four-fold increase. All eight post-divested corporations have significantly outperformed the S&P 500.

As the major industrial economies undergo restructuring, telecommunications services become more central to the competitiveness of all businesses. The future structure, prices, services, and stability of the U.S. telecommunications industry will steadily gain importance in determining how well other businesses will compete in a global economy. The Clinton administration has placed telecommunications policy and the development of a national information super highway at the center of its infrastructure renewal program. Universal service and the appropriate role for government in guaranteeing all Americans access to the global network is once again a major issue for public debate.

Market Structures and Employment Trends

Telecommunications is composed of two basic industries: telephone equipment manufacturing (SIC 3661) and telephone communications services (SIC 481). Prior to divestiture, vertically integrated AT&T dominated both the equipment and service markets. In this section, we examine each major industry's current structure and employment.

Equipment

AT&T remains the world's leading telecommunications equipment manufacturer; in 1991, worldwide sales of telecommunications products and systems generated approximately one-quarter of its total revenue. However, its leadership position is challenged by the French telecommunications giant, Alcatel. In the U.S., AT&T competes with six other multinational firms: Northern Telecom (Canadian), Siemens (German), Alcatel (French), Ericsson (Swedish), NEC (Japanese), and Fujitsu (Japanese). AT&T and Northern Telecom control about 70% of the U.S. digital equipment market. Siemens, the third largest manufacturer in the American market, operates in the U.S. under its own name and through its subsidiary companies, Stromburg-Carlson, Rolm, and Siecor—a joint venture with Corning. Each of the major multinational companies has opened or purchased U.S. manufacturing facilities.

During the 1980s, foreign-owned equipment manufacturers were major beneficiaries of divestiture and open equipment markets. Since 1984 the U.S. has run trade deficits in telecommunications equipment totaling $14 billion. The deficit fell to $557 million in 1991 (Wood 1992:21). With the entry of large multinationals, telecommunications equipment has become the most competitive market in the industry (Crandall 1990). In the global equipment market there are seven or eight major suppliers with AT&T and Alcatel taking a substantial lead; however, the world market cannot be accurately described as fully competitive. Each major telecommunications multinational corporation controls its own monopoly market, while competing for its global market share. AT&T retains its equipment monopoly with AT&T long distance; Alcatel has the market at France Telecom; Siemens has a special relationship with Deutsch Telekom; and Northern Telecom has its common ownership link with Bell of Canada.

The $60 billion annual U.S. domestic telephone equipment industry is comprised of four major market segments: (1) the network equipment market is primarily electronic digital switches and peripherals, transmission equipment, and fiber optic cable accounting for $11 billion in annual sales; (2) the customer premises equipment (CPE) market ($15.6 billion in annual sales) is primarily the $13 billion business equipment market, which includes PBXs, key telephone systems, call/voice processing equipment, teleconferencing equipment, FAX, and computer-telephone integration equipment; (3) the data and networking communications equipment market accounts for $16.8 billion total sales; and

(4) wireless communications equipment is rapidly growing at a rate in excess of 20% annually and represents $8 billion in sales. Table 2 reports 1992 market shares in the U.S. equipment market and the market share rankings of the leaders in the global equipment market. Network equipment is used in the operation of the nation's 26,000 central offices and in transmissions over the 3.2 billion circuit miles. In 1993, AT&T had a 42% share of the U.S. central office switch market, 29% of the PBX market, and 21% of the key telephone system market, while it dominated the fiber optics and cable transmission market. Motorola controlled the cellular user market with, for example, over 84% of the pager market. AT&T and Motorola together supplied over 80% of the cellular network equipment market.

TABLE 2

Leading Telecommunications Equipment Manufacturers

A. Ranked by U.S. Market Share

U.S. Central Office Equipment Market (1991) Market ($5.3 Billion):

AT&T	U.S.	40%
Northern Telecom	Canada	39%
AG Communications (AT&T-GTE)	U.S.	9%
Siemens & Stromberg-Carlson	Germany	8%

U.S. Electronic PBX Market (1991) Market ($2.8 Billion):

AT&T	U.S.	28%
Northern Telecom	Canada	23%
Siemens-Rolm	Germany	17%
NEC	Japan	6%

U.S. Key Telephone Systems and Hybrids (1991) Market ($1.8 Billion):

AT&T	U.S.	26%
Northern Telecom	Canada	13%
Executone	U.S.	12%
Toshiba	Japan	12%

B. Top Global Telecommunications Equipment Manufacturers

Leaders in the Global Equipment Markets: 1991 (Revenues in Billions):

AT&T	U.S.	$15.9
Alcatel	France	$15.5
Siemens	Germany	$11.0
Northern Telecom	Canada	$8.2

Source: North American Telecommunications Association

Employment in U.S. telephone equipment manufacturing has steadily declined from its peak level in 1970. In that year, Western Electric alone had 215,380 employees (Bell System Statistical Manual 1983:702). The 1970s decline was due mainly to technological advances; divestiture, however, accelerated this downward trend in the 1980s.[4] Now Motorola and AT&T are the only major U.S.-based telecommunications equipment manufacturers.

Since 1984, total telephone manufacturing employment has declined by 42% to 112,000 employees. Women comprise approximately one-half of all manufacturing employees today, down from 71% at divestiture. In addition, production worker employment has dropped sharply.[5] With the closure and downsizing of unionized AT&T and GTE facilities and the opening of nonunion foreign-owned plants, union coverage has dropped by approximately one-half. These sizable employment reductions and shifts, however, cannot be solely attributed to divestiture or deregulation. Also responsible are new electronic technologies. Their potential for new competition was a major force propelling the Justice Department to seek the divestiture of Western Electric in the first place.

In the early 1970s, telecommunications equipment manufacturers began to incorporate advances in microelectronics. This technology requires a less complex assembly process, since the chips encode connections that were previously hand wired. In many ways the evolution of the telephone equipment industry has mirrored developments in the electronics industry. Essentially no low-end consumer telecommunications products are currently manufactured in the U.S. Manufacturers in Korea, Singapore, Thailand, Taiwan, and China are the principal suppliers to the U.S. under a variety of ownership, joint venture, and distribution arrangements.

Complex telecommunications products such as digital switches are manufactured domestically. All digital switches are electronic. The manufacture of digital switching has rapidly evolved.[6] In addition to digital switches, manufacturers are also developing new digital transmission and network management systems.[7] The new digital network systems create demand for software and software programmers to support flexible multiproduct networks. Software has replaced hardware as the main source of value added in digital systems. Digital switches are designed with basic operating systems and software platforms that can be readily expanded. Each year new software upgrades are marketed to enhance the digital switching capabilities, often allowing new services to be offered without making any hardware changes. Sales of system software upgrades to the RBOCs exceeded $1.2 billion in 1992. These new products have created a demand for programmers, technicians, and software engineers as software factories are set up to supply the digital networks. At the same time, the shift from hardware to software renders obsolete many workers and engineers who possess primarily electrical or mechanical skills.

Services

During the Bell System era, telecommunications services led all service industries in productivity growth. Between 1950 and 1984 labor productivity growth in telecommunications services averaged 6% annually, and during the last decade of the Bell System, annual productivity growth rose to 6.9%. Since 1950 rapid advances in technology resulted in a massive accumulation of capital and great reductions in labor which radically increased the industry's capital-labor ratio. Econometric studies consistently demonstrated overall economies of scale in the network, specific output economies of scale, single supplier costs advantages, and economies of scope at AT&T and Bell of Canada (Kiss and Lefebvre 1987).

Since divestiture, productivity growth has significantly fallen below its postwar trend (See Chart 1). According to our calculations, using three different output measures, annual labor productivity growth has fallen to 3.5% from 4%. This drop in productivity growth is an unintended consequence of competition. The Justice Department thought divestiture would usher in an era of competition based on decentralizing technologies such as microwave and satellite communications (Rosenberg 1994). Microwave, however, was obsolete by the time divestiture was implemented. Instead, divestiture accelerated the deployment of new digital broad-band network technologies. The "systemness" of these centralizing technologies demand higher levels of network integration and inter-operability. Consequently, the digital network systems no doubt exhibit greater economies of scale and scope than the analog network they replaced. These economies, however, cannot be fully realized, because of the structural separations contained in the consent decree and because of the triplication of long-distance network facilities. This long-distance oligopoly market structure has produced considerable excess capacity. For example, even though AT&T accounts for almost two-thirds of the long-distance traffic, its competitors alone could readily serve the entire nation's long-distance demand (Allen 1993). In addition,

CHART 1
Productivity Growth in Telecommunications Services

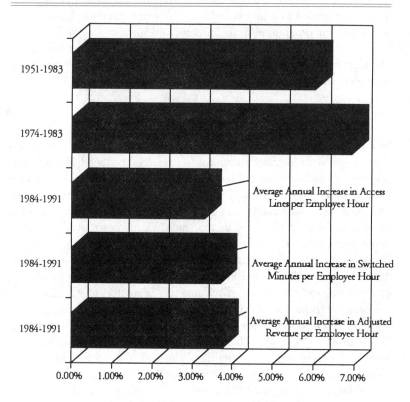

Sources: U.S. Department of Labor, Bureau of Labor Statistics. *Productivity Measures for Selected Industries and Government Services.* Bulletin 2421. April 1993, and Federal Communications Commission, *Statistics of Common Carriers.* 1991/1992 Edition.

the new competition requires that long-distance carriers devote an increasing proportion of their resources to advertising programs which add no value but employ large numbers of low-wage call-servicing representatives. Furthermore, competition led to the breaking of the social contract between the Bell companies and their employees that has resulted in a steady decline of both manager and worker morale.

The telecommunications service industry is divided into five major market segments: long distance, local area toll calls, local exchange service, cable TV, and wireless communications. AT&T, MCI, and Sprint divide the long-distance market. The seven RBOCs and GTE constitute the core of the local exchange service, local toll service, and the cellular telephone service markets. GTE has transformed itself into the "eighth RBOC" by selling its interests in Sprint and manufacturing and by merging with Contel. GTE is now the third largest local telephone holding company with over 18 million access lines.[8]

Each service market has varying degrees of regulation by the FCC and state regulatory commissions. In fact, regulatory oversight has undergone a revolution during the last decade. Similar to the long-distance market, cross-subsidies are being eliminated through rate reform and competitive entry. Incentive regulations, price caps on bundles of services, and deregulation have virtually replaced traditional rate of return regulation. In 35 states, long-distance carriers are permitted to compete with the BOC or GTE in intrastate toll markets. In 1992 the cable TV industry, which operated without regulatory oversight since 1984, was brought under FCC regulation; the FCC implemented two rate roll backs, reducing cable TV revenue by an estimated $2 billion annually. Although the FCC has opened cable TV markets to the regional Bells and local telephone service to the cable companies, current regulations prevent the RBOCs from providing cable TV in their local telephone service regions, and cable TV companies may not build switched voice networks in their TV franchise areas. While a new competitive environment is emerging in local telephone and cable TV service markets based on fiber optic technology, oligopoly or duopoly exists in most long-distance, intrastate toll, and wireless service markets. However, important regulatory and technical issues remain unresolved, creating uncertainty. Such decisions will determine the future configuration of networks and the convergence of cable TV and telephone.[9]

To upgrade their facilities for interactive media, the RBOCs will need to make massive investments. Their financial performance has been strong since divestiture, greatly helped by lower interest rates and the 1986 changes in federal tax laws. Shareholder wealth (share price plus dividends) has grown by more than 300% at each regional company.[10] They are also expanding into new unregulated businesses through fully owned subsidiaries. These new businesses now account for 20% of the RBOC total revenue and are steadily growing in importance. Their fastest growing new businesses are cellular services and international operations.

Cellular telephone grew from no subscribers in 1981 to 14 million in 1993. In December 1994 the FCC will auction off radio bandwidths for the new wireless communication networks, personal communications services. These new digital wireless networks will substantially reduce the cost of mobile communications, greatly accelerating the use of wireless communications for voice and data. All this creates uncertainty for broad-band cable investment, however, since it will eventually substitute for some unknown volume of cable-based telecommunications. The potential substitution of wireless for broad-band cable services may slow the pace of investment in new fully fiber optic networks.

As Congress considers new telecommunications legislation, companies and regulators are anticipating industry's restructuring and are attempting to shape the new framework through their own actions, producing considerable turmoil in this market.[11] Not surprisingly, with all the organizational, technical, and regulatory turmoil in the local service market, no company is ready to fully commit its resources to replace the existing copper wire or coaxial cable networks. As a result, local service providers represent the biggest barrier to a national broad-band ISDN conversion (Botler et al. 1990). The current, as well as some of the proposed frameworks, could easily produce duplicate ISDN services in high-volume areas of the country, and no ISDN services in low-traffic/low-income regions. This prospect, coupled with other network uncertainties, has stimulated the Clinton administration to search for a national policy on how to build an information highway with universal access.

Yet while technological advances are changing the structure of the service industry, as they did in the equipment manufacturing industry, the resulting employment effects are somewhat different. Compared to the major employment declines in telecommunications equipment, the 10% employment decrease in services since divestiture is relatively modest.[12] The regional Bells, the major employers in the industry, have reduced their net employment by 12% (approximately 72,000 jobs) since divestiture (see Table 3), but these net employment figures understate the amount of restructuring that has occurred. Unionization remains stable at the RBOCs with two-thirds of all employees covered by collective bargaining agreements, although most of the new subsidiaries operate on a nonunion basis. Union coverage in the overall telecommunications service industry, however, has declined by 20% since divestiture. Approximately one-half of the industry's current employees work under a collective bargaining agreement. The 40,000 jobs generated by the growth of the nonunion long-distance carriers, MCI and Sprint, is one major cause of declining union coverage in the industry.

TABLE 3
Changes in Employment and Unionization in the Former Bell System

A. Regional Bell Operating Company: Employment and Unionization

	1984	1991	Employment Change 84-91	Union Membership	Union Density 1991
Ameritech	79,000	73,964	-6%	49,250	67%
Bell Atlantic	80,000	76,200	-5%	50,795	67%
BellSouth	99,100	96,975	-2%	58,214	60%
NYNEX	98,200	83,514	-15%	57,000	68%
Pacific Telesis	82,000	62,532	-24%	39,327	63%
Southwestern	74,700	59,460	-20%	38,500	65%
US West	75,000	64,206	-14%	41,000	64%
Total	588,000	516,851	-12%	334,086	65%

B. AT&T: Employment and U.S. Unionization

	AT&T-NCR Global	AT&T U.S. only	AT&T only	AT&T Management	AT&T Nonmanagement	AT&T U.S. Union	AT&T Union Density
1984	435,000	405,000	373,000	111,432	261,568	250,000	67%
1990	328,900	281,773	253,773	115,851	137,920	130,039	46%
1992	312,700					117,000	

The convergence of cable TV and local telephone service creates some serious problems for both the IBEW and CWA. Although some local cable TV companies are unionized, CWA estimates that of the 108,700 union-eligible cable TV workers, only 5% are union members. The largest cable operator, TCI, is aggressively antiunion. Since 1990, TCI has sponsored six decertification elections—successfully decertifying CWA in four units. The substantial pay discrepancies between unionized telephone workers and nonunion cable employees creates the potential for whipsawing as the unionized employers compete for future cable modernization work.

New Business Structures and Strategies: Their Implications for Labor Relations

The Bell System supplied a basic, homogenous product: dial tone. Dial tone was accessed by a leased telephone set manufactured by

Western Electric. Bell's universal service mission created an engineering organization capable of long-term capital and network planning. Scale economies were the source of productivity growth, decreasing service costs, and stability. The company exemplified stability; its organizational structure originated in 1909 and remained basically unchanged for over seventy years.

Since divestiture, AT&T and the RBOCs have reorganized to respond to new customer markets and service demands. In 1988 AT&T moved to a multidivisional corporate organization with strategic business units serving each major market segment; each business unit's performance is evaluated on standard financial criteria. Several RBOCs have recently adopted this horizontal business structure and the others are in transition. They are shifting their focus from responding to the regulators' concerns about the rate of return earned on their rate base to serving their customers on a profit and loss basis. The companies are in the process of reducing layers of bureaucracy from seven to four or five, increasing the span of supervisory control, creating multiple profits centers, pushing decision making down the organization, eliminating work through automation, and forming cross-functional market teams by process management and reengineering (Batt 1993a:12).

At AT&T, business restructuring has broken the social contract on employment security. The company reduced its U.S. employment by one-third and eliminated 55% of its union-represented jobs since 1984 through early retirements, voluntary severance, and massive layoffs. The regional Bells have started downsizing since 1991, relying mostly on voluntary separations. Their employment in 1995 is projected to be reduced to two-thirds of their 1990 levels.

Although these are leaner organizations, their bureaucratic control systems remain omnipresent. Computers and other electronic technologies used by workers on their jobs now often perform the monitoring, scheduling, information gathering, and coordinating functions formerly done by supervisors and managers. Consequently, many workplaces have less direct supervision, but more managerial control (Vallas 1993).

To summarize, in 1984 the AT&T consent decree divided the industry into regulated and competitive sectors. The company became the dominant business in the competitive equipment and long-distance markets. Its major competitor in equipment has been Northern Telecom, and in long-distance service MCI is number two. The seven RBOCs are the major organizations in the regulated market; however, each has adopted its own post-divestiture strategy toward regulation. In the following section, we will profile AT&T, Northern Telecom, MCI, Sprint, NYNEX, and BellSouth and identify links between their respective business strategies and their labor-management relations.

AT&T at the Crossroads

After divestiture, AT&T lost market share in its traditional markets. In both manufacturing and long-distance service, it held on to its analog systems, as the competition introduced digital equipment and built digital networks.[13] In its most lucrative market, long-distance service, AT&T's market share had declined to two-thirds of its pre-divestiture level by 1991. Until 1987, the FCC kept AT&T rates artificially high until the competition gained equal network access capability. In 1988, in response to growing digital competition from MCI and Sprint, AT&T wrote down $6.7 billion of obsolete analog network equipment, producing the first annual loss in the corporation's 112-year history. Its corporate revenue has been basically flat, growing at 1% annually between 1987 and 1992, largely due to stagnant revenues in long-distance services, manufacturing products sales, and the inability to grow new profitable lines of business. When adjusted for inflation, revenues declined by 19% between 1984 and 1992 (Keefe 1994). To improve profitability, AT&T has consequently focused on reducing operating costs, which has led to the vigorous downsizing of its traditional businesses.

As part of the process to become more competitive, the company has been transforming itself from a predominantly unionized employer (67% organized) into a nonunion employer (46% organized in the U.S.). It has acquired and launched nonunion businesses while downsizing its unionized core operations. AT&T developed two new major nonunion businesses, American Transtech, the largest U.S. telemarketing service, and AT&T Universal Card, the second largest credit card company. It has also acquired two antiunion equipment manufacturers: Paradyne (data communications equipment—about 42% of the union eligible are represented by CWA) and, most recently, NCR. NCR is the sixth largest computer company with 1,300 locations in 130 countries. Approximately 1,000 of NCR's 12,000 domestic union eligible employees are organized.

As a consequence of restructuring, AT&T employees have become demoralized. Our October 1991[14] AT&T Employment Security Survey data indicate that bargaining unit employees are profoundly pessimistic about their future employment prospects. In 1981 a Bell System survey found that 68% of nonmanagement employees felt that the company was providing job security and only 8% did not; by 1991 the numbers had more than reversed themselves with over 73% feeling that there was little job security. In some business units less than 4% of the non-management employees felt there was any job security. Less than 20% of the employees surveyed had confidence in management's ability to lead and solve the corporation's competitive problems. Over two-thirds felt they were unable to influence events that affect their employment. More than one-half of the employees surveyed had been surplused (their job abolished) at least once. The surplused employee group, on average, had been surplused two and one-half times.

When compared with attitude data collected at other traumatized organizations, the intensity of AT&T employees' pessimism goes beyond the negative attitudes found in many of those organizations. There are probably five reasons for these catastrophic-like responses. First, many employees chose to work at the company because of the Bell System's commitment to employment security, and now they face chronic insecurity. Second, downsizing has been a protracted ordeal that started in 1984 and still persists today. Third, the average bargaining unit survivor is immobile with family commitments; he or she is white, 43 years old, married with children at home, a homeowner, a high school graduate with some college, and a CWA member who has 18 years of AT&T service and annually earns $26,000 with good benefits. Some 87% of the survey respondents want to keep their current jobs until they retire, but less than 10% of them believe that there is any opportunity for advancement at the company. Fourth, employees use the former Bell System employment standards, which have remained largely intact at the local BOCs, to judge the new AT&T's employment practices. Fifth, the company conducts a continuous public relations campaign emphasizing the strengths of the corporation; the campaign permeates all corporate activities and appointments. In fact, the executive vice-president for human resources has a background in public relations, not labor relations or human resource management. AT&T is widely recognized as a progressive, innovative employer for its retraining, outplacement assistance, employee participation, and family leave programs. Many employees find it difficult to reconcile the company's positive public image with their recent personal experiences. Also, this positive image enables corporate executives to engage in denial about the human consequences of their downsizing decisions. Employees systematically underestimate (by 60%) the amount of AT&T downsizing that has occurred.

Several examples illustrate the difficulties encountered by the company and its employees in the post-divestiture environment. On January 1, 1984, divestiture caused the nearly one million employees of the Bell System to be divided among eleven companies.[15] AT&T soon retreated from its long-term commitment to employment security for telephone service employees and accelerated its plant closings in manufacturing. During the first two years of post-divestiture operations, its head count was reduced by 40,000 positions; approximately one-third of these cuts were made in management. This downsizing involved a gross reduction of 56,000 people, but in that process only about one-fourth were laid off. The remainder left through attrition, voluntary severance and early retirement programs, transfers, or retreats back to the BOCs. This was the prelude. Between 1984 and 1990, there was a net total employment reduction of 123,227, from 377,000 to 253,773 total U.S. employees. During this same period, however, the number of managers increased by 4,400.

After divestiture, the company was free to compete in the customer equipment market. Managers and union leaders were confident that under the leadership of the current CEO, Robert Allen, ATTIS would not only be an effective competitor in telecommunications business systems, but would quickly gain a share of the computer market. But in August 1985, AT&T announced a 24,000 job reduction at ATTIS. The job cuts would reduce $800 million from ATTIS's billion dollar operating losses. Because of vigorous protests, including a nationwide CWA strike vote, the company scaled back its job reductions. However, downsizing during the next six years eliminated employment for all systems technicians with less than twenty years seniority. Computer sales and service were eventually transferred to NCR in 1991, and AT&T business systems did not break even until 1992.

Facing aggressive competition in the consumer telephone markets, AT&T consolidated and automated production in its Shreveport, Louisiana plant. In 1985 the newly formed Consumer Products Division adopted "Business Passion" and "Shared Values" as its guiding vision. Taking a stakeholder view of the organization, management emphasized training and development and implemented a fine system for referring to its people as "employees." Consumer Products, however, was unprofitable. AT&T corporate told the Consumer Products management to fix the business or exit the market. In 1986, the manufacture of consumer telephone equipment was moved to Singapore to save 30% on production costs. All the bargaining unit members/employee stakeholders were laid off. Consumer Products has since opened plants in Thailand, Indonesia, and Mexico achieving even greater savings than in Singapore. Today, no consumer telephones are manufactured by AT&T in the U.S. The Shreveport plant's employment declined from 7,000 to 2,000 employees. Accompanying these employment reductions were declining employee attitudes toward job security and management leadership.

With growing competition from MCI and Sprint in the data private-line long-distance market, AT&T decided to replace all electromechanical and analog electronic switches with new digital toll switches. The cutover to the new switches was completed by 1991. The most senior technicians had maintained the electromechanical switches and had never received digital switch training. On January 1, 1991, some 4,400 senior technicians were transferred to a new business unit. Layoffs soon followed. The senior technicians were unable to bump the junior technicians back in the other business unit. The CWA filed a grievance. In April 1992, an arbitrator upheld the grievance and ordered back pay and the reinstatement of some 1,500 communications technicians, whose average weekly earnings were $750.

AT&T's modernization program encountered customer service difficulties as well. The network experienced four major system failures in 1990 and 1991. The most disruptive occurred in September 1991 when a power failure at a New York central office knocked out the switching center, disrupting communications in the Northeast, crippling the financial markets' voice communications, and closing down the FAA's East Coast air traffic control system.[16] An FCC report was highly critical of corporate management, alluding to internal problems caused by poor management, aging equipment, and possibly low employee morale caused by company layoffs. The FCC, however, failed to pursue the allegations of low employee morale, believing that these issues should be left to collective bargaining. Its report did criticize the company's management for oversight problems and questioned whether AT&T was focusing on its network operations. Shortly after the New York failure, the company lost a $1 billion FAA contract when the FAA switched to MCI. In spite of these problems, the quality of the long-distance service provided by AT&T remains superior to MCI and Sprint, according to customer complaint data compiled by the utility commissions (Keller 1992:1). Since 1984 the company has downsized the bargaining unit at an average rate of 1,000 jobs a month. As a consequence, bargaining unit employment declined from 250,000 at divestiture to 117,000 workers in 1992, representing a 53% reduction in union jobs. In 1991 it reduced employment by 11,800, and in 1992, another 14,000 jobs were eliminated. Between 1990 and 1993, CWA lost 7.4% of its AT&T membership, while the IBEW lost 12.3% of their AT&T members to downsizing. As downsizing continues, we estimate that bargaining unit employment will fall below 100,000 full-time jobs in 1995 (a 60% reduction). If this trend of eliminating 1,000 jobs per month is not disrupted, we project that the bargaining unit will disappear by 2004.

In 1990 AT&T classified 147,563 employees as nonmanagement; 97,206 were represented by CWA (66%) and 24,402 were represented by the IBEW (16%), which yields an 82% union density for the union-eligible work force. The decline in union coverage at AT&T to only 46% of the employees, however, cannot be explained by the growth of new nonunion hourly employment or the depopulation of traditionally unionized jobs. Primarily, deunionization is occurring at the upper boundary of the bargaining unit, as management has expanded the scope of supervisory and managerial job titles and employment. Approximately 47% of employees are classified as either managerial or supervisory, compared to 29% in 1980.

The AT&T Turnaround

In 1992 AT&T stock soared by 30%, adding $17 billion in market value. The company's financial success reflected major improvements in its operating performance. Since 1991, its long-distance market share has stabilized to produce $30 billion in revenue on domestic long-distance and $10 billion on its rapidly growing international service. The company won two Malcolm Baldrige National Quality Awards, awarded to AT&T Universal Card and AT&T Transmission Systems.[17] Most importantly, the recently reorganized Global Business Communications Systems, which employs 26,000 people, stopped losing money, ending years of multimillion dollar losses in business equipment. The $12.6 billion purchase of McCaw Cellular, the nation's largest cellular company puts AT&T in the leading position in the cellular market. And, AT&T remains a leading corporation in R&D investment.[18] Finally, the company earned 24% of its revenue in its growing international businesses in 1992; its top strategic objective is to transform itself into a global corporation.[19]

During 1992 the relationships between the company and its two unions improved. A three-year agreement was negotiated that creates a new framework for labor-management relations, called Workplace of the Future. The structure permits the unions to participate in Business Unit Planning Councils, and the contract requires that the unions select bargaining unit participants for the program. Through this involvement, the unions are able to develop plans to empower employees to provide quality service to the customer, influence restructuring and downsizing, and shape the structure and format for participative teams. If a planning council's program conflicts with existing contract language, it can apply for an exemption from the national Constructive Relationship Council. On March 8, 1993, the CWA and AT&T held a conference for 1,000 managers and union representatives to kick off Workplace of the Future. An enthusiastic Secretary of Labor, Robert Reich, commended the parties for their shared vision in his keynote speech. A similar conference was held with the IBEW in June 1993.

Recent developments have further encouraged the union leadership that AT&T is reversing its nonunion direction. The 1992 contract allows union members to transfer to nonunion subsidiaries (except NCR, which has been renamed AT&T Global Information Solutions). The union gained neutrality and card check provisions at those subsidiaries, and disputes over neutrality are arbitrable. Furthermore, in spring 1993, when the antiunion directors of Universal Card and NCR stepped down, they were replaced by executives who have good working relationships with the unions.[20]

However, opponents to Workplace of the Future also remain in powerful positions at both unions and the company. Four members of the CWA executive board oppose the union's participation in the program. At AT&T, engineering and finance managers remain committed to major cost reductions, further downsizing, part-timing, and subcontracting of bargaining unit work. Downsizing continues, particularly at Consumer Communications Services (residential long-distance), where several thousand full-time operator jobs are scheduled for elimination because of office consolidations, part-timing, new voice recognition technology, and volume reductions. Less than 5% of the company's long-distance calls now require an operator's assistance. In 1987, there were 28,000 full-time operators employed, and by 1995 there will be less than 8,000 remaining. Whether the bold Workplace of the Future vision can become a reality in a downsizing environment remains at best uncertain.

Northern Telecom: The Aggressive Challenger

Northern Telecom is AT&T's most formidable competitor in the U.S. telecommunications equipment market.[21] Until the 1956 AT&T-Justice Department consent decree required divestiture, NT (formerly Northern Electric) was part of AT&T's Bell System; Western Electric owned 44% of NT's stock and AT&T owned 24% of Bell of Canada. Today, the independent Bell of Canada Enterprises owns 53% of NT's shares; the rest are publicly traded. Northern Telecom is Canada's leading multinational enterprise.

Northern Telecom developed the first digital central office switch in 1976 and gained a substantial first-mover advantage. AT&T did not offer a network digital switch until 1982, and it did not reach volume production until 1985. After divestiture the RBOCs rapidly began replacing their electromechanical switches with new digital equipment. NT was the major beneficiary of their modernization program. In the U.S., NT sells digital switches to the independents, the RBOCs, MCI, and Sprint. In addition, it has entered into joint ventures or distribution agreements to sell its PBX equipment.[22] The corporation has cultivated its public image by pursuing honors such as the Award for Export Achievement (U.S.), Business Excellence in Industrial Design (Canada), Telecommunications Achievement (Japan), and the *1990 Canada Award for Business Excellence in Labor-Management Relations*. There is irony in Northern Telecom's 1990 Canada Award for Business Excellence in Labor-Management Relations. NT has reduced its Canadian unionized work force by 25%, laying off 2,000 hourly employees between 1988 and 1991, while its Canadian operations increased total employment by 4%. Between 1981 and 1992, NT's union density in Canada declined from 61% to 38%. About half of the reduction in employment came in the two years after the U.S.-Canada free trade agreement was signed. The company shifted work from Canada to nonunion U.S. facilities in right to work states such as North Carolina, Tennessee, Florida, Georgia, and Texas. In 1992, NT's U.S. employment had grown to 22,000, nearly equal to its Canadian work force.

NT sought to compete with AT&T based on its lower cost for manufacturing. NT's U.S. operations have followed a textbook deunionization strategy. Its Nashville plant opened in 1975 as runaway facility, which resulted in the closing of its Michigan (UAW) plant. CWA began organizing in 1976 and was recognized in 1980. The company hired King, Ballou & Little to orchestrate its antiunion campaign; they dragged out negotiations for a year, hired 200 new employees (including a large number of political refugees), and then encouraged decertification. The union lost the decertification election. During the union suppression campaign, the company engaged in illegal wiretapping and monitoring of employee conversations through hidden microphones. CWA filed a lawsuit in federal court and agreed to a favorable settlement with Northern Telecom in February 1992.

After decertifying CWA in 1981, NT went on to win five other decertification elections between 1983 and 1988. However, its last decertification effort failed. The company used concessionary demands to force a two and one-half month strike by 500 East Coast technicians in 1989. The union was able to hold out. In October 1991, the Canadian Auto Workers and CWA cosponsored an international trade union conference in Toronto to launch an international organizing campaign of Northern Telecom's worldwide facilities.

At this time, Northern Telecom relies on digital switching for the majority of its sales. As the RBOC's electromechanical switch replacement program approaches completion, NT's largest customers are reducing demand for switches. The company is shifting resources to its digital switch software development to serve its embedded base hardware. Its antiunion low-cost manufacturing strategy may lose its relevance as the company focuses on software development and sales. NT is experiencing difficulty in making the transition to a software value added environment. In the second quarter of 1993, it posted a $1 billion loss.

MCI

MCI was founded in 1964 to break into AT&T's long-distance monopoly in private-line services. MCI skillfully used regulatory and judicial proceedings to achieve its objectives, while marketing itself as the competitive underdog out to slay the lumbering giant. During this early period it frequently faced bankruptcy, which deeply influenced its corporate culture. In 1975, it introduced Execunet Service, directly entering into competition with AT&T for publicly switched long-distance service. John DeButts, chairman of AT&T, ordered the disconnection of MCI from the network. The FCC upheld AT&T and prohibited MCI from entering the heavily cross-subsidized long-distance market. However, in 1978 Federal Judge Skelly Wright reversed the FCC and permitted MCI to enter the long-distance business, disrupting the entire telephone rate structure. Ironically, DeButts' decision to disconnect MCI from the AT&T network was later used as evidence in the Justice Department's antitrust case to demonstrate AT&T's predatory behavior toward MCI.

Between 1968 and 1992, MCI's Chairman was William McGowan, the son of a union organizer. McGowan hated bureaucracy; he resisted manuals, procedures, permanent committees, and most vehemently, union contracts. MCI's organization, during his tenure, bordered on anarchy. Annual turnover often exceeded 30%. The company is aggressively antiunion and moves work whenever a union organizing drive might be successful. For example, in 1987 CWA organized a majority of 200 telemarketing representatives in an outbound MCI office in Detroit, most of whom were college-educated African-American women. As MCI haggled over an NLRB certification election, they closed the office and moved the telemarketing work to Iowa. The 200 service representatives were immediately laid off and instructed to report to one of six area motels for their final paychecks. The services representatives were told that if they wanted to retrieve their personal items from the office, they needed to schedule an appointment. When they arrived for their possessions, they were escorted by armed guards.

In addition, MCI pays its operators little more than minimum wage (less than half of the AT&T rate) by internally subcontracting the work and vigorously resisting unionization. The only unionized division of MCI is Western Union International represented by the Teamsters; this division was purchased from Xerox in 1982.

MCI is the second largest long-distance service provider in the U.S. and the sixth largest international common carrier. During the early 1980s, it was America's fastest growing company. Revenues grew at a 26% compounded annual rate. The company has earned the reputation as the best mass marketer in telecommunications with its "Friends and Family" discount program. By 1992, it had captured a 17% share of long-distance revenues from AT&T and 13% of the customer-declared presubscribed lines, with nearly 10 million customers.[23]

MCI, once a small entrepreneurial company, now employs 31,000 people in 65 international locations. Under a second generation of executives, its success is producing the bureaucracy so despised by its founders.[24]

Sprint

Sprint is the only company in the U.S. to provide long distance, local, and cellular telephone service. In long distance, Sprint is the number three company and has not experienced MCI's success. Sprint long-distance service remains a financial under-performer yielding 5% net operating income in 1992, considerably below the 23% generated by its local service. Sprint long distance continues to change owners. Originally owned by Southern Pacific, it was sold to GTE and United as a joint venture. GTE sold its stake to United Telecommunications. United changed its name to Sprint Communications and has recently merged with Centel. The United-Sprint independent local telephone holdings are unionized by CWA (approximately 25% of Sprint's employees are union represented). Centel is also a unionized local independent telephone company. CWA and the IBEW supported the merger between unionized Centel and union-hostile Sprint. The unions may have contributed the margin of victory in a contested proxy vote in December 1992. Sprint's long-distance operations have resisted unionization; they are now the target of a CWA organizing drive. The union has established the Sprint Employees Network with some 400 members. Sprint has resorted to a union suppression campaign, including firings and office closings.

NYNEX

NYNEX was the worst performing RBOC during the late 1980s, as it became ensnared in scandal and bitter labor relations. Its misbehavior included systematically overcharging itself for supplies and inflating its rate base, executives throwing wild sex parties using company funds, and being the first company criminally indicted for violating the Modified Final Judgment. Historically, NYNEX has had the worst labor-management relationship in the industry. In 1989, a dispute over health insurance produced a bitter four-month strike that the company lost.

New York Telephone, a NYNEX subsidiary, accounts for 65% of the corporation's revenue. It operates in a hostile regulatory environment under the supervision of one of the toughest state commissions. New

York City's local service market is the most competitive in the country. Teleport and Metropolitan Fiber compete with New York Telephone in downtown Manhattan's $3 billion local service market, while MCI is using a Time-Warner cable franchise on a trial basis to bypass New York Telephone's local service.

Since 1991 NYNEX has been trying to engineer a major turnaround. It unloaded a number of poor performing new ventures, including the NYNEX Business Centers and some real estate holdings. The company negotiated an agreement with the state regulators, effectively separating its competitive and regulated businesses. Then the company reorganized itself into two major groups: the Telecommunications Group (87% of employment) and the competitive Worldwide Services Group. Similar to the other RBOCs, it aggressively lobbies for deregulation, fearing that the federal and state regulators will permit open entry into its markets while it is tied to a cross-subsidy rate structure that could prevent it from matching competitive prices.

In 1991 NYNEX hired James Dowdall from AT&T to change its relationship with the unions. New labor agreements covering 57,000 workers were negotiated eleven months early, settling in September 1991. But hostile labor-management relations have a long history at New York Telephone dating back to the wildcats in the 1960s.[25] Without centralized control from AT&T, many years of acrimonious relations exploded. In 1986 there was a ten-day strike over health benefits, which ended when the company withdrew its demands. In 1989 NYNEX insisted on moving to a preferred provider organization for basic health coverage. CWA spent 18 months prior to the contract expiration mobilizing its membership to resist any health benefit concessions. In August 1989 the strike began. Both sides dug in. The CWA and IBEW conducted an effective corporate campaign against NYNEX and were able to intervene in the regulatory process postponing rate increases. After four months the company eventually conceded on the major issue, health insurance, although it paid the smallest wage increases (1% per year) during the life of the agreement.

CWA's District 1 leadership has challenged NYNEX in all venues. For example, the union has allied itself with consumer groups to fight telephone deregulation in New York State. The union has won, through its militant tactics, the largest deferred wage increases in the 1991 contract and held on to the most expensive health benefits package in the industry. NYNEX is the only former Bell Company that has maintained its traditional health insurance coverage. In 1991, the four-year agreement provided 4% annual wage increases over the life of the agreement, more than any other contract in the industry. The union also resisted contingent pay.

The District 1 leadership opposes all cooperative programs with the company. Joint meetings are used to challenge management to grant more concessions. Union critics charge that the leadership's adversarial posture only gives the company stronger incentives to downsize the unionized work force and also prevents the union from participating in the inevitable industry restructuring. Fighting deregulation may only serve to weaken New York Telephone and strengthen the nonunion competition. NYNEX's labor relations, however, has implemented a number of joint programs with the union locals.

NYNEX began major downsizing efforts in 1991. The September 1991 contract provided an early retirement incentive program. By the end of that year, 7,300 craft employees had opted for the enhanced retirement package. Some 3,400 management jobs were eliminated that required layoffs. In contrast, bargaining unit force reductions have relied on voluntary methods, although the union mobilized against this downsizing. At the end of 1992, the company had eliminated 12,000 jobs in less than two years, and its net income returned to its 1988 level.

On December 20, 1993, the New York Public Service Commission told NYNEX to cut telephone rates in the state by 3% and improve service quality in Brooklyn, Queens, and the Bronx. Several days later the *Wall Street Journal* reported that the company would reduce operating costs by 30% over the next three years by downsizing its work force by 22,200 jobs with 14,100 to be eliminated at New York Telephone and 7,100 to be reduced at New England Telephone.

Shortly after this announcement, CWA and the company entered into negotiations. In March 1994, the parties reached agreement that extends the existing contract through August 1998. New contract provisions contain the most far-reaching employment security framework in the industry. The contract provides a special retirement incentive that adds six years to both service and age, and it also includes a 30% social security supplement until age 62 or a $500 bonus, whichever is greater. The incentive program is aimed at voluntarily eliminating 16,800 jobs and is expected to cost $2 billion or $77,000 per participating employee.

While a major portion of this program is aimed at voluntarily inducing workers to leave the company, other components seek to create a future for the surviving work force. A major innovation is the creation of a two-year Associate's Degree program in telecommunications technology, which is open to all craft workers. The employees will work four days a week and go to school the fifth day on company time. All educational expenses will be paid by the company. Upon graduation, employees will receive a $50-a-week increase. NYNEX recognizes that it is a high labor cost supplier and hopes to offset this cost disadvantage with a highly educated, flexible, and productive work force.

In addition, all employees with five years of service are eligible to take a two-year educational leave and receive $10,000 per year for education expenses while retaining full benefits, seniority, and a guaranteed job when they return. The contract also creates a job bank and a new job sharing provision. Union workers are guaranteed access to all new company ventures in the information industry. New subsidiaries will start up by offering union workers the opportunity to bid into the new jobs. Neutrality and card-check recognition will apply in any nonunion NYNEX entity. Wage increases are 4% in 1994 and in 1995, 3.5% in 1996, and 3% in 1997, with an additional 3.23% in stock and cash bonuses over the term. Cost-of-living protection kicks in if inflation should exceed 8%. The fully paid medical plan is maintained for the life of the agreement.

NYNEX and the CWA have created a framework that can dramatically turn around their relationship. By creating a future for the incumbent work force while humanely reducing employment, the parties will hopefully avoid the more than a decade of employee trauma that AT&T has experienced.

BellSouth

In contrast to NYNEX, BellSouth and the CWA have maintained the best labor-management relationship in the post-divestiture industry. Interestingly, a violent strike was a catalyst for constructive change. In 1955, CWA conducted a 72-day strike at Southern Bell over the appropriate scope of arbitration and the right to strike during the term of the contract. Both the union leadership and corporate management were astonished by the ferocity of the strikers who dynamited exchanges, shot up telephone cables, and even shot a scab off a telephone pole. Confrontations between strikers and the police were commonplace across the South as many strikers were jailed. Employees were fired for strike-related misconduct and over 200 strike-related disciplinary arbitration cases were eventually heard. Once the strike was settled, the disciplinary cases adjudicated, and normalcy returned, both the union and management leaders vowed that there would never be another episode like the 1955 strike. For the relationship to improve, management had to accept the legitimacy of the union's representative role. Both parties have worked hard since then to develop a constructive relationship based upon mutual understanding and respect. Consequently, after divestiture this strong relationship has brought about considerable change, peacefully.

In the telecommunications industry, BellSouth is the most advanced organization in transforming its industrial relations system. It is reshaping its practices to respond to environmental pressures, as predicted by the transformation proponents. Kochan, Katz, and McKersie (1986) describe a shift away from traditional "New Deal" industrial relations to a new system that puts greater emphasis on strategic and workplace issues and processes. Some of the key industrial relations practices in this new system are found at BellSouth. They include contingent pay, team systems of work organization, worker employment security and career development, and worker and union participation in business and strategic decisions. At the workplace level, QWL programs continued after divestiture, and in 1989 some 600 QWL teams were merged with the company's total quality program. Employment and union security are the quid pro quo for the union's participation in the total quality program (Batt 1993b:15-18).

At the strategic level, BellSouth and CWA teamed up to advocate state deregulation of services. Fearing competitive entry, BellSouth has sought to gain pricing flexibility so it can respond to any incursion into its local service markets. Recognizing that a hamstrung BellSouth stuck in the old regulatory regime could potentially cost the members their jobs, the union supported deregulation. As a result BellSouth is the only RBOC that has removed traditional rate-of-return regulatory control and replaced it with more flexible incentive regulations in every state within which it operates.[26] Deregulation has allowed the company to restructure itself along lines of business, rather than remaining primarily in state organizations needed for regulatory accounting purposes.

Employment security remains the major labor relations challenge facing BellSouth and the CWA. The company is the largest RBOC with 97,112 total employees, of which 58,214 are CWA bargaining unit employees. The parties have entered into an Employment Security

Partnership, which provides open access to training and transfer opportunities, but does not place any restrictions on the company's ability to adjust its staffing levels. BellSouth has negotiated union institutional security language for its telephone subsidiaries; however, there is no neutrality language for its nontelephone businesses, which now employ almost 15,000 people.

In November 1993 BellSouth announced a force reduction of 10,800. This announcement was followed by the company's decision to invest in QVC. The increasingly competitive local service environment will test the limits of the parties' constructive relationship as the company adjusts to market forces rather than regulatory stability.

CWA's Strategic Responses to Industry Restructuring

The CWA has been heralded as a union that engages in strategic planning (Dunlop 1990). Prior to divestiture, under the leadership of President Glenn Watts, the union created the Committee on the Future in July 1981. In March 1983 a special convention adopted ten resolutions and two constitutional amendments proposed by the committee.[27] The administrative reforms improved the union's internal operations. In 1986 and 1987, to further improve its operating effectiveness, CWA further streamlined its governing structure.

In the legislative arena, the CWA has joined with the RBOCs in promoting legislation that would allow them to enter the domestic equipment manufacturing business and long-distance service. These reforms are opposed by AT&T. The CWA and the IBEW also support the RBOCs' effort to supply cable TV, video, and information services. Morton Bahr, president of CWA, sits on the national Democratic Party's leadership committee and serves on Vice-President Gore's influential Council on the National Information Infrastructure.

At the state level, union policies on deregulation vary by district. In the South, District 3 supports deregulation, while in the Northeast, Districts 1 and 2 oppose telephone deregulation. The CWA and the IBEW, however, are currently working together to develop an effort to join with consumer groups to contain the most damaging effects of deregulation, based on the twin goals of preserving union jobs and universal telephone service at reasonable rates.

CWA's major strategic goal is "wall-to-wall" unionization in the information industry. Since divestiture, CWA has added 85,000 new members in the industry through organizing and mergers (Table 4). Mergers with several telephone independent unions after the divestiture announcement added 40,000 members. In 1987 CWA merged with the International Typographical Union, as America's oldest union (founded in 1852) grappled with declining membership as a result of the diffusion of computerized typesetting. In 1993 it merged with the National Association of Broadcast Employees and Technicians with members in the broadcast and cable TV industries.

TABLE 4
CWA's Post-Divestiture Merger and Organizing Outcomes

Year	Organization	Members
Mergers:		
1982-85	Telephone Independent Unions in New York, Pennsylvania, and Delaware	40,000
1987	International Typographical Union	25,000
1993	National Association of Broadcast Employees and Technicians	10,000
Organizing Under Neutrality Agreements:		
1986	AT&T various locations	5,000
1992	US West	1,800
1992	Ameritech	1,000
1986	Pacific Telesis	1,000
1986	Southwest Bell Cellular, Publishing, and Voice Messaging	200
1989	NYNEX Cellular	50
1989	Bell Atlantic Business Systems	50
Organizing in the Face of Suppression Campaigns:		
1989	Sprint Employees Network	400
1992	National Association of NCR Employees	400
1984	45 Cable TV organizing campaigns and decertifications	2,000
1987	MCI organizing stopped after terminations	
1980	Northern Telecom decertification campaign	500

Since divestiture the union has organized 5,000 AT&T employees under neutrality provisions. CWA is currently organizing at NCR and American Transtech, both AT&T subsidiaries. At NCR, it is organizing field engineers at 20 locations. For this national campaign the CWA set up the National Association of NCR Employees (NANE) and by early 1994 approximately 400 field engineers had joined. The union runs an electronic bulletin board to keep members and organizers informed, while allowing them to communicate with each other. CWA has also undertaken a corporate campaign to press AT&T for neutrality and access rights. NCR has vigorously resisted the organizing drive, hiring Jackson and Lewis to organize their response. In the spring of 1994, NANE met with NCR's human resources vice-president and presented him with postcards of support from over 500 field engineers. In June 1994, the NLRB ruled that AT&T-NCR's Satisfaction Councils were employer-dominated labor organizations and ordered that they be disbanded.

In contrast, Transtech is being organized under the limited neutrality provisions first negotiated in the 1992 collective bargaining agreement. Transtech employs 1,500 managers, 600 staff workers, and 3,500 temporary employees. The Transtech Employees Association is organizing both 600 staff employees and the 3,500 temporary employees that are contracted through eight employment agencies. The temporary employees earn about $8 an hour with no benefits. They move from project to project for employment. The union is demanding that these workers be made regular AT&T employees. Under neutrality the union has negotiated card check recognition, managerial neutrality, access to non-work areas, and instant arbitration if any of these privileges are violated.

CWA has developed a sophisticated organizing program in telecommunications. Each year union organizers mobilize employees on their personal time to get a union recognized. However, they have not achieved much success at the new aggressively antiunion competitors, such as MCI, Sprint, or Northern Telecom. At the local level, CWA has conducted 45 organizing campaigns in cable TV. Although some cable TV franchises have been organized, the major corporations maintain an aggressively anti-union posture. The growth of this nonunion sector has the potential to destabilize collective bargaining in the unionized core.

In collective bargaining, the CWA has sought to maintain a loose pattern on major economic issues. The union seeks to prevent any substandard agreements in the industry, which could then become a pattern setter for other contracts. The CWA has been successful in keeping a pattern together. To advance its interest, the union has engaged in strikes, developed a member mobilization program, and used workplace campaigns. In 1983, 1986, and 1989 it undertook strikes to oppose concessions on health insurance. Concessions are difficult to sell to the membership, particularly when the companies are earning higher profits than ever possible under the regulated Bell System. However, the growth of nonunion competition in virtually every market segment is putting downward pressure on wages and benefits.

In August 1988 CWA launched its Mobilization Program in preparation for 1989 bargaining. Mobilization is grassroots organizing that involves members in one-on-one communication on important issues at the work site. The program's basic aim is to involve all union members in actively representing their collective interest.[28] The campaigns are designed to connect "the bonds of worker solidarity" through collective action. Mobilization tactics include petitions, one-on-one postcard messages, wearing common colors, expressing solidarity through rallies, arm bands, and stand-ups, work-to-rule campaigns, organizing non-members, picket lines, electronic picket lines, community support activities, and strikes.

The mobilization programs have steadily improved in their effectiveness since 1988 and were particularly useful in 1992 bargaining. Rather than strike, CWA continued to bargain after the contract expirations at AT&T, Bell Atlantic, Pacific Telesis, and US West. The membership was mobilized to support the union's bargaining objectives. Electronic town meetings, conference calls, and taped telephone messages kept members involved and informed about bargaining progress. At AT&T the unions threatened an electronic picket line by getting all their supporters to pledge switching their long-distance phone service to another carrier until a contract was signed. Some CWA locals demonstrated their mastery of information technologies in getting the union's story out to their members and to management. CWA is also developing its in-workplace strategies. The union believes that these tactics will grow in power as employers rely more and more on a committed and involved work force to provide high-quality customer service.

The industrywide force reductions have serious implications for the stability of CWA's governing coalition. The telephone installation and central office crafts have been the main pillar of political power within the union, often in coalition with operators. Each of these groups has experienced massive downsizing. Local, district, and national leadership in CWA historically have come from the ranks of telephone installation and central office crafts with one major exception, the president of the union. Joseph Beirne worked in Western Electric sales in New Jersey and New York; Glenn Watts started out representing the C&P Commercial Department in Washington, DC; and Morton Bahr began with the independent MacKay Radio in ship-to-shore radio on Long Island.

Because each of these leaders began in groups with little influence over union affairs, each became effective coalition builders. With the decline of the traditional union power bases, a new female leadership is emerging at the local, district, and national level. The recently elected Secretary-Treasurer Barbara Easterling and District Vice-Presidents Sue Pisha (District 7-US West) and Janice Wood (District 9-Pacific Telesis) are indicators of the changes underway inside CWA. Also, two-thirds of the union's senior organizing staff is female, which is another indicator of the future union membership.

Local Unions

Grievance administration remains the primary function of the local unions in the telephone industry. The local unions' representation provides a buffer for workers who can easily be caught between the formal bureaucratic control system and the informal (but widely followed) work practices. Research evidence indicates that effective grievance representation, particularly winning grievances, remains the single most important activity in building the membership's commitment to their local union. Employee participation and work restructuring that reduces traditional methods of bureaucratic control and legitimizes informal practices also have the potential to build the local union. Research suggests that union participation in work reform improves member loyalty and does not undermine the union (Eaton, Gordon, and Keefe 1992; Vallas 1993).

Post-Divestiture Restructuring and Collective Bargaining

Prior to divestiture, AT&T and its BOCs bargained at two levels. At the first level, called "national bargaining," Bell System-wide agreements were reached on wages, benefits, and employment security. As a result, a telephone technician working in New York City received the same wage increases whether he or she worked for the local operating company, New York Telephone, or AT&T. The cents-per-hour component of the cost-of-living escalator tended to compress the wage structure throughout the Bell System (Keefe 1989). In a similar manner, vacations, pension benefits, health care coverage, and insurance benefits became more standardized across the system, regardless of the employing BOC. This standardization aided human resource planning and forced adjustments by facilitating personnel movement among the companies. At the second level of bargaining, "local" bargaining, the individual BOCs bargained with local union leadership over work administration and work rules. Local bargaining issues included overtime policy, posting of schedules, steps in the grievance process, health and safety, and absence pay. Local bargainers, however, could not address issues that were on the national bargaining table. With divestiture came a restructuring of labor-management relations. Shortly after divestiture, AT&T sought to remove itself from the common expiration dates established in telephone bargaining. As a result, cross-company comparisons would not be made, and the pressure to conform to a potentially more expensive RBOC pattern would be lessened. In 1985 AT&T and its two unions met under the auspices of the bargained-for Common Interest Forum, and discussions were opened to bargain off cycle. Those negotiations stalled, in part because of the change in leadership at the CWA. President Glenn Watts was retiring; his successor, Morton Bahr, was not officially in place as president. The company and its unions, however, were later able to renegotiate the termination date of its 1983 contract from August 9 to May 31, 1986. This removed AT&T from the contract termination deadline of August 9, 1986, faced by the RBOCs. Thus, some modicum of differentiation was achieved.

Since the core business of the RBOCs had remained relatively unchanged, the expectations about bargaining were similarly unchanged. Initially, CWA sought to maintain a national bargaining structure (Koch, Lewin, and Sockell 1988). When that proposal was rejected, the union pressed for continuance of the two-tier structure, with the first tier at the RBOC level and local bargaining remaining at the operating company level. Eventually, all the RBOCs but Ameritech opted for this two-tier structure; Ameritech negotiates at the local operating company level. Bargaining has taken place in this new structure in 1986, 1989, and 1992. However, at BellSouth, US West, and NYNEX, regional bargaining has expanded its scope as the RBOCs standardize procedures across the local companies to improve operating efficiency.

With the restructuring of the RBOCs away from regulated state organizations toward market-oriented businesses, pressures are building to change local bargaining structures. As service deregulation advances, the state organizations of the former BOCs have diminished importance as regional Bells reorganize along their lines of business. We anticipate this will create a demand to change the local bargaining structures at the RBOCs shifting local negotiations away from state-based BOCs to the lines of business divisions. US West and CWA developed a separate agreement for its customer service division, Home and Personal Services Division in 1992. AT&T's Workplace of the Future represents an interim step in a similar process, where the CWA and IBEW representatives meet with business unit executives in planning councils to discuss workplace programs. The unions have also agreed to meet with AT&T in 1994 to discuss the appropriate bargaining structure for the future negotiations. However, while local structures may change, we believe that economic issues will remain relatively centralized in regional bargaining for the RBOCs and in national bargaining for AT&T.

Pressures for the Centralization of Bargaining

CWA maintains a loose pattern bargain across the industry on economic issues, receiving considerable assistance from AT&T and the RBOCs. Although the newly competitive AT&T was permitted to escape the common expiration date starting in 1986, it remains not only a participant in the loose pattern, but on some issues it has become a pattern setter for the RBOCs, for example, on wages. Only NYNEX negotiations in 1989 and 1991 produced patternbreaking agreements. AT&T and the RBOCs, however, have faced different problems. Employment security has been the most difficult bargaining issue at AT&T, whereas health insurance has been a strike issue at four RBOCs.

Because of increasingly stringent financial scrutiny by Wall Street, strategic economic issues exert a centralizing influence on the industry's post-divestiture bargaining structure. Deferred wage increases have averaged 2.78% annually, and COLAs have been either eliminated or highly restricted, while each company, except NYNEX, has obtained some form of contingent pay, most commonly profit sharing. In either 1986 or 1989 all companies but NYNEX adopted preferred provider organizations to deliver their basic health insurance. Most agreements contain expanded transfer rights, retraining, early retirement incentives, and severance pay enhancements to address employment security. Only Pacific Telesis and Southwest Bell, however, made no layoff commitments during this period. As the companies restructure, the tradition of broad-banded occupations with common wage schedules facilitate force adjustments. This informally centralized system of bargaining remains a source of work force flexibility, cost containment, and stability in labor-management relations.

In contrast, union institutional security and work administration issues arising from business reorganizations, new technologies, nonunion competition, and work restructuring exert a decentralizing influence on local bargaining structures. A 1992 CWA survey indicated that there were over 30 different local participative programs in operation at AT&T. Some of these programs had union participation and others did not. In the former Bell System companies, Quality of Work Life (QWL) became known as a "labor" program, since it was negotiated by labor relations. QWL always had union involvement, while Total Quality is often viewed as a management participative program, because it is not negotiated and rarely has union involvement (Batt 1993a). All the RBOCs and AT&T have adopted workplace reforms such as QWL, quality teams, project teams, and self-managed teams with varying degrees of commitment and institutionalization. The latest generation of joint involvement programs focus most often upon continuously improving customer service. Strategically for the unions, retaining the loyalty of the embedded customer base is essential to preserving jobs in the newly competitive markets. US West and BellSouth are the leaders in these joint labor-management, workplace redesign, and participative programs (see Hilton 1993 on US West). They are also the corporations that have agreed to the most far-reaching union security provisions including broader bargaining unit recognition and accretion. Corporate commitments to union institutional security, employment security, and union and worker participation to improve performance are tied closely together in the industry. Security is exchanged for participation in improving performance (Batt 1993b).

Our review of collective bargaining in the post-divestiture industry examines wages, health insurance, employment security, and union institutional security agreements and trends. An overview of participative programs is beyond the scope of this chapter; however, we believe that their pervasiveness may indicate a third level of informal bargaining is emerging at the workplace level.

Wages

Relative wages in telecommunications have not declined in the post-divestiture period (Hendricks and Sasslos 1990). The union wage differential may have increased after divestiture with the influx of non-union companies and contractors (Peoples 1990). Spalter-Roth and Hartmann (1992) report a significant union wage effect for women in the industry, originally reported by Ehrenberg (1978) for female-dominated occupations.

Labor and management have bargained not only over the amounts of pay increases but over pay methods as well. The unions want deferred wage increases with a cost-of-living adjustment (COLA), while management has proposed lump sums and different forms of contingent pay, such as performance bonuses and profit sharing. In the Bell System, three annual base wage increases accompanied by two cost-of-living adjustments were the norm in national predivestiture wage settlements. In 1986 at the conclusion of AT&T's first set of post-divestiture negotiations with its unions, base wage increases were maintained, but the COLA was suspended. Although the parties had jointly participated in win-win negotiations training, it was the distributive issue of wages that caused the negotiations to reach an impasse and CWA to undertake a 26-day strike. Complicating matters for the union, three weeks into their strike the IBEW *accepted* AT&T's final offer and settled without a work stoppage. The IBEW settlement left little room for further negotiations with CWA. When the CWA finally settled, it too had an agreement with a suspended COLA and the same base wage offer as the IBEW. The suspended COLA subsequently impacted the wage negotiations for the RBOCs later that summer. Not only did AT&T's wage increase set a standard or, more accurately, a "ceiling" on RBOC negotiations, it also changed expectations for continuing a COLA. Generally, the wage increases bargained were in the range of 6% to 7% over three years, but some of these increases were paid in the form of lump sum or ratification bonuses. There was also a trend to restructure COLA. If the COLA was not entirely replaced by some form of profit sharing, it was restricted, paid in a lump sum, or both. In other RBOCs, COLA was limited but paid in the base. In the contracts negotiated in 1992, only two agreements pay COLA increases; BellSouth will pay an estimated 1.4% over the agreement, and Bell Atlantic's formula will yield less than 1% over the contract term. NYNEX maintains COLA, but it pays out only if inflation (CPI) exceeds 8%.

Table 5 reports negotiated wage changes since divestiture. Deferred wage increases have been negotiated for each year at AT&T and the RBOCs; the post-divestiture trend shows a steady increase over the three successive contracts. AT&T is the pattern leader in wage changes. Each company has pursued some form of contingent pay based on business performance including profit sharing, team awards, and success sharing, which is either linked to increases in stock prices or is a stock award. The unions have resisted contingent pay methods in negotiations,

TABLE 5

Post-Divestiture Wage Bargaining Outcomes

Company	Base Wage Increases (Percent):									
	1986	1987	1988	1989	1990	1991	1992	1993	1994	Average
AT&T	2	3	3	4	2.5	2.5	4	3.9	3.9	3.20
Ameritech	2	2	2	2	3	3	3.5	3.5	3.5	2.67
Bell Atlantic	2	3	3	3	2.25	2.25	4	3.74	4	3.03
BellSouth	2	1.5	1.5	4	1	1	4	1.68	1.68	2.04
NYNEX	2.5	1	1	3	1.5	1.5	4	4	4	2.50
Pacific Telesis	2	2	2	3.1	2.6	2.6	4	3.5	3.5	2.93
Southwest Bell	3	1.5	1.5	5	3	3	$5-$22	$7-$24	$7-$26	2.89
US West				5	2.5	2.5	5	3	3	3.00
Average Change	2.21	2.00	2.00	2.00	2.37	2.29	3.94	3.29	3.32	2.78

Cost of Living Adjustments			
	1986	1989	1992
AT&T	Suspended	Eliminated	None
Ameritech	In base and lump sum	Eliminated or no pay out	None or no pay out
Bell Atlantic	Restricted and lump summed	Restricted paid in base wages	Restricted paid in base wages less than 1%
BellSouth	Restricted paid in base wages	Restricted paid in base wages	Restricted 1.4% increase paid in base wages
NYNEX	Capped paid in base	Capped paid in base	Restricted pays CPI over 9%
Pacific Telesis	COLA eliminated	None	None
Southwest Bell	Capped and lump sum payment	Capped split between lump sum and base	Eliminated
US Bell	Eliminated	None	None

Contingent Pay			
AT&T	None	Profitsharing	Stock shares: $3500
Ameritech	None	Profitsharing	Profitsharing
Bell Atlantic	$300 lump sum signing bonus	Profitsharing	Profitsharing
BellSouth	Lump sum bonus	Team incentive bonus based on profit and quality	Team incentive bonus increased
NYNEX	None	None	None
Pacific Telesis	Team award	Team award	Team award
Southwest Bell	Team award	None	Profitsharing
US Bell	$600 signing bonus	Team award $600 signing bonus	None

treating them as company add-ons outside the basic economic package under negotiation. The firmness of union resistance to contingent pay, however, varies. The CWA at BellSouth expects to earn half of their pay adjustments during the 1992-95 contract through contingent pay, totaling up to 5% annually, whereas CWA at NYNEX and US West rejected contingent pay in 1992 negotiations. Their members will receive deferred wage increases of 4% annually at NYNEX and 5% in the first year and 3% in both the second and third year at US West. CWA at NYNEX in 1994, however, has accepted stock and cash bonuses amounting to 3.23% between 1995 and 1997 and base wage increases of 4%, 3.5%, and 3%.

The similarity of not only the unions' proposals but also AT&T's and the RBOCs' contingent pay and COLA proposals indicates that pattern bargaining on wage issues remains basically intact in the post-divestiture environment. When all forms of wage compensation are added together, wage increases have advanced at a similar rate, although the forms of payment vary.

Conflict and Scale Economies in Health Insurance Administration

In 1983 the round of negotiations just prior to divestiture, AT&T had sought to restructure health benefits. The company's objective was to have employees share some of the costs of providing health coverage. A strike occurred, in part, over this issue. In 1986 negotiations, three companies (Ameritech, BellSouth, and Southwestern Bell) successfully negotiated Preferred Provider Organization Plans (PPOs) or Managed Care Networks as their basic form of health insurance. These programs provide the companies with more power in dealing with the health care industry, and they slow the rate of increase in health care costs. In 1989 the other five remaining former Bell companies made similar proposals that ran into considerable union opposition, including strikes at the four RBOCs. Of the five, only AT&T settled for managed care without a 1989 strike. By 1989 it was apparent that the RBOCs were financially healthy, making health care or any other concessions difficult to accept. The unions struck at Bell Atlantic (one month), NYNEX (four months), Pacific Telesis (two weeks), and US West (one week) to defeat managements' demand to replace traditional health insurance with managed care or PPOs. Except at NYNEX management prevailed in these strikes. All former Bell companies, again except NYNEX, now have a managed care framework as their basic health coverage (Table 6). In

1991, NYNEX established a committee to move to a Preferred Provider Association (PPA); however, the traditional plan may remain in effect through 1998.

TABLE 6
Post-Divestiture Health Care Bargaining Outcomes

Preferred Provider Organization (PPO)

Company	1986	1989	1992
AT&T	None	Established as basic package	Continued
Ameritech	Established as basic package	Continued	New network
Bell Atlantic	None	Established as basic package after 1 month strike	Continued with joint CWA claims facilitators
BellSouth	Established	Expanded	Continued with joint CWA claims facilitators
NYNEX	None 10-day strike	Rejected after 4-month strike	Optional
Pacific Telesis	None	Established as basic package after 2-week strike and a contract rejection	Expanded
Southwest Bell	Established	Continued	Expanded with CPI adjusted co-pay and deductibles
US West	None	Established as basic package after 1-week strike	Expanded

The 1983 predivestiture national contract created a health care cost containment committee. This committee has been carried forward into most post-divestiture collective bargaining agreements. In 1989, after accepting management's PPO proposal, CWA bargained a health and wellness committee at US West and two joint committees at Bell Atlantic. One Bell Atlantic committee works on national health care reform, and the other serves as an advisory committee on health care administration.

In 1992 there were, for the most part, only minor adjustments bargained in health care packages. The Bell Atlantic and BellSouth contracts created CWA-appointed facilitators that work in the benefits office, assisting employees with their health claims. At Southwest, deductibles and copayment schedules were tied to movement in the medical component of the CPI.

The similarity of post-divestiture company proposals on health insurance is another strong indicator of continued pattern bargaining in the industry. As the RBOCs and AT&T pursue cost containment strategies for rising health insurance costs, they derived bargaining power and scale economies from the centralization of health insurance management. These economies, derived from forming large care networks and whipsawing health providers, are another force in centralizing the industry's economic negotiations.

Breaking the Bell System's Social Contract on Employment Security

While wages and health care costs have been important issues, by far the most contentious one for AT&T and its unions has been the issue of employment security. Prior to divestiture, Bell System employees, union-represented and management alike, had secure jobs. Employment security was achieved by careful human resources planning and managed deployment of labor-displacing technology. AT&T retained employees in whom it had substantial human capital investments. The employees were decidedly loyal to the Bell System and its mission of providing universal and reliable telephone service. The spirit of service was the guiding shared value. Furthermore, the union leadership readily accepted technological advances in the workplace. A job control unionism, seeking security through highly detailed job classifications, never emerged in the industry. Instead, most job classifications were extremely broad, making work assignments easier and the work force more flexible.

As a result of the basic Bell System's social contract, employment security issues were not paramount in predivestiture negotiations at the national level. There were several income protection programs bargained, notably the Supplemental Income Protection Program (SIPP) and the Voluntary Income Protection Program (VIPP), primarily to aid adjustment in Western Electric manufacturing. The former provided incentives for bargained-for employees to consider "early retirement"; the latter was geared to providing separation income to junior employees who opted to resign. Furthermore, in 1980, AT&T signed an understanding with its unions that it would not subcontract "traditional telephone work" where such subcontracting would directly result in layoffs, downgrading or part-timing of regular employees.

At the local level, contracts did contain language on force adjustments, layoff procedures and layoff pay. These provisions, generally, were "idle" in the contract, with the major exception of the employees in Western Electric's factories. This latter group of employees experienced the ups and downs of business cycles.

Immediately after divestiture, AT&T began to feel the press of competition, both in the manufacturing and in the service businesses. About 40,000 U.S. positions were lost in 1984 and 1985. This early downsizing increased the urgency for the unions for better employment security protection at the 1986 bargaining table.

As a result, AT&T and the CWA created a jointly owned Alliance for Employee Growth and Development; a similar fund was established by AT&T and the IBEW. In 1989 the IBEW program merged into the Alliance. Its mission is to provide training and career development for both displaced workers and active employees. The Alliance is a nonprofit corporation jointly owned by AT&T and the two unions, CWA and IBEW, that relies on over 300 workplace committees to deliver training that is custom designed to meet a wide array of employee training needs (Batt and Osterman 1992). Between 1986 and 1992, the Alliance provided services, such as career counseling and resumé writing, to over 59,451 union members (60% of whom were active employees) and has spent about $80 million or about $67 annually per bargaining unit member employed in 1986. When compared to AT&T's *annual* training budget of $300 million, the Alliance has been asked to perform a heroic task on a relatively small budget. Its current annual budget has been increased to over $20 million per year or almost $200 annually per bargaining unit member.

Besides the Alliance, AT&T has also bargained an automated employee transfer system (ATS). The system provides employees, both active and laid off, with real time information about job openings nationwide in AT&T. Furthermore, employees facing layoff are given priority placement in the company. ATS itself is a hallmark of advanced information technology. With it, the unions and the company overcame a host of inter-bargaining unit movement issues that heretofore appeared to be insurmountable obstacles. Unfortunately the system's reputation has suffered because the kinds of jobs that are available within the firm often do not match the pay, geographical constraints, or occupational skills of those who face displacement. To help increase the bank of available jobs, the company agreed to permit unionized employees to transfer into the company's nonunion subsidiaries, except NCR.

In addition to the Alliance, AT&T has bargained several other options for employees aimed at increasing "career" security. Employee relocation expense reimbursements have been improved, and employees' rehire rights have been expanded. Employees have access to special leaves of absence programs, in which the company will continue to pay medical benefits, as well as transitional leave of absence programs, enabling employees to accumulate seniority for pension eligibility. Tuition assistance has been enhanced, and even a "Transition to Teaching" program has been established, aimed at covering tuition expenses for employees who leave and obtain a teaching certificate.

In all, these different programs can broadly be subsumed under the category of "effects" bargaining. In essence, the ability to manage the size of the work force still is, relatively speaking, a sole right of management. However, this right has created several obligations for management to provide various forms of financial cushions for employees who are displaced as a result of those staffing decisions.

Perhaps the one divergence from the "effects" employment security packages, though, is the "Workplace of the Future" agreement. In this understanding, AT&T and its unions agree to work together "to develop new approaches to managing change in the workplace" and business units will "jointly give input on decisions that affect technology deployment, work organizations and jobs." The Human Resource Board, staffed by management and union personnel, will give input to AT&T's Management Executive Committee on "critical issues affecting people." It is conceivable that this broad agreement to manage people differently may move the unions closer to "decision" bargaining on force management.

Unlike AT&T, the RBOCs have managed change more gradually and most often voluntarily. Similar to AT&T, most of the RBOC provisions are the result of "effects bargaining" and do not contain any provisions regulating employment levels. As Lynch and Osterman (1989) show in their study of BellSouth, the contract provisions determine which workers go first in a downsizing and their eligibility for transfers, early retirements, and severance payments, but management maintains complete control over staffing levels and the volume of force reductions. (Table 7 summarizes employment security provisions at the RBOCs and AT&T.) Pacific Telesis represented the greatest departure from this pattern. In 1986 bargaining, it agreed to a no layoff clause during the life of

TABLE 7
Post-Divestiture Employment Security Bargaining Outcomes

Company	1986	1989	1992
		Training and Education	
AT&T	Joint alliance & ETOP programs established	Alliance funding increased; Broader tuition assistance	Alliance funding increased
Ameritech	No change	Increased tuition assistance; Training Opportunity Program	Educational sabbaticals TOP expanded
Bell Atlantic	$5 million training and development fund	$3 million for training fund	$3 million for training fund
BellSouth	Limited training and retraining	Training and retraining open to all	Educational sabbaticals added
NYNEX	No change	No change	No change
Pacific Telesis	Joint training fund	Joint training fund	$3 million for training fund
Southwest Bell	No change	No change	No change
US West	No change	Pathways retraining programs	Surplus priority access to training
		Severance and Voluntary Initiatives	
AT&T	Income protection program enhanced	Income protection program enhanced	Income protection program enhanced
Ameritech	No change	Expanded early retirement income	Increase in income protection
Bell Atlantic	No change	Income security plan	Income protection program enhanced
BellSouth	No change	No change	Improved early retirement income
NYNEX	Income protection program	Incentives for early retirement	Incentives for early retirement
Pacific Telesis	No change	No change	New early retirement severance increased
Southwest Bell	Incentives for voluntary separation	Early retirement income improved	Voluntary severance expanded
US West		Enhancements for voluntary separation	Enhancements for voluntary separation

TABLE 7 (*Continued*)
Post-Divestiture Employment Security Bargaining Outcomes

Company	1986	1989 Transfer and Recall Rights	1992
AT&T	Job information center	Automated transfer system-displaced priority	Access to nonunion subsidiaries for transfer
Ameritech	No change	Relocation allowance increased; Medical benefits of laid-off employees	Priority placements for displaced
Bell Atlantic	Job information center for displaced employees	Employee career resource centers	No change
BellSouth	Career continuation program	Employment security partnership	Joint committee on subcontracting
NYNEX	Priority placement for displaced employees	No change	No change
Pacific Telesis	No layoff agreement	No layoff agreement Transfer and relocation assistance improved	No layoff, automated transfer system
Southwest Bell	Career resource center; Notice increased to 90 days	No layoff agreement	No change
US West		Upgrade and transfer plan	Joint committee on skill needs

the agreement. No subcontracting would be allowed when surplused bargaining unit employees could perform the work. In 1989 and 1992 the agreement was extended, although there was considerable concern over how surplused employees were being reassigned, and a joint committee was established to investigate reassignments. In 1989 the RBOCs devoted more resources to various joint training centers, and in Southwestern, surplus employees were given a guarantee of an alternative job offer prior to being laid off. The 1992 negotiations saw the introduction of an automated transfer system in Pacific Telesis. By and large, however, the changes in employment security programs were generally geared either to "effects" protection or to encourage employees to quit voluntarily or retire early.

Some of the most innovative work force adjustment procedures have been bargained at AT&T, the company that has engaged in the most downsizing since divestiture. Most of the RBOCs have adopted similar programs, but on a smaller scale. Except for Pacific Telesis and Southwest Bell no other company has made a formal commitment to maintaining the Bell System's social contract on employment security.

Union Institutional Security Provisions

Management's intentions about its future relationship with the union are most readily conveyed by their willingness to negotiate union institutional security provisions. Since these provisions make it easier for the union to organize and gain representation rights, they reveal whether management wants a constructive long-term relationship with the union or prefers to restrict or possibly eliminate the union's representative role. Union institutional security arrangements are permissive subjects of bargaining, which cannot be brought to impasse, making them truly voluntary issues for management. Union institutional security agreements facilitate union organizing at large corporations, which have the capacity to choose their union status in today's legal environment (Kochan, McKersie, and Chalykoff 1986). Basically these provisions re-create the framework for organizing that prevailed prior to Taft-Hartley (1947), when unions achieved their greatest organizing successes.

Although each of the seven RBOCs and AT&T have created nonunion subsidiaries since divestiture, they have each granted some of these provisions. Their responses, however, differ as to the desirability of union representation for all their union eligible employees. A variety of union security provisions are contained in the 1992 collective bargaining agreements at AT&T and the seven RBOCs. The most prevalent provision is neutrality, where management agrees not to hire consultants or engage in a campaign to keep the union out of a nonunion workplace. At NYNEX, Southwest Bell, and AT&T (except for NCR), for example, these provisions cover the entire corporations, while the other neutrality language pertains only to the telephone subsidiaries. BellSouth and US West, the two companies with the best labor-management relations, granted the most important provisions from the standpoint of the union, broader recognition and accretion. Several hundred jobs at TechSouth were accreted into the BellSouth bargaining unit on January 1, 1993. As a result of BellSouth and CWA's joint review of management job titles and tasks, 500 jobs have been returned to the bargaining unit. At US West, 1,900 jobs have been accreted into the bargaining unit and the company has agreed to broaden the union recognition language to include all union eligible workers at US West Communications, except labor relations and legal affairs.

In 1992 negotiations, NYNEX and AT&T, the two companies working the hardest to improve their labor-management relationships, granted numerous institutional security provisions. The NYNEX agreement provides for neutrality throughout the corporation, transfer rights to its subsidiaries for a worker being displaced, a subcontracting review committee, the review of management job titles, card check recognition throughout the corporation, and the return of all splicing work to the bargaining unit. In 1994 the company agreed that union workers would be guaranteed access to jobs at all new NYNEX ventures in the information industry before hiring off the street. The 1992 AT&T contract provides for neutrality, card check recognition, transfer rights for displaced workers, and union access to hold group meetings at all subsidiaries except NCR. Subcontracting grievances must be arbitrated within 30 days, and regular reports are provided to the union on the use of outside contractors and temporaries. The goal is to reduce the use of outside contractors and temporaries. AT&T recently established an internal temporary service staffed by displaced bargaining unit employees. In addition, the union institutional security provisions in the AT&T contract are subject to instant arbitration, rather than forcing the union to rely on NLRB enforcement.

Union institutional security provisions enable the union to maintain its representation in the traditional telephone companies and allow it easier access to the nonunion subsidiaries. At the RBOCs, CWA and the IBEW have maintained their levels of unionization, while at AT&T the level has steadily declined in spite of the institutional security provisions that facilitated the organization of 5,000 new members. The unions, however, have been unable to organize many of the nonunion subsidiaries, even with the expanded protections contained in the contract provisions.

Conclusion: Labor Relations Under Regulated Competition

The future of labor-management relations in telecommunications is inextricably bound up with the resolution of the government's unsettled policy toward the industry. A decade after divestiture, telecommunications public policy remains in turmoil. Major policy questions are unanswered, concerning the future of ISDN, the integration of telephone and cable TV carriers, and the boundaries of telecommunications, information services, and home entertainment products. These questions remain in part because Congress has been unable to break two decades of gridlock and amend the Communications Act of 1934.

By default, the FCC and the federal courts have been the major architects of the new policy, one that has been accomplished by a radical reinterpretation of existing law (Stone 1989). Although the FCC initiated deregulation in the equipment industry in 1968 and long distance in 1969, federal judges have made or supervised the major industrial policy decisions ever since. In 1978 Federal Court Judge Skelly Wright unexpectedly decided to permit competition in the publicly switched long-distance network. Since 1982, Federal Judge Harold Greene has supervised the division of the industry into competitive and regulated segments under the Modified Final Judgment. Since divestiture, the FCC has continued to pursue its partial deregulation strategy, most recently with its co-location decision, getting considerable cooperation from state legislatures but opposition from state regulators. Most policymakers have rejected regulated natural monopoly in favor of a mixed regime of regulated competition or what some critics refer to as "contrived competition." Services are increasingly offered in duopolistic or oligopoly market structures. In exchange for limited entry the regulators and state legislatures have granted firms either indexed or total price deregulation. The regulators, however, have kept oversight on service quality and some special dominant carrier regulation to prevent predation that could eliminate the new competitors.

The decade after the AT&T divestiture, however, is most likely to be a transition period. Congress with the support of the Clinton administration is currently considering major reform legislation to promote competition. Supporting the reform process is the RBOC-led coalition, supported by the IBEW and the CWA, along with the other local telephone companies. Opposing most of these reforms is AT&T's Unity Coalition, which includes most of AT&T's direct competitors, such as Sprint and MCI, as well as most of the equipment manufacturers.

Will Employees Once Again Incur Major Costs in Restructuring?

Employees continue to bear major costs from the AT&T divestiture, as jobs are lost and large investments in firm-specific human capital go unrealized. One decade later, employee insecurity and fear remain pervasive. However, these outcomes were predictable. In the period leading up to the AT&T consent decree, the policy-making process did not provide even a forum for the consideration of employee interests.

Instead, their legitimate interests and their representatives were systematically excluded from the purview of the legal and regulatory processes that shaped the new telecommunications industrial policy. Once again, as Congress considers reform legislation, no bill addresses the labor, employment, or productivity effects of restructuring the industry. Between October 1993 and March 1994, the industry's major employers announced downsizing plans that will eliminate 98,000 jobs. Instead of ignoring this massive restructuring that will tragically disrupt many lives, public policymakers need to develop a framework to support employee adjustment. An industry adjustment system needs to involve employers, unions, and the appropriate federal and state agencies. In principle, incumbent employees should not suffer major or long-lasting costs as a result of the industry's restructuring. To achieve this objective requires the linking of private joint labor-management initiatives to the government's one-stop employment service, the diffusion of high-wage, high-skill, and high-performance work organizations, and financial support for workers experiencing dislocations. Policymakers also need to make the low-wage, low-skill alternatives, such as part-timing, subcontracting, and temporary employment, more expensive. To do this, they might require that employers provide these workers with decent wages and benefits, including health insurance, pensions, and access to education and training opportunities.

The invisible barriers to occupational mobility must be eliminated. The industry's lifetime employment frameworks allowed employers to invest heavily in training; however, the training was highly employer specific. Employees learned organizationally and technically specific languages and skills that make them highly productive within their incumbent organizations, which also supported their high wages. However, firm-specific human capital investments provide these employees with few valuable skills that can be realized on the labor market. Educational and training policies need to focus on more general skill sets that permit all employees to move laterally across labor markets. To facilitate this process the industry needs to develop industry-based skill standards and certification procedures, skill demand forecasts, and subsidized training and educational programs. Employer policies that block employee movement between bargaining unit and "managerial" positions or between union and nonunion employers need to be aggressively challenged and eliminated.

Institutional support for occupational mobility should be encouraged. This may include labor law reform that permits occupational labor organizations, rather than relying solely on site-specific recognition procedures. Occupationalization can also be supported by broad-band skill standards and the reform of training and educational institutions. A more effective U.S. Employment Service that links together labor market institutions is essential to any program to support occupational mobility.

Nevertheless, breaking the industry's social contract through uncoupling employee security from firm profitability could have serious long-term consequences for productivity, service quality, and stable labor-management relations. This new turbulent environment makes it difficult to connect employee efforts to outcomes that are meaningful to them. As a result, successfully implementing high-performance work organizations becomes even more difficult. If these innovative organizational efforts cannot be clearly linked to outcomes that are important to the performers, such as job security and higher wages and benefits, they will remain short-term experiments that are not institutionalized.

In the coming decade the regional BOCs will face increasing cost pressures from the new competition. Profits are already down and declining, according to Steven Albrecht of the CWA research department. Uncertainty about either integration or duplication of cable TV and telephone cable networks further complicates the financing and planning of local fiber optic installations.

The major issue for labor-management relations in telecommunications is whether the RBOCs and GTE can gain sufficient control over their environment to manage their restructuring or whether restructuring will result from a series of unanticipated shocks delivered by an errant or poorly managed public policy process. In addition, as the RBOCs undertake restructuring they learn from the AT&T experience. AT&T has accomplished a massive restructuring without a major strike or conflagration over employment security; however, its workers, technicians, and many managers are extremely demoralized. Yet, precisely because AT&T was able to accomplish its massive restructuring over a protected period, the RBOCs will probably not have that freedom. Their unions and the employees already learned from the AT&T experience that once involuntary layoffs start, they are considerably more difficult to stop. Consequently, they are more likely to move into opposition in the early stages of a massive downsizing. The RBOCs need to create a transitional framework that permits restructuring for new competitive lines of business while tending to the employment concerns of their work forces. The 1994 NYNEX agreement reflects a significant advance in this process.

Acknowledgments

We want to thank Anne Brasher for her research assistance and Rose Batt, Larry Cohen, Helmut Druke, Adrienne Eaton, Harry Katz, George Kohl, Brent Kramer, Frieder Naschold, Alice Stelmach, and members of the Telecommunications Consortium for their helpful comments on earlier drafts.

Endnotes

[1] First, US West announced the elimination of 9,400 jobs. In November, Bell-South said it was eliminating 10,800 jobs. In January 1994, GTE announced the elimination of 17,000 jobs and Pacific Telesis said it would downsize by 10,000 jobs at Pacific Bell by 1997. In February, AT&T declared that it will eliminate another 15,000 jobs on top of already scheduled force reductions of 6,000 operator and call servicing positions and 7,500 jobs at Global Information Solutions, formerly NCR. In March, Ameritech said it would reduce its work force by 6,000 and NYNEX after bargaining with CWA scaled back its plans to eliminate 22,500 jobs to 16,800 positions.

[2] Fixed costs of long-distance transmission had fallen from $125 before World War II to less than $2 per circuit mile by the late 1970s (Vietor 1994, p. 189).

[3] However, telephone service has expanded to 93.8% of U.S. households and remains relatively fixed at 2% of consumer expenditures.

[4] The newly formed AT&T Technologies, clinging to its electronic analog systems, immediately lost market share to Northern Telecom (NT), when NT introduced the first digital switches. AT&T's market share of equipment sales to the former Bell Companies fell from 79% in 1983 to 59% in 1988. It responded to the new market structure by closing 22 of 26 supply centers, which reconditioned leased telephone equipment, and shutting down several of its domestic factories, while it moved some production offshore. The company then raced into the digital market with its 5ESS local exchange switch and the 4ESS toll switch. GTE, the other major U.S. predivestiture manufacturer, has been selling off its electronics and telephone factories to concentrate on local services, and formed a joint venture with AT&T, AG Communications, to manufacture switching equipment, which eventually will be fully owned and integrated into AT&T. IT&T has exited the telecommunications. Motorola, on the other hand, has become a major international supplier of cellular equipment; its cellular sales reached $6.5 billion in 1991. In April 1992, Northern Telecom and Motorola formed a joint venture to distribute cellular network equipment, Motorola-Nortel.

[5] Production employment dropped by 50% since 1983 according to the Employment and Earnings data, the Current Population Survey indicates a two-thirds decrease between 1983 and 1992. Production worker employment is declining at a compound annual rate of 9%.

[6] In stage one, manufacturers focused on the unique hardware (e.g., circuit boards and chips) needed to develop a digital switch. In a rather short period of time, this hardware became standardized with most components now being bought on the open market. Standardization has steadily reduced the hardware's value. In the second stage, competitive developments centered on operating systems and software enhancements for new services. In the current stage, we see the service providers enhancing their own software or working with manufacturers to create software defined networks and software capable of delivering customized services for "intelligent networks." Advanced Intelligent Networks (AIN) will ultimately provide the end users with the flexibility to design their own network services.

[7] A digital environment creates the potential for increasingly fast data transmission. High speed data can be sent either over privately leased carrier circuits or through the public network using packet switching technologies. Packet switching methods divide data into small packets, permitting each packet to travel a different route. Identifying bits are attached to the packet that contain the destination's address and also allow it to be reassembled at the receiving end. Packeting speeds the transfer of data by eliminating queuing, error correction procedures, and flow control mechanisms. The latest standard is Asynchronous Transfer Mode or ATM which is a switching and transmission technique that can process video and data signals distributed through an integrated broad band fiber network at hundreds of megabits per second. ATM combines the advantages of both circuit and packet switching.

[8] In the U.S. there are 140 million local loops or access lines that are supplied by the local exchange carriers, approximately 90 million are residential lines and the other 50 million are business lines. In addition, the local market is supplied by cable TV with approximately 60 million cable TV customers and by cellular telephone service with 14 million cellular customers who gain access through their local cellular carrier.

[9] In both local and long-distance services, the major carriers are transforming their analog voice systems into broadband and integrated digital services networks (ISDN). ISDN is an engineering concept, not a technology; it signifies a digitally switched network that simultaneously can carry video, voice, data, and imaging transmissions. Fiber optics is the preferred broadband medium for this digital transmission. Light waves pulsed through an optical fiber can carry voice, data, imaging and video transmissions simultaneously over the same strand (integrated broad band) without any electrical distortion or "noise." Fiber makes existing cable TV and telephone networks technically obsolete. It is currently deployed on most long distance and toll routes with growing application as local exchange feeder cable. About 90% of the potential circuit usage of fiber, however, is in the local loop, or what is referred to in the industry as the "last mile" (Botler et al. 1990:173). It is this last mile that represents the single largest obstacle to a national digital broadband network. A complete broad band conversion is estimated to cost between $150 billion to $500 billion.

Several companies are committed to fiber optic trials in the local loop. U.S. West, for example, plans a test in Omaha. It will cost $1,500 to hook up a fiber optic subscriber compared to $1,200 to connect a regular telephone customer; however, projections indicate that the cost for fiber optic loops should fall to $1,000 within a few years. Alternately, Pacific Bell plans to use fiber optics only as feeder cable in its $16 billion interactive media upgrade in California. Pacific Bell will run fiber optic to a local access point and from there will use cheaper coaxial cable, used by cable TV companies, to supply two-way interactive services, while retaining their regular telephone lines. Bell Atlantic, on the other hand, will use its standard copper wires and a recent technology, ADSL or asynchronous digital subscriber line (also known as narrow band, ISDN-n), to transmit video over regular telephone lines, while it implements a major fiber optic upgrading of its local networks. Bell Atlantic in December 1992 won approval from the New Jersey legislature to build a fiber optic network throughout the state, which would deliver broad band services to every subscriber's curb. In addition, the major cable television interests, such as Tele-Communications Inc. (25% cable market share) and Time Warner (12% cable market share) and major competitive access provider companies, such as Teleport and Metropolitan Fiber Systems, are both battling and allying with the seven regional Bells and GTE to become major local ISDN suppliers.

The highly leveraged cable TV industry earns about 30% of the revenue of the RBOCs. Although Bell Atlantic's merger with TCI failed, it signaled that the leading cable TV company does not believe it has the financial resources to build a publicly switched interactive network capable of competing with the RBOCs. Other alliances are moving ahead. US West acquired 25.5% of Time-Warner's stock while it continues to pursue a possible interest in number four, Cablevision Systems; BellSouth has a proposed acquisition of Prime Management; Bell of Canada is purchasing 30% of the sixth largest cable company, Jones Intercable. Southwest Bell bought Hauser TV, but its merger with Cox Cable also collapsed.

[10] Providing basic local service remains the RBOC's single largest source of revenue ($40 billion), followed by $19 billion paid by the long-distance carriers in access charges to the RBOCs for use of their local networks in completing long-distance calls. The intrastate toll service is the third largest source of revenue for the RBOCs, accounting for 13% of their $82.4 billion revenue in 1992.

[11] In April 1994, Pacific Telesis divested its cellular telephone services, creating a new company, Air Touch, to escape regulatory burdens placed on it by the California regulatory commission. In January 1994, Pacific Telesis announced a 10,000 employee force reduction at Pacific Bell, and in November 1993, Pacific Bell released a plan for a major $16 billion broad band network modernization program for California.

In April 1994 AT&T's purchase of McCaw cellular was challenged by Judge Greene for violating prohibitions in the Modified Final Judgment, as the Justice Department considered filing for an injunction based on antitrust violations. In August 1993, AT&T purchased McCaw cellular, the nation's largest cellular service provider, for $12.6 billion in stock. In February 1994, AT&T announced the elimination of 15,000 jobs in the Long-distance Communications Services Group, which employs 96,500 people and generates $40 billion in revenue and most of its profits. In December 1993 it announced a major force reduction at NCR.

In March 1994 Ameritech, the Midwest's regional Bell, announced a 6,000 employee force reduction. In February 1993, Ameritech filed a plan with the FCC for complete deregulation. Ameritech proposes to surrender its local service monopoly in return for complete freedom to compete in all telecommunications markets, including cable TV, equipment manufacturing, and long-distance services.

In March 1994 US West said it would issue up to 5.6 million shares to settle a shareholder lawsuit alleging that the company withheld information and misled investors about a $560 million restructuring charge taken in 1991. In October 1993 US West announced the elimination of 9,400 jobs. In May 1993 US West invested $2.5 billion to purchase 25.5% of Time Warner, the second largest cable TV company. In February 1994 the FCC announced a 7% reduction in cable TV rates, following a 10% reduction in 1993.

In February 1994 Viacom won the bid for Paramount, with the support of $1.2 billion raised from NYNEX's purchase of Viacom preferred stock. In March 1994 NYNEX reached an innovative agreement with CWA to handle a force reduction of 16,800.

In February 1994 the FCC denied GTE's requests to continue an experimental cable TV venture, stating that the alliance between GTE and a local cable company was "an unnecessary affiliation." In January 1994 GTE announced an organizational consolidation and the downsizing of 17,000 employees.

[12] In 1992 the industry employed 872,000 employees, down from its peak of 965,000 in 1983. Nonsupervisory employment fell to 649,000, a 7% decline since 1983. Approximately one-half of the employees in the industry are female, a proportion that has remained relatively constant over the last decade.

[13] For instance, Northern Telecom and Siemens-Rolm steadily gained market share from AT&T in PBX equipment. In the important network switch market, AT&T lost its substantial lead when in 1988, for the first time, Northern Telecom shipped more network switches than AT&T. In addition, AT&T's marketing of business and computer equipment produced a series of billion dollar losses. Its joint computer venture with Olivetti failed to produce a distinctive computer, and AT&T was never able to establish itself as a profitable competitor in the computer business. The company eventually merged its computer business with NCR and sold the UNIX operating system software division to Novelle.

[14] In 1991 we undertook an employee survey at AT&T to evaluate the effectiveness of the negotiated employment security programs. The survey was mailed on September 24, 1991 by AT&T Transtech to a stratified random sample of 8,100 AT&T bargaining unit employees. A total of 3,160 employees responded to the single mailing, yielding a response rate of 39%.

[15] 377,000 were assigned to AT&T; 588,000 remained with the seven RBOCs; 10,000 were shifted to Bell Communications Research Corporation (Bell Core, the research lab jointly owned by the RBOCs); and Cincinnati and Southern New England Telephone were divested. Approximately 125,000 people were transferred from the Bell Companies to AT&T. Of these, approximately 69,000 went to AT&T Communications (Long Distance), and 56,000 to AT&T Technologies, primarily Information Systems or ATTIS (Computers and Customer Premises Equipment).

[16] A year before a cable crew mistakenly cut a working fiber optic cable in Newark, New Jersey, which disrupted telephone traffic along the East Coast corridor, including the FAA air traffic control system.

[17] The latter manufactures digital network equipment at the Merrimack Valley Works.

[18] Developed at Bell Labs, the new AT&T Hobbit chip will power the new generation of wireless personal service communicators; AT&T will jointly manufacture these communicators with Panasonic.

[19] To become a global competitor, the corporation plans to generate 50% of its earnings from international sales by the year 2000, up from essentially nothing at divestiture. AT&T employs 53,000 people or 17% of its work force overseas.

[20] For example, Jerre Stead moved from turning around GBCS to reorganize NCR; nonunion NCR has substantially downsized its U.S. work force since AT&T's acquisition. Also a senior labor relations manager has recently been hired from the Federal Mediation and Conciliation Service to run the operations side of labor relations.

[21] NT's revenues increased almost fivefold over the last decade from $1.7 billion to $8.4 billion in 1992. More than 50% of NT's revenue is earned selling network digital switches. And, over half of NT's sales were in the U.S., compared to 27% in Canada.

[22] Northern Telecom has also entered the European market with its recent acquisition of STC in Britain (where it now ranks third in the digital switching equipment business), and it has purchased a 40% stake in Matra, the French communications company. NT, with an 8% share of the $102 billion global equipment market, ranked 4th in 1991 sales. In 1989, North America accounted for 91% of NT's revenue, but by 1992 more than one-quarter of Northern Telecom's sales were outside the U.S. and Canada.

[23] In comparison, AT&T retained 62% of the revenue and 75% of the presubscribed lines. MCI's revenues exceeded $10.5 billion in 1992. Although long-distance rates have declined by more than 40%, costs have dropped faster, allowing MCI to earn $589 million in 1992. For the last three years, MCI's revenues have increased at more than 10% annually, while calling volume has annually risen by more than 15%. MCI derives over 90% of its revenue from the long-distance business.

[24] In 1990 MCI purchased the fourth largest long-distance carrier, Telecom U.S.A, for $1.25 billion. In 1993, British Telecom purchased 20% of MCI's stock, a deal that strengthens the international network capabilities of both firms. In addition, MCI has entered a strategic alliance with Stentor, a Canadian consortium, which includes Bell Canada, to create a seamless cross-border intelligent network. Following AT&T's purchase of McCaw Cellular, MCI purchased a 17% interest in Nextel, a mobile communications company, and MCI announced plans to build local bypass networks to circumvent the RBOC's local access charges.

[25] The defeated seven-month strike in 1971 embittered many rank-and-file workers. The national framework for negotiations proposed by AT&T in 1973 was partly motivated to prevent pattern-breaking strikes by New York Telephone workers.

[26] However, BellSouth still is required to serve all customers within its operating region and service quality is actively monitored by the state commission.

[27] However, the union's analysis of the changing environment was wrong. Following AT&T's lead, the CWA leadership thought that the newly competitive AT&T would be the dynamic growth area for employment and union membership, while the BOCs would be relatively stagnant with declining employment and membership.

[28] The term "career" security is to be distinguished from "job" security (security in one's job) and "employment" security (security with one's employer). Career security means that training will be available to each employee to insure that he or she can learn a marketable skill (i.e., security in the labor market). While AT&T and the CWA move from employment security to career security, the bargaining unit employees we surveyed have moved from expecting employment security to wanting job security.

References

Allen, Robert. 1993. Chairman of the Board and Chief Executive Officer, AT&T. Statement March 24, 1993. Hearings Before the House Subcommittee on Telecommunications and Finance. U.S. Congress. Edward Markey, Chairman. National Information Infrastructure. Serial No. 103-12, pp. 170-190.

Amidon, Jane, Suzanne Brennan, Richard Klugman, and William Rich. 1989. *AT&T: A Strategic Analysis*. New York: Northern Business Information.

Barbash, J. 1952. *Unions and Telephones*. New York: Harper and Row.

Batt, Rosemary. 1993a. *High Performance Work in Telecommunications*. Cambridge, MA: MIT, Sloan School of Management.

_____. 1993b. *Work Reorganization and Labor Relations in Telecommunications Services: A Case Study of BellSouth Corporations*. Cambridge, MA: MIT, Sloan School of Management.

Batt, Rosemary, and Paul Osterman. 1992. *Public Policy and Workplace Centered Training*. Washington, DC: Economic Policy Institute.

Beatie, Pat, and Marc O'Brien. 1992. *Inside AT&T: A Profile*. Alexandria, VA: Telecom Publishing Group.

Bogel, Walter. 1990. *Telecommunications Policy for the 1990s and Beyond*. New York: M.E. Sharpe.

Boroff, Karen, and Jeffrey H. Keefe. 1992. *AT&T Employment Security Survey*. New Brunswick, NJ: Institute of Management and Labor Relations, Rutgers University.

Bradley, Stephen, and Jerry Hausman, eds. 1990. *Future Competition in Telecommunications*. Cambridge, MA: Harvard Business School Press.

Brock, Gerald W. 1981. *The Telecommunications Industry*. Cambridge, MA: Harvard University Press.

Brooks, T.R. 1977. *Communications Workers of America*. New York: Mason Charter.

Cappelli, Peter, and Charles R. Perry. 1986. "Bargaining in Telecommunications after Divestiture." Wharton School Working Paper Series #628.

Cappelli, Peter, and Charles R. Perry. 1988. "Labor Relations in Telecommunications." University of Pennsylvania Discussion Paper #37.

Cespedes, Frank, and John Cady. 1992. *MCI Telecommunications Corporation.* *Harvard Business School Case: 9-582-106.* Cambridge, MA: Harvard Business School.

Coll, Steven. 1986. *The Deal of the Century.* New York: Atheneum.

Council on Competitiveness. 1993. *Competition Policy: Unlocking the National Information Infrastructure.* Washington, DC: Council on Competitiveness.

Coy, Peter, and Robert Hof. 1992. "The Baby Bells' Painful Adolescence." *Business Week.* October 5, pp. 124-34.

Crandall, Robert. 1991. *After the Break-up.* Washington, DC: Brookings Institution.

CWA Information Industry Reports. Communications Workers of America. George Kohl, Research Director. Washington, DC: CWA.

Dower, Rick, ed. Various dates. Report on AT&T Telecom Publishing Group. Alexandria, VA.

Dunlop, John T. 1990. *The Management of Labor Unions: Decision Making with Historical Constraints.* Lexington, MA: Lexington Books.

Eaton, Adrienne, Micheal Gordon, and Jeffrey Keefe. 1992. "The Impact of Quality of Work Life Programs and Grievance System Effectiveness on Union Commitment." *Industrial and Labor Relations Review,* Vol. 45, no. 3, pp. 591-604.

Ehrenberg, R.G. 1979. *The Regulatory Process and Labor Earnings.* New York: Academic Press.

Elton, Martin, ed. 1991. *Integrated Broadband Networks: The Public Policy Issues.* New York: North-Holland.

Federal Communications Commission. 1939. *Investigation of the Telephone Industry in the United States.* New York: Arno Press, reprint 1974.

_____. 1993. *FCC Common Carriers Statistics 91-92.*

_____. 1990, 1991. Various Reports of the Common Carrier Bureau on Network Disruptions. 1/15/90, 1/4/91, 11/5/91, 9/17/91, and 11/8/91.

_____. 1993. *Report on Long-distance Market.* June 29.

Gormley, W.T., Jr. 1983. *The Politics of Utility Regulation.* Pittsburgh, PA: University of Pittsburgh Press.

Grawe, O., and M. Kafoglis. 1982. "Regulation and Relative Wages and Earnings." In M.A. Crew, ed., *Regulatory Reform and Public Utilities.* Lexington, MA: Lexington Books.

Greene, Judge Harold. 1982. Consent Decree Opinion in US v. AT&T. United States District Court for the District of Columbia. August 11. (Reprinted by Western Electric.)

Gross, Joel. 1992. *MCI Communications: As the Tide Comes, the Boat Will Rise.* New York: Donaldson, Lufkin & Jenrette Securities Corporation.

Henck, Fred W., and Bernard Strassburg. 1988. *A Slippery Slope: The Long Road to the Breakup of AT&T.* New York: Greenwood Press.

Hendricks, Wallace. 1987. "Telecommunications." In D. Lipsky and C. Donn, eds., *Collective Bargaining in American Industry.* Lexington, MA: D.C. Heath.

Hendricks, Wallace, and Susan C. Sassalos. 1990. "Labor, Employment, and Wages." Mimeo, University of Illinois.

Hilton, Margaret. 1993. Pulling Together for Productivity: A Union Management Initiative at US West Inc. OTA-ITE-583. Washington, DC: US Congress, Office of Technology Assessment.

Horwitz, Robert. 1989. *The Irony of Regulatory Reform*. New York: Oxford University Press.

Huber, Peter. 1987. *The Geodesic Network: 1987 Report on Competition in the Telephone Industry*. U.S. Justice Department.

Katz, Harry. 1993. "The Decentralization of Collective Bargaining: A Comparative Review and Analysis." *Industrial and Labor Relations Review*, October.

Keefe, Jeffrey. 1989. "Measuring Wage Dispersion: An Application of Entropy Measures to Analyze the Former Bell System's Pay Structure." *Proceedings of the Forty-First Annual Meeting of the Industrial Relations Research Association*. Madison, WI: IRRA, pp. 539-48.

_____. 1994. *AT&T After Divestiture*. Rutgers University. Material for AT&T-CWA-IBEW Workplace of the Future.

Keller, John J. 1992. "Some AT&T Clinets Gripe That Cost Cuts Are Hurting Service: The Downside of Downsizing." *Wall Steet Journal*, January 24, p. 1.

Kiss, Ferenc and Bernard Lefebvre. 1987. "Econometric Models of Telecommunications Firms." *Revue Economique* (March), No. 2, pp. 307-74.

Koch, Marianne, David Lewin, and Donna Sockell. 1988. "The Effects of Deregulation on Bargaining Structure: The Case of AT&T." In *Advances in Industrial Relations* 4.

Kochan, Thomas A., Harry Katz, and Robert McKersie. 1986. *The Transformation of American Industrial Relations*. New York: Basic Books.

Kochan, Thomas, Robert McKersie, and John Chalykoff. 1986. "The Effects of Corporate Strategy and Workplace Innovations on Union Representation." *Industrial and Labor Relations Review*, Vol. 39, no. 4, pp. 487-501.

Lynch, Lisa, and Paul Osterman. 1989. "Technological Innovation and Employment in Telecommunications." *Industrial Relations*, Vol. 28, no. 2, pp. 188-205.

North American Telecommunications Association. 1992. Telecommunications Market Review and Forecast. Washington, DC: NATA.

_____. 1993-1994. Telecommunications Market Review and Forecast. Washington, DC: NATA.

Northern Business Information. Various dates. *Telecom Market Letter*. New York: McGraw-Hill.

_____. Various dates. *Telecom Strategy Letter*. New York: McGraw-Hill.

Northrup, H. 1979. *The Impact of the AT&T-EEO Consent Decree*. Philadelphia, PA: Wharton Industrial Research Center.

Norwood, Stephen H. 1990. *Labor's Flaming Youth: Telephone Operators and Worker Militancy 1878-1923*. Champaign, IL: University of Illinois Press.

Peoples, James. 1990. "The Impact of Regulatory Change on Wage Levels in Telecommunications." Mimeo, Rutgers University.

Phillips, Almarin. 1982. "The Impossibility of Competition in Telecommunications." In M. Crew, ed., *Regulatory Reform of Public Utilities*. Lexington, MA: Lexington Books.

_____. 1985. "The Reintegration of Telecommunications: An Interim View." In M. Crew, ed., *Analyzing the Impact of Regulatory Change in Public Utilities*. Lexington, MA: Lexington Books.

Pitt, Douglas, and Kevin Morgan. 1992. "Viewing Divestment from Afar." In Harvey Sapolsky et al., eds., *The Telecommunications Revolution*. New York: Routledge.

Rosenberg, Nathan. 1994. *Exploring the Black Box*. New York: Cambridge University Press.

Schacht, John. 1985. *The Making of Telephone Unionism 1920-1947*. New Brunswick, NJ: Rutgers University Press.

Spalter-Roth, Roberta, and Heidi Hartmann. 1993. *Women in Telecommunications: Exception to the Rule of Low Pay for Women's Work*. Washington, DC: Institute for Women's Policy Research.

Stone, Alan. 1989. *Wrong Number*. New York: Basic Books.

Straw, R.J. 1984. "The Effects of Divesture on Collective Bargaining." *Proceedings of the Thirty-Seventh Annual Meeting of the Industrial Relations Research Association*. Madison, WI: IRRA.

Telephony. 1992. "NYNEX Embarks on a New Road." *Telephony*, April 27, pp. 33-40.

Temin, Peter. 1987. *The Fall of the Bell System*. New York: Cambridge University Press.

Teske, Paul. 1990. *After Divestiture*. New York: SUNY Press.

United States District Court for the District of Columbia. 1982. Consent Decree Opinion. Judge Harold Greene.

Vallas, Steven Peter. 1993. *Power in the Workplace*. New York: SUNY Albany.

Verma, Anil, and Joseph Weiler. 1992. "Industrial Relations in the Canadian Telephone Industry." In Richard Chaykowski and Anil Verma, eds., *Industrial Relations in Canadian Industry*. Toronto: Dryden Press.

Vietor, Richard. 1994. *Contrived Competition: Regulation and Deregulation in America*. Cambridge, MA: Harvard University Press.

von Auw, A. 1983. *Heritage and Destiny: Reflection on the Bell System in Transition*. New York: Praeger.

Weinhaus, Carol, and Anthony Oettinger. 1988. *Behind the Telephone Debates*. New Brunswick, NJ: Ablex Publishing Corporation.

White, Wilda, and Joseph Badaracco. 1992. AT&T Consumer Products. Harvard Business School Case: 9-392-108. Cambridge, MA: Harvard Business School.

Wood, Robert. 1992. *Telecommunications: A Vital U.S. Infrastructure*. Mimeo, Washington, DC: IBEW.

Zuboff, Shoshana. 1988. *In the Age of the Smart Machine*. Chapter 9, "The Information Panopticon." New York: Basic Books.

Labor Relations in American Textiles

Richard P. Chaykowski
Queen's University

Terry Thomason and Harris L. Zwerling
McGill University

Editor's Abstract

Textile manufacture is a highly competitive industry. Products are relatively standard and a similar technology is available to all manufacturers. Labor costs are an important basis of comparative advantage. For these reasons, and also because of apparel and textile-led development strategies on the part of many nations, U.S. textile manufacturers have faced increased international competition in recent years. This has occurred primarily in the market for cloth to be used in the manufacture of apparel, which is moving increasingly offshore. Increasingly, U.S. textile producers are specializing in the high end of the market: carpeting, drapes, upholstery, sheets, towels, and other linens.

Low unionization of the textile industry, historically and at present, can be explained by (1) employer resistance motivated by competitive product markets and labor intensive production processes; and (2) the characteristics of the textile work force in terms of personal characteristics, location, and skill levels. The location of the industry in small employer-dominated towns in the Southeastern states, a history of racial and gender divisions in the labor force, plant closures, and an absence of good local labor market alternatives for many workers have all contributed to difficulties in organizing this industry. Chaykowski, Thomason, and Zwerling argue that the key factor preventing unionization has been fierce, sometimes illegal employer resistance. They document its nature in four cases: Darlington-Milliken, J.P. Stevens, Cannon Mills, and S. Lichtenberg. Ironically, large textile firms are the least organized and probably the worst law violators. The limitations of current labor law and its enforcement are demonstrated convincingly in this part of the chapter.

The authors also suggest that long-run technological and market trends may eventually contribute to more textile unionization. Technological innovation has been eliminating the lowest-skill jobs and raising capital requirements for firms. Firms now must be larger than in the past. With the concentration of U.S. producers in the high end of the market, there is a concurrent need for a more skilled, "flexibly specialized" work force. An important innovation that is making U.S. producers more competitive in the high value-added fashion markets, with their frequent style changes, is "quick-response" (QR) systems that link textile manufacturers to clothing makers and retailers. The U.S. industry is changing in a way that may eventually make it more amenable to organization.

However, in the short run, technologically induced increases in productivity, the import situation, and a wave of mergers/acquisitions in the 1980s have all contributed to declining industry employment. Over the 1970s and 1980s, wages have been stable in real terms but low (at 73% of the average for manufacturing). There is little evidence that unions have much bargaining power in the textile industry. This explains in part their continuing organizing difficulties despite very innovative organizing strategies, including corporate campaigns and the creative use of litigation. In 1993 ACTWU experienced a wave of organizing success, but it is unclear whether this trend will persist.

o   o   o

The modern textile industry traces its beginnings to a number of 18th century inventions, including the spinning jenny, the flying-shuttle, and the water-powered drawframe. These inventions permitted mechanization of textile production and led to the establishment of the first industrial factory by Richard Arkwright in England in 1770 (Thomas 1982). The American textile industry began with an act of industrial espionage when Samuel Slater, on a visit to the Arkwright mill in 1789, learned the (up to then) closely guarded secrets of mechanized textile manufacture. A year later, Slater, with the aid of Philadelphia businessman Moses Brown, constructed the first American textile mill in Pawtucket, Rhode Island (Tindall 1984). Today the industry accounts for more than $65 billion in sales and employs more than 650,000 workers. While commonly regarded as an aging and technologically stagnant "sunset" industry, primary textiles have undergone a technological revolution in recent years prompted in part by longstanding global competition.

Historically, labor relations in the textile industry has been among the most confrontational in the U.S. Textile management has vigorously opposed union organization for more than 90 years, and today the textile industry is essentially unorganized. Only about 15% of the industry's work force is unionized, a density level that is one of the lowest among manufacturing industries. Nevertheless, the economic ground appears to be shifting. Technological progress has reduced the importance of labor costs as a comparative advantage in global trade and has increased the minimum efficient scale, thereby raising entry barriers. At the same time, technological innovations have increased industry skill requirements. These changes could be creating favorable conditions for union organization.

This chapter examines labor relations in the American textile industry. The chapter is divided into two sections. In the first section we discuss economic and technological factors affecting primary textiles, including the industry's economic structure, international trade, production processes, and the nature of the labor market. In the second section we discuss the state of labor relations in the textile industry, in particular, the history of recent organizing campaigns, factors affecting union organization, and the collective bargaining agenda in unionized firms.

Economic Context

Economic and Market Structure

The primary textile industry produces a wide variety of goods, including yarns and fabrics for use in apparel; household goods such as carpets, drapes, bed linen, curtains, towels, and upholstery; and industrial products such as filters, parachutes, fire hoses, adhesive tape, automobile tires, and storage tanks. These products are made from synthetic fibers such as rayon or polyester or from natural fibers such as cotton, wool, silk, jute, or flax.

Textile manufacture is a highly competitive industry with a large number of small to medium-size firms. At the same time a few large, vertically integrated firms, such as Burlington Industries, Capital, Spring Industries, Fieldcrest-Cannon, Milliken, and West Point-Pepperell, have captured substantial market shares in some product lines. Two factors contribute to the competitive nature of the industry. First, products are relatively standard and easily substitutable. Second, technology is embodied in machinery that is available to all manufacturers. However, escalating capital requirements associated with recent technological innovations have raised entry barriers.[1]

The diversity of the industry is partially illustrated with the data reported in Table 1. These data show that there is substantial sectoral variation with respect to establishment size and productivity. In general, weaving and yarn mills are the largest firms in the industry—the four largest firms control about 40% of the market, while finishing and dyeing companies are typically small firms that work on a contract basis for weaving and yarn producers. Similarly, knitting firms also tend to be smaller because they require smaller capital investments for efficient scale relative to weaving or spinning firms. In addition, technological change has been less significant for knitting than for either weaving or spinning processes.

TABLE 1

Employment, Payroll, Establishments, and Value of Shipments, By Subsector, 1987

Sector	Establish-ments	Employment Total (000s)	Per Estab.	Payroll Total (mil. $)	Per Employee	Value of Shipments Total (mil. $)	Per Employee
Total	6,412	672	105	11,410	16,979	62,786	93,432
Brd. cotton fabric	301	72	239	1,260	17,500	5,508	76,500
Brd. manmade fabric	441	88	200	1,596	18,136	8,049	91,466
Brd. wool fabric	119	14	118	236	16,857	1,051	75,071
Narrow fabric	277	19	69	296	15,579	1,136	59,789
Knitting	2,130	203	95	2,988	14,719	13,531	66,655
Finish, except wool	971	56	58	1,036	18,500	7,042	125,750
Carpets and rugs	477	53	111	1,039	19,604	9,795	184,811
Yarn and thread mills	610	114	187	1,850	16,228	10,277	90,149
Misc. textile goods	1,086	53	49	1,109	20,925	6,398	120,717

Source: *Statistical Abstract of the United States*, U.S. Bureau of the Census, 1991 (Table 1303, p. 740).

The industry underwent a dramatic restructuring in the 1980s as operations were rationalized and the industry became increasingly concentrated (Office of Technology Assessment 1987). Plants were closed, product lines were discontinued, and operations were consolidated. From 1977 to 1987, the number of textile establishments declined by more than 11%, from 7,202 in 1977 to 6,412 ten years later. During this same period, industry employment fell by nearly 25% from 876,000 to 672,000 employees. Most of these plant closings occurred in the mill towns of the southeast Piedmont. The U.S. Office of Technology

Assessment (1987) estimates that more than 85% of the spindles and 95% of the looms that were taken out of production between 1983 and 1985 were eliminated from mills in South Carolina, North Carolina, and Georgia. Plant closures in these states had a particularly high human cost, since the mill was often the principal (or only) employer in the locality. Workers were left with little or no alternative employment opportunities, while the closure devastated the local government's tax base (Long 1982c).

This restructuring occurred in the context of a wave of mergers, hostile takeovers, and leveraged buyouts (LBOs) that were motivated by favorable financial conditions in some industry firms (Long 1982b; Guyon 1981). These firms were typically selling at discounts relative to their book value, had little debt, and substantial cash or other liquid assets. In many cases, takeover attempts were led by investors with no previous experience in the textile industry.[2]

The most dramatic (and destructive) takeover attempt during this period occurred in 1987 when Dominion Textile, the dominant Canadian textile firm, and Asher Edelman, a New York investment broker, tried to acquire Burlington Industries, the nation's largest textile manufacturer.[3] This attempt was defeated when Burlington's management purchased the company in a leveraged buyout that was partially financed by Morgan Stanley & Co., a New York investment firm. In 1990, Burlington's ESOP acquired majority ownership of the company, making Burlington the largest employee-controlled manufacturing firm in the U.S.

In the two months between the initial Edelman-Dominion proposal and the Morgan Stanley buyout, Burlington management staged a vigorous defense. Burlington brought legal action against Edelman-Dominion, claiming that Edelman-Dominion had based their initial offer on confidential, insider information and that the proposed merger of the two companies constituted a violation of antitrust laws. Furthermore, the company obtained political assistance from the North Carolina state legislature, which passed a restrictive anti-takeover law, and from North Carolina's two U.S. senators, Terry Sanford and Jesse Helms, who initiated an SEC investigation of Edelman and Dominion Textiles.[4] The ferocity with which Burlington's management battled the Edelman-Dominion buyout is reminiscent of industry struggles with organized labor (see below).[5]

These takeover attempts frequently left the surviving company saddled with substantial debt, which was difficult to either service or retire out of operating revenue. Companies were forced to dispose of substantial parts of their business in order to relieve the debt load. For example, following the Edelman-Dominion takeover attempt, Burlington was forced to eliminate its research and development facility (with more than 550 employees) and to divest 20 subsidiaries valued at more than $1 billion. These subsidiaries, which included Burlington's denim operations (acquired by Dominion Textiles in November 1987), were among the company's most profitable divisions (Waldman and Freeman 1987) and yet were sold at a substantial discount (Cohen and Williams 1987). Between 1987 and 1990, Burlington's work force was reduced from 44,000 to 27,500 employees. By 1991 the employee-owned company, still coping with the debt incurred in the takeover attempt, was considering filing for bankruptcy. However, in 1992 the company recapitalized with a public offering of 57 million shares of common stock at $14. The proceeds from this offering were used to retire a substantial portion of the debt incurred in the LBO (Brannigan 1992).

The financial machinations of the 1980s led to several legal actions by aggrieved employees and former employees of companies involved in the merger wave. In 1989 a class-action suit was filed on behalf of 6000 employees of the 20 former subsidiaries of Burlington that were sold to reduce the debt incurred by the LBO. This action, which claimed that the former employees were entitled to their pensions when they left Burlington rather than when they retired from the companies that bought the subsidiaries, was settled for $70 million in February 1993 (*Wall Street Journal* 1993). A second suit, initiated in June 1992 with the aid of the Amalgamated Clothing and Textile Workers Union (ACTWU), claimed that management had violated its fiduciary responsibilities with respect to the company's ESOP by diluting the value of Burlington stock, which fell from $37.80 per share in 1989 to $14 at the time of the public offering (Ruffenach and Anders 1992).

International Trade

Since the 1950s, international trade in textiles has expanded, leading to a long-term shift in the global economic structure. Developing nations, particularly in the Pacific Rim, have begun to replace industrialized nations as major textile producers. This shift is, in part, attributable to economic factors such as easily transferrable technology, relatively low capital requirements, comparative advantage in labor costs in a labor-intensive industry, and in some cases, proximity to raw materials.

However, this shift may also be attributed to a "clothing-led" industrialization strategy. Pioneered by Japan, developing countries pursued an import-substitution policy in the clothing industry, with the goal of becoming clothing exporters. Importing textiles initially, a backward-integration strategy allowed these countries to establish a primary textile industry. In so doing, they increased the domestic content of their clothing exports, reduced costs, and achieved comparative advantage in the international clothing market (ILO 1991a).

Growing competition from developing nations and an erosion of domestic markets have led to restrictions on foreign imports by industrialized nations. The fundamental regulatory framework is the Multi-Fiber Agreement (MFA), which was first negotiated in 1974 and has since been renegotiated on three different occasions, most recently in 1986.[6] The MFA allows industrialized nations to restrict textile imports through unilateral action, following failed attempts to negotiate a bilateral agreement. The MFA was initially designed as a temporary measure to protect industrialized nations from market disruptions due to textile imports, while at the same time permitting a progressive liberalization of international textile trade, as prescribed by the General Agreement on Tariffs and Trade (GATT). However, successive renegotiations have led to increasingly restrictive protocols. The most recent version (MFA—IV) extended restrictions to textiles made from ramie, silk, and linen and allowed importing nations to limit import growth to an annual rate of 1%, compared to the previous limit of 6%.

By 1990 the U.S. had negotiated bilateral agreements to regulate trade covering more than 100 textile products with more than 35 exporting nations. Nevertheless, trends in imports (Table 2) show the increasing share of the American textile market held by foreign producers since the mid-1970s. These data indicate that textile imports grew by more than 12% annually between 1976 and 1988, while the domestic market grew at less than half that rate during that same period (approximately 7% per annum). Import penetration, which was less than 4% of the domestic market in 1976, increased to almost 7% by 1988.[7]

Increased import penetration during the 1980s was encouraged in part by the free-trade policies of the Reagan administration, which were continued by George Bush. Congress passed legislation restricting foreign textile imports in 1985, 1988, and 1990, yet each time, this legislation was defeated by presidential vetoes that Congress was unable to override. In the most recent GATT and MFA negotiations, the Reagan and Bush administrations advocated phasing out MFA restrictions over

TABLE 2

Textile Products, Shipments, Exports, and Imports

Year	U.S. Shipments (1)	Exports (2)	Domestic Shipments	Imports (2)	Apparent U.S. Market (AUSM)	Exports/ U.S. Shipments (%)	Imports/ AUSM (%)
1975	31,064						
1976	36,389	1,451	34,938	1,392	36,330	4.0	3.8
1977	40,551	1,407	39,144	1,490	40,634	3.5	3.7
1978	42,281	1,466	40,815	1,832	42,647	3.5	4.3
1979	45,136	2,130	43,006	1,820	44,826	4.7	4.1
1980	47,255	2,488	44,767	2,023	46,790	5.3	4.3
1981	50,262	2,326	47,936	2,466	50,402	4.6	4.9
1982	47,515	1,766	45,749	2,201	47,950	3.7	4.6
1983	53,358	1,559	51,799	2,524	54,323	2.9	4.6
1984	55,489	1,541	53,948	3,469	57,417	2.8	6.0
1985	53,277	1,462	51,815	3,616	55,431	2.7	6.5
1986	55,349	1,653	53,696	4,136	57,832	3.0	7.2
1987	62,786	1,891	60,895	4,697	65,592	3.0	7.2
1988	64,768	2,339	62,430	4,458	66,888	3.6	6.7
1989	65,951	2,810	63,141	7,294	70,435	4.3	10.4
1990	65,706	3,635	62,071	6,807	68,878	5.5	9.9

Source: (1) U.S. Bureau of the Census, Census of Manufacturers 1987, and 1989, 1991 Annual Survey of Manufacturers.
(2) U.S. Bureau of the Census, 1976-88, Highlights of the U.S. Export and Import Trade; 1989, U.S. Merchandise Trade.

a 10-year period, during which time bilateral quotas would gradually be replaced by a single, global quota for each product. At the end of the period, the global quota would itself be eliminated (The Economist 1990). Finally, in an effort to create a North American Common Market, the Reagan-Bush administrations negotiated the Free Trade Agreement (FTA) with Canada in 1988 and the North American Free Trade Agreement (NAFTA) with Mexico and Canada in 1991.[8]

Producers from industrialized nations (and especially the U.S.) have maintained markets through a combination of technological innovation and a comparative advantage in capital formation, which have allowed them to substantially increase labor productivity. In addition, there has been a segmentation of the global textile market. Producers from developing nations have captured the "low end" of the market, particularly apparel fabrics, while industrialized nations have developed the "high-end" market, including specialty high-fashion apparel fabrics as well as home furnishing and industrial products (ILO 1990b).

Technological Innovations

Textile technology changed very little in the first 200 years since Arkwright's mill helped inaugurate the industrial revolution. However, over the past 25 years the industry has witnessed a revolution in the development of both product and process technologies. The manmade fiber industry continues to develop synthetics with superior performance characteristics relative to natural fibers and older synthetics. These new fibers have led to improvement of existing products as well as the creation of new products and markets such as geotextiles. In addition, enhancements to textile machinery have increased machine speeds and output and have either eliminated or automated various stages of the production process. As a result, productivity and minimum capital requirements have increased, while labor content has been reduced. Furthermore, these technological innovations have fundamentally transformed work organization, market strategies, and skill requirements in the textile industry.

Panel A of Table 3 indicates that there has been a substantial expansion in new machinery investment during the 1980s as the level of real annual expenditures increased by more than 53% from 1982 to 1989. Over that same period, the level of real annual expenditures on new buildings increased modestly (approximately 24% from 1982 to 1989). These trends suggest that manufacturers were improving productivity rather than expanding capacity. Similarly, the data in Panel B indicate that textile producers reduced real annual spending on used capital equipment from $150 million in 1982 to $115 million in 1989. As a result, textile productivity increased dramatically, while labor productivity increased by approximately 8% annually from 1982 to 1989 (refer to Panel C). From 1975 to 1985, textile mill productivity grew 5.6% annually, compared to an annual growth rate of 2.4% for manufacturing as a whole (MIT Commission on Industrial Productivity 1989).

Industry process innovations include enhancement of basic textile machinery, the introduction of microelectronic technology, and the automation of formerly manual operations. Among the most dramatic of developments are the substitution of open-end spinning for older ring spinning machines and the introduction of shuttleless looms. Open-end technology eliminates two processes in yarn production and increases output relative to ring spinning.[9] This technology, which was pioneered in the 1960s, accounts for an increasingly larger share of American textile

TABLE 3

Textile Products, Capital and Repair Expenditure, and Productivity, 1982-1989
(millions of current dollars)

	1982	1983	1984	1985	1986	1987	1988	1989
			Panel A: New Capital Expenditures					
Buildings	241.8	207.0	305.9	269.3	228.8	283.2	329.8	300.3
Mach. & Equip.	1,284.0	1,373.3	1,717.3	1,594.0	1,369.5	1,744.5	1,912.9	1,976.5
Subtotal	1,525.9	1,580.3	2,032.2	1,863.3	1,598.3	2,027.7	2,242.7	2,276.8
			Panel B: Used Capital Expenditures					
Buildings	28.2	24.5	55.5	33.2	49.0	50.1	18.3	37.9
Mach. & Equip.	150.1	153.3	148.0	132.8	190.4	159.0	91.2	115.0
Subtotal	178.2	177.8	203.5	166.0	239.4	209.1	109.5	152.8
Total	1,704.1	1,758.1	2,226.7	2,029.3	1,837.7	2,236.8	2,352.2	2,429.6
			Panel C: Productivity					
Value added ($ mil.)	18,550.2	21,333.4	22,110.4	20,693.3	22,232.3	25,660.1	26,333.4	27,368.1
Value per prod. worker (act. curr. $)	30,138.4	34,188.1	36,216.9	36,605.9	40,079.9	44,618.5	46,077.7	48,370.6

Source: U.S. Bureau of the Census, *Census of Manufacturers* 1987 and *Annual Survey of Manufacturers*, 1983, 1985, 1987, 1989.

production. The share of domestic shipments produced by open-end machines increased from 21% in 1984 to more than 38% five years later (Isaacs 1990a). Similarly, shuttleless looms are more productive, with a higher weft insertion rate and the ability to weave wider fabrics and produce higher quality fabric than the shuttle looms that they are gradually replacing.[10] From 1973 to 1990, the number of shuttleless looms in the U.S. increased from 13,000 to 70,000 (Isaacs 1990c).

In addition, new technology has automated links between processes, eliminating human labor that would formerly upload and download material into and from machines as well as transport it between processes. Two examples are automatic bale feeders and chute-fed carding. Automatic bale feeders eliminated the need to manually separate cotton bales into layers, feed those layers into opening and picking hoppers, and remove waste from these machines. Chute-fed carding has eliminated the need to hand-carry the cotton lap produced from the opening and picking process to the carding machine.[11] These technologies have not only increased productivity and reduced labor costs, but they have also enhanced the quality of output from these intermediate stages, thereby reducing defects and downtime in upstream processes.

Finally, the 1980s was a period of increasing use of computers and microelectronic technology in all aspects of the textile business including production. This technology, which was first introduced in the textile production process to monitor machines, has gradually evolved to include diagnostic and control functions (Bonham 1991). Microelectronics reduce machine downtime and labor costs and improve product quality. Manufacturers have also begun to introduce computer-aided design technologies into the weaving and finishing processes, which substantially reduces the delay between the creation of a new design and its introduction into market. These innovations have substantially transformed textile manufacture into a process technology; the industry envisions a future where "lights out" spinning and weaving operations have all but eliminated the textile mill work force (Isaacs 1990a, 1990b).

Combined with the threat of global competition, technological innovations have begun to have a significant impact on work organization as well as business and marketing strategies in the industry. Competition from low-cost foreign producers, who have been able to capture a large portion of the low-end commodity market, has forced American manufacturers to adopt a "niche" marketing strategy (Kilman 1986). This strategy requires that textile producers quickly respond to changes in market conditions and evolving market opportunities. The industry has developed a program called "quick response" (QR) that uses computers to link primary textile manufacturers to clothing-makers and retailers (Sease 1985). Electronic data-interchange technology provides textile and clothing producers with real-time information on the state of the market, thereby allowing manufacturers to more quickly adjust production and reduce stock-outs, markdowns, and inventory carrying costs.[12]

As indicated, QR allows manufacturers to exploit market niches, particularly in the high value-added fashion markets that are subject to frequent style changes. An effective QR program also gives domestic manufacturers a comparative advantage in the domestic market, which is the largest in the world. Since American manufacturers are physically closer to domestic retail outlets, they have a competitive advantage with respect to delivery time (Sease 1985). In addition, developing nations as yet lack the communications infrastructure to effectively create electronic links with American retailers (ILO 1991a).

Niche marketing and QR may require more flexible forms of work organization than those traditionally found in the textile industry, whereby firms attempted to achieve economies of scale through mass-production manufacturing. The industry is slowly beginning to recognize the need to change old habits. A survey of "world class manufacturers," conducted by the Institute of Textile Technology in 1989, recommended that textile manufacturers shift to smaller plants (or to modular production within existing facilities), reduce layers of management, and move to "operator-controllable" production (Isaacs 1989). Industry analysts also foresee the need for team production, pay-for-knowledge compensation systems, and group (as opposed to individual) bonus systems (*Textile World* 1990). However, few of these innovations in work organization or personnel practices have actually been introduced into the workplace.

Technological innovations in the textile industry have altered the comparative advantages that have shaped global trade for the past 35 years. The production function has fundamentally changed so that labor costs are a much less significant economic factor, while capital requirements have become more important. Developing nations do not have the necessary infrastructure to effectively use newer communication technologies; in addition, manufacturers in these countries, which lack a domestic capital base and which have less stable political systems, are at a comparative disadvantage with respect to capital formation.

The Textile Market

The American textile industry began in the New England states, where it was primarily located until the mid-1920s. After the Civil War, Southern manufacturers began to build mills in small towns in the Piedmont region of Virginia, North Carolina, South Carolina, Georgia, and Alabama. Lower production costs and newer, more productive technology provided Southern manufacturers with a competitive advantage which, in combination with a depressed textile market, led to the eventual dominance of Southern mills (Wright 1986).[13] As of 1983, more than 72% of industry employment was located in the Southeast and more than 55% was located in the three states of North Carolina, South Carolina, and Georgia (Rowan and Barr 1987).

Textile manufacture has traditionally been a low-wage, low-skill and primarily white male industry. In recent years the work force has become increasingly black and female, and although the intra-industry occupational distribution has changed—so that a relatively more highly skilled work force is employed—the industry remains largely low skill, low wage.[14] The increasing proportion of African-American and female workers may be attributed to increasing opportunities outside the textile industry for white male workers in the South (Penn and Leiter 1991).

Table 4 presents data concerning employment and wages in the textile industry from 1970 to 1989. These data indicate that there has been a substantial reduction in employment of 36% over this twenty-year period. Most of this reduction occurred in the 1980s. Furthermore, textiles is a low-wage sector compared to other manufacturing industries; textile wages are approximately 70% of the wage rate for manufacturing as a whole. In addition, labor costs as a share of production costs steadily declined from 1978 to 1988 by approximately 1% per year. Finally, real wages in the textile industry declined over the late 1970s and early 1980s and increased only modestly thereafter, despite the fact that the industry experienced substantial productivity growth over this period.

Technological innovations described in the previous section should increase work force skill requirements in the textile industry (Bailey 1988). Modern textile machinery is more expensive than the machinery that it replaces; consequently, machine downtime due to human error is more costly. In addition, flexible manufacturing requires that workers be able to perform a wider variety of tasks so that they can be easily moved from one job to the next as production requirements change. Finally, microelectronic technology that is increasingly built into textile machinery and production processes requires basic literacy and numerary skills that were previously unnecessary. The rapid pace of change associated with this technology makes these skills even more important.

American textile manufacturers are beginning to recognize that increased skilling of their work force is necessary for global competitiveness. John Eapen, director of process engineering and automation for Fieldcrest-Cannon, states:

> Everyone in the world is buying the same machinery, so you don't get ahead having the latest; you merely stop falling behind. What really makes the difference is the skill in manufacturing (cited in Isaacs 1989:72).

Importantly, textile management may see the need for changing long-standing human resource practices. Among other things, manufacturers have become increasingly concerned with education and training as a means of upskilling their work force (Bailey 1988).

In addition, manufacturers are placing more emphasis on employee retention. A recent survey of "world class manufacturers" made the following recommendations as a means of "stabilizing textile talent" (Isaacs 1989:76):

TABLE 4

Textile Products, Employment, Wages, and Salaries, 1970-1989

Year	Total Textile Employment (000s) (1)	Production Workers (000s) (1)	Textile Production Workers' Hourly Wage (Curr. $) (2)	Textile Production Workers' Hourly Wage (Const. $) (2)	Total Employee Payroll (mil. $) (Curr. $) (1)	Total Employee Payroll (mil. $) (Const. $) (1)	Textile Labor Costs as Share of Shipments (%)	All Mfg. Production Workers' Hourly Wage (Curr. $) (2)	All Mfg. Production Workers' Hourly Wage (Const. $) (2)	Hourly Wage Textiles/All Mfg. (%)
1970	924.5	812.9	2.45	6.28				3.35	8.59	73.1
1975	835.1	724.9	3.42	6.32				4.83	8.93	70.8
1976	875.9	765.3	3.69	6.45				5.22	9.13	70.7
1977	875.4	764.6	3.99	6.55	7,881	12,942	19.4	5.68	9.33	70.2
1978	861.8	752.5	4.30	6.55	8,368	12,756	19.8	6.17	9.41	69.7
1979	842.1	732.3	4.66	6.37	8,824	12,070	19.5	6.70	9.17	69.6
1980	816.1	706.2	5.07	6.12	9,228	11,132	19.5	7.27	8.77	69.7
1981	785.2	678.5	5.52	6.04	9,574	10,475	19.0	7.99	8.74	69.1
1982	717.4	615.5	5.83	6.02	9,046	9,336	19.0	8.49	8.76	68.7
1983	723.3	624.0	6.18	6.19	10,061	10,081	18.9	8.03	8.05	77.0
1984	709.5	610.5	6.46	6.25	10,192	9,866	18.4	9.19	8.90	70.3
1985	658.4	565.3	6.70	6.27	9,967	9,324	18.7	9.54	8.92	70.2
1986	644.3	554.7	6.93	6.38	10,306	9,490	18.6	9.73	8.96	71.2
1987	672.0	575.1	7.17	6.56	11,410	10,439	18.2	9.91	9.07	72.4
1988	668.5	571.5	7.38	6.46	11,554	10,117	17.8	10.19	8.92	72.4
1989	652.7	565.8	7.67	6.43	11,837	9,930		10.49	8.80	73.1

Source: (1) U.S. Bureau of the Census, *Census of Manufacturers 1987* and *1989 Annual Survey of Manufacturers.*
(2) U.S. Bureau of the Census, *Statistical Abstract of the United States, 1971-1991.*

(1) Make sure wages are competitive with the local industries and not just with the textile industry. (2) Increasingly, World Class Manufacturing plants are moving toward pay policies which assure production personnel a certain degree of income security. Sometimes, all plant personnel are paid on salary, but this is not a universal practice. (3) Take a hard look at work schedules. Worldwide, and especially in the U.S., people are becoming increasingly conscious about having a quality life style (cited in Isaacs 1989:76).

Whether the industry will implement these or similar changes remains to be seen. On the basis of past history we are skeptical, but the fundamental economic forces motivating change may prove to be irresistible.

Textile Labor Relations

Unions and Union Organization

The two principal unions in the textile industry are the United Textile Workers of America (UTWA), which was organized in 1901 by the AFL, and the Amalgamated Clothing and Textile Workers Union (ACTWU). The ACTWU was formed by the merger of the Amalgamated Clothing Workers Union (ACWU) and the Textile Workers Union of America (TWUA) in 1976. The TWUA was founded in 1939 and arose from the Textile Workers Organizing Committee, which was formed by the CIO in 1934 for the purpose of organizing the previously unorganized Southern textile mills (Marshall 1967:171).[15]

Primary textile manufacture has traditionally been and remains a largely unorganized industry. Table 5 reports membership data for the two major textile unions. Since the ACTWU represents members in both the textile and clothing industries, we cannot determine exact textile membership in the ACTWU. However, using 1975 data, we estimate that in 1989 approximately 76,000 textile workers were represented by these two unions, or 12% of total employment.

There is substantial variation in union density between sectors in the industry. In general, mills owned by large vertically integrated textile firms, such as Burlington, Milliken, Fieldcrest-Cannon, etc., have proven more resistant to union organization than smaller firms. This is evident from data presented by Kokkellenberg and Sockell (1985:Table 3), who report that in 1980 union density in knitting mills was 15.5%, density in the finishing and dyeing sector was 30.3%, and membership in yarn and fabric mills was estimated to be 10.4% of total employment.

TABLE 5

Major Textile Unions, 1955-1989
Membership (000s)

Year	ACWU	TWUA	ACTWU	UTWA
1955	210	203	—	49
1957	273	190	—	43
1959	288	173	—	37
1961	290	142	—	34
1963	288	122	—	33
1965	288	123	—	36
1967	288	125	—	37
1969	285	122	—	38
1971	270	117	—	37
1973	257	117	—	37
1975	232	105	—	36
1977	—	—	301	31
1979	—	—	301	31
1981	—	—	233	28
1983	—	—	253	26
1985	—	—	228	23
1987	—	—	195	20
1989	—	—	180	20

Key: ACWU—Amalgamated Clothing Workers' Union
TWUA—Textile Workers' Union of America
ACTWU—Amalgamated Clothing and Textile Workers' Union
UTWA—United Textile Workers' Union
Source: Gifford, Courtney D., *Directory of U.S. Labor Organizations*, biannual.

As noted earlier, finishing and dyeing firms tend to be among the smallest in the industry, while the yarn and fabric mills are among the largest. Attempts to organize these large mills have been singularly unsuccessful.

Factors Explaining Union Organization

Two explanations have typically been advanced to explain the lack of organization in the textile industry: (1) employer resistance motivated by competitive product markets and labor-intensive production processes and (2) worker characteristics and attitudes.

Employer Resistance. In their survey of managers from 28 Southern textile companies, Rowan and Barr (1987:95) found that a "unique feature in the organization of personnel management in the textile industry is the major emphasis on keeping the plants nonunion." The reasons are not surprising. The industry has traditionally been highly competitive, with few entry barriers, and labor intensive. Textile companies have employed the traditional array of techniques for avoiding and suppressing unions, ranging from paternalistic benefits programs (designed primarily for attracting labor to remote workplaces) to unlawful campaigns of antiunion coercion. Very early textile mill villages provided firms with several means for exercising control over their employees. In these rural company towns, workers' homes, stores, and churches were owned by the firm. Companies that subscribed to "welfare work" sponsored numerous social activities for their employees which were generally designed to promote loyalty to the firm (Jacoby 1985). In addition, whole families would typically work in the mills. However, this paternalism was inextricably intertwined with the more coercive features of textile labor relations. The pervasive involvement of company management and its agents in the working and nonworking activities of employees provided excellent opportunities for surveillance. The threat of eviction of an entire family of employees (deemed to be unreliable or disloyal) from these relatively privileged, racially segregated enclaves provided a substantial disincentive to engage in union activity. However, after passage of the Fair Labor Standards Act in 1938, companies found maintaining these villages to be less economically feasible, so they began to sell them off. Hall, Korstad, and Leloudis (1986:285) suggest that the subsequent dispersion of textile workers into the rural surroundings of the mills, which was facilitated by proliferation of the automobile, has also hindered organizing.

Vestiges of paternalism remain in many communities where the textile industry is still the principal employer. Even after textile firms divested themselves of the proprietary aspects of their civic authority, they continued to exercise a disproportionate influence in communities that depended on the industry (Zingraff 1991:205; *Textile World* 1977). It was not simply a matter of economic dependence, since textile firms continued to play a critical political and social role in these communities. The implicit (and sometimes explicit) threat of plant closure or relocation creates substantial community pressure against union activity due to its enormous potential costs.

There is a long history of extraordinarily bitter confrontations between textile interests and union organizers, many of which were marked by violence, threats, or coercion. Large-scale organization of Southern textile workers began in the 1920s when wage cuts and implementation of the "stretch-out" led to three spontaneous and generally unorganized walkouts in the Carolina Piedmont in 1929 (Marshall 1967:101-110). Collectively known as the Textile Revolt, these demonstrations were singularly unsuccessful. Striking workers were discharged, arrested *en masse*, and killed or wounded in clashes with police or the national guard; organizers were either arrested or kidnapped. None of these actions led to lasting organization, and further efforts were discouraged by extensive use of the blacklist. These events were substantially repeated in 1934 when the UTW, attempting to capitalize on the more favorable political environment of the New Deal, called an industrywide strike involving 450,000 workers (Marshall 1967:166-174). Once again much blood was shed and several deaths ensued as strikers clashed with local law enforcement and the national guard. In Georgia striking workers and their families were held in camps behind barbed wire after Governor Eugene Talmadge declared martial law. Ultimately, this strike was no more successful than the earlier Textile Revolt in building permanent labor organizations.

While resistance to union organizing became less physically violent, employers remain intractable in their opposition to labor unions up to the present day. The nature of this resistance can usefully be illustrated by an examination of several of the most recent organizing attempts.

• Deering-Milliken: The TWUA launched its drive to organize the Darlington Manufacturing plant in March of 1956. The company strenuously resisted, interrogating employees and threatening to close the plant if the union succeeded. Roger Milliken warned both workers and supervisors at the mill that they would lose their jobs if workers organized (Sparks 1975:762-763). Stories of previous closures were circulated to remind employees that the Milliken chain had closed other plants in response to unionization and union activities. Despite these tactics, on September 6, 1956, a majority of Darlington workers chose to have the union represent them in collective negotiations. Six days later Darlington's board of directors voted to liquidate the company. That plant permanently closed in October.

The Darlington mill closure began one of the most highly publicized and protracted cases in the history of the NLRA.[16] The NLRB eventually found that the Darlington mill was part of Milliken's single integrated enterprise and that its closure was for the discriminatory purpose of chilling unionism in Milliken's other plants, thus violating Section 8(a)(3)(b) of the National Labor Relations Act.[17] Despite this decision, Milliken's actions effectively chilled union organization efforts throughout Southern textiles for the next two decades. For example, management at other textile concerns continued to remind their own employees of the potential dangers of unionization by posting newspaper articles about the Darlington closure on bulletin boards in the workplace (Sparks 1975:763).

- J.P. Stevens: In 1963, the TWUA and the AFL-CIO's Industrial Union Department (IUD) launched a drive to organize J.P. Stevens and Company (Hodges 1991). At that time J.P. Stevens was the nation's second largest textile manufacturer with more than 36,000 workers employed at 53 plants. The company engaged in an all-out battle against unionization by firing, coercing, and intimidating prounion employees (Hodges 1991). As a result, the TWUA lost 11 of 12 representation elections held for the employees at various plants owned by J.P. Stevens from 1963 to 1975 (Mullins and Luebke 1982:82). The outcomes of five of the elections were set aside due to company unfair labor practices.

The union's only success in organizing J.P. Stevens came in a 1974 election held for a unit comprised of the company's seven plants located in Roanoke Rapids, North Carolina (Mullins and Luebke 1982:82). However, this 1974 victory did not result in a contract since the company refused to bargain. Nevertheless, certification allowed the union to recast the J.P. Stevens campaign from a traditional organizing drive to a broad-based campaign using a variety of innovative tactics, including a consumer boycott as well as an extensive legal and "corporate" campaign. Among other actions, the ACTWU initiated antitrust litigation, claiming that J.P. Stevens and other major textile firms conspired to suppress wages through their antiunion efforts. Extensive discovery demands placed on other firms were designed to isolate J.P. Stevens from the rest of the industry (*Textile World* 1978).[18]

Central to the ACTWU's organizational efforts was the "corporate campaign," which involved two basic strategies: (1) harassment of J.P. Stevens' management and stockholders through picketing and the proposal of prolabor resolutions at annual stockholder meetings and (2) isolation of J.P. Stevens from companies with which it did business or had interlocking directorial relationships (Bronson and Birnbaum 1980b). The ACTWU pressured outside directors to resign from the board of directors of J.P. Stevens and to force the officers of J.P. Stevens to resign from other boards (Mullins and Luebke 1982:83).

By 1978 the union forced James Finley, then chairman of J.P. Stevens, from the board of Manufacturers Hanover Trust primarily as the result of the union's threat to withdraw an estimated $1 billion in assets from Manufacturers Hanover (Mullins and Luebke 1982:84). Later that year the union threatened to run dissident candidates for the board of directors of the New York Life Insurance Co., forcing Finley to resign from the New York Life board and forcing the chairman of New York Life to quit the Stevens board (Bronson and Birnbaum 1980b). A similar tactic used against Metropolitan Life Insurance forced Finley into early retirement in 1980. Subsequently, Metropolitan's chairman, Richard Shinn, met privately with the new Stevens' chairman, Whitney Stevens, to inquire about the progress of J.P. Stevens' negotiations with the ACTWU. At the time, Metropolitan held nearly one-half of the company's long-term debt. (Bronson and Birnbaum 1980a).

In October 1980 J.P. Stevens and the ACTWU negotiated a two and one-half year contract covering approximately 3,200 employees at ten plants. In return for a contract that included arbitration, a dues check-off, and retroactive wage increases, the ACTWU agreed to end the consumer boycott and corporate campaign (Bronson and Birnbaum 1980a). In 1983 J.P. Stevens and the ACTWU settled all of the union's pending unfair labor practice complaints (Lublin 1983). The settlement required the company to pay $1 million to the union as well as back pay to 18 employees who had been fired or harassed during the organizing drive (Lublin 1983). The agreement also required that Chairman Whitney Stevens draft a letter to NLRB General Counsel William Lubbers pledging that J.P. Stevens personnel would refrain from conduct that infringes on employee rights (Lublin 1983). For its part, the union was reassured by the relatively uneventful renewal of its collective agreements, J.P. Stevens' new investments in its unionized plants, and the company's conduct during more recent organizing campaigns, which was characterized as "remarkably clean" by Arthur Goldberg, the union's general counsel (Lublin 1983). Despite its considerable achievements in overcoming J.P. Stevens' fierce resistance, the ACTWU was unable to organize more than 10% of the textile manufacturer's employees before the firm was split up in 1988.

• Cannon Mills: Since 1974, the ACTWU (or its predecessor, the TWUA) have attempted to organize employees of Cannon Mills in Cabarrus and Rowan Counties, North Carolina on three separate occasions. In the first attempt, while the union lost the largest representation election ever held in the textile industry, it was nonetheless able to garner more than 45% of the 15,000 votes cast.[19] A second organizing drive began in 1984 after Cannon Mills was sold to David Murdock. The ACTWU hoped to capitalize on perceptions that conditions in the mills worsened since that time; at the time the campaign began, Murdock had permanently laid off 2,000 workers and further downsizing was planned (Williams 1985). This second drive resulted in another election loss as the union was defeated 5,692 votes to 3,534 (Rowan and Barr 1987:83).

According to Bruce Raynor, the ACTWU's southeast regional director, Cannon "ran an incredibly vicious campaign. Even the Stevens family never came down and personally threatened to close the mill" (cited in Rowan and Barr 1987:83). In a letter to Cannon Mills employees dated two months before the election, Murdock stated his absolute opposition to unionization. The appeal was a mixture of familiar themes. Murdock pointed out the company's contributions to plant communities, noting particularly the millions spent on community projects in Kannapolis, North Carolina, where Cannon Mills is located (Zingraff 1991:213). He also stated that the company was losing money and was "in serious trouble" (p. 212). Although he admitted to holding merger talks with other textile producers, he flatly denied a union charge that the company was about to be sold. This approach likely contributed to the victory for the company by nearly a 2 to 1 margin.

The third campaign began in June 1991 (BNA 1991a). After another campaign marked by ULP charges, the union lost 3,443 to 3,053 (BNA 1992a). The ULP charges, which are still before an NLRB administrative law judge, allege, in part, that management discharged and suspended union supporters, while also threatening plant closures and benefits reductions if the union won (BNA 1991c, 1992a, 1992b).[20]

The ACTWU represents about 4500 employees of the parent company, Fieldcrest-Cannon. As a result of the Cannon Mills campaign, Fieldcrest-Cannon initiated a fight with the union at these organized mills (Raynor 1992). The company fired a chief steward and refused to settle grievances. More than 40 grievances have gone to arbitration, and the union has won most of these. However, Fieldcrest-Cannon has refused to honor the arbitral awards. The ACTWU also filed bad-faith bargaining charges against Fieldcrest-Cannon after the company refused to match the 5.5% wage increase it granted to nonunion employees (BNA 1992b). According to an NLRB regional attorney, (1) the company had indicated that nonunion workers were receiving a larger increase because they had remained nonunion, and (2) the company had traditionally paid the same increase to union and nonunion employees.

• S. Lichtenberg: In 1987 the ACTWU began its drive to organize two rural Georgia drapery manufacturing plants—Samsons Manufacturing of Waynesboro and Delila Manufacturing of Louisville, both owned by S. Lichtenberg and Co. of New York (BNA 1991b, 1992c). Despite a campaign that the ACTWU characterized as having "massive and fla-grant violations of labor law to punish workers," the union won the April 1988 representation election (BNA 1991b). Subsequently, an adminis-trative law judge found that the employer had unlawfully interrogated workers about union activities, threatened closures, job losses as well as other forms of reprisal, changed job duties, and reduced wages. The administrative law judge ordered S. Lichtenberg to rehire 120 workers with approximately $1 million in backpay.

Legal pressures on the employer continued to mount, culminating in a January 1992 decision by the 11th U.S. Circuit Court of Appeals that reversed a district court and thereby enabled the NLRB to obtain an interim injunction against Lichtenberg under the NLRA's Section 10(j). The injunction forbade Lichtenberg from continuing to unilaterally change work rules and refuse to bargain. Within months Lichtenberg and the union settled the ULP case when the company agreed to rein-state and pay $950,000 to 267 employees who were fired or laid off for union activity (AFL-CIO News 1992). The parties also reached a three-year collective agreement covering workers at both plants.

In June of 1992, the ACTWU also settled a race and sex discrimina-tion suit it had filed against Lichtenberg as part of its legal campaign against the company. The suit argued that the theory of comparable worth was applicable to racial discrimination (Hayes 1992). The union claimed that Lichtenberg had discriminated against its black female production employees by paying them less than their white male super-visors even though the jobs in these two classifications required similar skill levels. While the settlement precluded a test of the viability of this legal argument, the case's central factual contentions concerning race, gender, and pay inequity point to factors that may be crucial to the future success of union organizing in the Southern textile industry.

Worker characteristics/attitudes. The failure to organize Southern textile workers has been attributed to their social, human capital, and demographic characteristics, including age, docility, race, gender, skill levels, and the lack of good labor market alternatives (Simpson 1981:385-388). The Southern textile worker has been alleged to be more docile and complacent than other blue-collar employees.

The relationships between these demographic characteristics and worker attitudes toward unions and union membership were analyzed in three empirical studies that were based on a 1980 survey of 127 non-supervisory production workers from four of J.P. Stevens' unionized

Roanoke Rapids plants. Reif, Schulman, and Belyea (1988) found that younger, black, lower-paid, and dissatisfied workers found unions to be more instrumentally valuable than other workers. They found that more educated workers were more likely to be members, although less likely to see the union as an effective advocate in obtaining gains in wages and working conditions. Schulman, Zingraff, and Reif (1985:199) found blacks favored unions more than white workers. Leiter (1986:969) found that white, higher-paid, and more senior workers were more supportive of the company than the union. He also found no gender-based differences. Leiter (p. 970) interprets this to mean that workers who support management do so out of perceived self-interest rather than docility. He concludes that successful opposition to the company by young, lower-paid, black workers is diminished by their lack of labor market opportunities and the ease with which they can be replaced.

MacDonald and Clelland (1984) surveyed more than 200 nonunion textile workers in Georgia. Their results suggest that senior and female employees have more negative sentiments toward unions. Both higher-skilled and younger employees are less deferential toward management, while deference is negatively related to union sentiment. However, they also indicate that prounion sentiments in their sample did not differ substantially from that found in a national Quality of Employment Survey of unorganized blue-collar workers.

The use of limited samples in these studies precludes broad generalizations based on the results. However, this research does suggest that explanations of the persistent low levels of textile unionization based on the greater supposed docility of Southern workers are less and less tenable, as the younger workers, who tend to be more favorably disposed to unionism, replace older employees, and as the industry work force becomes more educated, more black, and more highly skilled.

In considering the reasons why Southern textile workers have not unionized in substantial numbers, it is useful to consider a basic cost/benefit analysis of the decision to unionize. Given the nature of product market competition in the textile industry, it is unlikely that unionization can deliver significantly enhanced economic benefits. While unionization can provide due process protection and a more equitable treatment of employees, these benefits are more abstract, intermittent, and subjective. In contrast, the substantial and immediate costs of union activism in the form of employer resistance coupled with slow, meager legal remedies for illegal managerial actions, would seem to tip the balance against union support, except in rare or egregious circumstances.

Trends in Collective Bargaining

As previously noted, global competition and technological innovations created an impetus for changes in job content, job classifications, and skilling requirements for textile workers (ILO 1991b). Consequently, we would expect significant changes both in human resource practices in nonunion environments as well as in collective bargaining outcomes in unionized settings. However, the low level of union density has limited unions' ability to lead change, given the twin pressures of remaining competitive with the dominant nonunion portion of the industry and coping with import competition. In fact, despite significant increases in productivity, wage freezes or reductions were observed in large bargaining units in the 1980s, and real wages actually declined in the 1980s (ILO 1991a:83). Further, advance notice or severance payments related to the disemployment effects of technological changes appear very limited (ILO 1991b:17).

In order to explore whether or not meaningful changes have occurred in non-wage collective bargaining outcomes, we follow Katz and Keefe (1992) in examining the prevalence of contract provisions based on the Bureau of National Affairs (BNA) publication *Basic Patterns in Union Contracts*. In what follows, we examine trends in collective bargaining contract outcomes over the 1975 to 1992 period in the textile industry in each of the following areas: wages and overtime, vacations and holiday, employment security, benefits and safety, seniority, and union security. We also note major differences between trends in the textile industry and the broader manufacturing industry (including textiles).

There are several limitations to the use of these BNA data. First, the textile industry contract data form a small subset of the total BNA contract sample of 400 contracts. Consequently, tests of statistical significance of differences in the prevalence of contract provisions across years in the textile industry are not appropriate. Further, the contract provision frequency data that are available for the textile industry do not always include the same issues or areas as the data available for "all industries," which is the industrial group discussed in Katz and Keefe (1992). This resulted in an inability to conduct direct comparisons with the conclusions reported by Katz and Keefe. Finally, it is not possible to determine the degree of "(un)favorableness to the union" of any given clause that may appear. Therefore, it is not always possible to determine whether or not changes in union contracts represent gains or losses to the union. Taken together, these issues suggest that caution must be exercised when drawing conclusions of meaningful changes in contract outcomes.[21] Since a minority of the textile industry is unionized, collective bargaining may be less likely to pattern. Rather, it is likely that bargaining outcomes may instead reflect conditions at individual firms, particularly as competitive pressures in the industry increased. Therefore, major changes in the frequency of provisions across years are likely to represent significant bargaining developments. In what follows, we outline some of the major changes in the frequency of contract provisions in the textile industry.

Wages and overtime provisions. In the area of wages and overtime provisions, there have been substantial changes in the proportion of contracts with clauses dealing with wage reopening (increase), wage progression (increase), job classifications (decrease), and both sixth- and seventh-day overtime (increase) (refer to Appendix Table). Increases in clauses dealing with wage reopeners and decreases in clauses relating to job classifications appear aimed at increasing financial and workplace flexibility. Interestingly, the substantial changes in the number of contracts with wage reopener and job classification clauses in textiles are in marked contrast to the trends in broader manufacturing, where the frequency of contracts with these clauses remained relatively stable. The observed increase in overtime clauses clearly suggests gains by the unions.

Vacation and holiday provisions. Between 1975 and 1992, the percentage of textile contracts providing vacations that total each of two, three, four, and five weeks unambiguously increased (refer to Appendix Table). This trend appears to follow the increase in the broader manufacturing sector, although the changes in manufacturing are much less striking. In addition, the number of common holidays allowed in 100% of the sampled textile contracts increased from three in 1975 to five in 1992, with a decline in frequency appearing for only one common holiday (Washington's Birthday). This trend toward a broader range of common holidays occurring in all contracts appears to run counter to trends in manufacturing. Taken together, these descriptive data suggest that there has been a steady expansion of vacation and holiday provisions in the textile industry.

Employment security. Employment security provisions have assumed great importance across manufacturing industries during the

1970s and 1980s as a consequence of employment dislocations brought on by restructuring and the introduction of labor-saving technologies. There were substantial increases in the frequency of textile contracts which contained key layoff provisions, including allowing exceptions to seniority and specifying recall, while there were decreases in income maintenance and severance provisions (Appendix Table). Importantly, for each of these employment security provisions, the trends in textiles were generally not reflective of changes that occurred in the broader manufacturing sector. In the textile industry these trends suggest that unions lost ground in this key area over the 1970s and 1980s.

Insurance benefits. With the exception of accidental death and dismemberment benefits, the relative number of contracts with a range of insurance benefits (such as hospitalization, doctor's visits, and major medical) declined over the 1975 to 1992 period (Appendix Table). In each case the trend was reflective of similar trends occurring in the manufacturing sector. This trend in textiles is consistent with interview information (Raynor 1992) that suggests that firms are attempting to limit or cut back benefits.[22]

One issue here is whether comprehensive medical packages are replacing these individual insurance benefits as an offsetting trend. The data are not conclusive on this.

Safety and health benefits. One of the long-run areas of concern to management and unions has been health and safety. Technological change has been a major factor in improving working conditions by reducing airborne particulant and noise levels (Mika and Carroll 1992; ILO 1991:84; Dumas and Henneberger 1988:35).

Unions appear to have made substantial gains in a number of key areas related to safety and health (Appendix Table). Between 1975 and 1992, the relative frequency of contracts with provisions in each of the following key areas increased: general provisions, general statement of responsibility, company to comply with laws, and safety committees. Trends for these provisions in textiles appear to follow similar trends in manufacturing.

Seniority provisions. Unions have clearly made significant gains in negotiating a range of clauses related to the application of seniority (Appendix Table). These trends reflect similar increases in the frequency of contracts with these clauses in manufacturing.

Union security. With the exception of check-off clauses (which increased dramatically), the data suggest little change in the frequency of contracts with various union security provisions (see Appendix Table). The lack of union security clauses is consistent with the location of most textile firms in right-to-work states (Raynor 1992).

Taken together, these data are consistent with the view that unions have not been able to achieve major gains in key areas related to wages and employment. Wage levels have not changed significantly through the 1980s, and employers have actually achieved some degree of increased flexibility in contracts. Despite significant downsizing, gains in employment and income security were not achieved as they were in some manufacturing industries such as automobiles, where innovative programs such as the Job Opportunity Bank and SUBs were negotiated (Kumar and Meltz 1992:65).

Conclusion

Labor relations in the textile industry are substantially determined by the fact that the industry has been and remains predominantly nonunion. This reality may be explained by a number of factors including readily transferable technology, traditionally labor-intensive production methods, and a highly competitive product market. In the early part of the twentieth century, a nonunion strategy on the part of employers led to the location of the industry in the southern Piedmont. This allowed textile manufacturers to benefit from a work force with few economic alternatives and a population unsympathetic to unions. Combined with aggressive employer resistance to unionization, as evidenced by the actions of major firms such as J.P. Stevens, organizing drives have had little success. Furthermore, since unions have organized only a small proportion of the industry, their ability to raise wages and benefits above the levels prevailing in nonunion establishments has been very limited.

However, conditions seem to be rapidly changing on both the demand and the supply sides of the labor market in the textile industry. Leiter (1988) has suggested that three major factors have had a significant impact on the ability of unions to organize the industry: innovation in production technology, an increasing proportion of African-American workers, and a shift in ownership from privately held, family-owned firms to publicly held corporate enterprises.

Technology has changed the production function so that relative to labor, capital is a more significant factor of production. Consequently, labor costs are becoming less important as a determinant of industry competitiveness. In addition, technological change has raised entry barriers, as capital costs have increased substantially. Finally, new technologies and associated changes in work organization, production methods, and marketing strategies (e.g., quick response) have led to increased skill and training requirements (Benton, Bailey, Noyelle, and Stanback 1991:50-53). Consequently, resulting productivity increases should sustain wage growth under unionism (Leiter 1988:20), and the increasing importance of skilled workers could reduce the possibility of substituting nonunion labor once the work force is organized.

There is some evidence that African Americans in the textile industry are more favorably inclined to support unionism and that the proportion of African-American workers is increasing. This demographic shift should assist union attempts to organize textile workers (Leiter 1988:18). However, Leiter also suggests that white workers, who tend to occupy skilled positions, remain the key to organizing the work force (p. 21).

Leiter also points out that the rise of corporate ownership, while perhaps favoring unionization due to the increased economies in organizing or greater potential for mounting effective national campaigns, is also associated with several disadvantages, including having the financial resources either to shift production away from union plants (including closure) or to withstand strikes (p. 18).

Another factor substantially influencing the environment for union organizing is increased industrial development in the southern Piedmont. This trend has expanded job opportunities in the region and appears to have been accompanied by shifts in worker attitudes toward unionization. As employment opportunities outside the industry improve, workers have become less attached to textile firms and more willing to challenge managerial authority.

But perhaps the most significant factor determining future textile labor relations is whether or not the labor movement continues to be willing to organize workers. Over the course of 90 years of organizing there have been few victories, but many defeats, and managerial hostility to unionism has diminished slightly, if at all. Furthermore, the industry has undergone considerable corporate restructuring and employment downsizing since the early 1980s, leading to hopelessness in some quarters about organizing.

Nonetheless, at present ACTWU seems committed to continuing its attempt to organize the Southern textile industry. In 1993, ACTWU was successful in 11 out of 12 Southern textile bargaining unit representation elections—increasing representation by 3,400 workers. Ironically, corporate cutbacks in full-time employment, wages, and benefits seem to have contributed to union success (*AFL-CIO News*, Nov. 1, 1993). Hence, while the future prospects for textile unionism may well continue to reflect the failures of the past, one cannot dismiss labor as long as ACTWU remains dedicated to the difficult task of organizing.

Acknowledgments and Authors' Note

The authors thank Edward E. Carroll, Keir Jorgenson, Harold M. McLeod, W. J. Mika, and Bruce Raynor for helping us understand the industry; Mark Pitt for comments on a previous version of this chapter; and Tiza Soledad Flores, Michel Greiche, and Brian Lewis for superlative research assistance. The authors are listed alphabetically. Equal contributions were made by each.

Endnotes

[1] In addition, since commodity prices fluctuate considerably, large cotton textile manufacturers are able to reduce raw material costs by purchasing large quantities when prices are low (Office of Technology Assessment 1987).

[2] This movement began when David Murdock, following an unsuccessful bid to acquire Dan River, Inc., purchased Cannon Mills in 1982. (Cannon Mills had been the object of an unsuccessful takeover attempt by a group headed by Harold Geneen, the former chairman of International Telephone and Telegraph, during the previous year.) Murdock sold Cannon's sheet and towel division to Fieldcrest Mills in 1985, a few weeks after the ACTWU was defeated in an attempt to organize Cannon employees. In 1983 the management of Dan River fended off a takeover attempt by Carl Icahn (who later purchased TWA) by selling Dan River to an employee-owned holding company established by the company's employee stock ownership plan (ESOP). One year later the management of Cone Mills took the company private in a leveraged buyout using ESOP funds.

[3] In the previous year, Dominion Textiles had unsuccessfully attempted to acquire Avondale Mills, an Alabama textile concern that was eventually purchased by Walter Monroe Mills.

[4] Political concern stemmed from the notion that Edelman intended to break up Burlington and sell off the pieces.

[5] The acquisition movement continued the following year. A takeover attempt by West Point-Pepperell led to the dismemberment of J.P. Stevens, which divided its assets between Bibb Co., Oddessey Partners, and West Point-Pepperell. West Point-Pepperell was later acquired by William Farley, with junk bonds financed by the investment banking firm of Drexel, Burnham, Lambert, Inc. Farley surrendered control of West Point-Pepperell after he was unable to make interest payments on the debt incurred in his takeover. Joe Lanier, Jr., the former chairman of West Point-

Pepperell who had contested the Farley acquisition, led a buyout of Dan River in 1989.

[6] The origins of the MFA can be traced to the 1950s when imports of Japanese cotton products began to threaten American textile manufacturers. This led to the negotiation in 1956 of a bilateral treaty limiting Japanese exports. However, an expansion of textile imports from other nations (in particular, Hong Kong) led to the negotiation of the Short-Term Arrangement on Cotton-Textiles in 1961 and the Long-Term Arrangement (LTA) in 1962, which permitted industrialized nations to restrict the import of cotton textiles. The MFA extended the principles of the LTA to manmade fibres, wool, or blended fibre textiles.

[7] It is important to remember that: (1) these numbers refer to primary textiles only and not wearing apparel and (2) low-wage exporting nations have specialized in high-volume, low-cost textiles, so that in volume terms (square feet of cloth or feet of yarn) these import penetration figures are much higher.

[8] Canada, with a similar or less advantageous cost structure, does not pose a significant threat to American textiles (Thomason, Zwerling, and Chandra 1992). While Mexico does not currently have a large textile sector, low-wage rates in that country place American manufacturers at a potential comparative disadvantage. Illustrating the potential risks of NAFTA for American textile workers, in March 1993 Cone Mills and Compania Industrial de Parras, Mexico's largest denim maker, agreed in principle to launch a joint venture to build denim manufacturing facilities in Mexico. While management of Cone Mills stated that this venture would not affect employment at their American plants, union officials were skeptical (*Wall Street Journal* 1993).

[9] Open-end systems can produce approximately 4.5 times more yarn than ring-spinning machines. However, ring-spinning produces higher quality yarn than open-end machines, although the quality of open-end spinning has improved in recent years (Isaacs 1990).

[10] Shuttleless looms are also less noisy than shuttle looms, reducing noise from over 100 dB to the 90-95 dB range.

[11] Opening and picking, whereby cotton bales are broken up into small tufts and blended together, is the initial process in yarn production. Carding, the next process in the chain, takes the material produced by opening and cleans and straightens the cotton fibers and orients them in a parallel direction. The "lap" is a thin sheet of cotton produced by the opening and picking process under older technology. Under older technologies, human labor in the opening and carding rooms was among the most arduous and dirty in the yarn mill. Chute-fed carding and automatic bale feeders have eliminated this back-breaking work and have reduced exposure to cotton dust by enclosing these processes.

[12] Adoption of QR has slowed in recent years (*Textile World* 1991). The principal roadblock to the implementation of QR has been the difficulty in forging alliances between textile, apparel, and retail companies, who have had longstanding adversarial relationships (Bonham 1991).

[13] Production costs were lower in the South for the following reasons: (1) southern wages were lower for a variety of reasons, including the absence of unions; (2) since southern mills were closer to raw material sources (cotton), transportation was less expensive; (3) taxes were lower; and (4) since the Southern mills had been built more recently, they had more modern equipment (Marshall 1967).

[14] For example, Rowan and Barr (1987) note that as a proportion of total textile employment, white-collar employees increased from 14.1% to 20.6% from 1966 to 1984. Most of this growth was due to increasing numbers of managerial, professional, and technical employees; together these three classifications grew from 7% to 12.6% of total employment during this period. Furthermore, skilled craftsmen grew from 17.2% to 19.8% of total blue-collar employment, while the proportion of operatives and laborers declined.

[15] The UTW was a charter member of the CIO and TWOC. However, a dispute between Francis Gorman, president of the UTW, and Sidney Hillman, president of the AWCA and chairman of the TWOC, caused Gorman to lead a handful of UTW locals (with only 1,500 members) out of the CIO in 1938. The AFL reconstituted the UTW in 1939 using the remaining UTW locals and several federal locals (Hodges 1986:176).

[16] In all, the Darlington litigation lasted more than 24 years, from the initial filing of ULP charges in 1956 until the backpay settlement was reached in December 1980 (Wall Street Journal 1980a). By July 1981, Milliken and Company's $5 million payment was distributed to the former Darlington employees, who actually received $3 million after taxes; 144 of approximately 550 discharged workers were deceased as of this date. No former employees were reinstated (Eames 1974). To date, Milliken has no unionized employees (Rowan and Barr 1987).

[17] Darlington Manufacturing Co. v. NLRB, 165 NLRB 1074 (1967), 397 F. 2d 760 (4th Cir. 1968), cert. denied, 393 U.S. 1023 (1969).

[18] The union also sued J.P. Stevens for electronically eavesdropping on organizers' motel rooms in Wallace, North Carolina and for invading organizers' rights to privacy, free speech, and association by spying on them in Milledgeville, Georgia (Lemner 1980).

[19] On the heels of the TWUA's victory at the J.P. Stevens at Roanoke Rapids, the close vote in the Cannon election raised concerns that southern textile workers were no longer hostile to unionism. One unnamed management observer elaborated on this concern: "Today's textile worker is more mobile, more vocal, and more independent than his parents. And increasingly, he is young and black." (Textile World 1974:23).

[20] Ronald Morgan, an NLRB attorney in the Winston-Salem office, stated that this was one of the largest unfair labor practices cases processed in that region since the J.P. Stevens litigation of the 1970s (BNA 1992b).

[21] In this discussion, changes in the frequency of sampled contracts (as a percentage of industry contracts) that were on the order of 15 to 20 percentage points were considered important.

[22] One recent development in employee benefits is the negotiation of Section 401(k) retirement plans, which are similar to Individual Retirement Accounts (IRAs), where employers match employee contributions. Section 401(k) plans have begun to replace defined benefit pensions that were common in the industry but generally paid low levels of benefits. The merger wave of the 1980s also led to the negotiation of ESOPs. For example, recently ACTWU negotiated a collective agreement with Cone Mills that creates a Section 401(k) plan into which employees can receive common stock and can transfer ESOP funds (BNA 1992d).

References

AFL-CIO News. 1992. "ACTWU wins $950,000 at S. Lichtenberg." Vol. 37, no. 13 (June), p. 12.

_____. 1993. "ACTWU on Win Streak in the South." Vol. 37, No. 23 (November), p. 12.

Bailey, Thomas. 1988. "Education and the Transformation of Markets and Technology in the Textile Industry." National Center on Education and Employment, Technical Paper No. 2.

Benton, Lauren, Thomas R. Bailey, Thierry Noyelle, and Thomas M. Stanback, Jr. 1991. *Employee Training and U.S. Competitiveness: Lessons for the 1990s*. Boulder, CO: Westview Press, Inc.

Bonham, Julia C. 1991. "Robotics, Electronics and the American Textile Industry." In J. Leiter, M. Schulman, and R. Zingraff, eds., *Hanging by a Thread: Social Change in Southern Textiles*. Ithaca, NY: ILR Press, pp. 163-180.

Brannigan, Martha. 1992. "Loss is Reported for Burlington Industries Equity." *The Wall Street Journal*, May 7, p. B6.

Bronson, Gail, and Jeffrey H. Birnbaum. 1980a. "Labor Milestone: How the Textile Union Finally Wins Contracts at J.P. Stevens Plants." *The Wall Street Journal*, October 20, p. 1, 24.

_____. 1980b. "Rogers' Tough, Unorthodox Tactics Prevail in Stevens Organizing Fight." *The Wall Street Journal*, October 21, p. 37, 42.

Cohen, Laurie P., and Linda Williams. 1987. "Companies Provide Illustrations of Problems in Buy-Out Business." *The Wall Street Journal*, November 6, 1987.

Bureau of National Affairs (BNA). 1991a. "ACTWU Attempts to Unionize 9,000 at North Carolina Textile Plant." *Daily Labor Report*, June 21, p. A2.

_____. 1991b. "Georgia Firm Ordered by ALJ to Pay $1 Million in Back Wages." *Daily Labor Report*, April, p. A1.

_____. 1991c. "Results of Fieldcrest Cannon Election Uncertain Due to 538 Challenged Ballots." *Daily Labor Report*, August 23, p. A7.

_____. 1992a. "ACTWU Loses Fieldcrest Cannon Vote." *Daily Labor Report*, October 29, p. A12.

_____. 1992b. "NLRB Hearing Scheduled on ACTWU Complaints Against Fieldcrest Cannon." *Daily Labor Report*, March 9, p. A1.

_____. 1992c. "NLRB Obtains Interim Injunction in First-Time Ruling by Eleventh Circuit." *Daily Labor Report*, February, p. A4.

_____. 1992d. "ACTWU Workers Approve Two-Year Pact at Three Cone Mills Plants in North Carolina." *Daily Labor Report*, June 10, pp. A2-A3.

Dumas, Mark, and J. Edwin Henneberger. 1988. "Productivity Trends in the Cotton and Synthetic Broad Woven Fabrics Industry." *Monthly Labor Review* (April), pp. 34-38.

Eames, Patricia C. 1974. "The History of the Litigation of Darlington as an Exercise in Administrative Procedure." *University of Toledo Law Review*, Vol. 5, pp. 595-607.

The Economist. 1990. "Jousting for Advantage." September 22, pp. 6-39.

Guyon, Janet. 1981. "More Offers for Textile Concerns Are to Follow Geneen Group Bid for Cannon Mills." *The Wall Street Journal*, January 8, p. 39.

Hall, Jacquelyn Dowd, Robert Korstad, and James Leloudis. 1986. "Cotton Mill People: Work, Community, and Protest in the Textile South, 1880-1940." *American Historical Review*, Vol. 91, pp. 245-86.

Hayes, Arthur S. 1992. "Law: Minnesota Court Eliminates Case Backlog." *The Wall Street Journal*, June 8, p. B8.

Hodges, James A. 1986. *New Deal Labor Policy and the Southern Cotton Textile Industry, 1933-1941.* Knoxville, TN: The University of Tennessee Press.

_____. 1991. "J.P. Stevens and the Union: Struggle for the South." Paper presented at the Southern Labor Studies Conference, Atlanta, Georgia.

International Labour Organization (ILO), Textiles Committee. 1991a. *General Report, Twelfth Session.* Geneva: International Labour Office.

_____. 1991b. *Vocational Training and Retraining in the Textiles Industry.* Geneva: International Labour Office.

Isaacs, McAllister, III. 1989. "World Class Manufacturers Cut Labor Needs in Half." *Textile World* (October), pp. 71-76.

_____. 1990a. "Automation and Quality Key Spinning in the '90s," *Textile World* (January), pp. 45-55.

_____. 1990b. "Weaving in the '90s: More Air, Automation." *Textile World* (September), pp. 45-49.

_____. 1990c. "Manufacturing: Pace of Change is Breathtaking." *Textile World* (October), pp. 21-30.

Jacoby, Sanford M. 1985. *Employing Bureaucracy: Managers, Unions, and the Transformation of Work in American Industry, 1900-1945.* New York: Columbia University Press.

Katz, Harry, and Jeffrey Keefe. 1992. "Collective Bargaining and Industrial Relations Outcomes: The Causes and Consequences of Diversity." In D. Lewin, O. Mitchell, and P. Sherer, eds., *Research Frontiers in Industrial Relations and Human Resources.* Madison, WI: IRRA.

Kilman, Scott. 1986. "Textile Companies Rapidly Stake Out Niches: Merger Wave Promises Fewer but Stronger Mills." *The Wall Street Journal*, February 5, p. 6.

Kokkelenberg, Edward C., and Donna R. Sockell. 1985. "Union Membership in the United States, 1973-1981." *Industrial and Labor Relations Review*, Vol. 38, No. 4, pp. 497-543.

Kumar, Pradeep, and Noah Meltz. 1992. "Industrial Relations in the Canadian Automobile Industry." In R. Chaykowski and A. Verma, eds., *Industrial Relations in Canadian Industry.* Toronto: Holt, Rinehart and Winston.

Leiter, Jeffrey. 1986. "Reactions to Subordination: Attitudes of Southern Textile Workers." *Social Forces*, Vol. 64, pp. 948-974.

_____. 1988. "Prospects for Southern Textile Unionization." *Labour Studies Journal*, Vol. 14, No. 4, pp. 13-23.

Lemner, Urban C. 1980. "Southern Hospitality? As Union Organizers Get to Milledgeville, GA, the Mayor Holds an Unusual Welcoming Party." *The Wall Street Journal*, February 29, p. 42.

Long, Jody. 1982a. "In a Company Town Like Kannapolis, NC, Selling the Company Brings Lots of Worries." *The Wall Street Journal*, February 4, p. 33.

_____. 1982b. "Textile Stocks Are Getting Unusual Attention as Bargain Hunters Take Substantial Positions." *The Wall Street Journal*, March 25, p. 49.

_____. 1982c. "Textile Town Is Hit Hard by Recession." *The Wall Street Journal*, October 25, p. 33.

Lublin, Joann S. 1983. "J.P. Stevens Agrees to Spend $1.2 Million to End 20-Year War With Clothing Union." *The Wall Street Journal*, October 21, p. 60.

Marshall, F. Ray. 1967. *Labor in the South*. Boston: Harvard University Press.

McDonald, Joseph A., and Donald A. Clelland. 1984. "Textile Workers and Union Sentiment." *Social Forces*, Vol. 63, pp. 502-522.

Mika, W., and E. Carroll. 1992. Interview: Dan River Company.

MIT Commission on Industrial Productivity. 1989. "The U.S. Textile Industry: Challenges and Opportunities." Working Paper.

Mullins, Terry W., and Paul Luebke. 1982. "Symbolic Victory and Political Reality in the Southern Textile Industry: The Meaning of the J.P. Stevens Settlement for Southern Labor Relations." *Journal of Labor Research*, Vol. 3, pp. 81-88.

Office of Technology Assessment. 1987. *The U.S. Textile and Apparel Industry: A Revolution in Progress*. Washington, DC: Government Printing Office.

Penn, Roger, and Jeffrey Leiter. 1991. "Employment Patterns in the British and U.S. Textile Industries: A Comparative Analysis of Recent Gender Changes." In J. Leiter, M. Schulman, and R. Zingraff, eds., *Hanging by a Thread: Social Change in Southern Textiles*. Ithaca, NY: ILR Press, pp. 139-162.

Perry, Charles R. 1987. *Union Corporate Campaigns*. Philadelphia, PA: Industrial Research Unit, Wharton School, University of Pennsylvania.

Raynor, Bruce. 1977. "Unionism in the Southern Textile Industry: An Overview." In G. Fink and M. Reed, eds., *Essays in Southern Labor History*. Westport, CT: Greenwood Press, pp. 80-99.

_____. 1992. Interview: ACTWU.

Reif, Linda L., Michael D. Schulman, and Michael J. Belyea. 1988. "The Social Bases of Union Support: An Analysis of Southern Textile Workers." *Journal of Political and Military Sociology*, Vol. 16, pp. 57-75.

Rowan, Richard L., and Robert E. Barr. 1987. *Employee Relations: Trends and Practices in the Textile Industry*. Philadelphia, PA: Industrial Relations Research Unit, Wharton School, University of Pennsylvania.

Ruffenach, Glenn, and George Anders. 1992. "Big Textile Firm Is Accused in Suit of 'Gutting' ESOP." *The Wall Street Journal*, June 4, B7.

Schulman, Michael D., Rhonda Zingraff, and Linda Reif. 1985. "Race, Gender, Class Consciousness and Union Support: An Analysis of Southern Textile Workers." *The Sociological Quarterly*, Vol. 26, No. 2, pp. 187-204.

Sease, Douglas R. 1985. "Move to Fight Apparel Imports Is Set: Textile, Garment, Retail Concerns to Join Forces." *The Wall Street Journal*, December 17, p. 6.

Simpson, Richard L. 1981. "Labor Force Integration and Southern U.S. Textile Unionism." In R. Simpson and I. Simpson, eds., *Research in the Sociology of Work*, Vol. 1, Greenwich, CT: JAI Press, pp. 381-401.

Sparks, Philip. 1975. "The Darlington Case: Justice Delayed Is Justice Denied." *Labor Law Journal* (December), pp. 759-766.

Textile World. 1974. "Cannon, 'Yes,' Union, 'No': Here's What It Means," November, pp. 23-24.

_____. 1977. "Can the Union Win the 1-Million Worker Tug-O-War?," March, pp. 39-42.

_____. 1978. "Is the Union Trying to Isolate J.P. Stevens?," August, pp. 23-24.

_____. 1980a. "Corporate Campaign No Factor, Says Stevens," November, pp. 23-24, 27.

_____. 1980b. "Full Text of the Stevens-ACTW Union Agreement . . .," November, pp. 27, 30-32.

_____. 1983. "Stevens, ACTWU Strike an Accord," November, pp. 23, 27.

_____. 1990. "Textiles in the '90s: A Decade of Change," January, pp. 42-45.

_____. 1991. "QR Update: Technology's There, Partners Aren't," May, p. 26.

Thomas, Hugh. 1982. *A History of the World, Revised and Augmented Edition*. New York: Harper Torchbooks.

Thomason, Terry, Harris L. Zwerling, and Pankaj Chandra. 1992. "Labour Relations in the Canadian Textile Industry." In R. Chaykowski and A. Verma, eds., *Industrial Relations in Canadian Industry*. Toronto: Holt, Rinehart, and Winston, pp. 244-283.

Tindall, George Brown. 1984. *America: A Narrative History*, Volume 1. New York: W.W. Norton.

Waldman, Peter, and Alan Freeman. 1987. "Burlington Industries' Denim Plant Sale Catapults Old Rival to Near Top of Field." *The Wall Street Journal*, November 9, p. 7.

Wall Street Journal. 1980a. "Milliken Agrees to Pay Ex-Textile Workers $5 Million Settlement." December 4, p. 2.

_____. 1980b. "Stevens, Union Made Major Concessions to Stitch Together an Accord to End Row." October 20, p. 24.

_____. 1993a. "Business Briefs." February 8, p. B3.

_____. 1993b. "Business Briefs." March 30, p. B4.

Williams, Linda. 1985. "Textile Union Is Struggling to Organize Cannon Mills Workers as Ranks Shrink." *The Wall Street Journal*, January 16, p. 12.

Wright, Gavin. 1986. *Old South, New South: Revolutions in the Southern Economy Since the Civil War*. New York: Basic Books.

Zingraff, Rhonda. 1991. "Facing Extinction?" In J. Leiter, M. Schulman, and R. Zingraff, eds., *Hanging by a Thread: Social Change in Southern Textiles*. Ithaca, NY: ILR Press, pp. 199-216.

APPENDIX TABLE

Collective Agreement Provisions
(Frequency Expressed as Percentage of Industry Contracts)

	1975		1989		1992	
	Manuf.[a]	Textile[a]	Manuf.[b]	Textile[c]	Manuf.[b]	Textile[c]
1. Wage Provisions						
Deferred increase	91	61	75	50	89	50
Cost-of-living	43	6	33	NA	33	NA
Lump sums	NA	NA	25	10	29	10
Wage reopening	8	28	6	60	5	50
Two-tier system	NA	NA	29	10	27	NA
Wage progression	43	22	42	40	48	40
Reporting pay	85	100	91	100	93	100
Call-back, call-in	71	28	76	50	77	50
Temporary transfer	60	83	74	80	75	80
Wage incentive, piecework	49	83	49	70	45	70
Time Study	35	56	NA	NA	NA	NA
Job classification	65	89	93	90	93	90
Shift differential	92	89	93	90	93	90
Travel expenses	12	NA	16	NA	16	10
Hazard pay	5	NA	7	NA	7	NA
Work clothes	10	6	19	10	21	20
Tools	7	NA	17	NA	20	10
2. Overtime Provisions						
Provisions	99	100	99	100	99	100
Premium Pay for:						
Daily overtime	99	100	99	100	99	100
Weekly overtime	71	83	70	70	74	80
Sixth day overtime	19	22	25	40	25	40
Seventh day overtime	21	28	32	50	30	50
Saturday overtime	65	61	64	60	64	60
Sunday overtime	78	72	78	80	75	80
Layoff to avoid prohibited	24	6	25	NA	26	NA
Pyramiding prohibited	73	61	75	90	74	70
Advance Notice required	28	11	36	NA	40	NA
Distribution procedures	68	33	74	70	76	70
3. Amount of Vacation						
Percentage of contracts providing vacations totalling:						
1 week	80	78	79	80	79	90
2 weeks	89	83	97	100	96	100
3 weeks	88	50	97	100	96	100

APPENDIX TABLE (*Continued*)

Collective Agreement Provisions

(Frequency Expressed as Percentage of Industry Contracts)

	1975		1989		1992	
	Manuf.[a]	Textile[a]	Manuf.[b]	Textile[c]	Manuf.[b]	Textile[c]
4 weeks	82	44	93	90	94	90
5 weeks	45	22	66	40	66	50
6 weeks or more	12	NA	24	NA	25	NA
4. Common Holidays						
New Year's Day	97	89	98	100	98	100
Washington's Birthday	24	22	28	20	27	10
Good Friday	61	28	67	30	70	40
Memorial Day	96	72	95	60	96	70
Independence Day	100	94	98	90	97	100
Labor Day	100	100	99	100	99	100
Veterans Day	14	17	11	NA	11	
Thanksgiving	100	100	99	100	98	100
Day after Thanksgiving	60	28	78	30	80	30
Christmas Eve	68	50	70	100	99	100
Christmas	99	100	99	100	99	100
New Year's Eve	37	6	45	10	48	10
Employee's Birthday	10	0	16		15	10
Floating	14	6	17	20	17	20
5. Layoff Provisions						
Seniority applied in layoffs	93	94	95	100	96	100
Exceptions to seniority allowed	61	56	64	90	62	80
Advance notice of layoff required	52	22	57	20	57	20
Recall specified	80	67	90	90	96	90
Bumping permitted	63	50	72	90	75	80
Worksharing permitted	24	28	24	20	23	20
Provision for tech. displacement	8	17	NA	NA	NA	NA
Income maintenance provision	53	39	54	20	54	20
Work or pay guarantee	8	6	6	10	7	10
Severance	45	33	45	10	45	10
SUB	21	NA	13	NA	20	NA
6. Employee Insurance Provisions						
Life insurance	98	100	90	100	99	100
Accident, disability, and death	66	78	74	83	76	100
Sickness and accident	88	89	91	100	90	100
Transition and bridge	15	0	NA	NA	NA	NA

APPENDIX TABLE (*Continued*)

Collective Agreement Provisions

(Frequency Expressed as Percentage of Industry Contracts)

	1975		1989		1992	
	Manuf.[a]	Textile[a]	Manuf.[b]	Textile[c]	Manuf.[b]	Textile[c]
Hospitalization	97	100	65	33	64	29
Surgical	94	94	65	33	54	29
Doctor's benefits	53	44	42	17	32	14
Major medical	65	61	60	33	47	29
Maternity benefits	69	61	NA	NA	NA	NA
Miscellaneous medical expenses	61	56	53	17	47	29
Comprehensive medical	NA	NA	35	67	47	71
Dental	NA	NA	41	NA	39	NA
7. Safety and Health Provisions						
Provisions	85	78	94	100	96	100
General statement of responsibility	56	56	68	100	68	100
Company to comply with laws	24	11	33	30	35	30
Company provides safety equip.	38	NA	49	30	49	40
Company provides first aid	23	11	25	10	26	10
Physical examinations	24	6	34	10	33	NA
Accident investigations	15	11	24	NA	26	NA
Hazardous work provisions	13	NA	26	20	29	20
Safety committees	47	17	62	40	65	40
8. Seniority Provisions						
Probationary periods	80	77	92	90	93	100
Lists required	67	83	82	100	80	100
Vacancies posted	57	50	72	80	74	80
Layoffs in seniority	93	94	83	80	81	80
Promotions in seniority	76	78	95	100	96	100
Transfers in seniority	53	56	69	70	68	70

Source: Bureau of National Affairs, Basic Patterns in Union Contracts, 8th edition; 12th edition; 13th edition; Washington, DC: BNA 1975, 1989, 1992.

[a] Number of contracts is not available.

[b] Number of contracts is 245.

[c] Number of contracts is 18.

CHAPTER 10

Developments in Collective Bargaining in Construction in the 1980s and 1990s

STEVEN G. ALLEN
North Carolina State University
and National Bureau of Economic Research

Editor's Abstract

This review of labor relations in the construction industry is focused on the rise of the open shop over the past two decades. In the mid-1960s, half of all construction employees were union members. Today, fewer than one-fourth are union.

The economic context has been one of boom and bust since 1979. High interest rates had disastrous consequences for employment and output in the early 1980s. Starting in 1984, construction recovered in the residential and commercial areas, but highway, industrial, and government work remained depressed. This lasted until 1989. Then overbuilding in the commercial sector took its toll and resulted in an early 1990s downturn in construction activity. In sum, the boom was modest (industry unemployment never fell below 10% for the entire 1980s) and biased toward nonunion work—residential construction which is heavily nonunion and commercial construction which is increasingly so, especially outside urban centers.

After reviewing the institutional structure of collective bargaining in construction, Allen examines various explanations for declining unionization. He ultimately concludes that the primary onus rests on judicial and NLRB interpretation of labor law that facilitated double-breasting, especially after 1977, with a secondary explanation being increased management willingness to use nonunion construction contractors. Key decisions included *Kiewit* (1977) which facilitated "double-breasting" (establishment of a nonunion subsidiary by a union contractor), *R.J. Smith* (1971), and *Deklewa* (1987) which allowed contractors to escape prehire agreements at their expiration.

Allen considers and rejects two alternative explanations, both related to the idea that a rising cost differential made union construction less competitive. First, he considers trends in compensation. He finds that a rising wage gap between union and nonunion labor in the late 1960s and early 1970 may have provided an impetus to the initial increase in attempts by contractors to go nonunion. However, non-union wages rose more rapidly than union wages in the 1980s. Hence compensation trends are not a plausible explanation for union decline. Second, Allen examines productivity differentials. Early in the 1970s, union construction workers were so much more productive than non-union workers that their productivity entirely justified their higher earnings. However, the productivity gap narrowed somewhat between 1972 and 1977, perhaps because well-trained union members were increasingly working on nonunion jobs. Nonetheless, productivity differences have apparently stayed constant since 1977. Hence the explosion of nonunion work cannot be explained by a rising cost differential over the 1980s.

The union decline has stabilized since 1986, perhaps because the building trades unions are pursuing efforts at labor-management cooperation (strikes are down sharply) and are exploring job targeting—whereby union contractors are paid part of the wage differential between union and nonunion labor. Organizing is up in some locales, sometimes through "salting" the work force of nonunion contractors with union loyalists and, then, either organizing the project or disrupting it. Allen argues that labor law is unlikely to be changed sufficiently to reverse the phenomenon of double-breasting and the associated union decline in construction. The unions will come back only if they become even more competitive by capitalizing on their strongest asset: training.

o　o　o

Firms in the construction industry build and renovate structures. The industry has four major sectors: residential, commercial (mostly retail and office space), industrial, and heavy and highway. Most construction is done by independent contractors who must continuously compete for new projects. Some are general contractors who bid for an entire project. Some general contractors hire all employees directly, but the more common practice is to subcontract most of the work to specialty trade contractors. This means that the mix of firms and employees working on a project is constantly changing from the initial stage of groundclearing until the final touch-up of the interior.

Construction work has a number of unique characteristics that are reflected in its industrial and work organization. Construction jobs on a particular site are of relatively short duration. Over the course of a year, a construction worker may literally be employed at dozens of different locations. Job instability is exacerbated by technological and financial forces. Most of the work is done outside, so work schedules are often interrupted by the weather. A large share of construction projects is financed with borrowed money, making the industry extremely sensitive to interest rates and credit availability.

Construction work calls for a wide range of skills. Some tasks done by laborers require absolutely no training or previous work experience, whereas much of the work done by electricians requires years of training. Because most jobs are short term, employers have no incentives to provide training unless the costs can be shifted to another party. Most construction skills also are marketable outside the industry.

Industry Developments

Value added from the construction industry directly accounted for 5% of the nation's output and employment throughout the 1980s. The value of construction projects put in place accounts for 9% of national output. This larger figure reflects the fact that output and employment in many other industries—most notably lumber, cement, stone products, metal products, and machinery—is directly used as an input in construction.

The industry has gone through a bust-boom-bust cycle since 1979. Inflation soared to double-digit levels in that year, partly because of increased oil prices. Lenders required higher interest rates to offset the greater loss in purchasing power. The prime rate rose from 9% in 1978 to 13% in 1979 and 15% in 1980. To reduce inflation, the Federal Reserve Board pushed interest rates up even further. The prime rate peaked at 19% in 1981 and declined only modestly to 15% in 1982 (modest because inflation had dropped to 4% in that year). Other interest rates, including home mortgages, followed a similar pattern.

The consequences of high interest rates for the construction industry were disastrous. Real GNP in construction dropped by 8.4% in 1980, followed by further declines of 2.0% and 6.2% in 1981-82. Employment fell by 2.6% in 1980, 3.7% in 1981, and 7.0% in 1982. Unemployment for construction workers is always higher than in other sectors because of time needed to search for new work in between jobs. It increased from 10.1% in 1979 (compared to 5.8% for all experienced workers) to 14.4% in 1980 and 20.1% in 1982—the highest rate in any major sector of the economy since World War II.

The industry recovered along with the rest of the economy in the next four years. Output grew by 3.7% in 1983 and 9.1% in 1984. Most of the boost in 1984 came from two sectors: residential and commercial. Later in the 1980s state and local construction also picked up. Federal construction stayed level throughout the decade and industrial construction activity stayed below its 1982 level for most of the decade. By 1985 construction employment had risen above its 1979 peak and continued growing through 1989.

Construction activity fell in both 1990 and 1991, and at the time this was written, output remains below the 1989 level.[1] Value put in place declined from an annual rate of $464.4 billion in March 1990 to $394.3 billion in June 1991. Employment dropped by 1.0% in 1990, 9.0% in 1991, and 1.8% in 1992. The unemployment rate for construction workers jumped upward in 1991 and 1992 to 15.4% and 17.1%.

The biggest decline in construction activity occurred in the commercial sector. This was a consequence of overbuilding that took place in the 1980s, fueled by favorable changes in the tax treatment of structures in 1981 (later reversed by the tax reform bill in 1986) and speculative lending by savings and loan associations. Square footage put in place in commercial and industrial construction combined was lower in 1991 than in any year since 1961; almost all of this decline took place in the commercial sector. There also was a sharp drop in residential construction in 1990 and 1991.

The most notable trend in the composition of the industry is the rising share of commercial construction in the 1980s. This sector, which represented about 10% of all activity before the 1980s, grew to 17% in the latter part of that decade. Industrial construction has declined in importance. There also has been a slow but steady drop in the share of public construction from 30% in the late 1960s to 20% for much of the 1980s. Most of this drop comes from construction by state and local governments. The federal government's direct share fell by one percentage point in the 1980s. The change in its indirect share is impossible to gauge because there is no breakdown in the state and local construction series by whether the projects are fully or partially funded by the federal government.

What implications do these developments in the construction industry have for industrial relations? The most significant fact is that despite the growth in output and employment that took place between 1983 and 1989, economic conditions largely have checked the pressure for wage increases. Unemployment in the industry never got below 10% in the 1980s, in contrast to 1966-69 when it got down to 6%. The peak year for commercial and industrial construction was 1985, but square footage put in place that year was below the previous peak in 1979 and comparable to the level observed at the 1973 peak. This indicates that even in the healthiest sector of the industry, there was less pressure on wages than in previous expansions.

Second, the declining share of public-sector construction implies that a smaller share of construction jobs are being covered by prevailing wage laws.[2] These laws still frequently require union wage scales to be paid to all workers, thereby discouraging nonunion contractors from bidding for this type of work. With fewer jobs being covered by these laws, the competitiveness of the nonunion open shop increased.

Third, even though increased commercial construction normally would mean more jobs for union workers, this may not have been the case in the 1980s. Much of the new office and retail space was put in place in new suburbs and almost all of this work was done by the open shop.

The Workers

Changes in worker characteristics in the construction industry are reported in Table 1. Construction workers became younger, with the average age declining from 37.0 to 35.7 between 1977-78 and 1989. The trend in the overall labor force runs in the opposite direction because of the aging of the baby boomers. Construction is an exception because of a large drop-off in the percentage of workers 45 and over (from 31.1% to 23.7% of the labor force).

The racial mix of employment is an especially sensitive issue in construction. Even after the passage of the Civil Rights Act of 1964, many union locals continued to engage in overt discrimination by race. A number of policies were implemented to deal with this issue, including increased enrollment of blacks in apprenticeship programs, regulations setting minimal ratios for minority employment in publicly funded projects, set-aside programs for minority contractors, and of course, litigation.

Despite these efforts, there was very little change in the racial composition of the construction labor force in the 1980s. The percentage of black employees did not change between 1977-78 and 1989. The union sector of construction has made very modest progress in hiring minorities, but there has been absolutely no progress in the open shop. The percentage of union employees who were white did drop modestly from 90.6% to 89.0%, whereas the percentage of nonunion employees who were white was exactly 91% in both periods.[3]

Schooling and occupation are signals of the skill level of the work force. Schooling levels for workers in the industry rose in the 1980s. In

TABLE 1

Percentage Distribution of Construction Industry Employees
by Age, Gender, Race, Schooling, and Occupation

	May 1977-78	1989
Age		
Under 20	6.7	5.2
20-24	16.6	13.8
25-29	14.4	18.4
30-34	12.0	16.7
35-44	19.2	22.2
45-54	17.8	14.1
55-64	11.1	8.4
65 and over	2.2	1.2
Gender		
Male	93.0	90.4
Female	7.0	9.6
Race		
White	91.4	90.5
Black	6.6	6.5
Other	1.9	2.9
Years of Schooling		
Under 12	35.4	24.4
12	43.5	50.5
13-15	14.7	17.0
16 or more	6.4	8.0
Major Occupations		
Executive, administrative, and managerial	11.6	8.0
Professional specialty	1.8	2.5
Technicians and related support	0.7	1.1
Sales	0.4	0.9
Administrative support	6.4	6.5
Services and other	0.8	0.8
Precision production, craft, and repair	52.0	55.1
Machine operators, assemblers, and inspectors	1.7	1.7
Transportation and material moving	9.4	9.3
Handlers, equipment cleaners, helpers and laborers	15.1	14.1
Selected Crafts		
Brickmasons and stonemasons	2.5	2.2
Carpenters	16.7	13.3
Drywall installers	1.5	1.6
Electricians	4.1	5.5
Painters, construction, and maintenance	5.6	4.0
Plumbers and pipefitters	4.6	4.1
Roofers	1.7	1.9
Total, selected crafts	36.8	32.6

Source: CPS public use tapes.

1977-78, 35.4% of the workers had not completed high school; this figure had dropped to 24.4% in 1989. A smaller share of workers is employed as managers and laborers, whereas a larger share is employed in skilled crafts.[4] Because of changes in the occupational code used by the Census Bureau, it is possible to make exact comparisons for only a limited set of occupations.[5] Carpenters dropped from 16.7% to 13.3% of the labor force and painters dropped from 5.6% to 4.0%, whereas electricians increased from 4.1% to 5.5% of the labor force. More importantly, the combined share in the traditional skilled occupations categories dropped from 36.8% to 32.6%. Although a larger share of construction workers were employed in skilled production jobs, a smaller share was employed in the traditional building trades. This is indicative of a transformation in the nature of work across traditional occupational lines. Further evidence in support of such a trend is the increase in the share of workers in a skilled trade but no specific occupation from 0.2% to 2.1%.

Labor Institutions in Construction

Historical Background

The birth of today's union movement in the building trades can be traced to Peter McGuire's launching of the United Brotherhood of Carpenters and Joiners in 1881. Most other international unions in the building trades were organized by the end of the 19th century. Union growth depended on organizing efforts and employer resistance. The building trades offered workers improved wages, hours, and working conditions, often along with benefits in case of illness or death, in return for an initiation fee, union dues, and loyalty.

Union growth in this era hinged not only on overcoming employer resistance, but also on ability to compete with other unions. This was an especially touchy issue in the building trades because of the jurisdictional issues that arose from their craft structure. Disputes over which union had jurisdiction over which types of construction work were the main reason that the American Federation of Labor created its Building and Construction Trades Department (BCTD) in 1908.

Although there are numerous historical accounts of the origins of the building trades unions, most of the focus is on personalities, strategies, and ideologies within the union movement itself; relatively little is written from the standpoint of the employer. Most shops were very small and many employers had been union members themselves. In areas where most workers in a trade were organized, employers had little choice but to deal with the union and its business agent. Agents were quick to size up the opportunities in a situation of such asymmetric bargaining power—union racketeering became a serious problem in a number of cities.[6] Secondary boycotts were frequently used when the building trades needed additional leverage. Segal (1970:53) argues that the relationship was beneficial in some ways for the employer. The plumbers union provided lobbying support on issues such as building codes and licensing; it also helped limit competition by setting uniform wage rates and limiting labor supply. Employer associations gradually were formed on a craft basis in most major urban areas, and these became bargaining units.

Well before the Wagner Act, the prehire agreement was the principal instrument to commit contractors to use union labor. Under such an agreement, a contractor or an association of contractors would agree to hire union members at given wage rates and work rules over a specific time horizon. This practice continued to prevail even after passage of the Wagner Act because of the logistical difficulties of using elections to gauge employee preferences for union representation in the construction industry. High turnover precludes the stable attachment between a group of workers and an individual contractor that is necessary for an NLRB election; most construction jobs would be over long before the NLRB ever got around to counting the ballots.

Technically speaking, prehire agreements violated the Wagner Act because recognition was given to the union without the consent of the precise set of individuals who would be the contractor's actual employees. This issue was ignored from 1935 to 1947. In 1948 the NLRB carried out a pilot program of construction elections and found, to no one's surprise, that the costs were staggering. Eventually prehire agreements were legally authorized when Title VII of the Landrum-Griffin Act of 1959 added Section 8(f) to the NLRA.

The Unions

Almost all unionized workers in the construction industry are represented by one of the 15 national unions in the BCTD.[7] Since the time of the last IRRA-sponsored survey of industrial relations in the construction industry by Mills (1980), there have been two mergers within the building trades. On August 16, 1979, the International Union of Wood, Wire, and Metal Lathers merged with the United Brotherhood of

Carpenters and Joiners of America. On November 10, 1988, the Tile, Marble, Terrazzo, Finishers, Shopworkers, and Granite Cutters International Union merged with the Carpenters and Joiners. A former member of the building trades—the Teamsters—rejoined the fold in 1987, when the Teamsters reaffiliated with the AFL-CIO. The building trades are listed in Table 2, along with their membership in 1979 and 1989 as reported by the unions to the AFL-CIO.

TABLE 2

Membership of Unions in the Building and Construction Trades Dept., AFL-CIO
(1000s)

Union	1979	1989	Change
Asbestos workers	13	12	-1
Boilermakers	129	75	-54
Bricklayers	106	84	-22
Carpenters	619	613	-6
Electrical workers (IBEW)	825	744	-81
Elevator constructors	16	22	6
Engineers, operating	313	330	17
Iron workers	146	111	-35
Laborers	475	406	-69
Painters	160	128	-32
Plasterers	50	39	-11
Plumbers	228	220	-8
Roofers	28	23	-5
Sheet metal workers	120	108	-12
Teamsters	°	1161	°
Tile, marble, terrazzo	7	°°	°°
Sum, excluding Teamsters	3235	2915	-320

° Teamsters, Chauffeurs, Warehousemen, and Helpers of America affiliated on 11/1/87.

°° Tile, Marble, Terrazzo, Finishers, Shopworkers, and Granite Cutters International Union merged with United Brotherhood of Carpenters and Joiners of America on 11/10/88.

Source: Gifford (1990).

Excluding the Teamsters, membership in the building trades unions dropped by 320,000 in the 1980s, a 9.9% decline. In absolute terms, the unions suffering the largest drops in membership were the electrical workers (81,000), the boilermakers (54,000), and the laborers (69,000). (Many of the losses of the first two unions took place in manufacturing.)

In proportional terms, the unions losing the most members were the boilermakers (42%), bricklayers (21%), iron workers (24%), painters (20%), and plasterers (22%).

There are some notable exceptions to this overall pattern of declining membership. Two unions actually became larger in the 1980s: the elevator constructors (6,000 increase) and the operating engineers (17,000). Two very large unions—the carpenters and the plumbers—saw their membership decline only slightly.

Management Organizations

Most contractors are too small to have their own labor relations staff. If they join their local general or specialty contractor association, they get representation in contract negotiations and assistance with the resolution of grievances. Local contractor associations also help administer apprenticeship programs and provide services outside the labor relations arena such as lobbying, public relations, and legal advice.

There are about 65 national associations that represent general or specialty contractors.[8] The most visible associations include the Associated Builders and Contractors, an open-shop organization of mostly specialty contractors; the Associated General Contractors, a group that is about two-thirds union; the National Association of Home Builders, the largest organization that is mostly open shop; and the National Construction Employers Council, a confederation of 16 associations that are mostly or exclusively union. In addition to assisting their local chapters, these national organizations provide public relations, research, and lobbying services.

The interests of the owners of construction projects were first represented in 1969 with the formation of the Construction Users' Anti-Inflation Roundtable, consisting of 200 of the nation's leading chief executive officers. This group merged in 1972 into the Business Roundtable, a broader organization that maintains a Construction Cost-Effectiveness Task Force. The Business Roundtable has encouraged any and all steps that it feels would lower construction costs, including opening up bidding to open-shop contractors and bargaining to make adjustments in union contracts.

Bargaining Structure

The unionized portion of the industry is concentrated in the commercial, industrial, and heavy-and-highway sectors. In most cases, especially in commercial construction, bargaining takes place at the local level between an association of contractors and either a local union or a district council of locals. Usually local negotiations are limited to a single trade. When contracts for the various crafts expire at different times of the year, there is a heightened risk of a strike or lockout relative to other industries. A number of institutional mechanisms have evolved to deal with this risk, including formal negotiations involving several trades at once and contracts that expire at the same time across different trades. In the late 1960s and early 1970s the staggered structure of bargaining in construction was blamed for unusually high wage settlements. Many locals followed a practice called "leapfrogging," where the negotiated settlement in one trade creates pressure for even larger settlements in negotiations for other trades in that area and in nearby areas.

Although local agreements are the most common practice, they are not universal. Often there is a statewide agreement for heavy and highway construction. The bargaining unit is national in pipeline and elevator construction, as well as some industrial construction projects.

Even when wages are negotiated locally, most unions have a national contract that applies to traveling contractors. These contracts tend to be short statements that the contractor will use union labor both directly and through all subcontracts and will pay union scale, either as specified in the local agreement or, if no such agreement exists, the national agreement. This arrangement protects the contractor from being required to pay above normal rates, and it relieves the local unions from the risk of being unable to organize the project. Local unions and contractor associations have been known to complain, however, if during a strike or lockout an outside contractor continues working under the national agreement.

A practice that has become increasingly more common in the building trades is the project agreement. These agreements usually cover very large projects such as industrial or power plants construction where work goes on for many years. Typically these contracts are designed to make union labor more competitive by including a no-strike pledge with specific procedures to settle any disputes along with concessions on work rules. Between 1979 and 1981 there were 92 project agreements granted or pending, covering 83,344 employees. By 1986 there were 265 such agreements covering 117,185 employees.[9]

Human Resource Practices

Must workers complete an apprenticeship to enter a union in the building trades? Do unionized employers have to hire everyone through the hiring hall? Researchers who interview contractors find widespread misconceptions about which human resource practices actually are followed, not to mention their effectiveness.[10]

Training. Virtually all skills in the building trades are marketable across a wide range of employers. The employer has an incentive to train only (1) if the costs of training can be passed to the worker via lower wages and benefits or (2) no trained labor is available in the market, in which case the training cost is a substitute for a general wage increase. One unique aspect of apprenticeship programs is that they encourage investments in training by shifting some of the costs of training from the worker to other parties. Apprentices start at 50% of journeyman scale, with increases as they move through the program. Pay tends to be below productivity in the first year or two of the program but above productivity near the end, so that the employer and the trainee share the costs. In addition, administrative costs are paid by taxpayers and all union workers, who are assessed a fee for each hour worked to fund apprenticeships.

Apprenticeship programs traditionally have produced well-rounded, highly skilled workers. Most programs run from three to five years and involve a combination of on-the-job and classroom training. A substantial majority of the programs in the building trades are affiliated with the unionized sector. The unions recognize that their members must be very skilled to command the wages specified in the contract. If the skills of newly hired workers fall relative to those of experienced workers, the common wage scale cannot be maintained. At the same time, unions recognize that the apprenticeship program's size must be controlled. The size of today's program is a key determinant of future labor supply. In addition, unions have been wary that employers will use apprenticeship programs as a cheaper substitute for experienced labor.

Repeated studies have shown that most union members have not completed union apprenticeship programs. Apprenticeships are the main source of entry for bricklayers, plumbers, sheet metal workers, and electricians but not for carpenters and ironworkers. In the most carefully done quantitative study of this issue, Marshall et al. (1975) found that the two most important alternative sources of training were working as laborers or helpers on union job sites or informal on-the-job training in the open shop.

Union apprenticeship programs remain the most important source of training in the industry today, but this does not exempt them from criticism. Northrup (1984) argues that relatively few jobs require the multifaceted skills taught in the programs. The Business Roundtable (1982b) study of apprenticeship programs criticized the practice of advancing through the programs based on time in the program rather than on skills mastered. It also criticized federal and state regulation of apprenticeship programs for setting standards that often limit government support to union programs.

Traditionally most workers in the open shop have received their training on the job. Business Roundtable (1982c) found that although the open shop had 60% of the construction market, it accounted for merely 10% of the expenditures on training. Apprenticeship programs are administered by the Associated General Contractors (AGC) and the Associated Builders and Contractors (ABC), but these remain relatively small. Large open-shop contractors such as BE&EK, Brown & Root, and Flour Daniel have conducted their own task-oriented programs for some time. Similar approaches have been developed by many ABC chapters via the Wheels of Learning program in the 1980s and the current programs being operated by the Merit Shop Foundation.

Hiring. Most hiring by union contractors is done through informal mechanisms such as applications "at the gate" and contacts made through friends and relatives. Contracts often call for all hiring to be done through the hiring hall, but in practice the hiring hall is most likely to be used when informal mechanisms fail to yield enough applicants. Hiring halls usually are capable of providing adequate numbers of workers who meet minimum competency standards, thereby reducing recruiting and screening costs for union contractors.

Business Roundtable (1982a) criticized certain aspects of hiring procedures in the union sector, arguing that some locals impose restrictions on the selection of supervisors or use the hiring hall to put pressure on contractors by limiting the quantity or quality of referrals. The National Construction Employers Council and the Building and Construction Trades Department of the AFL-CIO (1985) addressed the foreman issue in its *Market Recovery Program Handbook*, which encouraged locals to give contractors responsibility for decisions involving foremen. Their 1986 study found that between 1980 and 1985 the share of local agreements that allowed management to choose foremen increased from 82% to 92%, whereas the share of contracts with no specified ratio of foremen to journeymen rose from 50% to 61%.

Obviously, employers in the open shop face no restrictions on their choices of recruiting methods or their selection of employees. Open-shop contractor organizations have experimented with hiring halls, but most hiring is done through informal methods in smaller firms and through state-of-the-art screening methods in the largest ones.

Work organization. Work at union jobsites is organized around the principle of craft jurisdiction. Under this work system, each task is allocated to one of the building trades, in effect giving that trade property rights over a range of work assignments. The only benefit to employers from this system is that as long as the local maintains its skill and training standards for membership, it provides some protection against shoddy workmanship (e.g., if a worker falsely claims he has a particular skill). This benefit is rather meager relative to the costs. Jurisdictional rules sometimes dictate that skilled journeymen do work that could have been done by semiskilled and unskilled labor. In addition, they restrict flexibility in work assignments when two different trades are close substitutes.

Union contracts sometimes specify minimum crew sizes, forbid supervisors to pick up tools, or restrict the ratios of helpers and apprentices to journeymen. When these provisions are enforced, they can increase construction costs considerably. The case study evidence on this issue indicates that these provisions often are ignored and, even when they are enforced, tend to affect costs only on small projects. The Business Roundtable (1982a) estimated that crew size restrictions raise costs by $42 million per year. Econometric evidence in Allen (1986c) shows that restrictions on substitution between different types of labor increases project costs by 2%.

In a few areas the building trades have restricted management from using the best available technology. In the early 1970s only 12% of union contracts contained limits on prefabricated components or on tools and equipment. However, more than 70% of the contracts with plumbers and sheet-metal workers had restrictions on prefabrication and more than 80% of painters' contracts had limits on tools and equipment at that time. Ten years later, Business Roundtable (1982a) reported, "While a minor percentage of all contracts sampled contain prefabrication limits, these restrictive clauses were found in one-half of the pipefitter/plumber contracts." They estimated that across all types of construction these restrictions raised costs by $30 million.

In the open shop, contractors have complete flexibility in assigning tasks to workers and selecting materials, tools, and equipment. Without craft jurisdictions, workers are trained to learn skills that cut across a number of trades. Without ratios specified in the contract, the employer is free to use any mix of laborers, semiskilled, and skilled labor. This is always cited as the main competitive advantage of the open shop.

Union Density

The Current Population Survey has contained a question about union membership in the May survey in 1970 and from 1973 to 1981; a question on contract coverage was added in 1978. Since 1983, these questions have been part of the monthly survey. The same union membership question appeared in 1966 in the Survey of Economic Opportunity. In Table 3 this information was used to calculate an internally consistent series of the percentage of all employees in the construction industry who are union members or who are covered by collective bargaining agreements.

TABLE 3

Percentage Union Members and Percentage Covered
by Collective Bargaining in Construction, 1966-1991

Year	Percentage Union Members	Percentage Covered by Collective Bargaining
1966	41.4	
1970	41.9	
1973	39.4	
1974	37.2	
1975	37.0	
1976	35.7	
1977	35.7	
1978	31.9	37.5
1979	31.6	36.9
1980	30.8	34.8
1981	32.8	38.9
1983	27.7	30.1
1984	24.8	26.4
1985	23.5	25.2
1986	23.0	24.6
1987	22.0	23.7
1988	21.6	23.0
1989	22.0	23.3
1990	22.5	24.0
1991	22.5	24.1
1992	22.0	23.5

Sources: 1968-81, Allen (1988); 1983-1992, Hirsch and MacPherson (1993).

Between 1970 and 1992, union density (the percentage of employees who report themselves to be union members) in the construction industry has fallen almost by half. In 1970, 42% of the employees in the construction industry were union members; in 1992, only 22% were. The downward trend in union density has been steady—throughout the 1970s and the first half of the 1980s, it dropped by an average of one percentage point per year. Particularly large declines were observed between May 1977 and 1978 (4%) and May 1981 and 1983 (5%). This decline stopped after 1987; since then, union density has stayed at 22%. The pattern for coverage by collective bargaining agreements is quite similar.

Age

Union density follows a concave pattern with respect to age, growing rapidly for workers in their 20s and early 30s but then peaking out and remaining flat for workers in their 40s and 50s. This pattern reflects the fact that it takes three to four years to become sufficiently trained to become a union journeyman. Also, many young workers spend some time working in construction (especially as unskilled workers on open-shop residential projects) but do not make a career of it.

Union density dropped across all age groups during the 1980s, with the largest declines taking place among younger and middle-aged workers. There are two aspects to this decline that are important to understand: (1) union membership still increases with age, but at a much slower rate, and (2) union membership rates actually declined for most cohorts. Figure 1 breaks down the difference between union density in 1977-78 and 1989 for private wage and salary workers in blue-collar occupations into two components: (1) a within-cohort change, indicated by the distance between the line labeled "1989 actual" and that labeled "1989, no change within cohorts" and (2) an across-cohort change, indicated by the spread between the latter line and that labeled "1977-78."

Consider the drop in union density for workers aged 35 to 39 from 49% in 1977-78 to 26% in 1989. In 1977-78, 36% of all workers aged 25 to 29 were union members, so the within-cohort drop in union density is 10 percentage points. If the 1977-78 patterns for union density by age had held up, however, the union density rate for this age group would have been 49%. Thus the failure of union density to increase with age for this cohort accounts for another 13 points of the decline.

Figure 1 shows that for workers between 40 and 54 in 1989, the within-cohort change accounted for most of the drop in unionization, whereas for workers under 40 the across-cohort effects dominated. This

FIGURE 1

Percentage of Construction Working in the Private-Sector Who Are
Union Members, by Age Group, May 1977-78 and 1989

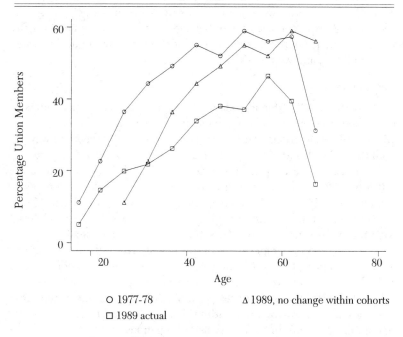

O 1977-78   Δ 1989, no change within cohorts
□ 1989 actual

indicates that the decline in union density in the building trades is being
driven by two very different forces. The odds that middle-aged and
older construction workers would be union members are lower than
they were for the same cohort 10 to 15 years ago. Although it is possible
that this results from mobility of workers from other industries who
were never organized, the more plausible explanation is that many of
the nonunion workers who are 40 and over are former union members.
The other force at work is that the new generation of construction workers has not been organized. Because many of them are now in their 30s,
it is unlikely that they will ever get the type of training that will qualify
them for union journeyman status. The building trades have probably
lost this generation of workers.

Other Personal Characteristics

The decline in union density was inversely related to education levels. Among workers who did not complete high school, union density

dropped by 20 percentage points, in contrast to a 15 percentage point drop for those with high school degrees and an 11 percentage point drop among those with some college. Union membership rates for whites and nonwhites were more or less the same in both 1977-78 and 1989. A higher percentage of men belong to unions than women in both years, but the proportional decline in union density was about the same for men (38%) and women (36%).

Occupation

In both the 1977-78 and 1989 samples, union density is much higher for skilled occupations than for handlers, helpers, and laborers. There are six craft occupations that (1) were defined in nearly the same way in both the 1977-78 and 1989 CPS and (2) had sample sizes of 100 or more in both years. The drop in union density is much larger for painters (30% to 11%) and roofers (36% to 11%) than for brickmasons and stonemasons (44% to 32%), carpenters (31% to 17%), electricians (58% to 40%), and plumbers and pipefitters (56% to 41%). This is consistent with the pattern in Table 1 where the declines in membership of the painters and roofers unions were proportionally larger than the decline across all building trades. Painting and roofing are generally considered to be less skill-intensive than masonry, carpentry, plumbing, and electrical work. Unless there are offsetting wage differentials, this would create a greater incentive for building owners and contractors to find nonunion substitutes in the less-skilled occupations.

Explaining the Decline in Union Density

Employers are most likely to sign and abide by collective bargaining agreements when three conditions hold. First, unions must have a near monopoly on the supply of skilled labor, which is most likely in areas with active union apprenticeship programs. Second, the union must have enough solidarity to make strike threats credible and costly to employers. Because of workers' ability to work for a wide range of employers (including those outside construction) and the high costs of delays to builders, union strike threats are quite powerful in a tight labor market. Third, union labor must be better trained and more experienced so that the employer gets higher productivity in return for higher wages. If this last condition does not hold, the employer has an incentive to renege on his relationship with the union.

The discussion here will examine four plausible explanations for the decline in union density: (1) wages and benefits have increased more for union than for nonunion workers, (2) the productivity advantage of union labor has eroded, (3) there is increased resistance by contractors and owners to unions, and (4) the interpretation of labor laws has changed in a manner favorable to employers.[11]

Wages and Benefits

Table 4 updates the estimates of union-nonunion wage gaps from Allen (1988a). The first column reports the estimates from that study for 1967, 1970, and May 1973-1983. The second column reports estimates for May 1973-1981 and the full year 1983-1986 from Linneman et al. (1990). The third column reports estimates for the full-year 1983-1992 that were generously provided by Barry Hirsch of Florida State University, using a data base he developed with his colleague David MacPherson. Even though the results are all obtained from the same data set (CPS), my estimates are somewhat larger than the others. This happens because of modest differences in control variables and model specification.[12]

The union-nonunion wage gap widened by a considerable margin in the late 1960s and the early 1970s. In 1967 union wages were 38% higher than nonunion wages, whereas by 1973 the gap had widened to 54%. Such a tremendous change in relative costs coupled with the weak attachments between workers and individual employers in the industry plausibly helped precipitate the decline in union density in the 1970s. In 1979 both sets of estimates drop by more than ten percentage points, but they increase in the early 1980s so that by 1983 both are higher than in 1979 although well below what they were in 1973-78. The Hirsch results show that the union-nonunion wage differential dropped by nine percentage points from 1986 to 1992.

The wage differential between union and nonunion labor is much lower today than it was in the middle of the 1970s and is comparable to the wage differential in 1967. If wage differentials were the only factor driving the decline in union density, then the unionized sector would have started recovering market share in the 1980s instead of continuing to drop. Although a widening wage gap was a key factor behind the initial decline in union density, we must look elsewhere for an explanation of why that decline continued in the 1980s.

There are no data on benefit costs in construction broken down by union status. The most expensive voluntary benefits are health insurance and retirement plans. The CPS supplements on benefit coverage for May 1979 and 1988 were used to calculate the proportion of union and

TABLE 4
Estimates of the Union-Nonunion Wage Gap, 1967-1992

Year	Allen	Linneman, Wachter, & Carter	Hirsch
1967	37.7		
1973	52.8	48.2	
1974	51.4	51.2	
1975	54.8	46.9	
1976	54.8	48.0	
1977	55.3	46.6	
1978	55.0	45.9	
1979	41.5	34.8	
1980	47.2	37.0	
1981	38.8	36.2	
1983	44.3	41.6	39.6
1984		42.5	41.0
1985		41.6	38.8
1986		40.4	38.3
1987			34.3
1988			31.8
1989			33.4
1990			28.8
1991			30.2
1992			29.0

Sources: Allen (1988a), Table 5, columns 2 and 3; Linneman, Wachter, and Carter (1990), Table 4, row 2; Barry Hirsch, personal correspondence.

nonunion workers in construction who work for employers that provide these benefits. There has been no change in pension coverage or participation rates for either union or nonunion contractors. Pensions are provided by the employer of 90% of union members and 33% of nonunion workers in both years. Health insurance coverage is down from 89% to 80% among union members. The share of nonunion contractors that provide health insurance has gone up from one-half to two-thirds. The critical element that is missing from these data is the generosity of the pension and health plans. A large increase in pension and health care costs per covered worker in union contracts relative to the open shop would offset the narrowing of the gap in health care coverage.

Productivity

The competitiveness of union labor depends not just on the wage differential with the open shop, but also on the productivity differential.

In an economywide study using data from the Census of Construction Industries, I found (Allen 1984) that in 1972 labor productivity is much higher in the unionized sector of the industry than in the open shop and that the estimated productivity difference between union and nonunion labor is about the same as the wage difference. This finding was further supported in my studies (Allen 1986a, 1986b, 1988b) of commercial office buildings, private hospitals, and retail space. However, in public construction my studies of schools and hospitals (Allen 1986a, 1986b) find no productivity difference between union and nonunion contractors, which I attribute to prevailing wage laws that shelter union contractors from the open shop and insensitivity of the owners of these structures to their cost.

All of these studies use data that were collected between 1973 and 1977. I reexamined the situation with economywide data for 1982 (Allen 1988a) and found evidence that the union productivity advantage had eroded. The best available data set for revisiting the question of how union and nonunion productivity compare is the 1987 Census of Construction Industries. In previous studies using the 1977 and 1982 Census data I was able to construct a data set in which each state would have three observations: one for each two-digit industry. The Current Population Survey no longer identifies the two-digit industry for construction employees and this information is often suppressed in smaller states in the Census reports. As a consequence, the sample used here consists of 51 observations: one for each state. To facilitate comparisons between 1982 and 1987, I reestimated the model for that year using the same aggregation scheme.

As long as the biases are the same in the 1987 and the aggregated 1982 data, the change in the union coefficient will indicate the direction in which the union-nonunion productivity difference is moving. The estimated productivity advantage of union over nonunion contractors in 1982 is 101%, but the margin of error in the estimate is quite large— plus or minus 38 percentage points. In 1987 the estimated productivity advantage is 76%, but the margin of error remains a sizable plus or minus 24 percentage points. The estimated decrease in the union productivity advantage is well within the range of imprecision of these estimates. Thus there is no solid evidence of a change in the union-nonunion productivity gap between 1982 and 1987.

Management Action

Partially in response to the high strike rates and rapid wage inflation of the late 1960s and early 1970s, the owners of construction projects and the contractors that they employ have taken a much more active role in controlling labor costs, steps that often involve switching from union to open-shop contractors. The Construction Users' Anti-Inflation Roundtable, which later evolved into the Business Roundtable, was established as a mechanism to help give large industrial firms better control over their construction costs.

The Roundtable has done two major studies highlighting problems in cost effectiveness in the industry. The 1974 study dealt exclusively with problems in the unionized sector of the construction industry: jurisdictional problems, hiring halls, scheduled overtime, and restoration of the role of management. The 1983 study was more wide ranging. Although it dealt with collective bargaining, it also examined project management issues relevant to union and open-shop construction, as well as construction technology and government regulation.

The Roundtable also has acted in a lobbying capacity to deal with legal and regulatory issues related to construction costs. Although the Roundtable has not explicitly called for project owners to switch to the open shop, it has engaged in a number of activities that increase the likelihood of such switches. These include sharing information about union activities and educating managers about strategies to deal with union issues. The impact of the Roundtable on union density cannot be quantified, but that does not mean it is negligible.

Many of the firms that decide to use union labor on a particular construction project do so to maintain good relations in their own collective bargaining arrangements. The overall decline in union density in the private sector has made it less likely that firms will unilaterally decide to use union labor when they build new offices and plants. This has happened in part because of simple shift-share factors and in part because the firms that still have unionized work forces are less likely to have company policies that automatically call for union contractors when construction needs arise.

Labor Laws and Their Interpretation

The premise at the time that prehire agreements were legally recognized by Landrum-Griffin was that if employees decided to change their representative or to become open shop, they would follow the same procedure as in other industries, namely to file a petition and have an election.[13] This introduced an asymmetry into the law with which employers were never comfortable. They were free to enter into a prehire agreement, but they had to go through an NLRB election to get out of one.

In *R.J. Smith Construction Co.*, 191 NLRB 693 (1971), the Board gave contractors a way out. Under this decision either party was allowed unilaterally to pull out of a prehire agreement unless a union had proven that it represented a majority of a contractor's employees. The timing of this decision reflects two factors: (1) Republicans returned to the White House in 1969 and, with a lag, were able to tilt the NLRB; and (2) rising union wage rates and an unprecedented number of strikes in the late 1960s had created more pressure for a shift in bargaining power toward employers. This doctrine was amended in *John Deklewa and Sons, Inc.*, 281 NLRB 184 (1987), to prevent unilateral repudiation during the period when the agreement was in effect. However, upon expiration, contractors remained under no obligation to bargain for a new agreement.[14]

The unions received another serious blow in *Peter Kiewit and Sons, Inc.*, 206 NLRB 562 (1973). Kiewit had an agreement with the operating engineers for highway construction in Oklahoma for years. In 1972 they brought in a subsidiary called South Prairie Construction Company, which started bidding for the same work in the same state on a nonunion basis. The subsidiary started getting contracts as Kiewit became increasingly reluctant to submit bids. The ruling in 1973 held that Kiewit had not violated the NLRA. The case then went to the Court of Appeals and the Supreme Court, which sent the case back to the NLRB.

The final NLRB decision (231 NLRB 76 [1977]) set up two tests to determine whether the practice of setting up a nonunion subsidiary, now called "doublebreasting," was legally permissible. First, when a contractor has union and nonunion subsidiaries, it must be determined whether a "single employer" exists. This is a purely qualitative test that depends on the interrelation of operations, common management, and centralized control of labor relations. Second, there is the question of whether the workers in the subsidiaries have a sufficient "community of interests" to be in the same bargaining unit. In making this decision, the Board is to consider "the bargaining history, the financial integration of operations, the differences in the types of work and skills of employees, the extent of centralization of management and supervision, particularly in regard to labor relations, hiring, discipline, and control of day-to-day operations, and the extent of interchange and contact between groups of employees" (*Kiewit* 1977).

Another interpretation of the Act that is used in some cases is known as the "alter ego doctrine." Suppose a company transfers its assets and business to a nonunion affiliate. Even though the original company has disappeared in a legal sense, all that essentially has changed is the name of the firm and, of course, its collective bargaining status. It has the same equipment, ownership, management, and customers, and sometimes, the same employees. Under this doctrine, the successor company is the alter ego of the original company and cannot escape its collective bargaining obligations, regardless of whether there is a community of interests for the employees.

At the time of *Kiewit*, the practice of doublebreasting was relatively rare in the industry. Northrup and Foster (1975) mentioned the appearance of the practice in a number of areas and predicted that it would become widespread. Their gift for prophecy is documented in Northrup's (1984) follow-up book. By 1983, 43 of the 50 largest contractors in the U.S. were unionized; of these 43, 22 had doublebreasted affiliates.

The *Smith*, *Deklewa*, and *Kiewit* decisions reduced the cost of terminating a collective bargaining relationship. In their aftermath, a new market developed under which contractors could buy legal and strategic advice on how to switch to the open shop.[15] The timing of these decisions coincides exactly with the beginning of the decline in union density. Except for the rather modest revisions to the *Smith* doctrine under *Deklewa*, the force of these decisions has not been diluted in subsequent years. They are clearly part of the explanation of declining union density because (1) they gave many employers an opportunity that they had long desired, and (2) even employers who preferred to stay with the union shop found themselves forced to go doublebreasted to meet rising competition from the open shop.

Allen (1993) presents econometric evidence that the impact of the *Kiewit* decision may be especially crucial. Before this case was finally resolved, the year-to-year variation in percentage union in the industry could be explained very well in terms of a single variable—the unit cost difference between union and nonunion labor. After the *Kiewit* decision, union density drops, and more critically, the correlation between relative unit cost and union density vanishes.

Despite these legal shocks and the cleverness of union-busting consultants, two other factors should not be overlooked. The construction industry has gone through two very depressed periods over the last 15 years and unemployment has been persistently high. In tighter labor markets, contractors who broke prehire agreements or went double-breasted would have faced damaging strikes. In the 1980s the threat to withhold labor was not a credible one.

The public image of the building trades is another factor that certainly has not helped in their fight against the open shop. Many baby boomers formed a highly unfavorable image when hardhats disrupted demonstrations against the Vietnam War. The reputation of discrimination against blacks and women remains despite data showing that the underutilization problem is slightly more severe in the open shop. A few locals have resorted to violence to try to intimidate owners, contractors, and project owners. Finally, in New York City and some other areas, locals remain corrupted by organized crime.[16]

The building trades have pushed repeatedly for labor law reforms to restore the long-term recognition of prehire agreements and to eliminate doublebreasting. These bills were approved by the U.S. House of Representatives in the 99th and 100th Congress but never made it through the Senate.[17]

The 1980s also saw a number of legislative battles over prevailing wage laws. Under Senate Bill 1171, introduced in 1983, the dollar threshold for coverage by Davis-Bacon would have been increased from $2,000 to $100,000 and the definition of prevailing wage would have been changed to greatly reduce the odds that it would be set at union scale.[18] This legislation met the same fate as the bills on doublebreasting and prehire agreements.

There has been more prevailing wage action at the state level. Until 1979, 42 of the states had their own prevailing wage laws covering public construction that fell outside the jurisdiction of Davis-Bacon. Since 1979, nine states have repealed their prevailing wage law: Alabama, Arizona, Colorado, Florida, Idaho, Kansas, Louisiana, New Hampshire, and Utah.[19]

Construction labor relations got some attention in the 1992 presidential campaign. In October 1992, President Bush issued two executive orders transparently designed to woo support from nonunion contractors. One suspended the Davis-Bacon Act in three states that suffered damage from Hurricane Andrew; the other barred contractors who enter into project agreements with unions from bidding on federal contracts. The lifting of both orders was one of President Clinton's first acts of office.[20]

Collective Bargaining Outcomes

Wage developments in the industry since 1973 are exhibited in Figure 2. The percentage increase in average hourly earnings for the

FIGURE 2

Percentage Change in Prices and Construction Wages, 1973-1991

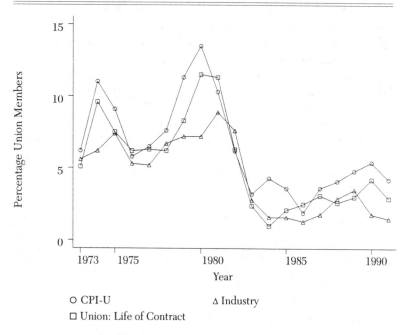

Year

○ CPI-U　　　　　　　　　△ Industry
□ Union: Life of Contract

entire industry wavered mostly between 5% and 7% through 1982, well below the inflation rate during that period. After 1982, wage growth was much slower, sticking between 1% and 3%, again somewhat below inflation. Between 1980 and 1992, average hourly earnings increased from $9.92 to $14.05, a 42% increase. At the same time the CPI-U increased by 70%, leading to a drop in real wages by 17%.

Benefits accounted for 29% of compensation in construction in 1991, costing $5.23 per hour. Legally required benefits cost construction employers $2.36 an hour, much more than the $1.40 average across all industries. Legally required benefits cost much more in construction mainly because of the greater cost of workers compensation in such a high-risk industry with relatively many small employers.[21] Between 1980 and 1991, total compensation per worker—including payroll taxes and benefits—grew by 58%, still below the rate of inflation.[22]

Wage adjustments in collective bargaining agreements covering 1000 workers or more in the construction industry were greater than the growth in wages for the industry as a whole through 1981, often much greater. In 1974, bargaining agreements called for increases above 10%, whereas average wages grew 6%. A similar pattern is observed in 1980-81. Since 1982 it has been a completely different ballgame. Union wage adjustments have tracked very closely with industrywide wage growth for the last 10 years.[23] These raw data are unadjusted for changes in worker or locational characteristics. Table 4 showed that the union-nonunion wage gap has declined substantially in the 1980s, implying larger increases in wages for open-shop than for union workers.

Important steps have been taken in the 1980s to remove contract provisions that make union labor noncompetitive. The Construction Labor Research Council (1992) found that the excess costs associated with constraints in collective bargaining agreements had been reduced by 40% from 1980 to 1992. The main improvements have come from reducing wage premiums for overtime and Saturday work and dropping provisions that call for pay when not working.

Relationships between unionized contractors and the building trades seem to have improved in the 1980s and 1990s. As described below in some detail, there have been a number of cooperative efforts between labor and management at the national level, including establishment of committees and elimination of burdensome work rules. There is indirect evidence at the local level in the form of a sharp reduction in work stoppages. Historically, the strike rate in construction has been higher than in most other industries. From 1968 through 1975, construction became much more strike prone—1% of estimated working time in construction was lost to strikes in contrast to 0.2% for all industries. This no doubt led many project owners and builders to seek alternatives in the open shop.

Since that time strikes have become low-probability events in the U.S. and this is especially true in construction. Strike activity has fallen along all major dimensions—number of strikes, workers involved, days idle, and percentage of working time lost. The percentage of working time lost to strikes fell to 0.3% between 1976 and 1981. Changes in the format used by the Labor Department to report strike statistics preclude precise comparisons for the industry before and after 1982. Through 1983 the strike rate remained higher (usually much higher) in construction than in all industries. Since 1984 this no longer has been true—the strike rate is now lower in construction than for the economy as a whole. Given the severe decline in the aggregate strike rate in the 1980s, this is a remarkable turnaround.

Strategies for Union Recovery

To recover market share, unions are following three strategies.[24] First, their tactics for dealing with the open shop have become much more competitive. Thomas Owens, director of organizing for the building trades, has developed a data base to track all major construction projects nationwide. This lets unions know about work that is to be contracted in their area and provides feedback about progress in competing against the open shop.

Another approach is to charge different wage rates for different types of work. In many parts of the country there has been a longstanding practice of charging lower rates for residential construction. This has been extended to more types of work including asbestos abatement.

Some unions have used a controversial tactic known as job targeting. Under this approach, the union gives a contractor a rebate covering part or all of the difference between union and open-shop rates so the contractor can land a particular project that otherwise would have gone to the open shop. This approach has proven popular in some locals because all members pay into the fund, thereby spreading the cost of the concession beyond those working at a particular job site.

In economic terms this practice is equivalent to price discrimination. It allows a seller with market power (in this case the labor union) to produce more than it would if a single price were charged to all customers, thereby making both parties better off. Even though price discrimination is a standard practice for businesses, job targeting has been challenged in court by the Associated Builders and Contractors, a mostly nonunion trade group, on the grounds that it is nothing more than a clever reincarnation of the kickback schemes used by corrupt business agents since the turn of the century. Metzgar (1988) points out that the subsidy "must be offered to whichever contractor wins the bid, whether union or nonunion; the union cannot pick and choose a specific contractor." Also those union members who will be affected by the subsidy must approve the practice. In 1989 the Wage and Hour Division of the Department of Labor ruled that job targeting violated the Davis-Bacon Act and cannot be used to obtain federally funded projects. The ABC has filed an antitrust case challenging the legality of job targeting for private-sector work.

When Toyota started to build its plant in Georgetown, Kentucky, in 1986 and refused to sign a project agreement, the unions launched a corporate campaign, described in Erlich (1988). The BCTD ordered all locals to refuse to work on the site, creating a shortage of labor in certain key crafts. The Kentucky Building Trades brought cases questioning the legality of the tax concessions that secured the plant. There were also mass demonstrations in a number of cities. After six months, Toyota signed a project agreement recognizing the costs of fighting the campaign. The same tactics are being followed to organize the BMW plant being built in Spartanburg, South Carolina.[25]

Some locals have "salted" the work forces of open-shop contractors with union members to either organize the project or disrupt it. A recent practice has been for union members to declare on job applications that they are union organizers, so that if they are not hired they can file unfair labor practice charges with the NLRB.[26] The company runs the risk of expensive back-pay assessments and penalties requiring preferential hiring on future projects if it does not have defensible hiring procedures and criteria.

The second strategy is labor-management cooperation. The unions have recognized that they need to work with contractors toward the common goal of building back market share. One step toward this was accomplished when the National Construction Employers Council signed an agreement with the BCTD to set up a "Market Recovery Program for Union Construction." One objective of this program was to develop "the collective bargaining program which . . . will assist in recapturing and maintaining the work for union construction."[27] This involves developing guidelines at the national level for how local contract provisions should be adjusted to make unions more competitive with the open shop. These include the standardization of work conditions across different trades (especially those involving work scheduling), elimination of inefficient work practices generated by either unions or management, reduction of down time, and special agreements for small commercial and industrial work.

A second objective of the program is to develop local labor-management committees. Most of the face-to-face interaction between unions and management traditionally has taken place in confrontational situations, mainly grievances and bargaining. A key purpose of the local committees would be to get the groups together to focus on common goals. The committees would monitor the size and growth of the open shop in their area, identify inefficient work practices, work to improve the collective bargaining process itself (e.g., contract duration, scope of bargaining units), and engage in public relations activities to win back project owners. The PRIDE program in St. Louis, which was set up in 1972, has been cited repeatedly as being successful in preventing erosion of market share. However, there is no systematic evidence on how these local efforts have worked out.

Another important step toward cooperation took place in 1987, when the National Constructors Association and the BCTD entered into the National Construction Stabilization Agreement. The agreement established a benchmark set of provisions to be used in project agreements. These provisions called for greater flexibility in work scheduling and assignments and a no-strike policy with financial penalties.[28]

The final strategy for dealing with the open-shop challenge is political. With Democrats controlling the White House and Congress, the odds that there will be labor law reforms favorable to the building trades have risen. Increased spending on infrastructure should lead to a greater share of jobs going to union members, thanks to prevailing wage laws. The unions received an extra advantage in securing contracts for public-sector work when the Supreme Court ruled in 1993 that state and local authorities were free to enter into union-only project agreements for publicly funded construction.[29] The case involved the $6.1 billion cleanup of Boston Harbor.

Two counties and three cities in the San Francisco Bay Area passed prevailing wage laws governing *private* construction within those localities. Under these laws, prevailing rates are to be set by the California Department of Industrial Relations. These laws have been challenged in state and federal courts. A federal judge struck them down in 1991, ruling that they were "impermissible interference in the collective bargaining process" under the NLRA and also violated the Employee Retirement Income Security Act.[30]

According to the Business Roundtable (1993), some local unions have been using the regulatory process to gain an edge on the open shop. For instance, union members can threaten to pack public permit hearings and voice (sometimes less than sincere) environmental concerns that are likely to delay a project as a tactic to win a union-only project agreement. They also can solicit inspections of open-shop job sites by OSHA or the state board for craft licensing. It is easy to understand management's apprehension about these tactics.

Despite these competitive, cooperative, and political efforts, union density is never likely to return to its 1970 level. The firms that have escaped their prehire agreements or have gone doublebreasted are unlikely to return, even under the most optimistic legislative scenarios. The key for a union comeback will be whether the building trades can capitalize on their strongest asset—training. This is especially critical now, given the lack of success the unions had organizing and training younger workers in the 1980s. Because of technological change and global competition, the demand for skilled labor is rising throughout the economy. This should give well-trained union labor a competitive advantage as long as there is no return to the huge wage increases and high strike rates of the late 1960s and 1970s.

Acknowledgments

Research support was provided by North Carolina State University. I am especially indebted to Barry Hirsch and David MacPherson for providing CPS estimates for 1983-1992. Herbert Northrup graciously provided access to his forthcoming work, along with helpful suggestions. I received helpful comments on earlier drafts from Quinn Mills, Bob Georgine, and Larry Cohen.

Endnotes

[1] At the time of this writing, the Commerce Department has suspended publication of its real output by industry series since 1989. To document the industry's situation in the early 1990s, I use instead the data on value and square footage put in place, published on a monthly basis by the Commerce Department.

[2] Prevailing wage laws set minimum wage rates that are usually well above the federal minimum wage for government-funded activities. The Davis-Bacon Act sets minimum wages for construction projects that are federally funded. Most states also have their own prevailing wage laws in construction. For discussions of the provisions of these laws and their economic impact, see Allen (1983) and Thieblot (1986).

[3] Ironically, underutilization of minorities in union construction is usually cited as an argument for repealing prevailing wage laws.

[4] The occupational code was changed between the 1977-78 and 1989 CPS. To make the codes comparable, the 1977-78 data were converted into the more recent coding scheme using a Census Bureau concordance mapping three-digit occupations under the old code to one-digit occupations under the new code.

[5] The mismatch rate in the concordance between the 1970 and 1980 codes for these occupations is 1% or less of the count of persons in those occupations. In terms of occupational shares, this amounts to an error rate that is well below 0.1% of all workers.

[6] See Christie (1956) for an account of union corruption at the turn of the century.

[7] The only other major union that bargains for workers in the industry is the United Steelworkers of America, which absorbed the United Mine Workers' District 50 in a 1973 merger. The union represents 8,450 construction workers, most of whom do heavy-and-highway work in Pennsylvania, West Virginia, Kentucky, and

New Jersey (*ENR*, April 26, 1990, p. 40). The union contains workers from all crafts, which it claims leads to greater efficiency by eliminating jurisdictional disputes.

[8] The January/February 1991 issue of *Construction Review*, published by the U.S. Department of Commerce, includes a directory of contractor organizations.

[9] National Construction Employers Council and the Building and Construction Trades Department, AFL-CIO (1986), p. 11.

[10] The most thorough and recent such study is Bourdon and Levitt (1980). The discussion below also draws from Mills (1972), Foster (1973), Northrup and Foster (1975), Marshall et al. (1975), Allen (1984), and Northrup (1984).

[11] Another possible factor, changes in worker and employer characteristics, was examined in Allen (1988a) and found to be unimportant. This conclusion did not change when I updated the analysis.

[12] Linneman et al. (1990) estimated a model across workers from all industries with different intercepts for union and nonunion workers in construction, whereas I estimate a model over workers in the construction industry only. In effect I have complete interactions between industry and all coefficients in the model, whereas they have an industry-intercept interaction. The other difference is that they include controls for overtime hours and a set of regional labor market characteristics in their model, whereas I do not. Hirsch restricts his sample to construction workers, but uses a different set of control variables. He includes part-time status and veteran status but does not include occupation.

[13] In writing this section of the paper, I have drawn heavily from Northrup (1989) and the testimony in U.S. Senate, Committee on Labor and Human Resources, *Construction Industry Labor Law Amendments of 1987*, Senate Hearing 100-220 (Washington, DC: U.S. Government Printing Office, 1987), especially the prepared statements of Arthur F. Rosenfeld, special assistant to the solicitor, U.S. Department of Labor, and Robert A. Georgine, president of the Building and Construction Trades Department, AFL-CIO.

[14] See Poltz (1990) for a more detailed discussion of *Deklewa*.

[15] For a good example of such advice, see the appendix by A. Samuel Cook, Esq. in Northrup (1984).

[16] See Northrup (1984:351-71) for a discussion of union violence and Ichniowski and Preston (1989) for an examination of union corruption and racketeering in New York City.

[17] Hearings were held for H.R. 281 in 1985 and 1987 and for S. 492 in 1987.

[18] For a complete discussion of these amendments, see U.S. Congress, Senate Committee on Labor and Human Resources, *Davis-Bacon Act Amendments, 1983*, Senate hearing 98-337 (Washington, DC: U.S. Government Printing Office, 1983).

[19] For details, see Thieblot (1986) and Northrup (1989).

[20] "Bush Lets Contractors in Three States Hire at Below-Union Rates," *Wall Street Journal*, Oct. 15, 1992:A4 (Western edition); "Clinton Cancels Bush Orders about Unions," *Wall Street Journal*, February 2, 1993:A2 (Eastern edition).

[21] The source of this information is U.S. Department of Labor, Bureau of Labor Statistics, *Employment Cost Indexes and Levels, 1975-91*, BLS Bulletin 2389 (Washington, DC: U.S. Government Printing Office, 1991).

[22] This information comes from BLS Bulletin 2389 and the October 1992 issue of *Monthly Labor Review*.

[23] The source of this information is various March issues of *Compensation and Working Conditions*, formerly *Current Wage Developments*.

[24] Some of the following discussion is drawn from "Toning up Union Muscles," *ENR*, April 26, 1990:36-40 and Business Roundtable (1993).

[25] "Unions Start BMW Plant Drive," *ENR*, April 12, 1993:6-7.

[26] See Northrup (forthcoming) for a thorough discussion of this practice.

[27] Building and Construction Trades Department, AFL-CIO, and National Construction Employers Council 1984:1.

[28] "Construction Industry Group, Labor Set Pact to Stem Job Losses to Nonunion Crews," *Wall Street Journal*, February 18, 1987.

[29] *Building and Construction Trades Council of the Metropolitan District v. Associated Builders and Contractors of Massachusetts/Rhode Island, Inc., et al.*, 61 U.S.L.W. 4221 (March 8, 1993); "Unions Win Case before Supreme Court for Control of Public Building Projects," *Wall Street Journal*, March 9, 1993.

[30] The sources of this information are L. Gordon Crovitz, "Stretching the Davis-Bacon," *Barron's*, April 15, 1991, p. 14, and "Private-Project Wage Laws Are Set Back," *Wall Street Journal*, June 26, 1991, p. B5 (Eastern edition).

References

Allen, Steven G. 1983. "Much Ado About Davis-Bacon: A Critical Review and New Evidence." *Journal of Law and Economics* (October), pp. 707-36.
_____. 1984. "Unionized Construction Workers Are More Productive." *Quarterly Journal of Economics* (May), pp. 251-74.
_____. 1986a. "Unionization and Productivity in Office Building and School Construction." *Industrial and Labor Relations Review* (January), pp. 187-201.
_____. 1986b. "The Effect of Unionism on Productivity in Privately and Publicly Owned Hospitals and Nursing Homes." *Journal of Labor Research* (Winter), pp. 59-68.
_____. 1986c. "Union Work Rules and Efficiency in the Building Trades." *Journal of Labor Economics* (April), pp. 212-42.
_____. 1988a. "Declining Unionization in Construction: The Facts and the Reasons." *Industrial and Labor Relations Review* (April), pp. 343-59.
_____. 1988b. "Further Evidence on Union Efficiency in Construction." *Industrial Relations* (Spring), pp. 232-40.
_____. 1993. "Unit Costs, Legal Shocks, and Unionization in Construction." Mimeo.
Bourdon, Clinton C., and Raymond E. Levitt. 1980. *Union and Open-Shop Construction*. Lexington, MA: Heath.

Business Roundtable. 1974. *Coming to Grips with Some Major Problems in the Construction Industry.* New York: Business Roundtable.

_____. 1982a. "Constraints Imposed by Collective Bargaining Agreements." Construction Industry Cost Effectiveness Project Report C-4, September.

_____. 1982b. "Government Limitations on Training Innovations." Construction Industry Cost Effectiveness Project Report D-2, March.

_____. 1982c. "Training Problems in Open Shop Construction." Construction Industry Cost Effectiveness Project Report D-4, September.

_____. 1983. *More Construction for the Money*, Summary Report of the Construction Industry Cost Effectiveness Project, January.

_____. 1993. "The Growing Threat to Competitiveness: Union Pressure Tactics Target U.S. Construction Owners."

Christie, Robert A. 1956. *Empire in Wood.* Ithaca, NY: Cornell University Press.

Construction Labor Research Council. 1992. "Cost Reducing Modifications to Construction Collective Bargaining Agreements."

Erlich, Mark. 1988. "Who Will Build the Future?" *Labor Research Review* (Fall), pp. 1-19.

Foster, Howard G. "The Labor Market in Nonunion Construction." *Industrial and Labor Relations Review* (July), pp. 1071-85.

Gifford, Courtney D. 1990. *Directory of U.S. Labor Organizations*, 1990-91 Edition. Washington, DC: Bureau of National Affairs.

Hirsch, Barry T., and David A. MacPherson. 1993. "Union Membership and Coverage Files from the Current Population Surveys: A Note." *Industrial and Labor Relations Review* (April), pp. 574-78.

Ichniowski, Casey, and Anne Preston. 1989. "The Persistence of Organized Crime in New York City Construction: An Economic Perspective." *Industrial and Labor Relations Review* (July), pp. 549-65.

Linneman, Peter D., Michael L. Wachter, and William H. Carter. 1990. "Evaluating the Evidence on Union Employment and Wages." *Industrial and Labor Relations Review* (October), pp. 34-53.

Marshall, Ray, Robert W. Glover, and William S. Franklin. 1975. *Training and Entry into Union Construction*, U.S. Department of Labor, Manpower Administration, Manpower R&D Monograph 39. Washington, DC: GPO.

Metzgar, Jack. 1988. "Buying the Job." *Labor Research Review* (Fall), pp. 51-57.

Mills, Daniel Quinn. 1972. *Industrial Relations and Manpower in Construction.* Cambridge: MIT Press.

_____. 1980. "Construction." In G. Somers, ed., *Collective Bargaining: Contemporary American Experience.* Madison, WI: Industrial Relations Research Association.

National Construction Employers Council and the Building and Construction Trades Department, AFL-CIO. 1984. *Market Recovery Program Handbook.*

_____. 1985. *Market Recovery Guidebook.*

_____. 1986. "Construction Industry Collective Bargaining in the 1980s."

Northrup, Herbert R. 1984. *Open Shop Construction Revisited.* Philadelphia, PA: Wharton School Industrial Research Unit.

_____. 1989. "Construction Doublebreasted Operations and Pre-Hire Agreements: Assessing the Issues." *Journal of Labor Research* (Spring), pp. 215-38.

_____. Forthcoming. "Salting the Contractors' Labor Force: Construction Unions Organizing with NLRB Assistance." *Journal of Labor Research.*

Northrup, Herbert R., and Howard G. Foster. 1975. *Open Shop Construction.* Philadelphia, PA: Wharton School Industrial Research Unit.

Poltz, Judith T. 1990. "Bargaining Obligations in the Construction Industry: An Outline of Recent Developments." *Labor Law Journal* (September), pp. 649-58.

Segal, Martin. 1970. *The Rise of the United Association.* Cambridge: Harvard University Press.

Thieblot, Jr., Armand J. 1986. *Prevailing Wage Legislation: The Davis-Bacon Act, State "Little David" Acts, the Walsh-Healey Act, and the Service Contract Act.* Philadelphia, PA: Wharton School Industrial Research Unit.

CHAPTER 11

Collective Bargaining in the Hospitality Industry in the 1980s

DOROTHY SUE COBBLE AND MICHAEL MERRILL
Rutgers University

Editor's Abstract

The Hotel Employees and Restaurant Employees International Union (HERE) represents individuals in both major parts of the hospitality industry. The union has had considerably more success in hotels than in restaurants, where unionization has virtually disappeared. Cobble and Merrill argue that the rebirth of unionism in the restaurant industry, as a whole, is impossible without a fundamental restructuring of the current legal and institutional framework—one that nurtures occupational as opposed to industrial organization. On the other hand, they predict that the recent decline in hotel unionism will level off and perhaps reverse itself. Hotels are immobile and have large numbers of long-term employees; moreover, especially in large cities and convention centers, they are vulnerable to strikes. Spurred by discontent with low wages, racial and gender discrimination, and deteriorating working conditions, HERE has used creative tactics and militant action to organize new members in some areas.

Cobble and Merrill review the substantial decline of hotel organization over the 1980s, from about 20% to 10%. Levels of unionization are still high in some major metropolitan areas, so the union still has bargaining power in those locales. HERE has generally been able to resist employer demands for reduced contributions to health care, although locals did often agree to change work rules in the 1980s. Employer moves to disband hotel association bargaining apparently backfired in some areas, such as San Francisco.

The union has had problems. Corruption has been an issue, although most locals are not corrupt. Moreover, the international is led primarily by older white men, despite a work force that is heavily female and minority. In recent years, a disproportionate number of Hispanics have entered the hotel and restaurant work force, where they join large concentrations of African Americans, Asians, and recent immigrants. Several important locals have had dynamic and progressive leadership, including ones led by women in San Francisco and Los Angeles. Boston's Local 26 has been especially successful in negotiating very innovative clauses in collective bargaining agreements. It has linked hotel occupancy rates with employee bonus payments, negotiated an employer-funded housing trust providing union members with loans and grants, won health benefits for extended family members and gay partners, and gained employer-financed English as a second language/literacy classes.

The hospitality industry has a generally poor record with regard to racial, sexual, and age discrimination. Lighter-skinned employees are more likely to work in the front-of-the-house customer contact positions, such as hotel desk clerks, waiters, or waitresses. Darker-skinned minorities are concentrated in cleaning, food preparation, and other non-contact positions. Younger women are also favored over older women. These discriminatory practices may increasingly be challenged in the hotel industry if the union overcomes its own somewhat uneven record with regard to racial and gender issues.

The prospects for collective bargaining in the hospitality industry are, therefore, mixed. The decline in hotel unionism has leveled off and may be reversed. But the future of unions in the restaurant industry is bleak, absent far-reaching legal and institutional changes that would foster the rebirth of occupational unionism.

o   o   o

For twenty-seven years, the West Hollywood coffee shop enjoyed labor peace and a loyal clientele. Yet when a new owner took over in 1984, he replaced the older unionized waitresses with younger help and ended the longstanding partnership with Local 11 of the Hotel Employees and Restaurant Employees International Union (HERE). The fired union members, ranging in age from fifty to seventy, organized as "the granny waitresses" and refused to go quietly. They picketed; they filed unfair labor practice charges; they reached out to customers and to labor and community organizations for support. Yet the new owner prevailed. The union could neither force the rehiring of the "grannies" nor organize the younger replacements.

In contrast, the Seoul-based, multinational Koreana Corporation failed in its 1992 bid to sever its Local 11 contract. The corporation had purchased the Hyatt Wilshire Hotel, fired all 125 union employees, and attempted to reopen as the newly refurbished and nonunion Wilshire Koreana. After less than a year of mass demonstrations, political pressure, and public relations efforts coordinated with the assistance of the AFL-CIO's Asian Pacific American Labor Alliance, Local 11 proudly called a press conference and announced the signing of a collective bargaining agreement with the hotel (Rosier 1992; Durazo interview 1993).

How typical are these examples? How representative are they of recent trends in collective bargaining in the hotel and restaurant industries? The union defeat at the West Hollywood coffee shop is certainly the more common story: Union coverage among hotel and restaurant workers dropped by half over the course of the 1980s. By some estimates, between 1980 and 1991 union density rates fell from 19.2% to 10% among hotel and motel employees and from 5% to 2% for restaurant workers (see Graphs 1 and 2).[1] In absolute numbers, union membership also declined throughout the 1980s, hitting a low of 269,000 by 1991, a loss of nearly 100,000 members from 1981 (AFL-CIO 1991; BNA 1988-89).

But the Koreana example represents a crucial subtext to the tale of overall decline. By the end of the 1980s, HERE was experiencing some success in resisting deunionization and by 1993 had even enjoyed a number of signal victories in organizing new establishments. Indeed, the 1992 HERE victory at the Wilshire Koreana may be indicative of a new mood in labor-management relations for the 1990s—a mood that has emerged in other sectors of the economy as well. In the aftermath of the drawn-out bloody confrontations of the 1980s—the most virulent in the industry since the late 1930s and 1940s—both labor and management are rethinking their strategies. HERE has taken steps to stem the hemorrhaging of union membership, becoming more responsive to employer calls for flexibility and creative problem solving, while simultaneously relying on such adversarial tactics as comprehensive or corporate campaigning, consumer boycotts, civil disobedience, mass sit-ins and "sip-ins," "walk and work" picketing, public relations gimmicks, and political leveraging.[2] In response, there is evidence that some employers, primarily those with some degree of unionism (such as the Hilton or Sheraton Corporation), have concluded that the costs of confrontation are too high. Others, however, remain committed to operating nonunion. Employers like McDonald's or the Marriott Corporation view collective bargaining as inimicable and the economic, social, and political consequences of a union-avoidance strategy minimal (*Washington Post* February 17, 1992; Fielder interview 1993).

The Koreana example also illustrates the current divergent realities for collective bargaining in the hotel and in the restaurant sector. Union density fell earlier in eating and drinking places than in hotels, and the drop was more precipitous. From a highwater mark of 20% to 25% in the 1950s, unionization dropped to 8% by 1970, and then to 5% by 1980. As the 1990s dawn, collective bargaining has virtually disappeared

GRAPH 1
Unionized Hotel Workers, 1970-1991
as % of Total Workforce

Sources: Richard Freeman and James Medoff, "New Estimates of Private Sector Unionism," *Industrial and Labor Relations Review* 32:2 (January 1979), 143-174; Edward C. Kokkelenberg and Donna R. Sockell, "Union Membership in the United States, 1973-1981," *Industrial and Labor Relations Review* 38:4 (July 1985), 497-543; Barry T. Hirsch and David A. Macpherson, "Union Membership and Coverage Files from the Current Population Surveys, 1983-1991," Department of Economics, Florida State University, Tallahassee, FL 32306-2045.

GRAPH 2
Unionized Restaurant Workers, 1970-1991
as % of Total Workforce

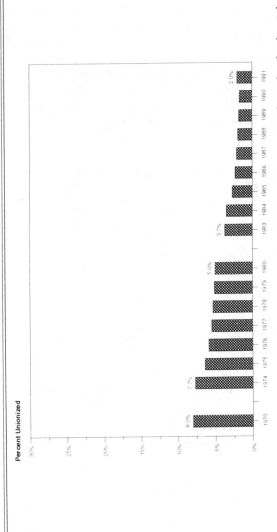

Sources: Richard Freeman and James Medoff, "New Estimates of Private Sector Unionism," *Industrial and Labor Relations Review* 32:2 (January 1979), 143-174; Edward C. Kokkelenberg and Donna R. Sockell, "Union Membership in the United States, 1973-1981," *Industrial and Labor Relations Review* 38:4 (July 1985), 497-543; Barry T. Hirsch and David A. Macpherson, "Union Membership and Coverage Files from the Current Population Surveys, 1983-1991," Department of Economics, Florida State University, Tallahassee, FL 32306-2045.

in eating and drinking places and is unlikely to return without a fundamental restructuring of the current legal and institutional framework for
employee representation. In contrast, the 1970s closed with one-fifth of
the hotel industry still unionized. And, despite the steep downward
national trends of the 1980s, collective bargaining in the hotel and motel
sector continues to have a major, if not decisive, impact in large urban
areas such as New York, San Francisco, Chicago, Los Angeles, Boston,
and Washington, as well as in gambling and entertainment centers such
as Las Vegas, Nevada and Atlantic City, New Jersey (Table 1A and Table
1B). Unions in the hotel and motel industry may have weathered the
worst. Certainly, HERE has demonstrated its resilience and may in fact
be well positioned for a rebound in the 1990s.

TABLE 1A

Changing Union Density Among Hotel and Motel Work Force in Most
Highly Unionized Regional Labor Markets (Percent)

	1980	1990	1992
Atlantic City, NJ	80	75	82
Boston	30	30	30
Chicago	75	70	70
Las Vegas	80	75	80
Los Angeles (County)	50	40	40
New York City	85	80	80
San Francisco	85	70	75
Washington, DC	80	50	50

Source: Union density estimates provided by HERE's Research Department and
various local union officials.

TABLE 1B

Union Membership in Selected HERE Locals, 1993

Local 226	Las Vegas	27,254
Local 6	New York City	17,573
Local 54	Atlantic City	14,302
Local 1	Chicago	11,530
Local 11	Los Angeles	8,389
Local 2	San Francisco	8,053
Local 100	New York City	6,217
Local 24	Detroit	5,799
Local 25	Washington, DC	5,373
Local 26	Boston	3,919

Source: Union membership estimates provided by HERE's Research Department and various local union officials.

The Hotel and Restaurant Work Force

Who works in the hospitality industry? What jobs do they hold?
What are those jobs like? As of June 1992, more than 8.5 million
employees depended on the hospitality sector for their livelihood—
6,679,000 in eating and drinking places and another 1,679,000 in hotels
and motels (USDL 1992:54). Eating and drinking places now employ
more workers than any other industry except health services. Moreover,
while hotel employment grew steadily over the 1980s, eating and drinking places added more new jobs than any other type of establishment in
the 1980s (Graph 3). This industry is now projected to have "the largest
numerical job growth of all industries from 1986 to 2000" (Emerson
1991:98; Silvestri and Lukasiewicz 1985:Table 5, 59; Plunkert 1990:12,
Table 5; Mencimer 1992; USDL 1988:6).

GRAPH 3
Hospitality Employment, 1958-1992

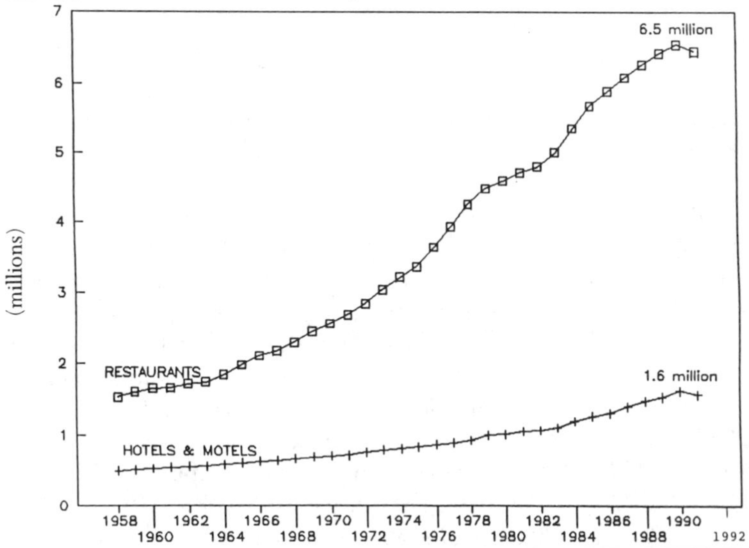

Sources: 1958-1990: Bureau of Labor Statistics, *Employment, Hours, and
Earnings, United States, 1909-1990,* vol. II, U.S. Department of Labor, Bulletin 2370,
March 1991, SIC 58 and SIC 701; 1991: *Employment & Earnings* (August 1992).

White male workers continue to be a shrinking minority within the
hospitality industry. In the first several decades of the twentieth century,

the vast number of new jobs in hotels, motels, and restaurants went primarily to women (Cobble 1991a). But the long-term trend toward feminization in the industry has slowed in the last two decades and appears finally to have halted. The dominance of women in the industry is not likely to be reversed, but neither is their share likely to increase at the rapid rate of past decades. In fact, during the 1980s the employment share of women in both hotels and restaurants fell from earlier in the decade to comprise 56% of all restaurant employees and 52.5% of all hotel employees (USDL 1989:98-9, Table 19, 98-9, 106-7; see Table 2).

TABLE 2
Female Employment, 1960-1990
(Percent)

Year	Eating and Drinking	Hotels
1960	54.7	46.0
1970	56.4	49.5
1980	56.3	54.2
1990	56.0	52.5

Source: Bureau of Labor Statistics, Employment, Hours, and Earnings, United States, 1909-1990, Vol. II, U.S. Department of Labor, Bulletin 2370, March 1991, SIC 58 and SIC 701.

The same cannot be said for the employment share of minorities in the hospitality industry. Between 1983 and 1991, overall restaurant employment increased by 8%, while the number of African Americans grew by 50% and the number of Hispanics by 123% (see Graph 4). A similar shift occurred in the hotel and motel sector. Overall, total employment in the industry jumped by 51% between 1983 and 1991, but the number of blacks rose by 63% and the number of Hispanics by 159% (see Graph 5; USDL 1989: Table 19, 98-9, 106-7). As a result, in 1983, minorities comprised 24% of hotel and motel workers and 15% of eating and drinking employees; by 1988 those percentages had risen to 31% and 20%, respectively. Indeed, this sector is now the nation's number one employer of minorities (USDL 1989:Table 19, 98-9, 106-7; Bernstein 1990:21).

What kinds of jobs do these workers have? Most workers hold non-supervisory, entry-level, service jobs. Ninety percent of all eating and drinking employees are in nonmanagerial occupations. Eighty-two percent are concentrated in food service jobs, working as waiters, cooks, kitchen workers, food counter workers, and bartenders (see

GRAPH 4

Restaurant Workforce, 1983-1991

Cum. Growth Rates by Race & Sex

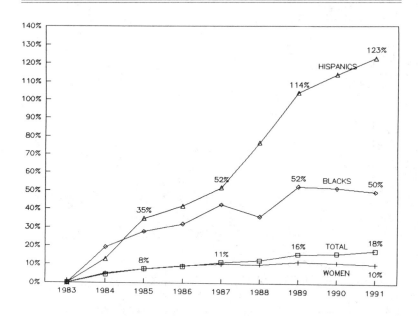

Sources: 1983-1988: Bureau of Labor Statistics, *Handbook of Labor Statistics.* U.S. Department of Labor, 1989, Table 19; 1989: *Employment & Earnings,* January 1990, Table 28; 1990: *Employment & Earnings,* January 1991, Table 28; 1991: *Employment & Earnings,* January 1992, Table 28.

Table 3). Three-quarters of hotel workers also occupy "low level" service occupations such as maid, janitor, food server, or hotel clerk (USDL 1990:56).

The hospitality industry now employs a disproportionate number of part-time and young workers. Over two-fifths of all wage and salary workers in restaurants are part-time, more than double the corresponding figure for private-sector workers (Personick 1991:20). But this pattern is of relatively recent origin. In 1940, only 21% of waitresses and 11% of waiters worked 34 hours or less. By 1980, however, the percentage of part-time food servers had leaped to 66% and 54%, respectively (see Graphs 6 and 7), and only one-fifth worked both year round and full time (see Cobble 1991a; Job 1980).

GRAPH 5
Hotel & Motel Workforce, 1983-1991
Cum. Growth Rates by Race & Sex

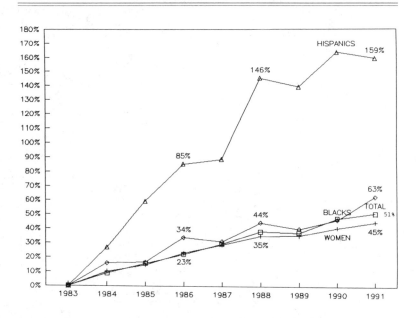

Sources: 1983-1988: Bureau of Labor Statistics, *Handbook of Labor Statistics.* U.S. Department of Labor, 1989, Table 19; 1989: *Employment & Earnings,* January 1990, Table 28; 1990: *Employment & Earnings,* January 1991, Table 28; 1991: *Employment & Earnings,* January 1992, Table 28.

A vast army of teenagers and college students in their twenties hold these part-time jobs. Eating and drinking places have a higher proportion of teenagers than any other retail sector. In 1990, 29% of all restaurant employees were between the ages of 16 and 19, compared to one-twentieth of the total private-sector work force (Hecker and Murphy 1985; Personick 1991:20).

Job segregation by race and sex is endemic in the industry. Women made some progress in the 1970s and 1980s, integrating such "non-traditional" areas as bartending, fine-dining food service, food supervision, and restaurant ownership (Cobble 1991a; Detman 1990; Hall 1989; USDL 1989; *Wall Street Journal,* March 8, 1986). But now, even when men and women have the same job title, women make less in wages and

TABLE 3

Eating and Drinking Places
Occupational Structure 1988

Occupation	Number	Percent
Managers, professionals, and administrators	393,780	6.1
Salespersons	409,860	6.3
Cashiers	359,180	5.5
All others	50,680	0.8
Clerks and secretaries	126,530	2.0
Food service	5,312,110	81.7
Supervisors	226,050	3.5
Hosts and hostesses	151,390	2.3
Bartenders	256,810	4.0
Waiters and waitresses	1,374,820	21.2
Waiter and waitress assistants	300,930	4.6
Counter and fountain workers	257,290	4.0
Cooks, restaurant or cafeteria	495,320	7.6
Cooks, fast food	532,770	8.2
Cooks, short order	150,980	2.3
Kitchen workers	1,505,640	23.2
Misc. food preparation	60,110	0.9
All other occupations	256,980	4.0
Total	6,501,260	100.0

Source: Bureau of Labor Statistics, *Occupational Employment in Selected Non-manufacturing Industries.* U.S. Department of Labor, March 1990, Table 21.

tips (Cobble 1991a; Mellor 1984; Mellor 1985; O'Connor 1971). Moreover, many of the most rapidly feminizing jobs have also been characterized by falling wages (whether as cause or effect is unclear). For example, between 1969 and 1979, as female bartenders became more common, the income of male bartenders declined by 50% and the income of female bartenders by 32% (Detman 1990:Table 12.3, 251). The same trends are evident in managerial positions. In the words of some researchers, middle management has now become a "velvet ghetto." Of equal importance, many of the lowest-paid jobs are still heavily female dominated. In 1991, women still comprised 82.9% of maids and housemen, 81.6% of waiters, 71% of counter and fountain workers, and 70% of kitchen workers (see Table 4 and Graph 8).

In contrast with the limited but perceptible entrance of women into some of the traditionally male jobs, job segregation by race has changed

GRAPH 6
Women's Weekly Hours, 1940-1980
Food & Beverage Servers

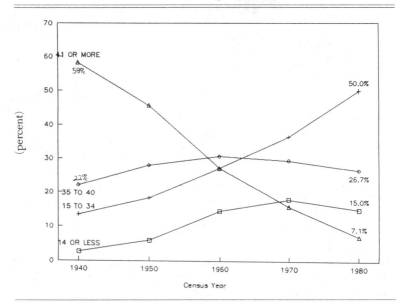

Census Year

Sources: 1940: U.S. Bureau of Census, *1940 Census of Population. Subject Reports: Occupational Characteristics*, Table 9; 1950: U.S. Bureau of Census, *1960 Census of Population. Subject Reports: Occupational Characteristics*, Table 14; 1960: U.S. Bureau of Census, *1960 Census of Population. Subject Reports: Occupational Characteristics*, Table 13; 1970: U.S. Bureau of Census, *1970 Census of Population. Special Reports: Occupational Characteristics*, Table 45; 1980: Bureau of the Census, *1980 Census of Population: Detailed Population Characteristics. Part 1: United States Summary*, Table 279.

little in the last decade. Historically, white workers occupied the visible or "front-of-the-house" positions such as maitre d', waiter, bartender, or hostess; African American and other non-European minorities were kept out of sight, working in "back-of-the-house" jobs cleaning and preparing food.[3] These historic patterns have persisted into the 1980s (Mencimer 1992; Bailey 1985; Graphs 9 and 10). African Americans are overrepresented in the lowest-paid, non-direct service jobs. In 1991, they constituted 27.2% of maids and housemen, 23.3% of short-order cooks, 18.3% of other cooks, and 16.6% of kitchen workers. And, significantly, with the exception of maids and housemen, their representation

GRAPH 7
Men's Weekly Hours, 1940-1980
Food & Beverage Servers

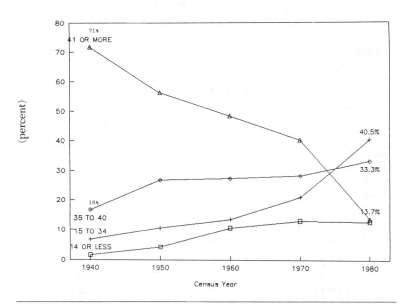

Sources: 1940: U.S. Bureau of Census, *1940 Census of Population. Subject Reports: Occupational Characteristics*, Table 9; 1950: U.S. Bureau of Census, *1960 Census of Population. Subject Reports: Occupational Characteristics*, Table 14; 1960: U.S. Bureau of Census, *1960 Census of Population. Subject Reports: Occupational Characteristics*, Table 13; 1970: U.S. Bureau of Census, *1970 Census of Population. Special Reports: Occupational Characteristics*, Table 45; 1980: Bureau of the Census, *1980 Census of Population: Detailed Population Characteristics. Part 1: United States Summary*, Table 279.

in these jobs had increased since the early 1980s. In contrast, African Americans *lost ground* or made no perceptible gains in some of the better-paying, more prestigious, direct service jobs such as bartending (falling from 2.7% to 2.0%) supervisory work, and table service (from 4.1% to 4.2%), *despite* their growing presence in the industry. The one exception appears to be "hotel clerk" where African Americans moved from 6.7% to 12.8% of the occupation (see Table 4 and Graph 9).

The picture for Hispanic workers, the second largest minority group in the hospitality industry, is more mixed. Although they too are disproportionately represented in "back-of-the-house" work (such as food

TABLE 4

Selected Occupational Groups, By Sex, Race, Hispanic Origins

	Women 1983/1991	African Americans 1983/1991	Hispanics 1983/1991
Hotel clerks	68.6/72.3	6.7/12.8	3.2/6.9
Maids and housemen	81.2/82.9	32.3/27.2	10.1/19.7
Bartenders	48.4/54.0	2.7/2.0	4.4/4.7
Cooks, except short order	50.8/46.9	1.6/18.3	6.8/14.4
Waiters and waitresses	87.8/81.6	4.1/4.2	3.6/7.7
Short-order cooks	38.5/28.9	12.9/23.3	2.4/11.7
Counter/fountain	76.0/71.0	9.1/10.9	6.7/7.9
Kitchen workers	77.0/70.6	13.7/16.6	8.1/13.8
Waiter & waitress assts.	38.8/38.5	12.6/15.3	14.2/20.6
Misc. food preparation	54.0/51.9	15.1/15.1	11.6/19.5

Source: 1983: Bureau of Labor Statistics, Handbook of Labor Statistics. U.S. Department of Labor, 1989, Table 18; 1991: Employment and Earnings, January 1992, Table 28.

preparation and house cleaning), they have a slightly greater range of occupational choice than do African Americans. The numbers of Hispanics in supervisory positions has increased in the last few years, for example, as has their representation in some of the direct public service jobs such as waiter, waiter assistant, and hotel clerk (see Table 4 and Graph 10).

Finally, the wages for jobs in the hospitality industry remain among the lowest paid anywhere in the economy (Henderson 1965; Hecker and Murphy 1985). Eating and drinking employees in fact are paid considerably less than are employees in *any other* nonagricultural industry (Emerson 1991:99, Table 4.15). According to the National Restaurant Association's 1992 survey of wages for hourly employees, only cooks and bakers earned over six dollars an hour. The hourly rates for non-tipped employees were shockingly low: $4.68 for fast food workers; $4.85 for dishwashers; and less than $5.35 for drivers, cashiers, cafeteria servers, and food checkers (National Restaurant Association 1992). Overall, eating and drinking employees averaged $5.24 an hour in 1991, hotel and motel $7.23 (USDL 1992:99).

The dismal wage situation shows little sign of brightening in the near future. Real hourly earnings dropped over the course of the 1970s and 1980s, especially in the restaurant sector (Table 5). Real weekly earnings declined as well, spurred in part by the steep downward slide in average weekly hours worked (see Graph 11 and Table 6). In restaurants and

GRAPH 8

Occupational Segregation 1983-1991
Women Workers

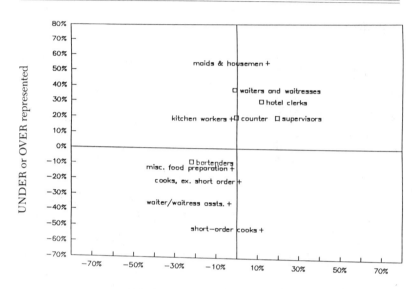

DECREASING or INCREASING parity

□ Front-of-the-house   + Back-of-the-house

Sources: 1983-1988: Bureau of Labor Statistics, *Handbook of Labor Statistics.*
U.S. Department of Labor, 1989, Table 19; 1989: *Employment & Earnings,* January
1990, Table 28; 1990: *Employment & Earnings,* January 1991, Table 28; 1991: *Employment & Earnings,* January 1992, Table 28. The vertical axis in Graphs 8, 9, & 10
show the degree to which women, African Americans, and Hispanics were under- or
over-represented in selected hospitality occupations in 1991. The degree of under- or
over-representation is equal to the difference between their actual representation in
the occupation and their overall representation in the industry. The horizontal axis
shows the amount of change in their position since 1983. Parity increased for groups
which became less under- or over-represented; it decreased where a group became
more under- or over-represented.

bars, real weekly earnings peaked in 1968, declining sharply from $153 a
week in 1968 to $95 in 1991 (see Graph 11). The earnings for hotel and
motel employees also fell, although not as precipitously. In 1972, the peak
year for real weekly earnings, hotel employees averaged $181 a week; in
1991 they averaged $160 (see Graph 11). Interestingly, however, real

GRAPH 9

Occupational Segregation 1983-1991
African American Workers

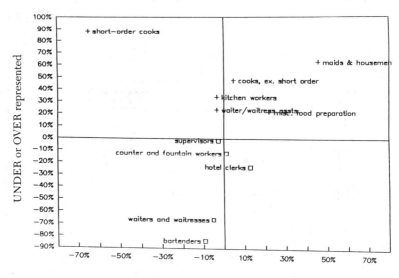

DECREASING or INCREASING parity
□ Front-of-the-house   + Back-of-the-house

Sources: 1983-1988: Bureau of Labor Statistics, *Handbook of Labor Statistics.* U.S. Department of Labor, 1989, Table 19; 1989: *Employment & Earnings,* January 1990, Table 28; 1990: *Employment & Earnings,* January 1991, Table 28; 1991: *Employment & Earnings,* January 1992, Table 28. The vertical axis in Graphs 8, 9, & 10 show the degree to which women, African Americans, and Hispanics were under- or over-represented in selected hospitality occupations in 1991. The degree of under- or over-representation is equal to the difference between their actual representation in the occupation and their overall representation in the industry. The horizontal axis shows the amount of change in their position since 1983. Parity increased for groups which became less under- or over-represented; it decreased where a group became more under- or over-represented.

weekly earnings in hotels and motels declined less than in manufacturing, and from 1982 to 1988 real earnings actually rose.

Moreover, few jobs carry a full array of benefits. The National Restaurant Association estimated in 1990 that "91% of eating and drinking place firms provided no health insurance for hourly or salaried employees."

GRAPH 10
Occupational Segregation 1983-1991
Hispanic Workers

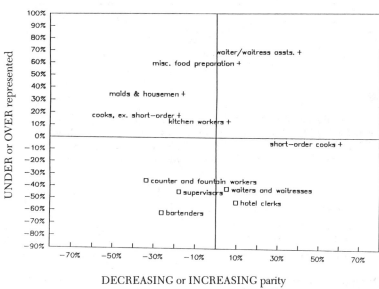

DECREASING or INCREASING parity
□ Front-of-the-house   + Back-of-the-house

Sources: 1983-1988: Bureau of Labor Statistics, *Handbook of Labor Statistics.* U.S. Department of Labor, 1989, Table 19; 1989: *Employment & Earnings,* January 1990, Table 28; 1990: *Employment & Earnings,* January 1991, Table 28; 1991: *Employment & Earnings,* January 1992, Table 28. The vertical axis in Graphs 8, 9, & 10 show the degree to which women, African Americans, and Hispanics were under- or over-represented in selected hospitality occupations in 1991. The degree of under- or over-representation is equal to the difference between their actual representation in the occupation and their overall representation in the industry. The horizontal axis shows the amount of change in their position since 1983. Parity increased for groups which became less under- or over-represented; it decreased where a group became more under- or over-represented.

Pensions, paid vacations, job-guaranteed leave, and other kinds of fringe offerings are even rarer (National Restaurant Association 1990:40-41).

The hotel and restaurant industry is diverse, however, and statistics can mask the reality of the lives of individual workers. Tips provide a good income for a small slice of the work force.[4] Others enjoy a living wage, job security, and fringe benefits because they work in the small

TABLE 5
Real Hourly Earnings, 1960-1990
(in 1982-1984 dollars)

Year	Eating and Drinking	Hotels
1960		3.91
1965	4.49	4.64
1970	4.95	5.45
1975	4.83	5.46
1980	4.24	5.22
1985	3.89	5.43
1990	[3.80]	[5.26]

Source: Bureau of Labor Statistics, *Employment, Hours, and Earnings, United States, 1909-1990*, Vol. II, U.S. Department of Labor, Bulletin 2370, March 1991, SIC 58 and SIC 701. Current earnings have been deflated to 1982-1984 dollars using the Consumer Price Index from the 1992 *Statistical Abstract of the U.S.*

unionized segment of these industries. The young, white, a la carte waiter in Washington's elegant Willard Hotel who earns $40,000 a year in wages and tips for a short work week, and the older black maid in New York who supports her family as a housekeeper at the unionized Ritz-Carleton both belie the statistics (Cobble 1991a; Mencimer 1992).

The Employers

Hotel and restaurant employers range from small independent restaurant entrepreneurs in far off places like Tucumcari, New Mexico to the corporate head of Marriott, who presides over thousands of hotels spread across the globe as well as such megachains as Big Boy and Roy Rogers. Another prominent type is the franchiser, a hybrid who is neither owner nor employee. A successful franchiser might expertly manage several outlets and reap a healthy profit; but like the sharecropper of days past, he must send rent, a guaranteed percent of the gross sales, and substantial user or service fees to the corporate landlord or parent company (Luxenberg 1985:13-50; Food and Allied Service Trades 1985:2-3).

Yet despite the variety among employers, some generalizations do emerge. Ownership in the hospitality industry is highly concentrated. The eating and drinking sector is dominated by a few large corporations. In 1982, the Department of Commerce reported that 14 big franchisors—McDonald's, Kentucky Fried Chicken, Dairy Queen, et al.— accounted for 53% of all restaurant sales (Food and Allied Service

GRAPH 11

Real Weekly Earnings, 1960-1961

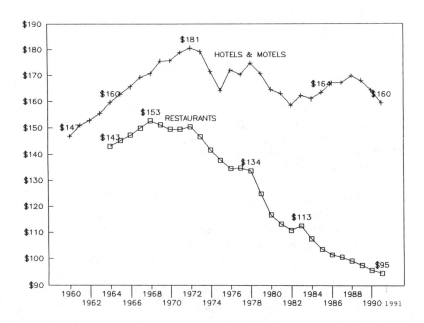

Sources: 1958-1990: Bureau of Labor Statistics, *Employment, Hours, and Earnings, United States, 1909-1990*, vol. II, U.S. Department of Labor, Bulletin 2370, March 1991, SIC 58 and SIC 701; 1991: *Employment & Earnings* (August 1992).

Trades 1985:10-12). Over the course of the 1980s, large chains and franchises such as Econo Lodge or Burger King have been gobbled up by even larger parent companies, further consolidating the industry. Indeed, the world's largest restaurant company is Pepsi Co. which now owns Pizza Hut, Taco Bell, and Kentucky Fried Chicken (Emerson 1991:25, 66). And, none of the executives interviewed by *Hotel and Motel Management* in 1990 disagreed with the prediction made by the Choice Hotels International CEO that "less than five global megachains will probably control 90% of the world's hotel market by the year 2000" (Food and Allied Service Trades 1985:13, 17; US Department of Commerce 1991; Geller 1990:22-23; Jesitus 1990:66).

Historically, hotels and restaurants clustered in urban centers, but that pattern changed dramatically with the rise of auto travel and the

TABLE 6
Average Weekly Hours, 1960-1990

Year	Eating and Drinking	Hotels
1960		39.9
1965	35.2	38.0
1970	31.2	34.6
1975	29.1	31.7
1980	26.1	30.5
1985	25.8	30.2
1990	25.2	30.8

Source: Bureau of Labor Statistics, Employment, Hours, and Earnings, United States, 1909-1990, Vol. II, U.S. Department of Labor, Bulletin 2370, March 1991, SIC 58 and SIC 701. Current earnings have been deflated to 1982-1984 dollars using the Consumer Price Index from the 1992 Statistical Abstract of the U.S.

move toward suburbanization in the post-World War II years. The industry thus became increasingly dispersed geographically, at the same time as it became more concentrated. The McDonald's Corporation provides a paradigmatic case of this process, but it is by no means the only instance of it. In 1991, McDonald's alone operated 8,600 separate restaurants in the U.S., spread out over the landscape almost like street lights. It also served clientele in 3,300 foreign outlets (BNA 1991).

A third long-term trend of considerable importance to the hospitality industry is the rise of more simplified, inexpensive service encounters. Restaurant spending, in particular, has shifted from full service to fast food during the last 20 years. The fast food share of industry sales rose from 26% in 1972 to 40% in 1989 (Personick 1991; US Department of Commerce 1991:40-42). Yet a substantial niche for specialized, upscale dining exists along with a large, middle ground of family restaurants. Similarly, although the lodging industry is moving toward more "limited service" hotels, the full-service hotel remains a permanent fixture. Customers continue to demand a variety of eating and lodging experiences (Food and Allied Service Trades 1985:10-12; Silvestri and Lukasiewicz 1985:54; Bailey 1985).

The diverse personnel practices of the industry are in part a response to this differentiated consumer market. Some employers—in particular the fast food operators—emphasize rationalization, predictability, and the substitution of technology for human output in work organization and labor relations. Their orientation is typically "mass market," aimed at turning out homogeneous products at the lowest possible cost to the greatest number of customers. Many use convenience and frozen foods prepared centrally in off-premise sites. They are prepackaged and pre-portioned, then dispersed to satellite operations for "finishing off." "Cooks" at Burger King do not slice, prepare or even flip their burgers—gas flames below and above sear the precut, uniform patties as the "cooks" place them on the assembly line. Machines add presliced pickles, premeasured condiments, and encase them in the buns. In this food factory, every hamburger theoretically emerges from the line like every other hamburger (Ritzer 1983; Wyckoff and Sasser 1978; Job 1980:41; Luxenberg 1985:83; Food and Allied Service Trades 1985:27-28).

In contrast, a still substantial part of the hospitality business focuses on quality rather than quantity, emphasizing innovation, individualized products and services, and employee skill enhancement. This segment of the industry believes that personal direct service to customers and "treating employees with respect," are the keys to business success in the 1990s. Experts here speak of "cross-training" employees, "the art of service," and the need for "batch-cooked" as opposed to mass-produced food.[5] The food service industry may have begun its "belated industrial revolution" in 1954 when Ray Kroc stumbled upon the McDonald brothers' San Bernardino hamburger stand, but the time-honored crafts of cooking and waiting, as well as the old "artisanal" workshops where the masters of each ply their trades, are not likely to disappear for a long time to come, if ever (Jacobs 1990; Luxenberg 1985:69; Powers 1974: 50).

The Unions

A single union, the Hotel Employees and Restaurant Employees International Union (HERE), historically has had jurisdiction over hospitality workers. The International Brotherhood of Teamsters, the International Longshore and Warehouse Union, the Service Employees International Union, and a handful of other unions also represent hotel and restaurant employees, but the vast majority belong to HERE.[6] Established in 1891 as a collection of individual craft locals comprised primarily of male bartenders, cooks, and waiters, HERE succeeded first in organizing skilled workers in elite restaurants (the so-called "tablecloth" end of the trade), and in neighborhood bars and eating places patronized by the working class. Hotel organizing awaited the industrial union boom of the 1930s. Union penetration reached its peak in the 1950s, when collective bargaining covered close to a fourth of the industry, and cities such as San Francisco, New York, and Detroit boasted unionization rates of 80% or more (Cobble 1991a:Chapters 3 and 4).

Two internal problems currently plague the union, both of which are rooted in its particular history and structure. HERE has been associated with organized crime since Prohibition days. In the 1920s and early 1930s, organized crime controlled the distribution of illegal liquor and often attempted to gain the cooperation of restaurant owners and employees. With repeal in 1932, organized crime shifted even more heavily into the bar and restaurant business in part to compensate for the revenue lost from bootlegging. In addition, certain structural factors heightened HERE's vulnerability to corruption. Decentralized unions that bargain in local, competitive markets such as the Teamsters, the construction trades, HERE, and others, have often been plagued by corruption.

In the 1930s and 1940s, socialist-influenced leaders such as Hugo Ernst and Jay Rubin successfully fought mob influence, defending the international presidency as well as key locals in New York City (Josephson 1956:216-33; Seidman 1935:199-213; Rubin and Obermeier 1943: 225-42). But in the mid-1970s, the corruption issue returned to haunt the union, both at the international and local levels. Since the election of Edward Hanley to the presidency of HERE in 1973, the Labor and Justice Departments have targeted the international and its officers for investigation. In 1984, the Senate's Permanent Subcommittee on Organized Crime issued a widely publicized report, singling out HERE as among the most corrupt international unions. Nevertheless, none of the top officers have been indicted, much less convicted.

At the local level, the vast majority of HERE's 151 locals remain relatively free of corruption, having neither warranted governmental suspicion nor surveillance. A few well-publicized cases, however, have shaped public perceptions of the union. For instance, in the early 1980s, the principal officer of Local 28 in Oakland, Ray Lane, was convicted of embezzling funds as well as requiring waitresses to perform sex acts in return for jobs from the union's hiring hall. In 1990, the Justice Department also used the RICO Act to remove the officers of Local 54 in Atlantic City, New Jersey, charging them, among other things, with unduly influencing certain laundry contracts in the beach-front casinos (Neustadt 1980:67; *Wall Street Journal*, April 29, 1985; *San Francisco Chronicle*, April 23, 1985; Swoboda 1990; *Los Angeles Times*, December 20, 1990; *New York Times*, December 20, 1990).

A second issue that has troubled HERE throughout its history is the degree to which union leadership has adequately reflected HERE's diverse membership in terms of gender, race, ethnicity, and even craft. Early HERE leadership corresponded to its primarily male, immigrant constituency. The sex and craft-based logic that guided local union structure also ensured representation for women and for minority occupations, both at the international and the local level (Cobble 1991a).

The demise of the craft and sex-based locals in the 1960s and 1970s and the creation of large, industrial-style locals representing all workers in the industry appears to have been a mixed blessing for the union in regard to female leadership. Initially, for example, female representation declined at both the international and local level, despite the continued majority presence of women in the industry (Cobble 1991a; Cobble 1990). By the 1980s, however, a new breed of local women leaders had emerged, elected to head mixed-gender organizations, not all-female divisions. Women now run some of the larger local unions, notably Local 2 in San Francisco and Local 11 in Los Angeles (Cobble 1991a; Hernandez 1989). But at the international level, the degree of female leadership has declined in the last two decades. In 1992, close to half of HERE's members were female, yet only one woman served on a General Executive Board of 28. (For contrasting earlier figures, see Cobble 1991a:184-86.)

Similarly, although minorities can be found at the helm of a number of pivotal locals, few are in elected or appointed positions at the national level. The lack of minority representation on the General Executive Board is particularly glaring in a union in which African Americans, Hispanics, and Asians probably comprise half of the membership or more (Del Vecchio 1988; Hernandez 1989). The unreflective character of HERE's leadership in terms of gender, race, and ethnicity is not only a problem of internal democracy but also is a serious liability for an organization that seeks to represent a work force that is approximately two-thirds female and minority.

Labor-Management Strife and the Breakdown of Multi-employer Bargaining

Throughout the 1980s hospitality management sought not only to deunionize where possible but to unravel many of the multi-employer bargaining associations established in the 1930s and 1940s[7] (Cobble 1991a). As the earlier Local 11 stories suggested, in the 1980s numerous union restaurants of long standing refused to sign contracts, managed to decertify the union, or closed down and reopened nonunion. In addition, in the restaurant sector, multi-employer bargaining virtually disappeared in the 1980s, even in such union towns as San Francisco and New York City. In San Francisco, the disastrous 1984 strike against the 200-member Golden Gate Restaurant Association ended with the dissolution of the employer association and the reinstatement, after fifty years, of bargaining between individual restaurants and HERE Local 2. Similarly, in New York, the Restaurant League of New York, which once represented a sizable number of prominent upscale restaurants in the city, ended formal bargaining with Local 100 in the late 1980s (Bureau of National Affairs 1988; Bitterman interview 1993).

Multi-employer bargaining in the hotel sector also fragmented in the 1980s, with individual hotels pulling out of employer associations and demanding their own individually tailored agreement. Yet by the late 1980s, many hotel employers began to reconsider their decision. The "divide and conquer" strategy attempted by the San Francisco hotels in the 1980s "backfired," according to Doug Cornford, former negotiator for the San Francisco Hotel Employers Association (HEA). The breakup of the HEA in Cornford's view actually "shifted the balance [of power] toward the union." Individual bargaining allowed the union to resort to their historically damaging whipsaw techniques, playing one hotel off against another. They could also choose to bargain first with the hotels most likely to accept their proposals, thus increasing pressure on the others to follow the pattern (Bureau of National Affairs [BNA] 1988, 1989).[8]

By the late 1980s, hotel employers also had begun to reconsider the costs of confrontation with the union. Union density in the industry continued to decline in the late 1980s as nonunion competitors proliferated and older union hotels went out of business or downsized. But, unlike restaurants, hotels could not shift ownership so easily and open with a nonunion crew, and few managed successful decertification campaigns (Keller 1984; Atkinson interview 1993). And, of equal importance, despite major strikes in the early and mid-1980s in union strongholds such as San Francisco, New York, and Las Vegas—many of which were the first such strikes since the 1930s and early 1940s—the hotels could not find a way of voiding their collective bargaining obligations.

In New York, for example, the industry weathered its first strike in 46 years. The 26-day walkout, affecting 165 unionized New York City hotels, ended with sizable wage increases for the 25,000 Hotel and Motel Trades Council (HMTC) members and more flexible work classifications for the employers affiliated with the New York City Hotel Association. The strike also demonstrated the resilience of both foes under fire. The hotels hired some 4,500 temps during the strike and proved they could continue to function, taking the union by surprise. Management misjudged their opponent as well, according to Vito Pitta, president of the HMTC. "They tried to break us, but they miscalculated" (Reid 1985; Smothers 1985; Berger 1985).

Similarly, in Las Vegas, the 67-day strike in 1984 failed for the first time to shut down the casinos, and union membership dropped precipitously as replacement workers decertified the union. Yet by 1992, HERE once again had 80% of the 38 Las Vegas casinos under contract and a membership of 35,000 (Taylor interview 1993; Franklin 1993). The 1980 hotel strike in San Francisco, the first since 1941, also left the labor-management relation deeply wounded but basically intact (Guma 1980; *Hotel & Motel Management*, September 1980:1, 22).

Bargaining Concerns in the 1980s

Over the course of the 1980s management pursued two primary bargaining goals: increasing worker "flexibility" and containing health care costs. In the early and mid-1980s, "flexibility" appears to have been the principal management bargaining mantra. In particular, they sought to alter the contract language requiring strict job classifications, a change that would allow for "cross-training," more team work, and labor intensification. They also pushed for the loosening of work rules governing scheduling and shift assignment; the freedom to hire outside the union hiring hall; and the institution of new worktime procedures which in some cases has meant longer work weeks and the elimination of overtime pay.

In large part, the employers prevailed in winning concessions on work rules. In New York's 1985 hotel strike, the employers won the right to shift employees from one classification to another. They also gained a modified two-tier wage scale in which new employees received 75% of scale for the first year (*New York Times*, June 28, 1985). The 1984 restaurant strike in San Francisco also revolved around loosening job classifications. In part, Local 2 lost the strike because they misjudged rank-and-file sentiment in the restaurants concerning work rules. Employees wanted the job security and workplace dignity that historically prompted the negotiation of these work rules. Like the employer, however, they also favored a more fluid definition of job descriptions and a broadening of work responsibilities (Cobble 1991a).

Management triumphed in other situations as well, even where employees strongly favored the retention of the specific work rules in question. HERE Local 28 in Oakland, California, and other HERE locals elsewhere relented in the face of Hyatt's demand for its infamous "Hyatt Work Week" (*Hotel and Motel Management*, July 10, 1989).[9]

In the late 1980s, however, employers were less able to impose new work rules unilaterally. In some instances, HERE adopted a more pragmatic problem-oriented stance. Rather than simply oppose the dissolution of the old rules across the board, the union demanded to participate in reshaping the rules. In 1989, Local 2 in San Francisco—partially chastened by the 1984 restaurant debacle and desirous of a quick settlement so they could focus on organizing the nonunion hotels—accepted an HEA proposal easing some overtime restrictions and allowing employees to change job classifications for a week without wage or other penalties. The union agreed to these changes in part "to help the city's unionized luxury hotels compete." But they also won the right to monitor the situation and insisted on certain other safeguards (Seal 1989a, 1989b). In other instances, HERE locals effectively resisted work rule changes. HERE Local 11, for example, embarked on a successful campaign of disruptive actions against Hyatt in 1989 and 1990 when the Hotel asked for a change in the work week (Seal 1990).

Soaring health and welfare costs have also concerned hospitality employers. (See HERE 1988 for estimates of costs.) Small restaurant owners felt the pinch most severely, prompting many throughout the 1970s and 1980s to seek relief, even if it meant enduring a strike and decertifying the union. Countless negotiations between individual restaurants and HERE locals broke down over the issue. Lowering benefit costs also was a major sticking point in the 1984 restaurant strike in San Francisco, the subsequent negotiations in 1988 with the remaining union restaurants, and the 1988 negotiations between the Restaurant League of New York and Local 100 (*Nation's Restaurant News*, September 24, 1984; *North California Labor*, April 4, 1988; *Restaurant Business*, December 10, 1988; Durazo and Atkinson interviews 1993; DelVecchio 1988).

Hotel employers also pursued lower benefits costs, but fewer sought deunionization over this issue. It did spark the 1991 strike against the

Frontier Hotel in Las Vegas, however, and was a "primary issue" in the recent round of hotel contracts signed in Los Angeles, Washington, Boston, and New York (*Catering Industry Employee*, February 1992 and September-October 1992; *Monthly Labor Review*, December 1989: 56; Rosier 1992, Keller 1984).

In general, hotel management made much less progress on gaining relief from soaring health care payments than on easing work rules, in part because both workers and the union viewed the retention of good health insurance as a top priority. In Washington, the union agreed to replace two of the health plans with preferred provider systems, but the hotels continued to shoulder all the costs (*Monthly Labor Review*, December 1989). In both the New York and Los Angeles negotiations, the hotels ended up promising to increase their financial contributions for health coverage. In Los Angeles, the union preserved the system "intact without worker co-payments" (*Hotel and Motel Management*, 1990; Rosier 1992). In Boston, where in 1988 Local 26 members had taken on an additional $17 in co-payments for health care, in the next round of negotiations in 1991, the union secured the "right to restructure its health and welfare fund" so it could offer benefits to "gay spouses and extended family members such as grandparents and aging parents" (*Boston Globe*, October-January 1990-91).

Not surprisingly, the union also sought to uphold living standards by pressing hard on wages. And in many cases, management often relented on this issue. Although national figures detailing the wage settlements among hotel and restaurant workers are not available, many of the most significant individual contracts for hotel workers have contained respectable increases. According to wage settlement data gathered by HERE's research department, the daily wages (in constant 1988 dollars) of unionized hotel workers in major cities rose considerably in the last two decades. To take one representative example, while the CPI rose 118% from 1975 to 1988, wages for room attendants increased by 168% in New York and 182% in San Francisco (HERE 1988). HERE also achieved wage advances after 1988, despite attempts by some hotel employers to seek concessionary relief from the "depressed and overbuilt hotel market" (Stuart 1993). The 1989 Disney World contract, for instance, called for wage increases averaging 7.6%, 6%, and 6% over the three years of the contract (*Monthly Labor Review*, February 1989:53-54). The most recent hotel pacts in New York City, Los Angeles, and Hawaii also granted substantial wage increases, especially to the non-tipped employees (*Hotel and Motel Management*, 1990; Rosier 1992; *Monthly Labor Review*, June 1990:69-70).

Other wage settlements from the late 1980s were more modest, but they signaled a willingness on the part of employers to allow employees to share in the profits once conditions in the industry picked up again. The 1991 contract negotiated by Local 26 and Boston hotel employers called for a wage freeze in the first year and low increases in ensuing years. In return, however, Local 26 gained employer approval to a provision linking hotel occupancy rates with employee bonus payments. When the hotel market in Boston rebounds, so will the pay checks of Boston's hotel employees (*Boston Globe*, October 1, 1991:35).

Local 26 in Boston also provides perhaps the best example of other innovative bargaining proposals used by HERE to maintain the overall living standards of their members. Although it represents only about 5,000 workers at 20 hotels in Boston, after a five-year struggle led by the formidable Domenic Bozzotto, Local 26 won an employer-funded housing trust providing union members with loans and outright grants. To use the fund, however, Local 26 had to secure an amendment to Section 302 (c)(7) of the Taft-Hartley Act, permitting unions to bargain a jointly administered housing trust. President Bush signed the amendment in 1990, and by mid-1991, the union had offered thousands of dollars in housing assistance to its members. The union made the housing fund their top bargaining issue because 98% of the members did not "earn the $60,000 needed to buy a median-priced home" in the Boston area and, according to some observers, because of "Bozzotto's belief in broadening the range of union activities as a way of empowering the underclass" (*Developments in Industrial Relations—1989 and 1990*:53; Baker 1991; Canellos 1990).

Other locals have used similar strategies to improve the living standards of those they represent. Local 2, for example, asked the city of San Francisco to impose fees on new hotels and motels to subsidize low-cost housing construction (*Catering Industry Employee*, July 1991:11).

Issues for the Future: Equity for Minorities?

Throughout the 1970s and 1980s, issues of equity for minorities surfaced sporadically at the bargaining table and bubbled up through the grievance machinery. Yet the problems of minority workers remained largely unresolved. In part because of the success of recent court cases and in part because of the increasingly vociferous nature of employee complaints, both labor and management will have to pay more attention to these issues in the 1990s.

HERE generally responded sympathetically to the complaints of female HERE members in the 1970s and 1980s. But it has neither positioned itself as an aggressive foe of sexual discrimination in hiring and promotion, nor become the champion of the rights of women in the industry as a whole. In national negotiations and in subsequent arbitration proceedings in the 1970s, for example, HERE and the Playboy Clubs International debated work rules about customer-bunny interaction, just how much of the server's body would be revealed by the bunny costume, and whether or not bunnies could be fired for "loss of bunny image." Some HERE locals also pursued the issue of discriminatory hiring practices, gender-specific uniforms, and other problems raised by female members. Yet most of the groundbreaking court cases of the 1970s and 1980s that challenged sex-segregated hiring and promotion policies and the wearing of sexually provocative uniforms occurred without the support of the union; moreover, in some cases, the plaintiffs named the union along with the employer as a defendant (Cobble 1991a:198-203; Spano 1986).

In the 1990s, HERE continued its generally sympathetic but non-aggressive approach to issues of sex discrimination. In 1991, Local 26 convinced the international to donate $50,000 for the production of a video on sexual harassment, and various other locals attended vigorously to the complaints of their female members in regard to discriminatory weight restrictions and uniform design (*Catering Industry Employee*, July 1991:27). Atlantic City's Local 34 debated the exact sheerness of pantyhose required by management, threatened a "pantyhose arbitration hearing," and considered a class-action suit against all 12 casinos alleging sexual harassment. Nevertheless, the union has yet to join with the Equal Employment Opportunity Commission in its recent systematic attempt to end Title VII violations in the hotel and restaurant industry or to publicly decry the severity of sexual harassment for hospitality employees.[10] (Batty 1993; Belluck 1992).

HERE has demonstrated a greater commitment to pay equity, however. The most celebrated HERE collective bargaining initiative in this regard involved its Yale University clericals, who staged a series of media-attended strikes in 1984, following years of internal organizing. They won a revised salary structure and wage increases of 35% over three years (Ladd-Taylor 1985:485). Two recent union court victories upgrading the pay of women cafeteria workers and maids also point to the heightened concern of the union over pay inequality between men and women. In August 1992, a Massachusetts court awarded $1.5 million in back pay to 41 HERE-represented women cafeteria workers to correct the discriminatory pay scales between female cafeteria workers and male custodians. In *Jancey v. Everett School Committee*, the court agreed with the plaintiffs that the 1945 Equal Pay Act barred differential sex-based pay scales between comparable jobs. Three months later, in an out-of-court settlement, 160 New York City hotels agreed to give the 10,000 maids in their employ millions of dollars in backpay and to equalize the wages of maids and housemen. The suit, initiated by Local 6 five years earlier, alleged sex-based wage discrimination under both the Equal Pay Act and Title VII.[11]

The union record in opposing discrimination based on race, ethnicity, and sexual orientation is similarly mixed. A number of HERE locals initiated programs oriented toward minority members in the 1980s, and the international union does pursue minimum wage increases; keeps abreast of Industrial Welfare Commission wage and hour regulations; and publicly favored the Civil Rights Reform Act of 1991. But given the gravity of the problem, HERE needs to pay more attention to equity issues in bargaining and initiate more aggressive legal, community-based, and legislative action.

The efforts of a few HERE locals on behalf of minorities have garnered results, however. A year before the expiration of its 1982 contract, Local 26 in Boston launched an explosive media campaign centered in part on the peculiar kinds of indignities suffered by minority workers. Billboards queried, "Dignity, Justice, and Respect: Too much to ask? Support Local 26, Boston Hotel Workers." When the hotels took the mops from female cleaners and asked them to scrub the floors on their knees the union drew national attention to their plight. The 1982 contract secured better promotion and seniority guarantees and proved to Bozzotto that bonds could be formed between "the front of the house and the back; the gratuity and the non-gratuity workers; the English speaking and the non-English speaking" (Sidel 1983). The Boston local closed the decade in high style, negotiating an employer-financed fund for literacy, English as a second language, and citizenship classes for its largely non-English speaking membership. Moreover, in the 1991 contract, they won the right to restructure the health and welfare fund to extend benefits to gay spouses (*Developments in Industrial Relations*,

1989:45; *Catering Industry Employee*, September 1992; *Boston Globe*, October 1, 1991:35).

The San Francisco and Los Angeles HERE locals, both under female leadership, also have repeatedly raised issues of workplace dignity for minority workers.[12] They have won contract clauses upgrading the low-end jobs into which most minorities find themselves shunted; setting up training programs aimed at promoting minority workers; securing time off for foreign-born workers who need to return home to visit their family or legalize their visas; and winning "protections and opportunities for promotions for illegal aliens." Local 2's Sherri Chiesa began her tenure in the mid-1980s by sponsoring advertisements on city buses showing 72-year-old minority waitress Silvana Osuna with the caption "Twenty years on your feet and they treat you like leftovers." The union's 1989 contract provides for employer contributions of five dollars per employee per month for an AIDS Fund to offset medical expenses for AIDS victims. The fund is expected to reach $3 million by 1994 (*Developments in Industrial Relations*, April 1989:42; Hernandez 1989; Cobble 1991a:202; Seal 1989b; *Wall Street Journal*, March 5, 1991).

But what about management attitudes toward the problems of women and minorities in the industry? They certainly are better positioned than the union to correct the problem. Industry journals now evidence a new rhetoric of concern about promotional opportunities for minorities and women and pay increased attention to the problem of sexual harassment. They also regularly devote space to keeping employers informed about changing legal obligations in regard to women and minorities, designed to help their readers avoid discrimination and, hence, litigation. Also, in an effort to diversify their management ranks, Kentucky Fried Chicken, Burger King's "Whopper College," and others now offer training programs for their hourly employees. McDonald's "Hamburger University," opened in 1983 at a cost of $15 million, is dedicated to "promote from within" (BNA 1985:6-18).

Yet the overall industry record, particularly in regard to minorities, is appalling. The startling governmental statistics detailed earlier in this chapter on the concentration of minorities in low-paying, low-status, dead-end jobs, not to mention the host of successful lawsuits against industry employers, suggest that hotel and restaurant management has not yet translated its new rhetoric into reality. Just recently, under pressure from an NAACP-backed lawsuit, Shoney's Big Boy agreed to pay out $105 million to those denied jobs or promotions because of their

race, gaining the honor of having made the largest retribution on record
in such cases (BNA 1992a; 1993).[13] Hospitality employers also make up
a disproportionate share of those cited for child-labor and wage-law violations—both illegal practices that heavily affect minority youth (Oliver
1982; BNA 1992b; Neustadt 1980:66).[14] Even the editors of *Nation's
Restaurant News* are beginning to chide their food service operator
patrons for the industry's slowness in providing "better training opportunities for hourly employees" and improved fringe benefits (November
18, 1991). Yet despite these problems, the foremost and certainly the
most aggressive lobbying arm of hospitality employers, the National
Restaurant Association, has forcefully opposed minimum wage increases, teen employment laws, mandatory parental leave and health
care coverage, and the Civil Rights Reform Act of 1990.[15]

The continuing level of anger among women and minorities makes it
clear that neither labor nor management have sufficiently addressed
their problems. Why does the industry still favor the "European look" in
hiring and promotion? Why does it tolerate the widening income
inequities between tipped workers (mainly white) and non-tipped
(mainly non-white)? Why should older women be fired or assigned to
the breakfast and lunch shifts while younger, more "attractive" women
or men work in the lucrative cocktail server and dinner jobs? Why
should the majority of supervisory positions go to those outside the
industry? Why not create more promotional ladders and training opportunities for the millions of women and minorities stuck in the hourly,
entry-level positions that are so characteristic of hospitality employment? Both sides have been blind to an enormous opportunity: whoever
takes on these critical concerns and becomes the champion of women
and minorities, will have gained a formidable ally for ensuring their
future (Mencimer 1992; Bailey 1985; Cobble 1991a; *50 Plus*, Feb.
1986:11, and Nov. 1987:16; Coultas 1986).

The Survival of Unionization in the 1990s and Beyond

Unions desire the continuation of collective bargaining in the industry, but it is unclear whether any but a handful of employers see it in
their interest. Nevertheless, the collective bargaining system in hotels
and motels is adjusting and will survive. There are signs that the trend
of the 1970s and 1980s has bottomed out, especially if the union continues its potent mix of pragmatism, militancy, and innovation. In restaurants, however, the decline began much earlier, has been steeper, and is

irreversible without a fundamental restructuring of the current legal and institutional framework for collective bargaining. Why would the future of collective bargaining be so divergent for these two sectors? Most importantly, as Cobble has argued elsewhere, the nature of the hotel and motel sector—its structure, size, the characteristics of its work force—make it much easier to organize and represent hotel workers under the current legal framework, which favors worksite unionism or the industrial union model. Hotels employ more workers per site; the tenure of their workers is relatively long term compared to restaurants; and their greater capital investment makes it more difficult for them to close down and reopen nonunion. All these factors help to make hotels easier to organize than restaurants using traditional NLRB procedures (Cobble 1992; Henderson 1965:30-42).

After the passage of the Wagner Act, unions penetrated the hotel sector more deeply and retained that momentum longer, than in restaurants. Twenty-five years ago many of the large urban hotel markets remained heavily unionized. Two decades of aggressive antiunionism by employers left them reeling—as it did unions in virtually every other sector of the economy. But by the end of the 1980s, hotel workers' unions had regained their equilibrium and reemerged, using more aggressive tactics. Relying on sophisticated corporate campaigns coordinated through the international's new research department (begun in 1987), and on civil disobedience, sit-ins, "soup-ins," vigils, noisy demonstrations at daybreak, round-the-clock "walk and work" picketing, and 400-member negotiation-support committees, the union cost hotels millions of dollars in convention business—and gained the attention and support of politicians, in part because of the potential political clout of a large number of angry urban minority voters (*San Francisco Chronicle*, September 24, 1992; *Catering Industry Employee*, July 1991; Hernandez 1989; Seal 1989a, 1989c, 1990; *Washington Post*, October 1, 1991; *Hotel and Motel Management*, September 1980:1, 22). These tactics also resonated well with the hotel work force, especially the predominantly back-of-the house minority workers. In contrast to restaurants, the identity between hotel employers and employees is minimal. The larger worksite and the lack of racial, ethnic or cultural identity between owner and worker encourages an adversarial posture.

Only recently, negotiations between Local 11 and the Los Angeles Hotel Employers Council demonstrated the vulnerability of hotel employers to the pressures of their large minority work force. In the wake of the Rodney King trial and the ensuing riots, a union-produced video ("City on the Edge") linking employer demands for lower wages and benefits with racial discrimination, poverty, urban decay and crime proved both prophetic and highly effective. Snatched up by the media, the video turned the public and the politicians against the hotels, threatened the fickle convention market, and intensified already troubled personnel relations in the hotels. The union soon had a generous contract (Rosier 1992; USDL 1992).

By the early 1990s, the union for the first time was positioned to turn the corner on hotel organizing and use their arsenal of tactics offensively as well as defensively. In 1985, HERE beefed up its organizing program, pumping new resources and staff into organizing campaigns and consolidating its efforts at the international level. In its initial forays, HERE won significant organizing victories at Chicago's Tremont Hotel and the Manhattan Beach Radisson Hotel in Southern California while suffering defeats at the Willard Hotel in Washington and Back Bay Hilton in Boston. Surprised by the animosity of the employer antiunion campaigns, HERE reassessed its strategy, according to Mark Atkinson, the assistant director of research for HERE. By 1988, HERE had improved its arsenal of weapons, becoming expert not only at communicating with hotel employees but in bringing pressures on hotel owners to behave with more neutrality in organizing. The significant 1993 victory at the PARC 55 in San Francisco, the first of San Francisco's new nonunion hotels built since 1985 to sign a contract, is one of the best and most recent illustrations of how HERE exerted pressure downward to achieve victory. In addition to marshaling strong local political and community pressure, they dampened consumer demand nationally by influencing travel agents, convention bureaus, and other organizations that structure the hotel business market, and they weakened the credibility of the "owners" in the eyes of potential investors (Atkinson interview 1993).

In contrast, HERE has had much less success in restaurant organizing. Fast food workers, for example, are notoriously difficult to organize. They are a young, part-time, high-turnover, relatively unskilled work force. They are scattered over countless sites and in many cases employed by multinational megachains (Charner and Fraser 1984; Food and Allied Service Trades 1985; BNA 1985:31; Bracker 1982). Yet outside the U.S., in Denmark, Finland, Australia, Mexico, and other countries, fast food workers at McDonald's and other chains have organized. And according to Michael Quinlan, Chair and CEO of McDonald's, unionization did not interfere with McDonald's vaunted service finesse. In fact, he admitted, morale improved and turnover declined (BNA 1991; *Boston Globe*, December 20, 1985:3; *Los Angeles Times*, December 20, 1985:1; *International Labour Reports* No. 24, Nov./Dec. 1987:24).

For fast food workers in the United States to repeat this success will require sweeping changes in labor law and the way American unions organize and represent employees. In Denmark, for example, unionized employees at milk shake supply centers, truckers, and printers all helped pressure McDonald's by refusing to produce and deliver goods for the chain. In the US, of course, such secondary boycotts are restrained under Taft-Hartley.[16] Streamlined employer recognition procedures would also make it easier to organize fast food workers. The long-drawn-out balloting procedures under Taft-Hartley penalize workers employed in establishments—like fast food chains—where employee turnover is high. Requiring employer recognition when a majority of current employees have signed union cards requesting representation, or simply allowing top-down organizing, as historically existed in the construction industry, would do much to make organizing possible. Finally, unions need to make a massive commitment to target and organize an entire chain or corporation rather than one or two units. In the 1930s, General Motors, the world's largest corporation at the time, agreed to collective bargaining, in part because auto workers struck plants across the country. The whole corporation felt the assault.[17]

The unions also need to rethink their approach to organizing fine-dining establishments. There have been some victories in elite restaurants: the recent contract at the Rainbow Room, atop the RCA Building in New York, or the organizing of Washington, D.C.'s Capitol Hill Club, the official watering hole of the Republican National Committee (*Catering Industry Employee*, Sept-Oct, 1992; *Washington Post*, January 29, 1991:A-17). But overall, HERE's restaurant campaigns have ended in defeat—in part because of the mismatch between the union's predominantly industrial-style orientation and the needs, self-perceptions, and aspirations of culinary workers in fine-dining establishments. The union's attempt to organize Berkeley's gourmet ghetto in 1985 is emblematic in this regard. Oakland's Local 28 anticipated a fairly easy organizing venture, since many of the owners of Berkeley's newest and finest restaurants were veterans of the left-liberal politics of the 1960s; some were even former union activists and organizers. What the union did not anticipate was the resistance of the employees. Food service workers at expensive eateries like Chez Panisse and the Santa Fe Bar and Grill bristled indignantly at union organizer rhetoric labeling them "urban farmhands." Others were simply indifferent to what the union offered. They already received a full range of benefits (with the exception of pensions—a benefit irrelevant to most of the younger work force), and employers provided them with what they most sought: access to training and exposure to a range of the culinary arts, whether cooking, knowledge of fine wines, or restaurant management. In fact, they feared unionization might actually make them worse off—lowering their tips (the bulk of their income) because incompetent workers would be retained; reducing craft and teamwork; and threatening the mutuality they felt with their employer (Weinstein 1985).

Ironically, returning to some of the "occupational" or craft practices that were once central to HERE's philosophy would make the union more appealing not only in Berkeley but elsewhere. The early culinary locals set standards for the occupation through apprenticeship and other training programs, through work rules specifying job performance criteria, and through enforcement of those standards at the worksite. The union in essence took over certain personnel functions such as hiring, training, discharge, and discipline. Locals served as semiprofessional associations intended to upgrade the status, prestige, and skill of the occupation as well as to maintain wages and good working conditions. The union also recognized a certain mutuality of interest between employer and employee: many employers had been former employees and would return to that status; the success of individual restaurants meant not only profits for the owner but directly impacted upon the level of tips for servers. Culinary workers have a direct financial relation to the customer and more customers can benefit everyone (Cobble 1991a; 1991b; 1991c).

For collective bargaining to revitalize in the hotel and restaurant industry—and if it is to expand into other service sectors—the system must recover some of its older diversity and flexibility. People have long done many different kinds of work; and the environment in which that work has taken place has also been diverse. In the past, unions have proved able to accommodate that diversity as the divergent practices of organizing and representation among construction workers, screen actors, janitors, teachers, and truckers attest. The test of unionism in the twenty-first century will be whether it can recover and extend its traditional flexibility.[18]

Endnotes

[1] In this chapter, we will be relying primarily on data gathered by the Census Bureau's decennial census as well as its Current Population Survey reports. In referring to the hotel industry, we will be using Standard Industrial Classification (SIC) Code 701, which includes virtually all hotel and lodging establishments. The term "hotels" will often be used to refer to all lodging accommodations. Generalizations about the restaurant sector rely on SIC code 581 which includes all eating and drinking firms engaged in the sale of prepared foods and drinks for consumption, with the exception of those in hotels and department stores. The terms "eating and drinking places" and "restaurants" will be used interchangeably.

[2] Some of these adversarial tactics are borrowed from the 1930s. "Sip-ins" refers to the union strategy of crowding a non-compliant restaurant with union sympathizers who only order coffee or soda and keep out better-paying customers. The "walk and work" picketing tactic involves "striking" employees picketing their own worksite during non-work hours, lunch and break times, but remaining on the job to prevent strikebreakers from being hired.

[3] One notable exception to this pattern was the disproportionate numbers of black waiters in the late nineteenth and early twentieth century. See Dorothy Sue Cobble, *Dishing It Out: Waitresses and Their Unions in the Twentieth Century* (Urbana: University of Illinois Press, 1991).

[4] Even in those occupations in which tipping is most common—food server, bartender, maid—many workers receive minimal tips, no tips, or must divide their tips with others (Cobble 1991a:40-44; O'Connor 1971).

[5] See the comments of various CEOs and industry analysts in the major industry journals. For example, *Hotel and Motel Management*, January 1980:19; *Lodging Hospitality*, December 1990:121-122; *Restaurants and Institutions*, March 17, 1990:9; *Nationals Restaurant New*, November 12, 1990:39. See also *New York Times*, September 4, 1985, June 30, 1986.

[6] The IBT, for example, has hotel clerks and other "front-end" workers in Las Vegas and other entertainment centers. The ILWU's catering industry membership is almost solely in Hawaii, where under Lou Goldblatt they organized the entire Hawaiian work force, including agricultural labor. The largest block of SEIU food industry workers are at Disney World. Electricians and other skilled workers in hotels and motels often belong to their respective international craft organizations. The world-wide federation representing workers in this sector is the International Union of Food and Allied Workers' Associations.

[7] Almost all hotel and restaurant bargaining occurs at the local level, with most contracts negotiated by a single local union. In a few situations, however, local unions from HERE and other internationals have organized multi-union bargaining councils. The leading examples are the Hotel Trades Council in New York City, which includes representatives from the electricians, painters, and stationary engineers; and the Service Trade Council, which negotiates for the 11,400 employees at Disney World and includes HERE plus locals of the International Brotherhood of Teamsters, Service Employees International Union, United Food and Commercial Workers, the Theatrical Unions, among others. The "management" sitting across the table

can be a single independent owner with one or more worksites or a multi-employer bargaining council representing multi-national corporations as well as independent hotel owners.

[8] Indeed, in the hotels a revival of multi-employer bargaining may be in store, in part because the union managed to manipulate the new, more chaotic bargaining system in its favor. In the restaurant sector, however, multi-employer bargaining appears unlikely to return until a substantial portion of restaurants are once again unionized.

[9] Under Hyatt's definition of work week, many employees lost the right to overtime pay and to refuse additional work after five consecutive work days; and Saturday and Sunday work no longer required extra compensations.

[10] Replicating Barbara Gutek's 1985 national study on sexual harassment, Eller (1990) found that a "higher proportion of hotel employees experience sexually harassing behavior in their workplace than do workers in society-at-large" (p. 85).

[11] Cobble was an expert witness on behalf of the plaintiffs in this case. The discussion here is based on files in her possession. See also *CLUW News* November-December 1992, announcing the settlement.

[12] Under the leadership of Jay Rubin, the New York Hotel Trades Council pioneered programs for upgrading minority workers in the 1950s and 1960s. They set up a payroll tax on the employer specifically allocated for training "Negro and Puerto Rican employees for more skilled jobs." See for example, *New York Times*, September 3, 1968. Training funds have also been won in Las Vegas and recently proposed by New York City's Local 100 (Atkinson interview 1993).

[13] In another example, the U.S. Court of Appeals cited Olsen's Dairy Queens Inc. in Houston for discriminatory hiring practices ignoring management's defense that "customers prefer to be served by persons of their own culture" (*DLR* April 29, 1993).

[14] In 1992, the Labor Department, for example, reached a $500,000 settlement of longstanding child labor law violations against Burger King Corporation, covering the company's approximately 800 restaurants (BNA 1992b).

[15] A distinct political agenda was not evident for unionized employers, but certainly there is some controversy over the conservative and aggressive employer lobbying that has burgeoned in the industry in the 1980s. For a view of the extensive grass-roots mobilizing of food-service and hotel proprietors, consult industry periodicals such as *Restaurants USA* (November 1990:11); *Hotel and Motel Management*, January 1980:19; *Restaurant Business*, December 10, 1988; and *Nation's Restaurant News* (January 1, 1990:29; September 3, 1990:21). Their agenda, according to the periodicals: repeal of the Civil Rights Act of 1990, blockage of family and medical leave and mandatory health care, preserving business meal deductions, sub-minimum and a training wage for teenagers, exemption from minimum wage for small companies, defining tips as wages for minimum wage purposes but repealing FICA taxes on tips.

[16] Some HERE locals are now attempting to use a form of secondary leverage in organizing, similar to that used by SEIU in the Justice for Janitors campaign. In-house cafeterias in downtown office buildings might be organized through union

pressure on the building owners who contract with individual eateries (Durazo interview 1993).

[17] As Cobble has argued elsewhere, greater commitment to providing worker training would also help unions win the loyalty of and maintain control over the young, transient fast food work force. And union hiring halls would not only offer locals a mechanism for regular, positive contact with transient members but they can perform an important service for small franchisors who desire a steady supply of competent, reliable labor.

[18] Unfortunately, since the 1950s collective bargaining has moved toward a single model of employee representation: more and more unions have come under Taft-Hartley; the exceptions to Taft-Hartley practices granted the construction trades and other sectors have been lost; NLRB rulings have encouraged uniformity and hence homogenization; and unions themselves, especially in the private sector, have moved toward an "industrial model" for all workers. Ironically, this industrial paradigm has spread even as the number of workers for whom it is appropriate has declined. Public policy is, in this regard, badly out of step with the needs and aspirations of employers and their workers.

References

AFL-CIO. 1991. *Report to the 1991 Convention from the AFL-CIO Executive Council*. Washington, DC.

Atkinson, Mark (Asst. Research Director, HERE). 1993. Telephone interview by Dorothy Sue Cobble. May 25 and June 1. New York City.

Baker, Bob. 1991. "Union Pioneers Home-Buying Aid For Members." *Los Angeles Times*. January 3.

Bailey, Thomas. 1985. "A Case Study of Immigrants in the Restaurant Industry." *Industrial Relations*, Vol. 24, no. 2 (Spring), pp. 205-221.

Batty, Jennifer. 1993. "Preventing Sexual Harassment in the Restaurant," *Restaurants USA*, Vol. 13, no. 1 (January), pp. 30-34.

Belluck, Pam. 1992. "For Waitresses, A Uniform Fight," *Philadelphia Inquirer*, October 14.

Berger, Joseph. 1985. "Tentative Pact Set in Walkout at City's Hotels." *New York Times*, June 27.

Bernstein, Charles. 1990. "The 1990 Civil Rights Act: Inequitable Legislation." *Nation's Restaurant News*, Vol 24, no. 35 (September 3), p. 21.

Bitterman, Brooks (Business Representative, HERE Local 100). 1993. Telephone interview by Dorothy Sue Cobble. February 5. New York City.

Bracker, Anne L. 1982. "Employment in the Fast Food Industry: The Myth of the Golden Arches." Unpublished paper, Vertical Files, Walter Reuther Labor Archives, Wayne State University, Detroit, Michigan.

Bureau of National Affairs. 1992a. "Class of Almost 30,000 Black Employees Certified in Discrimination Suit Against Shoney's." *Daily Labor Report* No. 123 (June 25).

_____. 1988. "Current Developments: San Francisco Hospitality Industry." *Daily Labor Report* (January 20), p. A8-A9.

_____. 1988-89. *Directory of Labor Organizations, 1988-89 Edition*, Rockville, MD.

_____. 1993. "Judge Approves $105 Million Settlement of Race Bias Suit Against Shoney's." *Daily Labor Report* No. 16 (January 27), p. 1.

_____. 1992b. "Labor Department, Burger King Reach Tentative Settlement of Child Labor Charges." *Daily Labor Report* No. 225 (November 20).

_____. 1991. "McDonald's Corporation Describes Keys to Succeeding With Overseas Employees." *Daily Labor Report* No. 33 (February 19).

_____. 1985. "Special Supplement: Employee Relations in the Fast Food Industry." *Retail/Services Labor Report*, Part II, Vol. 72, no. 23 (June 10), Rockville, MD.

Canellos, Peter. 1990. "Union's Activism Praised." *Boston Globe*, April 24.

Charner, Ivan, and Bryna Shore Fraser. 1984. *Fast Food Jobs*. Washington, DC: National Institute for Work and Learning.

Chazanov, Mathis. 1991. "Union Calls Rally at Canter's Deli to Mark Year of Picketing." *Los Angeles Times*, October 16.

Cobble, Dorothy Sue. 1991a. *Dishing It Out: Waitresses and Their Unions in the Twentieth Century*. Urbana: University of Illinois Press.

_____. 1991b. "Organizing the Postindustrial Work Force: Lessons From the History of Waitress Unionism," *Industrial and Labor Relations Review*, Vol. 44, no. 3 (April), pp. 419-436.

_____. 1991c. "Union Strategies for Organizing and Representing the New Service Work Force." *Proceedings of the 43rd Annual Meeting of the Industrial Relations Research Association*. J. Burton, Jr., ed. Madison, WI: Industrial Relations Research Association.

_____. 1990. "Rethinking Troubled Relations Between Women and Unions: Craft Unionism and Female Activism." *Feminist Studies*, Vol. 16, no. 3 (Fall), pp. 519-48.

Coultas, Carol. 1986. "We Fought Back and Won." *Good Housekeeping*. February, pp. 83-86.

Curme, Michael, Barry T. Hirsch, and David MacPherson. 1990. "Union Membership and Contract Coverage in the US, 1983-88," *Industrial and Labor Relations Review*, Vol. 44, no. 1 (October), pp. 5-11.

DelVecchio, Rick. 1988. "Bohemian Club, Union in Classic Battle for Power," *San Francisco Chronicle*, January 20.

Demaria, Alfred. 1988. "The Great Tipping Debate: Legal Implications," *Restaurant Business*, Vol. 87, no. 13 (September 1), pp. 180-81.

Detman, Linda A. 1990. "Women Behind Bars: The Feminization of Bartending." In Barbara F. Reskin and Patricia A. Roos, *Job Queues, Gender Queues: Explaining Women's Inroads into Male Occupations*. Philadelphia: Temple University Press, pp. 241-56.

"Developments in Industrial Relations." 1989. *Monthly Labor Review* (March), p. 45.

Durazo, Maria Elena (President, HERE Local 11). 1993. Telephone interview by Dorothy Sue Cobble and Michael Merrill. April 12. Los Angeles.

Eller, Martha. 1990. "Sexual Harassment: Prevention, Not Protection," *Cornell Hotel and Restaurant Administration Quarterly*, Vol. 20, no. 4 (February), pp. 84-9.

Emerson, Robert. 1991. *The New Economics of Fast Food*. New York: van Nostrand Reinhold.

Fielder, Jeff (Director, FAST). 1993. Telephone interview by Dorothy Sue Cobble. May 28. Washington, DC.

Food and Allied Service Trades Department, AFL-CIO. 1985. *A Profile of the Fast Food Industry*. Washington, DC: FAST Department, AFL-CIO (October).

Franklin, Stephen. 1993. "Hotel Union Gambles It Will Win out in Strike against Las Vegas Casino." *Chicago Tribune*, January 29.

Geller, Laurence. 1990. "Industry Must Adopt Global Approach to Succeed." *Hotel and Motel Management* (April 9), pp. 22-23.

Guma, Karen. 1980. "6,000 Strike City Hotels." *Union Wage* (September-October).

Hall, Elaine J. 1989. "Serving Side by Side? The Organizational Stratification of Waiters and Waitresses Between and Within Restaurants," Working paper, University of Connecticut.

Hecker, Daniel and Ludmilla Murphy. 1985. "Retail Trade: Millions of Jobs, No Experience Necessary." *Occupational Outlook Quarterly*, Vol. 29 (Summer), pp. 13-19.

Henderson, John P. 1965. *Labor Market Institutions and Wages in the Lodging Industry*. East Lansing, MI: Michigan State University.

HERE, Local 11. 1988. *Union's Pre-arbitration Brief and Documentary Evidence, In The Matter of Interest Arbitration Between HERE, Local 11 and Employers' Council of Southern California, Inc.* Los Angeles, California.

Hernandez, Marita. 1989. "Latina Leads Takeover of Union From Anglo Males," *Los Angeles Times*, May 6, Sec. 1, p. 1, 28.

Jesitus, John. 1990. "1990 Franchisor Survey: Global Showdown." *Hotel and Motel Management* (September 10), pp. 57-66.

Job, Barbara C. 1980. "Employment and Pay Trends in the Retail Trade Industry." *Monthly Labor Review*, Vol. 103, no. 3 (March), pp. 40-43.

Josephson, Matthew. 1956. *Union House, Union Bar: History of the Hotel and Restaurant Employees*. New York.

Keller, Bill. 1984. "No Room at the New Inns for Unions." *New York Times*, June 1, section A, p. 4.

Liedy, Carol (Sec.-Treasurer, HERE 54), 1993. Telephone interview by Sarah Ryan. June 9. Atlantic City, NJ.

Luxenberg, Stan. 1985. *Roadside Empires: How the Chains Franchised America*. New York: Viking.

Mellor, Earl F. 1984. "Investigating the Differences in Weekly Earnings of Women and Men." *Monthly Labor Review*, Vol. 107 (June), pp. 21-33.

_____. 1985. "Weekly Earnings in 1983: A Look at More than 200 Occupations." *Monthly Labor Review* (January), pp. 54-59

Mencimer, Stephanie. 1992. "Separate Tables: Where Are the Black Waiters in Washington's Fanciest Restaurants?" *Washington Post*, December 13.

National Restaurant Association. 1990. *Survey of Benefits for Hourly Employees in Foodservice as reported in Restaurants USA*, June-July 1990, pp. 40-41.

_____. 1992. *Survey of Wages for Hourly Employees in Foodservice as reported in Restaurants USA*, January 1993, p. 41.

Neustadt, David. 1980. "They Also Serve: Waitering, a Changing Union, and China-town Struggles." *Village Voice* (May 12), pp. 66-68.

O'Connor, Charles. 1971. "Wages and Tips in Restaurants and Hotels." *Monthly Labor Review*, Vol. 94, no. 7 (July), pp. 47-51.

Oliver, Myrna. 1982. "Cafe Agrees to Pay $297,000 in Settlement." *Los Angeles Times*, January 29.

"Pays and Perks, Does Lodging Fall Short?" 1989. *Lodging Hospitality* (October).

Personick, Martin. 1991. "Profiles in Safety and Health: Eating and Drinking Places." *Monthly Labor Review* (June), pp. 19-26.

Plunkert, Lois M. 1990. "The 1980s: A Decade of Job Growth and Industry Shifts." *Monthly Labor Review* (September).

Powers, Thomas F. 1974. "Industry Dynamics: An Institutional View." in *The Future of Food Service: A Basis for Planning*, T. F. Powers, ed. University Park, PA: Pennsylvania State University, Food Service and Housing Administration, June.

Reynes, David. 1986. "Labor Protest at Disneyland Hotel is Focus of Union Organizing Effort." *Los Angeles Times*, May 3, p. 32.

Ritzer, George. 1983. "The 'McDonaldization' of Society." *Journal of American Culture*, Vol. 6 (Spring), pp. 101-08.

Rosier, Sharolyn. 1992. "HERE Gains Hotel Pact as APALA Helps Bridge Cultural Gap," *California AFL-CIO News*, November 9.

Rubin, Jay, and M.J. Obermeier. 1943. *Growth of a Union: The Life and Times of Edward Flore*. New York.

Seal, Kathy. 1989a. "Hotels Sign Five-Year Union Pact." *Hotel and Motel Management*. September 25, p. 2.

_____. 1990. "Union Local Takes Non-Strike Action; Conducts 'Soup-In'." *Hotel and Motel Management*. January 15.

_____. 1989b. "Union Targets Hotel Investors in Organizing Drive." *Hotel and Motel Management*. January 1.

Seidman, Harold. 1935. *Labor Czars*. New York.

Silvestri, George, and John Lukasiewicz. 1985. "Occupational Employment Projections: The 1984-95 Outlook." *Monthly Labor Review*, Vol. 108 (November), pp. 42-57.

Smothers, Ronald. 1985. "Adversaries in Hotel Strike: Calm Under Pressure." *New York Times*, June 10.

Spano, John. 1986. "Suit Calls Provocative Outfits 'Harassment'." *Los Angeles Times*, May 28.

Stuart, Lettice. 1993. "In San Antonio, Hyatt Defies U.S.A. Trend." *New York Times*, February 17.

Sullivan, Joseph. 1990. "US Lawsuit Says Mob Controls Union in Atlantic City Casinos." *New York Times*, December 20, p. A1.

Swoboda, Frank. 1990. "Federal Suit Links Union Chief, New Jersey Local to Mob." *Washington Post*, December 20, p. 16.

U.S. Department of Commerce. International Trade Administration. 1991. "Outlook for 1991." *U.S. Industrial Outlook—Retailing* (January), pp. 40-2.

U.S. Department of Labor. 1992a. *Compensation and Working Conditions*. (October), Washington, DC: GPO.

_____. 1992. *Employment and Earnings*. (September), Washington, DC: GPO.

_____. 1991a. *Employment and Earnings.* (November), Washington, DC: GPO.

_____. 1991b. *Employment, Hours, and Earnings,* U.S. 1909-90. Vol. 11. Bulletin no. 2370 (March), Washington, DC: GPO.

_____. 1989. *Handbook of Labor Statistics #2340.* Washington, DC: GPO.

_____. 1990. *Occupational Employment in Selected Nonmanufacturing Industries.* Bulletin no. 2348 (March), Washington, DC: GPO

_____. 1988. *US Occupational Outlook Handbook, 1988-89 Edition.* (April), Washington, DC: GPO.

Weinstein, Harry. 1985. "Union Cooks Up An Organized Dish But Restaurant Workers Won't Bite." *Los Angeles Times,* September 30, p. 3.

Wyckoff, D. Daryl, and W. Earl Sasser. 1978. *The Chain Restaurant Industry.* Lexington, MA: Lexington Books.

CHAPTER 12

Collective Bargaining in Agriculture

PHILIP L. MARTIN
University of California, Davis

Editor's Abstract

In the late 1970s, many commentators believed that unions were about to make a breakthrough in the representation of agricultural workers. California had passed a statute (ALRA) modeled on the National Labor Relations Act (NLRA), but which was somewhat more favorable to unions. ALRA provided for rapid representation elections, a make-whole remedy for employer bad-faith bargaining, fairly extensive rights for unions to discipline their members to promote solidarity, some access for organizers onto private property, and more legal secondary activity than is permissible under the NLRA. Legislation occurred after the United Farm Workers (UFW), under the leadership of Cesar Chavez, had experienced rapid growth in union membership.

Martin explains why agricultural unions received major setbacks in the 1980s and 1990s and why farm workers remain largely unorganized today. He attributes primary causality to the continuing supply of large numbers of legal and illegal immigrants working for a short time in the industry before returning to Mexico or moving on to other U.S. employment. Farm employers have utilized their political influence to maintain this large supply of farm laborers at low wages. The growth of the farm labor contractors and "custom harvesters," along with other changes in farm ownership, also frustrated unionization. Federal regulation of farm labor contractors has not been effective. A large proportion of farm labor contractors violate employment laws, helping to depress labor standards.

Additional reasons for the frustration of collective bargaining include other weaknesses of ALRA in an era in which farm owners were politically better organized than farm workers. Funds for enforcing ALRA were insufficient. Even more fundamentally, unions were often unable to gain contracts once they won representation elections under the law. Their inability to win strikes, along with the declining effectiveness of the consumer boycott, weakened especially the UFW. Martin estimates that contracts are in force in less than 10% of units in which representation elections were won under ALRA. He also considers the internal problems which have plagued the UFW in the

1980s and discusses the failure of the "Grapes of Wrath" boycott at the end of the decade.

As a result, farm workers have experienced declining real farm earnings. In California, average hourly earnings in agriculture were approximately 55% of those in the rest of the private sector in the early 1990s. However, seasonal work and charges by farm labor contractors further reduce the relative incomes of farm workers.

The last section of the chapter surveys collective bargaining in agriculture outside California, including the tomato industry of Ohio and the plantation agriculture of Hawaii. Martin views the low organization of the industry as likely to continue in the current legal environment, with continuing high levels of legal and illegal immigration and expanding use of farm labor contractors. He contends that what has happened in California agriculture may presage the future of other situations in which immigrants without other job opportunities are a significant portion of the work force—industries such as janitorial services and residential construction.

o   o   o

Agriculture is one of the least unionized industries in the United States. There are about 2.5 million workers employed at least part of each year by some 800,000 farm employers, and fewer than 50,000 or 2% belong to a labor organization that has a contract on the approximately 400 farms with collective bargaining agreements. The large farms that employ most of the nation's hired workers do resemble factories in the fields, but the established farmworker unions that once represented workers on perhaps 1000 of these farms are in retreat.

Unions have been replaced as the major factor affecting the structure and functioning of the farm labor market by farm labor contractors (FLCs) and similar intermediaries who recruit and supervise recently arrived immigrant workers (Commission on Agricultural Workers 1992). The substitution of FLCs for unions, especially in the few labor markets where collective bargaining gained a foothold in the 1970s, contributed to falling real farm wages during the 1980s. In addition, FLCs tend to reduce the take-home pay of workers because they often charge workers more for housing and transportation than if workers were hired directly by growers. FLCs are likely to continue to expand their presence in farm labor markets at the expense of unions and collective bargaining in the 1990s.

Farming is the nation's oldest industry and, despite extensive government intervention and subsidies, the production of food and fiber is considered an American success story (Learn et al. 1986). Unions and collective bargaining were never expected to be important features on Midwestern family farms, but they were expected to be common on large fruit and vegetable operations in the West and South. For this reason, commentaries on collective bargaining in agriculture follow a familiar pattern: They review a history of union "failures punctuated by disappointments" and then focus on a fledgling organization that could blaze a new path. Books and articles written in the early 1980s concluded that the United Farm Workers (UFW) activities leave "behind a rich legacy of social change, not the least of which was the unionization of California farmworkers" (Jenkins 1985:227). Koziara (1980) echoed this theme; she explained the many obstacles the UFW union had overcome in California to achieve almost 500 election victories on California farms in the late 1970s, and she expected Cesar Chavez to spread the UFW to large farms throughout the U.S. during the 1980s. However, when Chavez died in 1993, the UFW was only a shell of its 1970s self (Bardake 1993).

This chapter explains why collective bargaining did not take root in agriculture during the 1980s. The emphasis is on events in California, since that state enacted an Agricultural Labor Relations Act (ALRA) in 1975 which incorporated several features that are being discussed as reforms needed in the National Labor Relations Act (NLRA), including mandatory quick elections, a make whole remedy for employer bad faith bargaining, and fairly extensive rights of unions to discipline their members in order to promote solidarity. What happened in California agriculture may also presage the effects of continued mass migration on collective bargaining in other industries in which immigrant workers without other U.S. job options are a significant fraction of the work force, such as janitorial services and residential construction (Martin and Midgley 1994).

The U.S. Food and Fiber System

Agriculture is considered to be the oldest and, by some measures, the largest industry in the United States (Box 1). The farmers and farmworkers who actually produce crops and livestock on farms are often described as the keystone of the larger food sector, which includes both the industries that provide farmers with fertilizer and equipment and the industries that process, transport, and distribute food to consumers. Most of the jobs and economic activity in the food sector is in the non-farm economy. Farming accounts for only 2% of U.S. jobs and less than 2% of GDP (Lipton and Manchester 1992).

BOX 1
Farming and Farm Employment

For purposes of the Census of Agriculture, a farm is "any place from which $1,000 or more of agricultural products were produced and sold or normally would have been sold during the census year," the years ending in 2 and 7. According to this definition, there were 2.1 million farms in 1991. About 20% of all farms are in Texas, Missouri, and Iowa. The largest 107,000 U.S. farms each sold farm products worth $250,000 or more, and they accounted for 56% of gross cash income. Exports of farm products in 1990 were $40 billion, or 11% of the total $366 billion in U.S. exports. U.S. imports of agricultural products were $23 billion, 5% of U.S. imports, leaving a net agricultural trade surplus of $17 billion. The U.S. is a net exporter of the fruits and vegetables that many hired workers pick.

About 4.6 million people lived on farms in 1990. However, most of the 2.5 million farm residents who are in the labor force are not employed in agriculture: 52% are employed off the farm. Most farmworkers live in towns and cities; although data are inadequate, it is believed that fewer than 10% of U.S. farmworkers live on farms.

The American farming system is often considered a crown jewel of the U.S. economy, a system which is envied around the world because it produces such an abundance of farm products that surpluses of food and fiber rather than shortages have been the major U.S. agricultural problem for over half a century. The United States is a net exporter of food and fiber, and this ability of the nation's farmers to produce more food than Americans need has helped to hold down domestic food prices. Americans devote only 12% of their expenditures for personal consumption to food and beverages, versus 15% to 20% in Western Europe, 42% in Japan, and over 50% in India (U.S. Statistical Abstract 1992:833). The average American family spends about $28,400 annually, including $4,300 on food.

Agriculture has long been a special-case industry. Producing or obtaining food is an essential task of all economic systems, and agriculture, which employed most Americans as recently as 70 years ago, is a special case in history, economics, and government regulation. The history of the United States is in large part the story of how an agrarian nation that believed family farmers were the backbone of democracy evolved into an industrial nation. Several million farmers selling wheat or corn made these markets a leading example of how competitive markets functioned, and the seemingly cruel fate of impersonal market forces leaving too many farmers and their families in poverty led to a variety of government programs that attempt to prop up farm prices and incomes. The federal government intervened in product markets to ensure that family farmers got fair prices and thus fair incomes, but government often refused to intervene in the farm labor market under the theory that family farms should not be bothered with rules and regulations just to employ a hired hand who would soon acquire land and be a farmer in his own right.

Agriculture has changed. Fewer and larger farms produce more of the nation's food and fiber; the largest 5% of all farms, each a significant business, account for over half of the nation's farm output, while the smallest two-thirds of the nation's farms account for 5% of all farm output. Farmers have become more integrated into the nonfarm economy; nonfarm businesses supply inputs to farmers that range from credit to chemicals, so that farmers are affected directly and indirectly by interest rate fluctuations and pesticide regulation changes. Farmers have also become more integrated into the world economy; exports of farm products account for almost one-fourth of the value of U.S. farm production, so changes in the value of the dollar and trade policies can swing agriculture from boom to bust.

Public policies have tried to help farmers and their families buffeted by these changes in the national and global economies. Government policies continue to increase and stabilize farm incomes by assuring guaranteed prices for major field crops such as wheat, corn, and cotton. Government policies have also helped farmers to understand the scientific and economic factors that affect their biological factories by establishing land grant universities and extension services to educate them. But in comparison to these efforts to educate and assist farmers, government efforts to help farmworkers represent a history of neglect.

Farm Labor: A History of Neglect

This neglect of farmworkers can be attributed to a number of factors. Family farms—defined by the U.S. Department of Agriculture (USDA) as those that can operate with less than the equivalent of one and one-half year-round hired hands—have been the goal of the American farming system since colonial times. Agriculture's job ladder imagined "hired hands" to be temporary additions to the farm family who would soon become farmers in their own right; for this reason, 19th century folklore often includes stories of youthful hired hands marrying farmers' daughters. When the farm population began to shrink after 1935, it was assumed that farmworkers could best be helped after they left the farm, so there was more emphasis on maintaining full employment and regulating the nonfarm labor market than on intervening to improve conditions in the farm labor market[1] (Taylor 1975).

As historians have noted, the neglect of farmworkers was rooted in more than the assumption that most would soon become farmers or nonfarm workers. A permanent class of farmworkers, especially in a country that offered free land to all who wanted to farm, was an uncomfortable topic in a nation founded on the ideals of equality. Slavery was the system initially used in the South to assure plantation agriculture a supply of labor to produce cotton, tobacco, and other crops for distant European markets. Farmers in the western United States depended on hired farmworkers, many of whom were immigrants who had no other U.S. job options, to help them produce crops for distant markets in the eastern states.

There was an explicit discussion in California of the need for farmworkers who had no other U.S. job opportunities. When the *California Farmer* in 1854 asked, "Where shall the laborers be found . . . to become the working men" on the state's large farms, there was an acknowledgment that "slavery cannot exist here." Nevertheless, farm work was described as "the work of the slave." The magazine repeated its question and offered a solution: "Then where shall the laborers be found? The Chinese! . . . those great walls of China are to be broken down and that population are to be to California what the African has been to the South" (Quoted in Fuller 1991:7). Furthermore, a California farm spokesman in 1872 observed that hiring seasonal Chinese workers who housed themselves and then "melted away" when they were not needed made them "more efficient . . . than Negro labor in the South [because] it [Chinese labor] is only employed when actually needed, and is, therefore, less expensive" than slavery (Quoted in Fuller 1942:19809). Neither slaves nor immigrant farmworkers were topics that fit easily into discussions of how to bolster the family farm way of life which linked Americans to the ideals of their founding fathers.

The dream of farm ownership proved to be elusive for many farmworkers, and they protested poor wages and working conditions (Jamieson 1945) Some of the most colorful and short-lived U.S. unions attempted to organize farmworkers, but they had no lasting success due to the lack of a federal statute that granted farmworkers organizing and bargaining rights, farmer opposition, and the continued arrival of immigrant workers seeking jobs (Daniel 1981).

The termination of the Bracero program in 1964—which had brought almost 5 million Mexican farmworkers into the U.S. during the previous 22 years—ushered in a golden era for some farmworkers. Union organizing and the general scarcity of farm labor raised farm wages sharply: California's average farm wage rose from $.95 per hour in 1965 to $2.43 in 1975, a 156% increase in 10 years. There were reports that construction-style labor markets were developing in at least parts of agriculture, marked by high wages when work was available, and unemployment insurance benefits when it was not.

Illegal immigration ended this golden era for farmworkers. The number of aliens apprehended exceeded one million in 1977, and then rose sharply after 1982, until 1.8 million aliens were apprehended in 1986. Many of the aliens apprehended were Mexicans who were trying to find farm jobs in the United States. Today, 60% of all farmworkers and 80% of the migrant farmworkers are Hispanic immigrants (Mines et al. 1993:12-13).

Agricultural Trends

During the 1960s there was a widespread expectation that mechanization would soon eliminate most of the nation's then three million farmworkers. Processing tomatoes is an oft-cited example of what happens to the demand for migrant or immigrant workers after mechanization. In 1960 a peak 45,000 workers (80% Braceros) were employed to handpick 168,000 acres of tomatoes. Thirty years later, about 5,500 were employed to sort four times more tomatoes harvested from 330,000 acres. Growers argued that "the use of Braceros is absolutely essential to the survival of the tomato industry," but the termination of the Bracero program in 1964 accelerated the mechanization of the harvest in a manner that quadrupled production to 10 million tons between 1960 and 1990 (Martin and Olmstead 1985).

A uniformly ripening tomato and a mechanical harvester permitted mechanization to save about 80% of the labor needed to handpick processing tomatoes. In addition, the tomato harvester changed the work force and the wage system; women paid hourly wages to sort machine-picked tomatoes replaced Bracero men who earned piece rate wages to handpick tomatoes.

The mechanization of the tomato harvest proved to be the exceptional type of labor-displacing change in fruit, vegetable, and horticulture (FVH) agriculture, not the rule. There have been important labor savings in FVH agriculture since the 1960s, but they are usually less visible than machines replacing hand harvesters. Changes in production practices have saved labor, such as drip irrigation (which saves irrigation labor), dwarf trees and vines trained for easier hand or mechanical pruning, and precision planting and improved herbicides which save thinning and hoeing labor.

There is also an important countertrend to labor-saving mechanization. Picking and packing grapes, vegetables, and melons in the field increases "farm" employment and reduces "nonfarm" employment because field packing crews both harvest and pack a commodity. The trend toward field packing is uneven, but it has been ascribed to both high wages in unionized packing houses and portable technologies that make it easier to pick and pack in the fields (Martin 1990).

Agricultural engineers note that machines are available to harvest practically every fruit and vegetable grown in the United States, but that machines replace hand pickers only when it is economically rational to make the switch, or when the cost of machine harvesting is cheaper than the cost of hand harvesting (Brown 1984). The cost of machine harvesting falls as technological improvements make machines more efficient, science makes crops more amenable to machine harvesting, and packing and processing facilities become capable of efficiently handling machine-harvested produce. Since the technology of hand harvesting tends to be static, farm wages are the best indicator of the cost of hand harvesting.

An index that compares farm wages to the price farmers pay for machinery shows clearly that there was little economic rationale to mechanize during the 1950s, the peak Bracero years (Figure 1). However, after the Bracero program ended in 1964, wages rose faster than machinery prices, explaining the 1960s expectation that hand-harvesting jobs would soon be eliminated by machines. Mechanization continued to be a priority for fruit and vegetable growers in the early 1970s, and they supported so many mechanization projects at land-grant universities that the universities were accused of being virtually private research labs for them (Hightower 1978). However, just as these complaints about growers manipulating university researchers to find machines that would replace troublesome unionized workers reached their peak in the late 1970s, growers lost interest in mechanization. The reason is clear; by the late 1970s, enough unauthorized alien workers were arriving so that using hand workers was preferred to adopting machines.

FIGURE 1

Ratio of U.S. Farm Wages Index to Index of Farm Machinery Prices 1945-90 (1910-14 = 100)

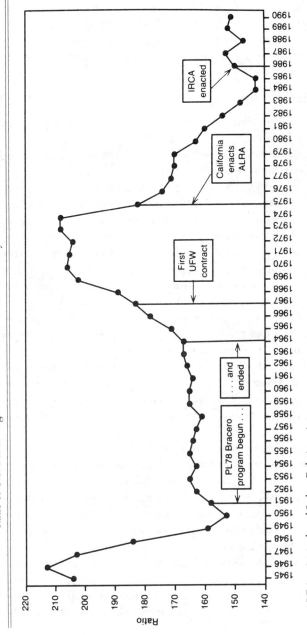

ALRA = Agricultural Labor Relations Act.
IRCA = Immigration Reform and Control Act.
UFW = United Farm Workers.
Source: U.S. Department of Agriculture, Economic Research Service, unpublished data.

Farm wages fell relative to the price of machinery throughout the 1980s, reaching a post-war low in 1983-84. Since the Immigration Reform and Control Act (IRCA) was enacted in 1986, the wage-machinery index has risen slightly, but not enough to prompt widespread interest in mechanization. As a result, the major fruits and many vegetables are still hand harvested today.

Expansion

Americans increased their per capita consumption of fruits and vegetables by 10% to 20% between 1970 and 1990 as a result of rising incomes, stable prices, and changing diets. The per capita consumption of fresh vegetables rose during the 1980s, for example, 23% to 136 pounds per person. This rising per capita consumption was especially noticeable for broccoli and cauliflower; the per capita consumption of fresh broccoli almost tripled from 1.6 to 4.5 pounds during the decade. The consumption of fresh fruit also rose sharply during the 1980s, led by increases in per capita consumption of apples, grapes, and strawberries. Despite these increases in per capita consumption, Americans have among the lowest levels of fruit and vegetable consumption among OECD countries, suggesting that this expansion may continue.

The U.S. consumption of most farm commodities increases about 1% annually, about the same as the rate of population growth, but the demand for FVH commodities might continue to increase by another 2% or 3% annually, or about as much as personal incomes typically go up, because Americans tend to spend about the same percentage more on FVH commodities as their incomes rise. For example, if personal incomes rise 2%, then expenditures on broccoli, cauliflower, and similar commodities also rise 2%.

Will Americans continue to increase their per capita consumption of especially fresh fruits and vegetables in the 1990s? Personal income growth has slowed, braking the rate of income-drive consumption increases. However, the government-endorsed "5-a-day" campaign that encourages Americans to eat five portions of fruits and vegetables daily, as well as the availability of many fresh fruits and vegetables year round, increased the per capita consumption of fresh fruits by 7% during the 1990-91 recession and helped to keep fresh vegetable consumption stable.

Americans can continue to increase their consumption of fresh fruits and vegetables that farmworkers harvest without increasing U.S. farmworker employment if more fruits and vegetables are imported. Imported fruits and vegetables account for less than 10% of the typical American's consumption, and most of these imports are fruits such as bananas that are not grown in the United States. Tomatoes, sometimes considered a symbol of the ability to produce a fresh vegetable far from where it will be consumed, are mostly produced in the United States— only 11% of the fresh tomatoes in 1992 were imported, including those imported from Mexico during the winter months.

Will the North American Free Trade Agreement (NAFTA) shift the production of fruits and vegetables to Mexico? Perhaps after the year 2000, but not during the 1990s (Martin 1993). Mexico's primary competitive advantage is climate; Mexico can produce fresh vegetables during the winter months when most U.S. production areas except Florida are not producing. But even if Mexico were to completely displace production in Florida, most fruit and vegetable production would remain in the United States because two-thirds of the production occurs in the summer and fall, when Mexico is not producing significant quantities. Mexico is unlikely to replace Florida soon as the source of most winter fruit and vegetables because, in many cases, low yields and low labor productivity make production there more expensive.

Mexican reforms and NAFTA are unlikely to spur a quick shift of production to Mexico. NAFTA eliminated tariffs on fruits and vegetables grown in Mexico. These tariffs were already low—the average U.S. tariff on the Mexican fruits and vegetables exported to the United States in 1990 was 8%, so that as a result of NAFTA, Mexican production costs may fall by 8%. But this tariff cost reduction could be dwarfed by the appreciation of the peso expected as NAFTA stimulates foreign investment in Mexico. One study projected a 29% increase in the real peso exchange rate due to NAFTA, and such a peso appreciation would raise Mexican production costs far more than tariff reduction lowers the U.S. price of Mexican crops (Hufbauer and Schott 1992:57).

NAFTA will not solve the other problems associated with producing in Mexico for the U.S. market—higher transportation costs, less public research on disease and other factors which reduce yields, and lower worker productivity. These Mexican disadvantages could be overcome with foreign investment and time, but Luis Tellez Kuenkler, Undersecretary in the Mexican Ministry of Agriculture and Water Resources, cautions that Mexican agricultural exports will not skyrocket overnight. He may have been correct when he predicted in 1991 that Mexican

FVH exports to the United States would rise, at most, by 40% within five years after a NAFTA is signed, or from $900 million in 1990 to $1.3 billion by 1998. U.S. FVH production by then is likely to be worth $35 to $40 billion annually, demonstrating that even increased trade with the country best suited to produce for the U.S. market should not eliminate the need for farmworkers in the United States.

Farmworkers

Immigrants from Mexico dominate the farm work force, and there is no reason to expect the characteristics of farmworkers to change in the 1990s. Farm labor data are notoriously unreliable, but the U.S. Department of Labor's National Agricultural Worker Survey (NAWS) found that the farm work force throughout the U.S. is coming to resemble the stereotype long familiar in California, Texas, and Florida, viz., most farmworkers are immigrants from Mexico (Mines et al. 1993).

The NAWS found that three-fourths of the workers employed on U.S. farms in the early 1990s are minorities, usually immigrants from Mexico who have been in the United States for less than 10 years (Figure 2). Many of these immigrants are Special Agricultural Workers (SAWs)—aliens who were illegally in the U.S. in the mid-1980s and who were legalized under special provisions of IRCA. There is a significant and growing percentage of unauthorized workers—despite the legalization of 1.1 million farm workers in 1987-88—estimates of the percentage of unauthorized workers who harvest particular fruits and vegetables today often range from 30% to 50% (Commission on Agricultural Workers 1992). These "new-new" immigrants include significant numbers of indigenous peoples from southern Mexico and Central America, such as non-Spanish speaking Mixtec Indians.

It is often believed that most farmworkers are migrants who "follow the sun," moving from farm to farm to harvest crops. This is not the case (Martin and Martin 1993). According to the NAWS, the average farmworker is employed on less than two farms during a typical year. While employed, farmworkers have average hourly earnings of about $5. Most find work seasonally, so average weekly earnings of $180 to $200 for 26 weeks of work leaves the average farmworker with earnings that are only three-fourths of the poverty-level income for an individual.

The farm work force portrayed in the NAWS is hard to organize into unions. Most workers are not U.S. citizens, and many are out of the U.S. for three or four months annually, making it hard to sustain a worker

FIGURE 2
NAWS Farmworker Profile: 1989-91

Demographic Characteristics: Most farmworkers are male, young, married, and immigrants with a SAW status
- 73% are male; 67% are 35 or younger (median age 33)
- 58% are married; 52% have children, and 60% do farm work accompanied by their families
- 60% are foreign born, including 55% who were born in Mexico
- 70% are Hispanic
- 29% are SAWs; they have a median 7 years of farm work experience
- 10% are unauthorized; these young workers (median age 23) have only 2 years of U.S. farm work experience
- 53% of all SAS workers have 8 or fewer years of education (median 8 years; 65% speak primarily Spanish
- 57% of the workers live with their families at the work site

Farm Work and Earnings: Most workers experience extensive seasonal unemployment and have low annual earnings
- Workers on average spend 50% of the year or 26 weeks doing Seasonal Agricultural Services work for 1.7 farm employers, 20% or 10 weeks unemployed, 15% or 8 weeks doing non-SAS work, and 15% or 8 weeks traveling abroad
- 75% of all crop workers are employed in fruits or vegetables
- 77% are hired directly by growers, usually to harvest crops
- Median hourly earnings were $4.85; work weeks averaged 37 hours, for SAS earnings of $180 and, for 26 weeks, $4,665
- Less than half of the workers have Unemployment Insurance and Workers Compensation coverage; 21% have off-the-job health insurance
- 28% live in employer-provided housing

Other Work and Income: Farmworkers are poor but not dependent on welfare
- 46% of all SAS workers have below poverty level incomes, the poverty rate is highest for unauthorized workers (77%)
- 36% also do non-SAS farm work; such work paid a median $4.50 per hour and is preferred to farm work
- 40% of the workers spend an average 19 weeks abroad each year
- Median individual incomes are $5,000 to $7,500; median family incomes are $7,500 to $10,000; 50% of the families are below the 1989 poverty line of $12,675 for a family of four
- 55% of the workers own assets, usually a vehicle
- 16% receive food stamps; 3% receive Aid to Families with Dependent Children

organization. Seasonal work and low earnings make it difficult for farmworkers to support themselves if they go on strike, while porous borders permit strikebreakers to quickly replace those who go on strike. These factors add up to a fundamental obstacle for unions; most farmworkers see especially seasonal farm work as temporary. They hope to improve themselves in their country of origin or in a nonfarm U.S. job, so it is hard to maintain support and commitment for a farmworker union.

Evolution of Farmworker Unions

Despite formidable obstacles, there have been numerous struggles between farmworkers and farm employers for the past century. Farmworkers seem at first blush to represent an attractive target for union organizers. Millions of workers who are receptive to unions because of low wages, often arbitrary supervision, and sometimes employer charges for housing, food, and other items needed to work in remote rural areas. But organized farmers managed to keep most farmworkers unorganized, largely because farmworkers saw hope for advancement outside of U.S. fields—it has been said that the only goal shared by seasonal farmworkers is the hope that, next year, they won't have to be in the fields.

Second, farm employers have proven to be formidable opponents of unions. Many organizing drives were led by nonfarm workers, and farmers were able to rally rural law enforcement personnel and urban business partners such as banks and food processors against these "outside agitators" (Daniel 1981). Farmers argued that their workers did not want unions to represent them because committed farmworkers wanted to climb the agricultural ladder to farm ownership. Furthermore, farmers argued that they must oppose unions because a farmworker union would be too powerful—a harvest time strike could cause them to lose an entire year's income.

Third, government has not been kind to farmworkers. Lawmakers have been more sympathetic to farmers than to immigrant and minority farmworkers who often cannot vote. Congress excluded farmworkers from the NLRA in 1935, and this exclusion from organizing and bargaining rights remains today. The American public is also sympathetic to farmers, seeing their family-run businesses that supply essential food as a continuing link to the founding fathers. Farmers with money and organization and a sympathetic public were able to use government far better than farmworkers whose wages and working conditions generated only periodic pangs of guilt.

There were three major waves of farmworker union activity: during and after World War I, during the 1930s Depression, and since the 1964 termination of the Bracero program. In all three periods, workers were usually spurred into action by decisions of farm employers, such as advertising for workers at a high wage and then cutting the wage when too many workers appeared. However, there is almost no link between past and present in farmworker union activities. The workers and leaders active in 1915 played no role in the strikes of 1933, and the workers and union leaders of the 1930s were absent from organizing activities during later decades. Finally, the major farmworker union to emerge in the 1960s, the UFW, differs from most American unions in its broad, civil rights for Hispanics agenda; its reliance on boycotts and political activities rather than more traditional worker organizing and strikes; and its reliance on relatives of founder Cesar Chavez for leadership.

The UFW

The United Farm Workers burst onto the farm labor scene in 1966 with a 40% one-year wage increase, and the UFW has continued to be considered the nation's major farmworker union since then. The UFW was founded in 1962 by Cesar Chavez, a former farmworker (Taylor 1975; Sosnick 1978). Chavez was helping Hispanic workers to deal with government agencies when, in 1965, the AFL-CIO-chartered Agricultural Workers Organizing Committee (AWOC) called a strike against California table grape growers.[2] Chavez's fledgling organization joined forces with the AWOC, but growers were able to harvest their grapes by using farm labor contractors to obtain strikebreaking workers.

Chavez broke with the past by trying to keep the pressure on grape growers during the winter months, when they were not producing grapes. The key, according to Chavez, was to enlist a public that had been made sensitive to the problems of poverty and discrimination by the War on Poverty and the Civil Rights movement. Chavez hoped to attract sympathetic Americans to his "La Causa" by persuading them not to buy the products of the conglomerates that incidentally grew table grapes. During the 1965 Christmas shopping season, Chavez and his supporters picketed liquor stores, asking Americans not to buy whiskey produced by a conglomerate whose grape subsidiary refused to grant wage increases to farmworkers.

High-profile visitors flocked to Delano, California, the small town where Chavez lived. U.S. senators, unions, churches, and student groups endorsed the boycott, generating free publicity. When Chavez and his supporters early in 1966 went on a 300-mile march to the state capital in Sacramento, the targeted conglomerate—Schenley Industries—agreed to negotiate a contract that included a 40% wage increase.

The UFW boycott then shifted to another large grape grower, leading to interunion conflict. The grower rebuffed the UFW with the announcement that its farmworkers were already represented by the Teamsters union. Chavez and his supporters cried foul, noting that there had never been an election to determine the preferences of the farmworkers. Under pressure, an election won by the UFW was held in August 1966. The UFW and the Teamsters signed a jurisdictional agreement that left field worker organizing to the UFW and nonfarm packingshed workers to the Teamsters.

After these initial successes the UFW sent letters to California table grape growers requesting that they recognize the UFW as the bargaining agent for their field workers. The table grape growers did not respond, and the UFW launched a successful national boycott that urged consumers not to buy California grapes. The UFW obtained endorsements of the grape boycott from unions, religious leaders, students, and urban politicians. Pressure on the grape growers increased as annual per capita grape consumption fell from 3.2 pounds in 1966 to 2 pounds per person in 1971 and 1972.

The breakthrough came in March 1970, when grape growers recognized the UFW and signed contracts that offered harvesters a $1.75 hourly wage plus a piece rate of 25 cents per box, a union hiring hall that would register and send workers as needed to unionized grape growers, pesticide protections, and a system to resolve worker grievances. However, UFW fortunes fell after these 1970 successes. The UFW followed its grape boycott strategy with California lettuce growers, but many of them responded by signing contracts with the Teamsters, in violation of the UFW-Teamsters jurisdictional agreement. The lettuce boycott which followed was not effective.

The UFW held its first constitutional convention in September 1973, when the UFW had 67,000 members, or about 10% of California's field workers. However, the UFW was losing contracts steadily to the Teamsters, the union preferred by growers, so that on the eve of the Agricultural Labor Relations Act (ALRA) in 1975, the Teamsters—with 300 contracts—had largely replaced the UFW as the major union representing California farmworkers.

The ALRA and ALRB in 1975

The 1974 California gubernatorial campaign was waged in part on the need for a legislative framework to end the violence in the fields.

The winning Democrat, Jerry Brown, supported a compromise bill that was eventually accepted by the UFW, growers, and Teamsters. A special session of the California legislature enacted the ALRA, which was signed on June 5, 1975, so that the first elections could be held during the peak harvest period in September 1975.

The UFW won most of the first ALRA elections. There were elections on almost 400 California farms during the first four months that the law was in effect, and the UFW won three-fourths of those in which a final vote was certified by the Agricultural Labor Relations Board (ALRB), the state agency established to oversee elections and to hear charges that the ALRA had been violated (ALRB Annual Report). This election activity depleted the ALRB's funding and, in what proved to be a familiar story, farmers and non-UFW unions unhappy with what they perceived to be an ALRB tilted in favor of the UFW persuaded the California legislature not to appropriate additional funds, forcing the ALRB to temporarily cease operations. The UFW countered with an initiative to amend the California constitution that would have required funding for the ALRB. The UFW initiative failed, but it illustrated the high-profile nature of the farmworker issue.

The UFW consolidated its position as the nation's leading farm worker union in the late 1970s. A March 1977 jurisdictional pact with the Teamsters again removed its major competitor from the fields. The UFW was certified as the bargaining representative for workers on over 300 farms, and 50,000 to 70,000 members were employed sometime during the year under 150 contracts. However, this monopoly in the fields allegedly encouraged the UFW to switch from organizing farm-workers to depending on the ALRB to redress grower infringements of worker rights—the number of organizers fell from 200 in the mid-1970s to a handful by 1980, while the legal and political staff expanded. The UFW moved its headquarters from Delano, a farmworker town in the area of California with half of the state's farmworkers, to a mountain top location far from most farmworkers. Widely reported purges of non-Hispanic union staff in the early 1980s left a UFW whose leadership was dominated by relatives of founder Chavez.[3]

The Demise of the UFW

In 1975, the average entry-level wage on unionized farms in California was $3.11 per hour,[4] so that a worker employed full-time (2,000 hours) could earn more than the poverty-level income for a family of four ($5,500). In 1979, when the first round of contracts signed under the ALRA was expiring, the UFW demanded a 40% wage increase, from $3.70 to $5.25 hourly. Growers resisted this UFW wage demand (Majka and Majka 1982). The union called strikes that reduced the supply of winter lettuce by about one-third, but the strike boomeranged and raised grower revenues because lettuce prices tripled (Carter et al. 1987).

The UFW eventually won the 40% one-year wage increase it demanded, raising entry-level wages to $5.25 hourly (the federal minimum wage was $3.10 hourly in 1980). This wage gain proved to be a Pyrrhic victory. Several corporate growers signed UFW contracts in order to go out of business, and others switched from being both growers and packers to being only nonfarm packers of vegetables grown for them by independent growers, who assumed the responsibility for getting broccoli or lettuce harvested. UFW membership plummeted as corporate growers went out of business, and the union was unable to negotiate agreements with successor growers. By some estimates, UFW membership dropped from 60,000 in the early 1980s to 6,000 a decade later.[5] The 1979-80 vegetable strike also led to judgments against the UFW; the union was forced to pay $1.7 million for damages caused to a lettuce grower during the strike.

Growers who had rocky relations with the UFW supported a Republican candidate for governor in 1982 who had promised to bring "balance" to the administration of the ALRB. After his election, the new general counsel changed the procedures through which worker charges that the ALRA had been violated were investigated, new board members included ex-legislators who had tried to eliminate the ALRB, and the UFW tried to have the agency defunded.

Growers also benefited from a series of court rulings that overturned key ALRB decisions. The ALRA differs from the NLRA in three important respects. It includes provisions that require elections to be held quickly, before migrant farm workers move on to another job; a unique remedy that requires farm employers who bargain in bad faith to "make their employees whole" for any wages or benefits they lost; and broader powers for unions to discipline their members (Box 2).

The make-whole remedy was most troublesome to growers. They charged that refusing to accede to UFW demands would lead to charges that growers were not bargaining with the union in good faith. According to growers, an ALRB sympathetic to such UFW charges gave

---

BOX 2
NLRA and ALRA Differences

There are three major differences between the NLRA and the ALRA: elections, bargaining, and internal union affairs. Since the ALRA was written to resolve differences between parties that distrusted one another, it is often more detailed than the NLRA. Unless specified in the ALRA or justified by unique agricultural circumstances, the ALRB is required to follow NLRB precedent when interpreting the ALRA.

Elections. The ALRA defines "employer" in a manner which generally makes the most stable entity, the landowner or farm operator, the union's bargaining partner. FLCs who bring only workers to the farm and then take direction from the farmer cannot be employers under the ALRA. All the workers on a farm are normally in one wall-to-wall bargaining unit, a provision meant to simplify matters for farmers and to prevent seasonal Hispanic workers from being isolated in their own units.

A union can be certified as the bargaining representative for workers only after a secret ballot election: recognition picketing and voluntary recognition are banned. Elections can be held only when a 50-50 rule is satisfied—at least 50% of the farm's normal peak employees must be at work, and a majority must sign authorization cards before a union can petition for an election. Once an election petition is filed, an election must be held within seven days (48 hours if a strike is in progress); disputes are then resolved after the election. Before the election, union organizers are permitted to "take access" to workers on the farm for up to three hours daily.

Bargaining. Farm employers are required to bargain in good faith with the union selected by their workers. If a farm employer fails to bargain in good faith, the employer can be required to make employees whole for any wages and benefits they lost during the bad faith bargaining period. The ALRB General Counsel proposes the hypothetical package that would have been paid (say $6 hourly), subtracts the wage actually paid ($5), and the employer then owes $1 for all hours worked during the bad-faith period. The ALRB initially issued make-whole orders routinely; California courts in the mid-1980s responded by ruling that several ALRB findings of bad-faith bargaining were actually legal hard bargaining. Another court ruled that before the ARLB could issue a make-whole order, the employer had to be given an opportunity to show that even with good-faith bargaining, no contract with higher wages would have been signed. Make whole has turned into a chimera for many farmworkers; most of the awards actually paid have come in the form of settlements between the union and the employer.

The ALRA permits more secondary activity than the NLRA. The NLRA permits workers in a dispute to boycott only the struck product at a neutral secondary employer; the ALRA, by contrast, permits vineyard workers to urge consumers, for example, to boycott both the wine and the store selling it.

Internal Union Affairs. The ALRA permits union shop clauses in collective bargaining agreements that require workers to join the union within five days and to remain union members "in good standing" to keep their jobs. Unlike the NLRA, the ALRA permits union-defined good standing rules to include "any reasonable terms and conditions" of membership. The UFW has over 30 good-standing terms and conditions.

Farm employers have charged that this broad good-standing rule permits unions to control members and thus their workers. There have been several decade-long cases involving growers who purportedly refused to sign contracts with the UFW because of this broad good-standing clause, although there have been fewer than three charges annually filed by disgruntled workers against their unions. The ALRB has ruled against the UFW in several of these cases.

Source: ALRA and ALRB court decisions, 1975-1993, and Martin et al. 1988.

the union two chances to win wage increases—once at the bargaining table, and again as the ALRB considered union charges that the employer was engaged in bad faith bargaining.

The UFW won several significant make-whole remedies from the ALRB in the early 1980s; remedies against individual lettuce growers arising out of the 1979-80 strike, for example, ranged from $2 to $20 million. However, in March 1984, a California court overturned many of them with a decision that farm employers had been engaged in lawful "hard" bargaining, not unlawful bad faith bargaining, and the "new" ALRB decided that the UFW, in one case, had engaged in bad faith bargaining with a major vegetable grower. A California court in 1987 dealt the make-whole remedy another blow. Even if the union convinced the ALRB that an employer had bargained in bad faith, the court ruled that farm employers must be given the opportunity to prove that, even if there had been good faith bargaining, the employer would not have agreed to higher wages for economic or other legitimate reasons, so no make-whole wages were owed to farm workers (Martin and Egan 1989). As a result, many employers reopened their make-whole cases, so that after almost two decades, there have been more than 50 cases in which the ALRB decided that farmworkers were owed make-whole, but in only five cases have farmworkers received board-ordered make-whole payments.[6]

The UFW had reduced its organizing activities and changed its leadership, and it was unprepared for these ALRB and legal setbacks. In order to regain momentum, the UFW in 1984 returned to the grape boycott—its 1960s success story. The UFW charged that five pesticides used on California table grapes caused illnesses among farm workers and their families and left residues on grapes that posed threats to customers. Instead of enlisting churches, students, politicians, and unions to provide pickets in front of grocery stores, the UFW launched a "high-tech boycott" that relied on a direct mail campaign that asked shoppers not to patronize stores that sold grapes. The UFW argued that the thin profit margins characteristic of the grocery business would persuade the store to drop grapes if just 5% to 10% of a store's customers responded to the boycott appeal.

This "wrath of grapes" boycott has received periodic boosts, such as occurred during the summer of 1988 when Cesar Chavez launched his "fast for life." Sympathetic religious, union, and political leaders agreed to "pass the boycott cross" from one to another, and cities and counties passed resolutions that prohibited the use of public funds to buy California table grapes for schools, jails, and other facilities. But table grape consumption has been rising despite the boycott; the average American ate over seven pounds of grapes in 1992-93, up from six pounds in 1984-85.[7] The UFW in 1993 had no table grape contracts. Cesar Chavez died in 1993. Amid the many accolades, there were frequent references to Chavez as the Hispanic Martin Luther King[8]—a person who "epitomized the spiritual and political goals of a people." The leader of the California Senate called Chavez "perhaps the greatest Californian of the 20th century," the legislature considered making his birthday, March 31, a voluntary state holiday, and legislation pending in Congress that would prohibit most U.S. employers from hiring permanent replacement workers was re-named the Cesar Chavez Worker Protection Act. The Kennedy family were longtime supporters of Chavez: Senator Edward Kennedy called Chavez "one of the most heroic figures of our times," and a Senate resolution honored Chavez as "one of the greatest leaders of human and civil rights advancement the United States has known."[9]

But the Chavez eulogized in 1993 had become an increasingly controversial figure. A newspaper series on "Fields of Pain" detailing the problems of California farmworkers was followed by "Fields of Betrayal," an indictment of the UFW and Chavez by farmworker advocates who charged that the UFW went into the fields only to block other unions seeking to represent farmworkers (*Sacramento Bee* December 8-11, 1991; February 23, 1992). News accounts of UFW activities during the 1980s focused more often on "people problems" within the union—10% of the 350 delegates to the 1981 constitutional convention walked out to protest Chavez's refusal to consider their nominees to the union's executive board—rather than on the boycott or the union's organizing and bargaining successes. Even though many of the Hispanic politicians in California today began with the UFW, the UFW lost its once formidable influence in state politics. UFW boycott tactics also subjected the union to judgments for damages: Chavez was in Arizona at the time of his death to testify in a case in which the UFW was ordered to pay a California vegetable grower $2.9 million for damages suffered in a five-year boycott.[10]

The recent focus on personalities and politics obscured two fundamental changes that have made it difficult for the UFW—or any other farmworker union—to organize farmworkers: the changing structure of agriculture and continued illegal immigration. Even though legislation guarantees farmworkers union rights in California, and there are more farmworker unions and farmworker organizations operating in California today than ever before, there are fewer contracts in the 1990s than there were in the 1960s.

Structural Changes in Agriculture

Unions have two major sources of bargaining power: withholding their labor in order to stop production, or discouraging the consumption of a product. Farmworker unions have rarely been able to prevent production with strikes; farmers have usually been able to secure replacement workers. For this reason, the UFW and several other farmworker unions have relied on actual or threatened consumer boycotts to bolster their position at the bargaining table.

This boycott strategy works best if a conglomerate that sells brand-name products also has a farming operation. In that case, a farmworker union protesting low wages can threaten to boycott (e.g., all Coca Cola products if Coca Cola does not agree to the wage demands of the orange pickers at its relatively small orange juice division). The UFW used the bargaining leverage that reflects "the importance of being unimportant" against major food, beverage, liquor, and retailing corporations during the 1960s and 1970s.

Many of these brand-name corporations sold their farming operations in the 1980s, or restructured so that they now simply pack and market commodities that are grown for them by "independent" farmers. (Villarejo 1989). This structural change hurts unions; the UFW can no longer threaten to boycott Seven-Up, for example, because Seven-Up no longer hires farmworkers to harvest lemons. Instead, it buys lemons produced by "independent" growers. Gallo, the wine company once targeted for a UFW boycott, today buys most of its grapes from independent growers.

The independent growers who produce most of the nation's fruits and vegetables are often large corporations—many have annual sales in the $20 million to $200 million range—but most have no labels recognized by consumers, and it is harder for a union to boycott an entire commodity such as grapes than a brand-name product like Gallo wine. In this manner, the structure of agriculture has evolved into many layers between the field and the grocery store, and unions are left fighting with the relatively powerless employers on the bottom layer. Nonfarm packers and retailers are usually exempt from boycott pressure if they do not employ farmworkers and if they buy commodities from several farms. Furthermore, the NLRB has recently complicated the boycott strategy by ruling that some field workers—those who pack crops in the field for custom harvesters—are nonfarm workers under the NLRA, so that a union bargaining for them could not engage in secondary boycotts.[11]

Many farms hire workers through farm labor contractors (FLCs) or custom harvesters, so that if there were to be a workplace dispute, it would be between the FLC-custom harvester and the workers, not the farmer and the workers. Farmworker unions generally, and the UFW in particular, see FLCs as their competitors—some expected the ALRA to reduce the influence of FLCs in the farm labor market (Mamer and Hayes 1976:80). FLCs typically organize farmworkers into crews of 20 to 50 workers, and each "crew boss" is responsible for ensuring, among other things, that the workers do not unionize (Box 3). The UFW knew that FLCs were often manipulated by growers, and some went out of business owing workers money. For these reasons, the UFW was able to get the ALRA written in a manner that considers the landowner or farm operator, not the FLC, to be the employer of farmworkers for collective bargaining purposes.

FLCs cannot be bargaining partners for unions, but custom harvesters can. Thus, many FLCs have acquired enough responsibility over when and where to harvest, and enough equipment to transport the commodity from the field to the packing house, to be considered custom harvesters rather than FLCs. Workers employed by these FLC-custom harvesters have been very difficult to organize; in one southern California citrus harvest, for example, FLC-custom harvesters replaced the UFW as "representative" of 5,000 workers between 1980 and 1985.

FLC-custom harvesters prevent unions from securing a foothold on many large farms, while other FLCs keep small crews of unauthorized workers under their thumb. Many older and established farmworkers with a van typically house the illegal immigrants who continue to arrive and provide them with rides to work. Even though an extensive body of federal and state regulations govern FLC activities, many of those involved do not register with authorities, and of those who do, many ignore the regulations. For example, a FLC must disclose in writing wages and working conditions at the time of recruitment—analogous to explaining conditions on the assembly line when an employment application is filled out—but workers who request written contracts are told

---

BOX 3
Farm Labor Contractors

Farm labor contractors (FLCs) are the intermediaries who match farm workers with jobs. Such intermediaries are common in labor markets in which immigrant workers are hired in crews for seasonal jobs. In these situations, the employer may want 20 to 40 crews, each with 30 to 40 workers, and the workers may need a bilingual contractor to find jobs for them.

FLCs in western agriculture were originally bilingual go-betweens. The Chinese workers who had been imported to build the transcontinental railroad in the 1860s were barred from urban jobs, and a bilingual "head boy" both worked and arranged seasonal farm jobs for his 20 to 30 compatriots. Japanese immigrants in the early 1900s also followed this intermediary-as-fellow-worker model, but in the 1920s, the FLC as an independent business person evolved. Farmworkers went on strike against farmers who insisted on hiring workers through FLCs.

The federal government began to protect farmworkers in the 1960s, and the first protective legislation was aimed at forcing FLCs to identify themselves by registering with the U.S. Department of Labor. Many states also require FLCs to register, and both federal and state governments seek to discourage unscrupulous FLCs by requiring in many states that FLCs be fingerprinted, bonded, and tested for their knowledge of labor and pesticide regulations. For example, in California a FLC must pay a $350 annual license fee, post a $10,000 bond, undergo a character investigation, and pass pesticide safety and labor law tests.

The intent of ever-stricter FLC regulation was to drive out of business those who could not operate lawfully. This strategy has not been successful: the 4,000 FLCs and their 8,000 crew bosses are as many as ever, and enforcement data suggest that labor law violations are common. Coordinated federal-state labor law enforcement in California in 1992-93 found major violations committed by nine of 10 FLCs inspected.

FLCs evade effective enforcement of labor laws for a simple reason: they know the workers they hire and, as the U.S. Industrial Commission explained in the early 1900s, can thus "drive the hardest kinds of bargain" with them (quoted in Fisher 1952:43). Under such circumstances, it is hard to get farmworkers to complain about labor law violations and, even if they do, the general absence of written contracts makes it hard for often illiterate and non-English-speaking workers to provide the evidence needed for effective enforcement.

Intermediaries are found in most seasonal farm labor markets. Not all are FLCs, but the workers' crew boss becomes in most instances the person on whom the worker depends. It is very difficult for a union to substitute for this often personal relationship.

---

they are not needed. Subsequent disputes are then hard to resolve, as when workers assert that they were promised $12 per bin to pick oranges, but were paid $12 for the first bin and then $10. Neither unions nor federal and state labor law enforcers have been able to protect workers at the bottom of the layered farm labor market.

Immigration

Most farmworkers are immigrants limited to seasonal farm jobs by language, skill, and other factors. As early as the 1960s, the UFW recognized the dangers posed by illegal immigration—it complained bitterly about grower use of illegal alien strikebreakers in the 1960s and 1970s. However, by the mid-1980s, the UFW changed its position—it opposed employer sanctions on the grounds that fines on employers who knowingly hire illegal alien workers would increase discrimination against Hispanic workers. Instead, the UFW became one of the few AFL-CIO affiliates to disagree with the federation and favor more effective labor law enforcement rather than sanctions.

The Immigration Reform and Control Act of 1986 was expected to usher in a new era in farm labor. Even though it included the sanctions that the UFW opposed, it also included a Special Agricultural Worker (SAW) legalization program for unauthorized farmworkers. Both the UFW and growers thought each had found a way to enlist worker loyalty. Each created organizations to help unauthorized farmworkers to apply for legal status; however, collectively, these organizations assisted fewer than 75,000 of the 1.3 million aliens who applied for SAW status.

SAW workers no longer facing competition from illegal immigrants were expected to be in the vanguard of a new round of collective bargaining and wage increases:

> By giving legal status to eligible farmworkers and stemming the supply of new unauthorized workers, IRCA could have increased the possibility of successful labor organizing in agriculture. (Commission on Agricultural Workers 1992:111).

This has not proved to be the case, primarily because IRCA's agricultural provisions unleashed a massive new wave of illegal immigration (Bean et al. 1990). The resulting surplus of farmworkers made legal SAW workers fearful that if they demanded higher wages or better working conditions, they would be replaced by desperate new arrivals (Box 4).

Instead of collective bargaining, IRCA seems to have spurred the growth of self-help organizations. The UFW recently merged its so-called "community union"—La Union del Pueblo Entero (LUPE), which claimed 20,000 members in the early 1990s—into the smaller UFW. LUPE and similar organizations help members with immigration and related problems, provide them with access to credit and other services, and advocate on their behalf in exchange for an annual fee.

BOX 4
IRCA and Farmworkers

The U.S. enacted the Immigration Reform and Control Act (IRCA) of 1986 to reduce illegal immigration by making it more difficult for unauthorized workers to find U.S. jobs and to offer legal immigration status to certain unauthorized aliens. IRCA included three major agricultural provisions: deferred sanctions enforcement, the SAW legalization program, and the H-2A and the RAW foreign worker programs.

Until IRCA, Immigration and Naturalization Service (INS) enforcement in agriculture often involved the Border Patrol driving into fields and apprehending aliens who tried to run away. Today a paper chase has replaced this people chase, as INS investigators match the number of 1-9 employment verification forms with payroll records. Unauthorized aliens and their employers can and do easily evade such enforcement with fraudulent work authorization documents.

IRCA created two legalization programs: a general program which granted legal status to illegal aliens if they had continuously resided in the U.S. since 1982, and the SAW (seasonal agricultural worker) program, which granted legal status to illegal aliens who did at least 90 days of farm work in 1985-86. A SAW applicant was permitted to apply for the SAW program with only an affidavit from an employer asserting that the worker named in the letter had done, for example, 90 days of work in virtually any crop. The burden of proof then shifted to the INS to overcome the alien's showing of claimed employment. Studies suggested that the majority of SAW applications were fraudulent (Martin 1990).

The H-2A program revised the pre-IRCA system through which U.S. farmers could obtain DOL certification that they needed temporary farmworkers to fill temporary U.S. jobs. Western farmers opposed to going through a DOL-controlled certification process also got a four-year Replenishment Agricultural Worker (RAW) program included in IRCA. Federal agencies estimated the demand for and supply of farmworkers and, if a shortage is anticipated, then RAW visas were to be made available to workers between 1989 and 1993. Because IRCA produced labor surpluses rather than shortages, no RAW visas were issued. Even if they had been, RAWs probably would not have added to the farm work force, since 95% of those who registered to participate were (presumably) illegal aliens with U.S. addresses.

California Farmworker Unions Today

The ALRB has certified nine unions to represent farmworkers in California agriculture since 1975. There have been 1,609 elections supervised by the ALRB, of which 775 resulted in a union being certified to represent farmworkers. There are, however, fewer than 300 contracts on California farms, suggesting that even a favorable legal framework cannot overcome a worker surplus to guarantee union success.

Collective bargaining in California agriculture began under different circumstances. Two-thirds of the California elections were held between

1975 and 1978, and a union was typically certified as the bargaining representative. Since 1981, however, the number of elections held to decertify an existing union has been about the same as the number held to certify a union representative.

Table 1 provides contract and membership data on California farmworker unions. The data are approximate, since the ALRA does not require unions or employers to file contracts with the ALRB. The UFW membership data are approximate—the 22,000 figure is the official UFW membership tally, although the UFW has never paid dues to state and national labor federations for more than 10,000 to 15,000 members (*AFL-CIO News* May 3, 1993). The table highlights the fact that the UFW has been unable to turn election victories into lasting collective bargaining relationships; the UFW today has one contract with a vegetable grower, four with citrus growers, and one with a mushroom farm; most of the rest are with usually small nurseries.

The longest (and largest) farmworker contract in California agriculture is that between Teamsters Local 890 and Bud of California, the Dole Fresh Vegetables subsidiary of Castle and Cooke. This three-decade-long agreement covers 7000 workers in California and Arizona.[12] The union with the most farmworker contracts is the Christian Labor Association (CLA) with 182, but each covers an average of three workers.

The major organizing activities in California fields today are those of self-help groups. As more indigenous migrants from southern Mexico and Guatemala arrive in the U.S., there has been a proliferation of ethnic organizations. Some have been recognized as unions by the ALRB. For example, the Mixtec and Zapotec Indians in California from the southern Mexican state of Oaxaca have formed "civic committees" in a number of California towns, and one of these committees won an election in 1991 at a San Diego packing house.

The declining number of contracts and union members is also reflected in declining real farm earnings. Average hourly farm earnings have ranged from 40% to 60% of private-sector nonfarm earnings over the past three decades. In 1992, for example, average hourly earnings for U.S. farmworkers were $6.06, or 54% of the $11.14 private-sector nonfarm average, and average hourly farmworker earnings in California were $6.41, or 55% of the $11.73 nonfarm average.[13]

There are two ways to evaluate this "50%" farm-nonfarm wage relationship. Because farmworkers are employed only seasonally, their

TABLE 1
California Farmworker Unions in 1993

Union	ALRB Certifications[a] 1975-1993	Current Contracts	Percent of Certifications	Jobs Covered[a]	Major Members[b]	Commodities	Region
United Farm Workers	442	23	5	6,000	6,000 to 22,000[d]	All	All
Independent Union of Ag. Workers	15	8	55	1,200	2,200	Vegetables	Oxnard, Salinas, Bakersfield
Fresh Fruit & Vegetable Workers Local 78-b	19	19	100	1,200	1,800	Vegetables and Packing Sheds	Salinas and Southern California
Christian Employees Union	182	182	100	585	585	Dairy	Central and Southern California
Teamsters							
Teamsters 63	28	28	100	250	250	Dairy	Chino, Barstow,
Teamsters 890		3	10	3,000	7,000	Vegetables	San Diego Bud-Dole multiregion contract
Totals	775[c]	263	34	12,235	21,835		

[a] Includes unions with 10 or more certifications.

Notes: Unions with 10 or fewer certifications include: Comite de Campesinos Unidos, Teamsters Local 87, 166, 389, and 624, United Stanford Workers, Dairy Employees Union Local 17, and the Wine and Allied Workers Union. Unions without certifications and other farm labor organizations include: American Friends Service Committee Proyecto Campesino, San Joaquin Valley Workers Organizing Committee, Laborers International Union of North America, Anti-Racist Farmworkers Union, Laborers International Union Local 304, and Trabajadores Agricolas Unidos Independientes.

Source: Telephone survey conducted in August 1993.

[a] Average employment on farms under contract.

[b] Persons who pay dues to the union sometime during the year.

[c] Includes certifications of unions not listed above.

[d] The UFW claims 22,000 members. It pays dues to state and federal union federations for 5,000 to 10,000 members.

hourly earnings might be expected to be higher to compensate for the fact that most farmworkers are employed fewer than 1,000 hours annually, rather than 2,000 as in manufacturing. Such reasoning suggests that farmworkers should be compared to construction workers, many of whose jobs are also seasonal. Construction workers in 1990 had average hourly earnings of $13.78; farmworker earnings were only 40% as much. Seasonality might suggest a farm wage premium, but labor surpluses in fact lead to lower rather than higher farm wages. It is not just that there are usually more workers available than farmers hire; it is also true that the immigrants available to do farm work have no other U.S. job options—they either do farm work, or they remain jobless. The availability of such workers without options has usually kept the wages of seasonal workers paid on an hourly basis near the minimum wage. Many harvest workers have piece-rate earnings—they are paid according to the units of work they perform—and these workers typically have higher than minimum wage earnings.

In 1976, when the federal minimum wage was $2.30 hourly, the average hourly earnings of California farmworkers were $3.20, and the entry-level general laborer wage in UFW contracts was $3.11 hourly. During the late 1970s, statewide farmworker earnings rose in step with UFW wages, suggesting that the UFW had statewide impacts on average farm wages. This relationship was broken in the early 1980s, when the UFW achieved 40% wage increases with a few employers, some of whom then went out of business. During the late 1980s, the UFW and other farmworker unions have been forced to accept wage and benefit reductions, so that in many cases, entry-level wages are at or below early 1980s levels.

The fact that hourly farm earnings are nearly 60% of average nonfarm earnings might suggest that farmworkers have fared no worse than nonfarmworkers despite IRCA. But hourly farmworker earnings can be a misleading guide to annual earnings and take-home pay. Worker and advocate testimony before the Commission on Agricultural Workers (CAW) in 1990-91 made frequent reference to the surplus of farmworkers limiting the hours that any worker can work, so that even if hourly farm earnings maintain their 50% relationship to nonfarm earnings, annual farmworker earnings can fall.[14] Second, as more farmworkers are brought to farms by FLCs, their take-home pay can fall. Workers hired directly by a farmer are often housed on the farm at a nominal cost; those brought to the farm by a FLC,[15] by contrast, often pay a daily housing charge of $5 to $7, and another $3 to $4 daily for rides to work, so that take-home pay can drop from $200 weekly to $150 weekly as a result of the housing and transportation charges associated with FLCs. Third, the growth of nonfarm earnings may be constrained by the rising cost of fringe benefits such as health care; farmworkers rarely get such benefits, so to the extent that nonfarmworkers are trading benefits for hourly wages, farmworkers are falling further behind rather than catching up.

Activities Outside California

Farmworker organizing and bargaining in other states is generally limited. Outside California, the most important farm labor states have very few union activities. The ten states with the most seasonal farmworkers include 80% of all such workers, yet the "bright spots" for farmworker activity are in states such as Hawaii, Ohio, and New Jersey, which have fewer than 5% of the nation's farmworkers.[16]

Hawaiian agriculture is dominated by a handful of multinational food companies that include Dole and Del Monte. When the longshoremen's union organized the dock and transportation workers who served these farms in the 1940s, they also "marched inland" and organized most of the state's field workers. Today, the 9,000 to 10,000 farmworkers in Hawaii have the highest average earnings in the country—an average $9.09 in 1992. These mostly Filipino workers are aging, however, and the pineapple industry—which employs half of Hawaii's farmworkers— has asked the U.S. government for permission to recruit temporary or permanent Filipino immigrants to replace them.

The Ohio-based Farm Labor Organizing Committee (FLOC) is considered by some observers to have the best chance to fulfill the dreams of the UFW. FLOC president, Baldemar Velasquez, refined the UFW's boycott strategy by threatening consumer boycotts of the pickle and tomato products produced by Vlasic, Heinz, and Campbells unless they persuaded the "independent" farmers who employed farmworkers to recognize FLOC as these workers' bargaining representative. After a seven-year quest for recognition that began in 1978, Campbells recognized FLOC and signed an unusual three-way agreement, under which farmers who grow crops for Campbells recognize FLOC as the representative of their farmworkers, and Campbells adjusts the prices it pays them to reflect the wages and benefits that FLOC negotiates. Disputes are resolved by a third-party neutral—John Dunlop (Harvard) has held this post since 1985. Velasquez in 1991 claimed 4,000 farmworker members employed on 100 farms (CAW Appendix II 1992:992).

FLOC maintains an office in Florida, where many of its members spend the winter months, but it is not actively organizing workers there. Before it can expand its activities, it must deal with the 1993 change in the status of many of its workers. These workers have been sharecroppers who received as payment for picking cucumbers 50% of the revenues they fetched when delivered to the processor. As sharecroppers, they could legally employ their children during the six to eight-week harvest, enabling a family to sometimes earn $1,000 or more weekly. The transition to employee status will increase labor costs, as workers compensation and unemployment insurance coverage begins, and FLSA rules will restrict the activities of children in the fields. Velasquez suggested that, once this conversion to employee status is completed in Ohio and Michigan, FLOC will try to negotiate agreements covering these food processors' work forces in other states.

In New Jersey, the supreme court found in the 1950s that the state's constitution permitted workers not covered by the NLRA to organize and bargain with employers without retaliation.[17] New Jersey farmers have long relied on seasonal Puerto Rican workers, and these workers formed organizations to protect their interests, such as lobbying the state legislature to raise the minimum wage. The largest such organization in 1984 established a union affiliate COTA (Comite Organizador de Trabajadores Agricolas), which in 1990 claimed 200 members and one contract covering 21 workers who were guaranteed at least $4.12 hourly. COTA won four of the five elections in which it participated, but has been slow to turn election victories into contracts because of employer resistance (e.g., one contract required one year to negotiate and a brief jailing of the employer).

Florida and Texas have unions and self-help organizations, but very few contracts. The UFW has a contract until 1994 that covers fewer than 5% of the harvesters who pick oranges for Coca Cola's Minute Maid division, but more typical is the Farmworker Association of Central Florida, which provides credit and related services for 3,000 members, but has no contracts. There is a UFW office in Texas, but no contracts between farmers and farmworkers in the state. In Oregon, the Northwest Treeplanters and Farmworkers United called a 1991 strike of 120 workers against one of the largest growers in the Willamette Valley of Oregon which resulted in a wage increase, but won no contract. Farmworker organizations in major farm states such as Washington, Michigan, and North Carolina have had similar experiences.

Conclusion

Collective bargaining has been a century-old unfulfilled promise for American farmworkers, and there are few prospects for change in the

1990s. The reasons why farmworker union activities have been "much ado about nothing" for so long are well known: diverse farm workers share one goal—quit doing seasonal farm work as soon as possible, farmers are well organized to resist farmworker unions, and the government has often put obstacles in the way of farmworker unions, including their exclusion from the NLRA in 1935, and governmental toleration of waves of immigrant workers.

The farm labor market has been "layered" in the 1990s, so that farmworkers are more likely to deal with a FLC or crew boss than the farmer or packer for whom the work is done. The rise of FLCs is linked to continued illegal immigration; both intermediaries and an influx of unauthorized immigrants make it very difficult for unions to organize farmworkers. The mid-1990s stand in sharp contrast to the mid-1960s "golden era" for farmworkers, when it was hoped that the UFW would do the long-overdue job of organizing the nation's largest group of poor and unorganized workers. But the UFW was never able to represent more than about 100,000 of California's one million—and the nation's 2.5 million—farmworkers, and today the UFW and all other farmworker unions have fewer than 50,000 members.

Farmworker unions have been in the vanguard in the fight for federal and state laws to regulate the farm labor market and federal programs that assist farmworkers. Farm labor contractors are today subject to extensive regulation, farm employers are required to provide sanitation facilities in the fields, and the federal government spends over $600 million annually to help farmworkers and their children with education, employment, and related problems (Martin and Martin 1993). But problems persist. There are still "harvest of shame" conditions in many areas, due in part to the presence of immigrants unaware of or fearful of complaining of labor law violations.

In this environment, farmworker unions are struggling for a strategy to help farmworkers. Most have a strong mutual benefit and, increasingly, immigrant and civil rights components; they aim to protect newly arrived immigrants and to integrate them in the United States. They must then grapple with the age-old issue of how to bargain for improvements in agriculture before members drift into nonfarm jobs.

Endnotes

[1] In California, state legislation tried to fill in some of these gaps. In 1961 California covered women and children employed in agriculture under minimum wage laws; coverage was extended to men on larger farms under federal legislation in

1966 and to most farmworkers in California in 1967. Overtime pay after 10 hours daily or 60 hours weekly was required in 1976, and Unemployment Insurance was required for all California farmworkers and for the workers employed on larger farms throughout the United States in 1978.

[2] Contemporaneous reports said that 500 of 2,000 table grape pickers did not pick in support of a demand for a raise from $1.20 and $0.10 per 25-pound box of grapes to $1.40 and $0.25. The strike was referred to in a grower newspaper as "one of the most widely publicized strikes that is not a strike." *The Packer*, Oct. 9, 1965.

[3] In a summary typical of one-time UFW allies, one reporter described the UFW as "not primarily a farmworker organization. It was a fundraising operation, run . . . far from the fields of famous Delano, staffed by members of Cesar's extended family and using as its political capital Cesar's legend and the warm memories of aging boycotters" (Bardacke 1993:F1).

[4] The federal minimum wage was $2.10 hourly in 1975.

[5] UFW membership data are inconsistent. In 1981 the UFW claimed a peak of 105,000 members, although an internal report discussed 30,000 "regular dues-paying members." One partial explanation for the discrepancy is that after UFW was decertified on a particular farm, the UFW continued to claim as members non-dues-paying members as long as the UFW pursued claims that the employer was unlawfully involved in the decertification election. See Martin et al. 1988. New UFW president Arturo Rodriguez claimed 22,000 members in May 1993 and announced that the UFW intended to add 10,000 "associate" members annually. *Sacramento Bee*, May 27, 1993, p. A18.

[6] There have been additional cases in which the employer and union have agreed to settle a make-whole case before the Board renders a final judgment on the amount owed and has the funds distributed to workers under its supervision. For example, the UFW and vegetable grower Saikhon agreed in August 1993 on a $2.5 million settlement of a make-whole case dating from the early 1980s.

[7] Grape consumption was 8.5 pounds per person in 1989-90. Table grape imports have more than doubled since the early 1980s, one explanation for rising per capita consumption. U.S. fresh grape exports also doubled.

[8] For example, Rep. Dixon said that "Cesar Chavez achieved a position of moral and political leadership equaled perhaps only by that of Dr. Martin Luther King, Jr., and Mahatma Gandhi." *Congressional Record*, May 4, 1993, p. E1201.

[9] U.S. Senate Resolution 121, June 15, 1993.

[10] These judgments against the UFW opened a window on its finances. The UFW has in recent years had an annual income of about $5 million, of which two-thirds comes from contributions and one-third from dues. Union officers are paid subsistence wages: Chavez earned less than $6,000 annually, and the highest-paid UFW employee was a printer in the union's printshop.

The UFW reported assets of $8 million to the U.S. Department of Labor in 1990, $6.4 million in 1991, and $2-2.5 million in mid-1993. So far, the UFW has paid only one judgment—$1.7 million to an Imperial Valley vegetable grower for damages caused in a 1979-80 strike. However, several other boycott damage suits have been filed against them.

[11] Growers have been advised that they face a trade-off. If at least 15% of what they harvest belongs to another grower, these workers can be considered nonfarm workers under the NLRB ruling. The grower does not face secondary boycotts, but does have the obligation to pay overtime wages after eight hours daily or 40 hours weekly, rather than the 10-60 rule for Californian farmworkers.

[12] This relationship has become more rocky as Dole insisted on wage cutbacks and the workers paying more of their health care premium. The union called a strike in September 1989 to protest an employer demand for a 30% wage cut, which the union accepted after a three-week strike. In November 1992 the union agreed to a six-year contract that maintains base lettuce harvesters' pay at $7.25 hourly for three years, and then grants 1-2% increases (Testimony of Crescencio Diaz, Dec. 6, 1990, CAW Appendix II:415, and *The Packer*, Nov. 28, 1992).

[13] In 1970 average farm earnings of $1.42 hourly were 42% of $3.35 manufacturing earnings, and in 1980 the $3.66 farm average was 50% of the $7.27 manufacturing average.

[14] A rule of thumb is that farmworkers work on average 1,000 hours at $5.00 for $5,000; nonfarmworkers earn $10.00 hourly for 2,000 hours or $20,000. If farmworker hours drop to 800, their annual earnings fall to $4,000 or one-fifth the nonfarm average.

[15] This same testimony suggests that the USDA hourly earnings data used to compare to nonfarm earnings are misleadingly high, since they emphasize the hourly earnings of workers hired directly by farmers and not the lower earnings of workers brought to farms by FLCs.

[16] The monthly Current Population Survey (CPS) collects data on whether workers in particular industries and occupations are union members. There are few unionized farmworkers. In 1992 the CPS reported that about 2.5% of the 1.5 million agricultural wage and salary workers were union members, and that 5% of the 1.8 million persons with farming, forestry, or fishery occupations were union members, reflecting the higher degree of organization in these latter two industries.

During the 1970s, the CPS reported no unionized farmworkers in major farmworker states such as Washington and North Carolina. Several Midwestern states had 3-5% of their "farmworkers" in unions, but these are more likely to be hired hands in integrated farming and grain elevator operations than seasonal field workers. The CPS in the 1970s reported that 7% of California farmworkers were union members.

Analyses of the effects of unions on wages using 1970s' CPS data often found large union wage premiums. Unionized farmworkers, these studies suggested, earned 40-60% more than nonunion farmworkers (Perloff 1986). However, sample sizes are so small that it is not clear to what subgroup the CPS data refer.

[17] New Jersey, New York, Florida, Missouri, and Hawaii have similar constitutional provisions that are "self-implementing" (i.e., the state legislature does not have to pass an ALRA to grant farmworkers organizing rights). The New Jersey Supreme Court upheld this constitutional provision for farmworkers in 1989.

References

ALRB Annual Report. Sacramento, CA.

Bardake, Frank. 1993. "What Went Wrong with the UFW?" *The Nation*, reprinted in the *Sacramento Bee*, Aug. 1, pp. F1, F6.

Bean, Frank, Barry Edmonston, and Jeffrey Passel, eds. 1990. *Undocumented Migration to the United States: IRCA and the Experience of the 1980s*. Washington, DC: The Urban Institute Press.

Brown, G.K. "Fruit and Vegetable Mechanization." 1984. In P. Martin, ed., *Migrant Labor in Agriculture: An International Comparison*. Berkeley, CA: Giannini Foundation, pp. 195-209.

California Employment Development Department, Labor Market Information Division. 1992. *Farm Labor Contractors in California*. Report 92-2, July.

Carter, Colin, et al. 1987. "Agricultural Labor Strikes and Farmers' Income." *Economic Inquiry*, Vol. 25, no. 1, pp. 121-33.

Commission on Agricultural Workers. 1992. *Final Report*. Washington, DC: U.S. GPO.

Daniel, Cletus E. 1981. *Bitter Harvest: A History of California Farmworkers 1870-1941*. Berkeley: University of California Press.

Fisher, Lloyd. 1952. *The Harvest Labor Market in California*. Cambridge: Harvard University Press.

Fuller, Varden. 1955. *Labor Relations in Agriculture*. Berkeley, CA: Institute of Industrial Relations.

_____. 1991. *Hired Hands in California's Farm Fields*. Berkeley, CA: Giannini Foundation.

Fuller, Varden, and John Mamer. 1978. "Constraints on California Farm Worker Unionization." *Industrial Relations*, Vol. 17, no. 2 (May), pp. 143-55.

Hightower, James. 1978. *Hard Tomatoes, Hard Times*. Cambridge: Schenkman Publishing Company.

Hufbauer, Gary, and Jeffrey Schott. 1992. *North American Free Trade: Issues and Recommendations*. Washington, DC: Institute for International Economics.

Jamieson, Stuart. 1945. *Labor Unionism in American Agriculture*. Bulletin 836. Washington, DC: U.S. Bureau of Labor Statistics.

Jenkins, J. Craig. 1985. *The Politics of Insurgency: The Farm Worker Movement in the 1960s*. New York: Columbia University Press.

Koziara, Karen. 1980. "Agriculture." In G. Somers, ed., *Collective Bargaining: Contemporary American Experience*. Madison, WI: Industrial Relations Research Association.

Learn, Elmar, Philip Martin, and Alex McCalla. 1986. "American Farm Subsidies: A Bumper Crop." *The Public Interest*, No. 84 (Summer), pp. 66-78.

Lipton, Kathryn, and Alden Manchester. 1992. *From Farming to Food Service*. Washington, DC: USDA Agricultural Information Bulletin 640.

Majka, Linda, and Theo Majka. 1982. *Farmworkers, Agribusiness, and the State*. Philadelphia, PA: Temple University Press.

Mamer, John, and Sue Hayes. 1976. "The California ALRA: Meeting Particular Requirements." *Proceedings of the 29th Annual Meeting*. Madison, WI: Industrial Relations Research Association, pp. 73-81.

Martin, Philip. 1983. "Labor-Intensive Agriculture." *Scientific American* (October).

_____. 1990. "The Outlook for Agricultural Labor in the 1990s." *UC Davis Law Review*, Vol. 23, no. 3 (Spring), pp. 499-523.

_____. 1993. *Trade and Migration: The Case of NAFTA.* Washington, DC: Institute of International Economics.

Martin, Philip, and Daniel Egan. 1989. "The Make Whole Remedy in California Agriculture." *Industrial and Labor Relations Review*, Vol. 43, no. 1 (October), pp. 120-30.

Martin, Philip, and Elizabeth Midgely. 1994. *Immigration to the United States. Journey to an Uncertain Destination.* Washington, DC: Population Reference Bureau.

Martin, Philip, and Alan Olmstead. 1985. "The Agricultural Mechanization Controversy." *Science*, Vol. 227, no. 4687 (February), pp. 601-06.

Martin, Philip, Suzanne Vaupel, and Daniel Egan. 1988. *Unfulfilled Promise: Collective Bargaining in California Agriculture.* Boulder, CO: Westview Press.

Mines, Richard, Susan Gabbard, and Ruth Samardick. 1993. *U.S. Farmworkers in the Post-IRCA Period.* Washington, DC: U.S. Department of Labor, Office of the Assistant Secretary for Policy, Research Report 4.

Martin, Philip, and David Martin. 1993. *The Endless Quest: Helping America's Farmworkers.* Boulder, CO: Westview Press.

Perloff, Jeffrey. 1986. "Union and Demographic Wage, Hour and Earnings Differentials in the Agricultural Labor Market." Working paper 387. Berkeley, CA: Department of Agricultural and Resource Economics.

Sosnick, Stephen. 1978. *Hired Hands: Seasonal Workers in American Agriculture.* Santa Barbara, CA: McNally and Loftin.

Statistical Abstract of the United States. 1992. (Data are for 1988), p. 833.

Taylor, Ron. 1975. *Chavez and the Farmworkers.* Boston, MA: Beacon Press.

_____. 1976. *Proceedings of the 29th Annual Meeting.* Madison, WI: Industrial Relations Research Association, pp. 67-72.

Taylor, Paul S. 1975. "Public Policy and the Shaping of Rural Society." *S.D. Law Review*, Vol. 20 (Summer), pp. 475-95.

Villarejo, Don. 1989. *Farm Restructuring and Employment in California Agriculture.* Working paper. Davis, CA: California Institute for Rural Studies.

APPENDIX 1
UFW Chronology: 1962-93

- 1962: Established as a mutual assistance organization in Delano

- 1965: Joined strike called by Filipino table grape harvesters; boycotted liquor products of conglomerate grape grower

- 1966: Marched to Sacramento; won first contract, with a 40% wage increase for grape harvesters

- 1968: Launched a consumer boycott of California table grapes "La Causa"

- 1969: UFW began union-operated medical plan

- 1970: Falling grape consumption forces table grape growers to recognize the UFW; UFW asks lettuce growers to recognize the union as bargaining agent for their workers; most responded by signing Teamster contracts

- 1972: UFW-Coca Cola contract covering orange pickers in Florida

- 1973: Teamsters largely replace UFW as bargaining agent for California farmworkers

- 1975: ALRA enacted in California; UFW wins most of the first wave of elections

- 1978: California extends unemployment insurance to almost all farmworkers

- 1979: UFW calls strikes in support of its demand for a 40% one-year wage increase; strike settled with an increase in the entry-level wage from $3.75 to $5 hourly in the fall of 1980

- 1982: Many of the large vegetable growers with UFW contracts went out of business; others bargained hard, so that their contracts were not renewed

- 1982-84: Republican governor elected; courts overturn some make-whole remedies in favor of the UFW, and there are internal changes within union leadership

- 1984: UFW launches "wrath of grapes" campaign, urging Americans not to buy California table grapes because they are tainted with pesticides

- 1988: Chavez fast brings publicity to the boycott effort

- 1993: Chavez dies; ALRB rules that the UFW's grape boycott is unlawful

Source: UFW; ALRB decisions

APPENDIX 2
U.S. and California Farm/Nonfarm Hourly Earnings: 1962-92

	1962	1965	1968	1971	1974	1977	1980	1983	1986	1989	1992
U.S.											
Private Nonfarm Earnings ($/hr)	2.39	2.61	3.01	3.57	4.42	5.68	7.27	8.83	9.73	10.48	°11.45
Farm Earnings ($/hr)	1.01	1.14	1.44	1.73	2.29	2.87	3.66	4.11	4.53	5.31	6.08
Ratio	0.42	0.44	0.48	0.48	0.52	0.51	0.50	0.47	0.47	0.51	0.53
California											
Private Nonfarm Earnings ($/hr)	2.54	3.09	3.57	4.26	4.98	6.01	7.71	9.52	10.37	11.24	°12.12
Farm Earnings ($/hr)	1.27	1.42	1.67	1.97	2.78	3.53	4.35	4.85	5.73	6.39	6.41
Ratio	0.50	0.46	0.47	0.46	0.56	0.59	0.56	0.51	0.55	0.57	0.53

Sources: Economic Report of the President, 1992:396, 458 using 1977 = 100; Employment and Earnings, June 1992:130.

Rough Terrain for Collective Bargaining: A Management View

ERNEST J. SAVOIE

Ford Motor Company

Collective bargaining is a process in which employers and unions respond to economic forces—and often powerful social forces as well—that are seldom of their own making. It is an ever-changing process that has experienced several distinct phases in this country. One of the most distinctive and important of these phases was rooted in the turbulent decade of the 1980s.

For many American unions and employers, the '80s was a decade "on the edge." They had to confront industry and corporate restructurings, resizing and relocation of operations, recessions and low growth, near-term survival, trade-related issues, regulatory and deregulatory actions, sweeping technological advances, deep changes in the organization and conduct of work, political and social upheavals all over the world, and a fundamental long-term global reshaping of economies and businesses. Inevitably, the collective bargaining process and its practitioners were tested.

It would be unfair, as well as untrue, to characterize the '80s as an era of bad feelings, though there were indeed some highly visible bargaining meltdowns and some noisy exchanges of harsh words. Neither was it a time of wholesale failure. For the most part, the settlements reached expressed the new realities that were shaping the decade. Understandably, few employers or unions were fully satisfied with the results. But while wrenching change usually stood center stage, it did not totally dominate the drama. In some sectors, business as usual and even growth still occurred. It was true, however, that collective bargaining was no longer the prime-time player it had once been, and it commanded relatively little national attention. The fabric of collective bargaining, if not shredded, was certainly tattered and showing wear and tear as the decade ended.

One result for labor-management relations was the splintering—the tribalization—of collective bargaining into factions with specialized issues. This phenomenon brought grave dilemmas to the parties as former patterns and touchstones no longer provided reliable justifications to members or to corporate stakeholders.

Each bargain seemed to have a life and a course of its own. Health care and pensions, fairly well-established fixtures of collective bargaining agreements, had to be revisited and paid for in more up-to-date currency than past promises. Economics affected the whole employee "team," not just represented workers. For the first time since World War II, large numbers of nonrepresented white-collar employees and managers found themselves subject to layoffs or to wage and benefit slowdowns. The psychological contract between people and the organization was loosening.

Even more shocking, at least to senior management and to human resource executives, collective bargaining finally made its way to the board room, and senior managers and labor relations directors who could not "deliver" were replaced. At one conference of leading companies, attendees reported that more than half of their companies had replaced key members of senior management in the preceding two years. And with many labor relations professionals it became a challenging game to identify the shifting executive labor relations lineup in some of the better known companies.

The economic imperatives of the '80s loomed so large that some on both sides of the bargaining table emphasized the lines that divide and overlooked the ties that bind. This group used the familiar tactics of confrontation, containment, and brute force to deal with bleak and complex times. Historians will have to trace and evaluate the long-term results.

Other practitioners hopefully, but no less painfully, turned to the new rather than the old. They began to explore partnership and common destiny as a new collective bargaining option. By now this new option of cooperation has been sufficiently chronicled, if not sufficiently practiced, and important lessons are available to those who would learn. In the fashionable parlance of the day, there is a compelling though relatively small number of exemplars, benchmarks, and best practices. Consultants, associations, and universities are all making a living from the cooperation—or partnership—option. Though the partnership option is not for everyone nor for every situation, it has proven itself sustainable where leadership is determined to see it through.

Ford Motor Company and the UAW have traveled this partnership path for 14 years. Starting with small steps, they took ever larger strides in negotiation after negotiation. Working first from general concepts and then from tested tenets, they constructed a living national and local framework of joint programs that encompasses quality, employee empowerment, flexibility, efficiency, health and safety, job and income security, employee development and training, profit-sharing, teamwork, continuous improvement, and a wide range of employee and family needs. The company and the union supported these initiatives with increasing levels of national and local funding and with new governance and institutional arrangements that have endured through major challenges, including business cycle fluctuations and changes in management and union leadership at both the national and local levels.

Bottom-line results, though never guaranteed, have been achieved at Ford with the new approach. They include dramatic increases in product quality and customer satisfaction, some of the most efficient auto assembly plants in the world, widely recognized product leadership, increases in market share, high profitability in prosperous years and lesser declines in downturn years, enhanced employee commitment and satisfaction, and no national strikes and very few local interruptions during a taxing and unpredictable decade.

None of these results was achieved easily. Traveling the partnership path requires direct leadership attention, constancy of purpose, flexibility, resource allocation, large doses of employee development and training, and just plain "soak time." To sustain a large-scale transformation, bargainers must deal in broad terms, leaving plenty of room for adjustments and course corrections. Experience indicates there is no fixed, all-purpose model. Even the best cooperative efforts need to be periodically recast, redirected, renewed, and revitalized.

But rather than examine the Ford-UAW partnership or the many varieties of labor-management cooperation that developed in the '80s, I will review some broad trends from that decade that are likely to affect collective bargaining as we proceed into the '90s.

The four trends I have selected to emphasize are the climate for bargaining, the expectations of employees and the organization and design of work, the changing structures of unions and of economic units, and leadership focus.

Climate for Bargaining

The climate for bargaining in the U.S. continues to hold the storm clouds of heavy competitive pressures—global, domestic, technological, and often in combination. These pressures will force more reorganizations and greater efficiency, resulting in fewer employees in the unionized private sector, particularly in manufacturing and manufacturing-related services. The nation will not be able to rely on manufacturing to deliver employment.

Both traditional bargaining and partnership bargaining will have to deal with crises, job security, limited income growth, the reformulation and refinancing of pension and insurance benefits. Companies will have to increasingly enlist worker effort to help their firms. To do this, both companies engaged in traditional bargaining and those opting for partnership bargaining will have to educate workers about economic forces, share information, and stimulate dialogue and feedback.

This task will be particularly difficult for traditional bargainers because there is often little ongoing contract or mutual education between the parties, and because "the state of the business" is often regarded as one-sided propaganda. Partnership bargaining, on the other hand, because of its structure and values, as well as its cumulative and reinforcing experiences, may be able to do a better job of creating necessary mutual understanding and common education on economic matters. It may, as a result, be better positioned to handle crises.

Partnership bargaining, however, is not absolved from economic hardship. We cannot expect that partnership bargaining will always generate success in terms of survival or profitability. After all, when organizations were all autocratic (if that were ever so), there were always winners and losers due to economic forces. And should all organizations be participative, there would still be winners and losers due to economic forces. But participation and partnership, because of their focus on common destiny and common linkages, will give a positive edge, even if only to secure extra years of survival than would otherwise be possible— no small achievement in terms of forestalling or cushioning human and community dislocation.

While the distinction between traditional (adversarial, if you wish) bargaining and partnership bargaining will continue to be observable, we are likely to see a movement on the continuum of bargaining to a more centrist position of "both/and." This will not be for ideological reasons; it will primarily be a pragmatic response. Untempered adversarialism in today's unforgiving economy will not generate many successes and may often contribute to long-term decline. But neither can we expect partnership bargaining to produce an unbroken string of clear, continuing victories. New entrants and new players, moreover, will bring their own goals and experiences to both tables. The result will be a mixture of approaches—a blending—and it probably will be difficult for researchers and the media to label the good, the bad, and the ugly.

Employee Expectations and the Organization of Work

The second major trend that affected collective bargaining in the 1980s and is likely to continue in the 1990s relates to the expectations of employees and the organization and design of work. A significant force here is the increasing realization by management that people are the ultimate source of competitive strength and that in order to meet customer expectations and provide the best value and the highest quality, there must be intensive and aggressive dedication to employee development, to organization and work systems design, and to reward and recognition systems.

Central to this realization are these clear facts:

• Motivation and stimulation of a trained and eager skilled work force will be an increasing priority.

• Employees want more meaningful work and a larger role in decisions impacting their work. They want to be able to contribute ideas and energy.

• Employees want both monetary and nonmonetary "rewards" from their company and union affiliations.

• Employees want a workplace that values and understands differences and that provides a sense of belonging and esteem.

• Employees want a workplace that respects privacy, provides fair treatment, seeks to accommodate changing family and individual responsibilities, eliminates unnecessary stress, and actively pursues health and safety.

• Employees want to be able to grow, to develop themselves, to have skills that they are proud of and that are wanted and respected by society.

These have not usually been the subjects of traditional bargaining. Many employers, in fact, regard them as their untouchable rights. Many unions, fearing they may be coopted to do management's work and lose their own identity, are also uncomfortable with these subjects. Traditional bargainers do not have expertise in these subjects, and there is no trained cadre they can rely on.

Partnership bargaining, on the other hand, has extended into many of these areas and is more attuned to addressing these employee desires and organizational needs. In partnership bargaining, there is a greater awareness of the external and internal customer chain of work flow and the necessity of value added at each link. Employee communication, deep and wide, is seen as a strategic tool for which both unions and employers have a vibrant, common responsibility. People recognize that loyalty to one group is not disloyalty to the other. Partnership bargaining accepts, educates, and shapes the duality.

Future organizations will prosper and grow only if they gather, cultivate, and spread organizational learning among all their members. An essential element of this learning is understanding systems relationships, process chains and linkages, and the push and pull of competing demands and values. Organizational learning between two linked but competing organizations, such as takes place in collective bargaining, is especially difficult to realize because each group has a natural need for its own self-actualization. Because of the wider and deeper interactions that occur in partnership bargaining, there is a greater likelihood of enhancing the organizational learning of each group, as well as of creating a learning base that is common to both. It would be interesting to have some research on this.

Another feature related to the organization and the design of work is what is currently labeled as the management of diversity. This goes far beyond the traditional topics of race, gender, sex, disability, age, or other such "notable differences." The proper understanding and treatment of diversity affects such matters as work force cohesion and performance, team effectiveness, flexibility, goal togetherness, and organizational loyalty. Historically, employers and unions have done little to jointly sponsor diversity, although it could be of mutual benefit to both organizations. This is not surprising in traditional bargaining where unions and employers are prototypical examples of separate forces, and when they meet only periodically to address areas of conflict.

In increasingly competitive environments, the proper management and valuing of diversity will be more and more important as work force composition changes and as pressures keep mounting for fair treatment and inclusivity. The relationship between management and the union and the degree to which they accept and respect their own differences in outlook, background, and function will affect how they jointly address (or do not address) diversity in the workplace. Partnership bargaining, with its greater focus on common objectives and human factors (thus creating an environment of respect for all people) should be able to do a better job of effectively using and nurturing diversity. But it must be admitted that there is not much evidence we can rely on. Indeed, many observers believe the "diversity movement" is more developed and more vibrant in the nonorganized than in the organized sector.

The Changing Structures of Unions and Economic Units

A third trend that accelerated in the 1980s and complicated life for collective bargaining is the reconfiguration and realignment of industries, companies, and the processes of production and distribution. Unions, too, continue to merge and reshape, and a number of formerly premier industrial unions now have substantial portions of their membership (sometimes the majority) in industries and occupations startlingly different from their traditional base. Some occupations (for example, nurses and health care professionals) are being organized by four or five different unions. Much more so than in the past, companies and unions alike are engaged in many different "industries," and often there is quite a fresh mix of bargaining partners.

In addition, the growing array of joint ventures, mega-alliances, partial equity financing, long-term supplier and dealer contracts, and similar arrangements has further diluted the notion of a freestanding economic unit. This has profound implications for bargaining unit power, and it has significant relevance for managerial accountability and decision-making authority. Transnational ownership and linkages only add more frustration to this picture.

It is not clear what the result of all these changing structures is on bargaining relationships or the balance of power. Sometimes it seems to diminish the clout of specific bargaining units as they are unable to invoke economic interruptions to achieve their goals. At other times, a union's power is increased when, because of its strategic position, it finds itself capable of affecting economic activity far removed from its immediate orbit of power.

What is clear is that all this reconfiguration makes for rough terrain for bargainers who must travel it to reach settlements. They now have to understand many more forces and interconnections than in the past. They must know who to operate with and the methods that will work, and they must answer to many more stakeholders and constituencies than ever before. Another structural change is occurring because employment growth in the U.S. is in small and medium-sized firms. The day of the 400,000-plus employee company and of five- and ten-thousand-person plants is fast disappearing. The continuing growth of the smaller-firm sector will make it increasingly difficult for unions to sustain collective bargaining patterns, which already have been severely weakened. This puts more pressure on bargainers for firm-specific accommodations, it increases bargaining workload, and it creates imbalances in the eyes of the membership as well as in the minds of competitors.

The wide variety, vast complexity, and decentralization of American collective bargaining and the worldwide realignment of economic units will, I believe, result in the continuing coexistence of adversarial bargaining, partnership bargaining, and mixed bargaining—sometimes within the same companies and with the same unions. This is clearly so today in the case of the Machinists, Teamsters, and Electrical Workers. What fits in one situation just will not be acceptable in another, and economic realities will eventually wash away whatever will not work. Explaining this coexistence should produce a rich research agenda, or perhaps it will be a missed opportunity, because we tend to like the scenario where there are clear winners and simple solutions.

Leadership

If we are to handle the preceding three trends—an unrelenting harsh climate for collective bargaining, new imperatives flowing from the expectations of employees and the organization of work, and the changing and more complex structures of economic units and of unions—it will require superior leadership interaction.

Indeed, the whole notion of labor-management leadership needs to be rethought. It will not be sufficient for employers and unions each to develop their own leadership separately and then to hurl their leaders at each other like case-hardened weapons. This old approach just will not work today no matter how capable the individuals are or how good a job would be done in such separatist development.

The task of collective bargaining has grown beyond the confines of wages, benefits, and major terms of employment. Former generations felt they could pay the price of labor, take it out of competition, and go on with the business. And to some extent, in the prevailing economic environment that formula worked. But this is no longer our reality. Our new leaders—both management and union—must learn about the business, about worldwide economies, about human motivation, about their respective institutions, about power and service, and about communities, governments, and the public weal. And they must learn a lot of this together.

Further complicating the learning task is this question: How do we reach the dominant small and medium-employer segment, the increasingly powerful local unions, and the leadership cadres within these groups?

I am not talking here of school-type learning, though we should not underestimate the contribution that properly organized formal learning can make. It obviously has a place in our broader learning initiatives.

But the learning we especially need is that which comes from working on problems together, from wide and frequent networking, face-to-face assessments, task forces, joint visits to competitors and to benchmark operations, going through critical incidents, making change happen together, listening, brainstorming, and celebrating together. Partnership bargaining can do this; adversarial bargaining cannot because there is insufficient interaction and the subjects of interaction are limited.

Partnership bargaining, especially when it includes extensive joint program creation and administration, provides leadership and learning experiences unattainable otherwise. When joint initiatives also include operating management and certain business strategic involvement, such as at UAW-NUMMI, UAW-Saturn, UAW-Ford, CWA-AT&T, and the Amalgamated Clothing and Textile Workers and Xerox, leadership development is maximized, as is the opportunity to effect significant change.

Smaller organizations frequently lack the means and the know-how to learn about and to create and sustain such partnership and joint program initiatives. That is why I have espoused creating a National Labor-Management Relations Academy where experienced people could systematically share their learning with national, industry, and local collective bargaining leaders. It should be federally and state funded as a social contribution to American competitiveness. To be effective, however, such an academy would have to be "owned" by labor and management. It would require active and continuing sponsorship by union and management groups and should have appropriate government and consumer representation. In many respects it would be a counterpart to the

National Labor Relations Board and other governing agencies that were established long ago to make the "old" collective bargaining work. The leaders of the successful organizations of tomorrow will have to foster transition and flexibility even as they generate commitment and stability. They will provide unifying themes so that people of different backgrounds and different views can share in important common efforts. They will share leadership widely through all levels, recognizing the human need to belong and achieve.

To sum up: Collective bargaining will not get any easier. The landscape has been distorted by powerful forces, and we can expect to have to traverse still more difficult ground as we move through the 1990s. But we can greatly increase our likelihood of successfully maneuvering the rough spots by taking along an improved toolkit.

My view is that while the bargaining will not be easier, we can make it better—better for individuals, for management, for unions, for communities, and for our country. The bargaining and the effort to do this, whether we call it partnership bargaining or something else, is much more demanding than traditional bargaining. It will require the best efforts of our best people.

References

Auerbach, James A., and Jerome T. Barrett. 1993. *The Future of Labor-Management Innovation in the United States*. Washington, DC: National Planning Association.

Bluestone, Irving. 1987. "Joint Action: The New Track of Labor-Management Relations," *Workplace Democracy*, No. 56 (Spring).

Cohen-Rosenthal, Edward, and Cynthia E. Burton. 1987. *Mutual Gains*. New York: Praeger.

Collective Bargaining Forum. 1988. *New Directions for Labor and Management*. U.S. Department of Labor, Bureau of Labor-Management Relations and Cooperative Programs, BLMR120.

————. 1988. *Labor-Management Commitment: A Compact for Change*. BLMR123.

Cooke, William N. 1990. *Labor-Management Cooperation*. Kalamazoo, MI: W.E. Upjohn Institute for Employment Research.

Cutcher-Gershenfeld, Joel. 1988. *The Case of Xerox Corporation and the Amalgamated Clothing and Textile Workers Union*. U.S. Department of Labor, BLMR123.

Gilmour, Allan B. 1992. "Union-Management Cooperation," *Labor Law Journal*, Vol. 43, No. 8 (August).

Hoerr, John R. 1988. *And the Wolf Finally Came*. Pittsburgh, PA: University of Pittsburgh Press.

Kochan, Thomas A., Harry C. Katz, and Robert B. McKersie. 1986. *The Transformation of American Industrial Relations*. New York: Basic Books, Inc.

Pestillo, Peter J. 1993. Statement to the Commission on the Future of Worker/ Management Relations. Washington, DC (July 28), and "Twelve Years of Workplace Cooperation: Ford and the UAW," paper prepared for the Commission.

Savoie, Ernest J. (with Joel Cutcher-Gershenfeld). 1991. "Reflections on the Governance of Joint Training Initiatives." In L. Ferman, M. Hoyman, J. Cutcher-Gershenfeld, and E. Savoie, eds., *Joint Training Programs: A Union-Management Approach to Preparing Workers for the Future*. Ithaca, NY: Cornell ILR Press.

Savoie, Ernest J. 1993. "Making the New Labor Relations Work." *Looking Ahead*, Vol. XIV, No. 4 (January). Washington, DC: National Planning Association.

_____. 1993. "New Leadership Imperatives in Industrial Relations." *Proceedings of the Forty-Fifth Annual Meeting*. Madison, WI: Industrial Relations Research Association.

_____. 1991. "Working with Diversity at Ford." In M. Smith and S. Johnson, eds., *Valuing Difference in the Workplace*. Minneapolis, MN: University of Minnesota and the American Society for Training and Development.

Starkey, Ken, and Alan McKinlay. 1993. *Strategy and the Human Resource: Ford and the Search for Competitive Advantage*. Oxford: Blackwell Publishers.

Retrospective on Collective Bargaining in the 1980s

LESLIE E. NULTY

United Food and Commercial Workers International Union[1]

The decade of the 1980s was indisputably an era of turmoil and stress, not only for collective bargaining but for the full gamut of labor-management relations. Across widely differing industries new kinds of provisions appeared in collective bargaining settlements: lump-sum payments replacing across-the-board hourly wage increases, negotiated wage cuts, two-tier systems in which workers doing the same jobs but differing only by date of hire are paid at different rates, loss of various types of premium pay, workers forced to pay a portion of previously employer-provided health care, and on and on. The decade also saw the expansion of contingent forms of compensation dependent on firm or individual performance, including profit sharing and gainsharing, pay-for-knowledge systems, etc. Numerous unions experimented with various forms of worker ownership, principally through ESOPs designed to rescue distressed firms and worker self-management through a variety of "team" structures.

Combined with a steady decline in the unionized proportion of the private-sector work force, these new phenomena are frequently taken to illustrate the weakness of unions (and of workers) in the U.S. today.

Some observers look at the record and draw the conclusion that unions, collective bargaining, and labor relations as they have developed over the entire post-World War II period are obsolete. That existing institutions have outlived their utility and so must be radically redesigned. This author considers that to be a dangerous misreading of the history of the 1980s. Rather, looking back over the political and economic forces bearing on labor-management relations in the U.S. during this decade, one wonders that unions have survived at all as effective representatives of workers' interests. Yet clearly they have; and from this review of the range and variety of circumstances to which they have had to respond, one must conclude that U.S. unions today are, in fact, among our most adaptable and creative social institutions.

This volume surveys collective bargaining experience among an extremely diverse group of sectors confronting a variety of major structural economic pressures during the past decade. Some of these industries were heavily impacted by public policy that promoted trade liberalization and increased imports during the 1980s—but many were not. Some sectors had to respond to rapid technological change impacting highly skilled labor forces—but many did not. Some were afflicted by intense takeover and merger activity, often accompanied by massive debt increases for the surviving firm—but some were not. Some faced stagnant or declining demand for their products or services—but some did not. Yet each of these powerful external forces (most with negative consequences for individual unionized firms) is represented in at least one case study. In numerous instances the union and industry in question had to contend with more than one of these.

Yet, there was also a common set of additional adverse conditions that all faced and that must be taken into account in understanding collective bargaining experience in the 1980s.

Few now recall that the last two years of the 1970s saw major changes in federal economic policy, which set the stage for the wider scale assault on workers and their livelihoods that characterized the policies of the 1980s. Faced with spiralling and apparently uncontrollable inflation, the Carter administration and Congress pushed through deregulation of air and land transportation. Deregulation of telecommunications followed in the first half of the 1980s. As part of its anti-inflation policy, the Carter administration also attempted to implement a system of "wage/price guidelines." In practice, this became a system for controlling union bargaining settlements, given that there was no effective way to monitor or enforce compensation changes in nonunion situations. Finally, an attempt to reform U.S. labor law in 1978 was defeated by a massive alliance of the largest U.S. firms, most of whom had participated reasonably harmoniously in the post-war norms of labor-management relations up to that point.

All that was followed by the election of Ronald Reagan, the breaking of the air traffic controllers union (PATCO), and the rewriting of labor law through the administrative and judicial tools of the NLRB and the Reagan-appointed federal judiciary. During the eight years of the Reagan administration, NLRB appointees allowed the labor law caseload backlog to mushroom, as employers fired union organizers, sympathizers, and strike leaders, while committing rampant violations of other aspects of the law. The impact of these direct and explicit efforts to trim union representation and power were reinforced by other government policies that weakened general worker protection. These included deliberate weakening of enforcement efforts in the areas of occupational safety and health, wage and hour laws, equal opportunity and affirmative action requirements, along with cutbacks in unemployment compensation and other components of the "social safety net." Further compounding the pressure cooker atmosphere was the general *laissez-faire* approach in matters such as antitrust enforcement, securities and banking law, and trade law. This changed the competitive terrain for many firms and industries, throwing them into an intensified and desperate "survival of the fittest and strongest" atmosphere. In the scramble to prevail in that atmosphere, companies typically turned to their labor force to counter pressures from increased market, financial, or competitive pressure. Those that succeeded in prevailing had the wherewithal to enforce adverse terms, not only on their employers, but frequently on suppliers as well.

All of these factors came to bear on nonunion as well as unionized firms. The effectiveness of this assault on workers and their earnings is manifested in the employment, earnings, and income statistics for the population as a whole. Full-time jobs with comprehensive health care and defined-benefit pension plans are no longer the norm. Consistent health care cost-shifting by employers who provided health benefits, forcing employees to bear an increasing proportion of the expense, and fewer and fewer nonunion employers who offered health benefits at all came to characterize the conditions available to job seekers. This reduction in fringe benefit compensation was compounded by the rapid shrinkage in the proportion of the employed population covered by employer-provided pension plans of any kind. These massive trends in the nonunion sector increased the compensation gap between union and nonunion workers and compounded the employers' aggressive stance at the bargaining table. As a result, the era that saw massive attacks on the institution of unions and the collective bargaining process also saw one of the most significant redistributions of income ever experienced in our nation. The two phenomena are not unrelated.

As we seek to evaluate how collective bargaining outcomes and the collective bargaining process evolved during this era, we do well to bear in mind that only a tiny proportion of private-sector incomes in the U.S. is in fact determined through collective bargaining. Yet the 1980s saw one of the most significant shifts in our time, in the relative shares of national income from capital versus labor and from the working class to the very highest income groups. Given this global trend, the changes in collective bargaining processes and outcomes documented in this volume largely reflect union experiments in managing the process to minimize harm. This aspect of their character is evident in the fact that some of the most controversial outcomes of the 1980s are proving to be relatively short-lived.

Several papers in this volume point to recent rounds of bargaining moving away from lump-sum payments and two-tier pay systems. While these concepts were unilaterally introduced by management and originally opposed by union bargainers, in many sectors in recent bargaining rounds employers have acquiesced to union demands to return to negotiated wage increases. In the supermarket industry for example, lump-sum payments were first introduced as a means of narrowing the gap between wage tiers. Higher-paid workers agreed to ratify agreements that granted them lump-sum payments instead of across-the-board wage increases, in order to provide for relatively generous increases for workers on the lower tiers. This strategy proved to be fairly successful. The Department of Labor reports that after reaching a high point in 1987 of 60% of all union supermarket workers being under contracts with lump-sum provisions, in 1992 the proportion had fallen to 18% (Sleemi and Brown 1993). According to the Bureau of National Affairs, lump-sum payments were found in only 7% of all contracts negotiated in the first half of 1993, compared to 10% in the first half of 1992 and fully 42% in first-quarter 1988 contracts when these pay structures were first reported (BNA 1993).

In some instances these employer-initiated attempts to create new, lower and more controllable wage structures have proved to be short-lived for several reasons. Employers who need or desire to operate with a fully engaged labor force—one that can be relied upon to deliver quality products and service, one that will be amenable to training and new forms of work organization—these employers have discovered that the economic pressure on the individual worker, wrought by the failure to provide hourly wage increases and the divisiveness of two-tier systems,

operates against other management objectives. This has proven especially true in service-oriented industries such as supermarkets where
employee morale has a measurable impact as a result of the direct customer contact required of the employees.

Other kinds of pressures have proven effective in reversing or slow-
ing down collective bargaining aggressiveness by employers. In the
meatpacking industry, employers who have been forced to address occupational safety and health abuses through better worker training and
investment in better-designed work stations and machines have had to
find ways to recoup that investment. It is very hard to do that while
maintaining a high-turnover, low-paid, low-skilled work force. In the
case of IBP, the union negotiated a complete occupational safety and
health overhaul with the firm. This has led to reduced turnover, reduced
costs, and a stronger union presence within the plant. Among others,
this example illustrates how union efforts to get better OSHA enforcement (whether directly or through better congressional oversight) also
helps to stabilize the labor force and builds a base for more effective
union representation in the future.

One aspect of collective bargaining in the 1980s that will endure,
absent major public policy changes, is the impact of health care cost
inflation. Throughout the 1980s the cost of health benefits for active
workers, not to mention retirees for whom the problem is even greater,
rose at two to three or more times the cost of other forms of compensation. The pressure exerted on wages and other components of the compensation package by this one factor cannot be exaggerated. Unions that
conducted pre-bargaining surveys routinely found that members felt
most strongly that their collectively bargained benefits should be protected, even at the cost of lowered wage increases. Particularly for lower
wage union workers, employer demands for higher employee copayments and deductibles posed a particular threat to the ultimate value of
their take-home pay. Thus many changes in premium pay that occurred
during the 1980s (holidays and wage settlements documented in this
volume) were driven not only by external industry pressures and employer aggressiveness but also by the need to accommodate this demand
from union members.

Another aspect of collective bargaining experience in the 1980s that
merits some attention is the relationship between organizing and bargaining ability. Most of the cases recounted in this volume explore the
downward drag on collective bargaining settlements exerted by unions'

loss of ability to "take wages out of competition" as a result of the erosion of union market share. Some reference is made to auto, paper, and steel unions failing to organize the newest entrants in their industries. Some of the successful tactics of the hotel and restaurant union and recent successes in meatpacking are discussed. In all cases where unions have been able to make slow but steady progress in organizing, that is reflected in similar progress in collective bargaining outcomes. This relationship has been taken very much to heart within the UFCW, where organizing is accorded a high status. (Fully half of all workers organized by all AFL-CIO unions during the 1980s have been organized by the UFCW.)

Research by Paula Voos and Dale Belman has found that in the supermarket industry, for every additional 10% of a major metropolitan market that is unionized, workers' wages are enhanced by 2.2% to 2.3% (Belman and Voos 1993). The UFCW is communicating these results throughout the union through shop steward training sessions, with the goal of building a higher level of organizing effectiveness. The ultimate aim is to help restore the union's ability to "take wages out of competition."

Dissemination of this information is deemed to be critical, as the union has learned that the most effective way to organize is by combining sophisticated experienced staff with rank-and-file "volunteer organizers" who are able to communicate with unorganized workers on a true peer basis. Recruiting those volunteers is not always easy.

In an effort to elicit a higher level of participation in organizing from its existing members, the Cleveland local of the UFCW attempted to explicitly link the bargaining agreement and organizing. The union agreed to language in its contract with the multi-employer group for the metropolitan area which provided that if the union failed to maintain pickets at any store competing with a unionized store but paying less, union wages in the competing store could be reduced to the levels of the nonunion operator. This put pressure on the union and its members to put pressure on low-standard nonunion stores. As a result, the union got a much better response to its volunteer organizer recruitment efforts and succeeded in preventing encroachment by nonunion operators. This strategy has many interesting aspects: (1) it forced rank-and-file members to recognize the link between organizing and bargaining results and to take action to protect their contract; (2) in so doing, the union alleviated some of the excessive competitive pressure on union employers so that competition could occur on a basis other than wages; (3) the union avoided contract concessions absorbed by locals in other areas where unionization rates dropped precipitously during the same period; and (4) the union's bargaining position vis-à-vis organized employers is now strengthened because it proved it could mobilize its members in defense of the high standards for wages, benefits, and working conditions provided by the contract.

A great deal of attention and press has been given to difficult collective bargaining episodes during the 1980s that eventually led to "corporate campaigns" against the employer involved (International Paper, Peabody Coal, Hormel, etc.). Yet not enough attention has been paid by unions, or by those who study them, to the impact of corporate or comprehensive campaigns when targeted at nonunion employers. From the Service Employees International Union's "Justice for Janitors," to the UFCW's exposé of abusive practices by Food Lion, these efforts also contribute toward the goal of "taking wages out of competition."

The official legal attack on the established institutions of labor-management relations in the 1980s led many unions to go beyond the collective bargaining norms that had prevailed previously. Only the as yet unwritten history of the 1990s will be able to tell whether and to what extent the holding actions of the 1980s is allowing strategic regrouping, or whether it in fact spells the end of the labor movement and labor-management relations as we have come to know them—as some are predicting.

The pessimistic view unfortunately overlooks the many examples of creativity and initiative demonstrated in unions' organizing and bargaining strategies during the 1980s and into the 1990s, some of which have been mentioned here. If the results do not yet appear as spectacular as some of the union accomplishments of the 1960s, the difference has more to do with the heightened complexity of the economic and political environment of today than with failings intrinsic to the labor movement as such. The structure of hours, wages, and benefits provided under collective bargaining continues to provide a standard of fairness and stability that is unfortunately becoming increasingly rare in nonunion settings.

These characteristics—flexibility, creativity, and high standards—make collective bargaining an institution that needs to be nurtured and extended. Failure to do so will threaten to produce a free fall in wages and working conditions in today's political and economic climate.